MERMAID SAGA
VIZ Signature Edition
Vol. 1

STORY AND ART BY
RUMIKO TAKAHASHI

TAKAHASHI RUMIKO NINGYO SERIES Vol.1,2
by Rumiko TAKAHASHI
© 2003 Rumiko TAKAHASHI
All rights reserved.
Original Japanese edition published by SHOGAKUKAN.
English translation rights in the United States of America, Canada,
the United Kingdom, Ireland,
Australia and New Zealand arranged with SHOGAKUKAN.

Translation & English Adaptation/Rachel Thorn
Lettering/Joanna Estep
Design/Yukiko Whitley
Editor/Amy Yu

The stories, characters and incidents mentioned in
this publication are entirely fictional.

Printed in Canada

Published by VIZ Media, LLC
P.O. Box 77010
San Francisco, CA 94107

10 9 8 7 6 5 4 3 2 1
First printing, November 2020

PARENTAL ADVISORY
MERMAID SAGA is rated T+ for Older Teen and
is recommended for ages 16 and up. This volume
contains nudity and violence.

VIZ MEDIA
viz.com

VIZ SIGNATURE
vizsignature.com

Rumiko Takahashi

The spotlight on Rumiko Takahashi's career began in 1978 when she won an honorable mention in Shogakukan's prestigious New Comic Artist Contest for *Those Selfish Aliens*. Later that same year, her boy-meets-alien comedy series, *Urusei Yatsura*, was serialized in *Weekly Shonen Sunday*. This phenomenally successful manga series was adapted into anime format and spawned a TV series and half a dozen theatrical-release movies, all incredibly popular in their own right. Takahashi followed up the success of her debut series with one blockbuster hit after another—*Maison Ikkoku* ran from 1980 to 1987, *Ranma 1/2* from 1987 to 1996, and *Inuyasha* from 1996 to 2008. Other notable works include *Mermaid Saga*, *Rumic Theater*, and *One-Pound Gospel*.

Takahashi was inducted into the Will Eisner Comic Awards Hall of Fame in 2018. In 2019, she won the Grand Prix at FIDB Angoulême. She won the prestigious Shogakukan Manga Award twice in her career, once for *Urusei Yatsura* in 1981 and the second time for *Inuyasha* in 2002. A majority of the Takahashi canon has been adapted into other media such as anime, live-action TV series, and film. Takahashi's manga, as well as the other formats her work has been adapted into, have continued to delight generations of fans around the world. Distinguished by her wonderfully endearing characters, Takahashi's work adeptly incorporates a wide variety of elements such as comedy, romance, fantasy, and martial arts. While her series are difficult to pin down into one simple genre, the signature style she has created has come to be known as the "Rumic World." Rumiko Takahashi is an artist who truly represents the very best from the world of manga.

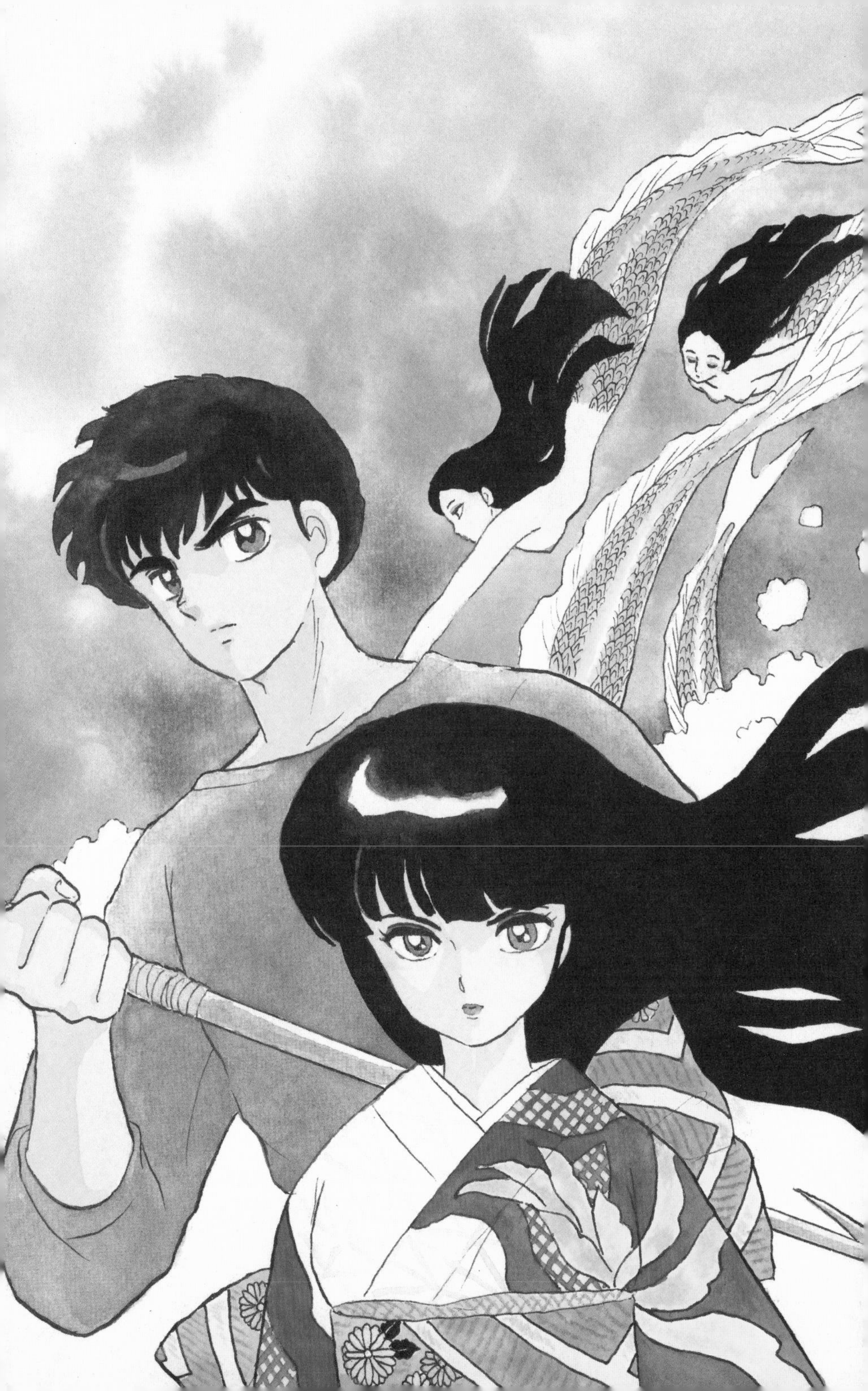

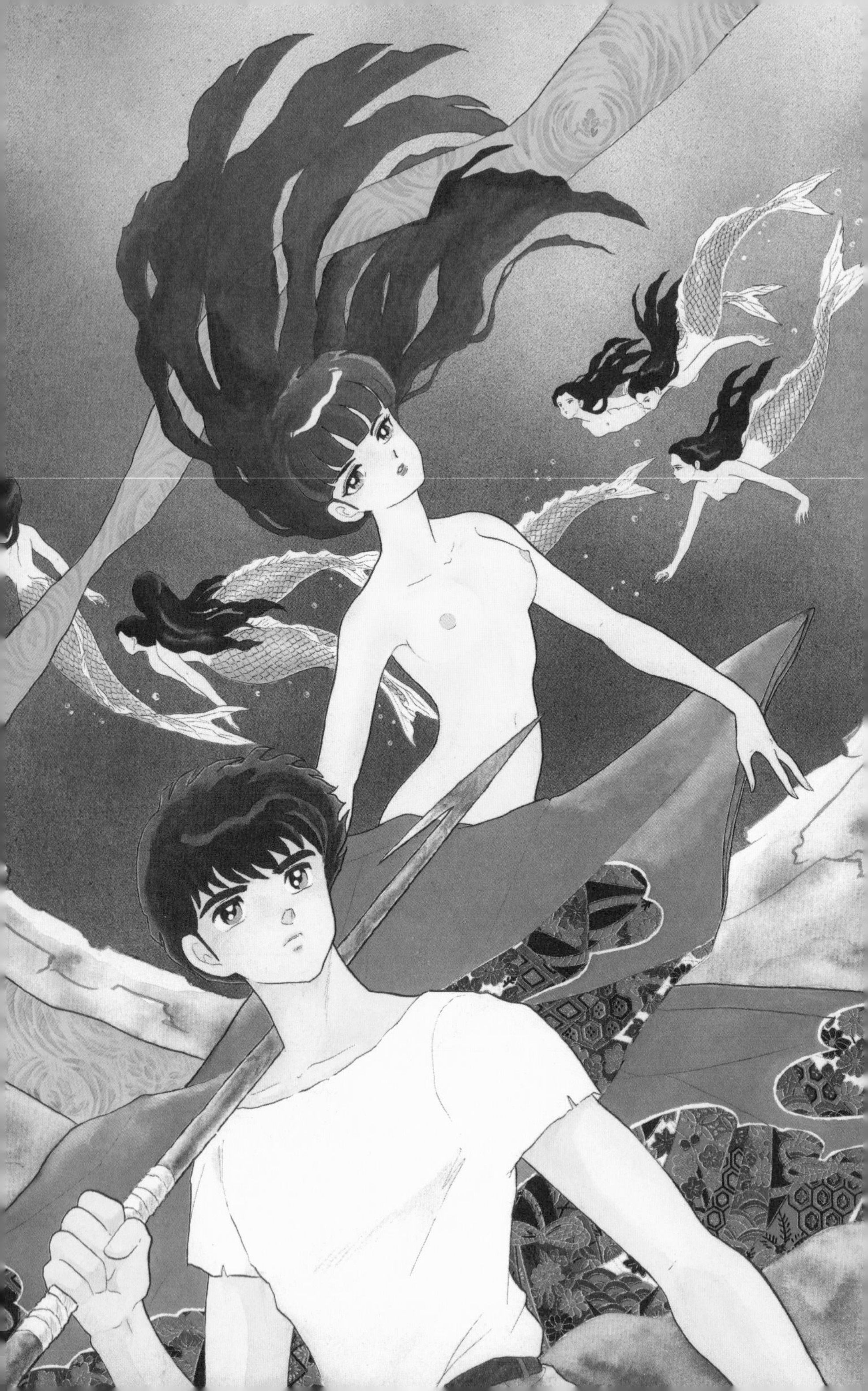

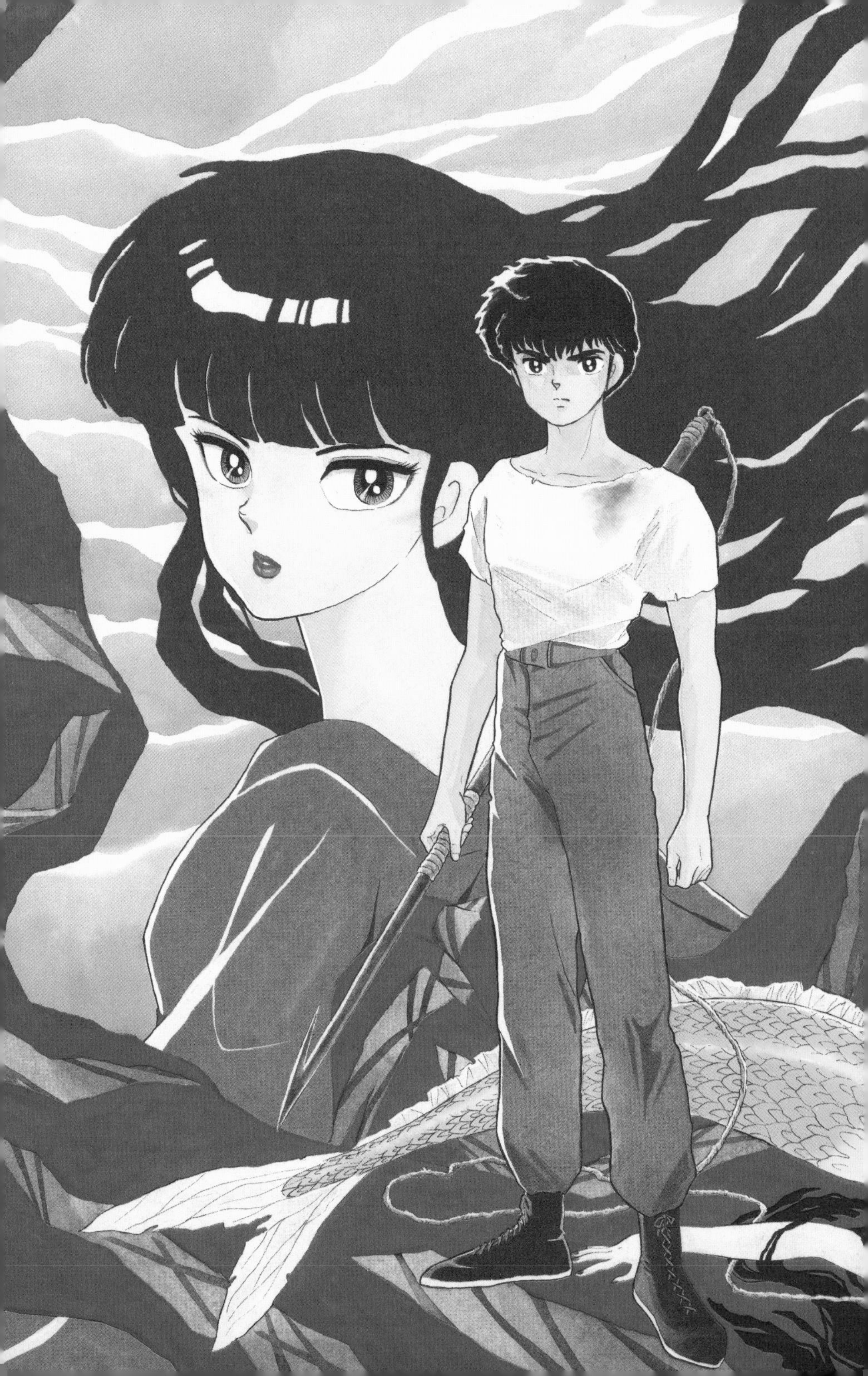

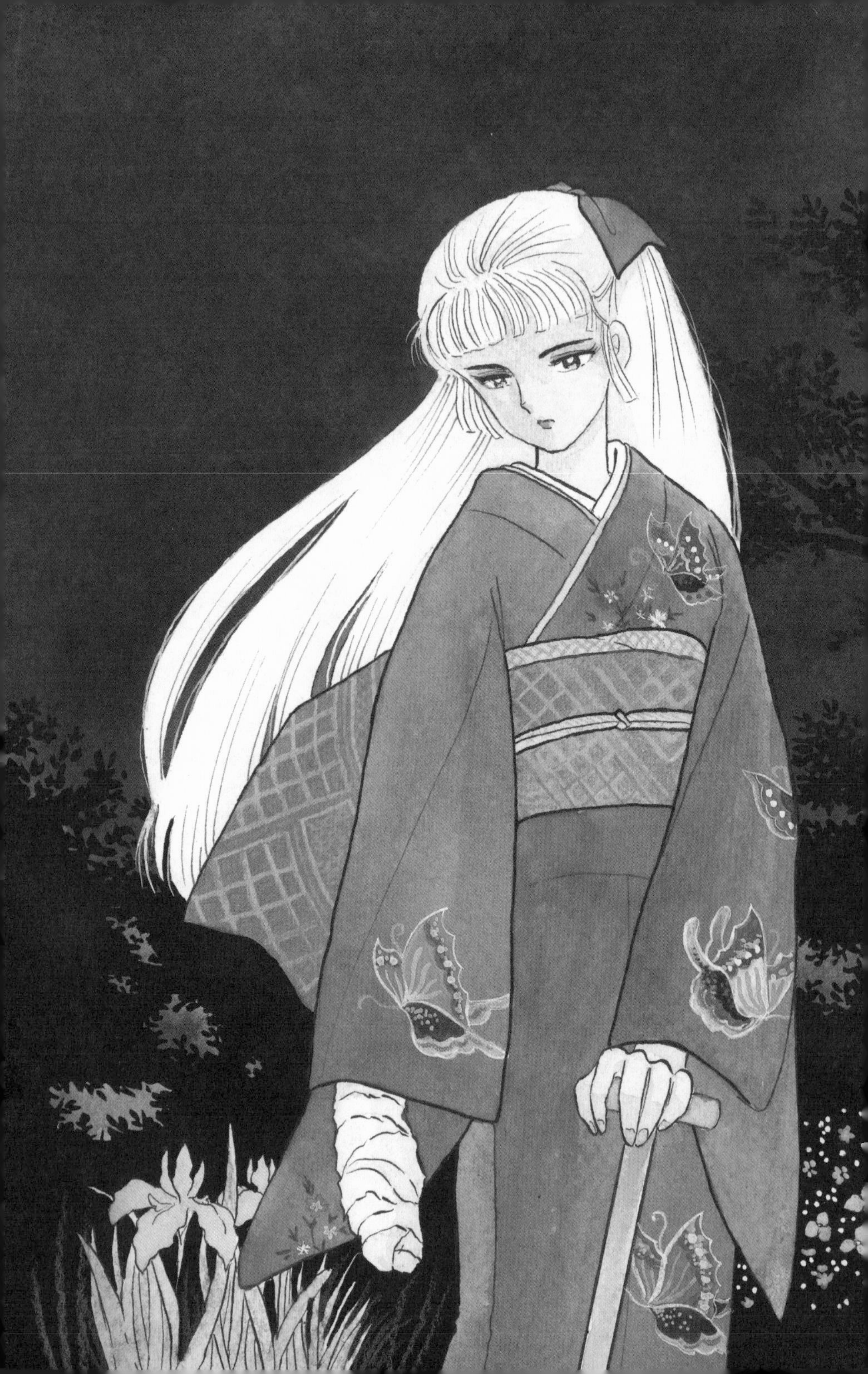

MERMAID SAGA

1

Story and Art by
Rumiko Takahashi

CONTENTS

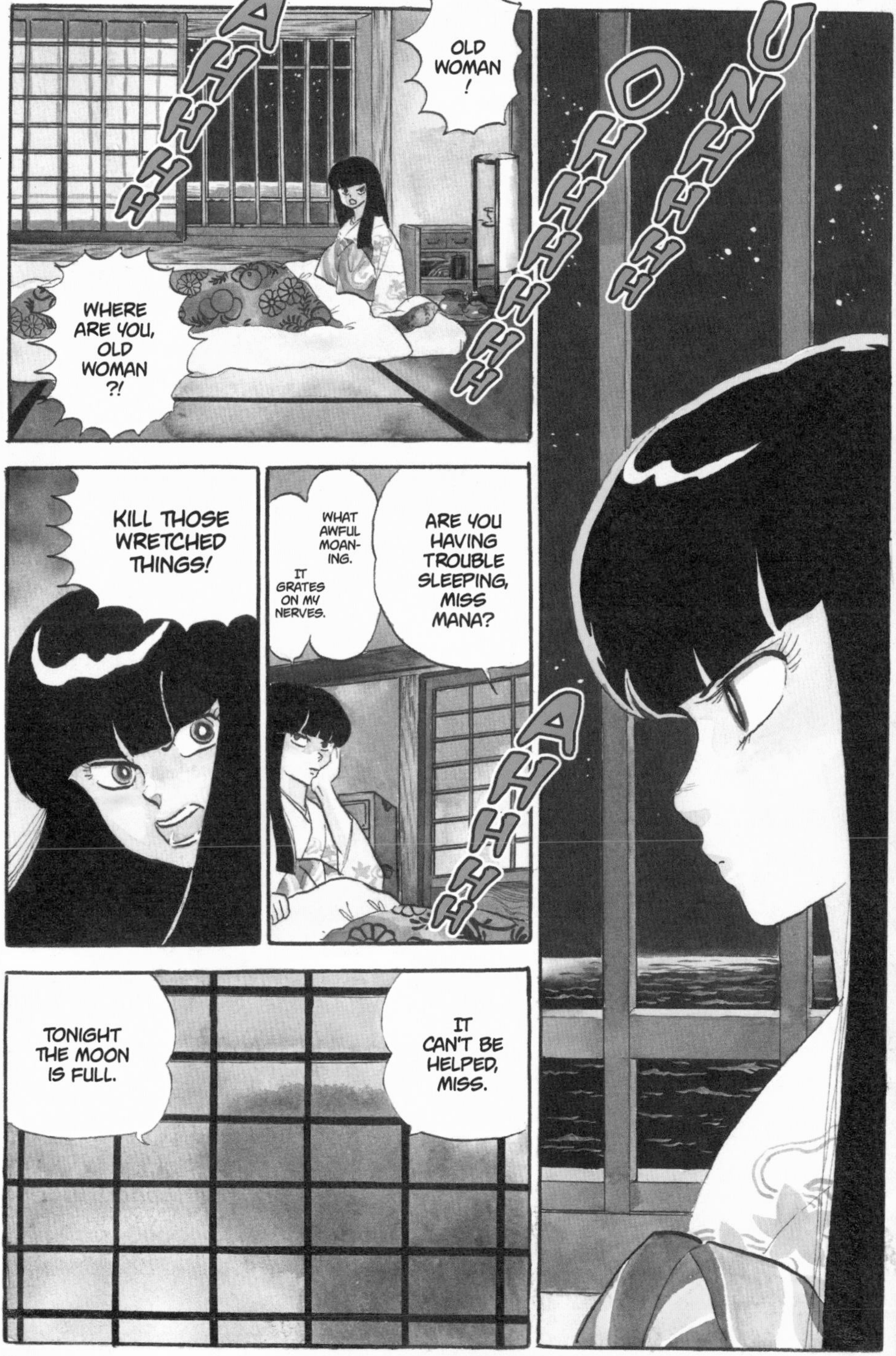
UNHHHHH
OHHHHHHHHH
AHHHHH
OLD WOMAN!
AHHHHHH
WHERE ARE YOU, OLD WOMAN?!
ARE YOU HAVING TROUBLE SLEEPING, MISS MANA?
WHAT AWFUL MOANING.
IT GRATES ON MY NERVES.
KILL THOSE WRETCHED THINGS!
IT CAN'T BE HELPED, MISS.
TONIGHT THE MOON IS FULL.

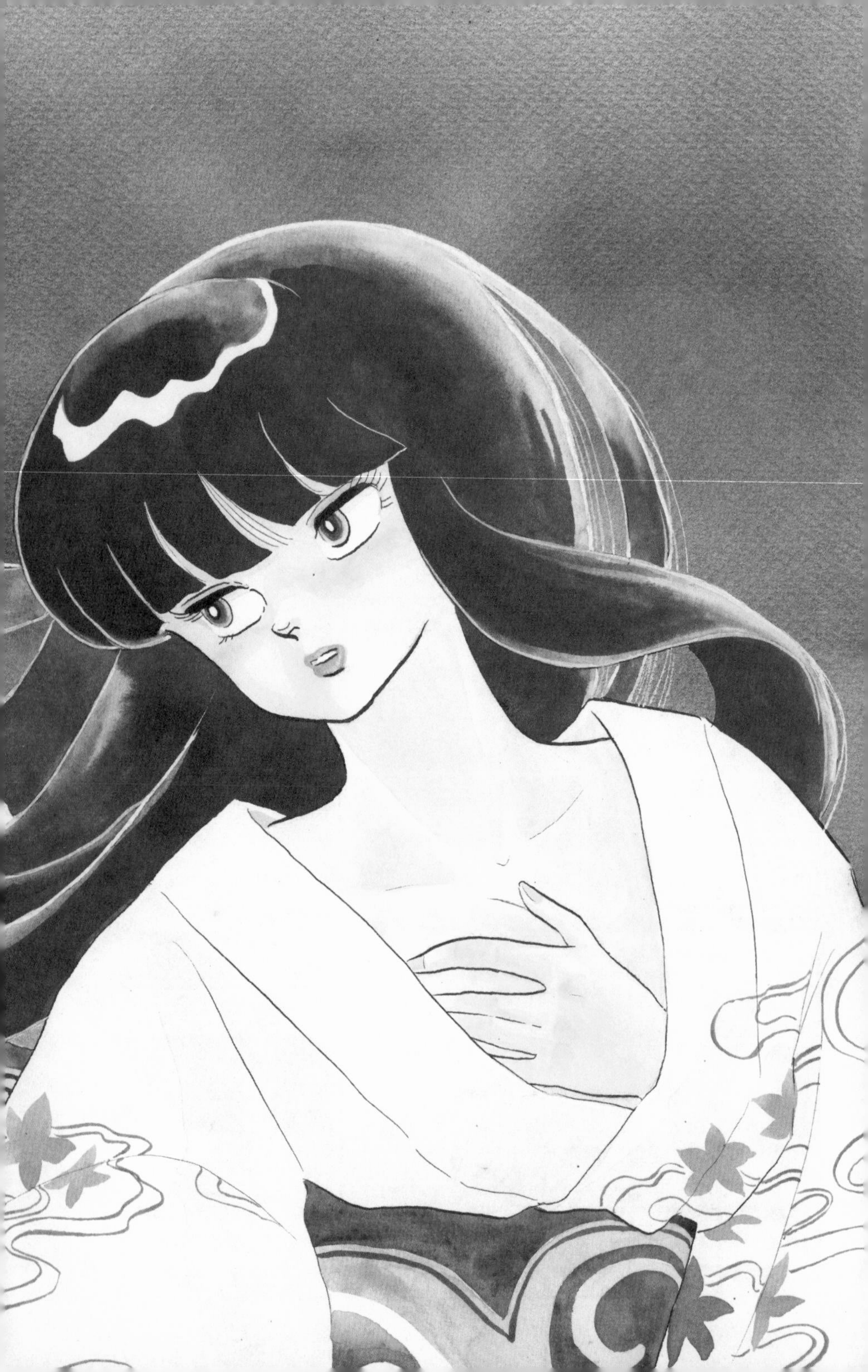

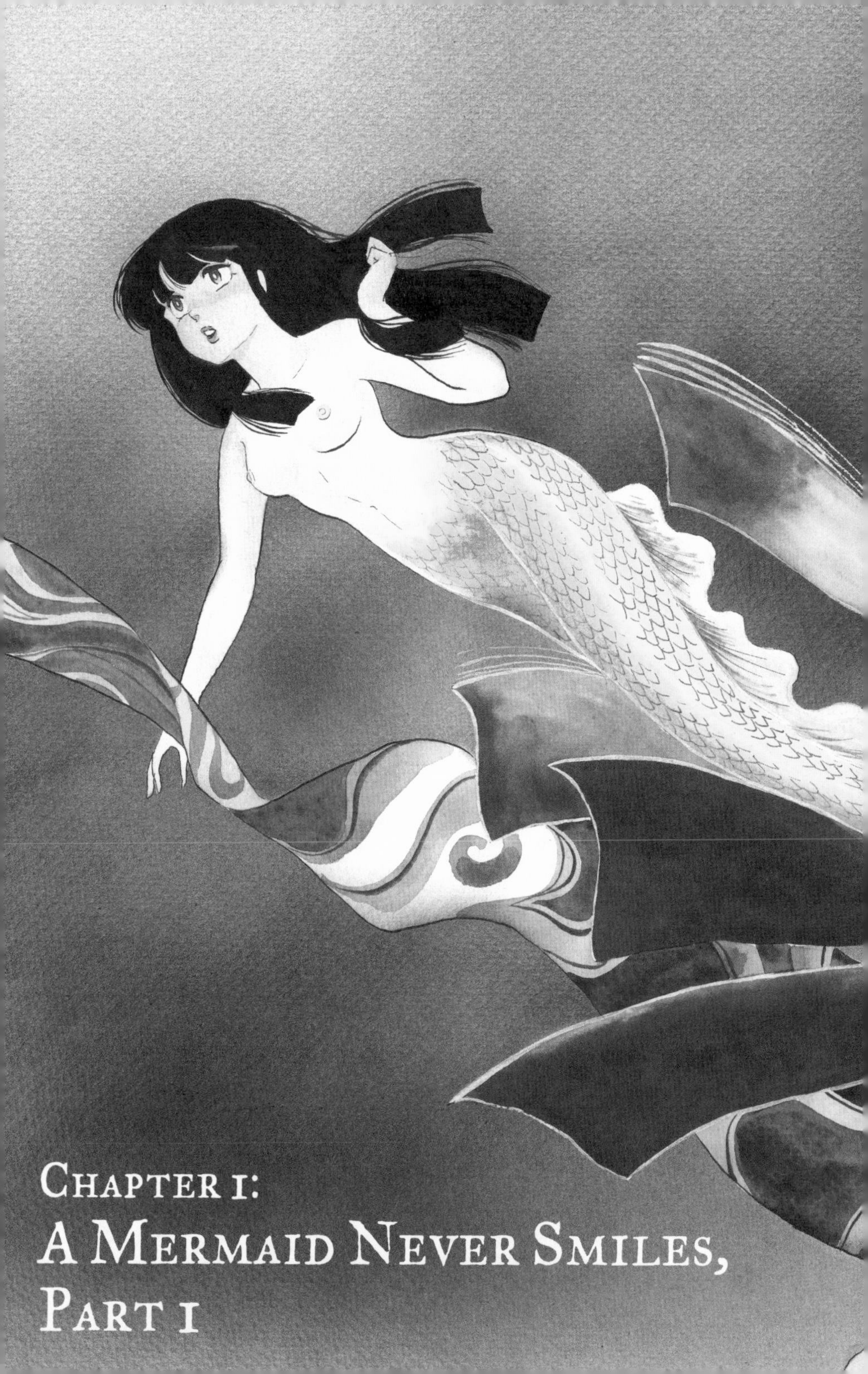

Chapter 1: A Mermaid Never Smiles, Part 1

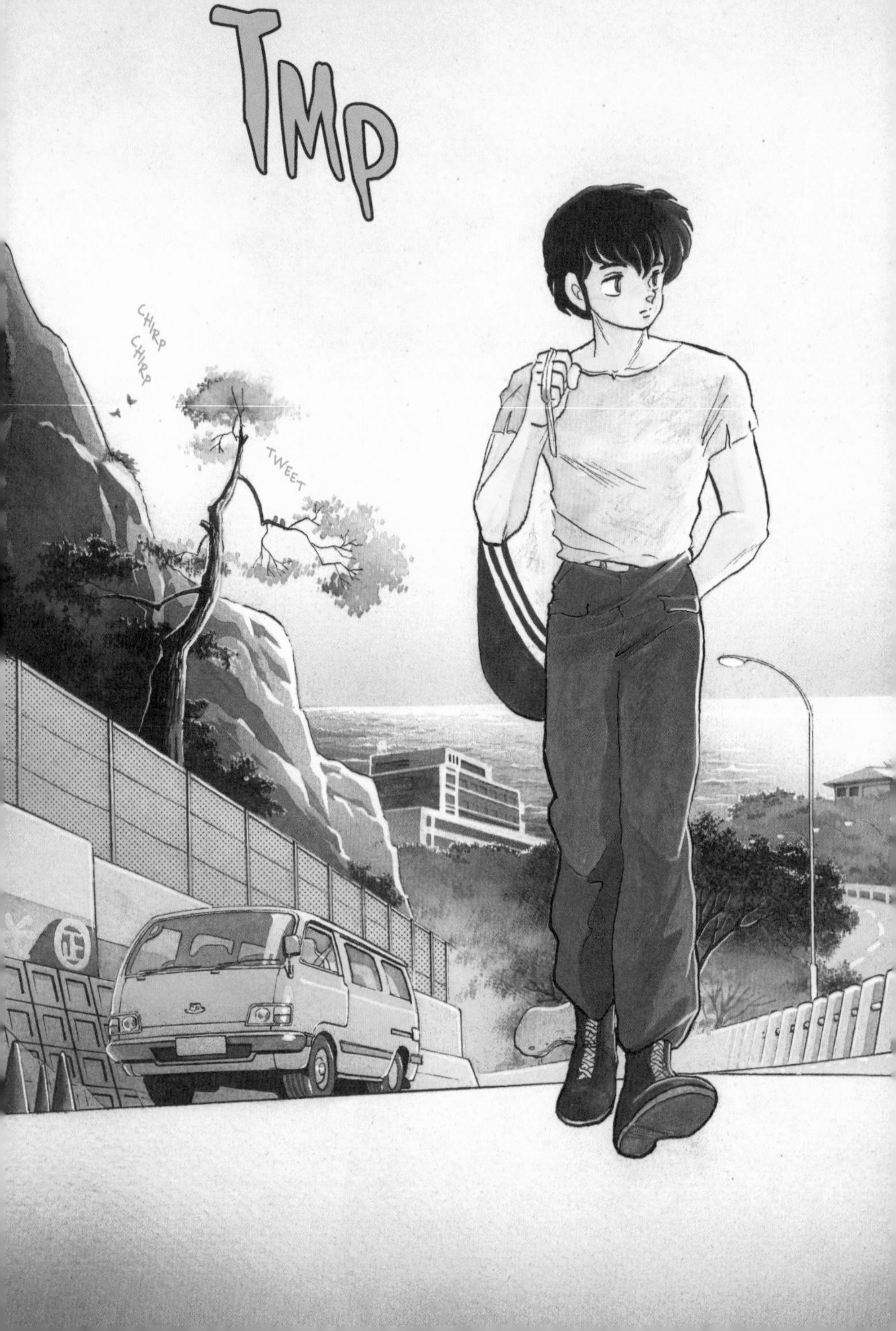
TMP
CHIRP
CHIRP
TWEET

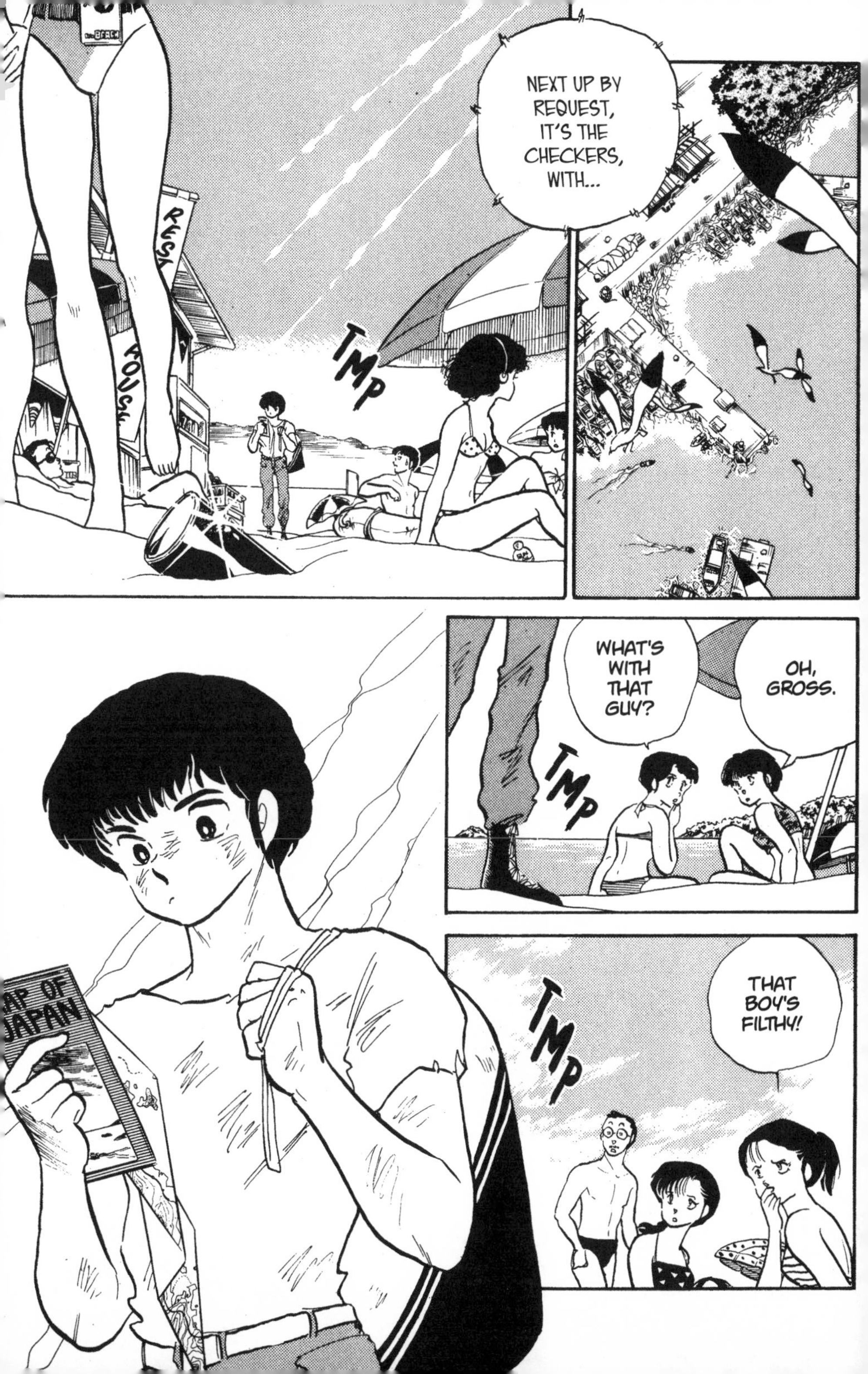
NEXT UP BY REQUEST, IT'S THE CHECKERS, WITH...
TMP
OH, GROSS.
WHAT'S WITH THAT GUY?
TMP
TMP
THAT BOY'S FILTHY!

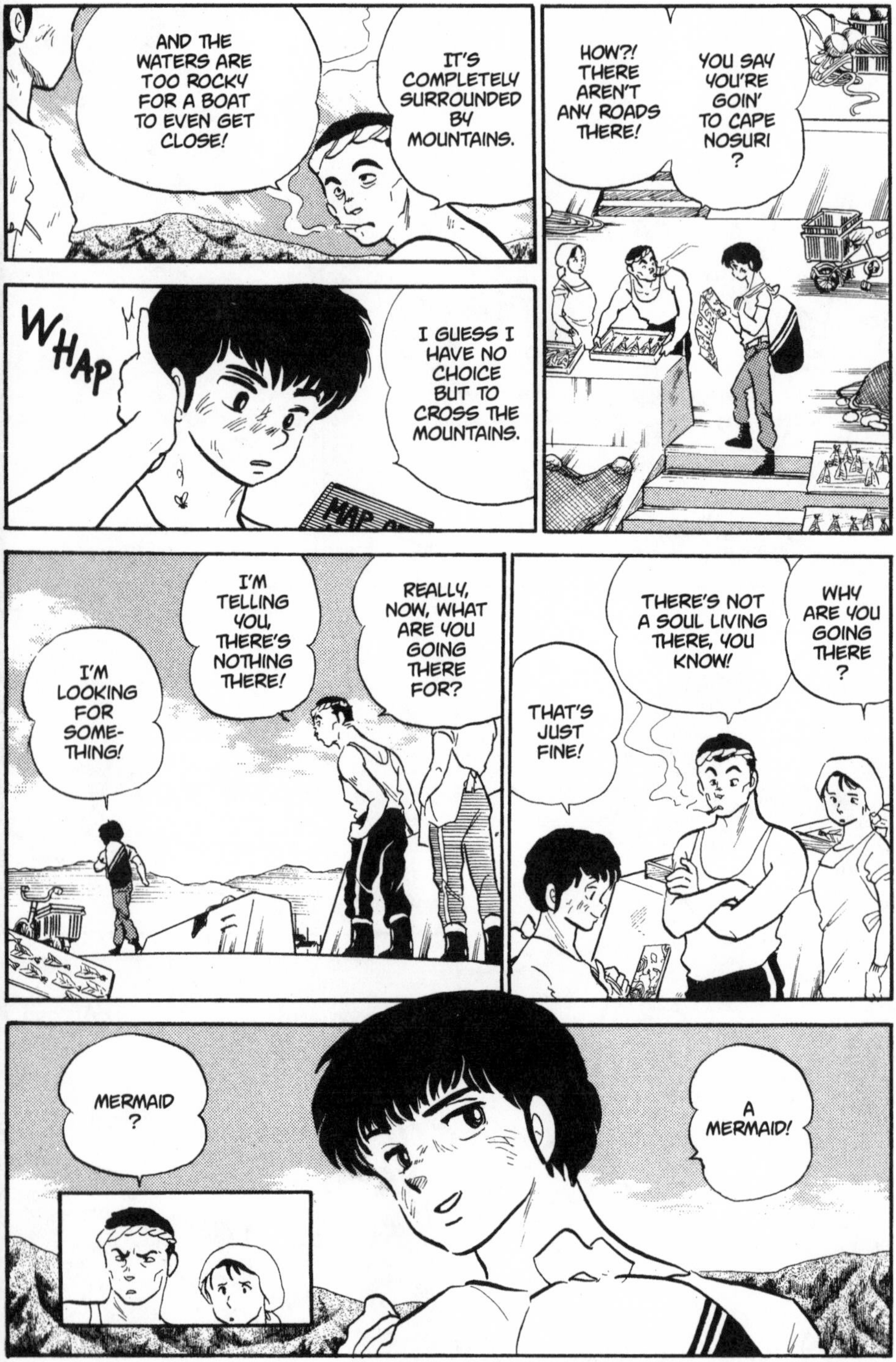
YOU SAY YOU'RE GOIN' TO CAPE NOSURI ?
HOW?! THERE AREN'T ANY ROADS THERE!
IT'S COMPLETELY SURROUNDED BY MOUNTAINS.
AND THE WATERS ARE TOO ROCKY FOR A BOAT TO EVEN GET CLOSE!
I GUESS I HAVE NO CHOICE BUT TO CROSS THE MOUNTAINS.
WHAP
WHY ARE YOU GOING THERE ?
THERE'S NOT A SOUL LIVING THERE, YOU KNOW!
THAT'S JUST FINE!
REALLY, NOW, WHAT ARE YOU GOING THERE FOR?
I'M TELLING YOU, THERE'S NOTHING THERE!
I'M LOOKING FOR SOME-THING!
A MERMAID!
MERMAID ?

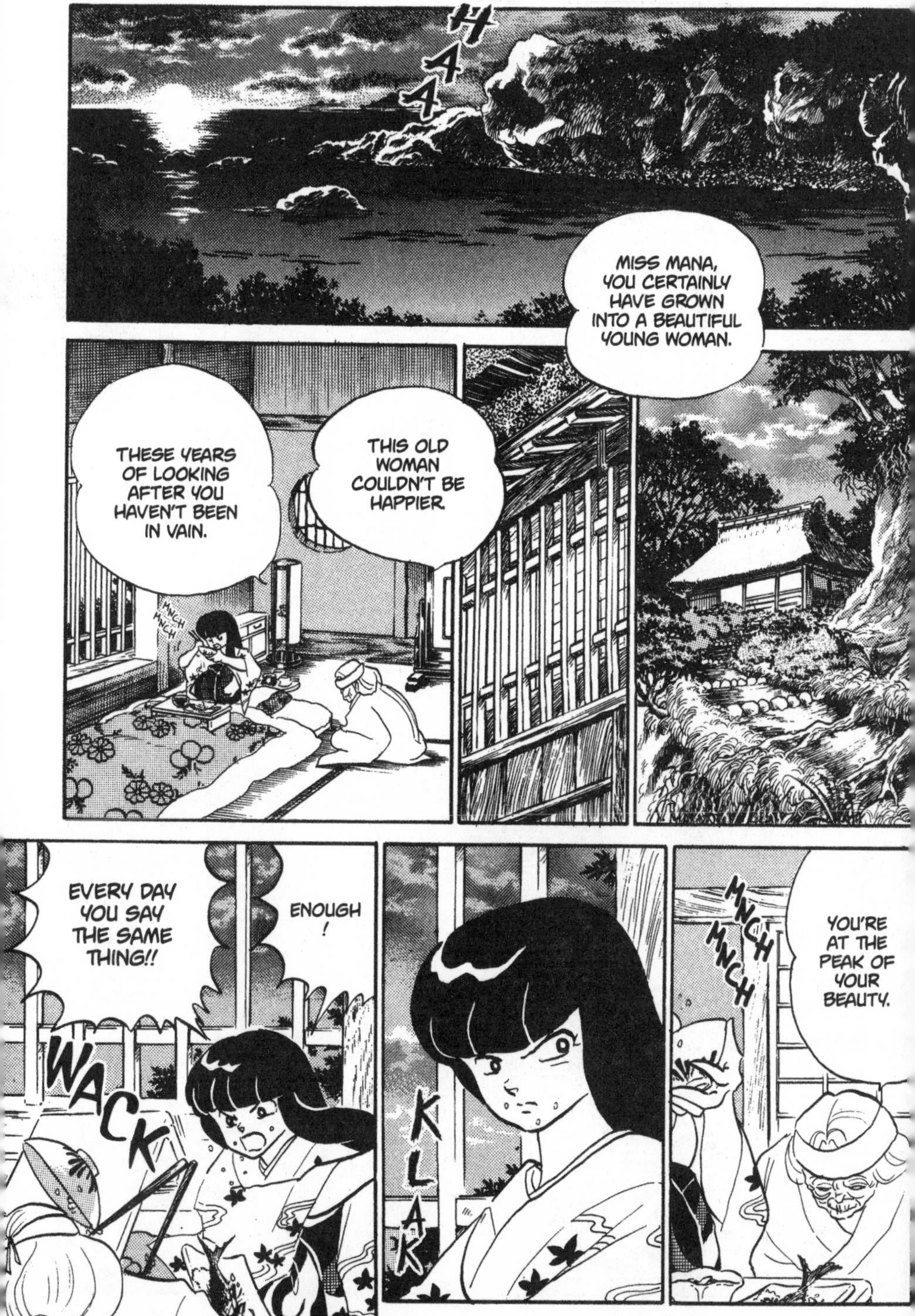
SHAAA
MISS MANA, YOU CERTAINLY HAVE GROWN INTO A BEAUTIFUL YOUNG WOMAN.
THIS OLD WOMAN COULDN'T BE HAPPIER.
THESE YEARS OF LOOKING AFTER YOU HAVEN'T BEEN IN VAIN.
MNCH MNCH
YOU'RE AT THE PEAK OF YOUR BEAUTY.
MNCH MNCH
KLAK
ENOUGH!
EVERY DAY YOU SAY THE SAME THING!!
WACK

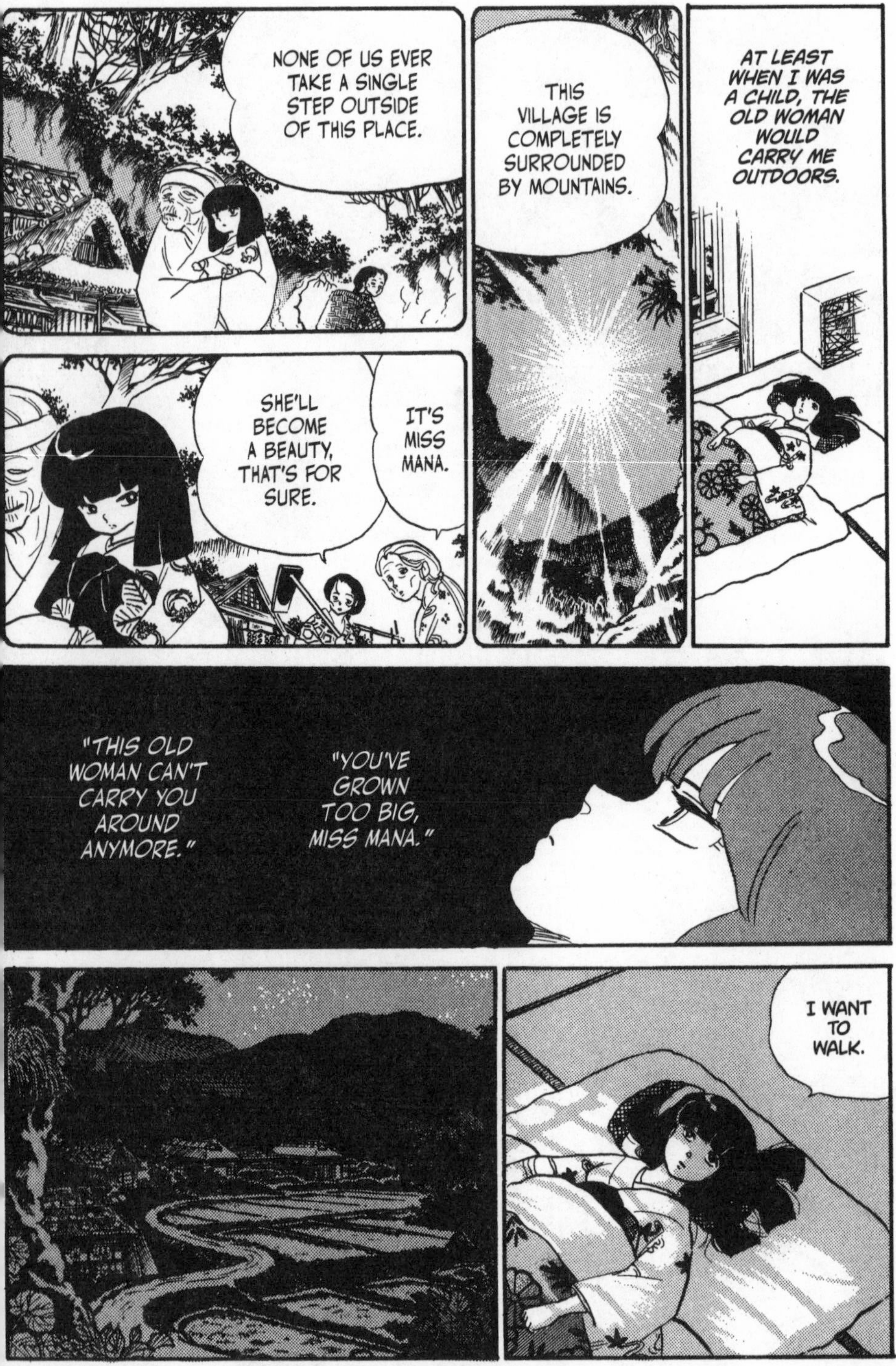
AT LEAST WHEN I WAS A CHILD, THE OLD WOMAN WOULD CARRY ME OUTDOORS.
THIS VILLAGE IS COMPLETELY SURROUNDED BY MOUNTAINS.
NONE OF US EVER TAKE A SINGLE STEP OUTSIDE OF THIS PLACE.
IT'S MISS MANA.
SHE'LL BECOME A BEAUTY, THAT'S FOR SURE.
"YOU'VE GROWN TOO BIG, MISS MANA."
"THIS OLD WOMAN CAN'T CARRY YOU AROUND ANYMORE."
I WANT TO WALK.

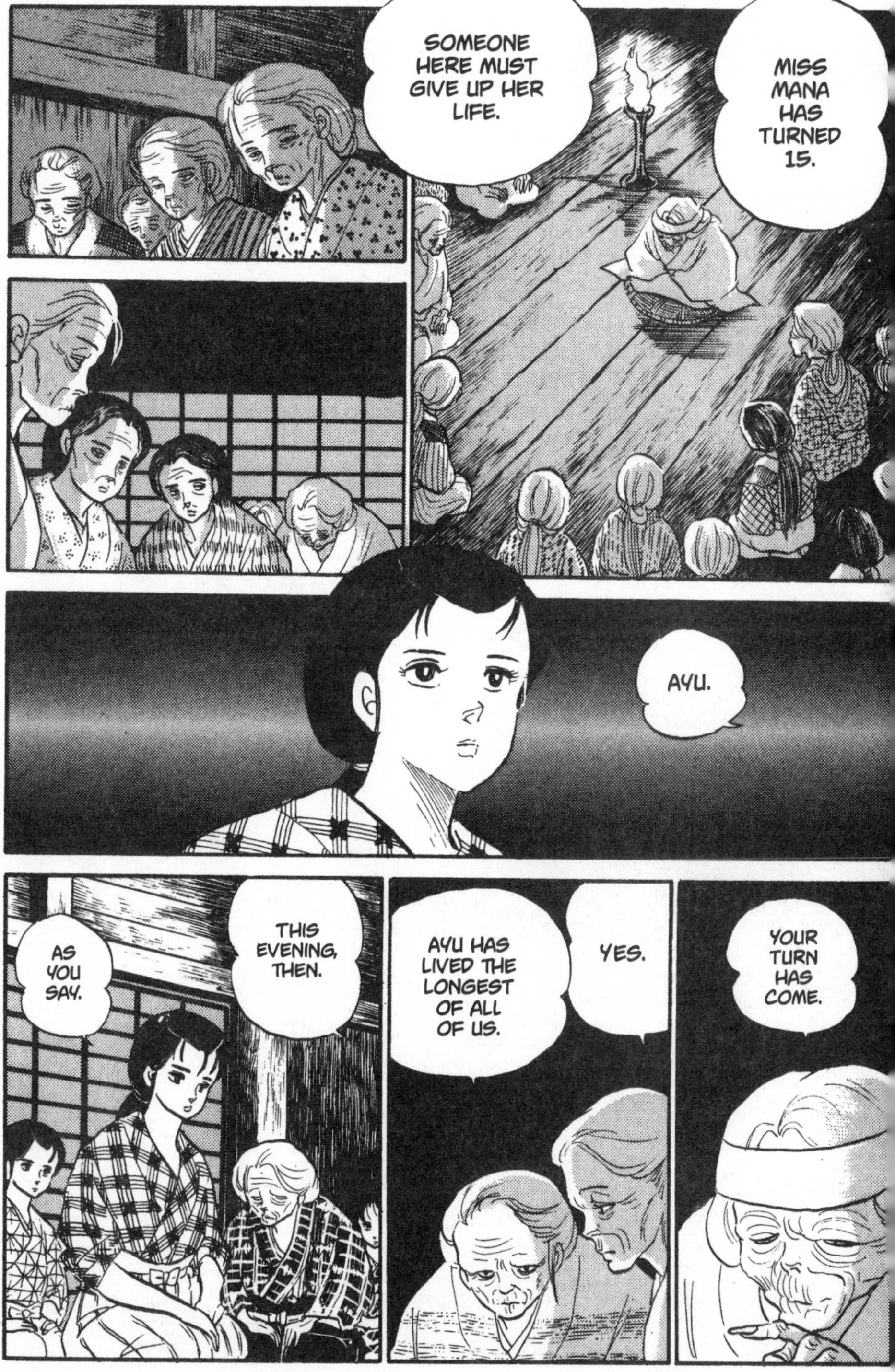
MISS MANA HAS TURNED 15.
SOMEONE HERE MUST GIVE UP HER LIFE.
AYU.
YOUR TURN HAS COME.
YES.
AYU HAS LIVED THE LONGEST OF ALL OF US.
THIS EVENING, THEN.
AS YOU SAY.

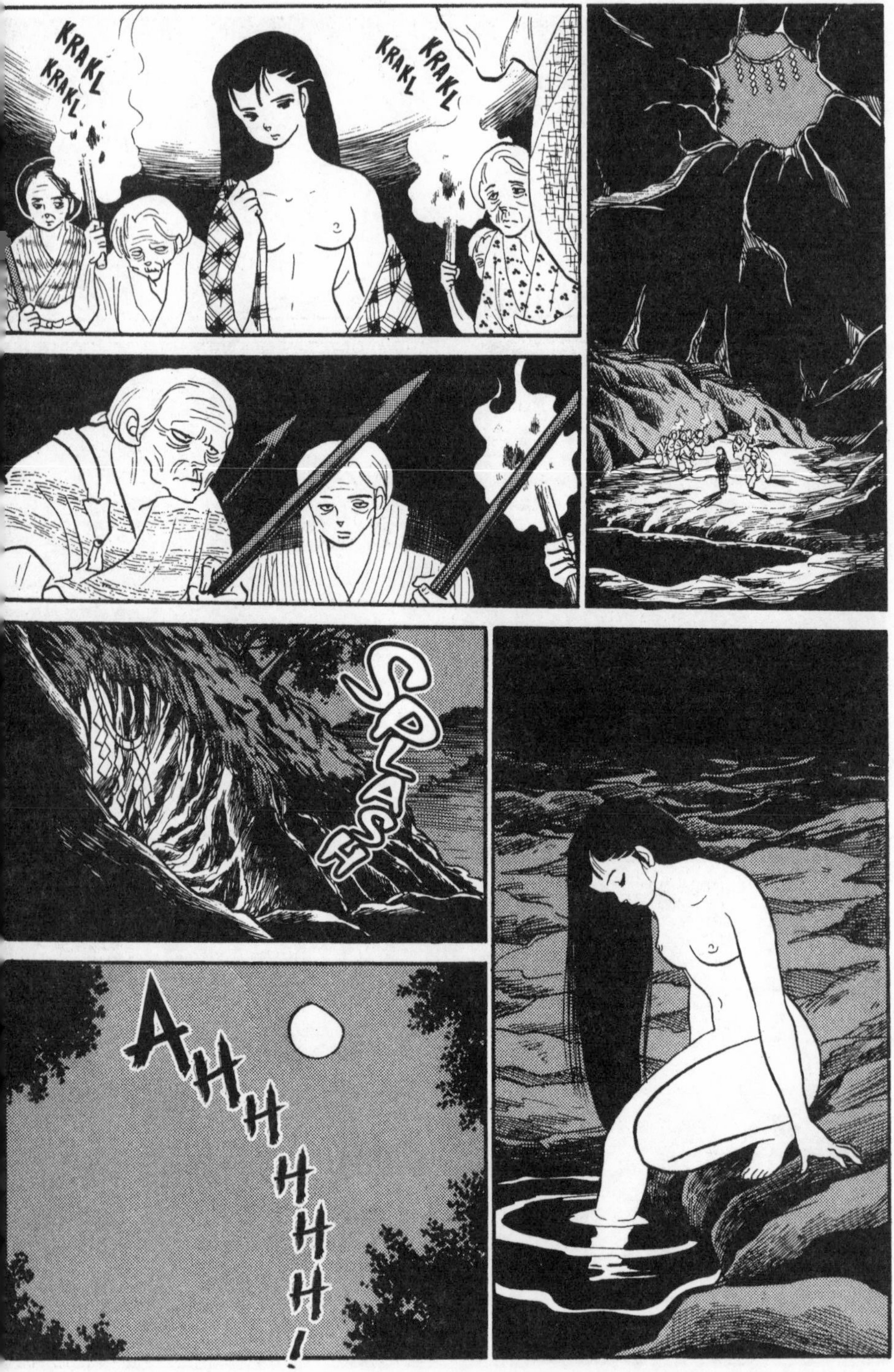
KRAKL KRAKL
KRAKL KRAKL
SPLASH
AHHHHHH!

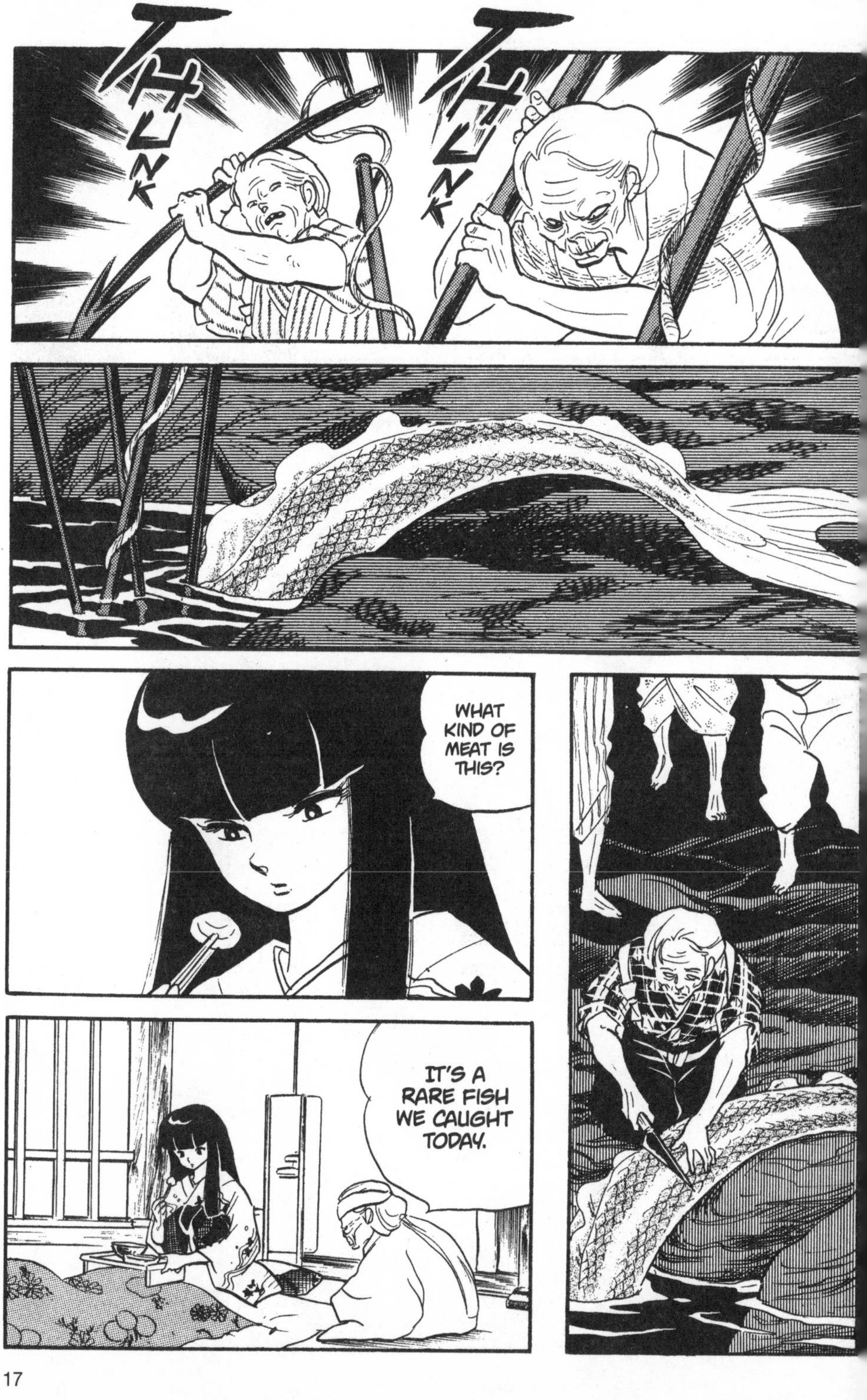
THUNK
THUNK
WHAT KIND OF MEAT IS THIS?
IT'S A RARE FISH WE CAUGHT TODAY.

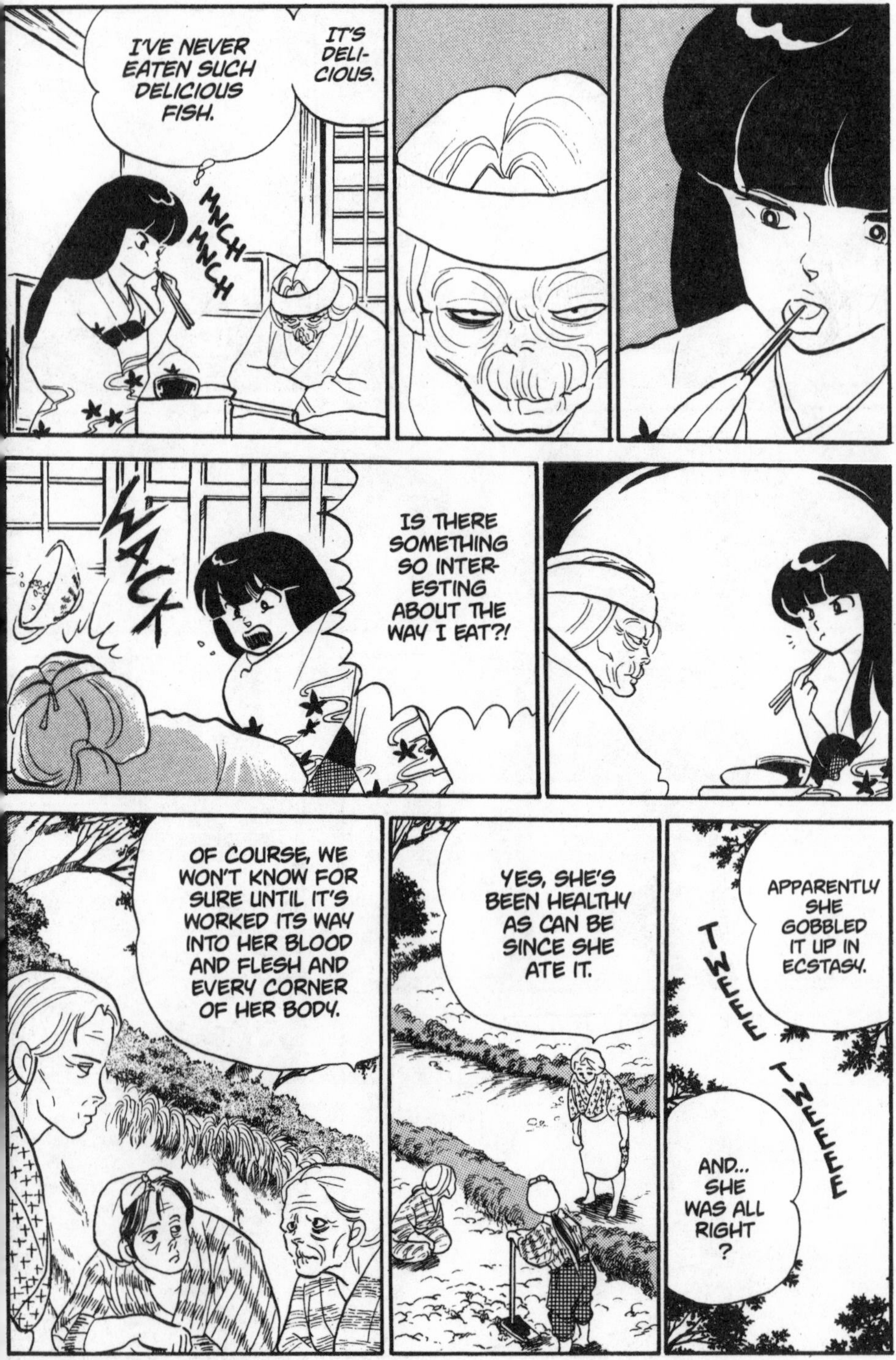
IT'S DELI-CIOUS.
I'VE NEVER EATEN SUCH DELICIOUS FISH.
MNCH MNCH
IS THERE SOMETHING SO INTER-ESTING ABOUT THE WAY I EAT?!
WACK
APPARENTLY SHE GOBBLED IT UP IN ECSTASY.
TWEEE TWEEEE
AND... SHE WAS ALL RIGHT?
YES, SHE'S BEEN HEALTHY AS CAN BE SINCE SHE ATE IT.
OF COURSE, WE WON'T KNOW FOR SURE UNTIL IT'S WORKED ITS WAY INTO HER BLOOD AND FLESH AND EVERY CORNER OF HER BODY.

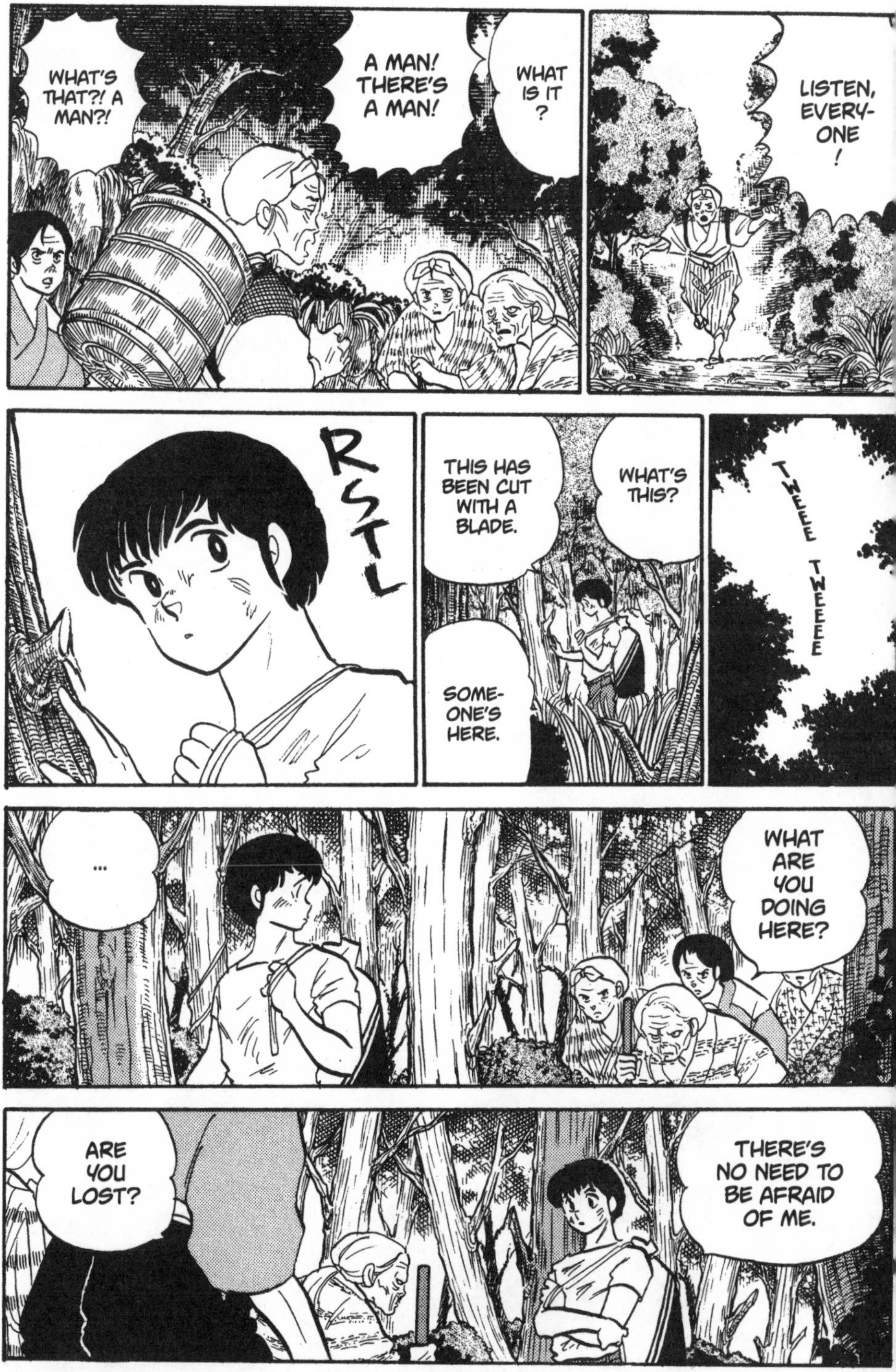
LISTEN, EVERY-ONE!
WHAT IS IT?
A MAN! THERE'S A MAN!
WHAT'S THAT?! A MAN?!
TWEEE TWEEEE
WHAT'S THIS?
THIS HAS BEEN CUT WITH A BLADE.
SOME-ONE'S HERE.
RSTL
WHAT ARE YOU DOING HERE?
...
THERE'S NO NEED TO BE AFRAID OF ME.
ARE YOU LOST?

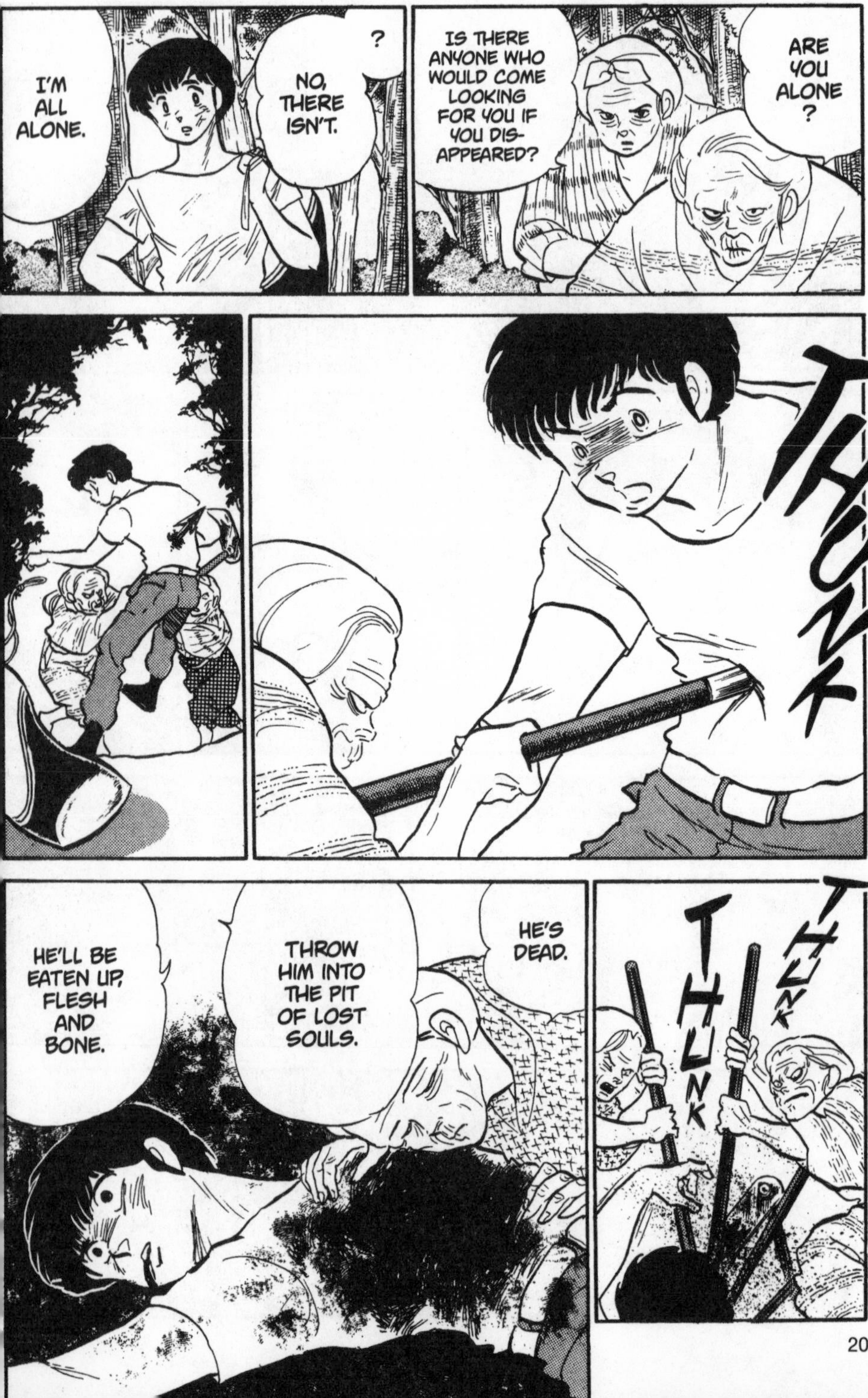
ARE YOU ALONE ?
IS THERE ANYONE WHO WOULD COME LOOKING FOR YOU IF YOU DIS-APPEARED?
?
NO, THERE ISN'T.
I'M ALL ALONE.
THUNK
THUNK
THUNK
HE'S DEAD.
THROW HIM INTO THE PIT OF LOST SOULS.
HE'LL BE EATEN UP, FLESH AND BONE.

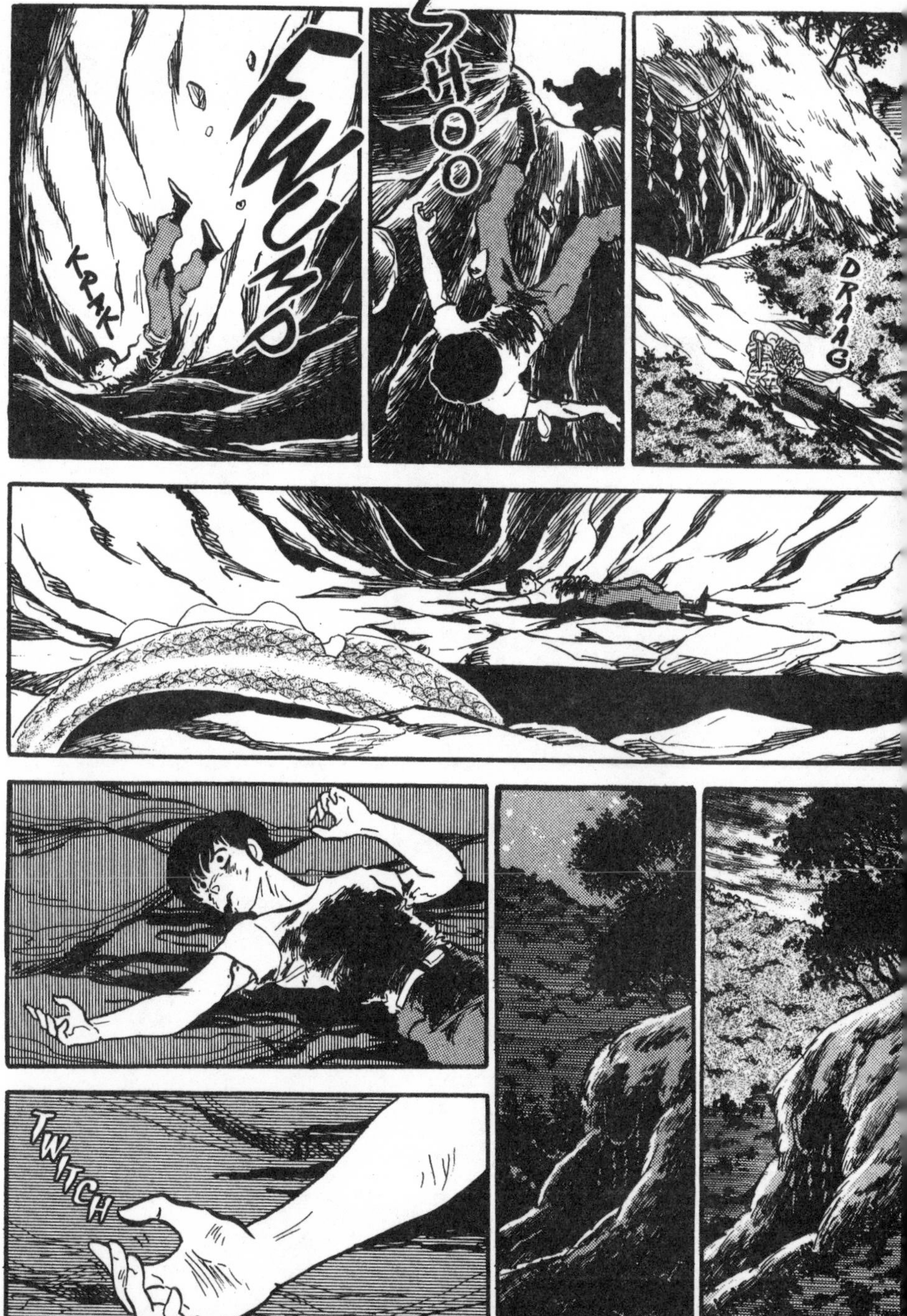
DRAAG
SHOOO
FWUMP
KRAK
TWITCH

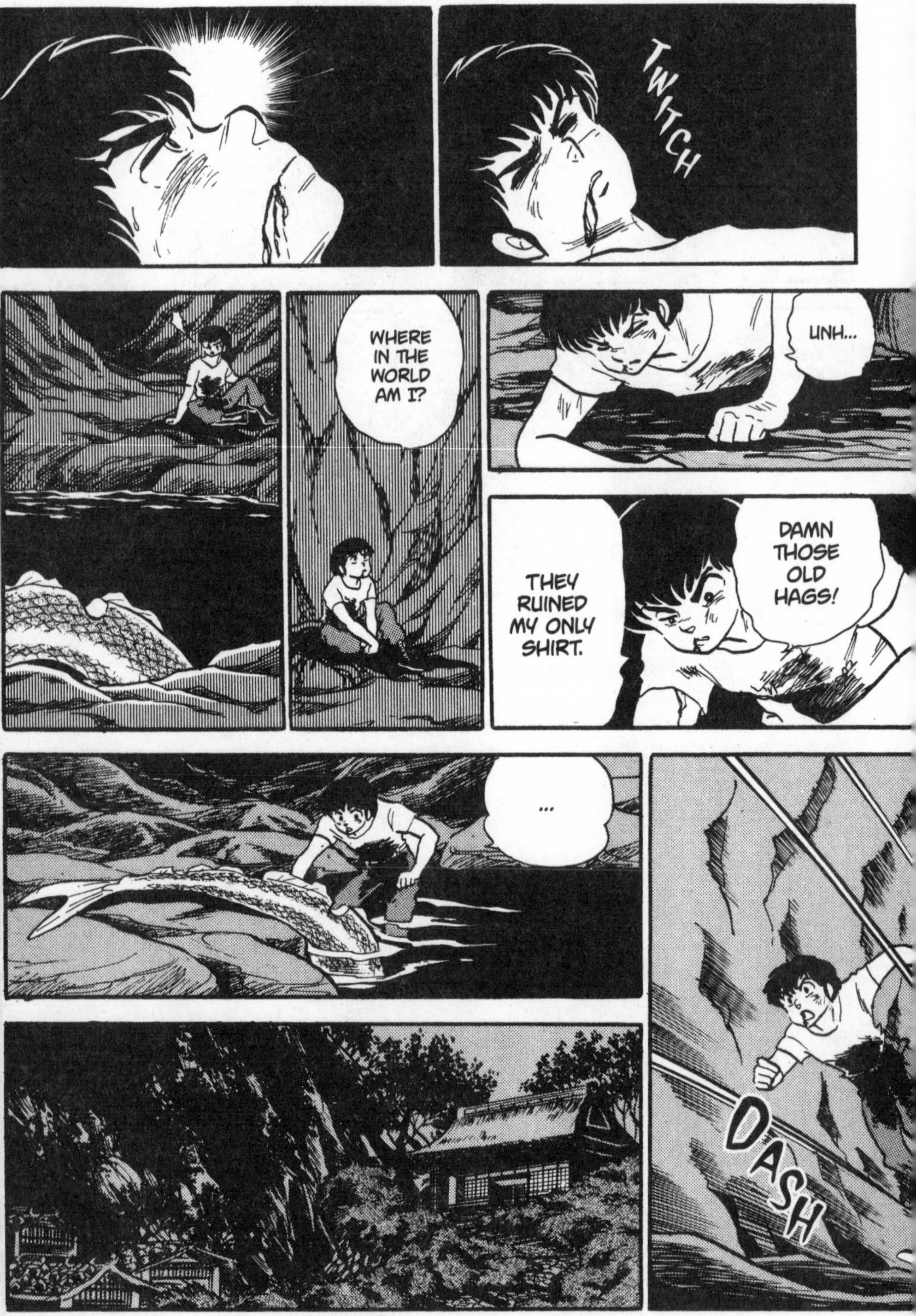
TWITCH
UNH...
DAMN THOSE OLD HAGS!
THEY RUINED MY ONLY SHIRT.
WHERE IN THE WORLD AM I?
DASH
...

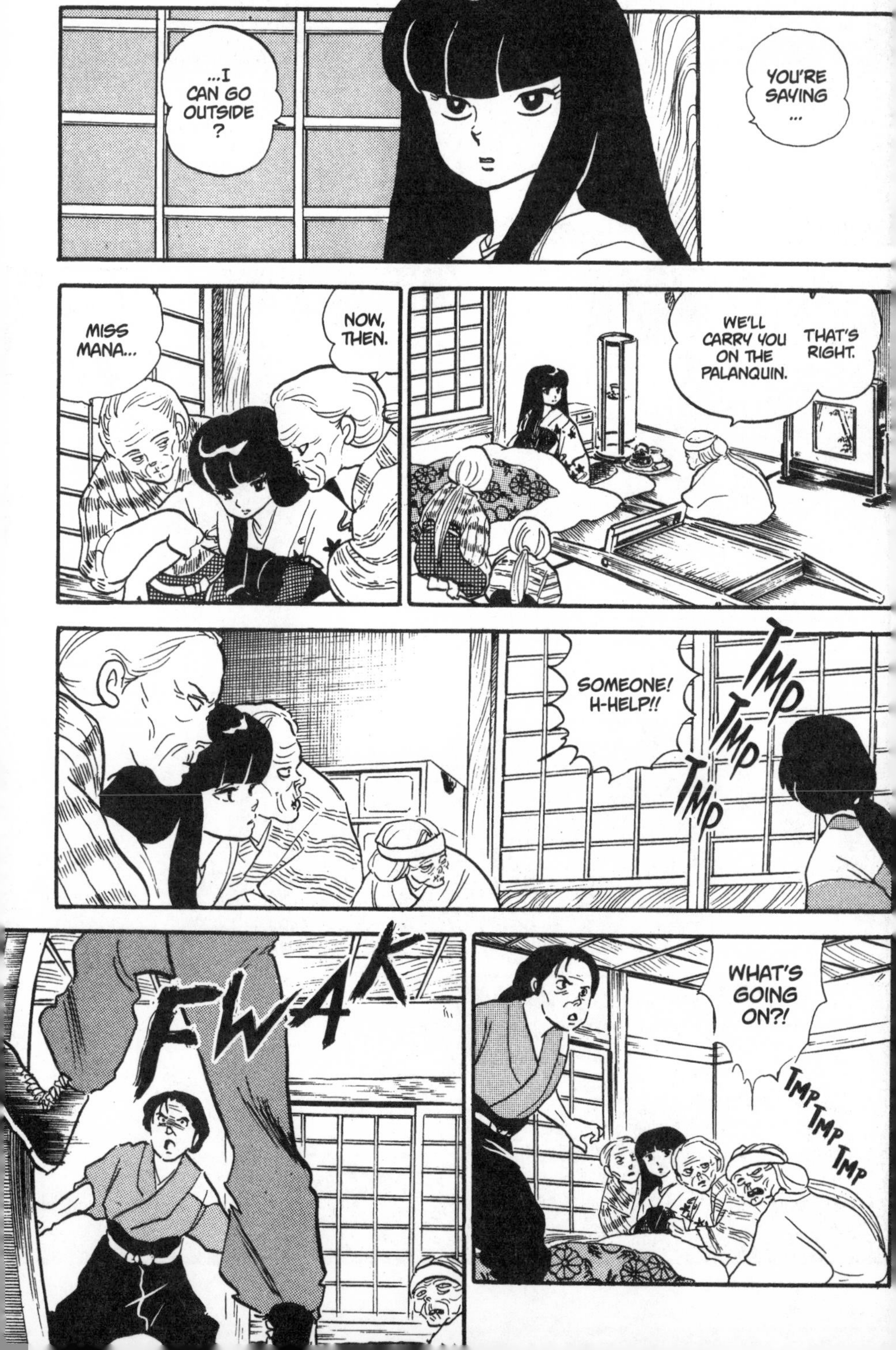
YOU'RE SAYING ...
...I CAN GO OUTSIDE ?
THAT'S RIGHT.
WE'LL CARRY YOU ON THE PALANQUIN.
NOW, THEN.
MISS MANA...
TMP TMP TMP TMP
SOMEONE! H-HELP!!
WHAT'S GOING ON?!
TMP TMP TMP TMP
FWAK

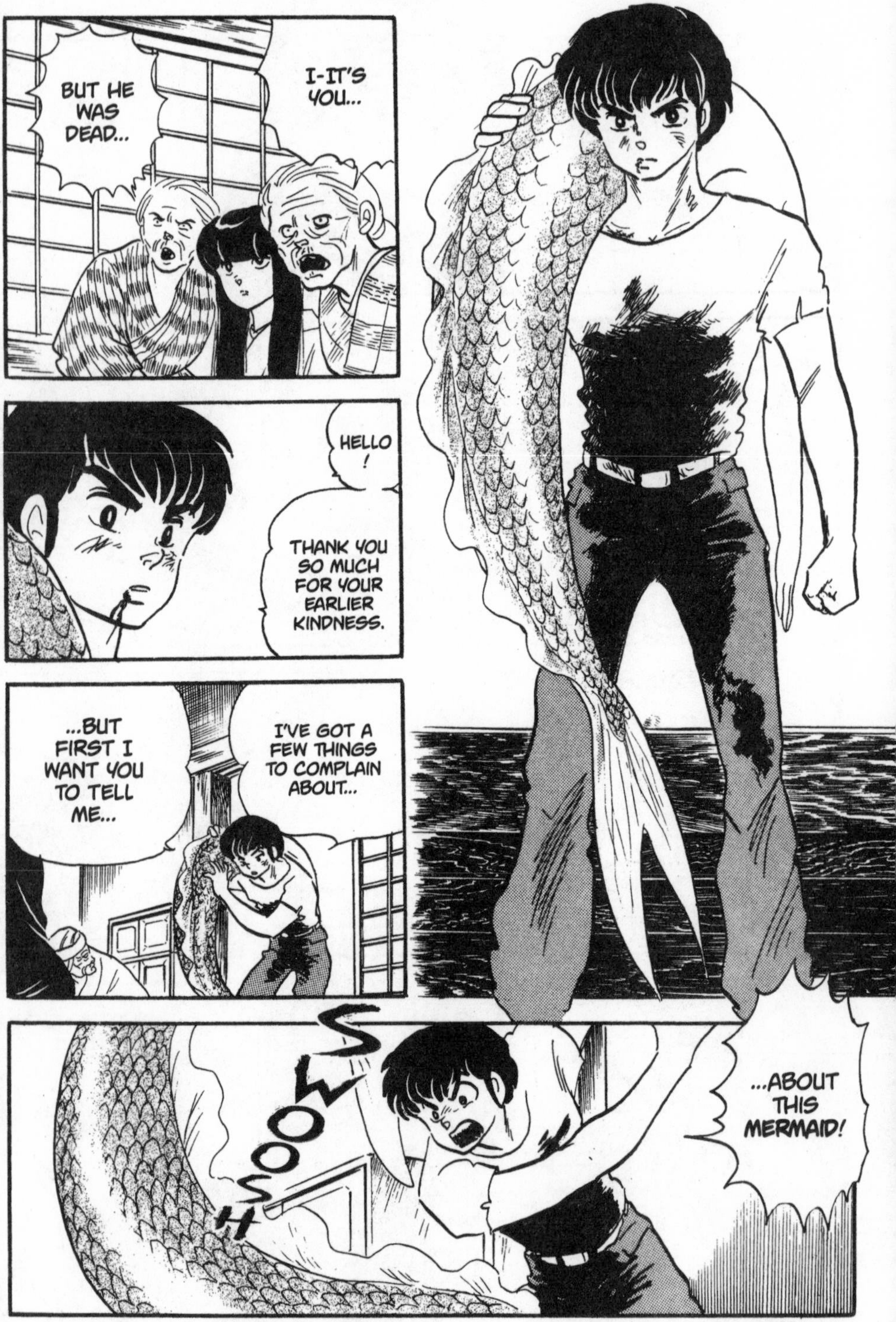
I-IT'S YOU...
BUT HE WAS DEAD...
HELLO!
THANK YOU SO MUCH FOR YOUR EARLIER KINDNESS.
I'VE GOT A FEW THINGS TO COMPLAIN ABOUT...
...BUT FIRST I WANT YOU TO TELL ME...
...ABOUT THIS MERMAID!
SWOOSH

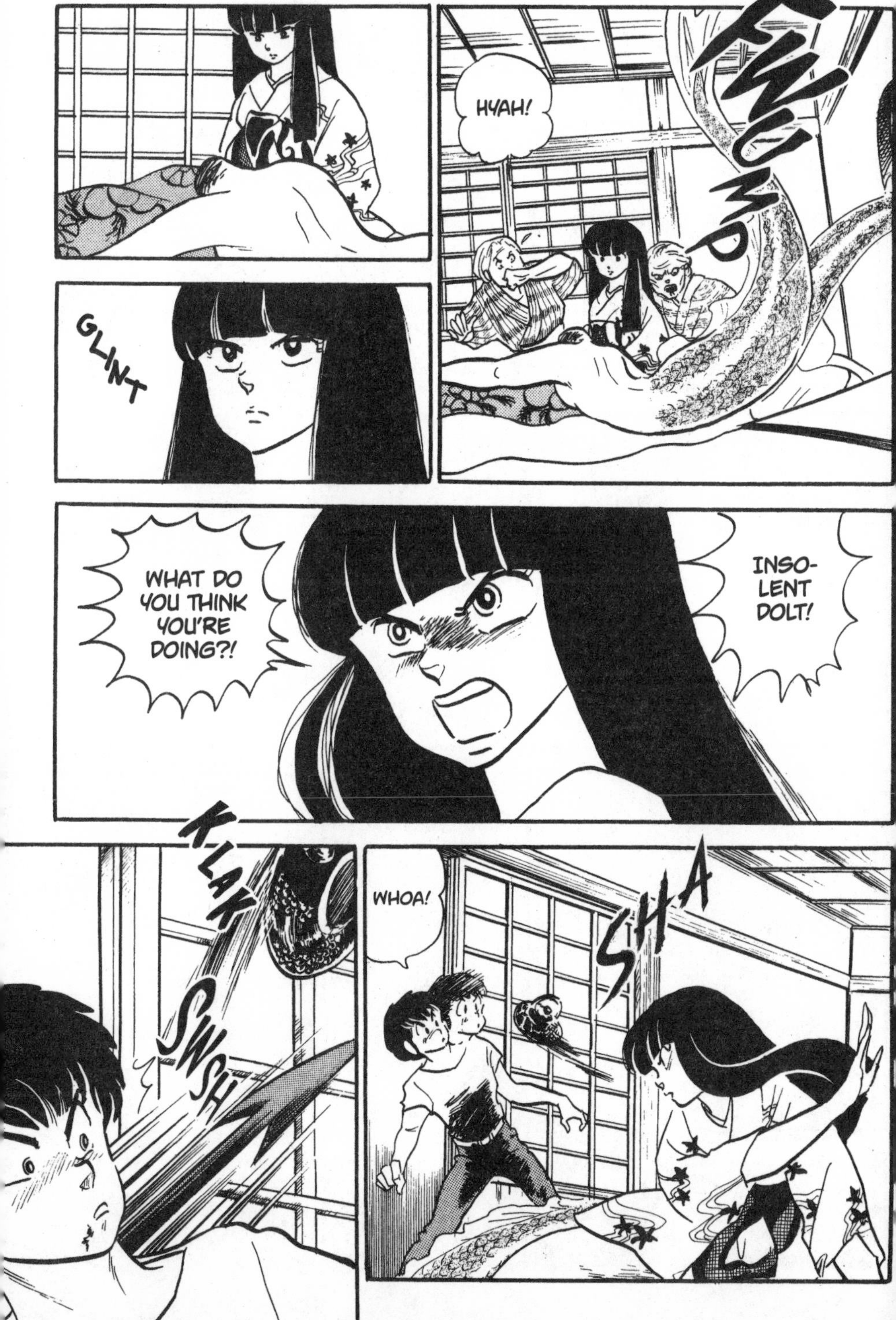
FWUMP
HYAH!
GLINT
INSO-LENT DOLT!
WHAT DO YOU THINK YOU'RE DOING?!
SHA
WHOA!
KLAK
SWSH

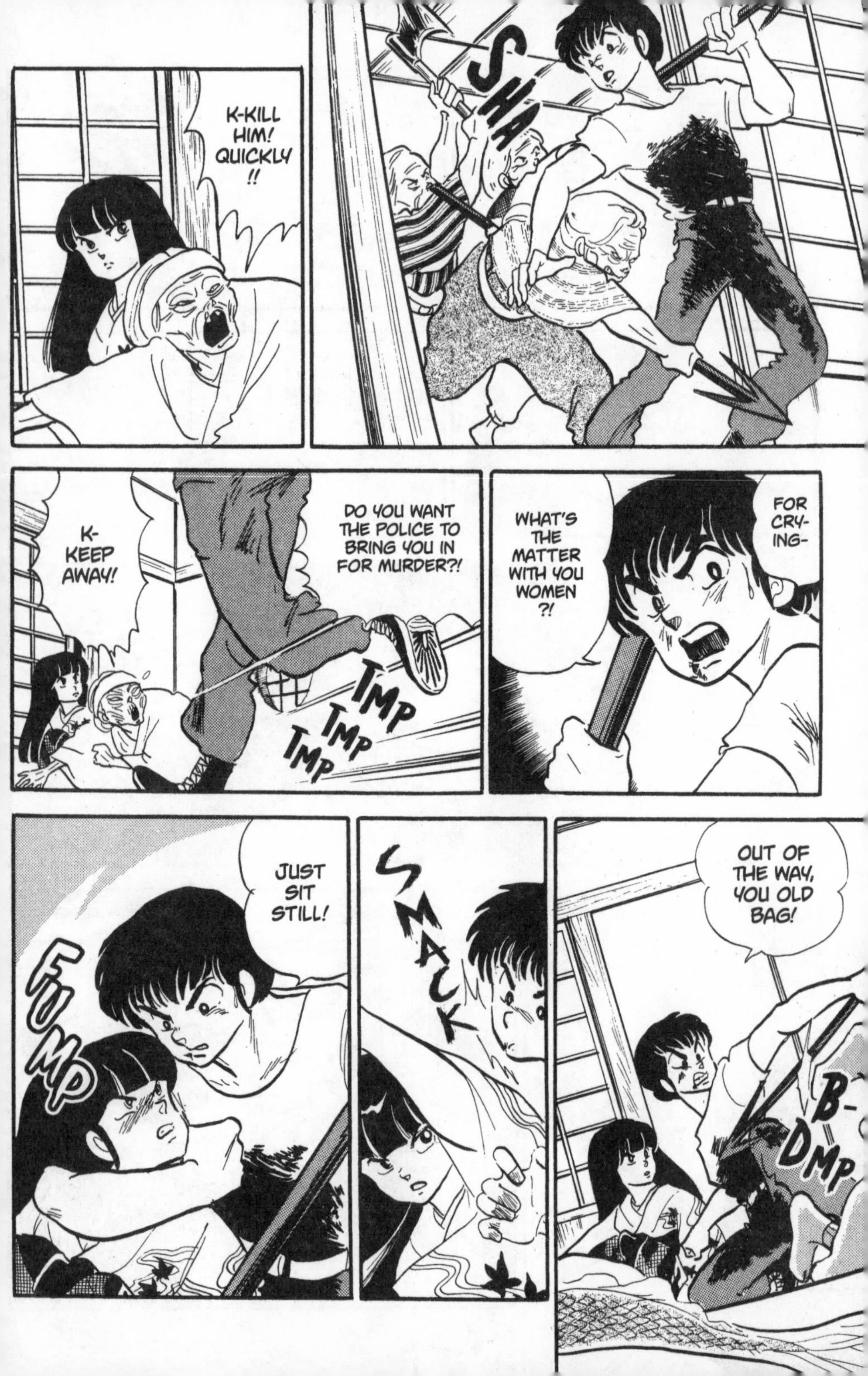
SHA
K-KILL HIM! QUICKLY!!
FOR CRY- ING-
WHAT'S THE MATTER WITH YOU WOMEN?!
DO YOU WANT THE POLICE TO BRING YOU IN FOR MURDER?!
K- KEEP AWAY!
TMP TMP TMP
OUT OF THE WAY, YOU OLD BAG!
B-DMP
SMACK
JUST SIT STILL!
FUMP

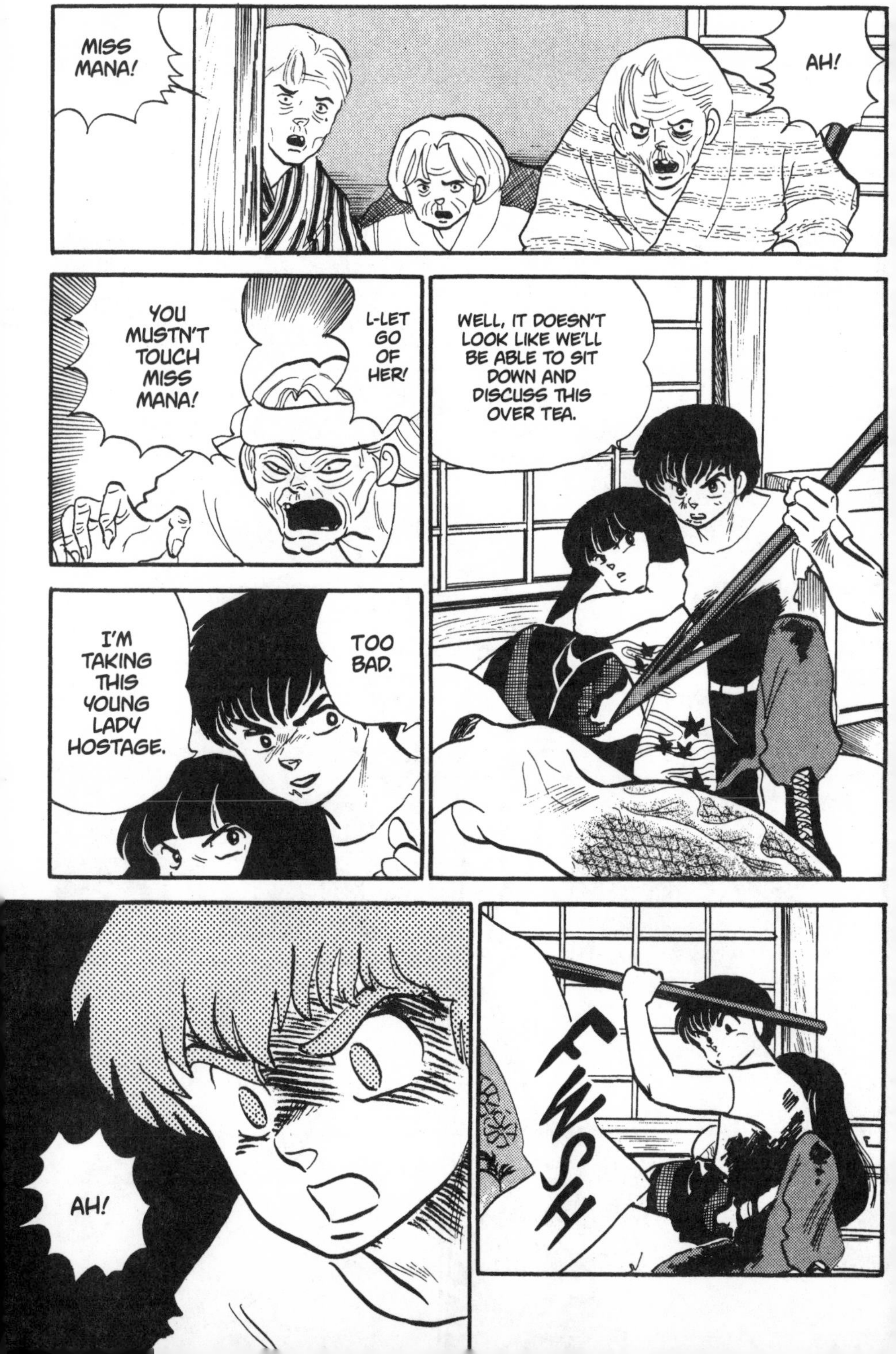
AH!
MISS MANA!
WELL, IT DOESN'T LOOK LIKE WE'LL BE ABLE TO SIT DOWN AND DISCUSS THIS OVER TEA.
L-LET GO OF HER!
YOU MUSTN'T TOUCH MISS MANA!
TOO BAD.
I'M TAKING THIS YOUNG LADY HOSTAGE.
FWSH
AH!

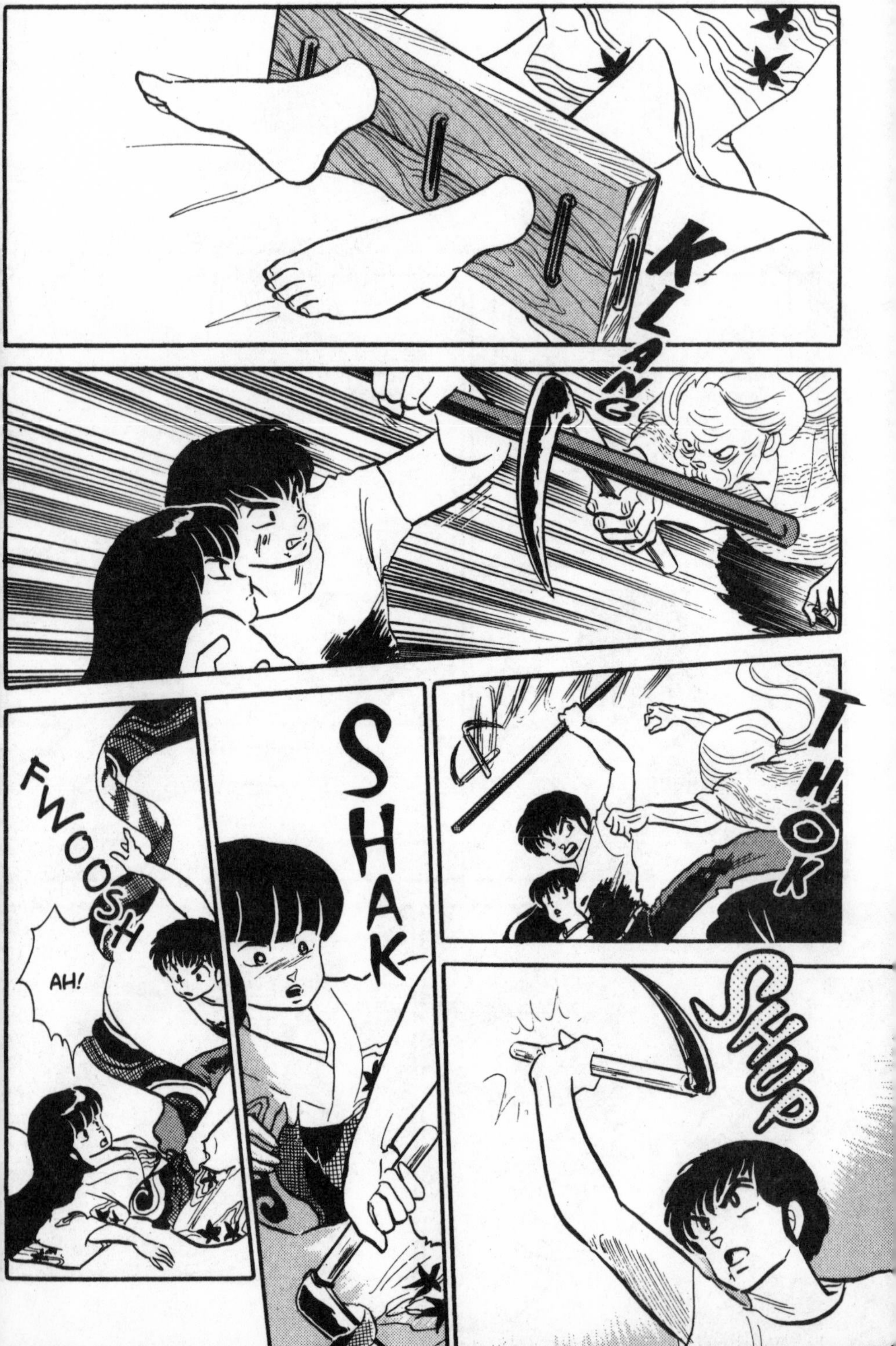
KLANG
THOK
SHUP
SHAK
FWOOSH
AH!

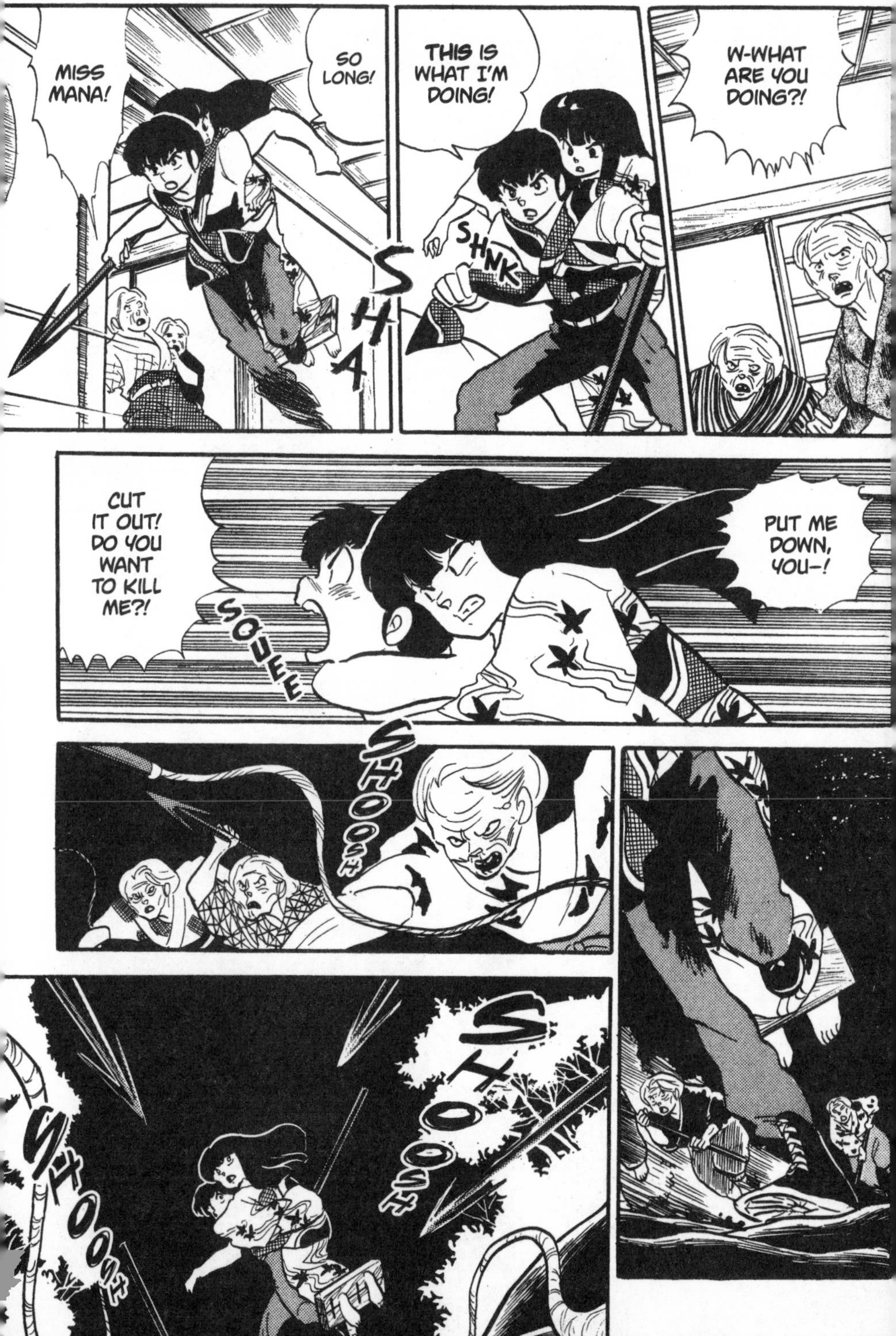
W-WHAT ARE YOU DOING?!
THIS IS WHAT I'M DOING!
SHNK
SO LONG!
MISS MANA!
SHA
PUT ME DOWN, YOU-!
CUT IT OUT! DO YOU WANT TO KILL ME?!
SQUEEE
SHOOOSH
SHOOSH
SHOOOSH

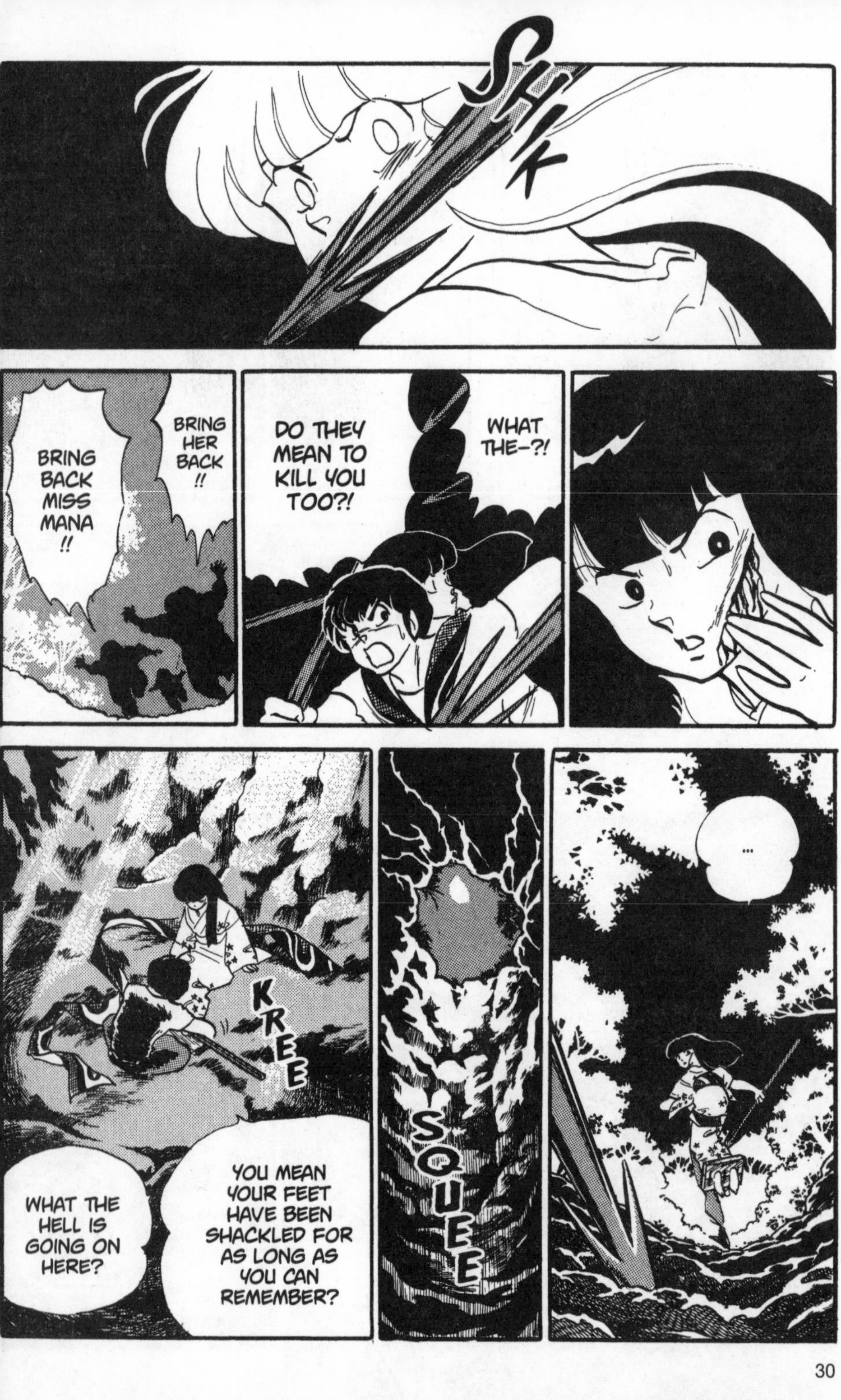
SHIK
WHAT THE-?!
DO THEY MEAN TO KILL YOU TOO?!
BRING HER BACK !!
BRING BACK MISS MANA !!
...
SQUEE
KREE
YOU MEAN YOUR FEET HAVE BEEN SHACKLED FOR AS LONG AS YOU CAN REMEMBER?
WHAT THE HELL IS GOING ON HERE?

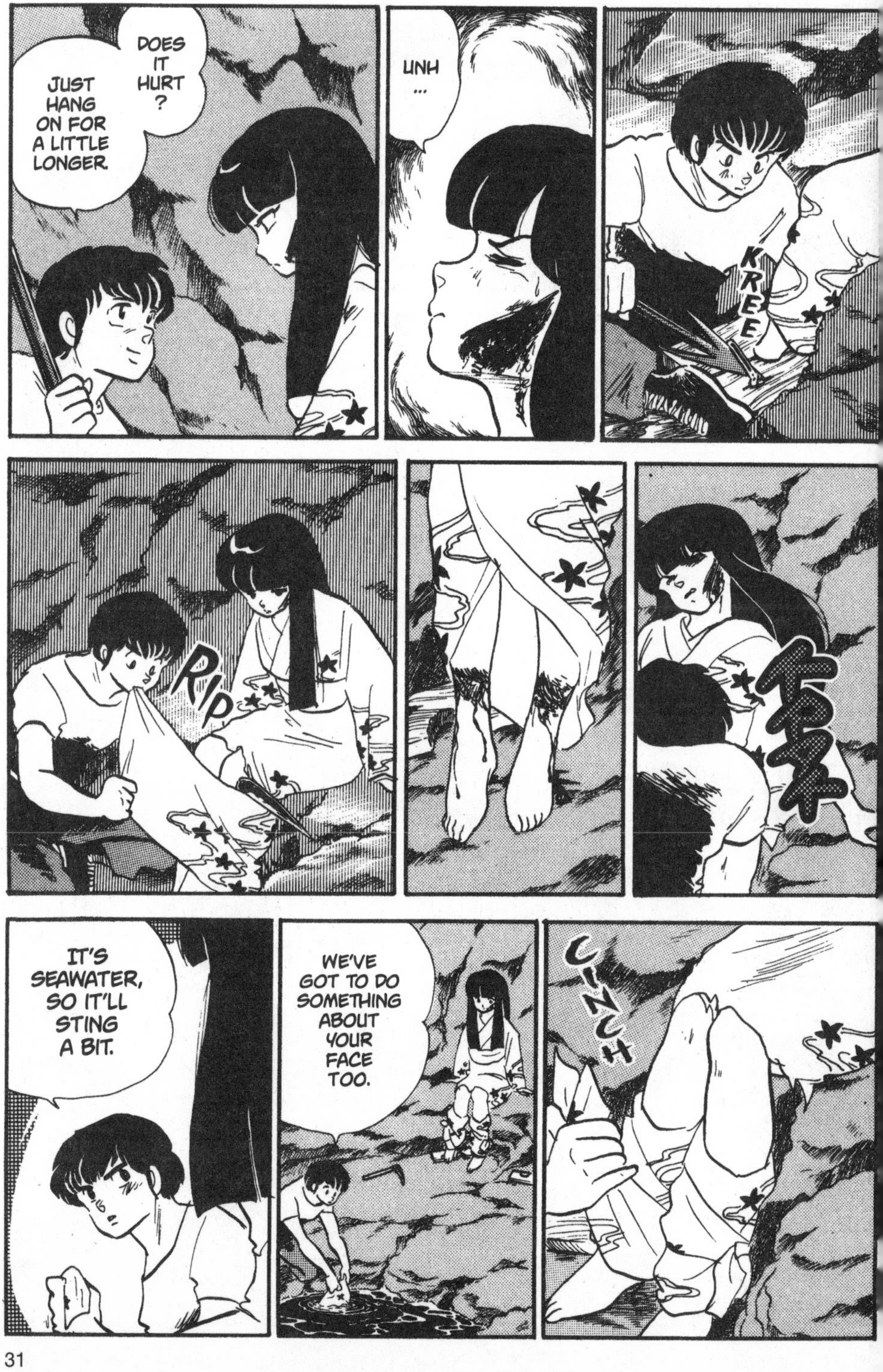
KREE
UNH ...
DOES IT HURT?
JUST HANG ON FOR A LITTLE LONGER.
RIP
CINCH
WE'VE GOT TO DO SOMETHING ABOUT YOUR FACE TOO.
IT'S SEAWATER, SO IT'LL STING A BIT.

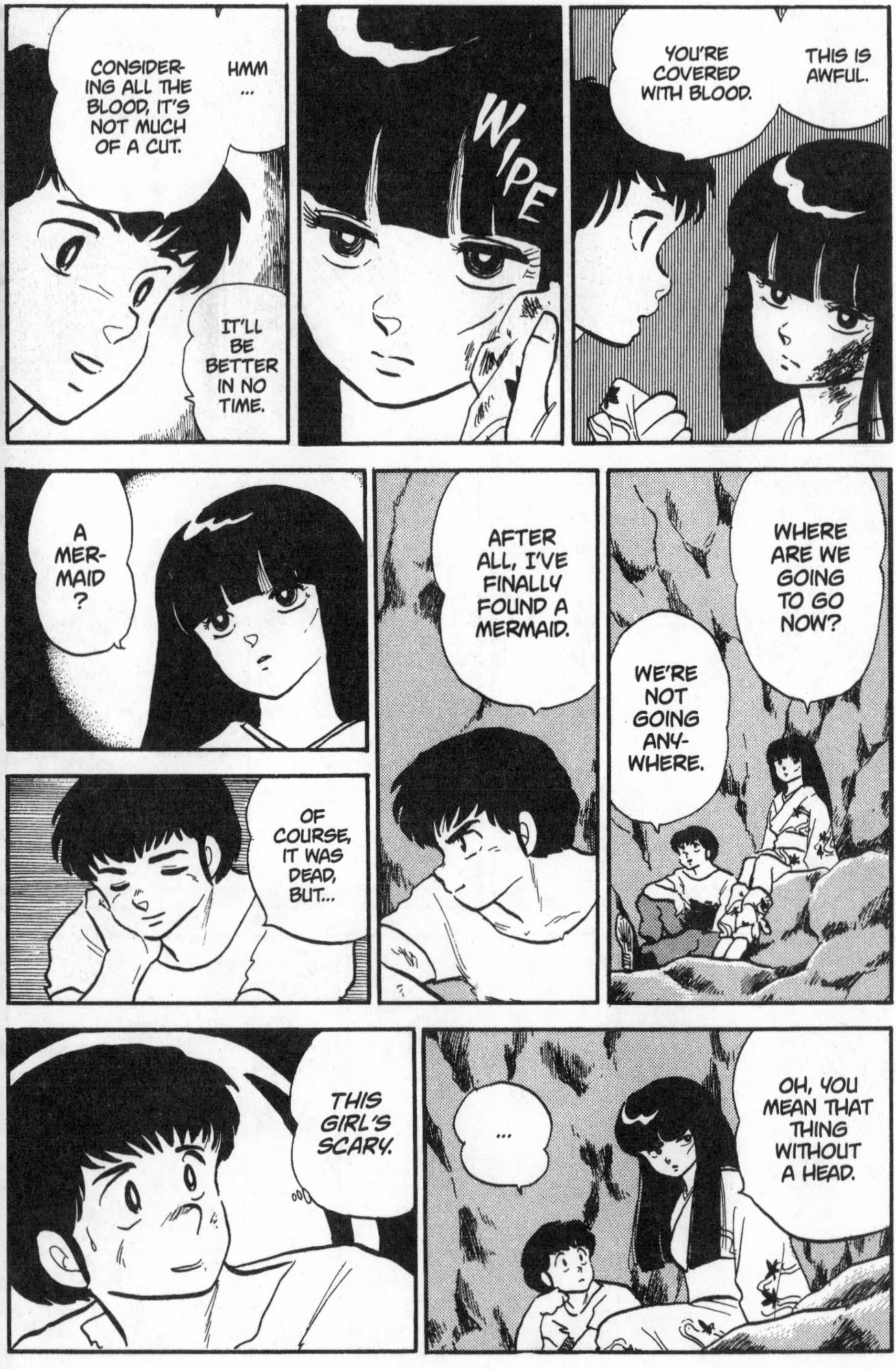
THIS IS AWFUL.
YOU'RE COVERED WITH BLOOD.
WIPE
HMM ...
CONSIDER-ING ALL THE BLOOD, IT'S NOT MUCH OF A CUT.
IT'LL BE BETTER IN NO TIME.
WHERE ARE WE GOING TO GO NOW?
WE'RE NOT GOING ANY-WHERE.
AFTER ALL, I'VE FINALLY FOUND A MERMAID.
A MER-MAID ?
OF COURSE, IT WAS DEAD, BUT...
OH, YOU MEAN THAT THING WITHOUT A HEAD.
...
THIS GIRL'S SCARY.

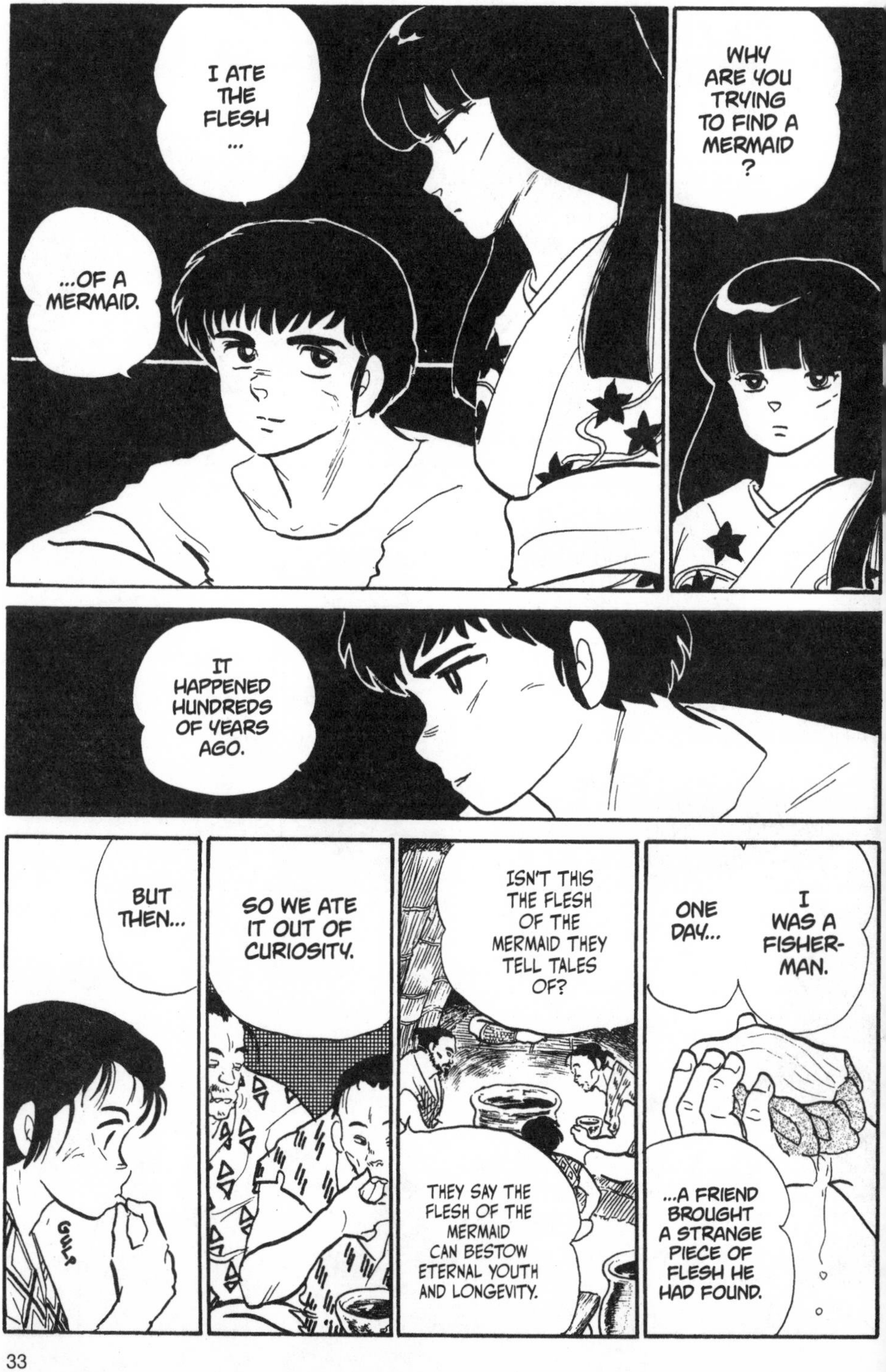
WHY ARE YOU TRYING TO FIND A MERMAID?
I ATE THE FLESH ...
...OF A MERMAID.
IT HAPPENED HUNDREDS OF YEARS AGO.
I WAS A FISHERMAN.
ONE DAY...
...A FRIEND BROUGHT A STRANGE PIECE OF FLESH HE HAD FOUND.
ISN'T THIS THE FLESH OF THE MERMAID THEY TELL TALES OF?
THEY SAY THE FLESH OF THE MERMAID CAN BESTOW ETERNAL YOUTH AND LONGEVITY.
SO WE ATE IT OUT OF CURIOSITY.
BUT THEN...
GULP

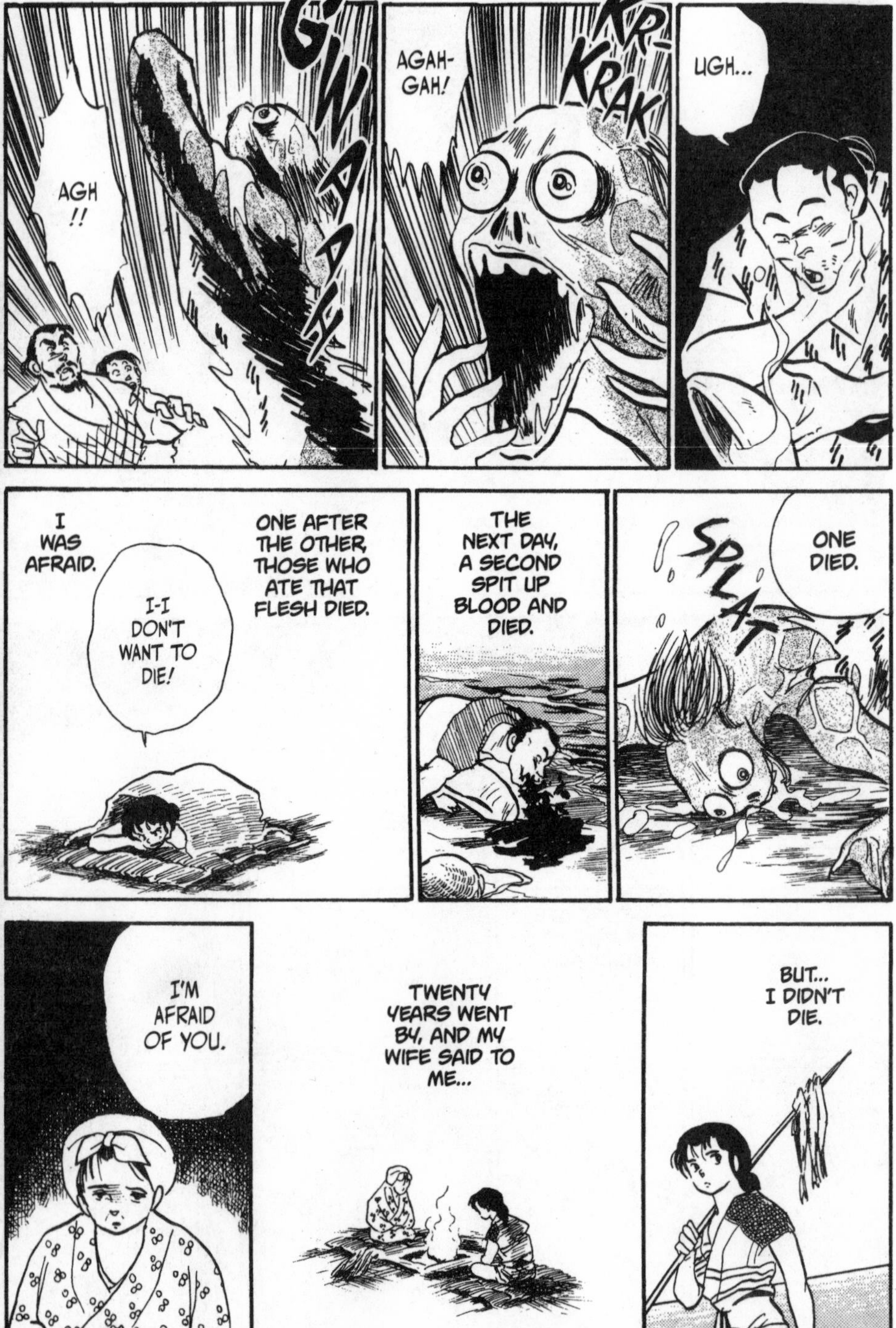
UGH...
KR-KRAK
AGAH-GAH!
GWAAAH
AGH !!
ONE DIED.
SPLAT
THE NEXT DAY, A SECOND SPIT UP BLOOD AND DIED.
ONE AFTER THE OTHER, THOSE WHO ATE THAT FLESH DIED.
I-I DON'T WANT TO DIE!
I WAS AFRAID.
BUT... I DIDN'T DIE.
TWENTY YEARS WENT BY, AND MY WIFE SAID TO ME...
I'M AFRAID OF YOU.

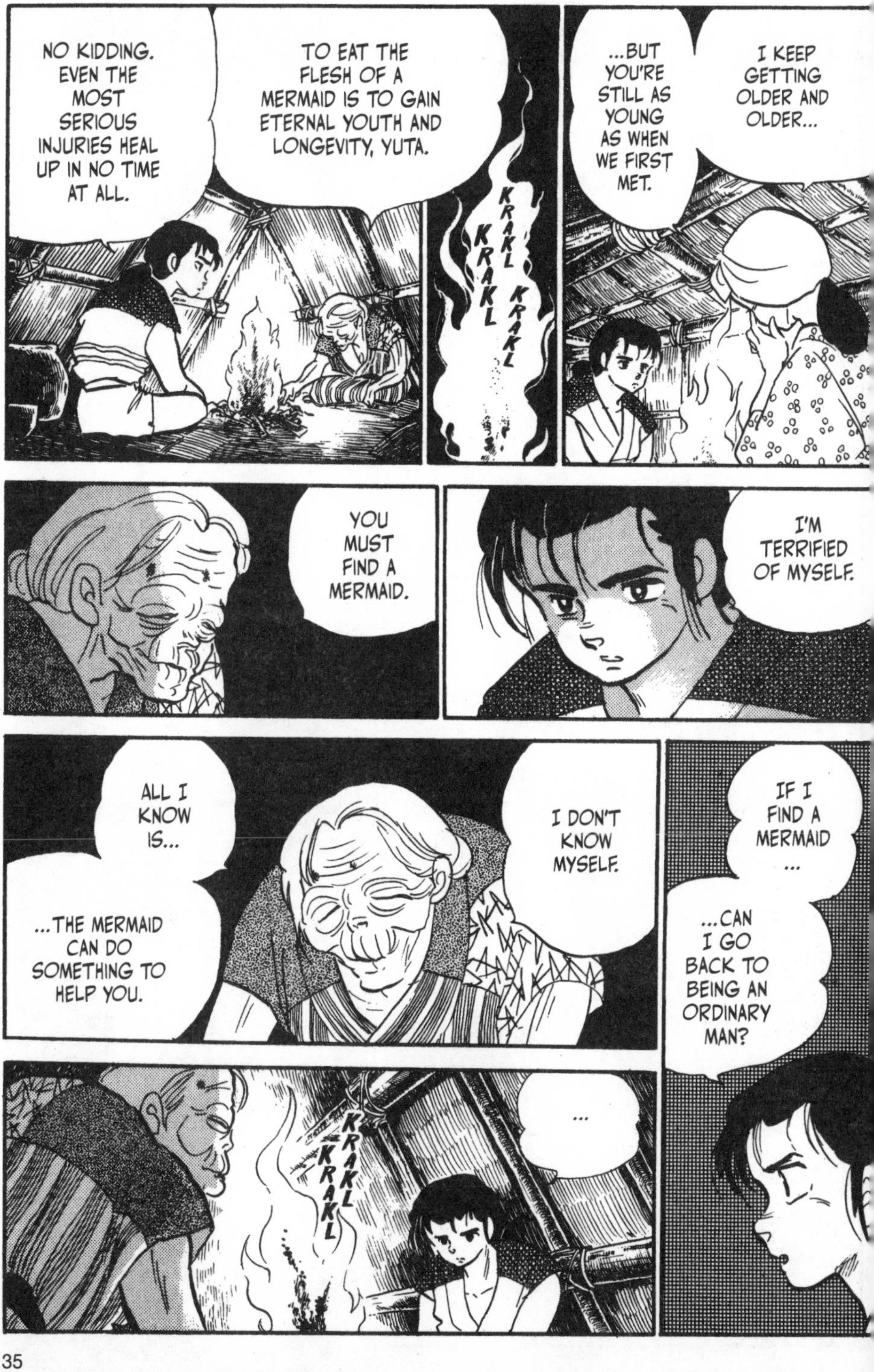
I KEEP GETTING OLDER AND OLDER...
...BUT YOU'RE STILL AS YOUNG AS WHEN WE FIRST MET.
KRAKL KRAKL KRAKL
TO EAT THE FLESH OF A MERMAID IS TO GAIN ETERNAL YOUTH AND LONGEVITY, YUTA.
NO KIDDING. EVEN THE MOST SERIOUS INJURIES HEAL UP IN NO TIME AT ALL.
I'M TERRIFIED OF MYSELF.
YOU MUST FIND A MERMAID.
IF I FIND A MERMAID ...
...CAN I GO BACK TO BEING AN ORDINARY MAN?
I DON'T KNOW MYSELF.
ALL I KNOW IS...
...THE MERMAID CAN DO SOMETHING TO HELP YOU.
...
KRAKL KRAKL

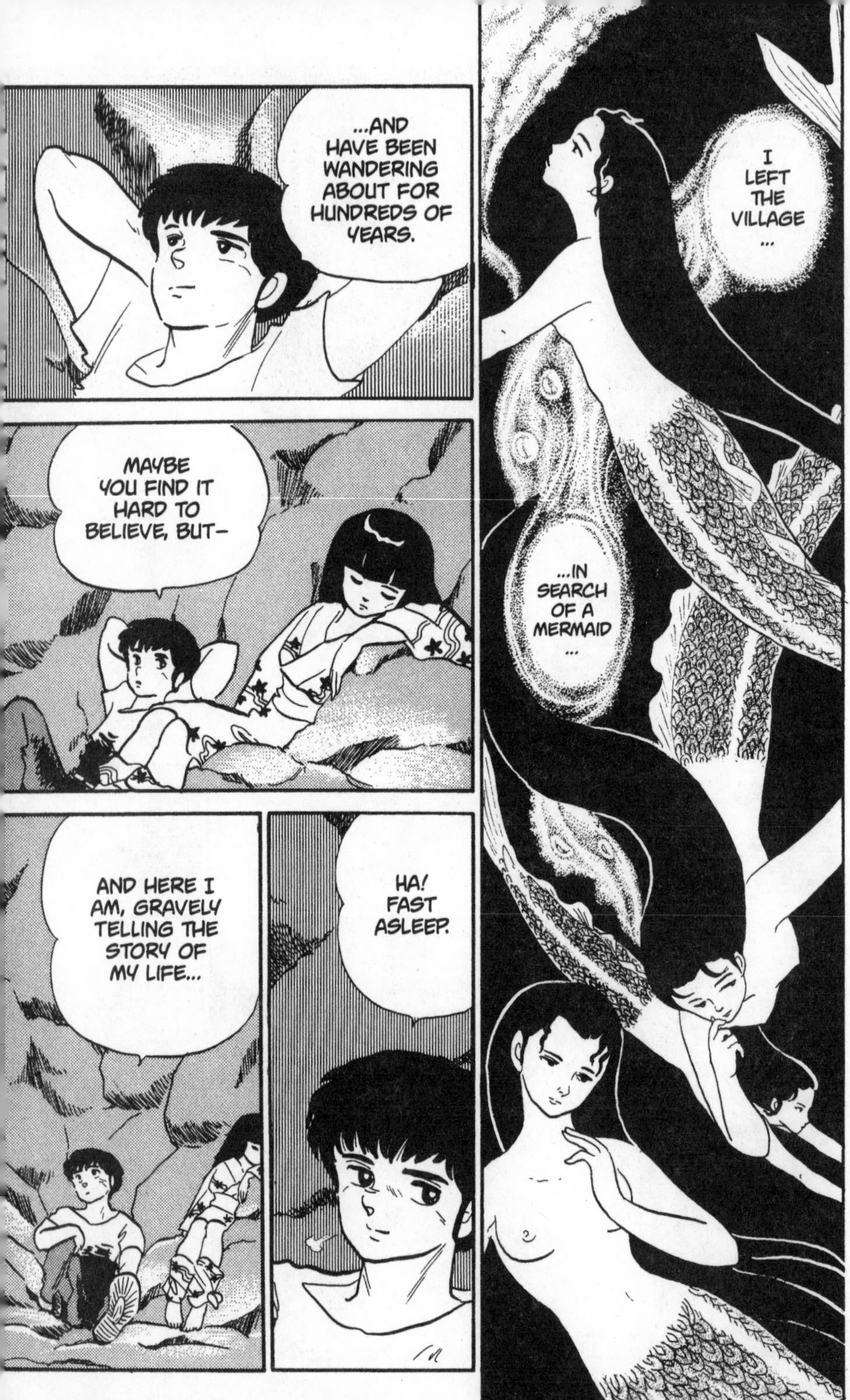
I LEFT THE VILLAGE ...
...IN SEARCH OF A MERMAID ...
...AND HAVE BEEN WANDERING ABOUT FOR HUNDREDS OF YEARS.
MAYBE YOU FIND IT HARD TO BELIEVE, BUT-
HA! FAST ASLEEP.
AND HERE I AM, GRAVELY TELLING THE STORY OF MY LIFE...

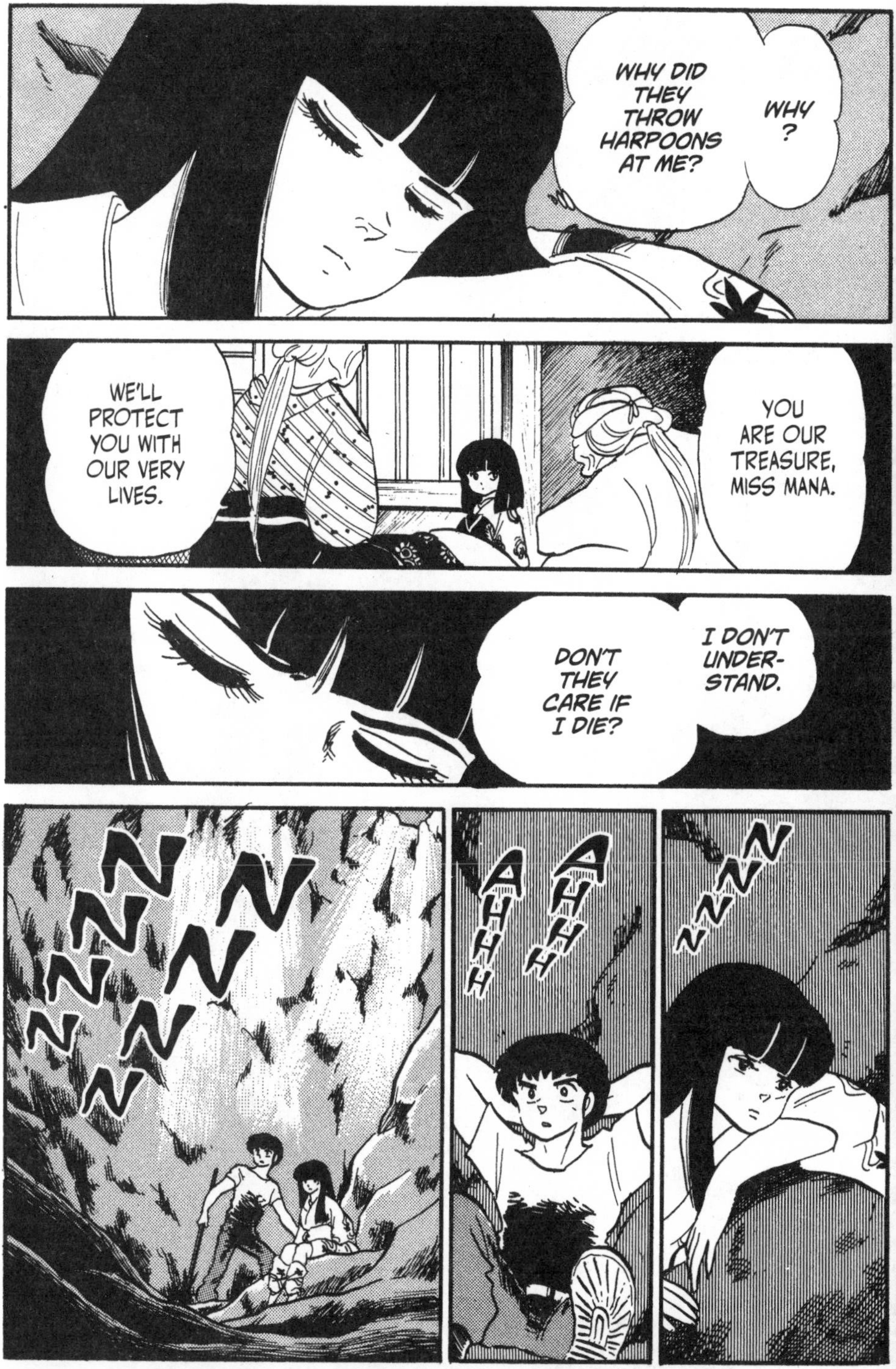
WHY ?
WHY DID THEY THROW HARPOONS AT ME?
YOU ARE OUR TREASURE, MISS MANA.
WE'LL PROTECT YOU WITH OUR VERY LIVES.
I DON'T UNDER-STAND.
DON'T THEY CARE IF I DIE?
NNNN
AHHHH
AHHHHH
NNNN
NNNN

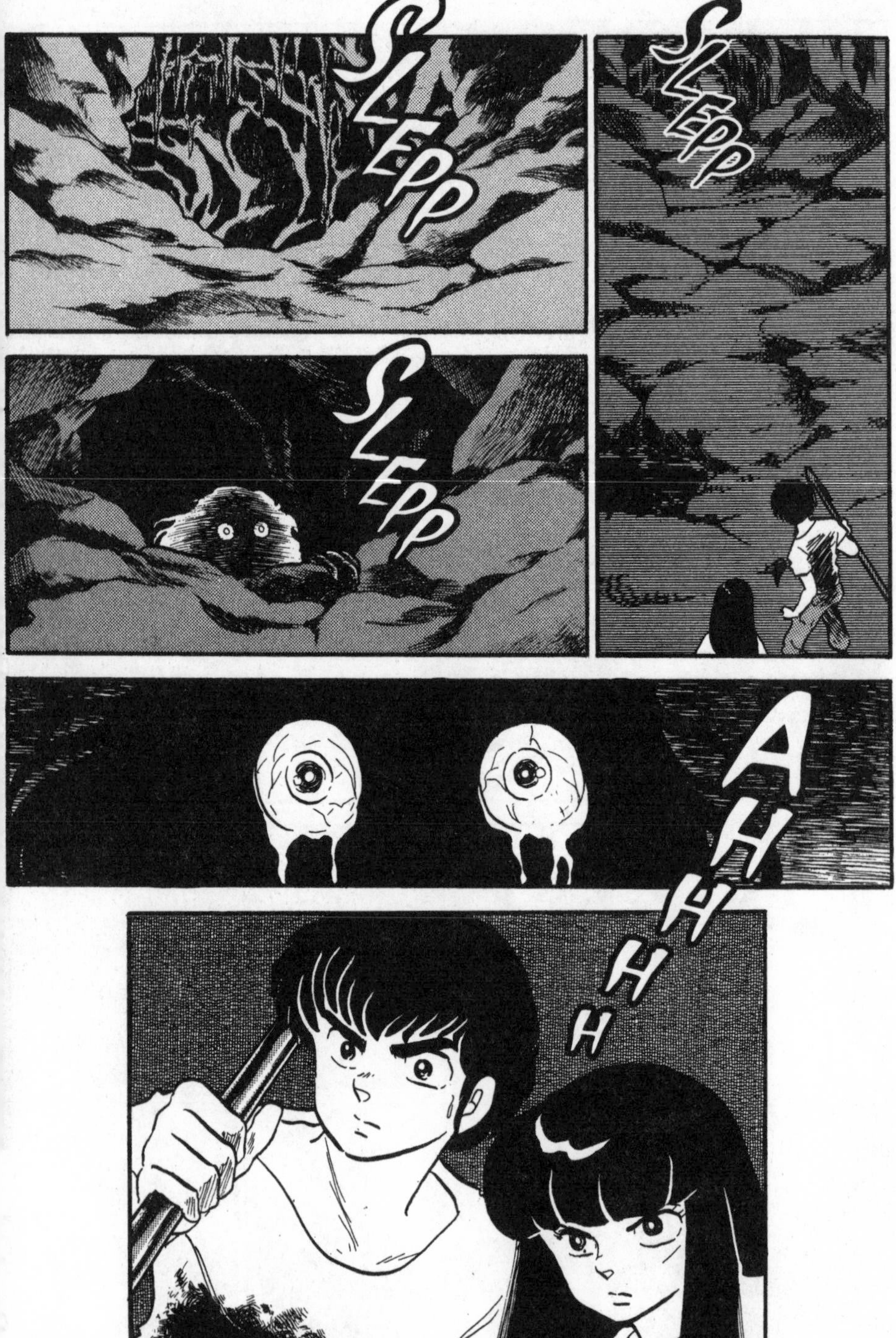
SLEPP
SLEPP
SLEPP
AHHHHH

Chapter 2: A Mermaid Never Smiles, Part 2

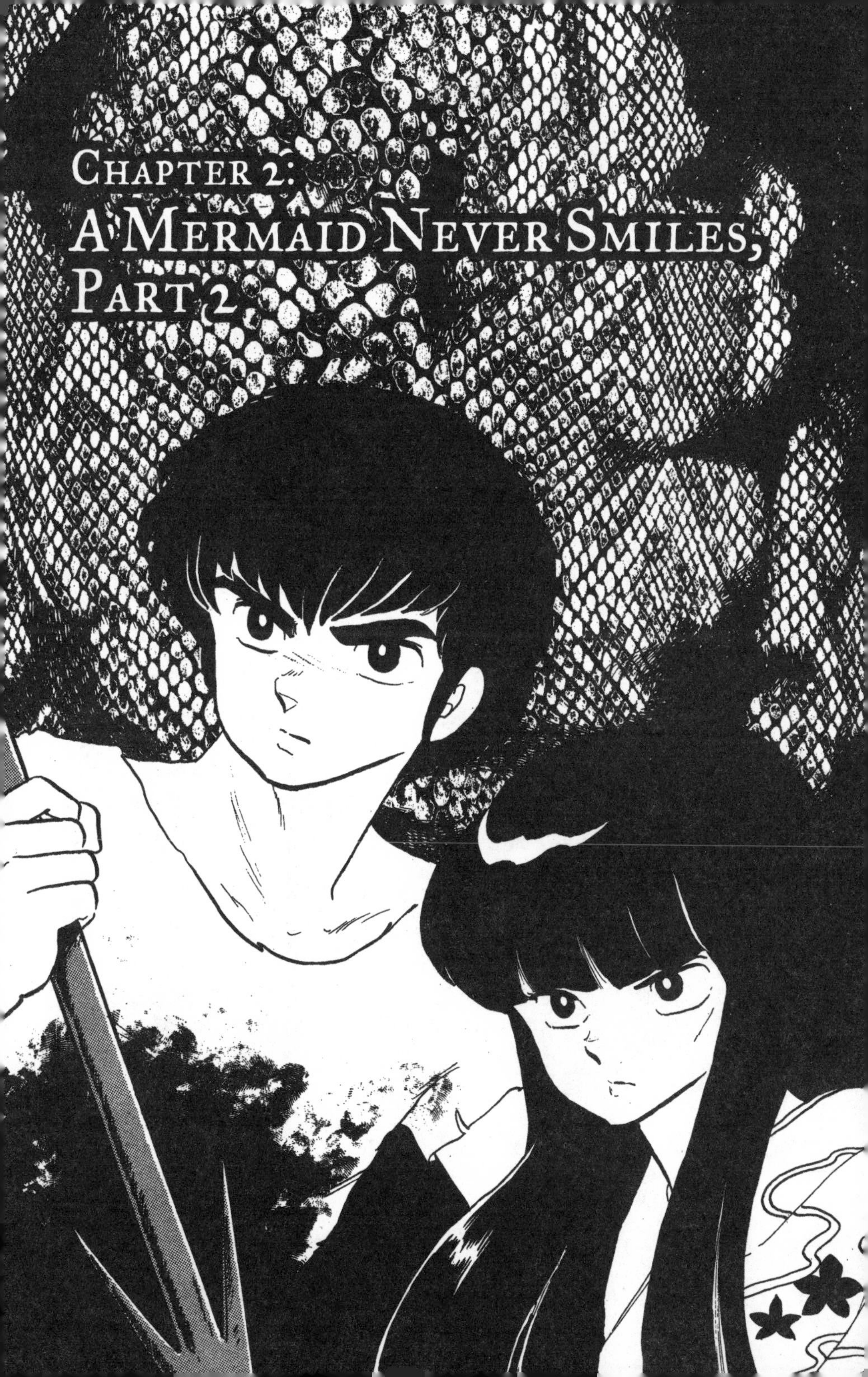

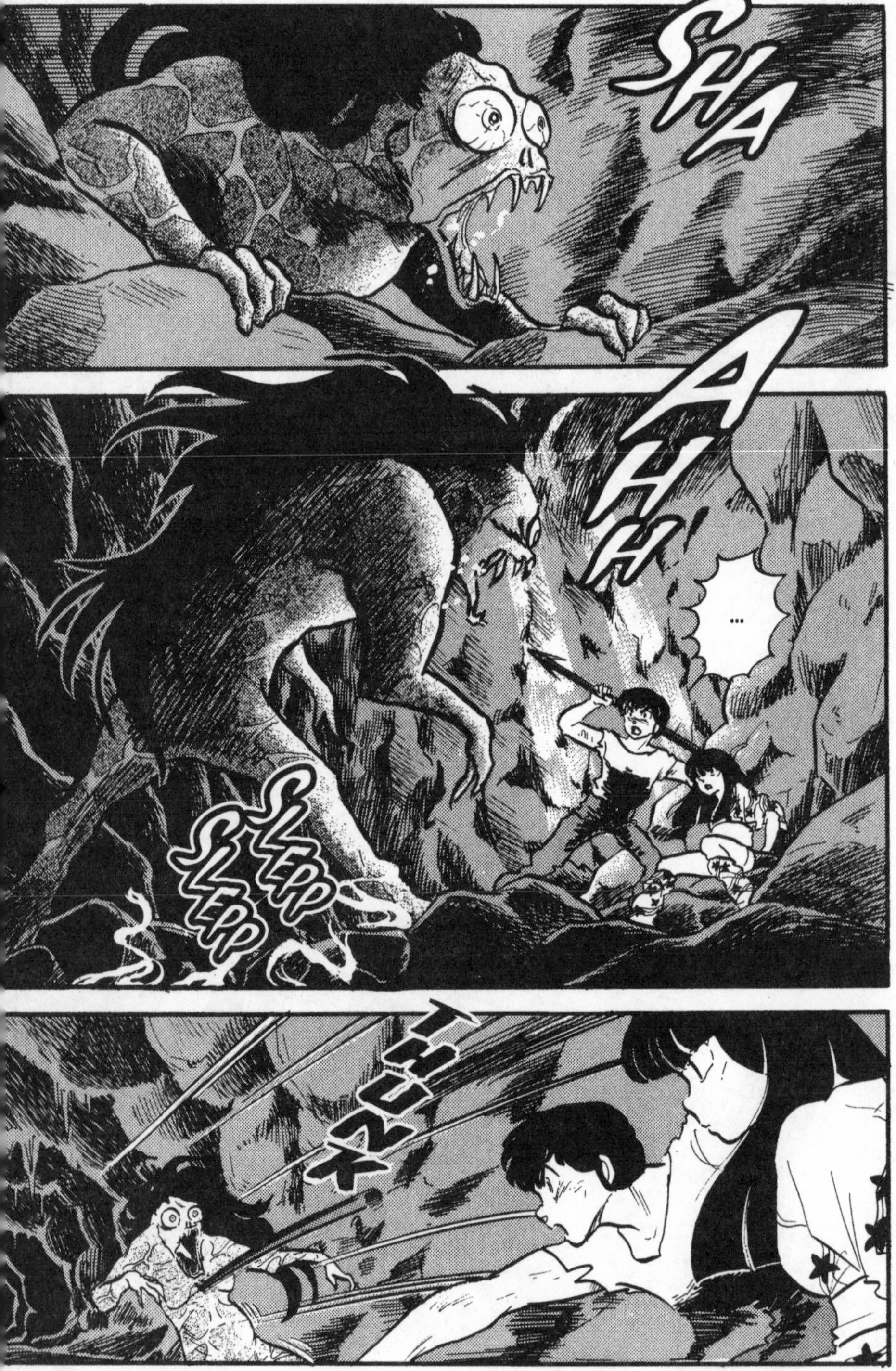
SHA
AHHH
...
SLEPP SLEPP
THUNK

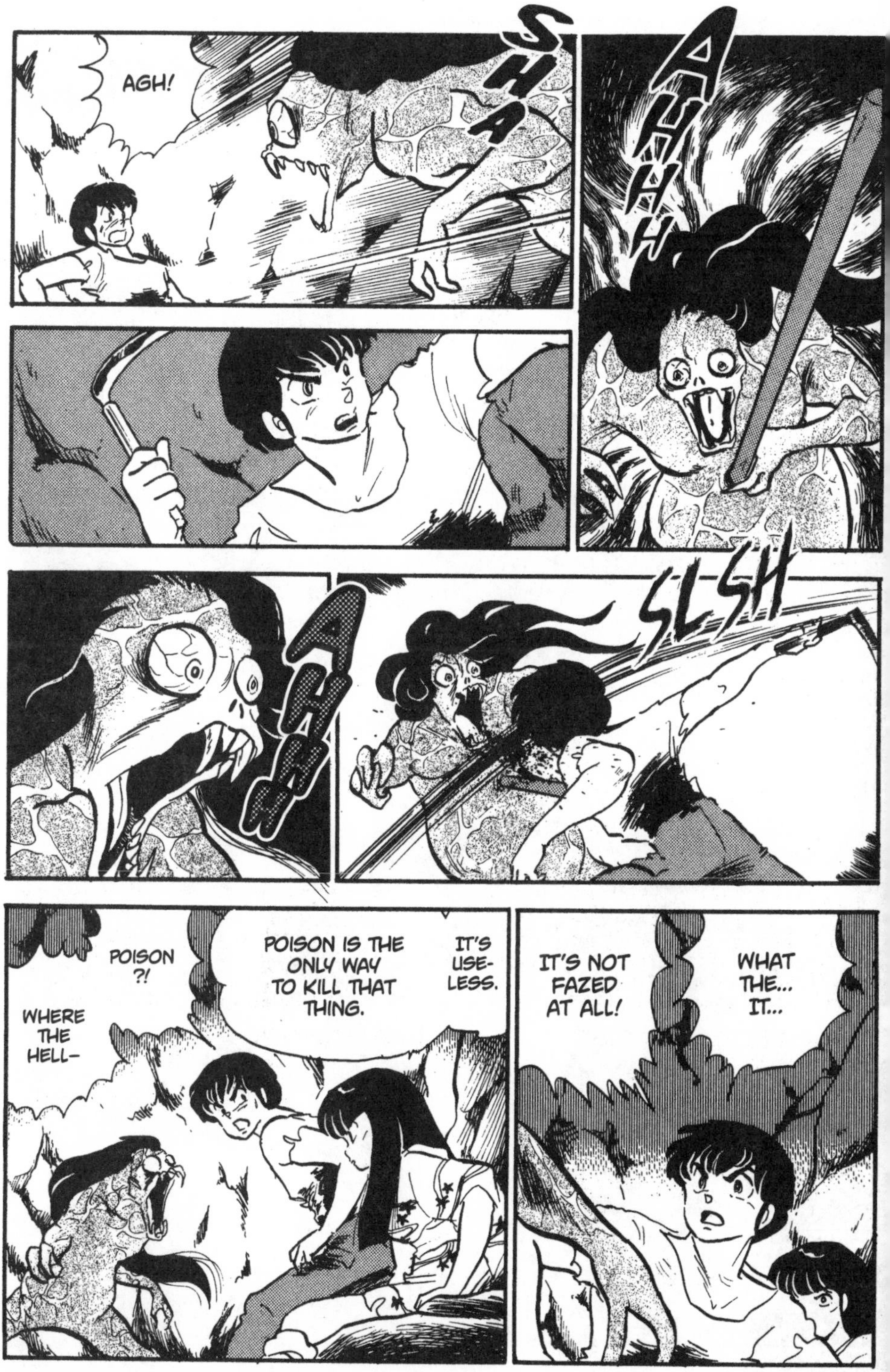
AHHHHH
SHHA
AGH!
SLSH
AHHHHH
WHAT THE... IT...
IT'S NOT FAZED AT ALL!
IT'S USE-LESS.
POISON IS THE ONLY WAY TO KILL THAT THING.
POISON ?!
WHERE THE HELL–

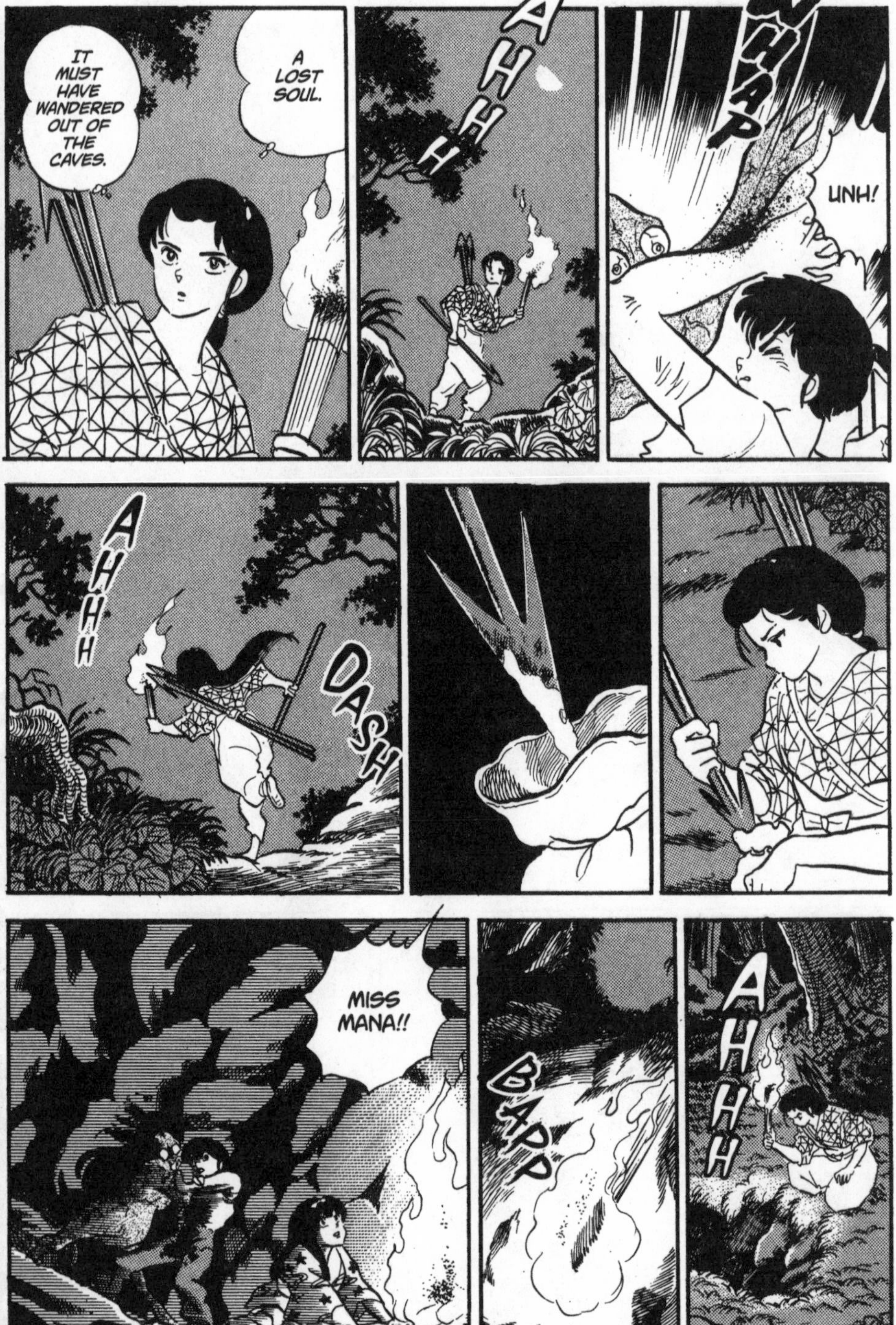
WHAP
UNH!
AHHHH
A LOST SOUL.
IT MUST HAVE WANDERED OUT OF THE CAVES.
DASH
AHHHH
AHHHH
BAPP
MISS MANA!!

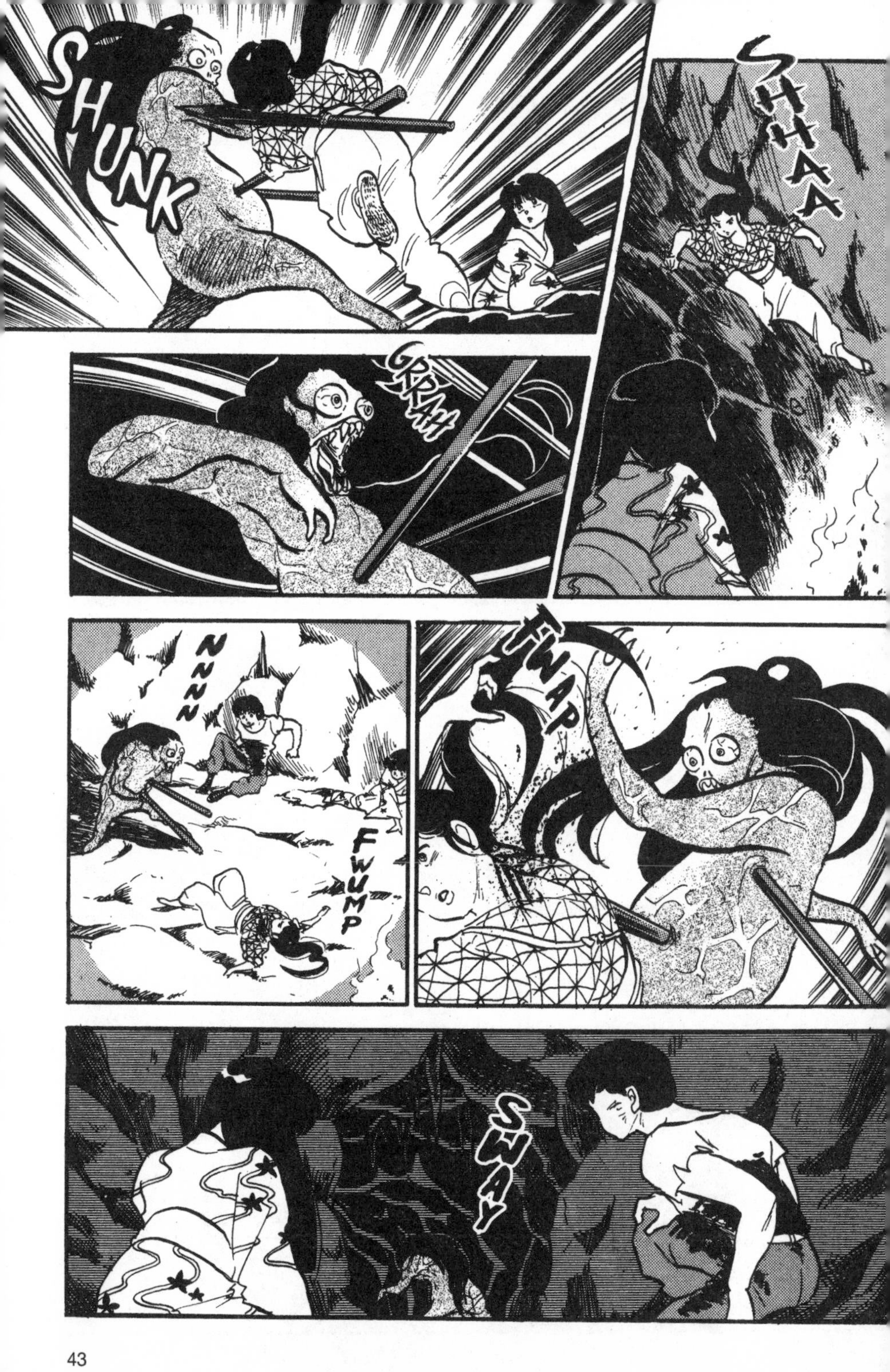
SHHAA
SHUNK
GRRAH
FWAP
NNNN
FWWUMP
SWAY

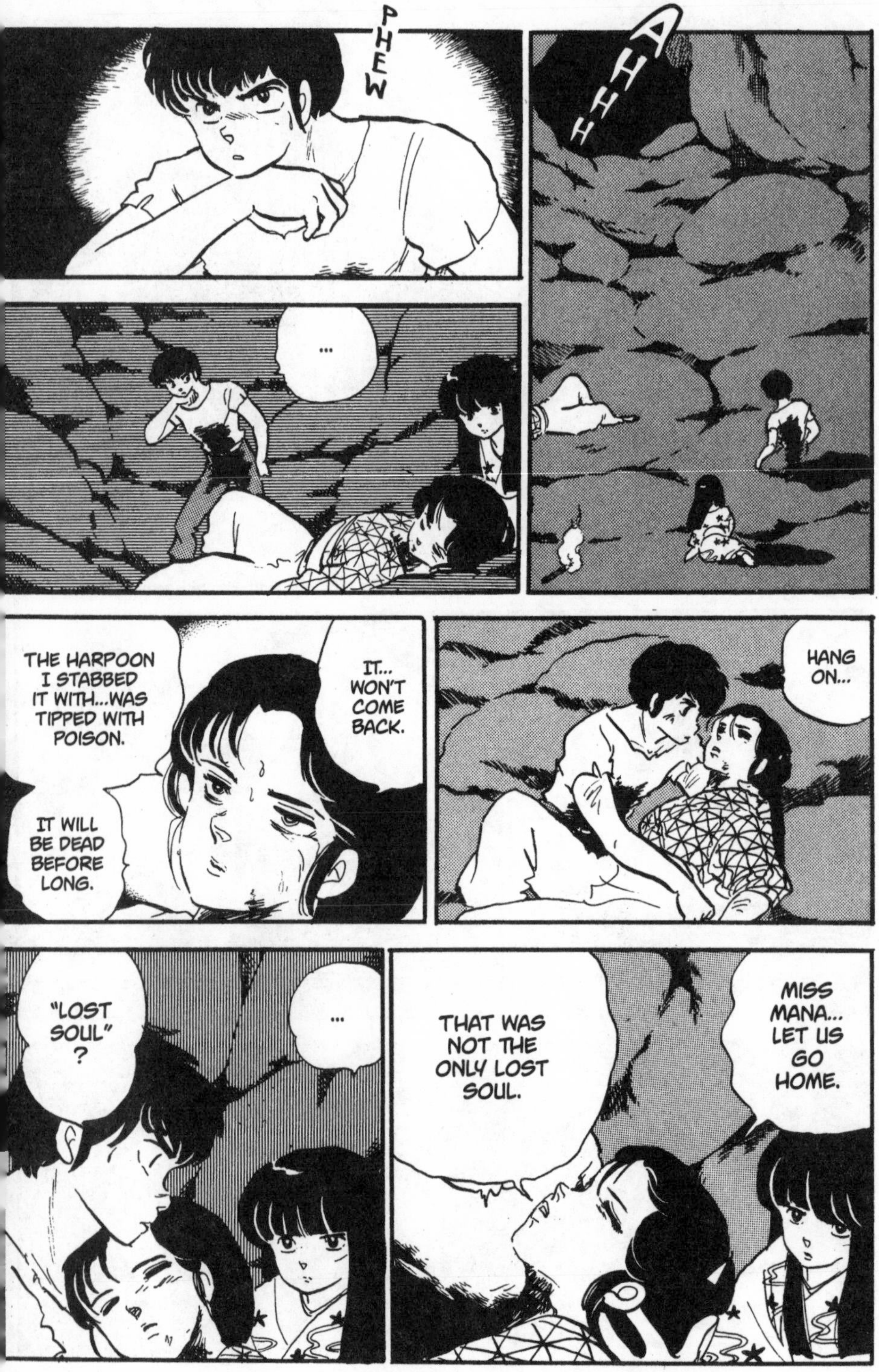
AHHHH
PHEW
...
HANG ON...
IT... WON'T COME BACK.
THE HARPOON I STABBED IT WITH...WAS TIPPED WITH POISON.
IT WILL BE DEAD BEFORE LONG.
MISS MANA... LET US GO HOME.
THAT WAS NOT THE ONLY LOST SOUL.
...
"LOST SOUL"?

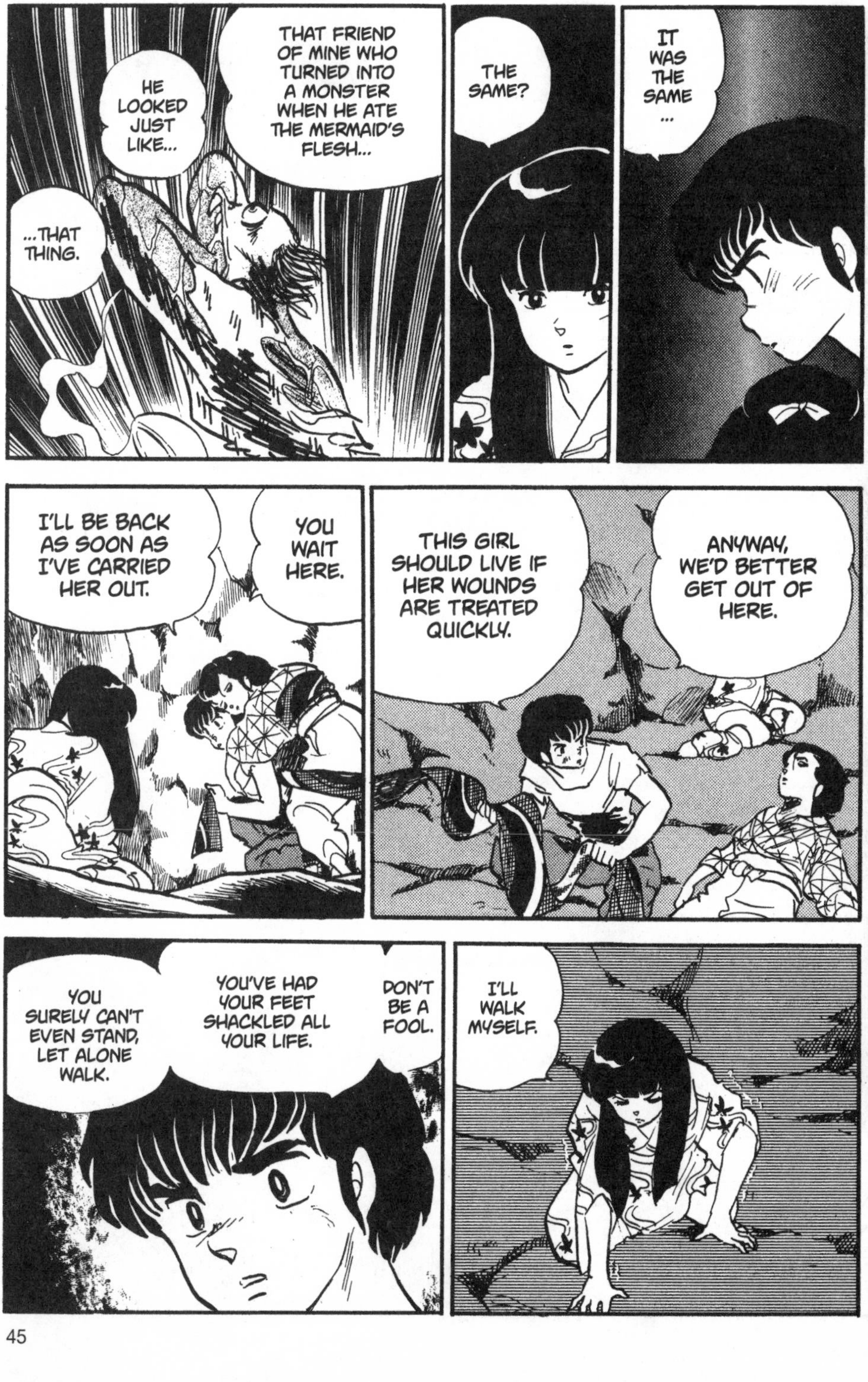
IT WAS THE SAME ...
THE SAME?
THAT FRIEND OF MINE WHO TURNED INTO A MONSTER WHEN HE ATE THE MERMAID'S FLESH...
HE LOOKED JUST LIKE...
...THAT THING.
ANYWAY, WE'D BETTER GET OUT OF HERE.
THIS GIRL SHOULD LIVE IF HER WOUNDS ARE TREATED QUICKLY.
YOU WAIT HERE.
I'LL BE BACK AS SOON AS I'VE CARRIED HER OUT.
I'LL WALK MYSELF.
DON'T BE A FOOL.
YOU'VE HAD YOUR FEET SHACKLED ALL YOUR LIFE.
YOU SURELY CAN'T EVEN STAND, LET ALONE WALK.

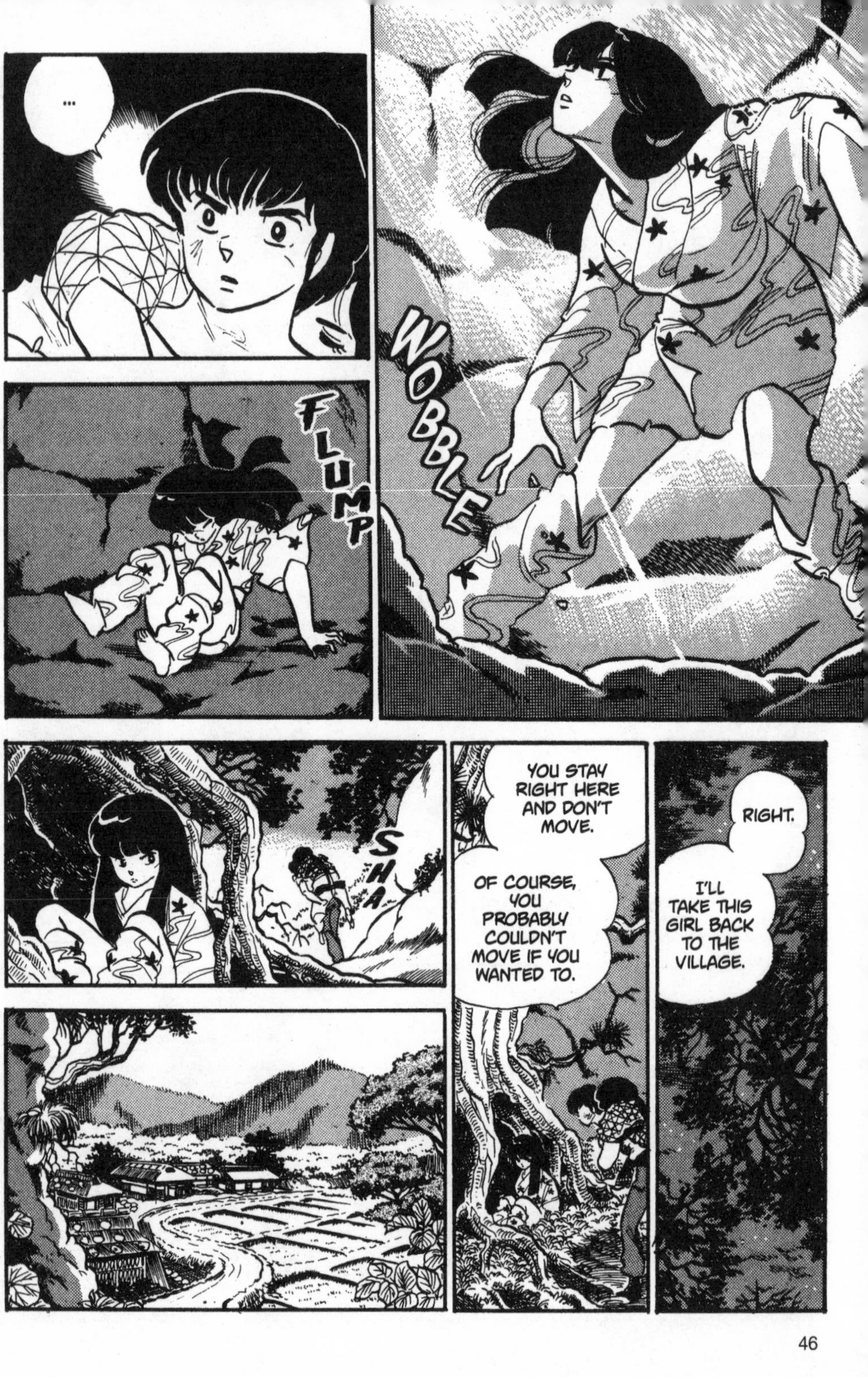
WOBBLE
...
FLUMP
RIGHT.
I'LL TAKE THIS GIRL BACK TO THE VILLAGE.
YOU STAY RIGHT HERE AND DON'T MOVE.
OF COURSE, YOU PROBABLY COULDN'T MOVE IF YOU WANTED TO.
SHA

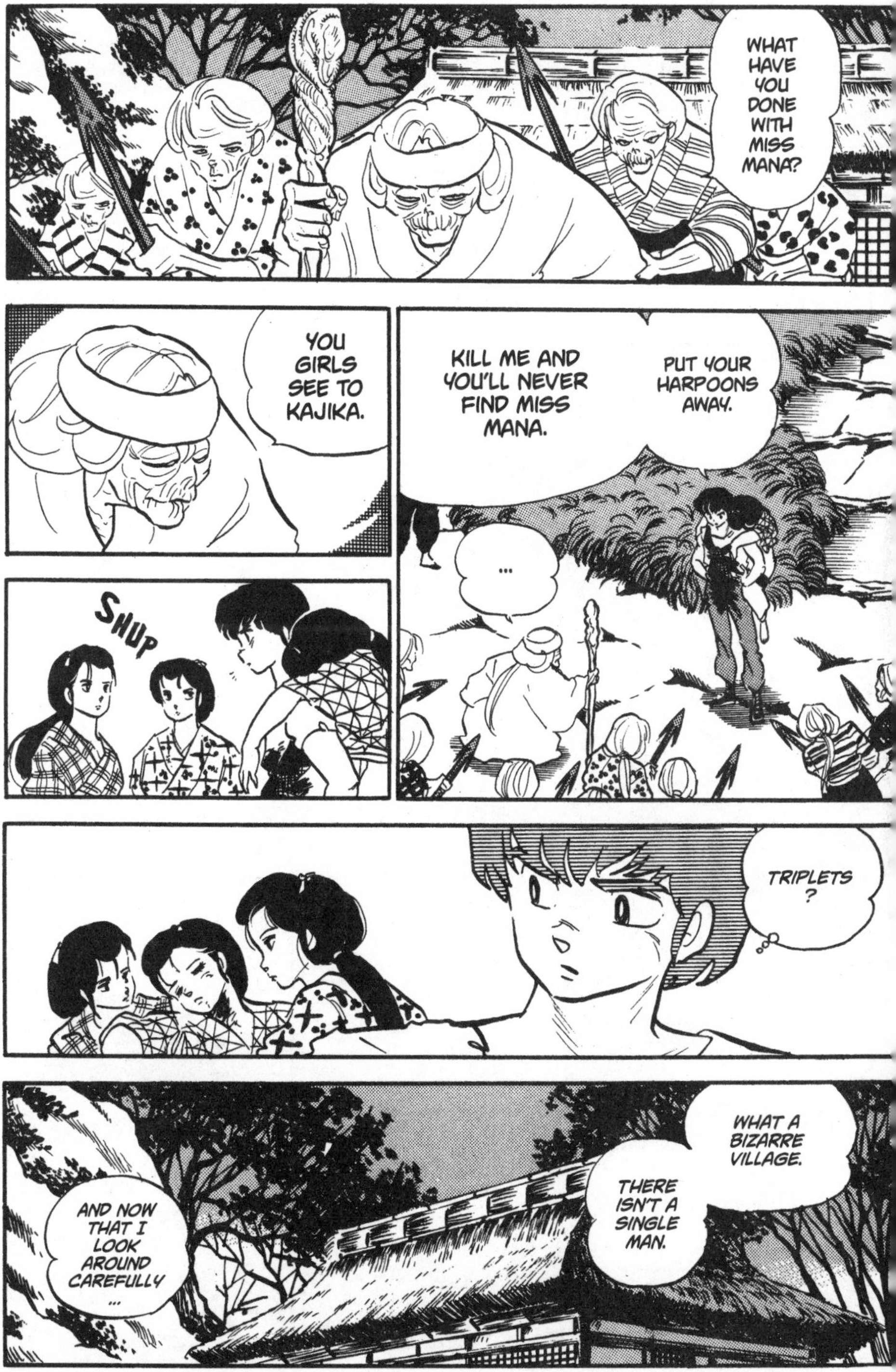
WHAT HAVE YOU DONE WITH MISS MANA?
PUT YOUR HARPOONS AWAY.
KILL ME AND YOU'LL NEVER FIND MISS MANA.
...
YOU GIRLS SEE TO KAJIKA.
SHUP
TRIPLETS ?
WHAT A BIZARRE VILLAGE.
THERE ISN'T A SINGLE MAN.
AND NOW THAT I LOOK AROUND CAREFULLY ...

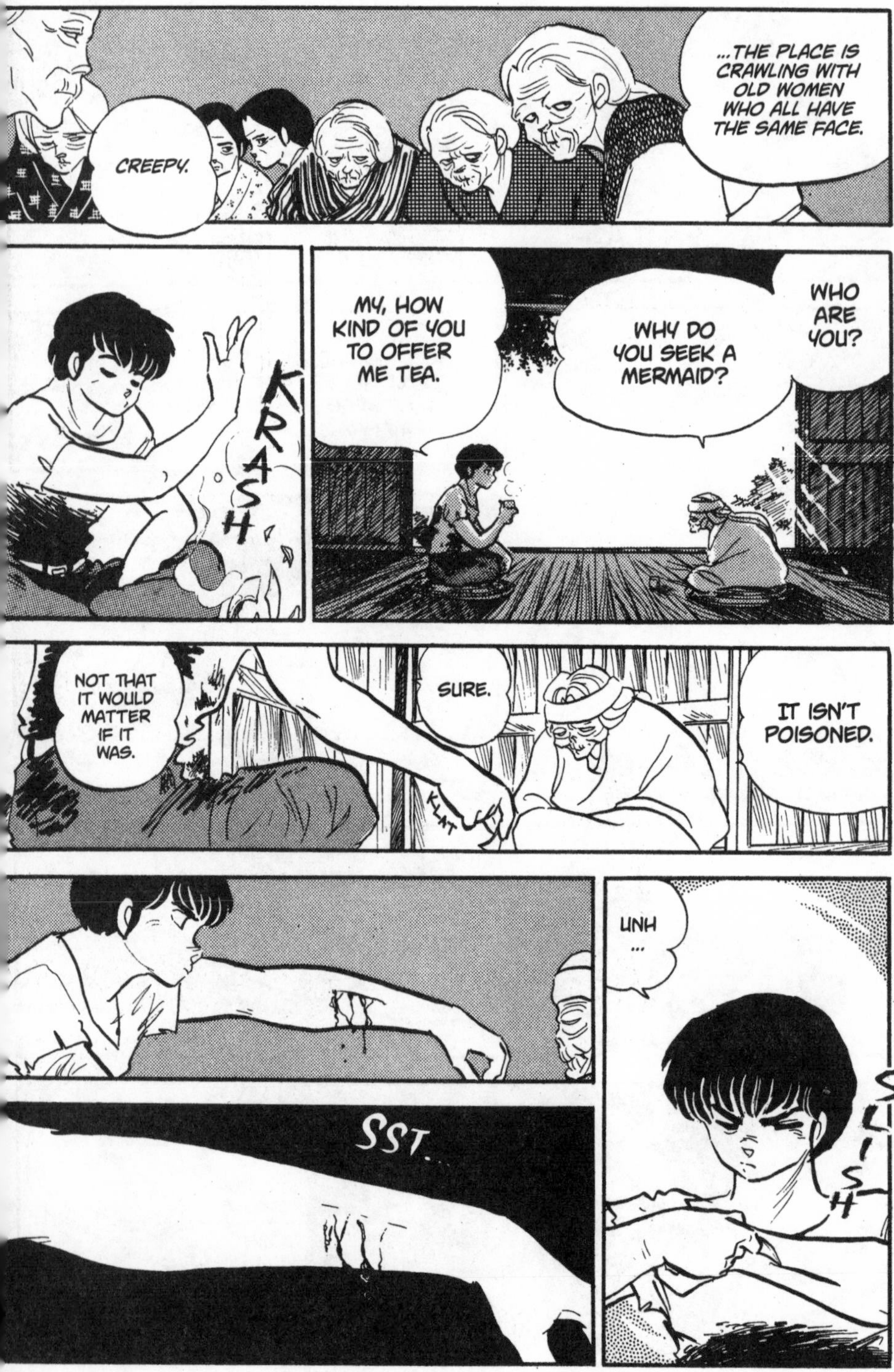
...THE PLACE IS CRAWLING WITH OLD WOMEN WHO ALL HAVE THE SAME FACE.
CREEPY.
WHO ARE YOU?
WHY DO YOU SEEK A MERMAID?
MY, HOW KIND OF YOU TO OFFER ME TEA.
KRASH
IT ISN'T POISONED.
SURE.
KLAT
NOT THAT IT WOULD MATTER IF IT WAS.
UNH ...
SLISH
SST...

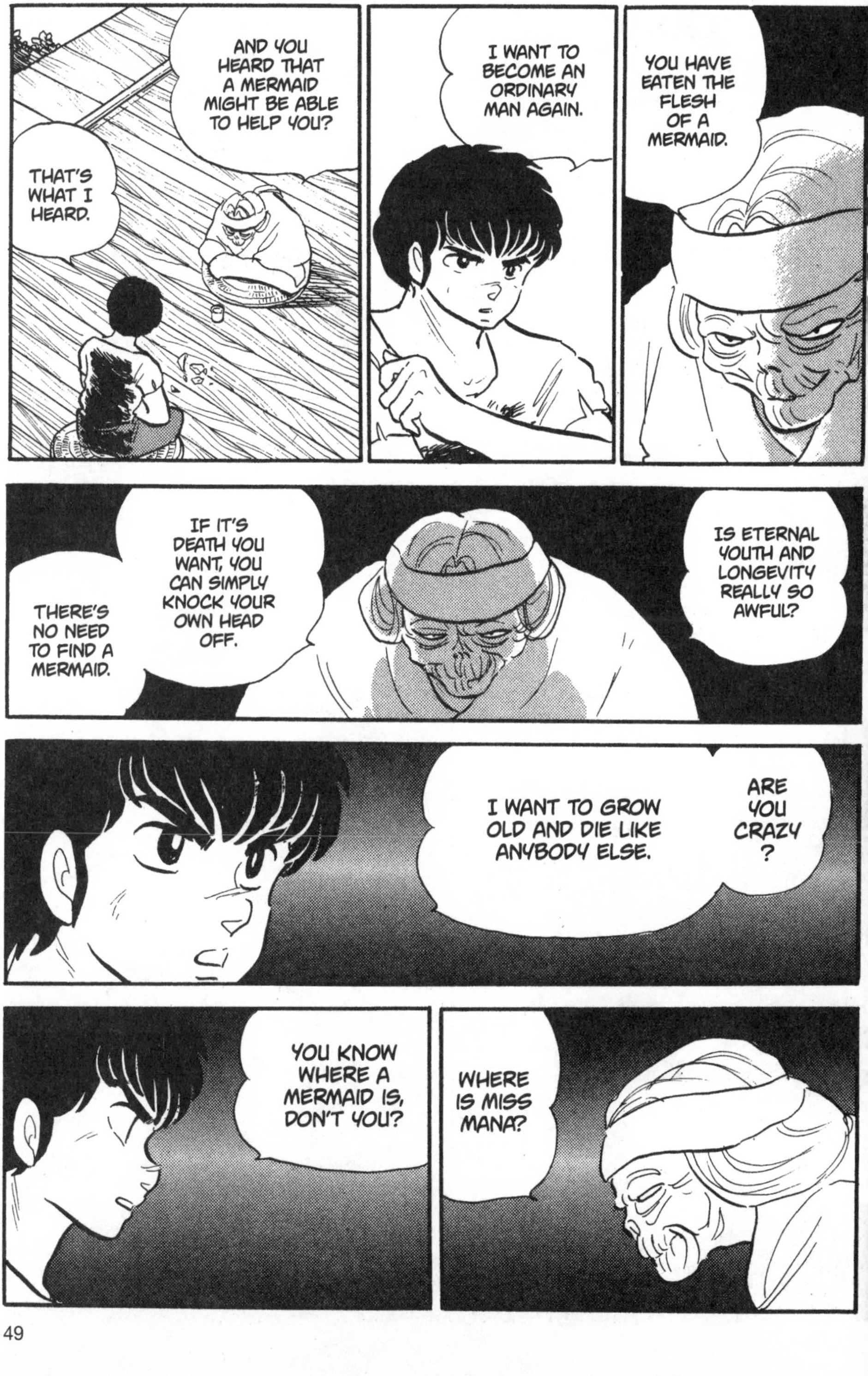
YOU HAVE EATEN THE FLESH OF A MERMAID.
I WANT TO BECOME AN ORDINARY MAN AGAIN.
AND YOU HEARD THAT A MERMAID MIGHT BE ABLE TO HELP YOU?
THAT'S WHAT I HEARD.
IS ETERNAL YOUTH AND LONGEVITY REALLY SO AWFUL?
IF IT'S DEATH YOU WANT, YOU CAN SIMPLY KNOCK YOUR OWN HEAD OFF.
THERE'S NO NEED TO FIND A MERMAID.
ARE YOU CRAZY?
I WANT TO GROW OLD AND DIE LIKE ANYBODY ELSE.
WHERE IS MISS MANA?
YOU KNOW WHERE A MERMAID IS, DON'T YOU?

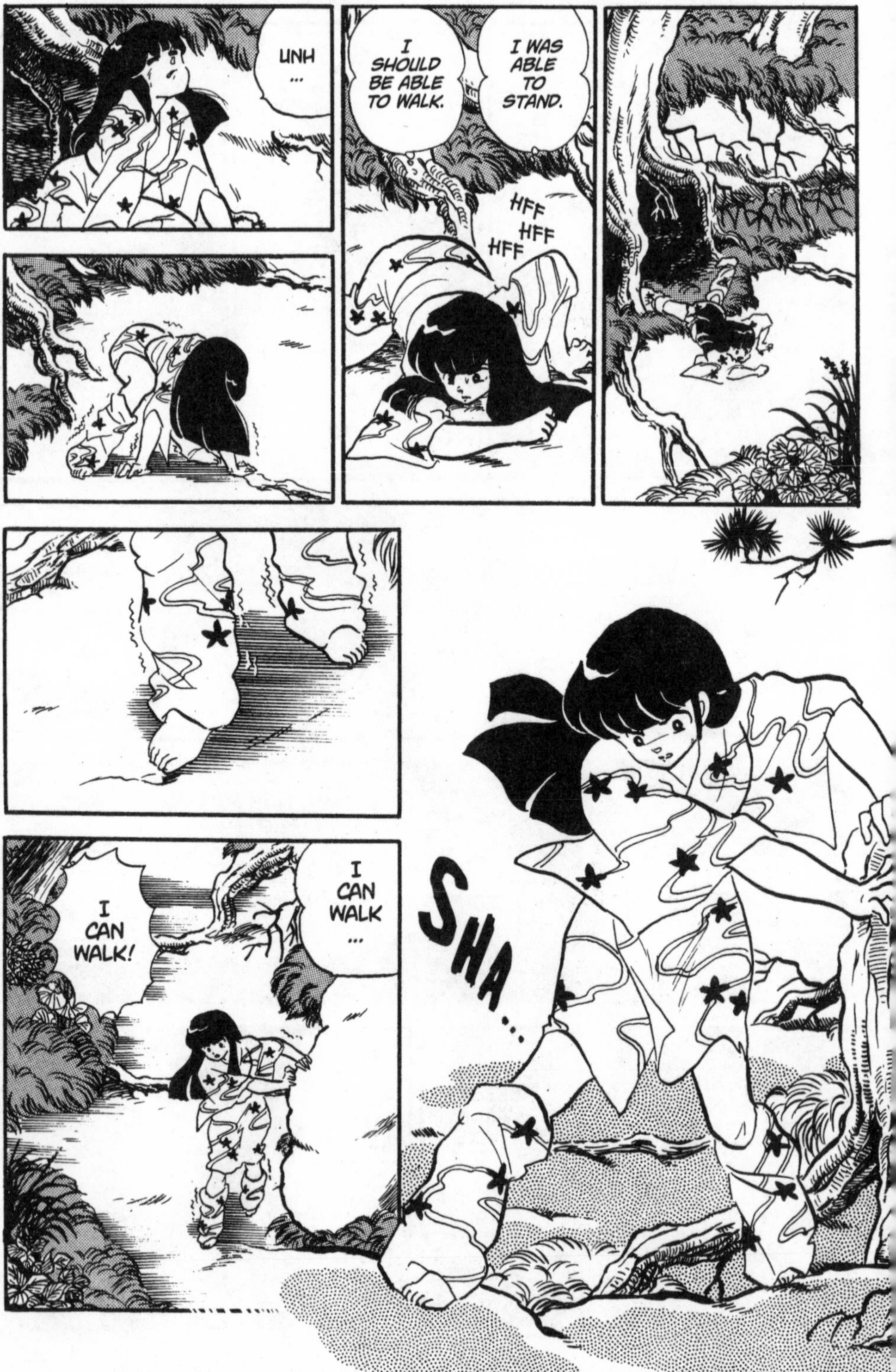

I WAS ABLE TO STAND.
I SHOULD BE ABLE TO WALK.
HFF HFF HFF
UNH ...
SHA...
I CAN WALK ...
I CAN WALK!

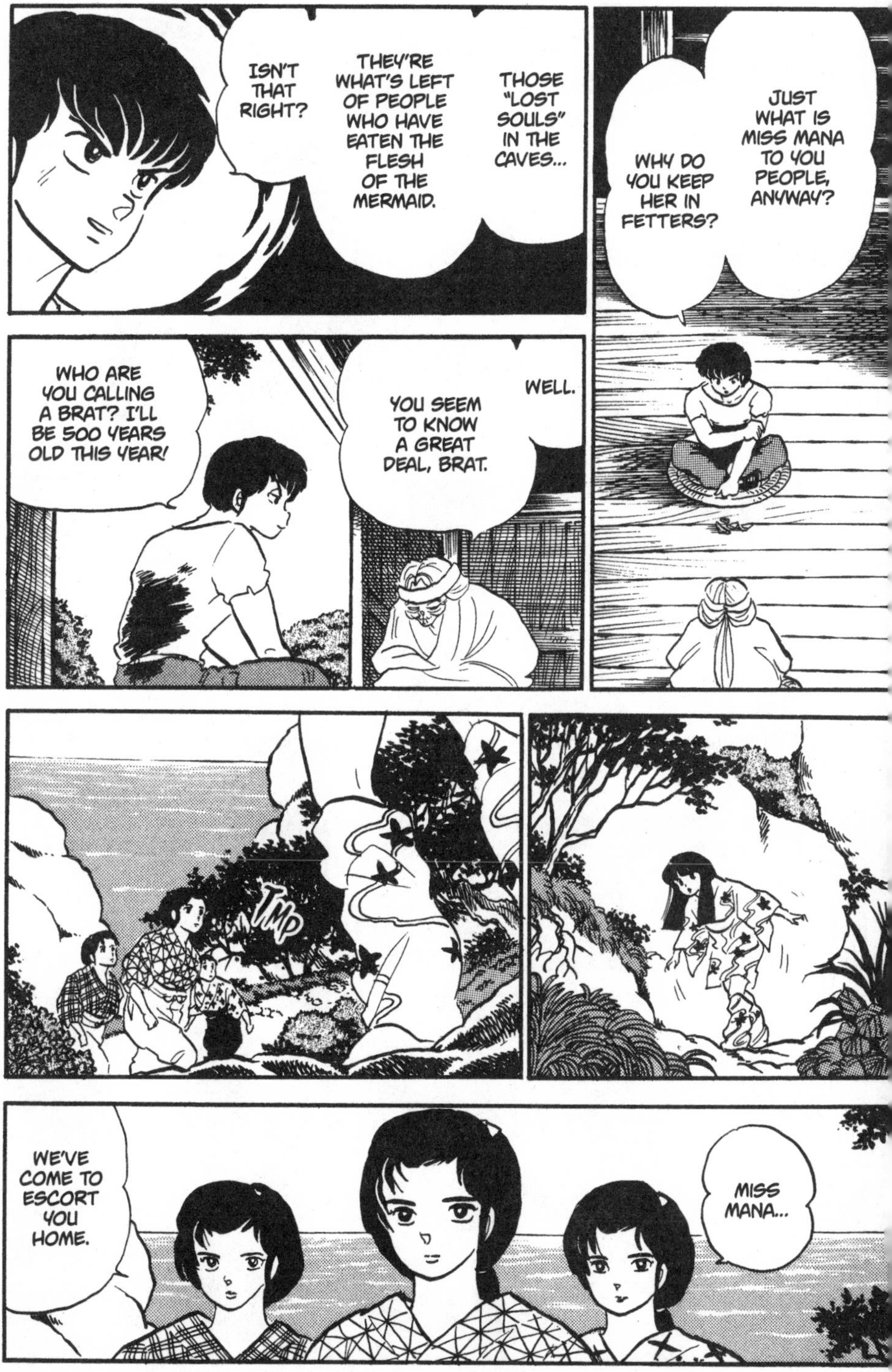
JUST WHAT IS MISS MANA TO YOU PEOPLE, ANYWAY?
WHY DO YOU KEEP HER IN FETTERS?
THOSE "LOST SOULS" IN THE CAVES...
THEY'RE WHAT'S LEFT OF PEOPLE WHO HAVE EATEN THE FLESH OF THE MERMAID.
ISN'T THAT RIGHT?
WELL.
YOU SEEM TO KNOW A GREAT DEAL, BRAT.
WHO ARE YOU CALLING A BRAT? I'LL BE 500 YEARS OLD THIS YEAR!
TMP
MISS MANA...
WE'VE COME TO ESCORT YOU HOME.

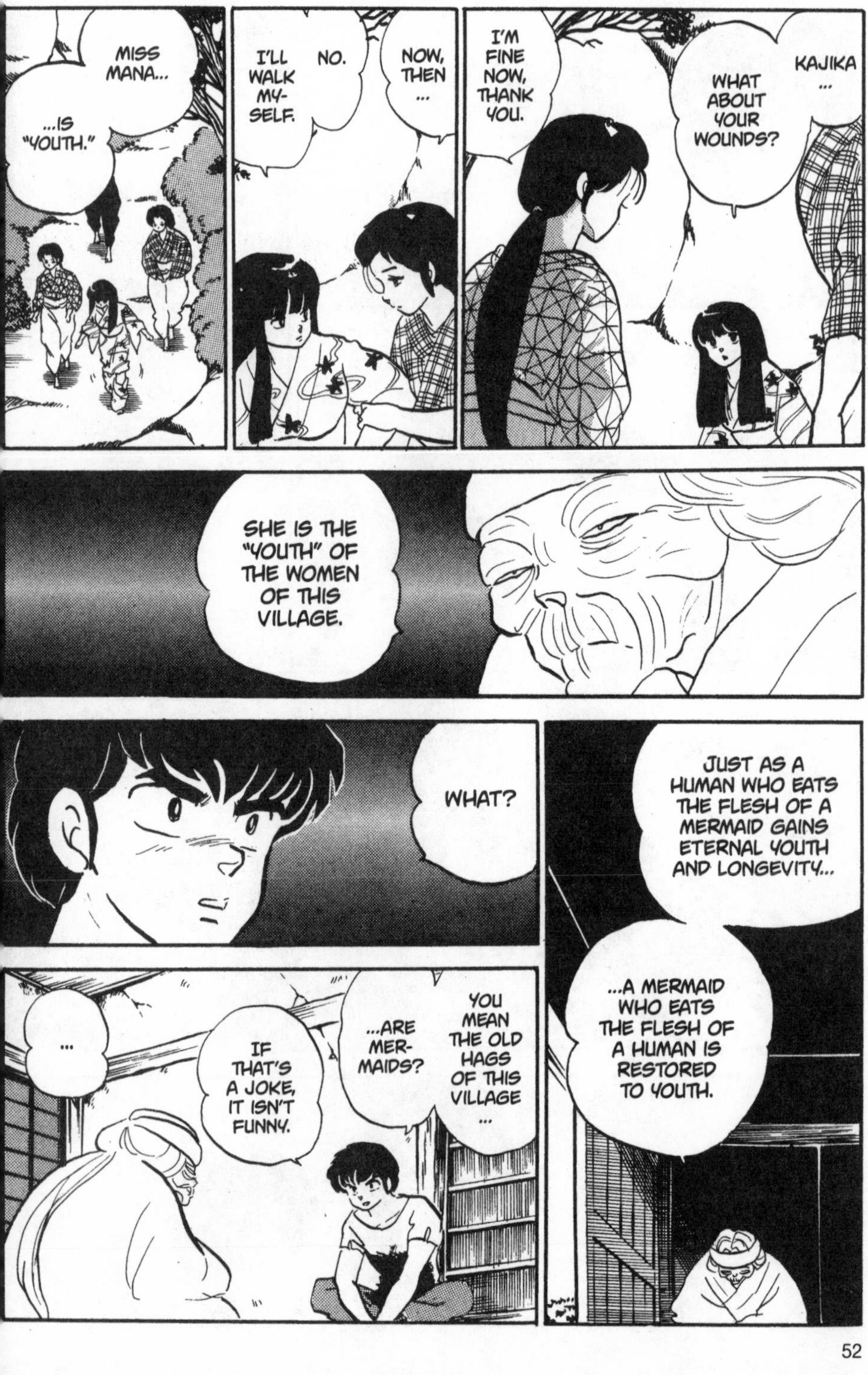
KAJIKA ...
WHAT ABOUT YOUR WOUNDS?
I'M FINE NOW, THANK YOU.
NOW, THEN ...
NO.
I'LL WALK MY-SELF.
MISS MANA...
...IS "YOUTH."
SHE IS THE "YOUTH" OF THE WOMEN OF THIS VILLAGE.
JUST AS A HUMAN WHO EATS THE FLESH OF A MERMAID GAINS ETERNAL YOUTH AND LONGEVITY...
...A MERMAID WHO EATS THE FLESH OF A HUMAN IS RESTORED TO YOUTH.
WHAT?
YOU MEAN THE OLD HAGS OF THIS VILLAGE ...
...ARE MER-MAIDS?
IF THAT'S A JOKE, IT ISN'T FUNNY.
...

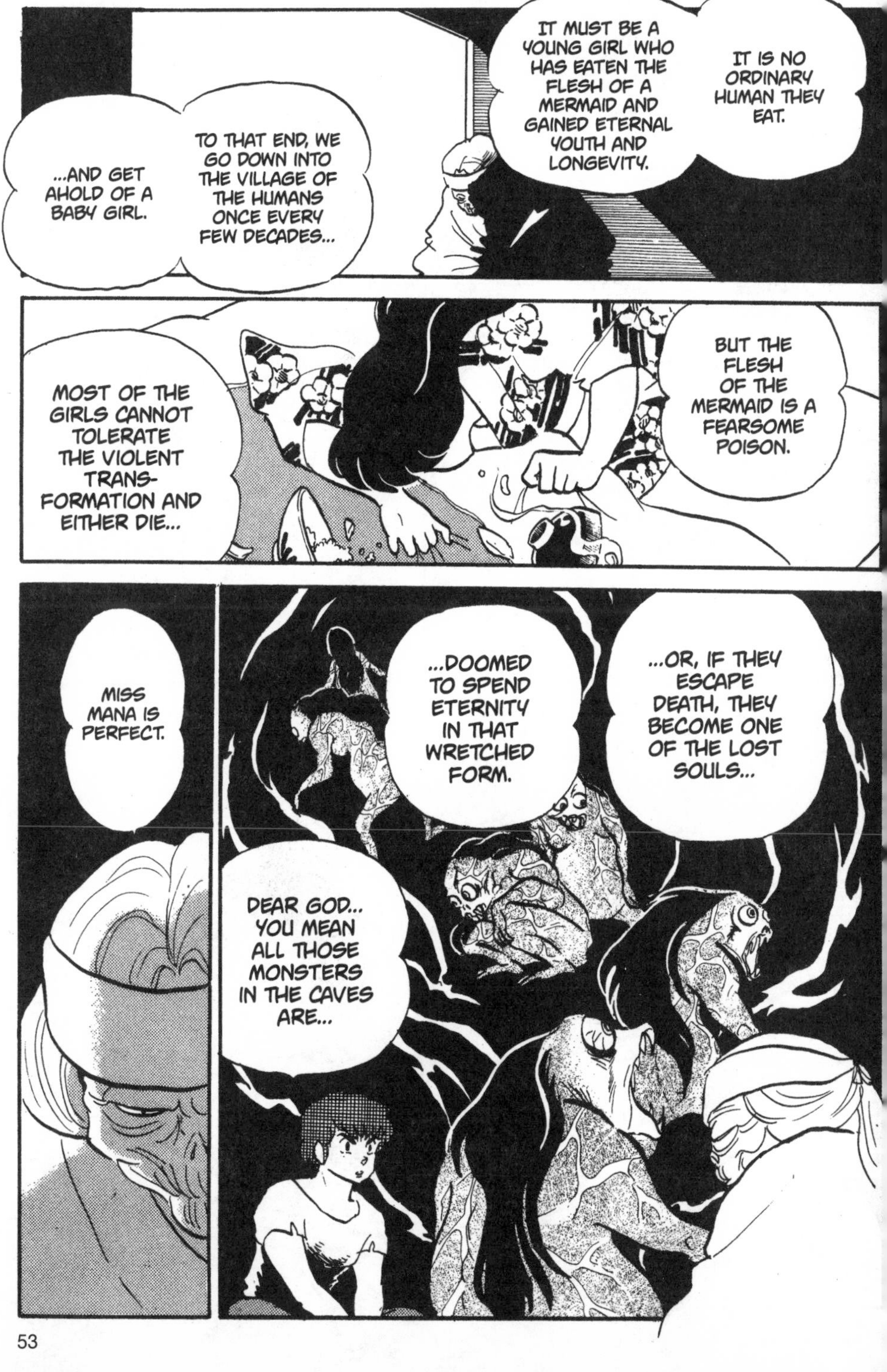
IT IS NO ORDINARY HUMAN THEY EAT.
IT MUST BE A YOUNG GIRL WHO HAS EATEN THE FLESH OF A MERMAID AND GAINED ETERNAL YOUTH AND LONGEVITY.
TO THAT END, WE GO DOWN INTO THE VILLAGE OF THE HUMANS ONCE EVERY FEW DECADES...
...AND GET AHOLD OF A BABY GIRL.
BUT THE FLESH OF THE MERMAID IS A FEARSOME POISON.
MOST OF THE GIRLS CANNOT TOLERATE THE VIOLENT TRANS-FORMATION AND EITHER DIE...
...OR, IF THEY ESCAPE DEATH, THEY BECOME ONE OF THE LOST SOULS...
...DOOMED TO SPEND ETERNITY IN THAT WRETCHED FORM.
DEAR GOD... YOU MEAN ALL THOSE MONSTERS IN THE CAVES ARE...
MISS MANA IS PERFECT.

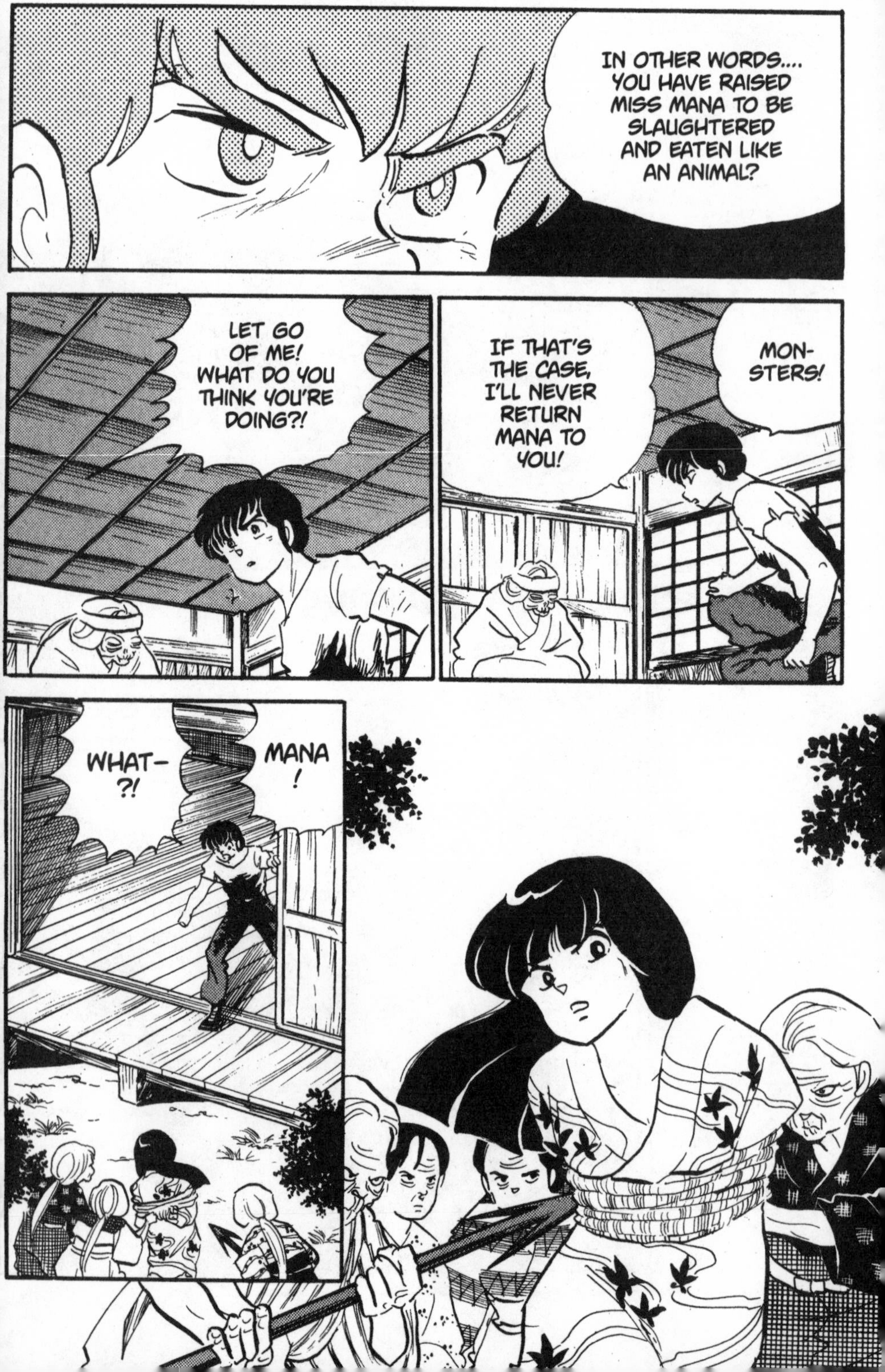
IN OTHER WORDS.... YOU HAVE RAISED MISS MANA TO BE SLAUGHTERED AND EATEN LIKE AN ANIMAL?
MON-STERS!
IF THAT'S THE CASE, I'LL NEVER RETURN MANA TO YOU!
LET GO OF ME! WHAT DO YOU THINK YOU'RE DOING?!
MANA!
WHAT-?!

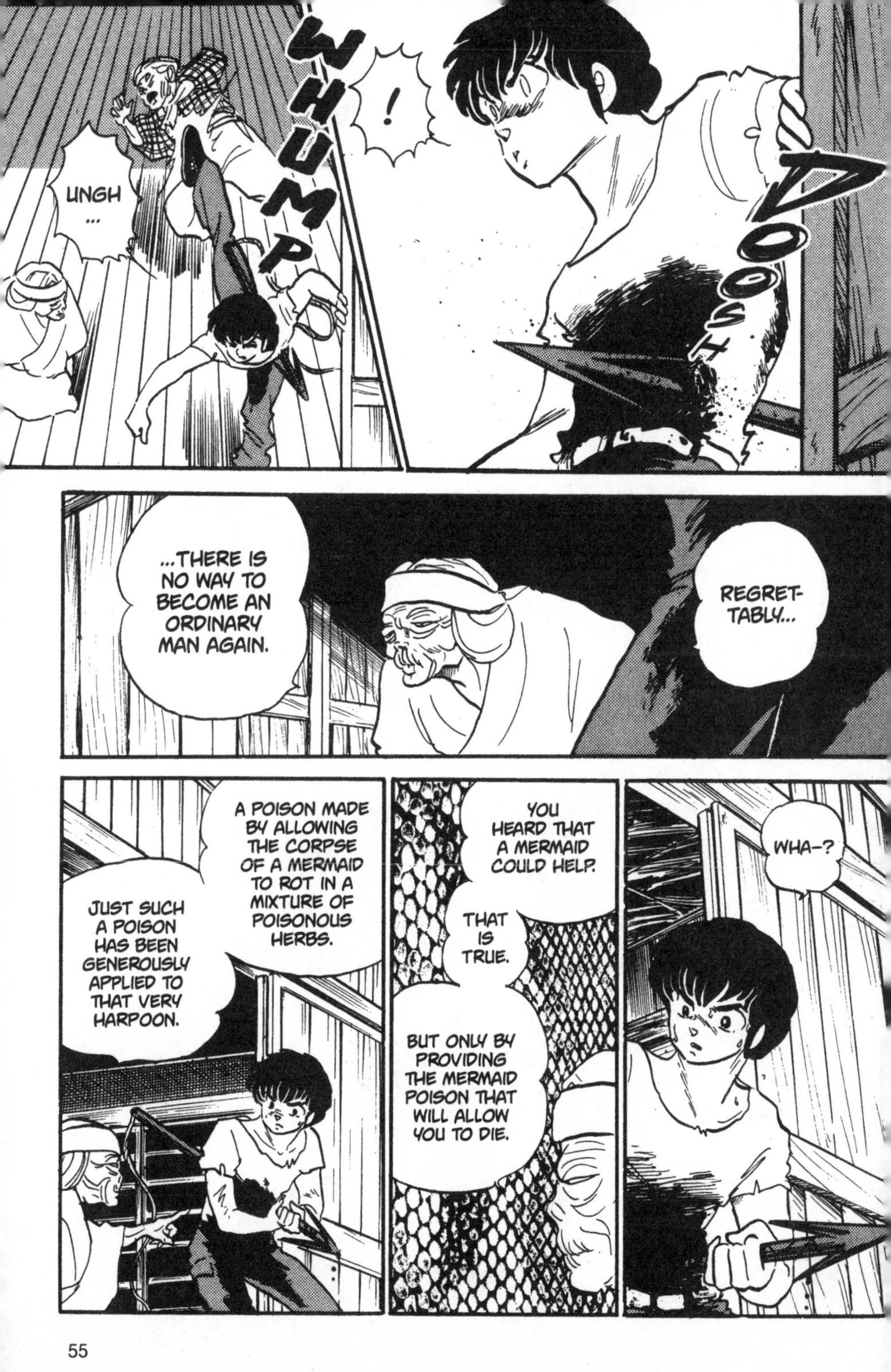
!
DOOSH
WHUMP
UNGH ...
REGRET-TABLY...
...THERE IS NO WAY TO BECOME AN ORDINARY MAN AGAIN.
WHA-?
YOU HEARD THAT A MERMAID COULD HELP.
THAT IS TRUE.
BUT ONLY BY PROVIDING THE MERMAID POISON THAT WILL ALLOW YOU TO DIE.
A POISON MADE BY ALLOWING THE CORPSE OF A MERMAID TO ROT IN A MIXTURE OF POISONOUS HERBS.
JUST SUCH A POISON HAS BEEN GENEROUSLY APPLIED TO THAT VERY HARPOON.

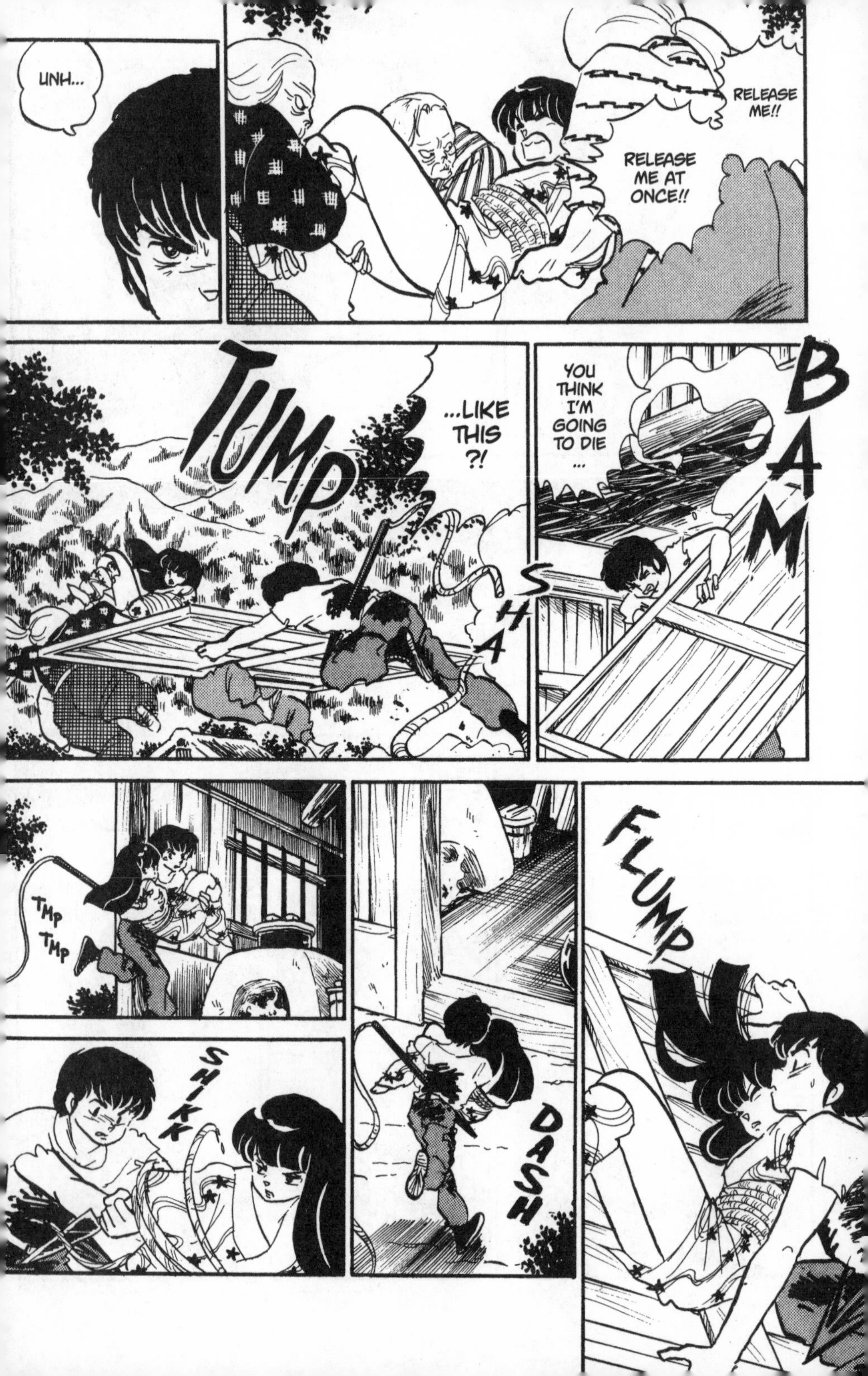
RELEASE ME!!
RELEASE ME AT ONCE!!
UNH...
YOU THINK I'M GOING TO DIE ...
BAM
...LIKE THIS ?!
TUMP
SHA
FLUMP
DASH
TMP TMP
SHIKK

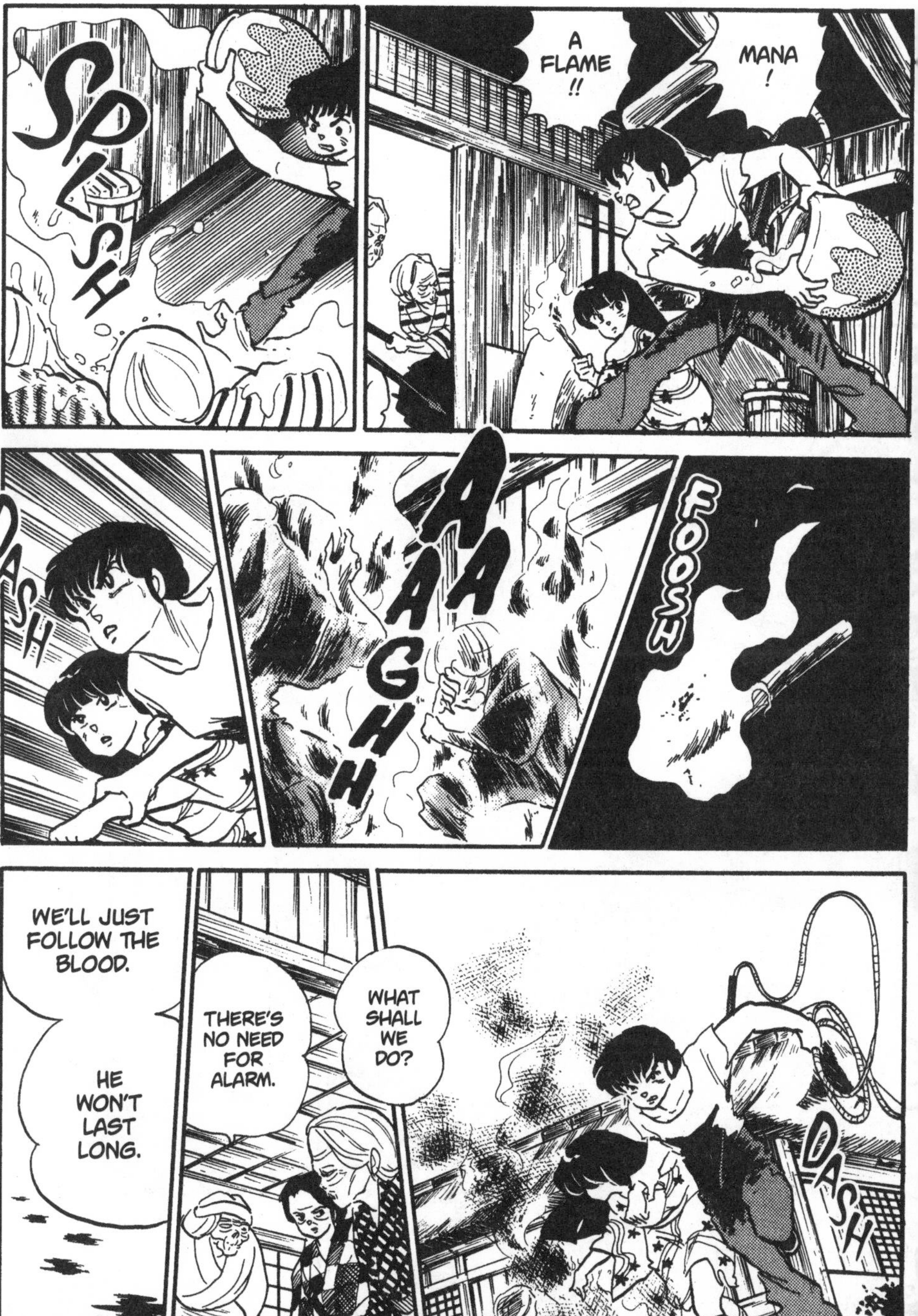
MANA!
A FLAME!!
SPLSH
FOOSH
AAAGHHH
DASH
DASH
WHAT SHALL WE DO?
THERE'S NO NEED FOR ALARM.
WE'LL JUST FOLLOW THE BLOOD.
HE WON'T LAST LONG.

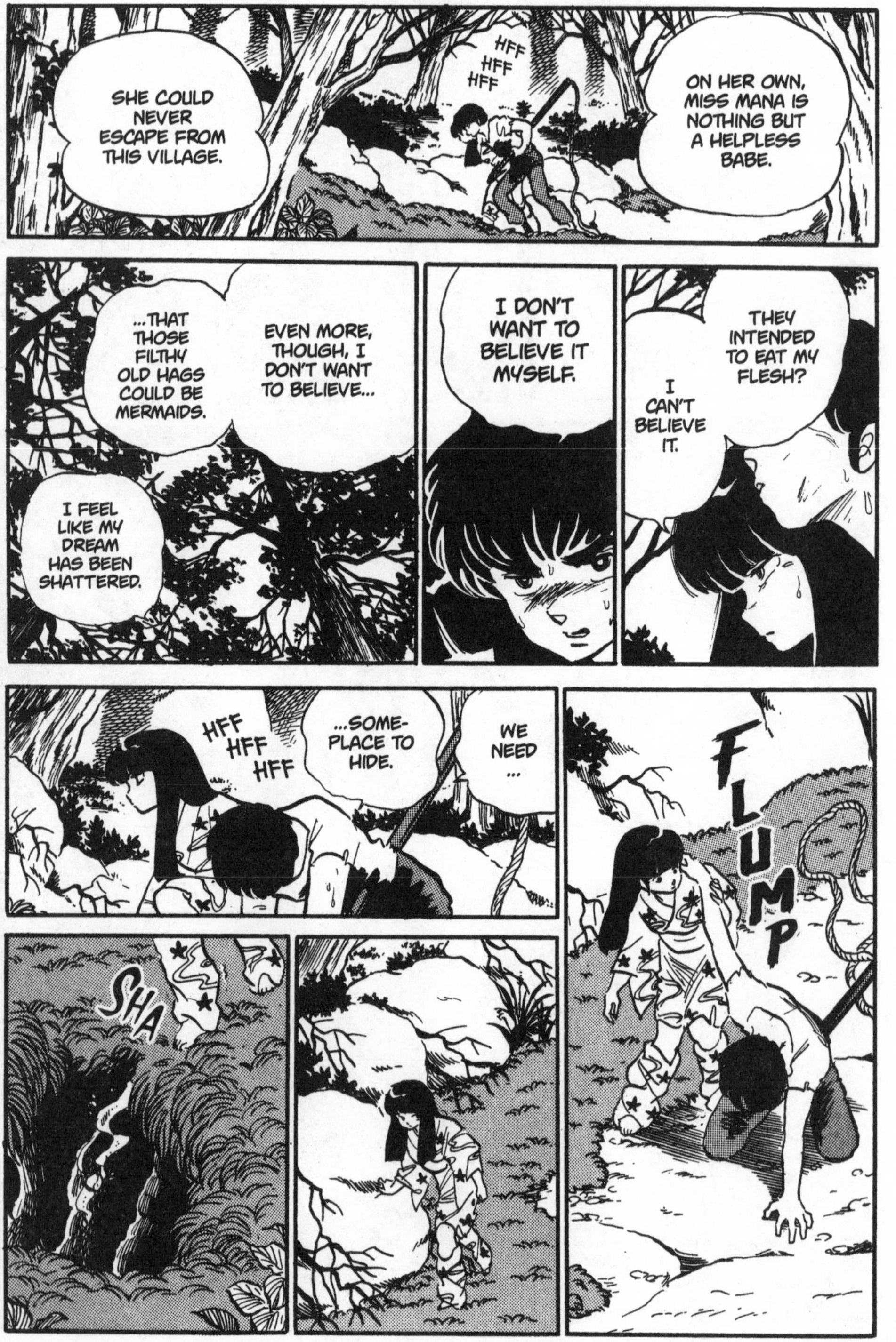
ON HER OWN, MISS MANA IS NOTHING BUT A HELPLESS BABE.
HFF HFF HFF
SHE COULD NEVER ESCAPE FROM THIS VILLAGE.
THEY INTENDED TO EAT MY FLESH?
I CAN'T BELIEVE IT.
I DON'T WANT TO BELIEVE IT MYSELF.
EVEN MORE, THOUGH, I DON'T WANT TO BELIEVE...
...THAT THOSE FILTHY OLD HAGS COULD BE MERMAIDS.
I FEEL LIKE MY DREAM HAS BEEN SHATTERED.
FLUMP
WE NEED ...
...SOME-PLACE TO HIDE.
HFF HFF HFF
SHA

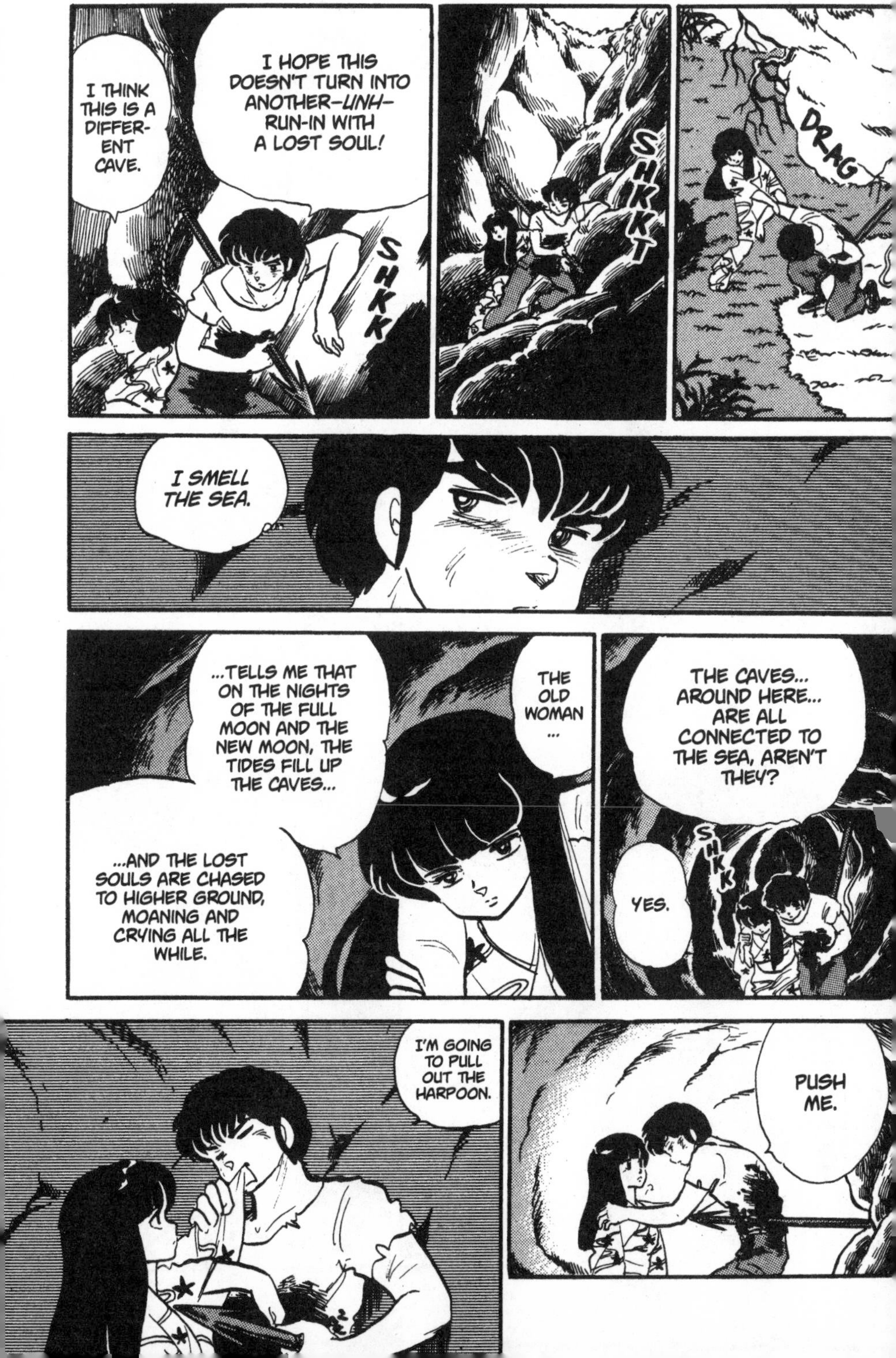
DRAG
SHKKKT
I HOPE THIS DOESN'T TURN INTO ANOTHER—*UNH*— RUN-IN WITH A LOST SOUL!
I THINK THIS IS A DIFFER-ENT CAVE.
SHKK
I SMELL THE SEA.
THE CAVES... AROUND HERE... ARE ALL CONNECTED TO THE SEA, AREN'T THEY?
SHKK
YES.
THE OLD WOMAN ...
...TELLS ME THAT ON THE NIGHTS OF THE FULL MOON AND THE NEW MOON, THE TIDES FILL UP THE CAVES...
...AND THE LOST SOULS ARE CHASED TO HIGHER GROUND, MOANING AND CRYING ALL THE WHILE.
PUSH ME.
I'M GOING TO PULL OUT THE HARPOON.

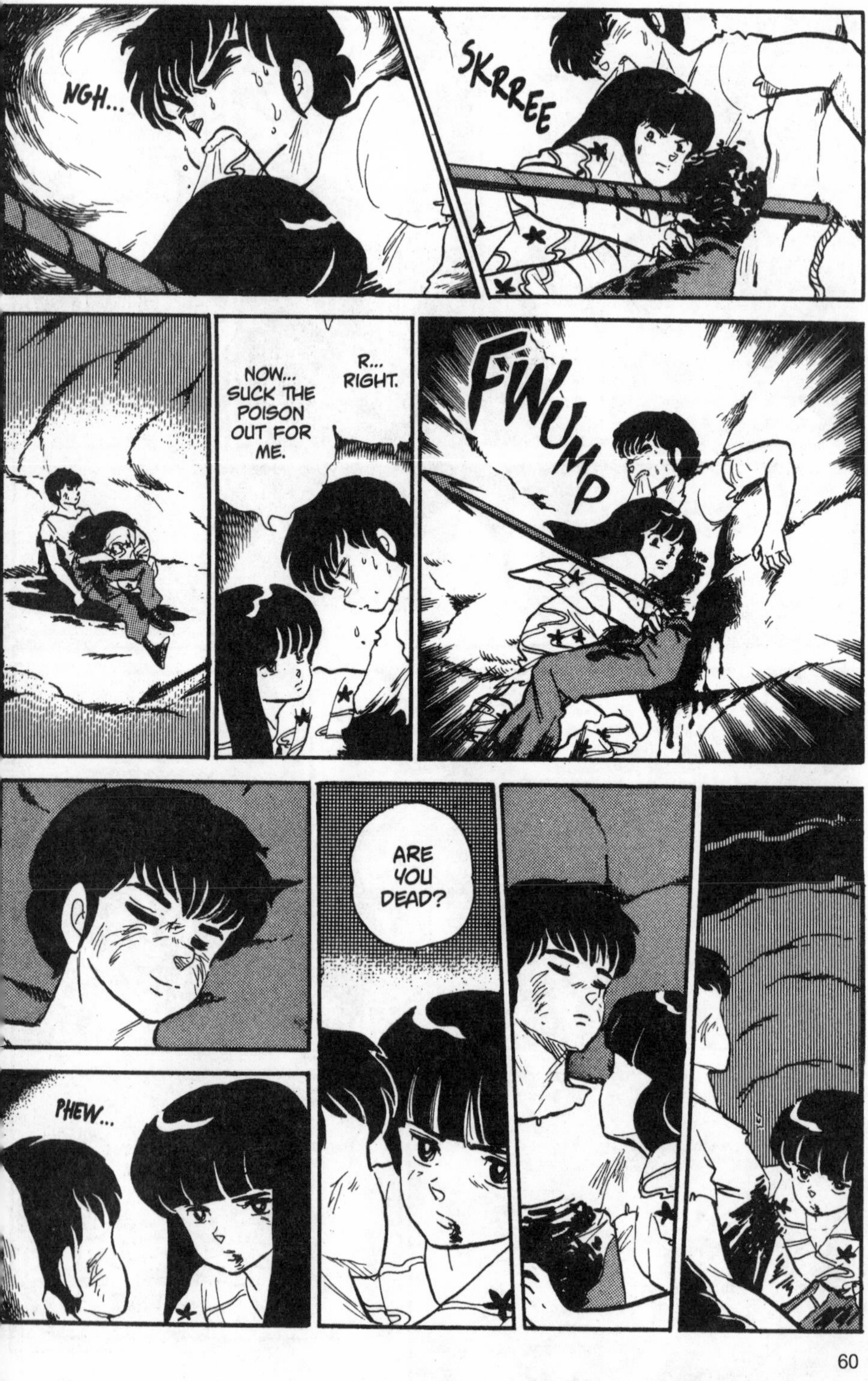
SKRREE
NGH...
FWUMP
NOW... SUCK THE POISON OUT FOR ME.
R... RIGHT.
ARE YOU DEAD?
PHEW...

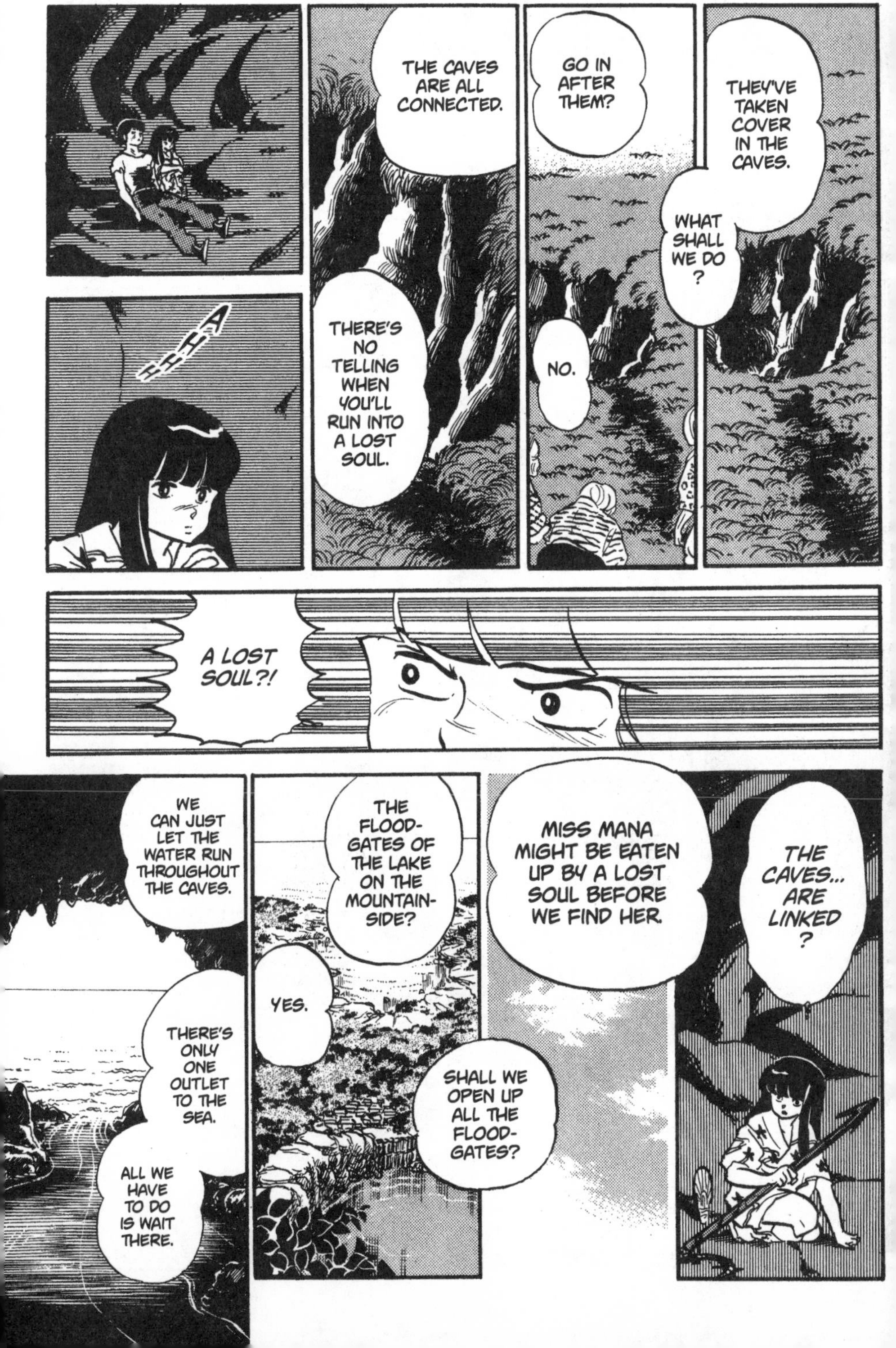
THEY'VE TAKEN COVER IN THE CAVES.
WHAT SHALL WE DO ?
GO IN AFTER THEM?
NO.
THE CAVES ARE ALL CONNECTED.
THERE'S NO TELLING WHEN YOU'LL RUN INTO A LOST SOUL.
A LOST SOUL?!
THE CAVES... ARE LINKED ?
MISS MANA MIGHT BE EATEN UP BY A LOST SOUL BEFORE WE FIND HER.
SHALL WE OPEN UP ALL THE FLOOD-GATES?
THE FLOOD-GATES OF THE LAKE ON THE MOUNTAIN-SIDE?
YES.
WE CAN JUST LET THE WATER RUN THROUGHOUT THE CAVES.
THERE'S ONLY ONE OUTLET TO THE SEA.
ALL WE HAVE TO DO IS WAIT THERE.

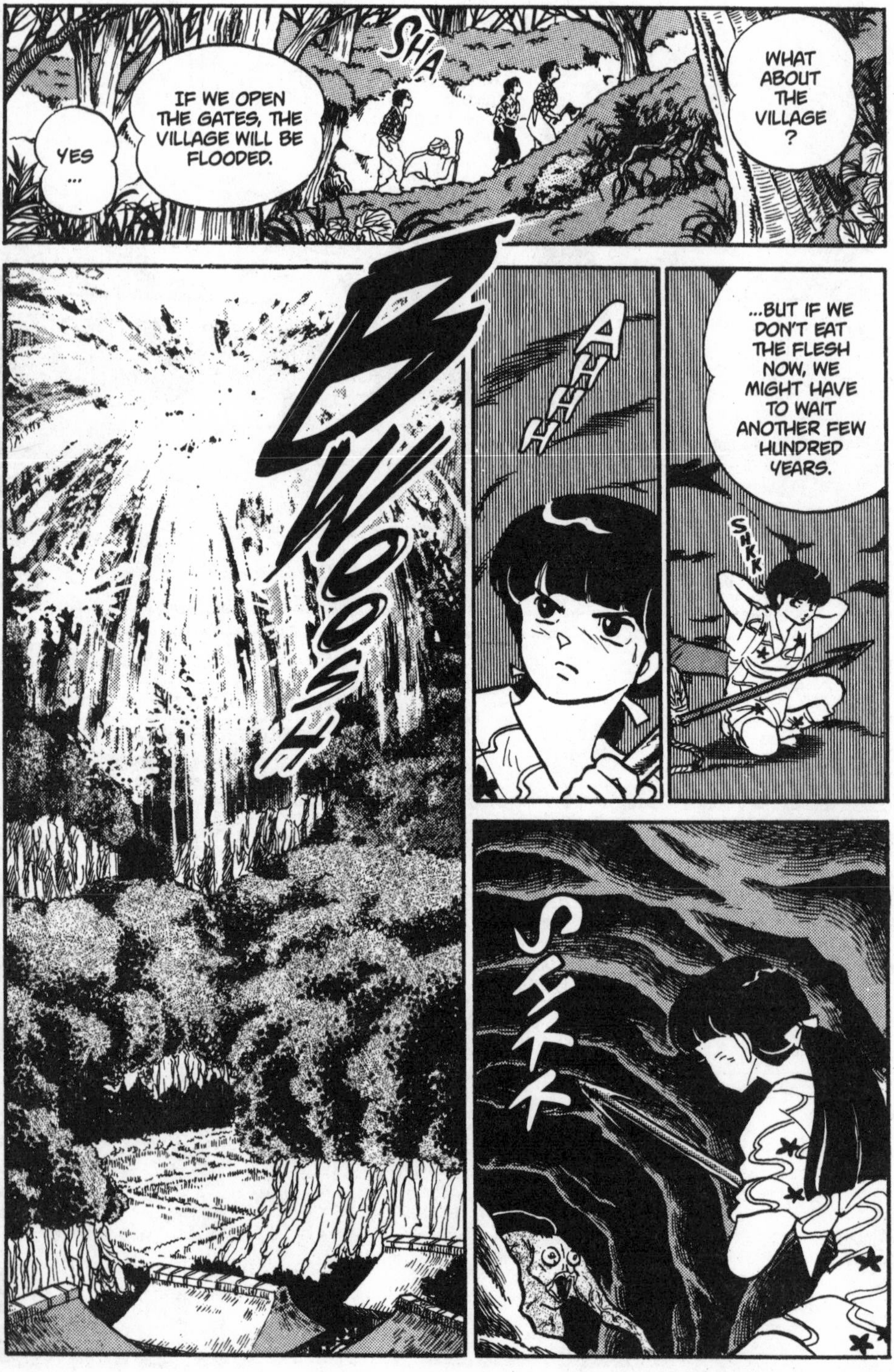
WHAT ABOUT THE VILLAGE ?
SHA
IF WE OPEN THE GATES, THE VILLAGE WILL BE FLOODED.
YES ...
...BUT IF WE DON'T EAT THE FLESH NOW, WE MIGHT HAVE TO WAIT ANOTHER FEW HUNDRED YEARS.
SHKK
AHHHH
SHKK
WHOOSH

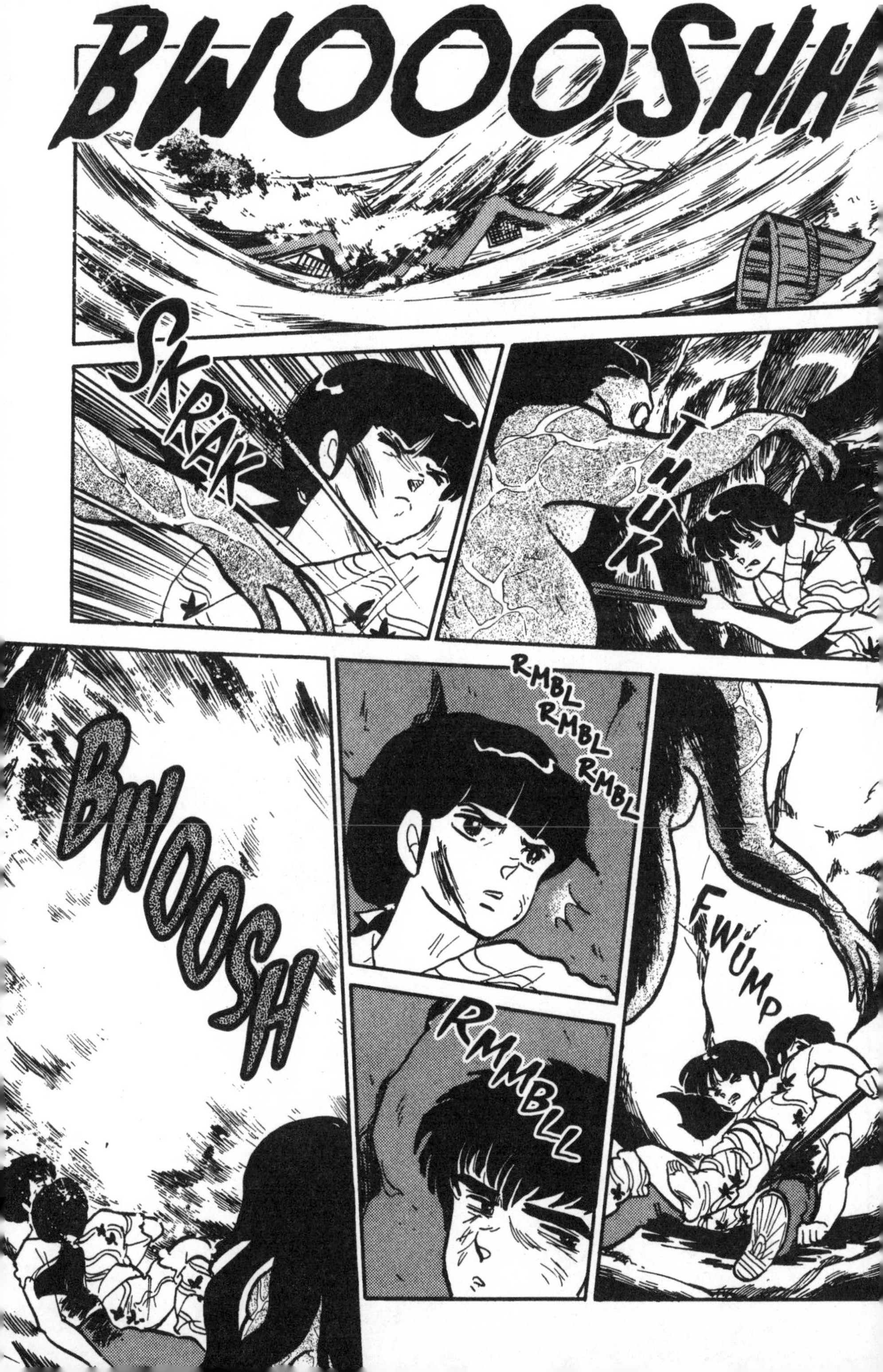
BWOOOSHH
THUK
SKRAK
FWUMP
RMBL RMBL RMBL
RMMBLL
BWOOSH

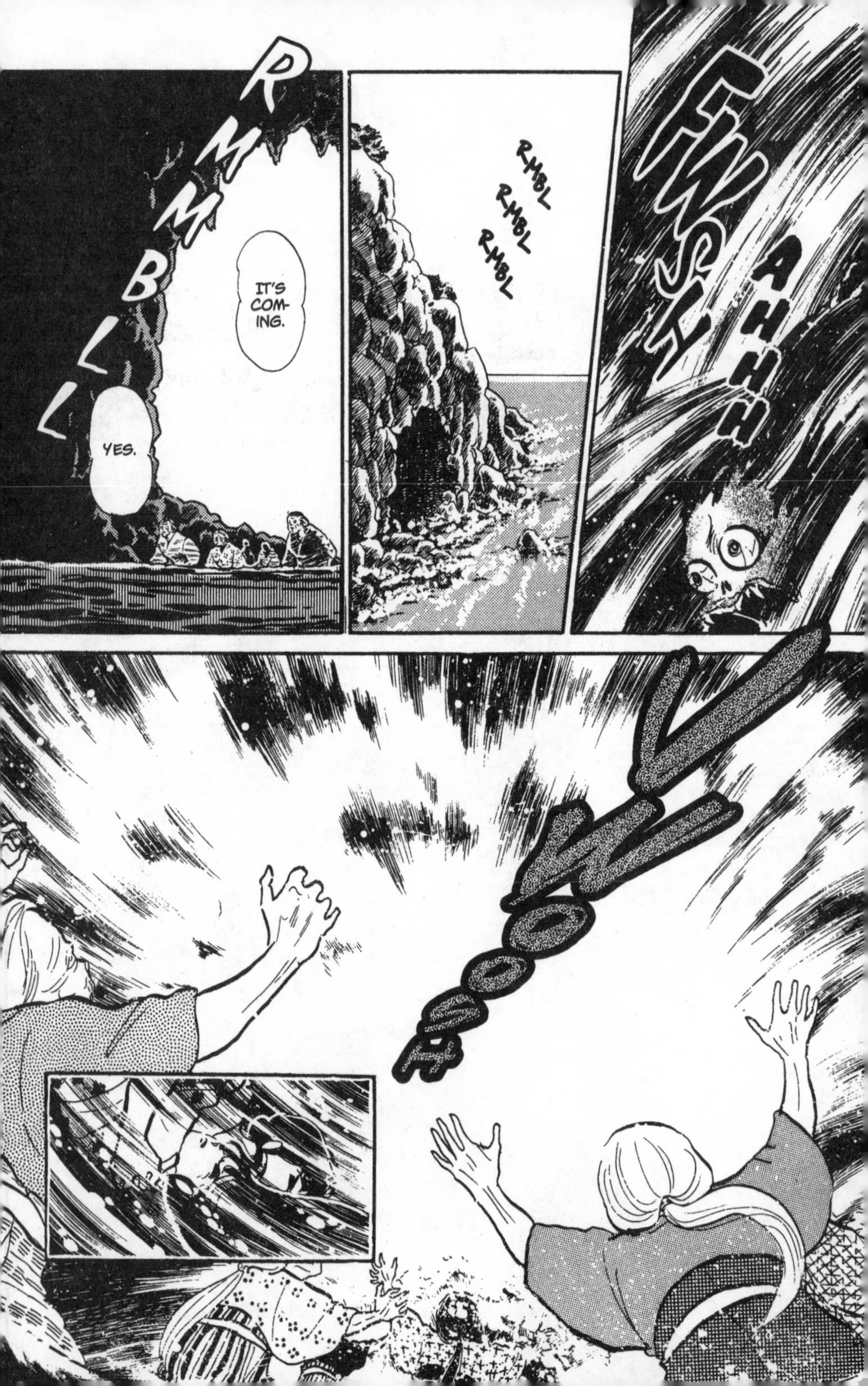
FWSHH
AHHHH
RMBL RMBL RMBL
RMMBLL
IT'S COMING.
YES.
VWOOSH

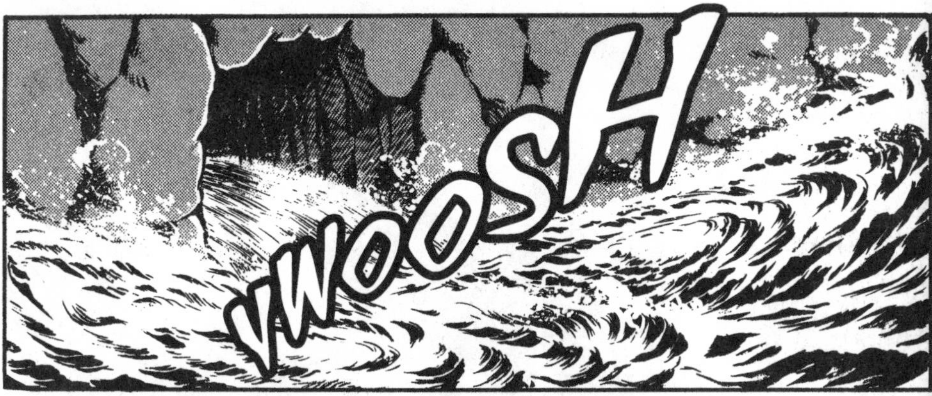
VWOOSH
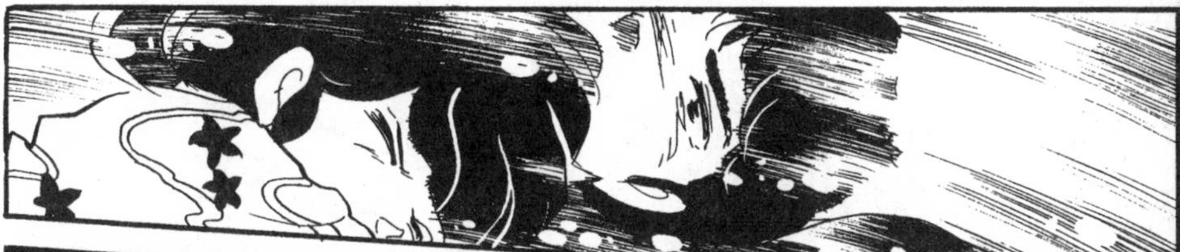
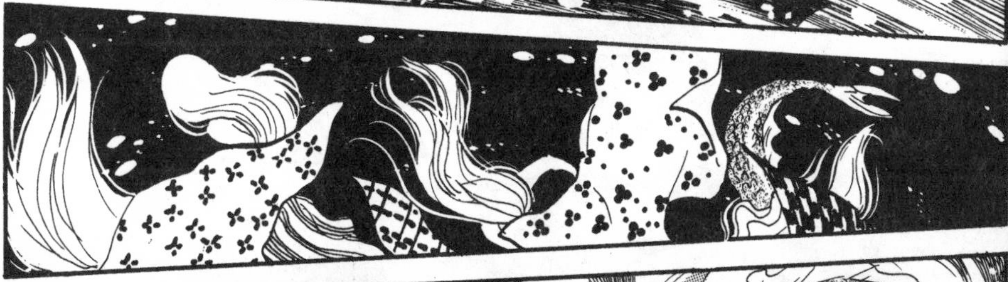
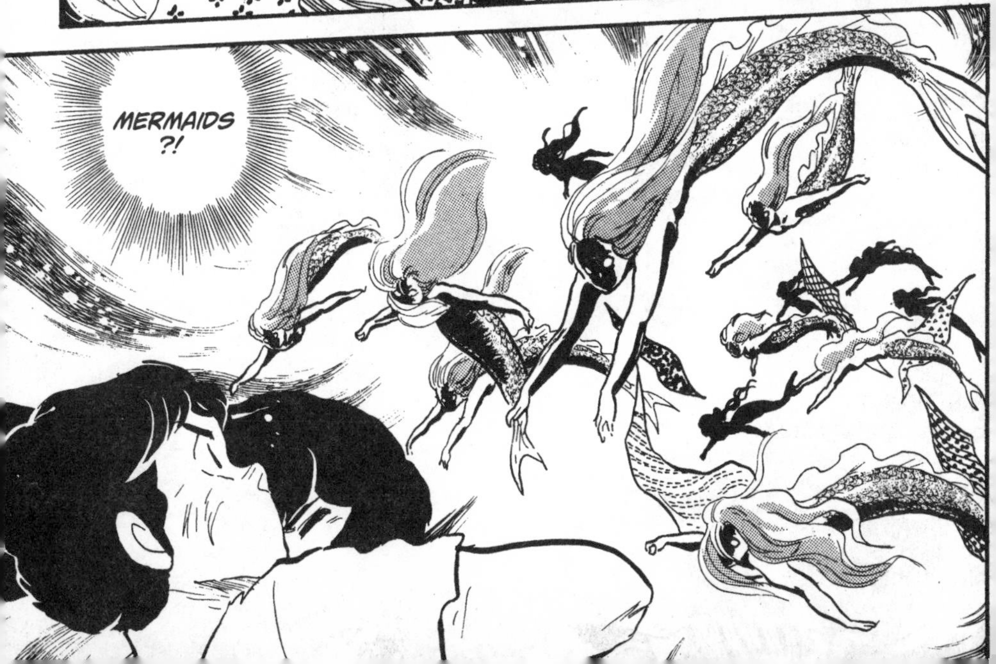
MERMAIDS ?!

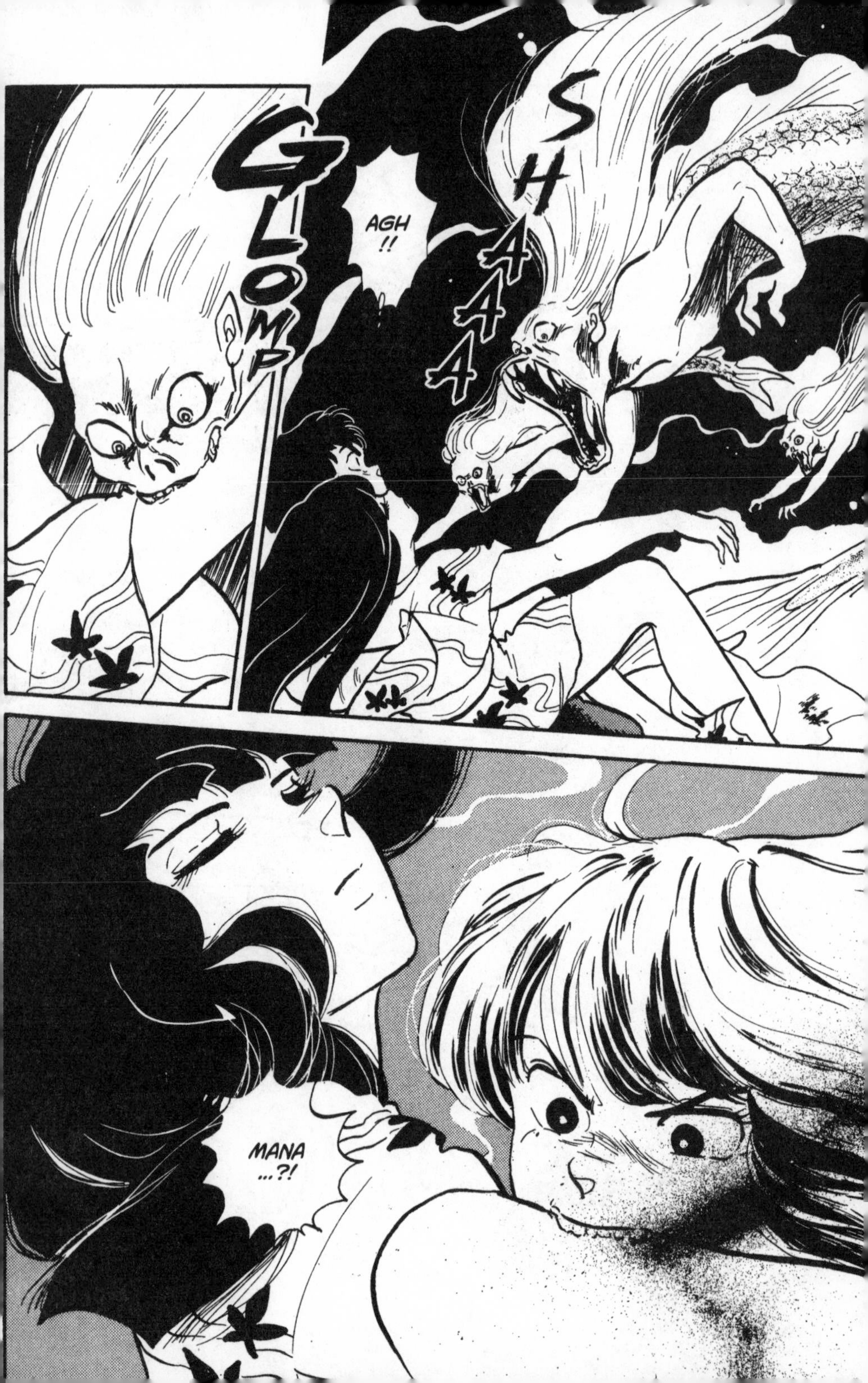
SHAAAA
AGH !!
GLOMP
MANA ...?!

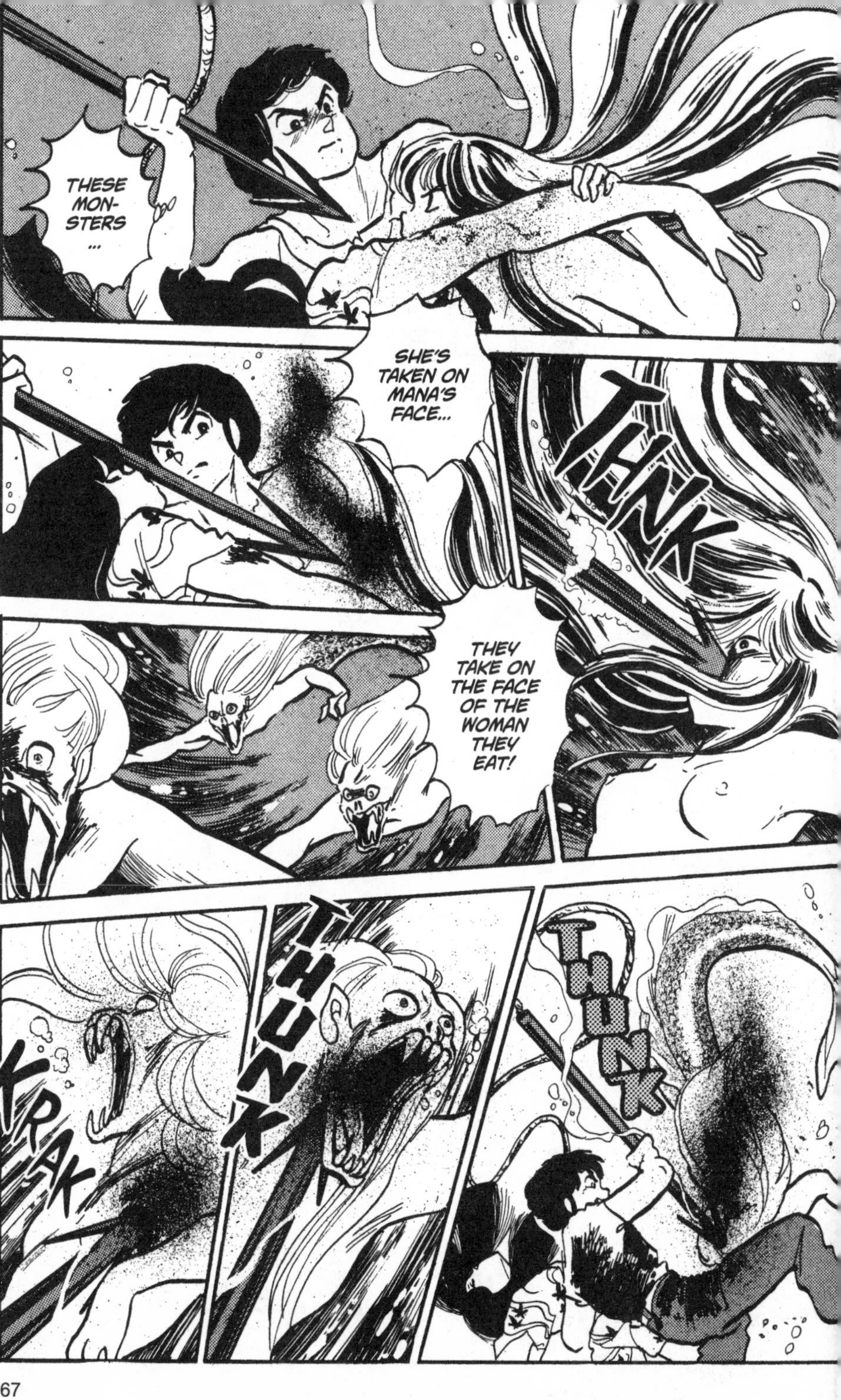
THESE MON-STERS ...
THNK
SHE'S TAKEN ON MANA'S FACE...
THEY TAKE ON THE FACE OF THE WOMAN THEY EAT!
THUNK
THUNK
KRAK

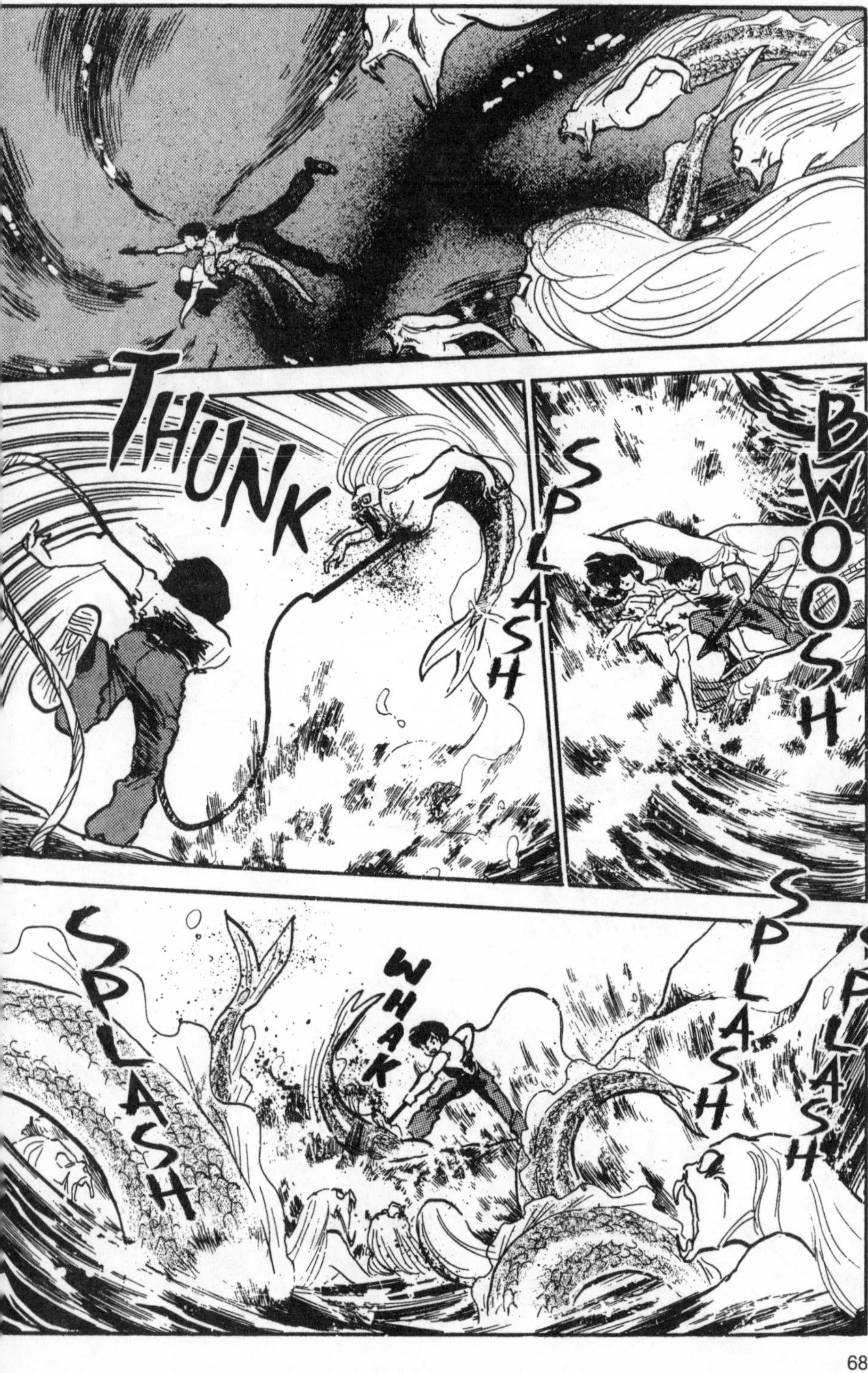
BWOOOSH
SPLASH
THUNK
SPLASH
SPLASH
WHAK
SPLASH

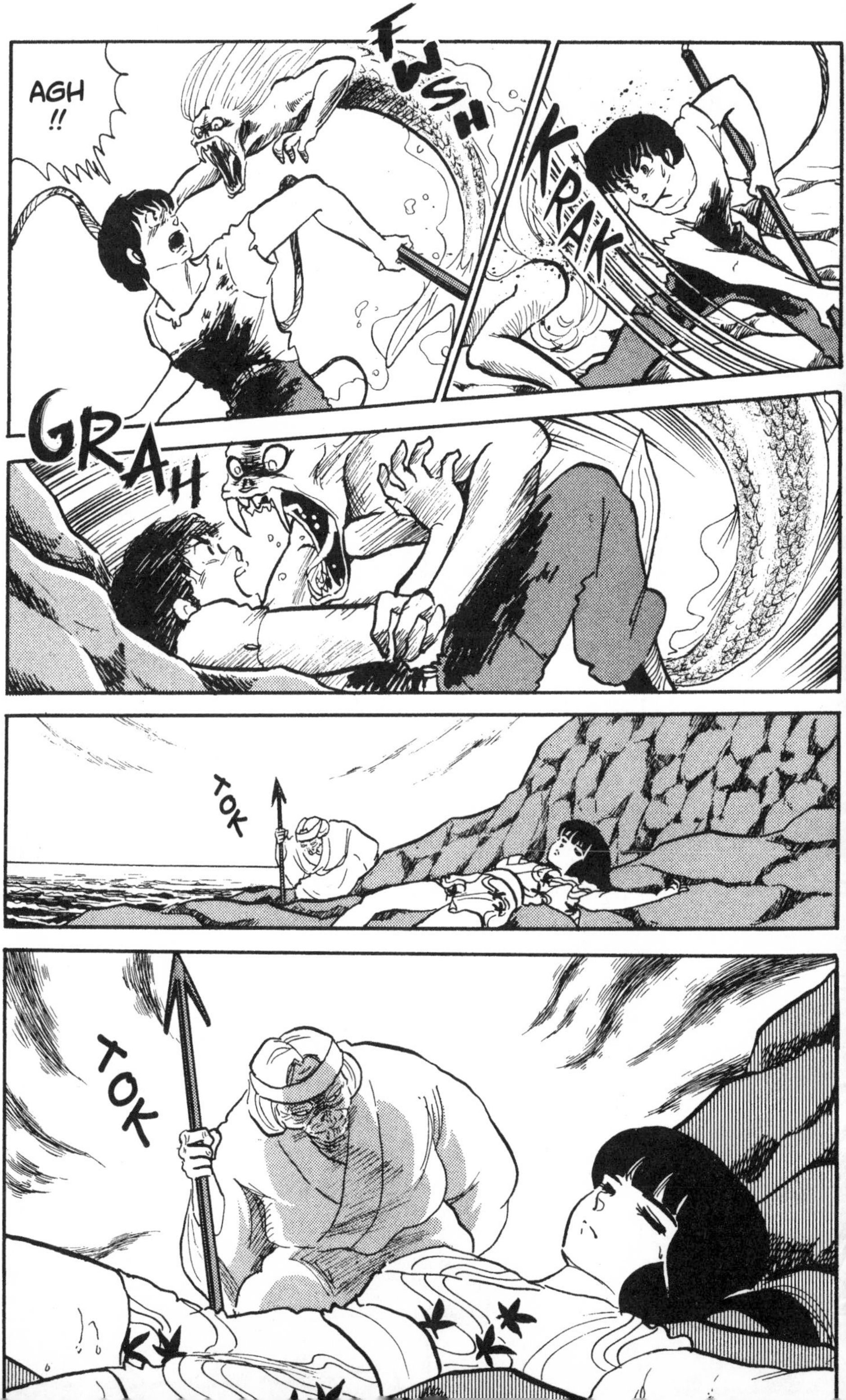
KRAK
AGH !!
FWSH
GRAH
TOK
TOK

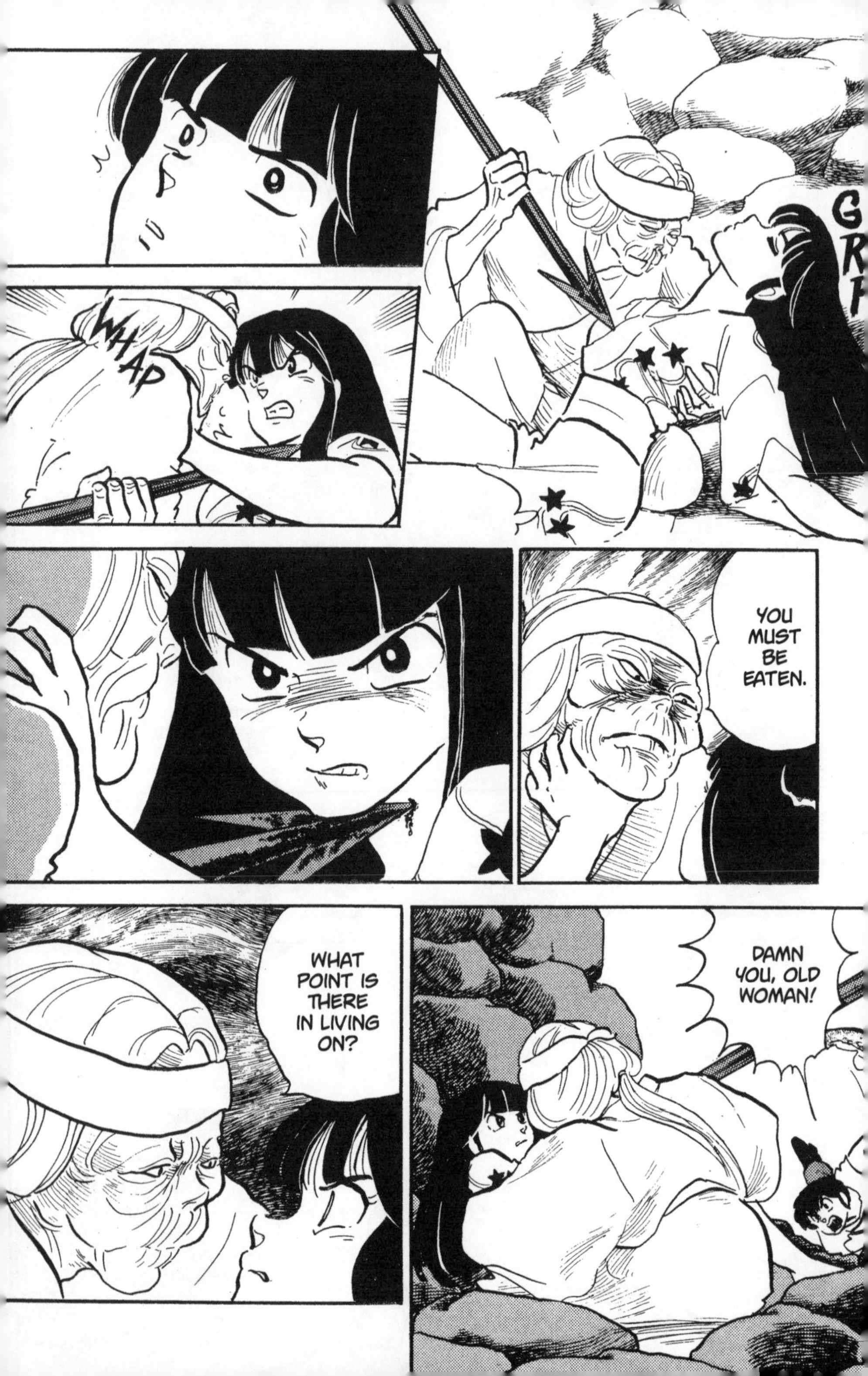
GRR
WHAP
YOU MUST BE EATEN.
DAMN YOU, OLD WOMAN!
WHAT POINT IS THERE IN LIVING ON?

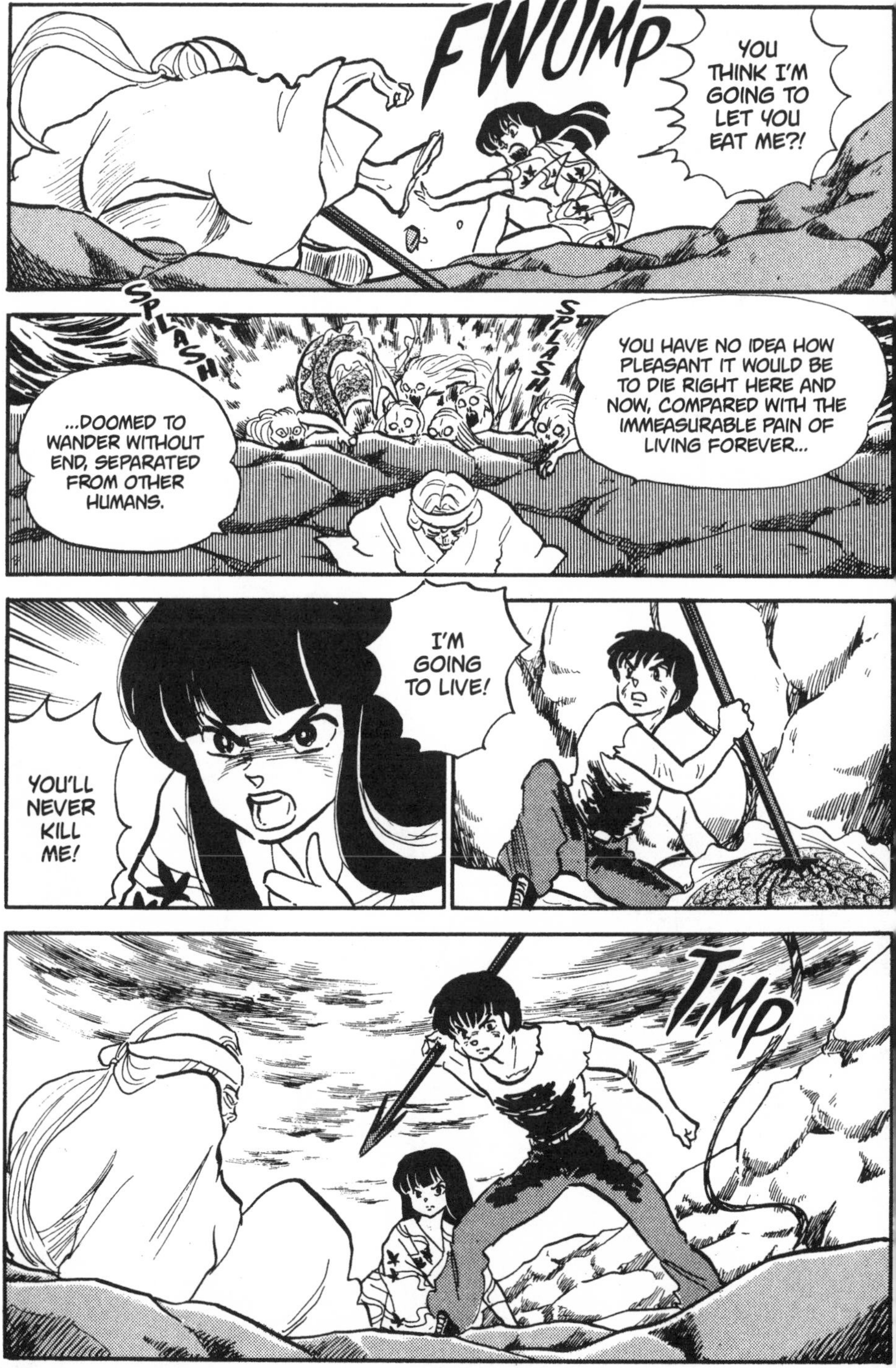
YOU THINK I'M GOING TO LET YOU EAT ME?!
FWUMP
SPLASH
YOU HAVE NO IDEA HOW PLEASANT IT WOULD BE TO DIE RIGHT HERE AND NOW, COMPARED WITH THE IMMEASURABLE PAIN OF LIVING FOREVER...
SPLASH
...DOOMED TO WANDER WITHOUT END, SEPARATED FROM OTHER HUMANS.
I'M GOING TO LIVE!
YOU'LL NEVER KILL ME!
TMP

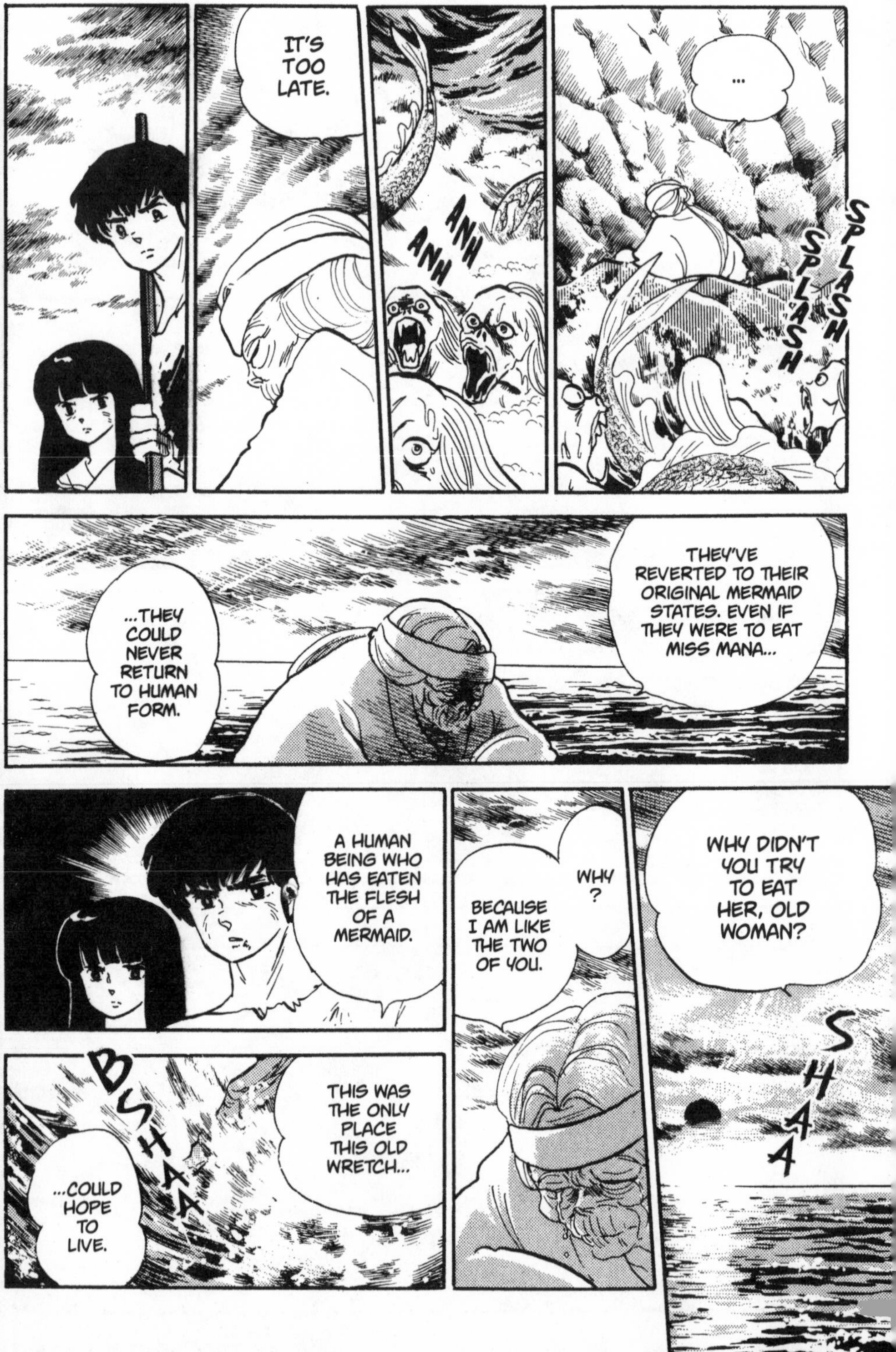
...
SPLASH SPLASH
ANHH ANHH
IT'S TOO LATE.
THEY'VE REVERTED TO THEIR ORIGINAL MERMAID STATES. EVEN IF THEY WERE TO EAT MISS MANA...
...THEY COULD NEVER RETURN TO HUMAN FORM.
WHY DIDN'T YOU TRY TO EAT HER, OLD WOMAN?
SHAA
WHY?
BECAUSE I AM LIKE THE TWO OF YOU.
A HUMAN BEING WHO HAS EATEN THE FLESH OF A MERMAID.
BSHAA
THIS WAS THE ONLY PLACE THIS OLD WRETCH...
...COULD HOPE TO LIVE.

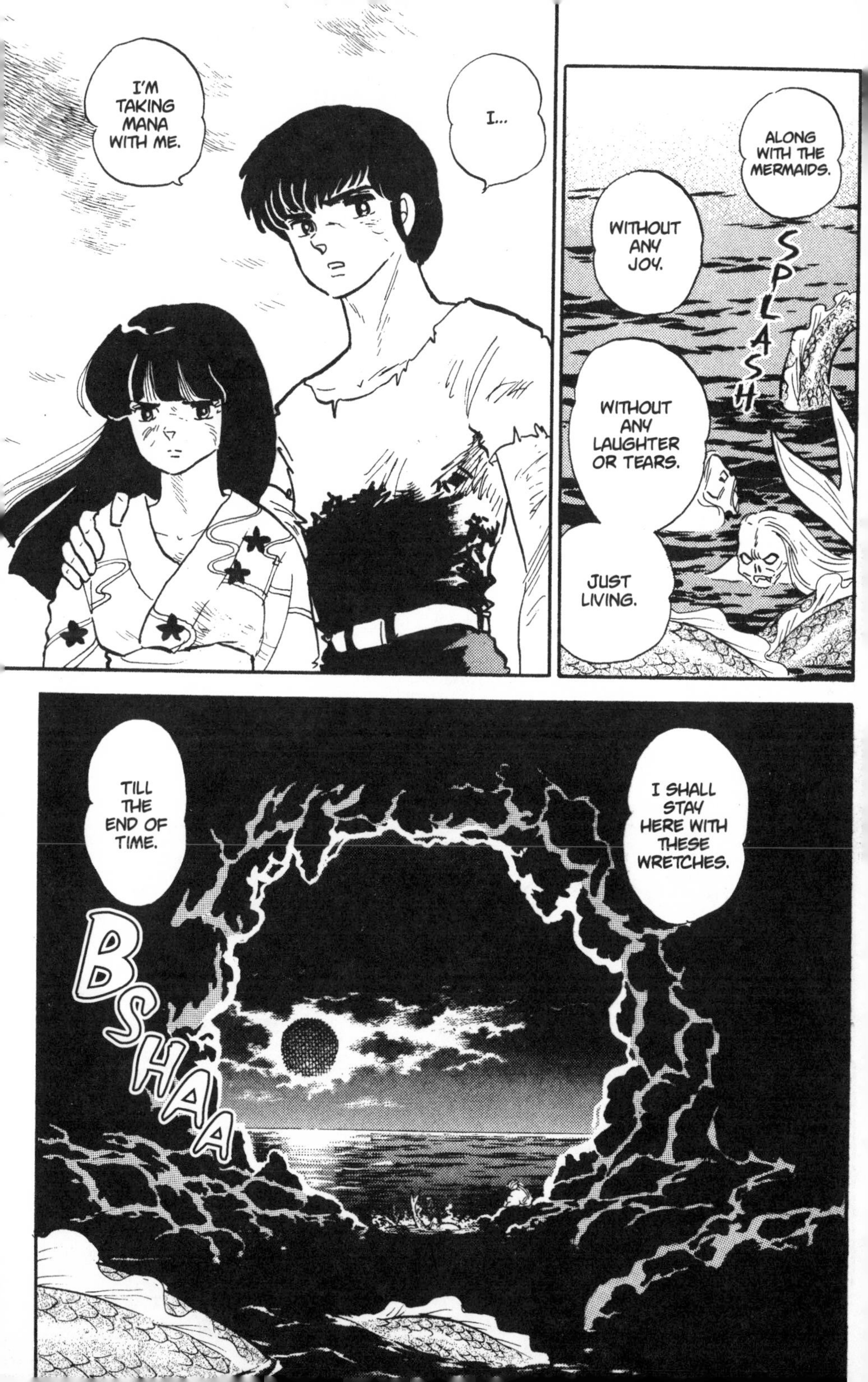
ALONG WITH THE MERMAIDS.
WITHOUT ANY JOY.
SPLASH
WITHOUT ANY LAUGHTER OR TEARS.
JUST LIVING.
I...
I'M TAKING MANA WITH ME.
I SHALL STAY HERE WITH THESE WRETCHES.
TILL THE END OF TIME.
BSHAA

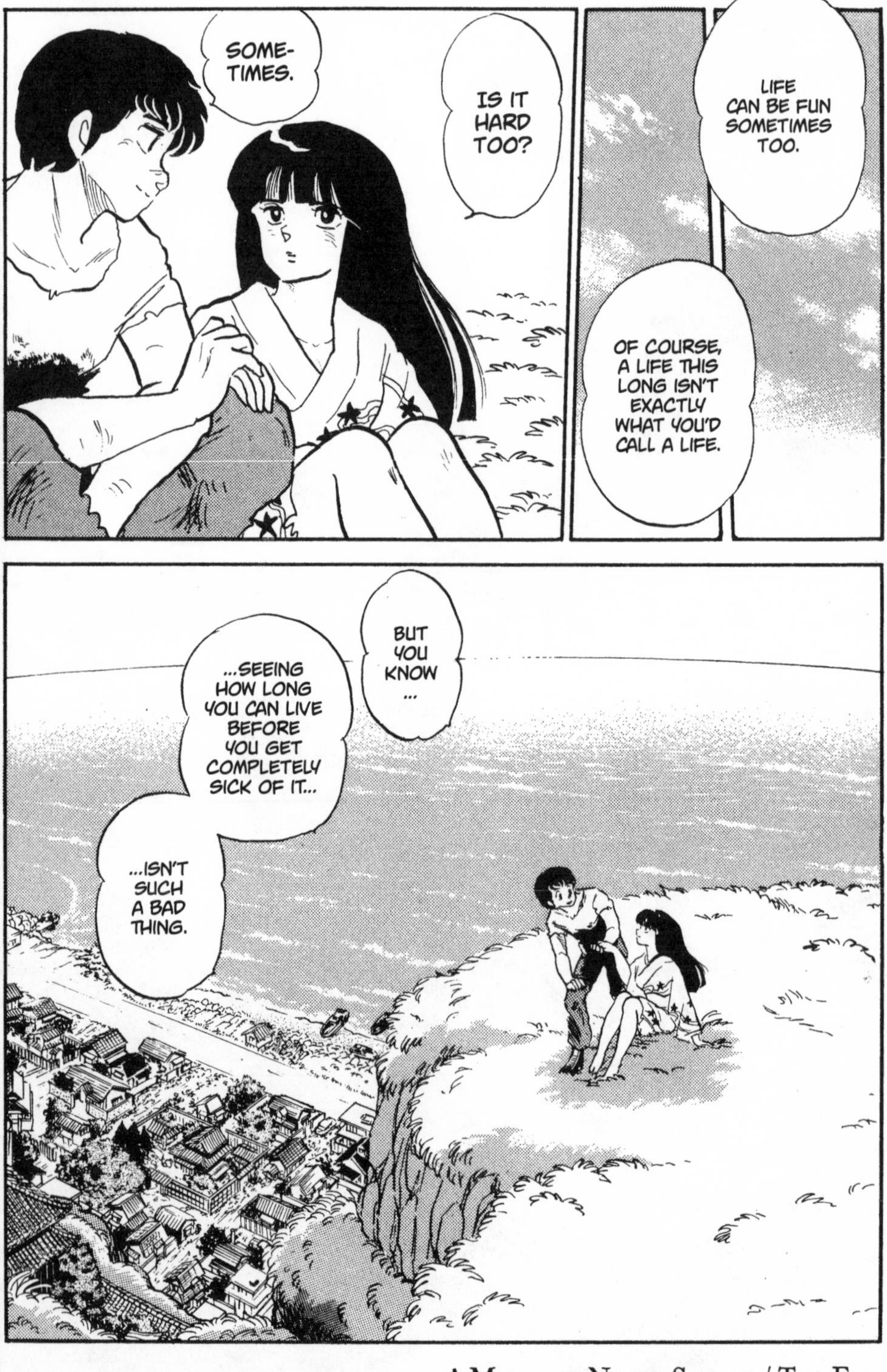
LIFE CAN BE FUN SOMETIMES TOO.
OF COURSE, A LIFE THIS LONG ISN'T EXACTLY WHAT YOU'D CALL A LIFE.
IS IT HARD TOO?
SOME-TIMES.
BUT YOU KNOW ...
...SEEING HOW LONG YOU CAN LIVE BEFORE YOU GET COMPLETELY SICK OF IT...
...ISN'T SUCH A BAD THING.

A Mermaid Never Smiles / The End

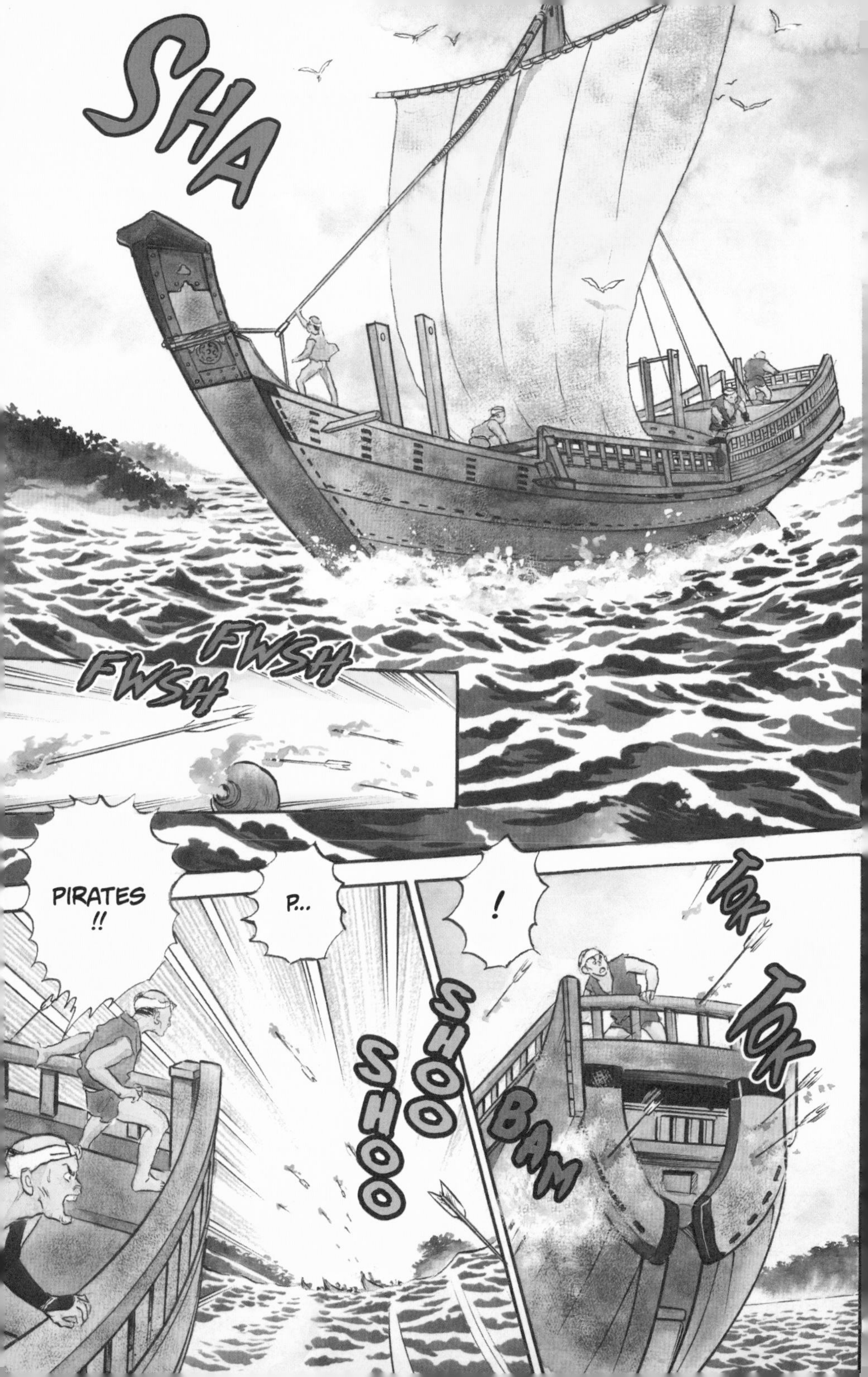
SHA
FWSH
FWSH
!
TOK
TOK
BAM
SHOO
SHOO
P...
PIRATES !!

Chapter 3: The Village of the Fighting Fish, Part 1

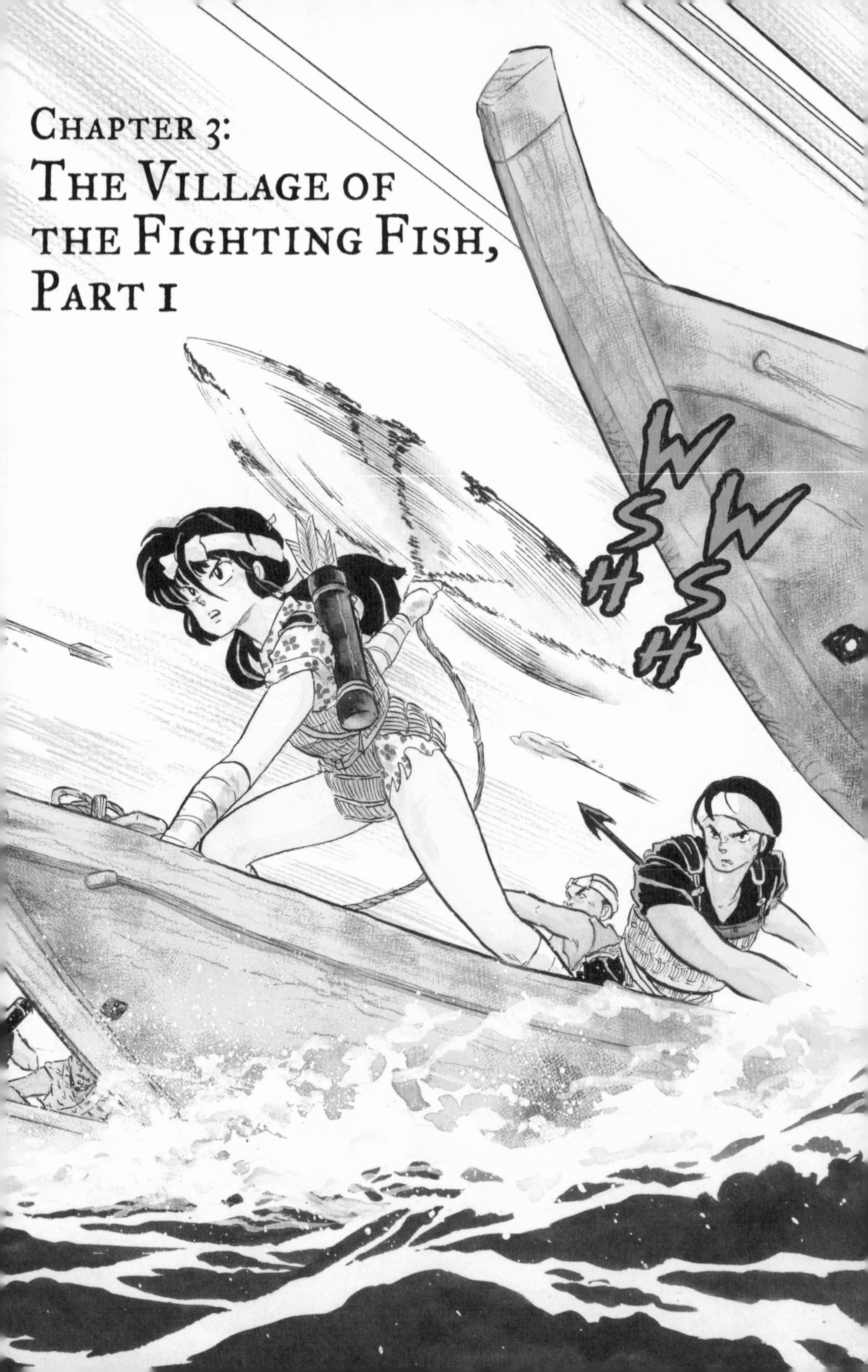
WSH
WSH

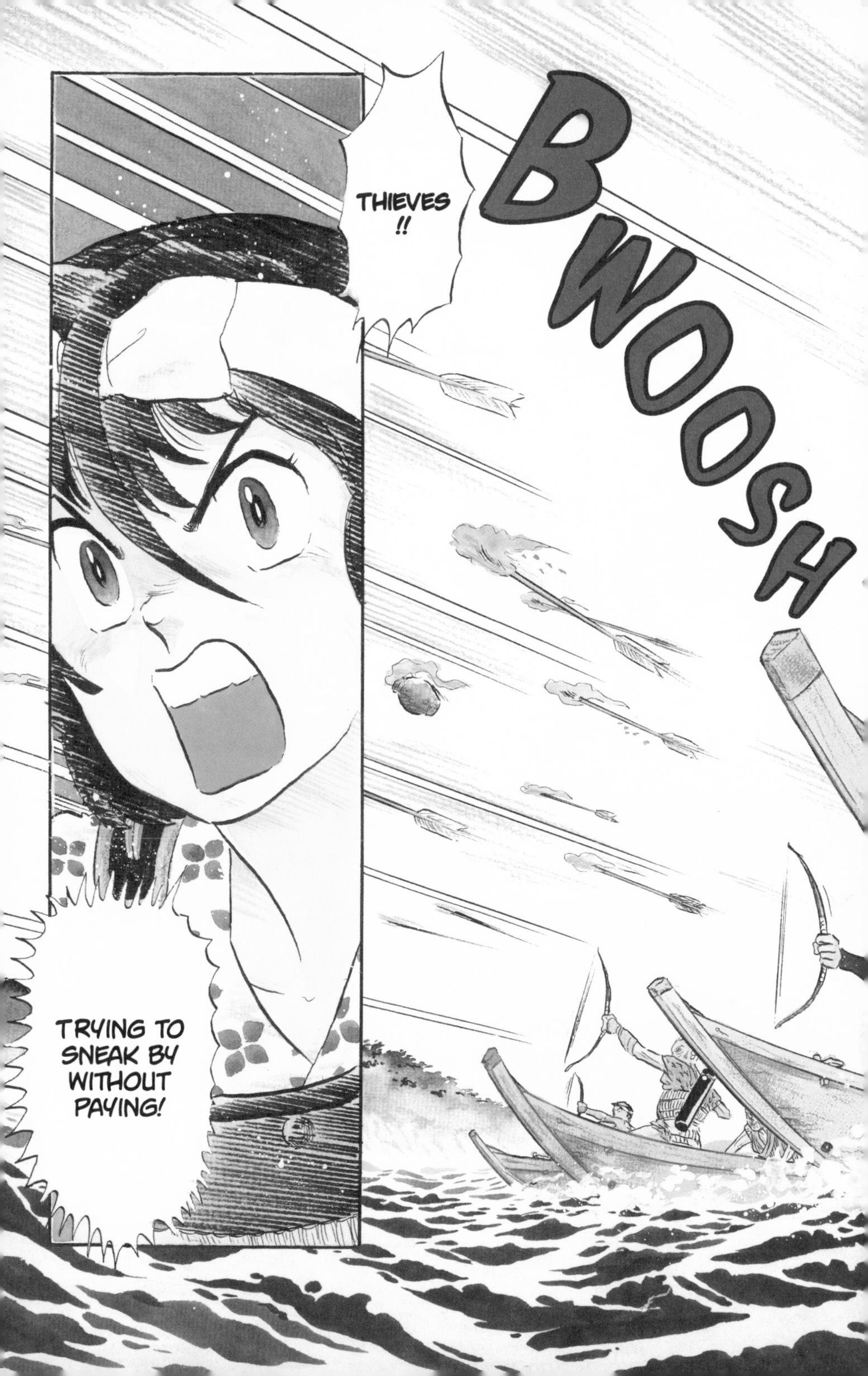
BWOOSH
THIEVES !!
TRYING TO SNEAK BY WITHOUT PAYING!

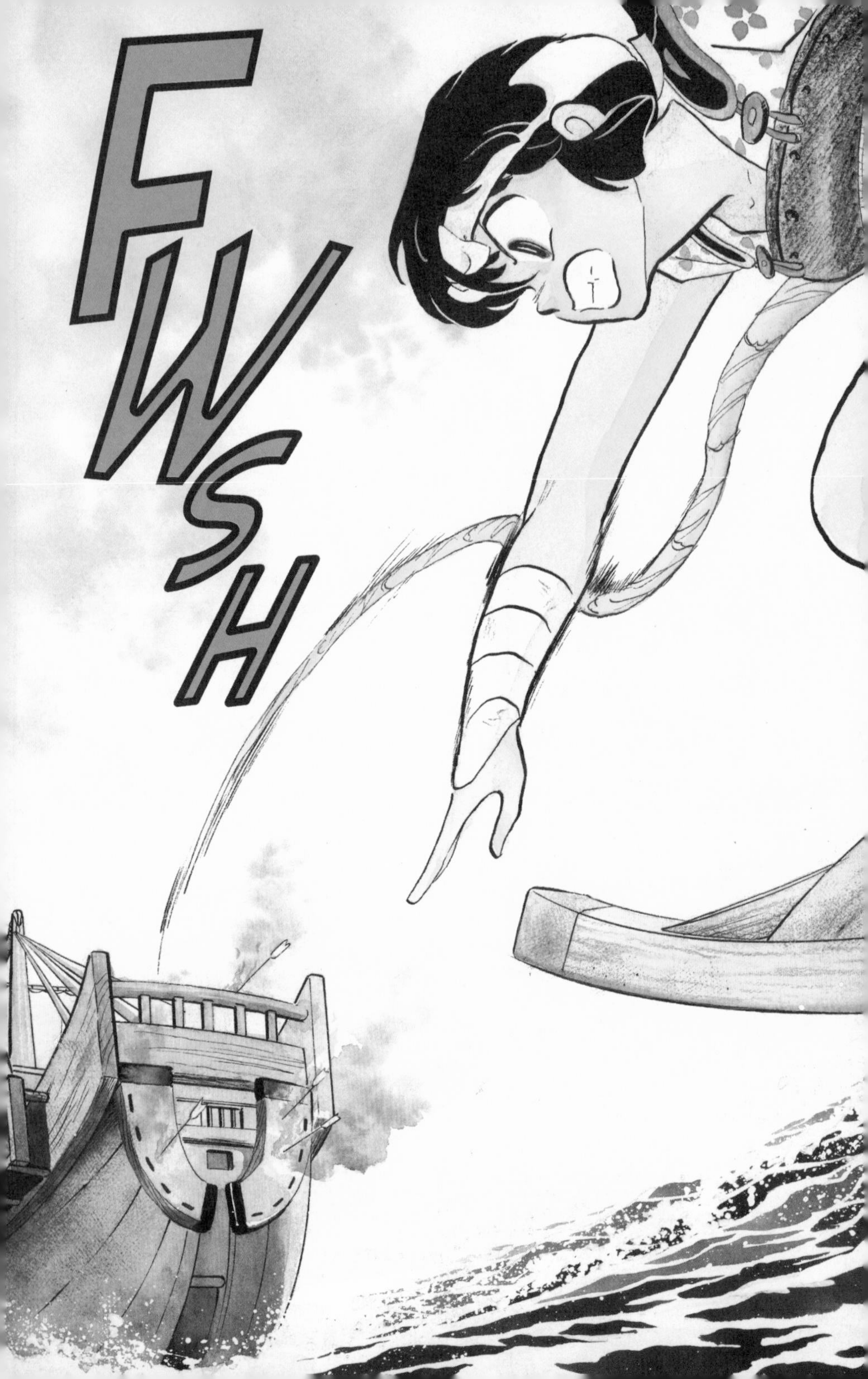
FWSH

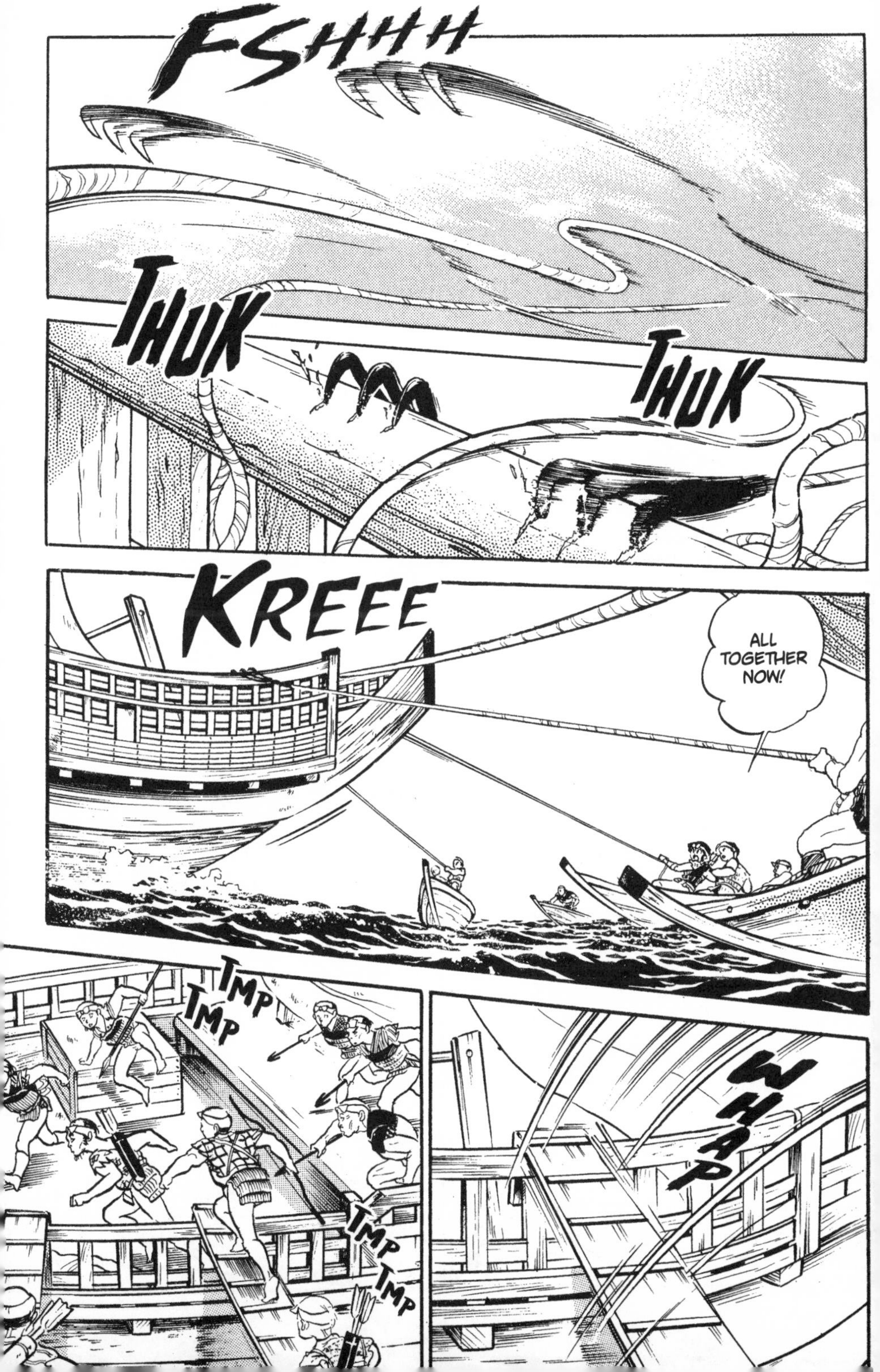
FSHHH
THUK
THUK
ALL TOGETHER NOW!
KREEE
WHAP
TMP TMP
TMP TMP

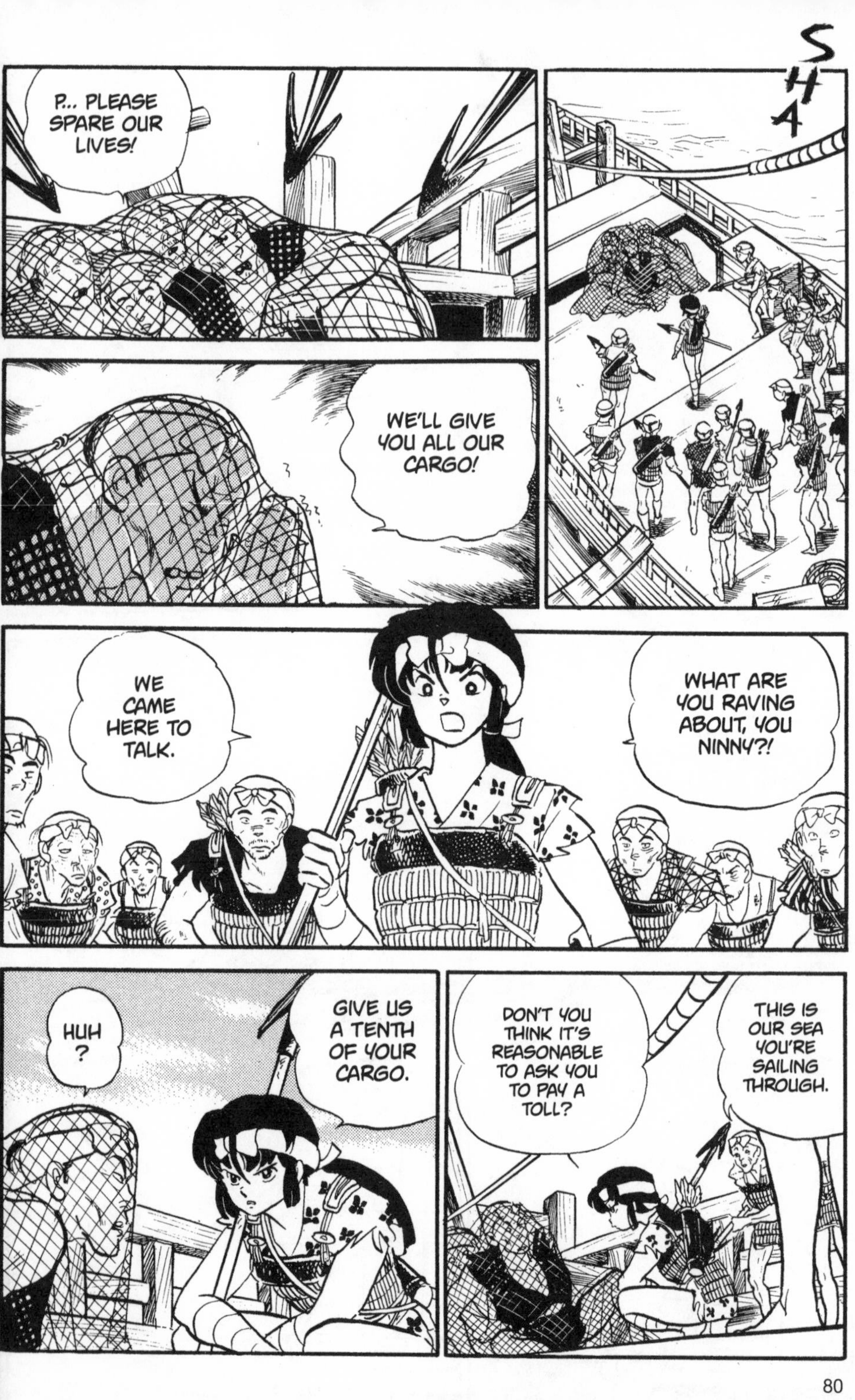
SHA
P... PLEASE SPARE OUR LIVES!
WE'LL GIVE YOU ALL OUR CARGO!
WHAT ARE YOU RAVING ABOUT, YOU NINNY?!
WE CAME HERE TO TALK.
THIS IS OUR SEA YOU'RE SAILING THROUGH.
DON'T YOU THINK IT'S REASONABLE TO ASK YOU TO PAY A TOLL?
GIVE US A TENTH OF YOUR CARGO.
HUH?

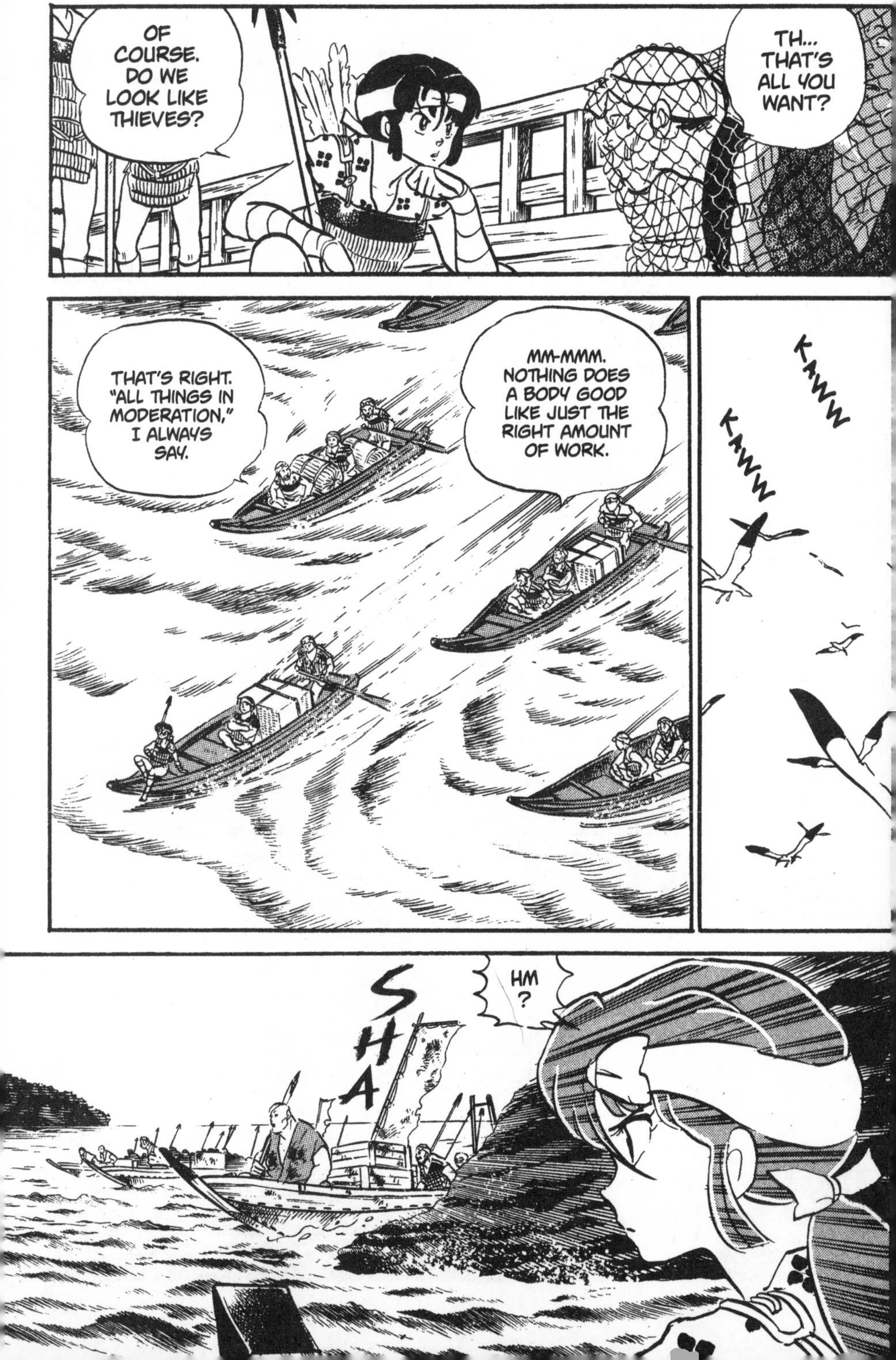
TH... THAT'S ALL YOU WANT?
OF COURSE. DO WE LOOK LIKE THIEVES?
KAWW
KAWW
MM-MMM. NOTHING DOES A BODY GOOD LIKE JUST THE RIGHT AMOUNT OF WORK.
THAT'S RIGHT. "ALL THINGS IN MODERATION," I ALWAYS SAY.
HM?
SHA

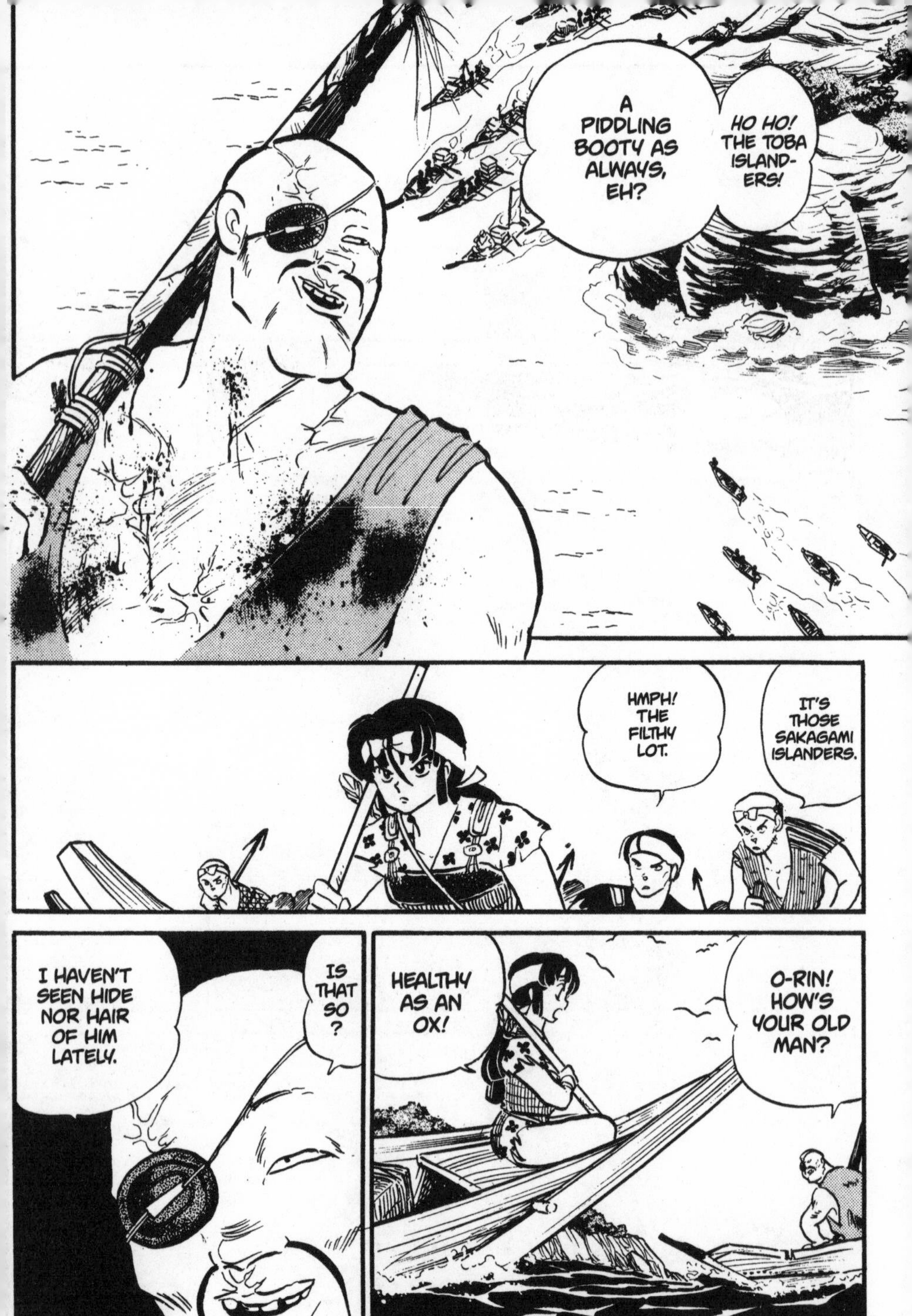
HO HO! THE TOBA ISLANDERS!
A PIDDLING BOOTY AS ALWAYS, EH?
IT'S THOSE SAKAGAMI ISLANDERS.
HMPH! THE FILTHY LOT.
O-RIN! HOW'S YOUR OLD MAN?
HEALTHY AS AN OX!
IS THAT SO?
I HAVEN'T SEEN HIDE NOR HAIR OF HIM LATELY.

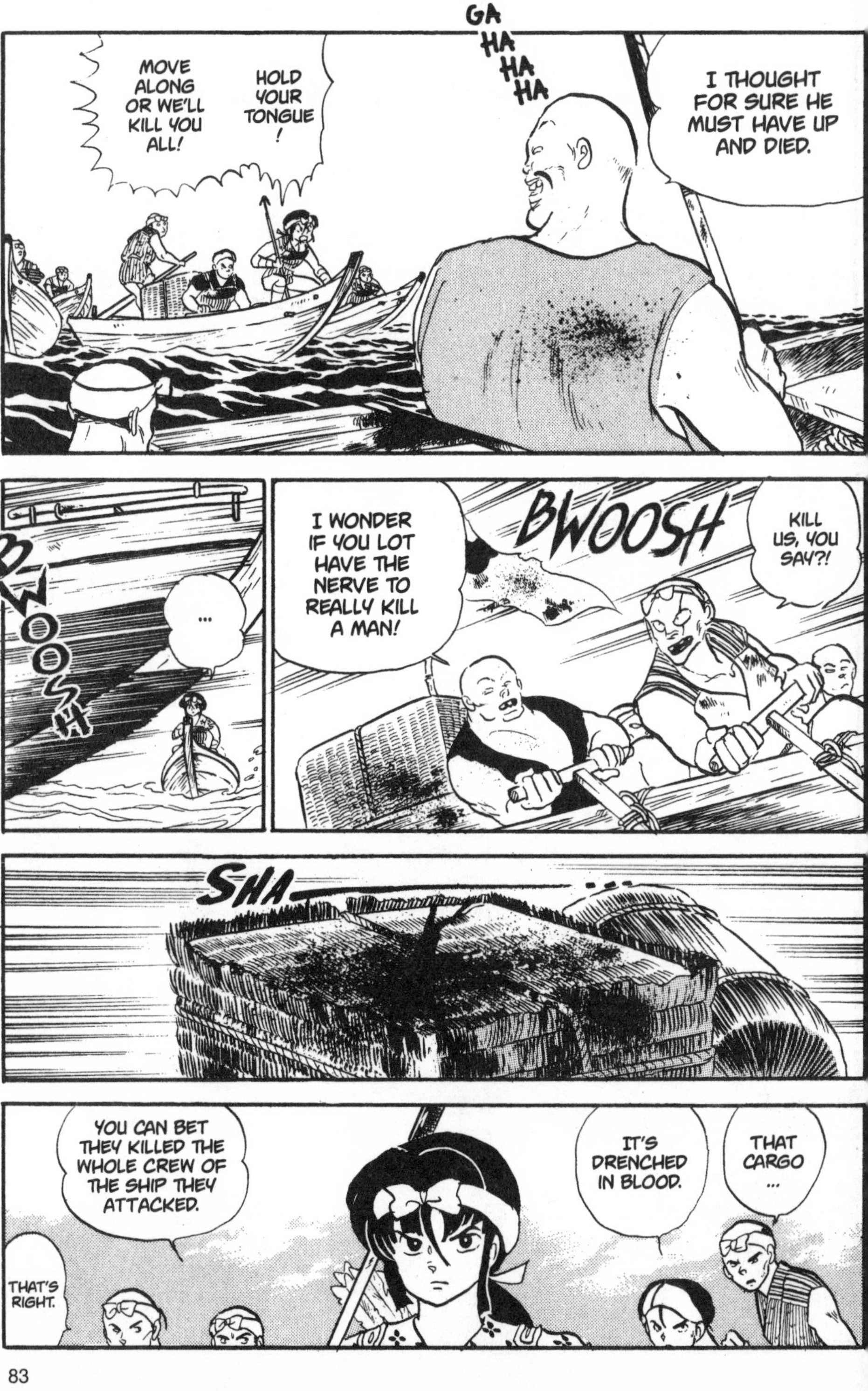
I THOUGHT FOR SURE HE MUST HAVE UP AND DIED.
GA HA HA HA
HOLD YOUR TONGUE!
MOVE ALONG OR WE'LL KILL YOU ALL!
KILL US, YOU SAY?!
BWOOSH
I WONDER IF YOU LOT HAVE THE NERVE TO REALLY KILL A MAN!
BWOOSH
...
SHA...
THAT CARGO ...
IT'S DRENCHED IN BLOOD.
YOU CAN BET THEY KILLED THE WHOLE CREW OF THE SHIP THEY ATTACKED.
THAT'S RIGHT.

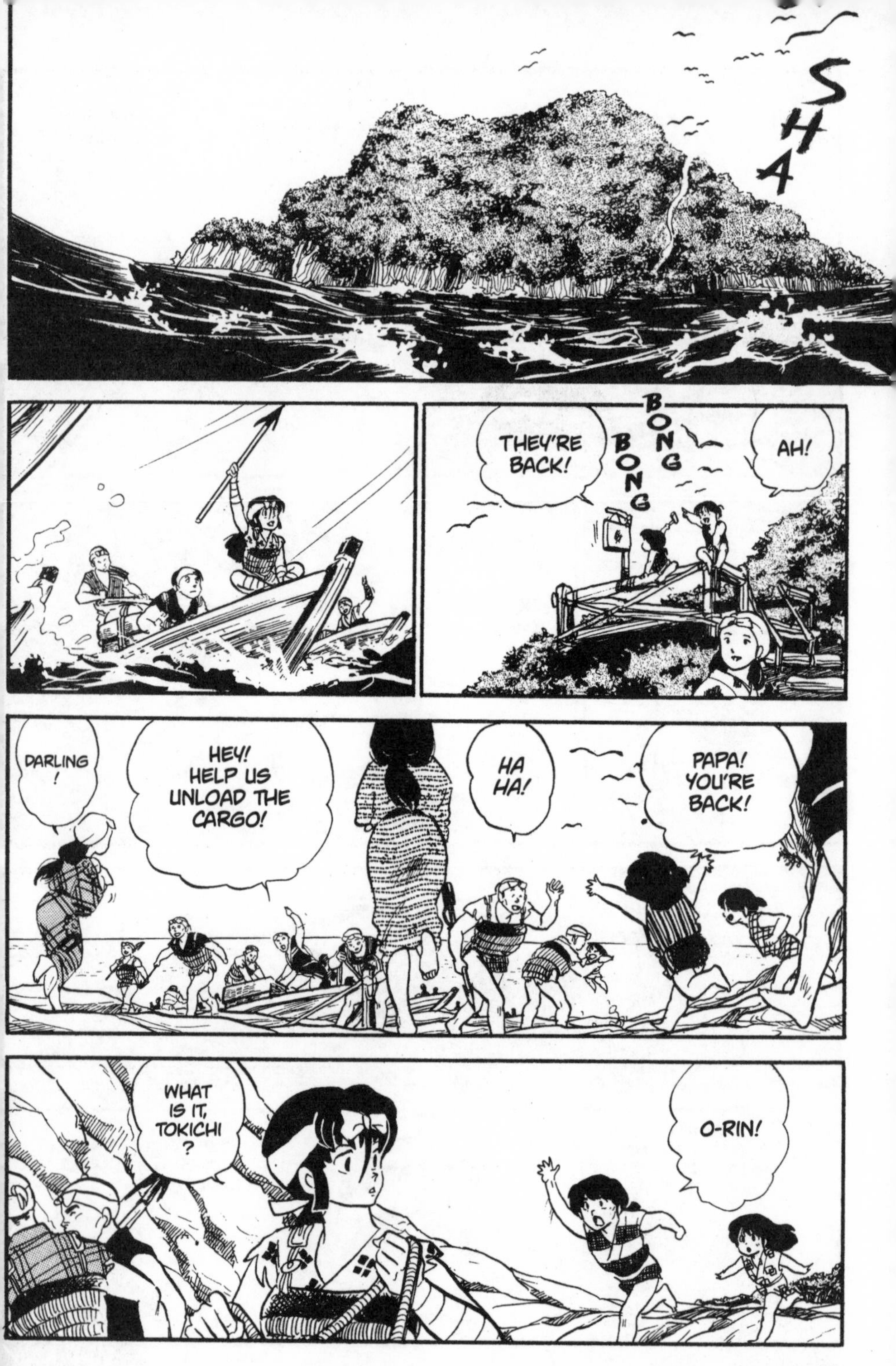
SHA
AH!
BONG
BONG
BONG
BONG
THEY'RE BACK!
PAPA! YOU'RE BACK!
HA HA!
HEY! HELP US UNLOAD THE CARGO!
DARLING!
O-RIN!
WHAT IS IT, TOKICHI?

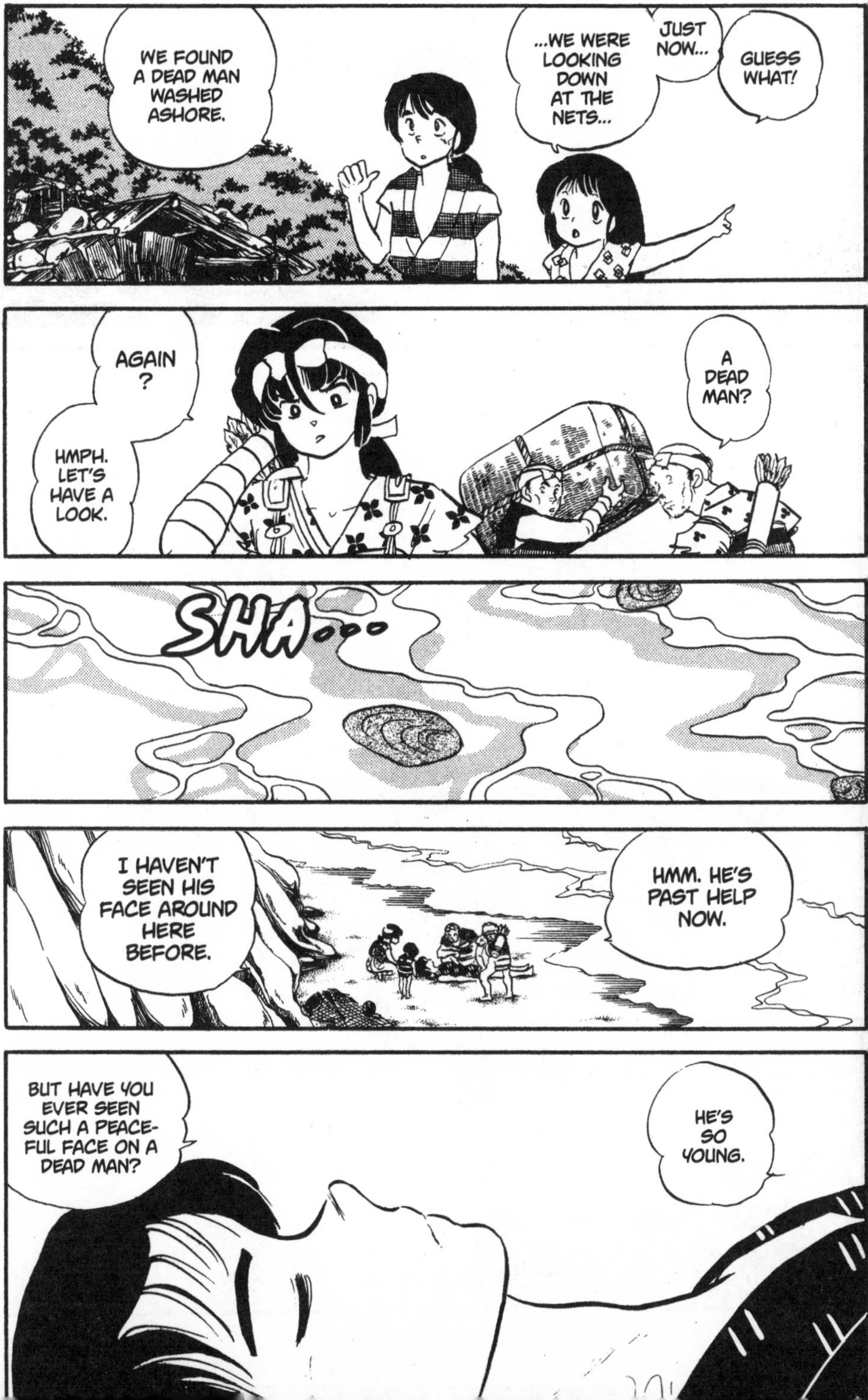
GUESS WHAT!
JUST NOW...
...WE WERE LOOKING DOWN AT THE NETS...
WE FOUND A DEAD MAN WASHED ASHORE.
A DEAD MAN?
AGAIN?
HMPH. LET'S HAVE A LOOK.
SHA...
HMM. HE'S PAST HELP NOW.
I HAVEN'T SEEN HIS FACE AROUND HERE BEFORE.
HE'S SO YOUNG.
BUT HAVE YOU EVER SEEN SUCH A PEACE-FUL FACE ON A DEAD MAN?

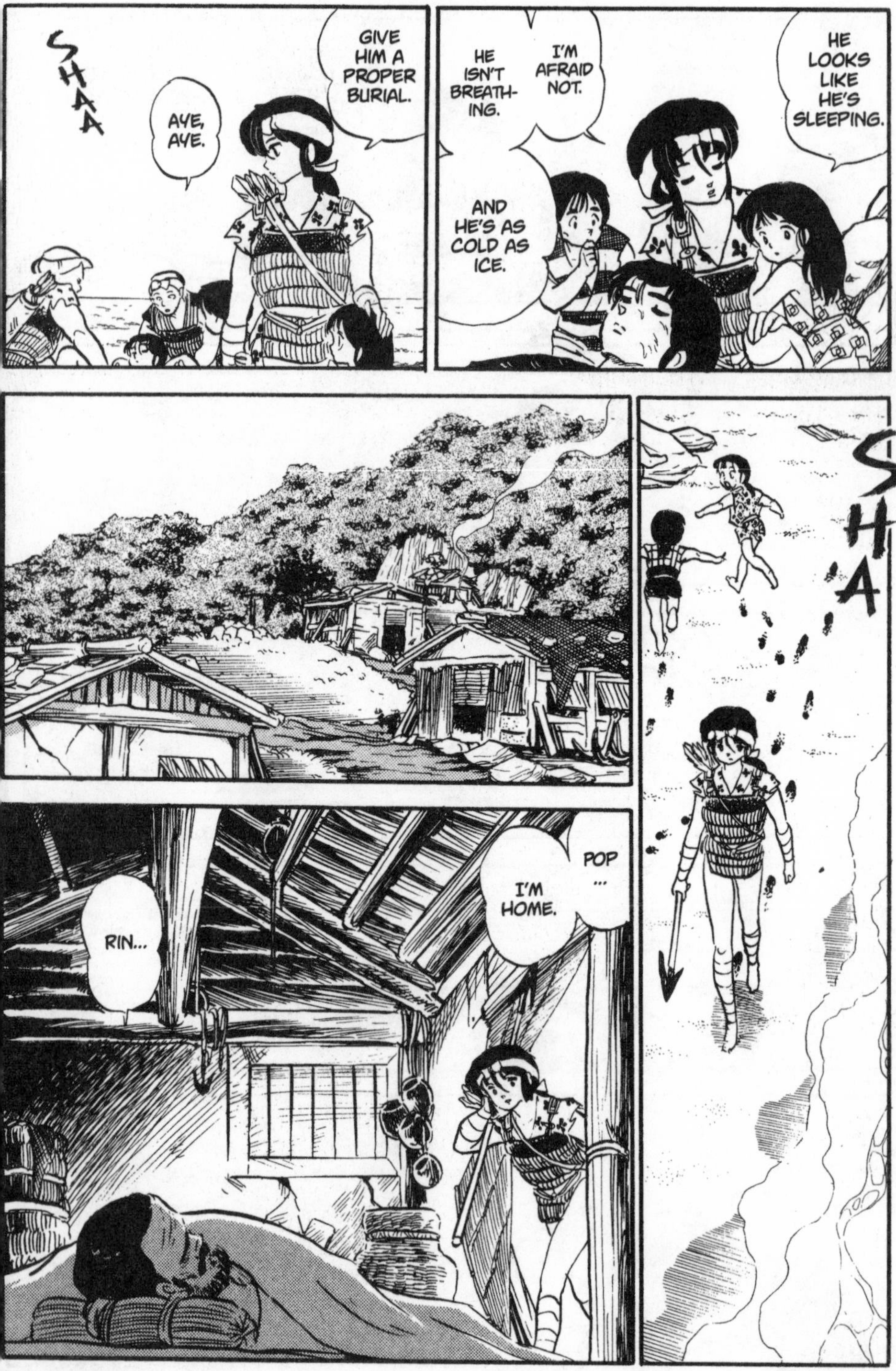
HE LOOKS LIKE HE'S SLEEPING.
I'M AFRAID NOT.
HE ISN'T BREATHING.
AND HE'S AS COLD AS ICE.
GIVE HIM A PROPER BURIAL.
AYE, AYE.
SHAA
SHA
POP ...
I'M HOME.
RIN...

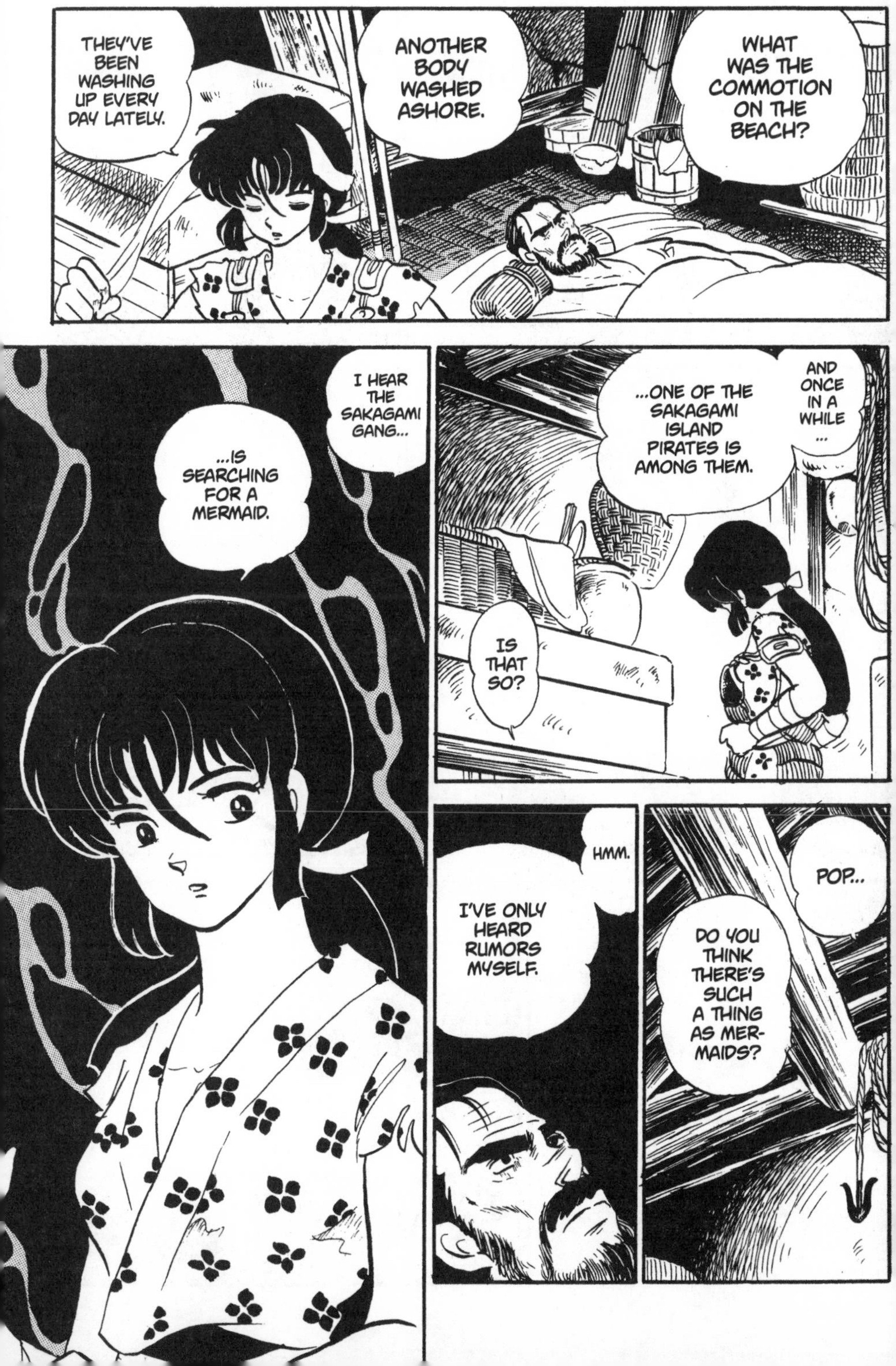
WHAT WAS THE COMMOTION ON THE BEACH?
ANOTHER BODY WASHED ASHORE.
THEY'VE BEEN WASHING UP EVERY DAY LATELY.
AND ONCE IN A WHILE ...
...ONE OF THE SAKAGAMI ISLAND PIRATES IS AMONG THEM.
IS THAT SO?
POP...
DO YOU THINK THERE'S SUCH A THING AS MER-MAIDS?
HMM.
I'VE ONLY HEARD RUMORS MYSELF.
I HEAR THE SAKAGAMI GANG...
...IS SEARCHING FOR A MERMAID.

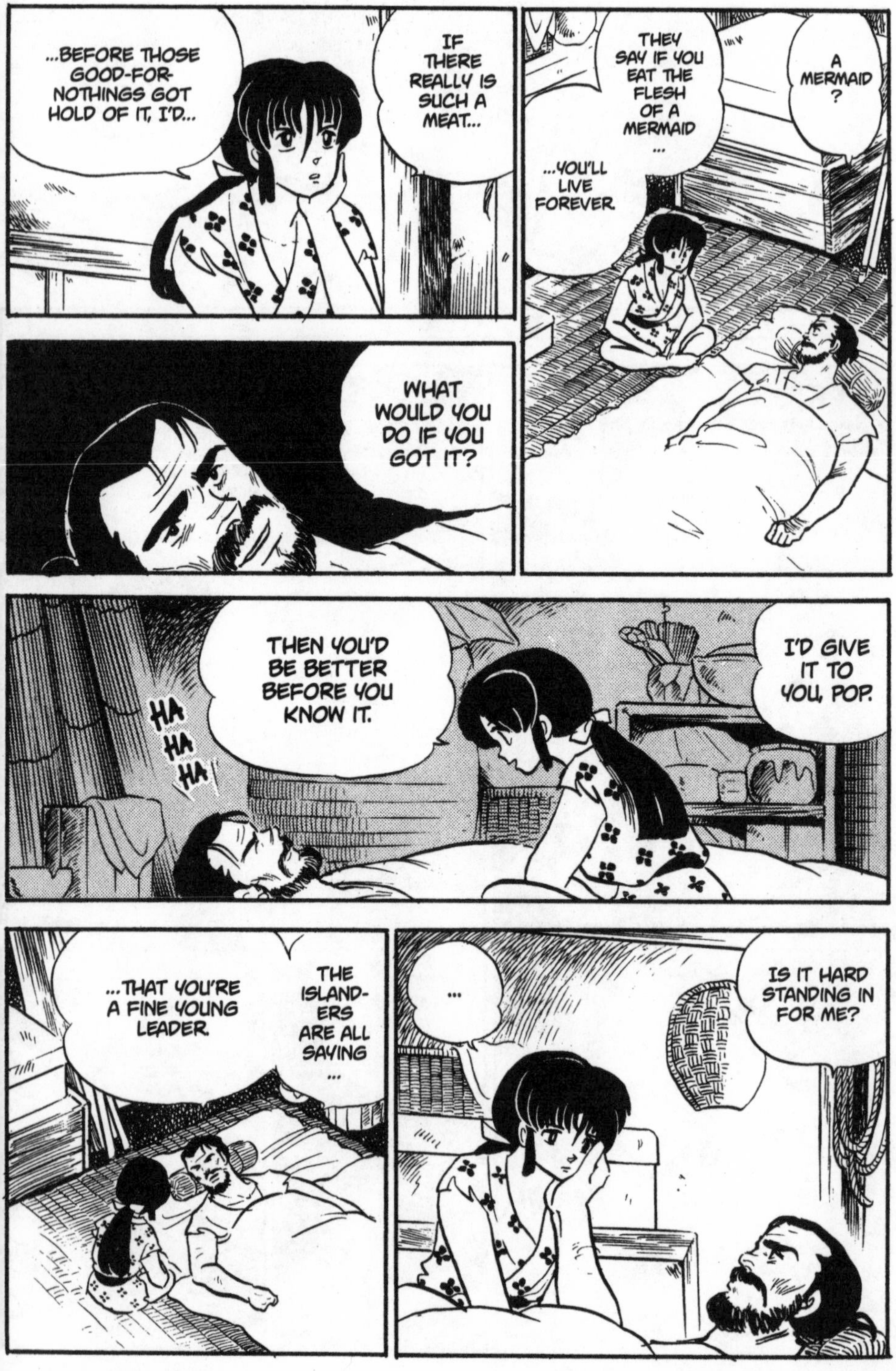
A MERMAID?
THEY SAY IF YOU EAT THE FLESH OF A MERMAID...
...YOU'LL LIVE FOREVER.
IF THERE REALLY IS SUCH A MEAT...
...BEFORE THOSE GOOD-FOR-NOTHINGS GOT HOLD OF IT, I'D...
WHAT WOULD YOU DO IF YOU GOT IT?
I'D GIVE IT TO YOU, POP.
THEN YOU'D BE BETTER BEFORE YOU KNOW IT.
HA HA HA
IS IT HARD STANDING IN FOR ME?
...
THE ISLANDERS ARE ALL SAYING...
...THAT YOU'RE A FINE YOUNG LEADER.

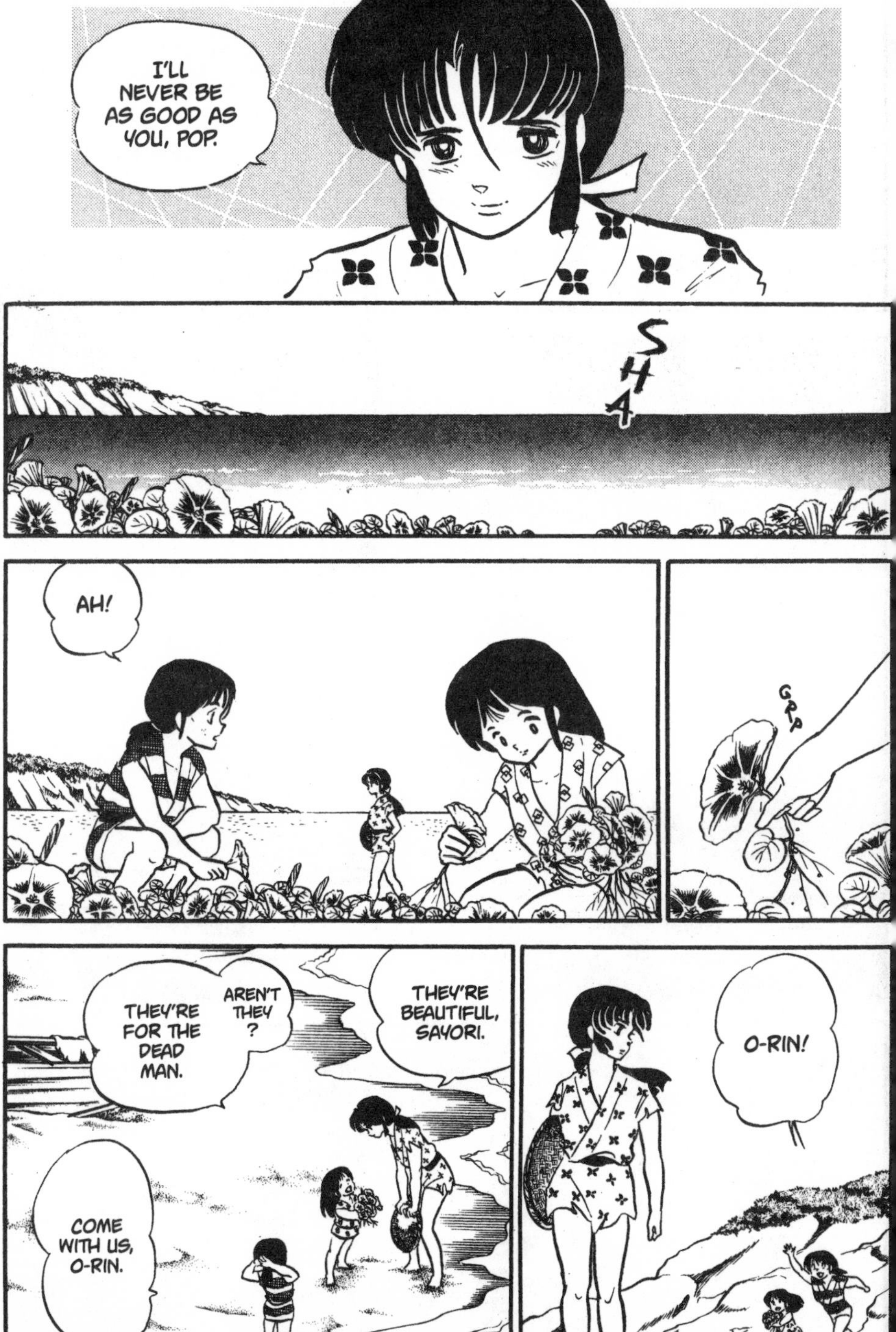
I'LL NEVER BE AS GOOD AS YOU, POP.
SHA
GRP
AH!
O-RIN!
THEY'RE BEAUTIFUL, SAYORI.
AREN'T THEY?
THEY'RE FOR THE DEAD MAN.
COME WITH US, O-RIN.

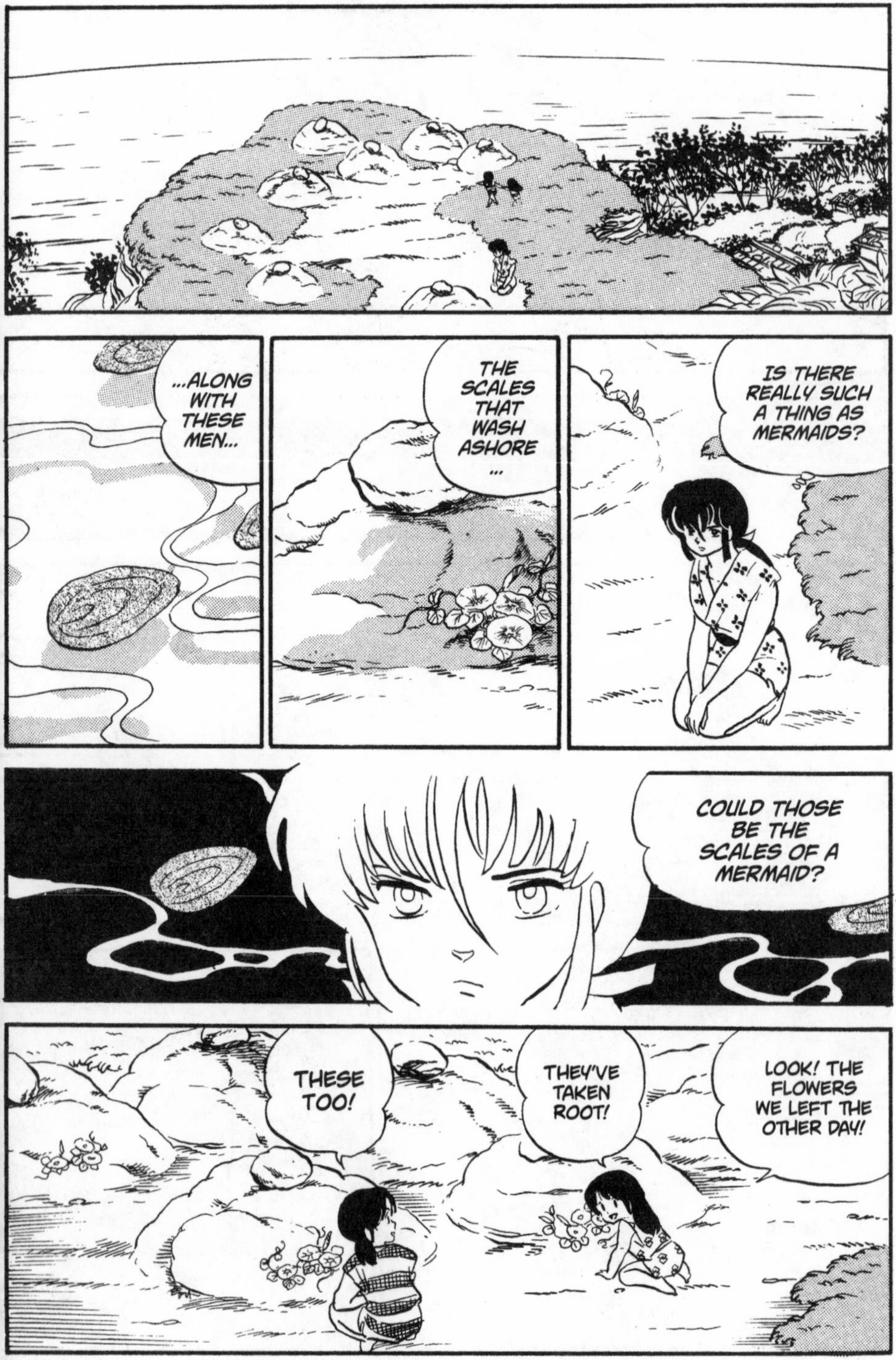
IS THERE REALLY SUCH A THING AS MERMAIDS?
THE SCALES THAT WASH ASHORE ...
...ALONG WITH THESE MEN...
COULD THOSE BE THE SCALES OF A MERMAID?
LOOK! THE FLOWERS WE LEFT THE OTHER DAY!
THEY'VE TAKEN ROOT!
THESE TOO!

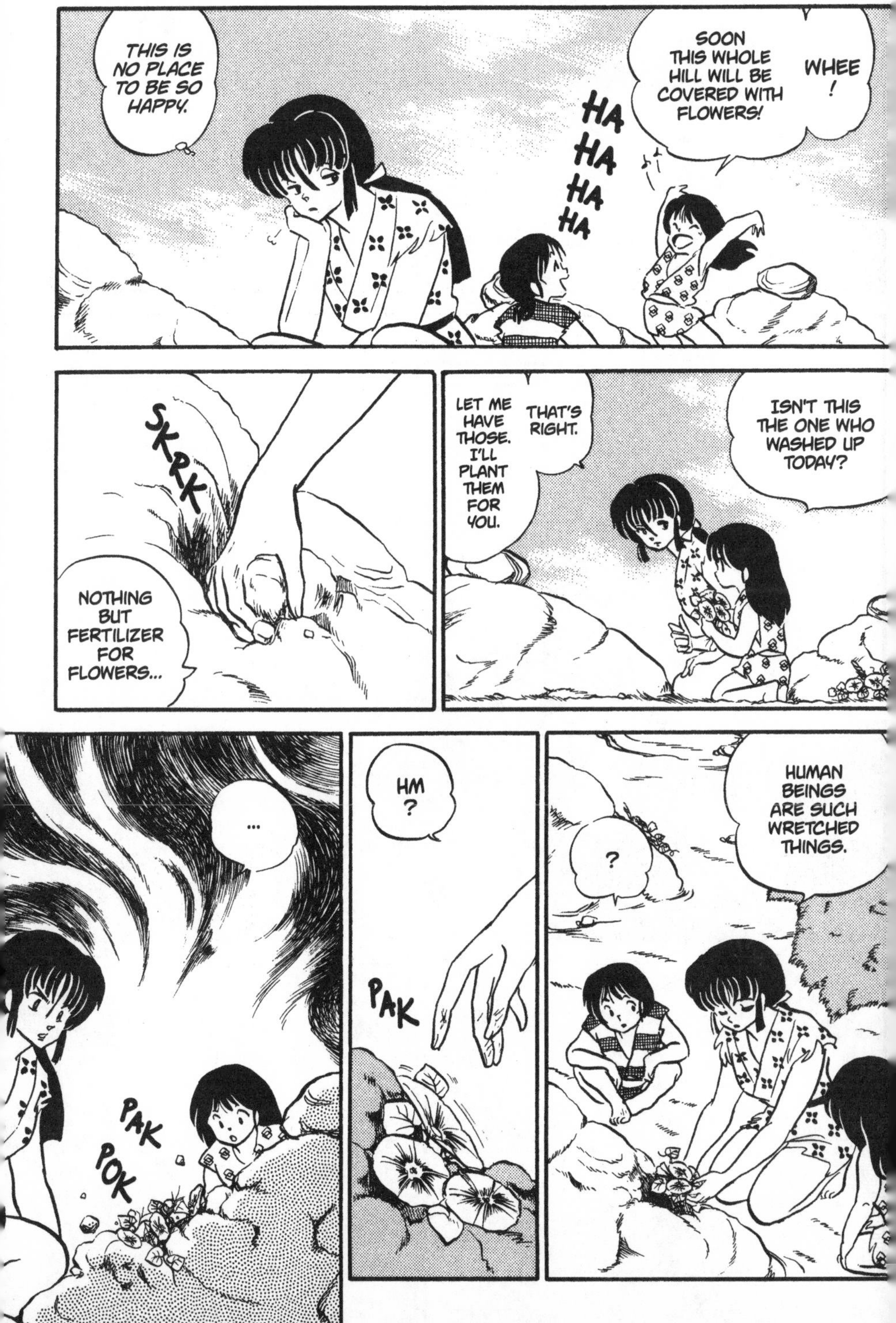
WHEE!
SOON THIS WHOLE HILL WILL BE COVERED WITH FLOWERS!
HA HA HA HA
THIS IS NO PLACE TO BE SO HAPPY.
ISN'T THIS THE ONE WHO WASHED UP TODAY?
THAT'S RIGHT.
LET ME HAVE THOSE. I'LL PLANT THEM FOR YOU.
SKRK
NOTHING BUT FERTILIZER FOR FLOWERS...
HUMAN BEINGS ARE SUCH WRETCHED THINGS.
?
HM ?
PAK
...
PAK
POK

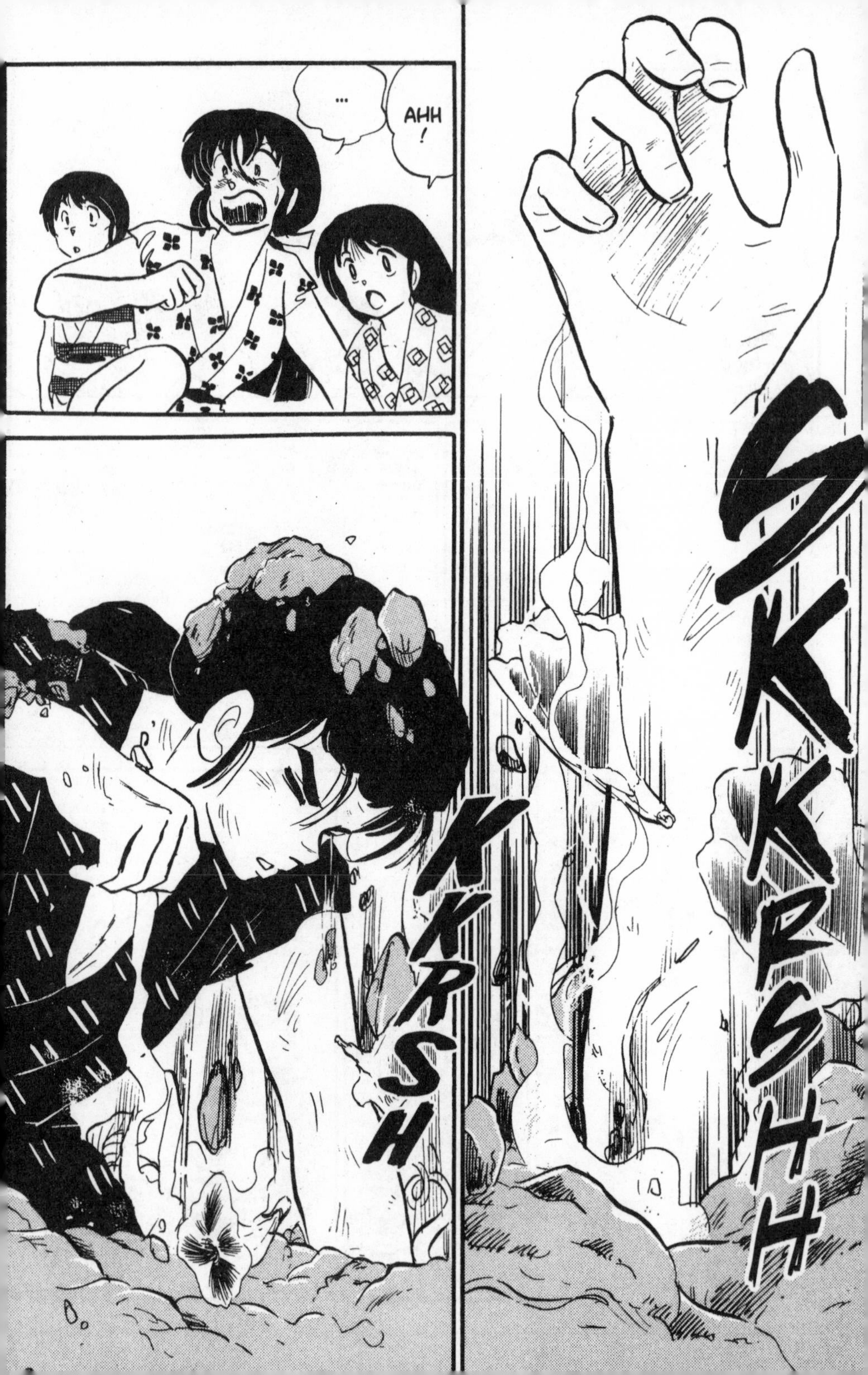
SKKRSHH
...
AHH!
KKRSH

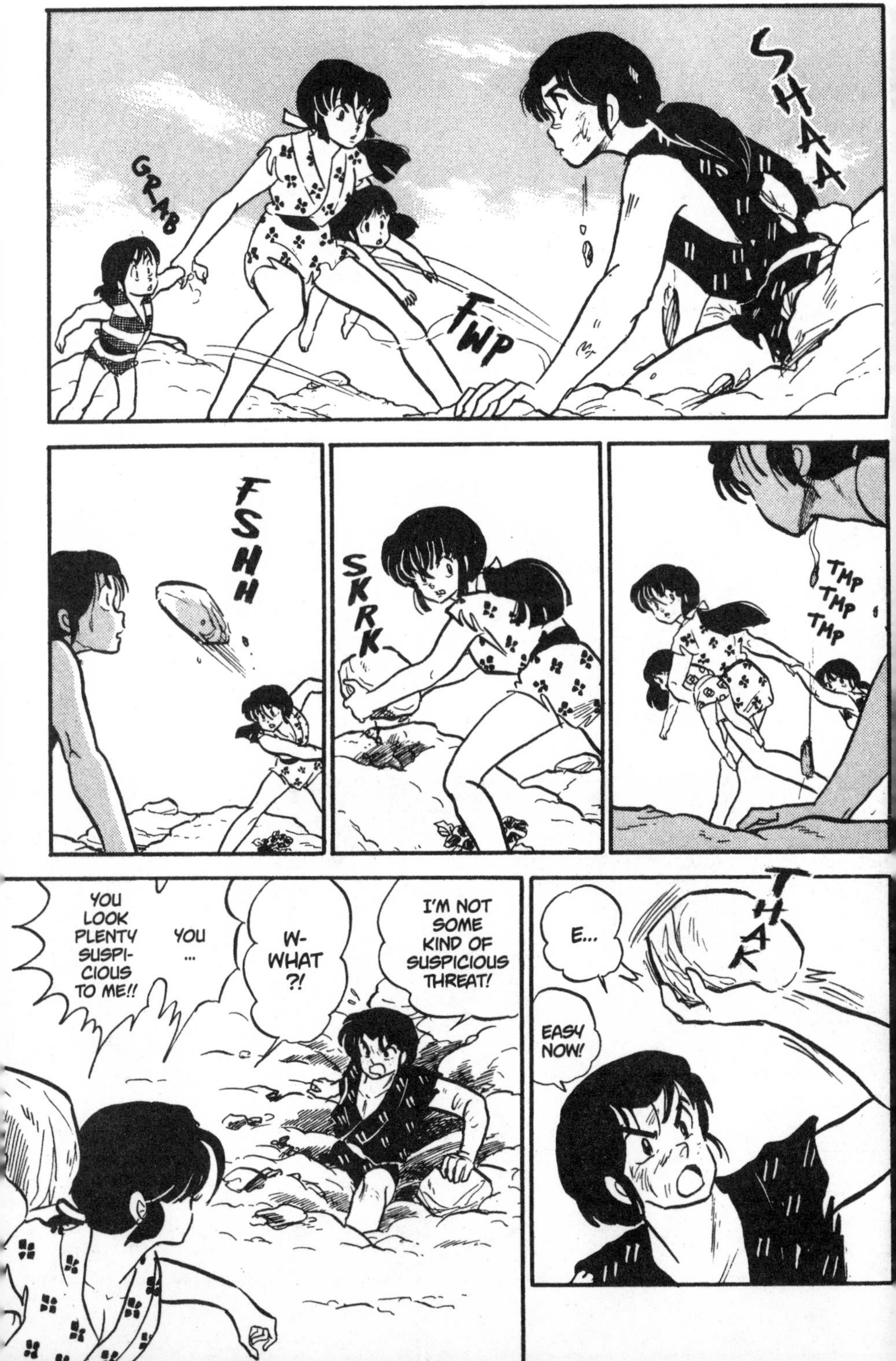
SHAA
FWP
GRAB
TMP TMP TMP
SKRK
FSHH
THAK
E...
EASY NOW!
I'M NOT SOME KIND OF SUSPICIOUS THREAT!
W-WHAT?!
YOU...
YOU LOOK PLENTY SUSPICIOUS TO ME!!

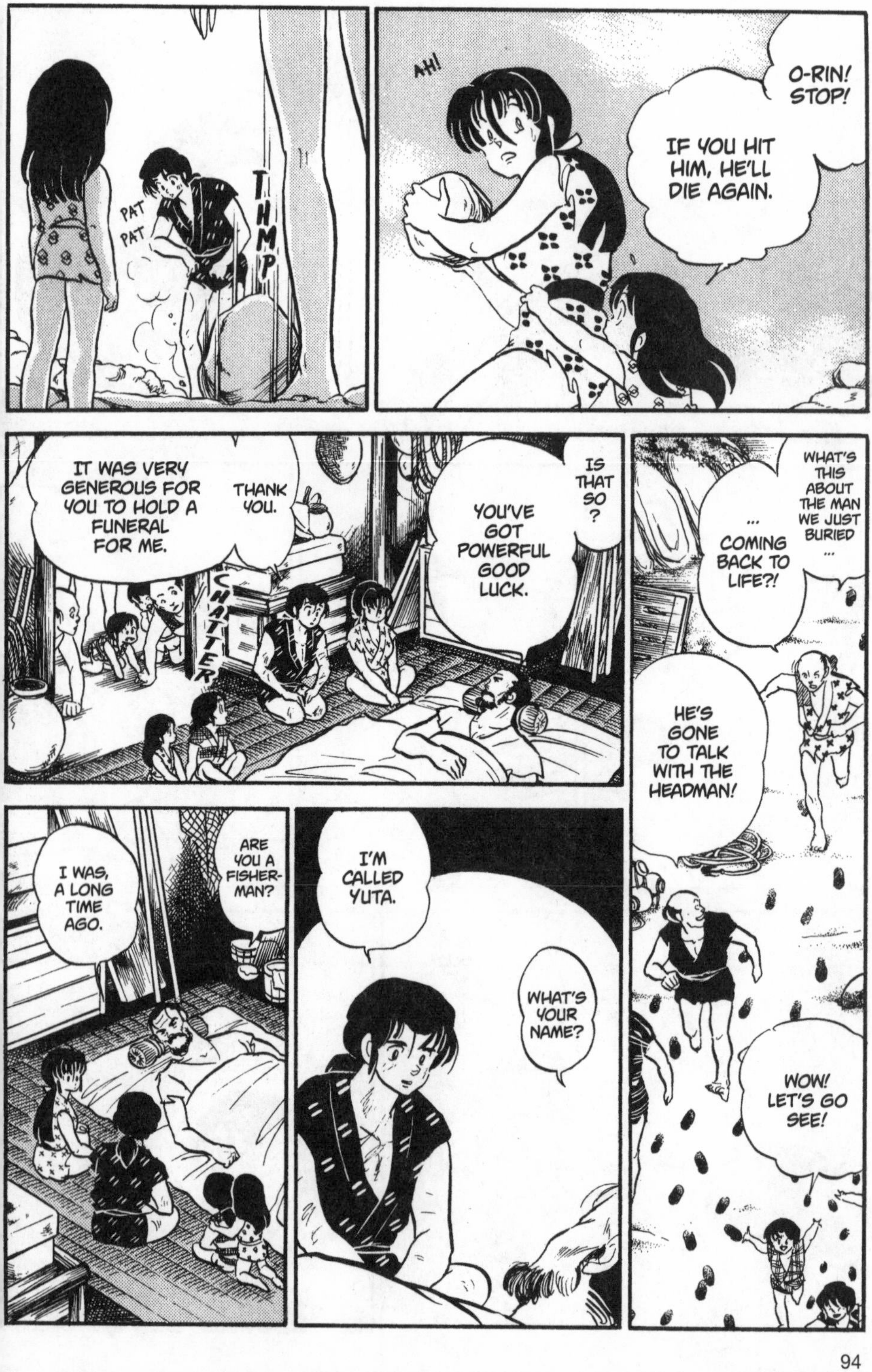
AH!
O-RIN! STOP!
IF YOU HIT HIM, HE'LL DIE AGAIN.
PAT PAT
THMP
WHAT'S THIS ABOUT THE MAN WE JUST BURIED ...
... COMING BACK TO LIFE?!
HE'S GONE TO TALK WITH THE HEADMAN!
WOW! LET'S GO SEE!
IS THAT SO?
YOU'VE GOT POWERFUL GOOD LUCK.
THANK YOU.
IT WAS VERY GENEROUS FOR YOU TO HOLD A FUNERAL FOR ME.
CHATTER
WHAT'S YOUR NAME?
I'M CALLED YUTA.
ARE YOU A FISHERMAN?
I WAS, A LONG TIME AGO.

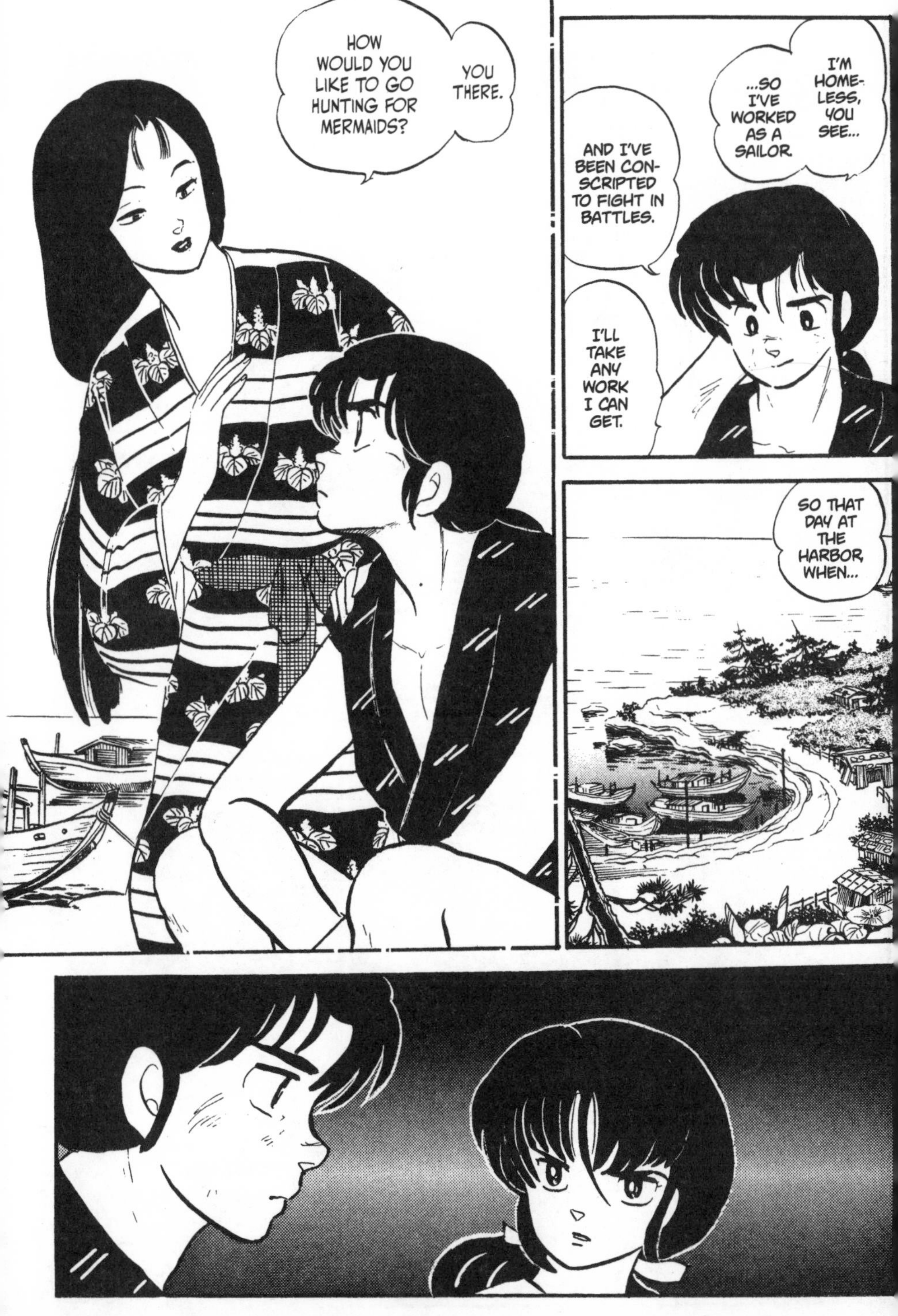
I'M HOMELESS, YOU SEE...
...SO I'VE WORKED AS A SAILOR.
AND I'VE BEEN CONSCRIPTED TO FIGHT IN BATTLES.
I'LL TAKE ANY WORK I CAN GET.
SO THAT DAY AT THE HARBOR, WHEN...
YOU THERE.
HOW WOULD YOU LIKE TO GO HUNTING FOR MERMAIDS?

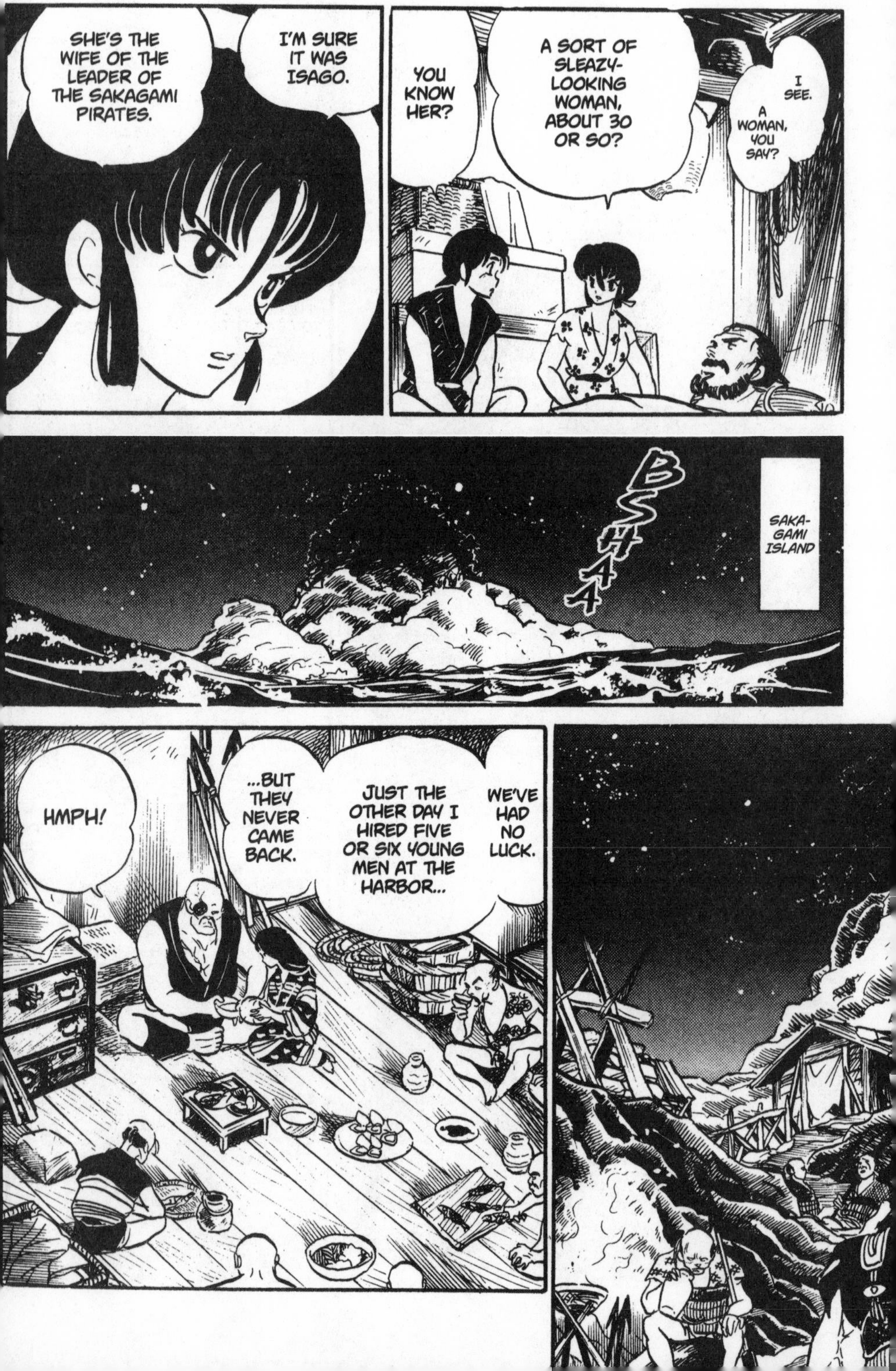
I SEE. A WOMAN, YOU SAY?
A SORT OF SLEAZY-LOOKING WOMAN, ABOUT 30 OR SO?
YOU KNOW HER?
I'M SURE IT WAS ISAGO.
SHE'S THE WIFE OF THE LEADER OF THE SAKAGAMI PIRATES.
SAKA-GAMI ISLAND
BSHAAA
WE'VE HAD NO LUCK.
JUST THE OTHER DAY I HIRED FIVE OR SIX YOUNG MEN AT THE HARBOR...
...BUT THEY NEVER CAME BACK.
HMPH!

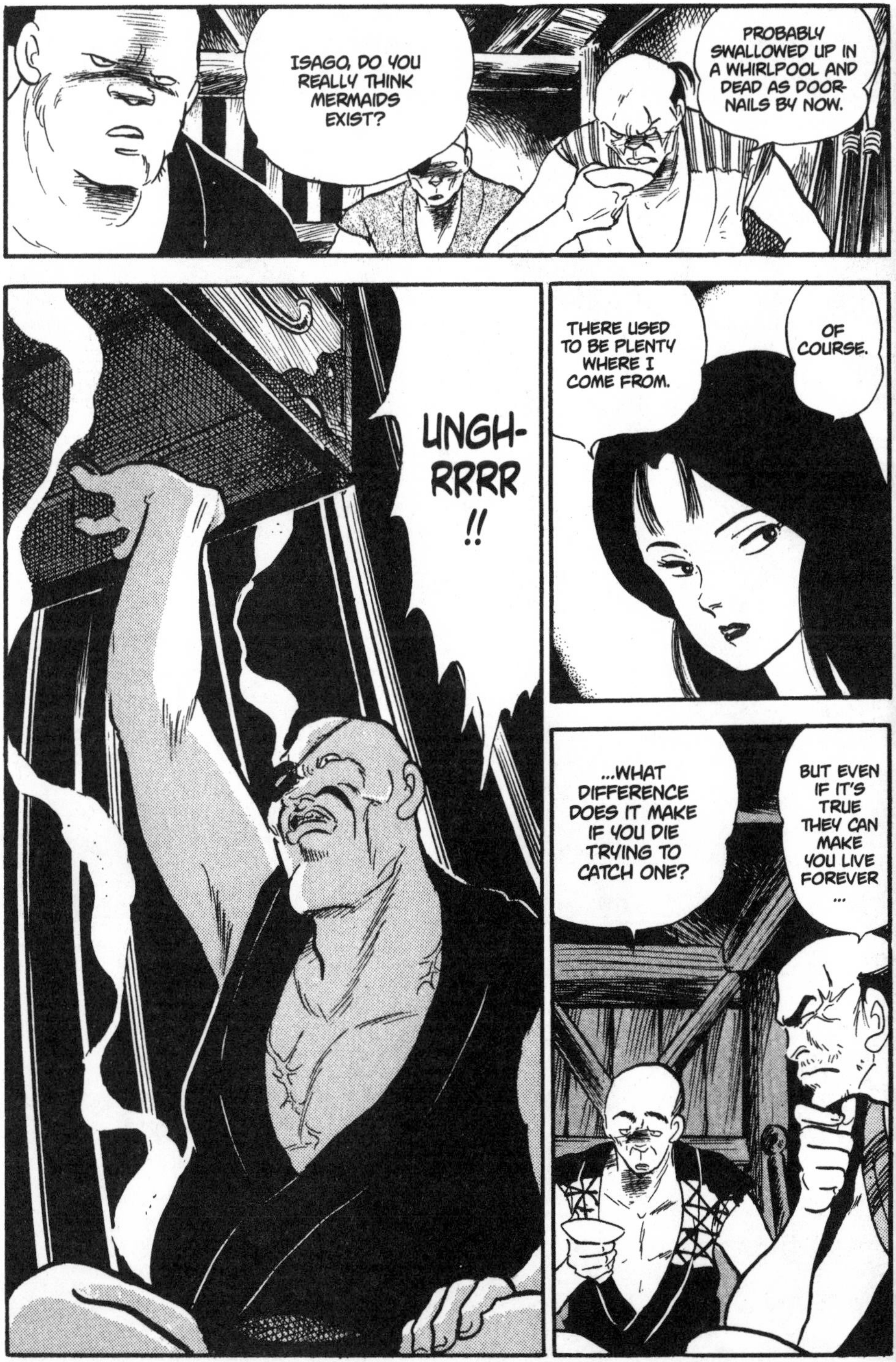
PROBABLY SWALLOWED UP IN A WHIRLPOOL AND DEAD AS DOOR-NAILS BY NOW.
ISAGO, DO YOU REALLY THINK MERMAIDS EXIST?
OF COURSE.
THERE USED TO BE PLENTY WHERE I COME FROM.
BUT EVEN IF IT'S TRUE THEY CAN MAKE YOU LIVE FOREVER ...
...WHAT DIFFERENCE DOES IT MAKE IF YOU DIE TRYING TO CATCH ONE?
UNGH-RRRR!!

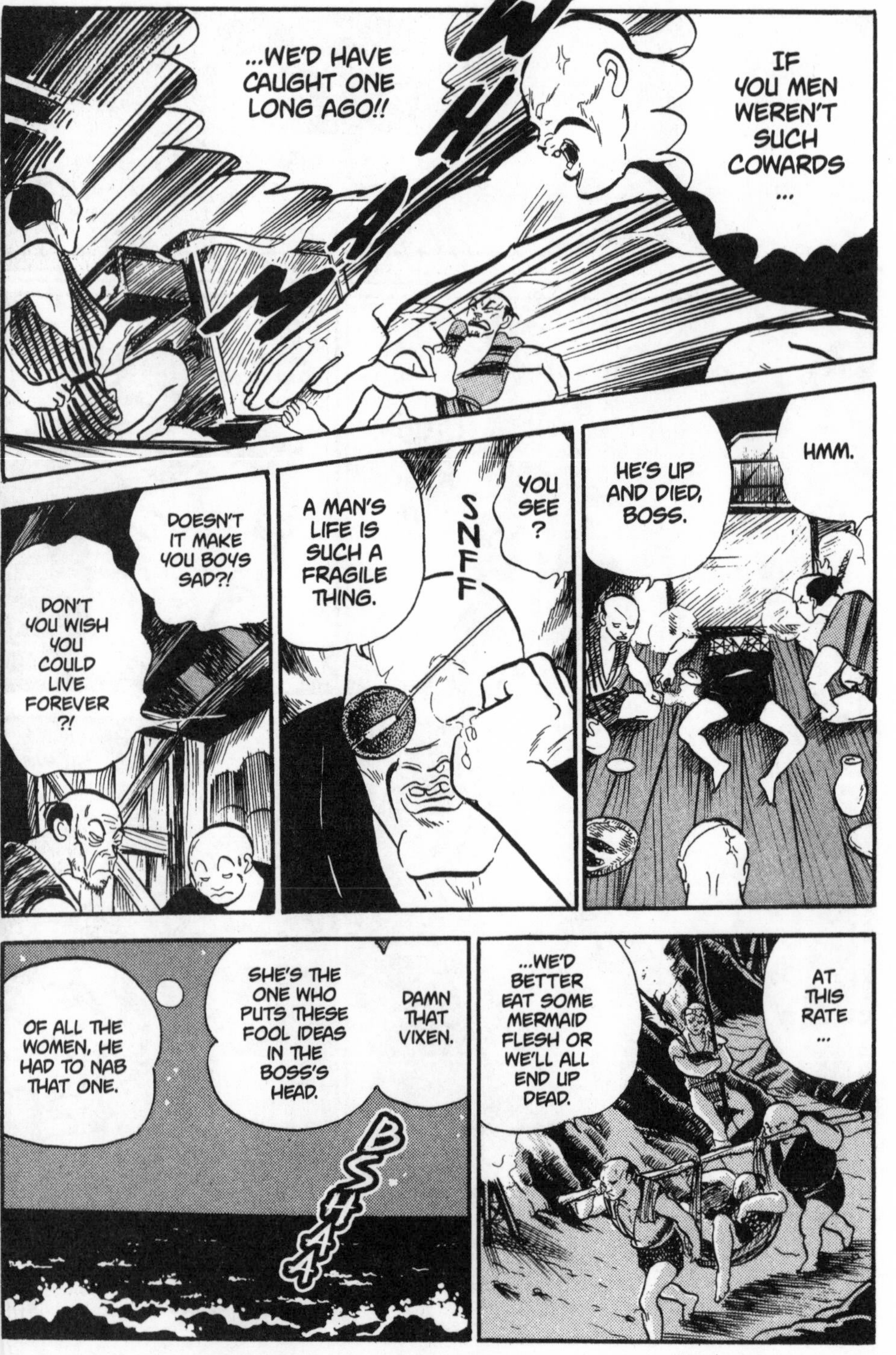
IF YOU MEN WEREN'T SUCH COWARDS ...
...WE'D HAVE CAUGHT ONE LONG AGO!!
WHAM
HMM.
HE'S UP AND DIED, BOSS.
YOU SEE?
SNFF
A MAN'S LIFE IS SUCH A FRAGILE THING.
DOESN'T IT MAKE YOU BOYS SAD?!
DON'T YOU WISH YOU COULD LIVE FOREVER?!
AT THIS RATE ...
...WE'D BETTER EAT SOME MERMAID FLESH OR WE'LL ALL END UP DEAD.
DAMN THAT VIXEN.
SHE'S THE ONE WHO PUTS THESE FOOL IDEAS IN THE BOSS'S HEAD.
OF ALL THE WOMEN, HE HAD TO NAB THAT ONE.
BSHAA

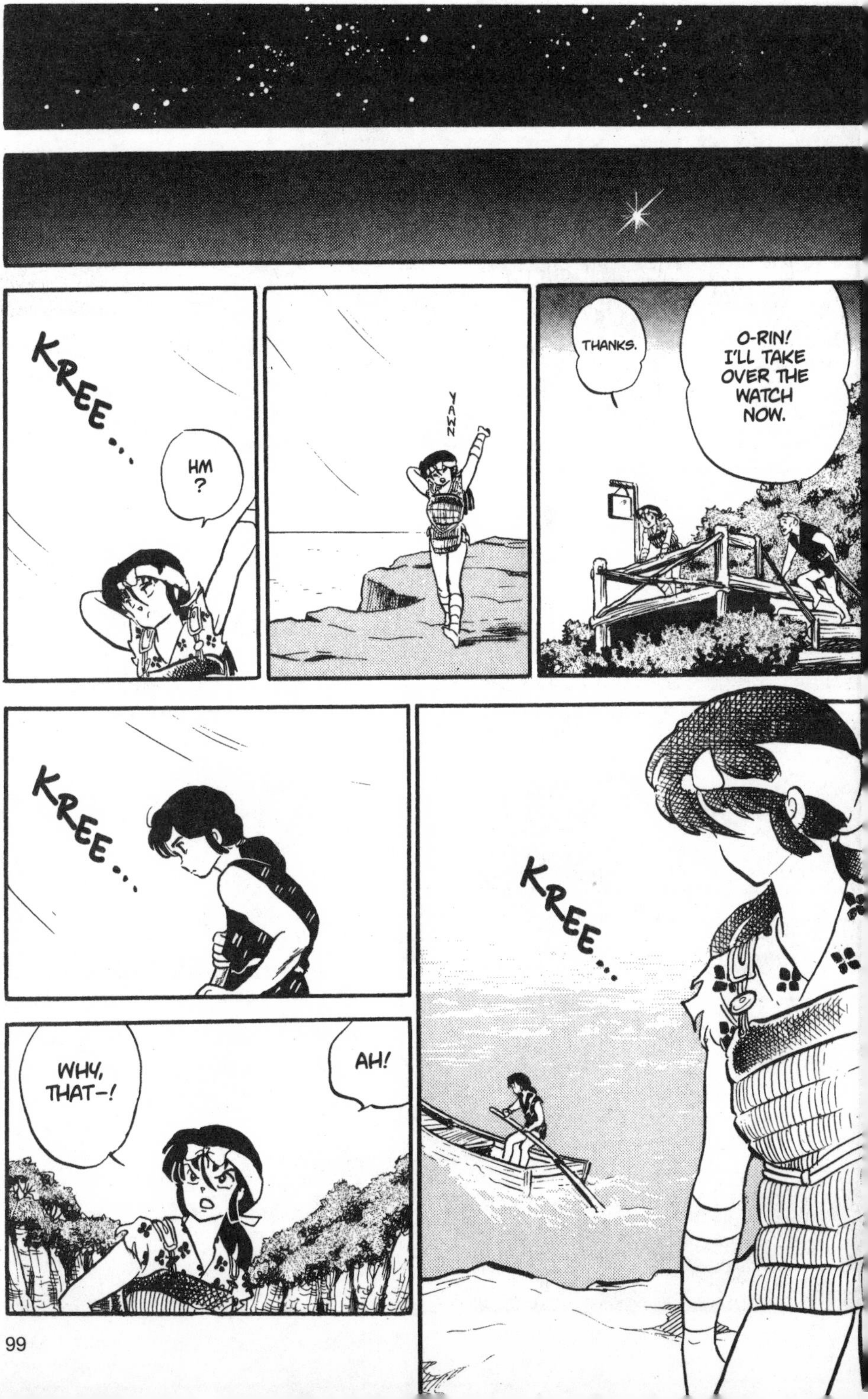
O-RIN! I'LL TAKE OVER THE WATCH NOW.
THANKS.
YAWN
KREE...
HM?
KREE...
KREE...
AH!
WHY, THAT-!

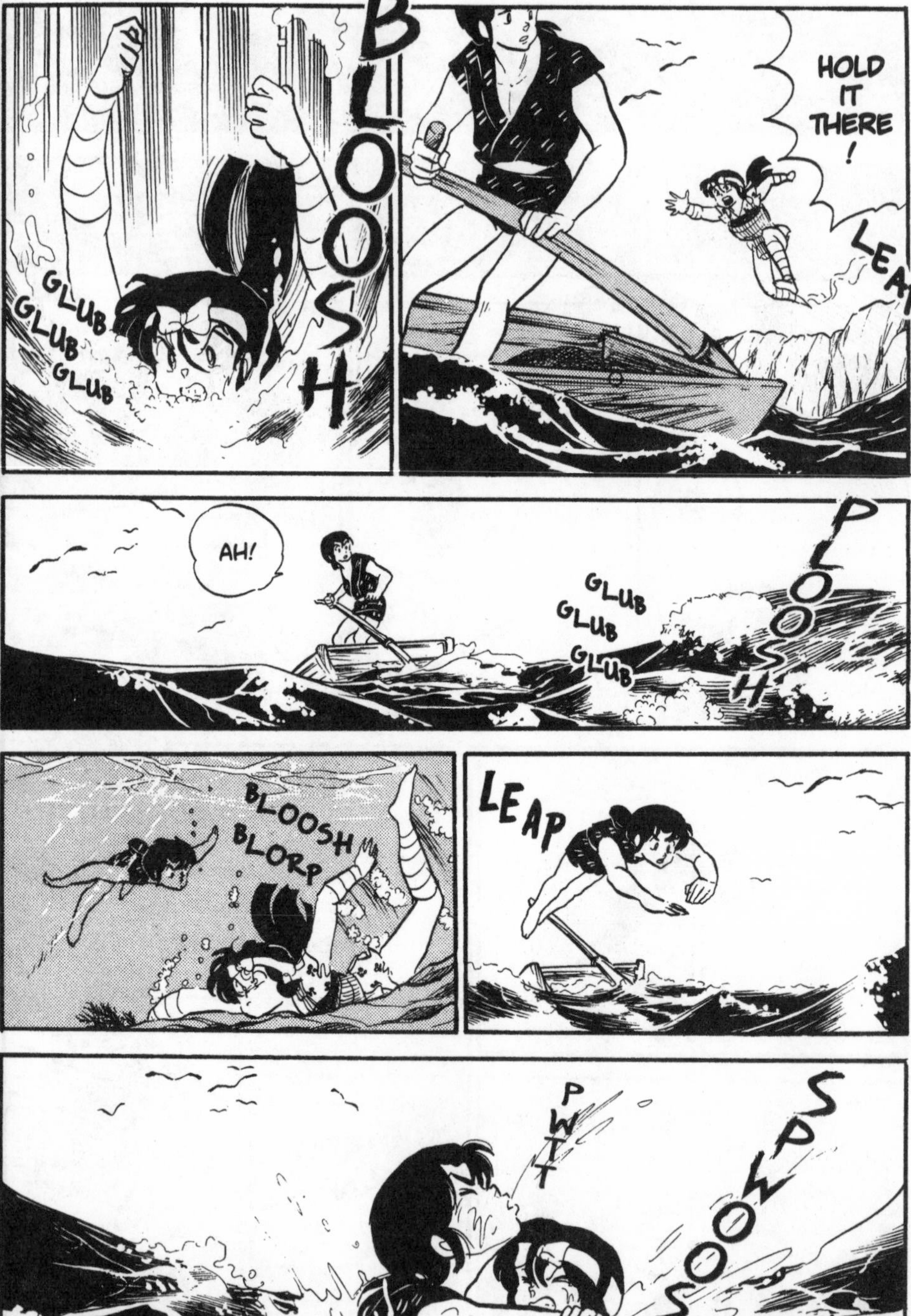
HOLD IT THERE!
LEAP
BLOOSH
GLUB GLUB GLUB
PLOOSH
GLUB GLUB GLUB
AH!
LEAP
BLOOSH
BLORP
SPWOOSH
PWIT

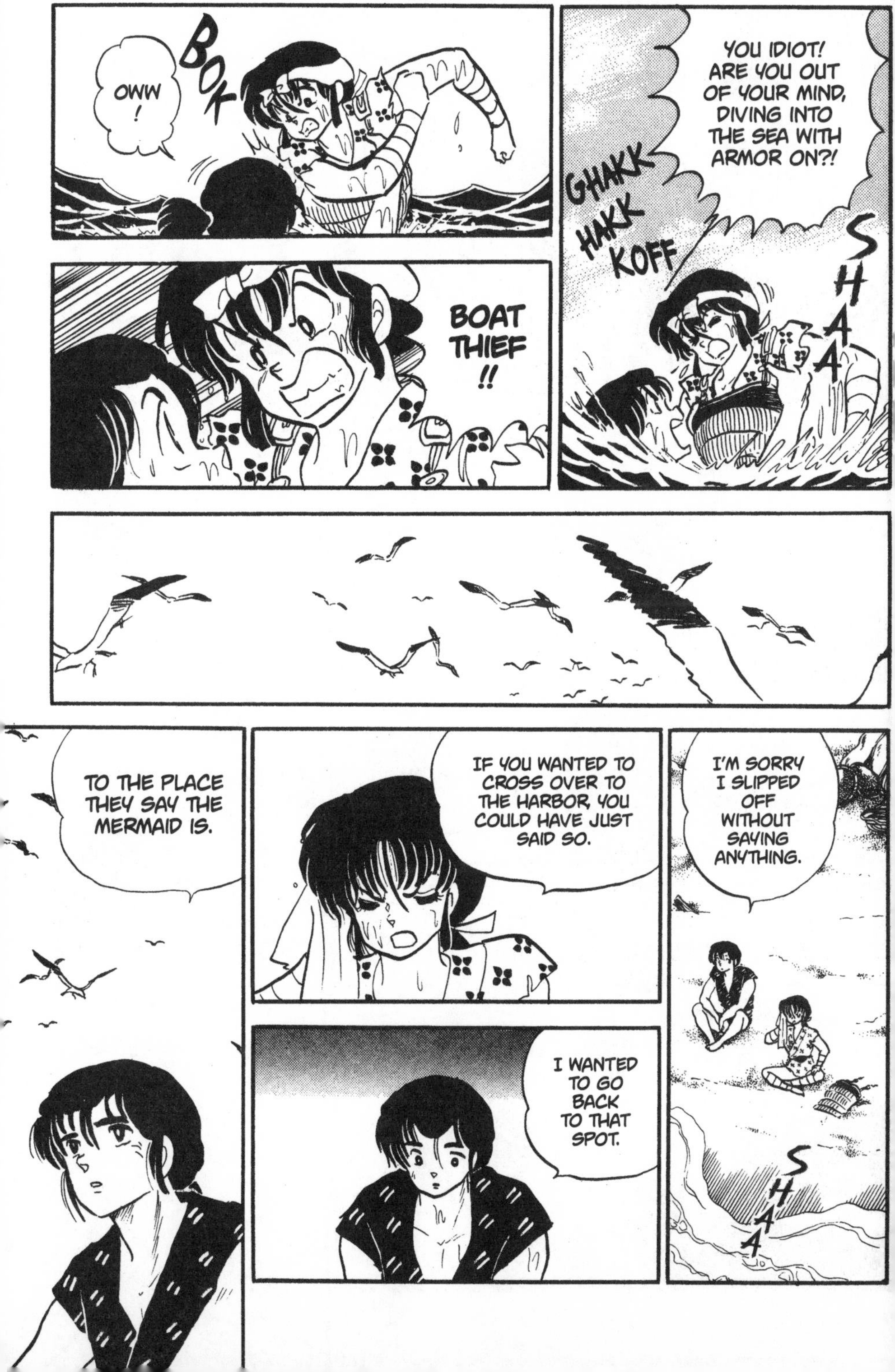
YOU IDIOT! ARE YOU OUT OF YOUR MIND, DIVING INTO THE SEA WITH ARMOR ON?!
GHAKK HAKK KOFF
SHAA
BOK
OWW!
BOAT THIEF!!
I'M SORRY I SLIPPED OFF WITHOUT SAYING ANYTHING.
SHAA
IF YOU WANTED TO CROSS OVER TO THE HARBOR, YOU COULD HAVE JUST SAID SO.
I WANTED TO GO BACK TO THAT SPOT.
TO THE PLACE THEY SAY THE MERMAID IS.

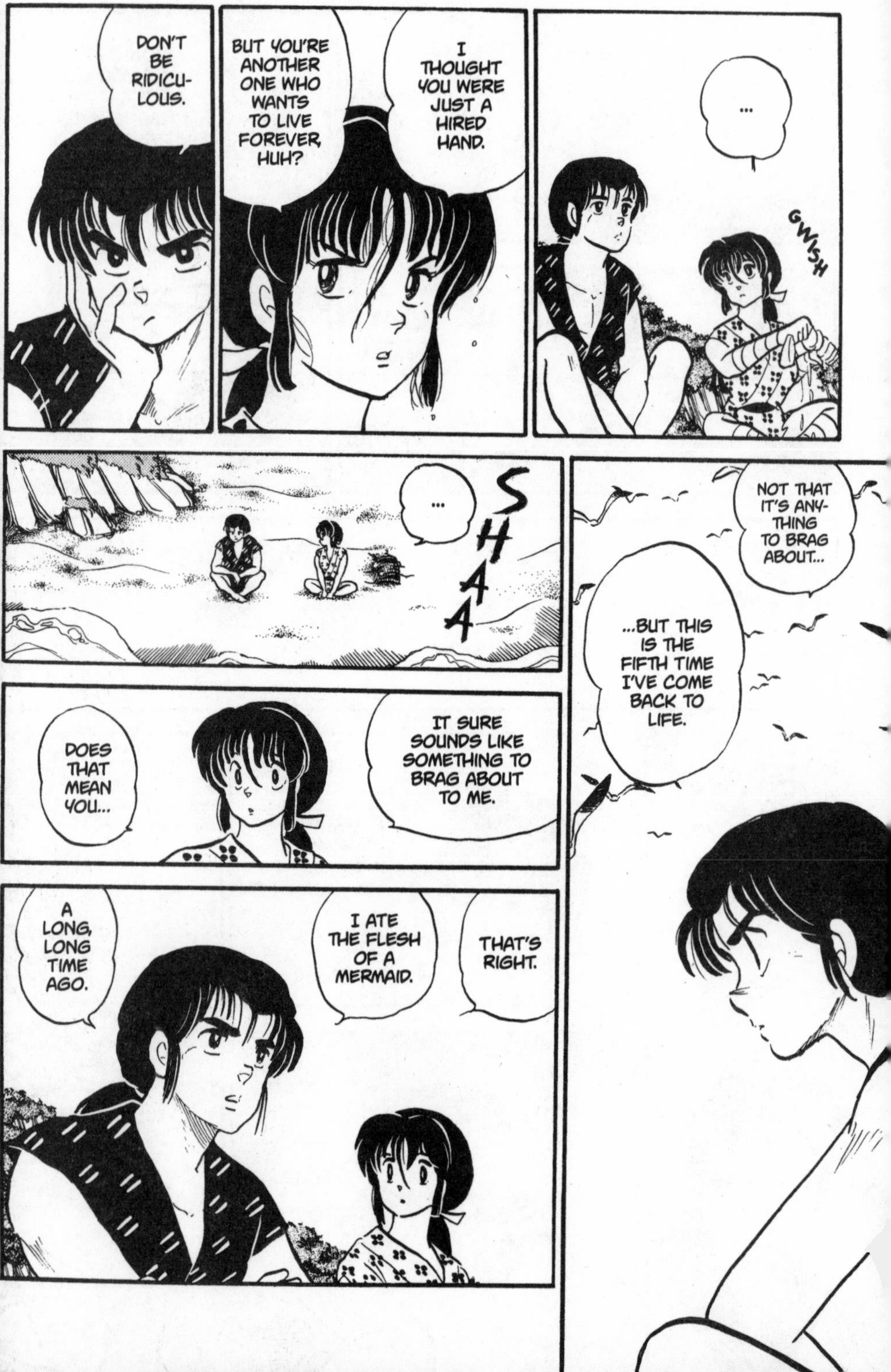
...
GWISH
I THOUGHT YOU WERE JUST A HIRED HAND.
BUT YOU'RE ANOTHER ONE WHO WANTS TO LIVE FOREVER, HUH?
DON'T BE RIDICULOUS.
NOT THAT IT'S ANYTHING TO BRAG ABOUT...
...BUT THIS IS THE FIFTH TIME I'VE COME BACK TO LIFE.
SHAAA
...
IT SURE SOUNDS LIKE SOMETHING TO BRAG ABOUT TO ME.
DOES THAT MEAN YOU...
THAT'S RIGHT.
I ATE THE FLESH OF A MERMAID.
A LONG, LONG TIME AGO.

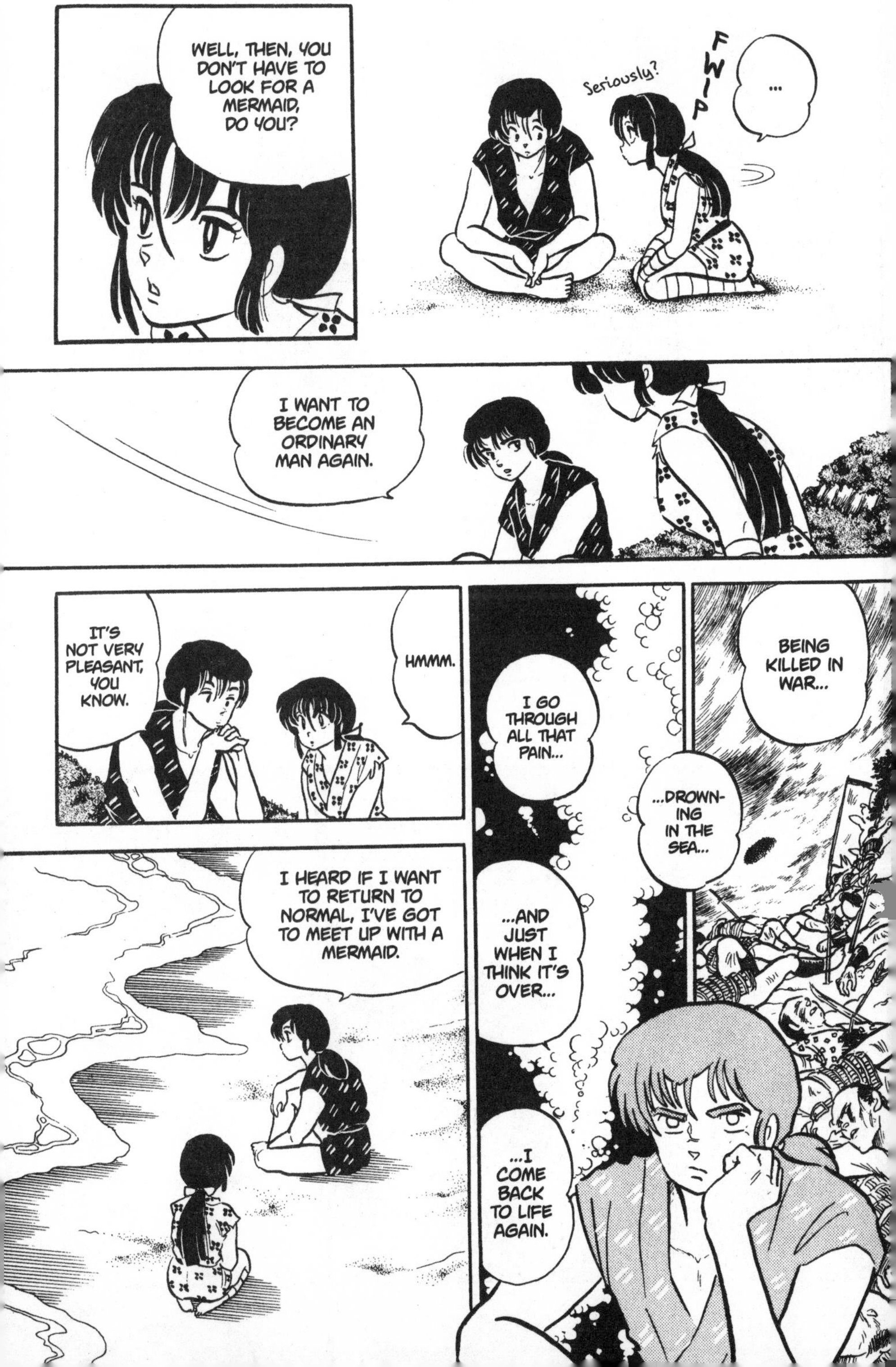
Seriously?
FWIP
...
WELL, THEN, YOU DON'T HAVE TO LOOK FOR A MERMAID, DO YOU?
I WANT TO BECOME AN ORDINARY MAN AGAIN.
HMMM.
IT'S NOT VERY PLEASANT, YOU KNOW.
BEING KILLED IN WAR...
...DROWN-ING IN THE SEA...
I GO THROUGH ALL THAT PAIN...
...AND JUST WHEN I THINK IT'S OVER...
...I COME BACK TO LIFE AGAIN.
I HEARD IF I WANT TO RETURN TO NORMAL, I'VE GOT TO MEET UP WITH A MERMAID.

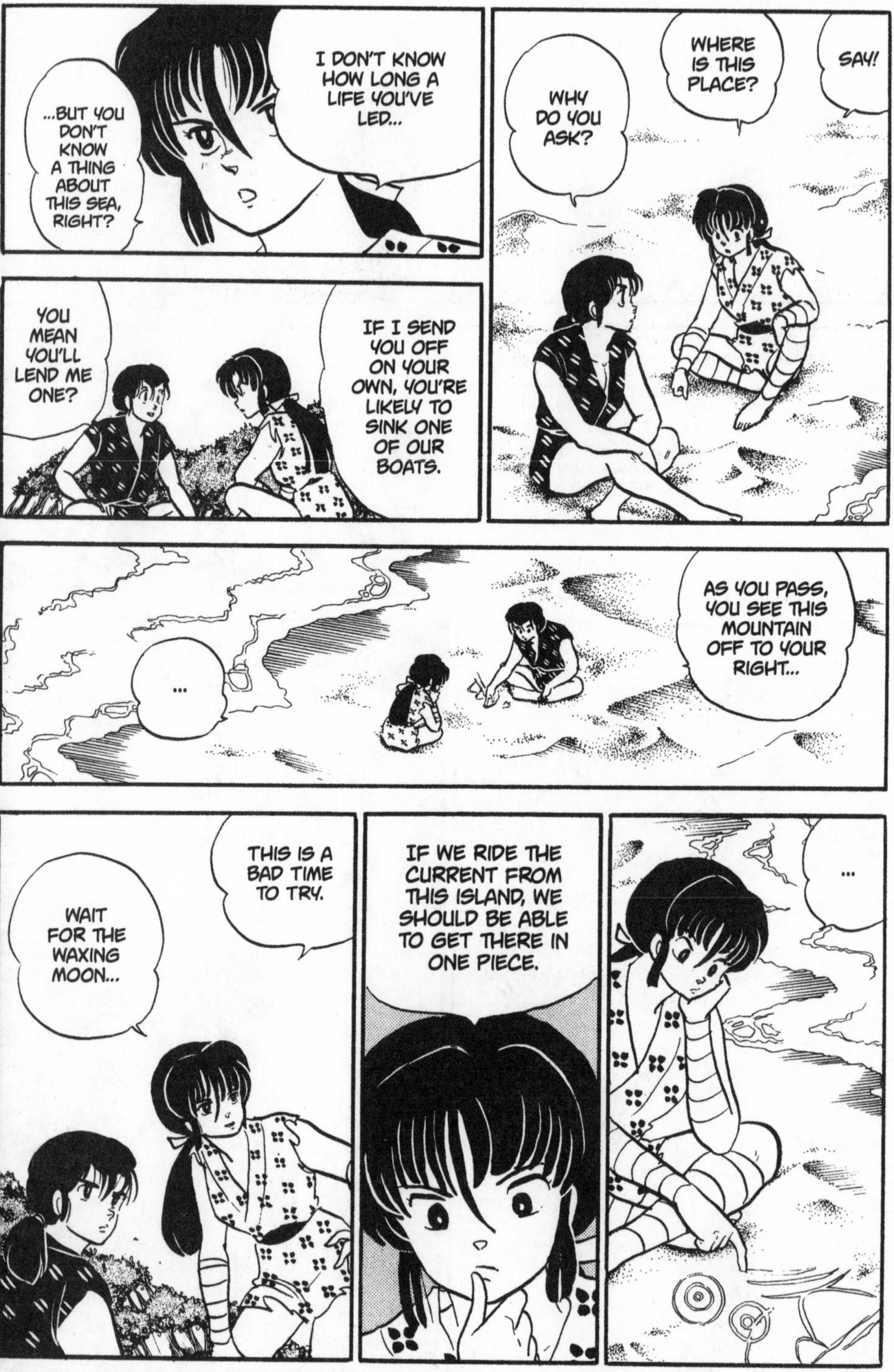
SAY!
WHERE IS THIS PLACE?
WHY DO YOU ASK?
I DON'T KNOW HOW LONG A LIFE YOU'VE LED...
...BUT YOU DON'T KNOW A THING ABOUT THIS SEA, RIGHT?
IF I SEND YOU OFF ON YOUR OWN, YOU'RE LIKELY TO SINK ONE OF OUR BOATS.
YOU MEAN YOU'LL LEND ME ONE?
AS YOU PASS, YOU SEE THIS MOUNTAIN OFF TO YOUR RIGHT...
...
...
IF WE RIDE THE CURRENT FROM THIS ISLAND, WE SHOULD BE ABLE TO GET THERE IN ONE PIECE.
THIS IS A BAD TIME TO TRY.
WAIT FOR THE WAXING MOON...

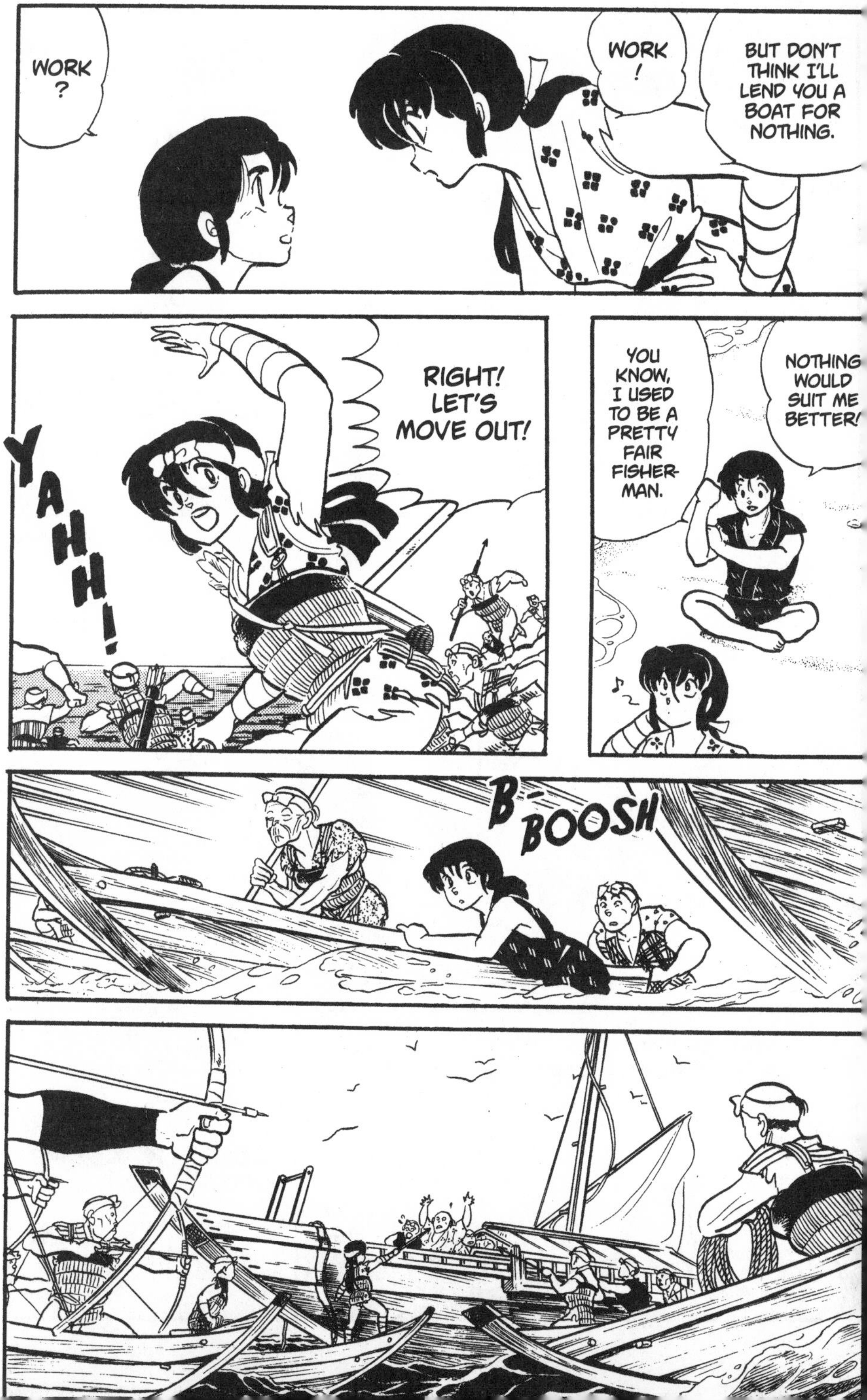
BUT DON'T THINK I'LL LEND YOU A BOAT FOR NOTHING.
WORK!
WORK?
NOTHING WOULD SUIT ME BETTER!
YOU KNOW, I USED TO BE A PRETTY FAIR FISHER-MAN.
RIGHT! LET'S MOVE OUT!
YAHH!!
B-BOOSH

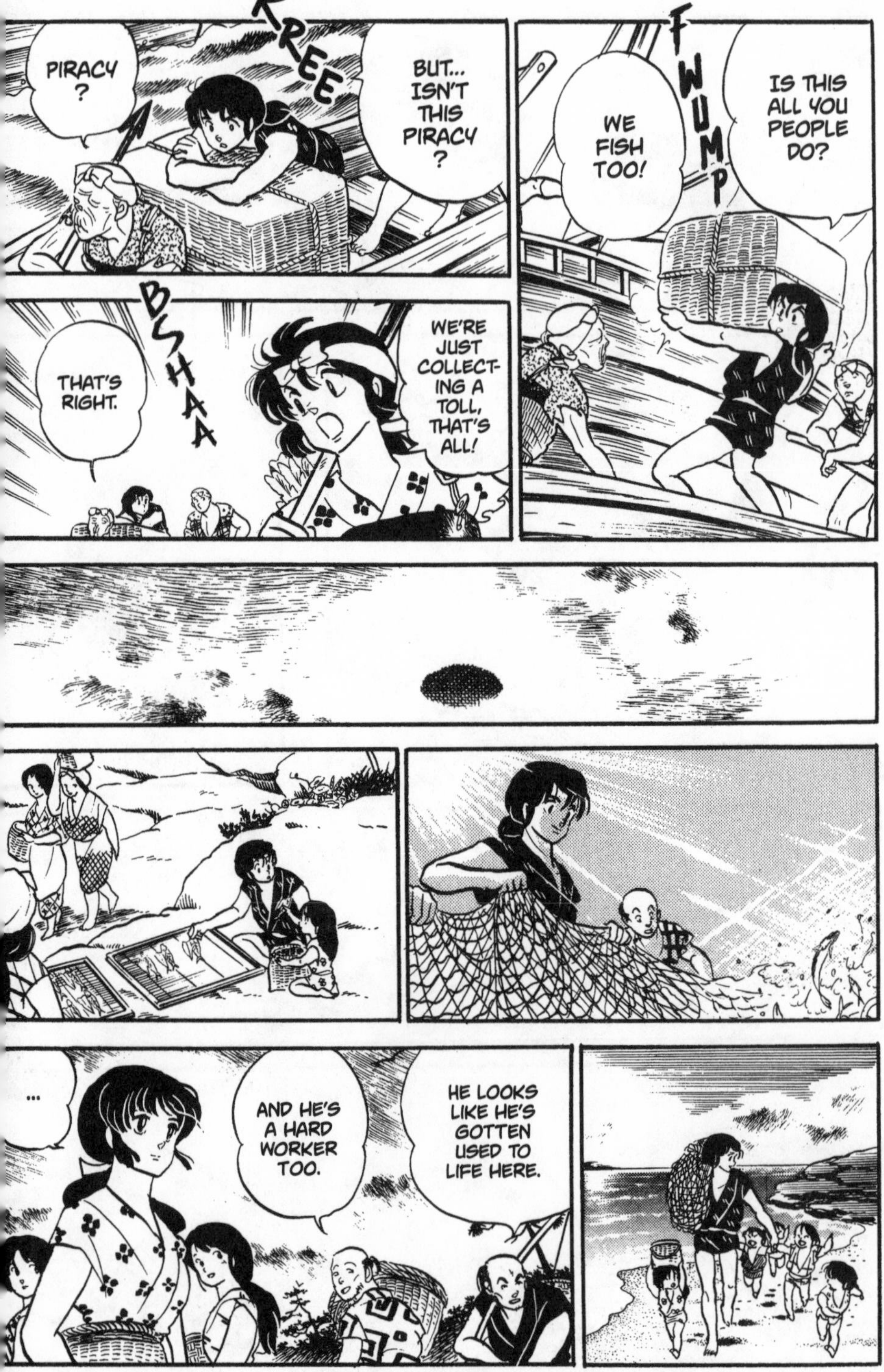
IS THIS ALL YOU PEOPLE DO?
FWUMP
WE FISH TOO!
BUT... ISN'T THIS PIRACY?
KREE
PIRACY?
WE'RE JUST COLLECTING A TOLL, THAT'S ALL!
BSHAA
THAT'S RIGHT.
HE LOOKS LIKE HE'S GOTTEN USED TO LIFE HERE.
AND HE'S A HARD WORKER TOO.
...

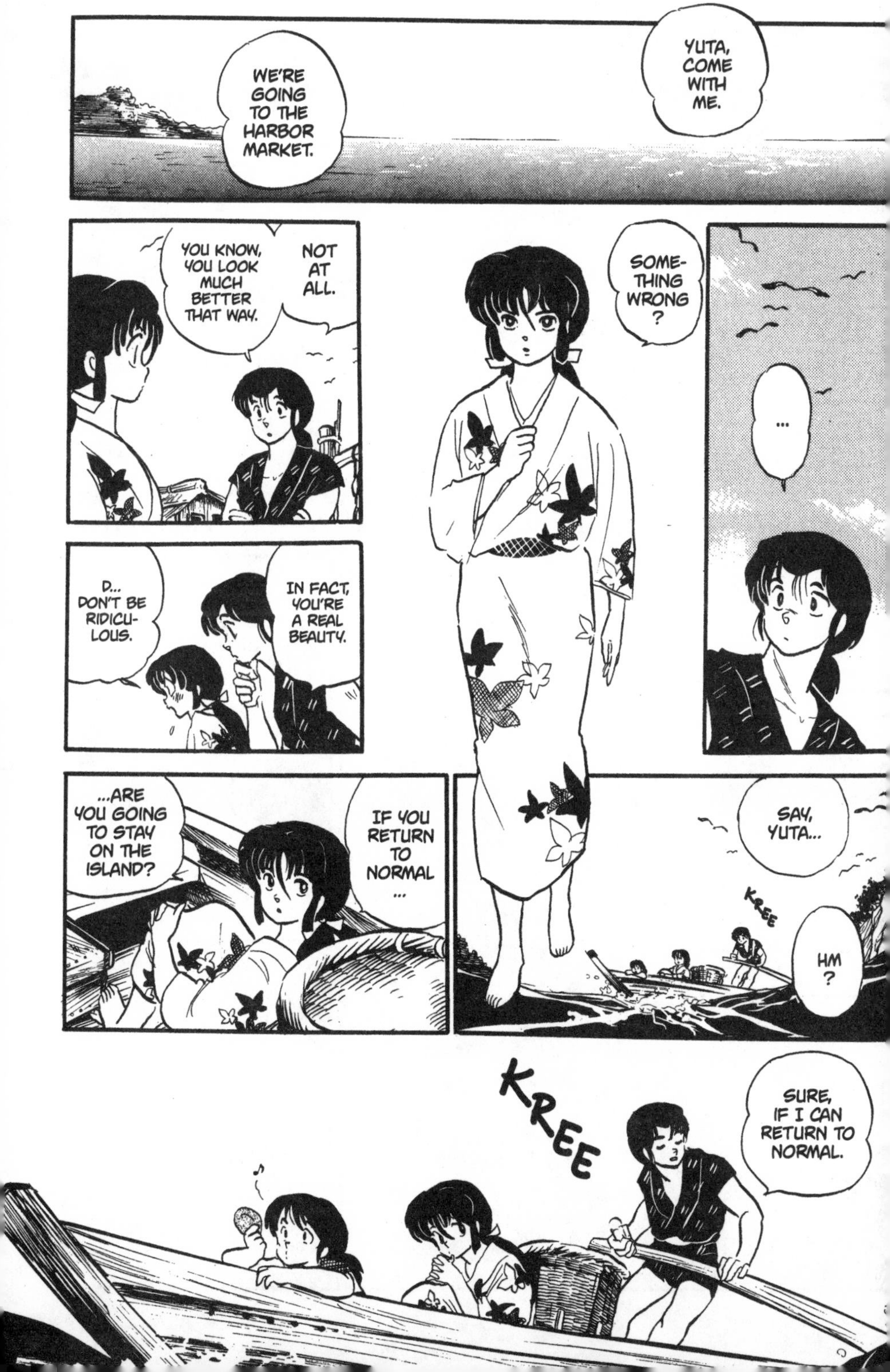
YUTA, COME WITH ME.
WE'RE GOING TO THE HARBOR MARKET.
...
SOME-THING WRONG?
NOT AT ALL.
YOU KNOW, YOU LOOK MUCH BETTER THAT WAY.
IN FACT, YOU'RE A REAL BEAUTY.
D... DON'T BE RIDICU-LOUS.
SAY, YUTA...
KREE
HM?
IF YOU RETURN TO NORMAL ...
...ARE YOU GOING TO STAY ON THE ISLAND?
SURE, IF I CAN RETURN TO NORMAL.
KREE

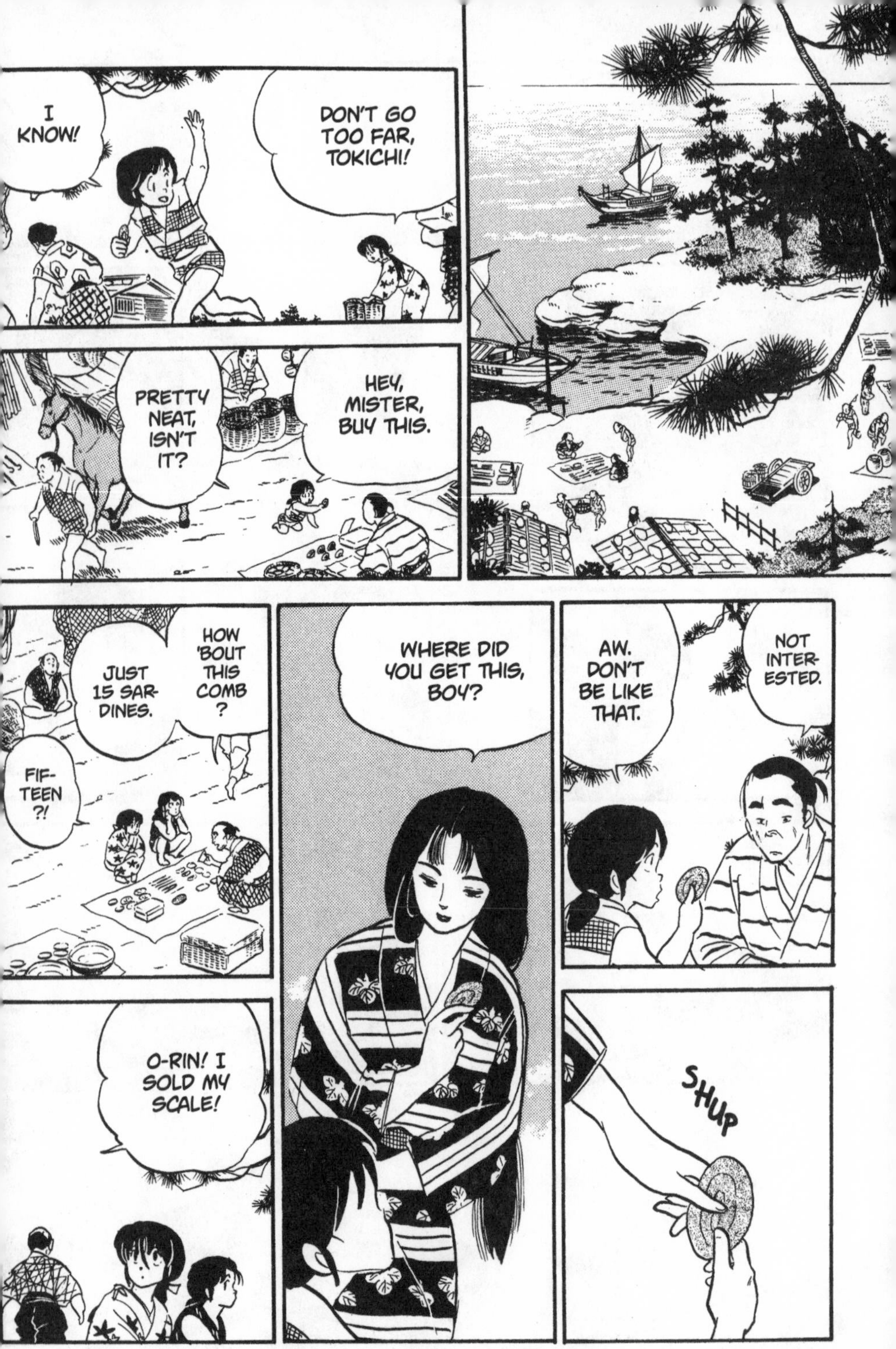
DON'T GO TOO FAR, TOKICHI!
I KNOW!
HEY, MISTER, BUY THIS.
PRETTY NEAT, ISN'T IT?
NOT INTERESTED.
AW. DON'T BE LIKE THAT.
SHUP
WHERE DID YOU GET THIS, BOY?
HOW 'BOUT THIS COMB?
JUST 15 SARDINES.
FIFTEEN?!
O-RIN! I SOLD MY SCALE!

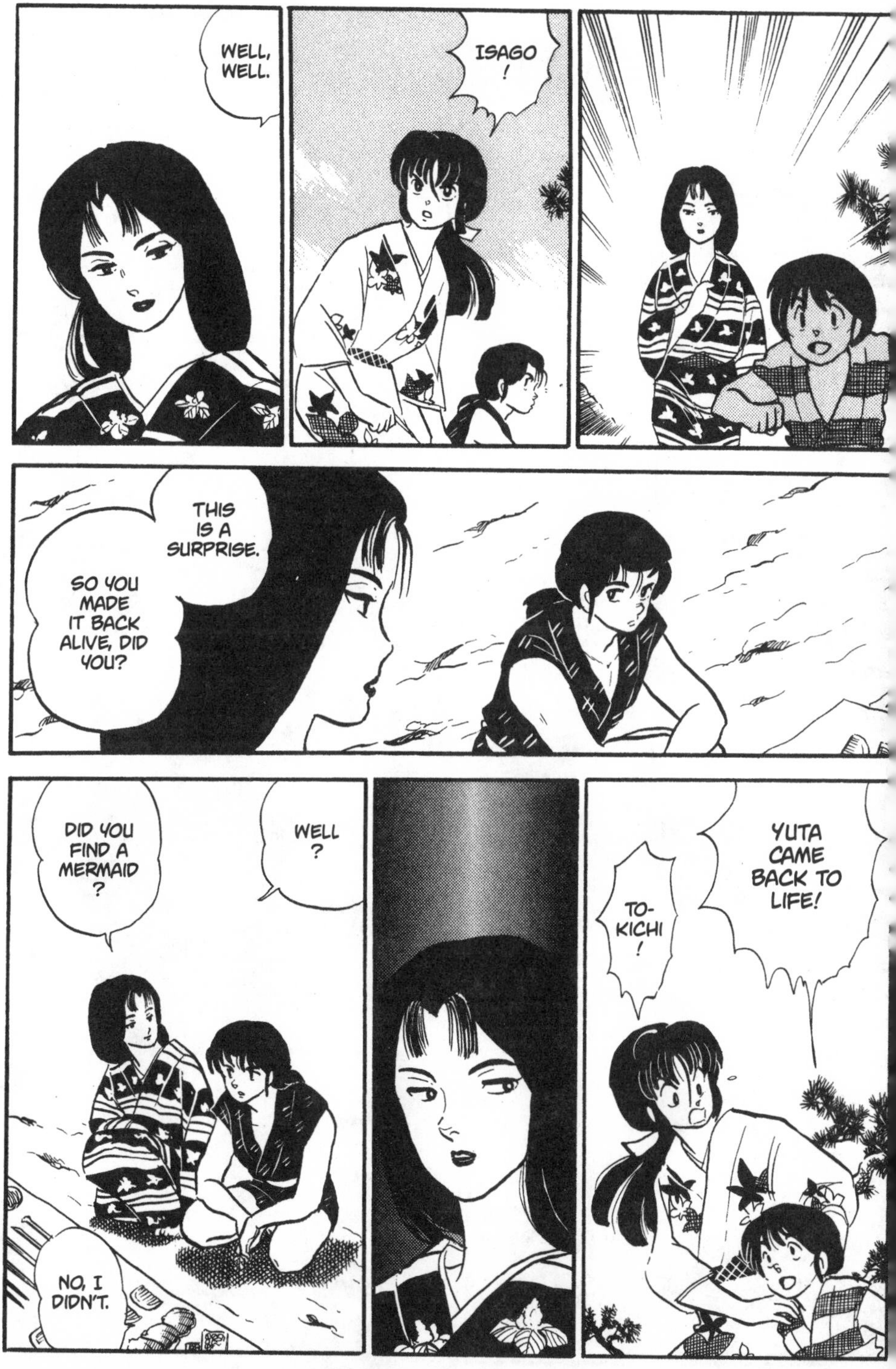
ISAGO!
WELL, WELL.
THIS IS A SURPRISE.
SO YOU MADE IT BACK ALIVE, DID YOU?
YUTA CAME BACK TO LIFE!
TO-KICHI!
WELL?
DID YOU FIND A MERMAID?
NO, I DIDN'T.

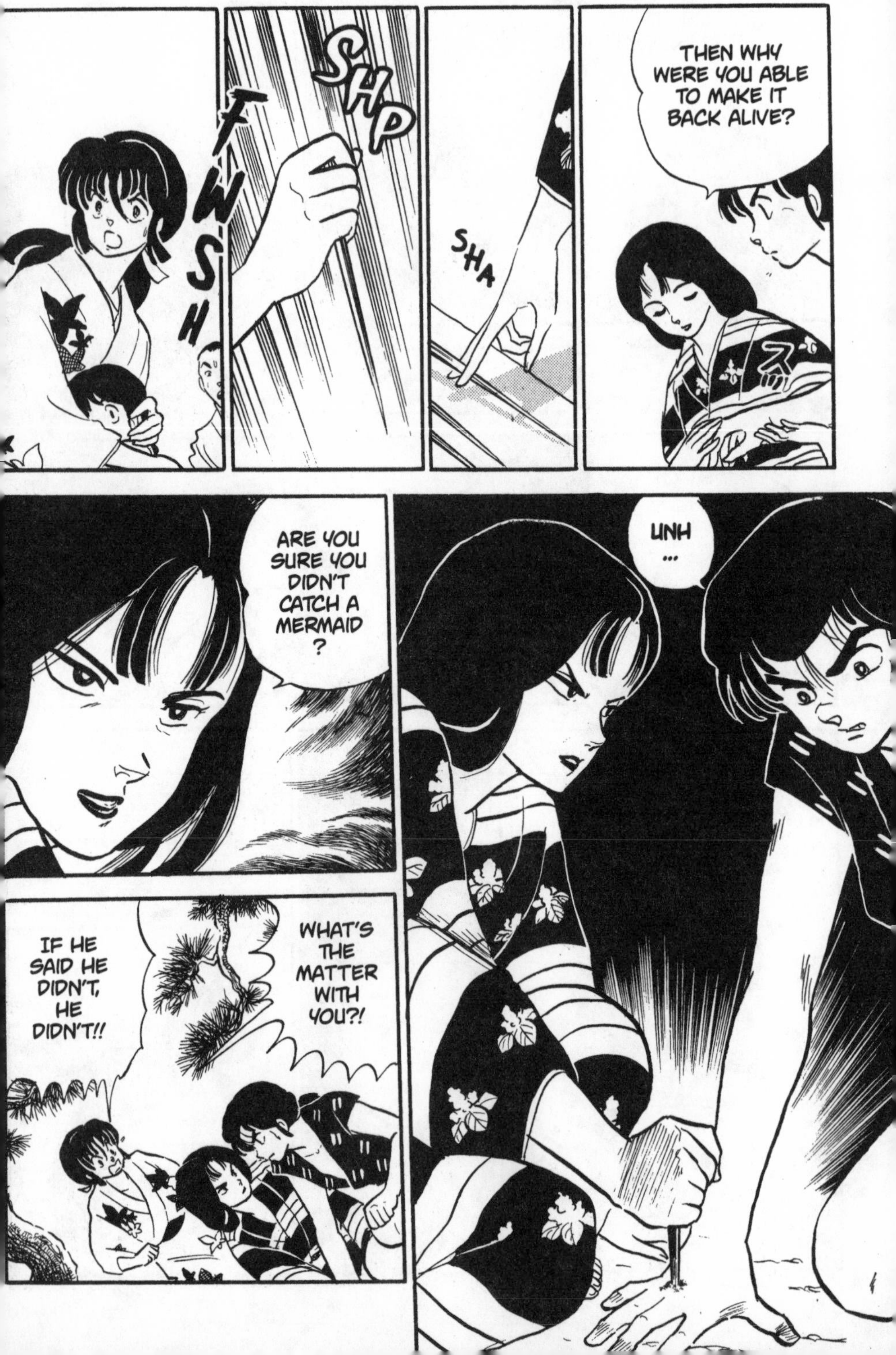
THEN WHY WERE YOU ABLE TO MAKE IT BACK ALIVE?
SHA
SHP
FWSH
UNH ...
ARE YOU SURE YOU DIDN'T CATCH A MERMAID ?
WHAT'S THE MATTER WITH YOU?!
IF HE SAID HE DIDN'T, HE DIDN'T!!

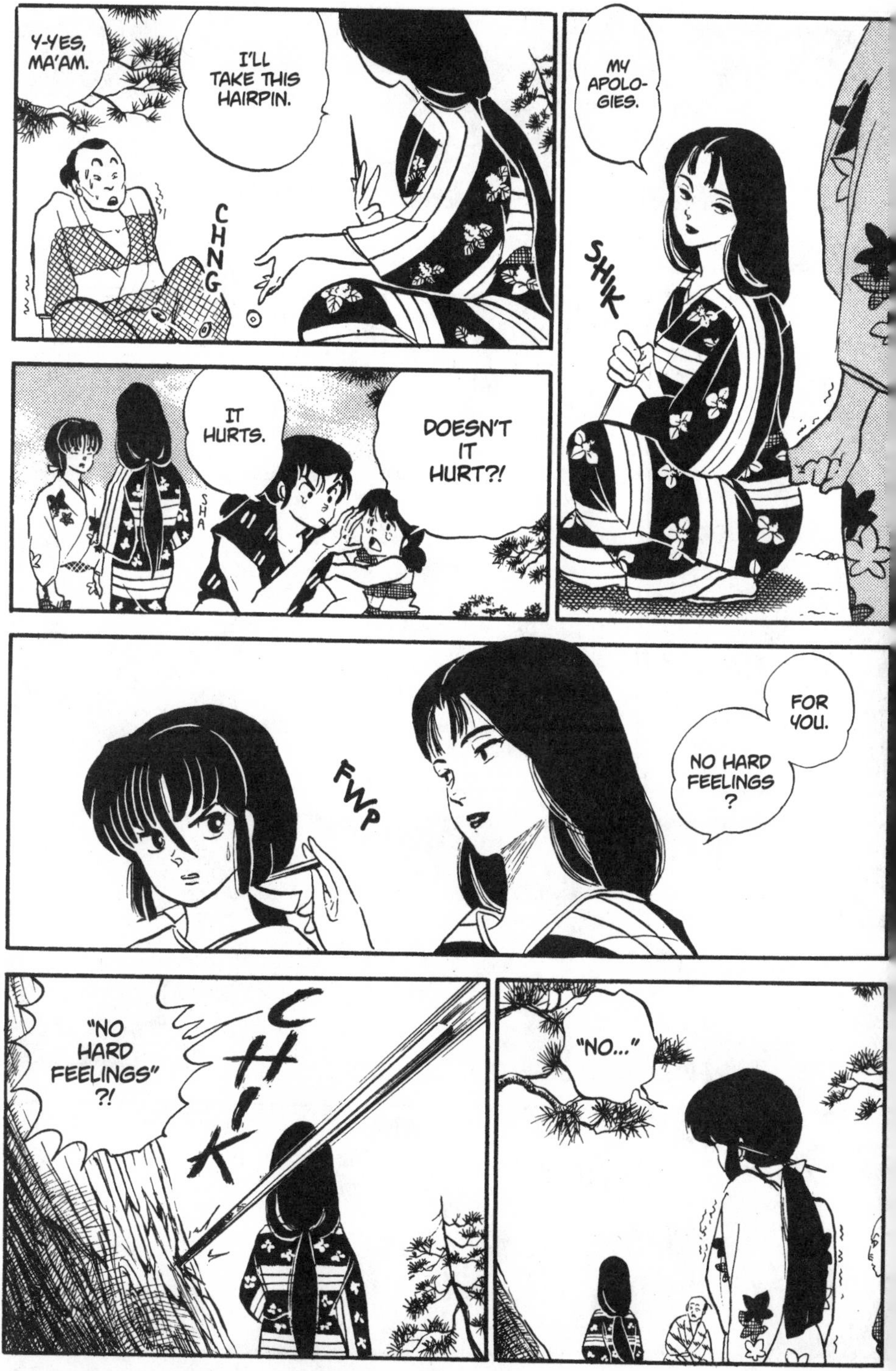
MY APOLOGIES.
SHIK
I'LL TAKE THIS HAIRPIN.
Y-YES, MA'AM.
CHNG
DOESN'T IT HURT?!
IT HURTS.
SHA
FOR YOU.
NO HARD FEELINGS?
FWP
"NO..."
"NO HARD FEELINGS"?!
CHIK

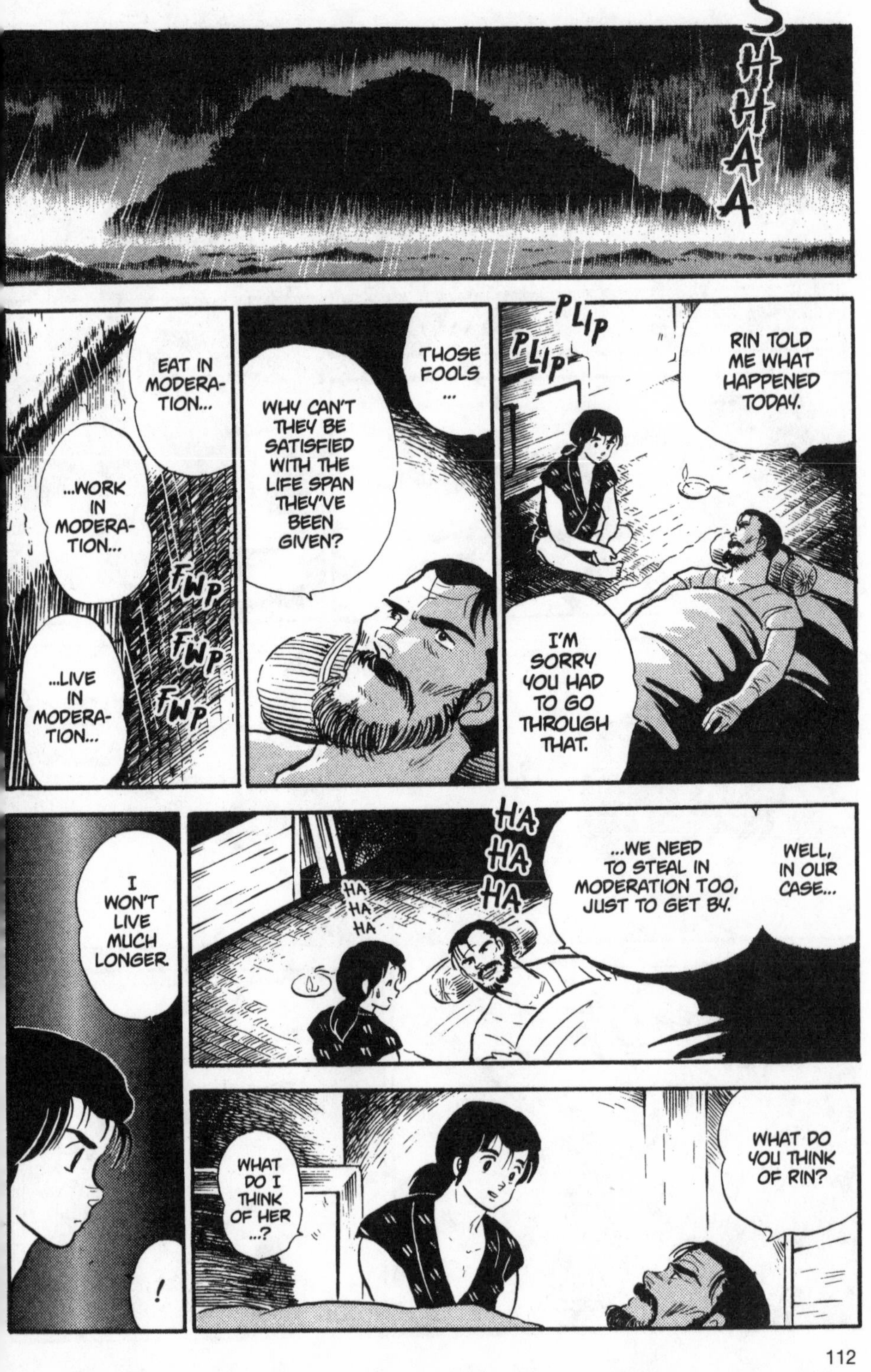
SHHAA
PLIP PLIP
RIN TOLD ME WHAT HAPPENED TODAY.
I'M SORRY YOU HAD TO GO THROUGH THAT.
THOSE FOOLS ...
WHY CAN'T THEY BE SATISFIED WITH THE LIFE SPAN THEY'VE BEEN GIVEN?
EAT IN MODERATION...
...WORK IN MODERATION...
FWP FWP FWP
...LIVE IN MODERATION...
WELL, IN OUR CASE...
...WE NEED TO STEAL IN MODERATION TOO, JUST TO GET BY.
HA HA HA
HA HA HA
WHAT DO YOU THINK OF RIN?
WHAT DO I THINK OF HER ...?
I WON'T LIVE MUCH LONGER.
!

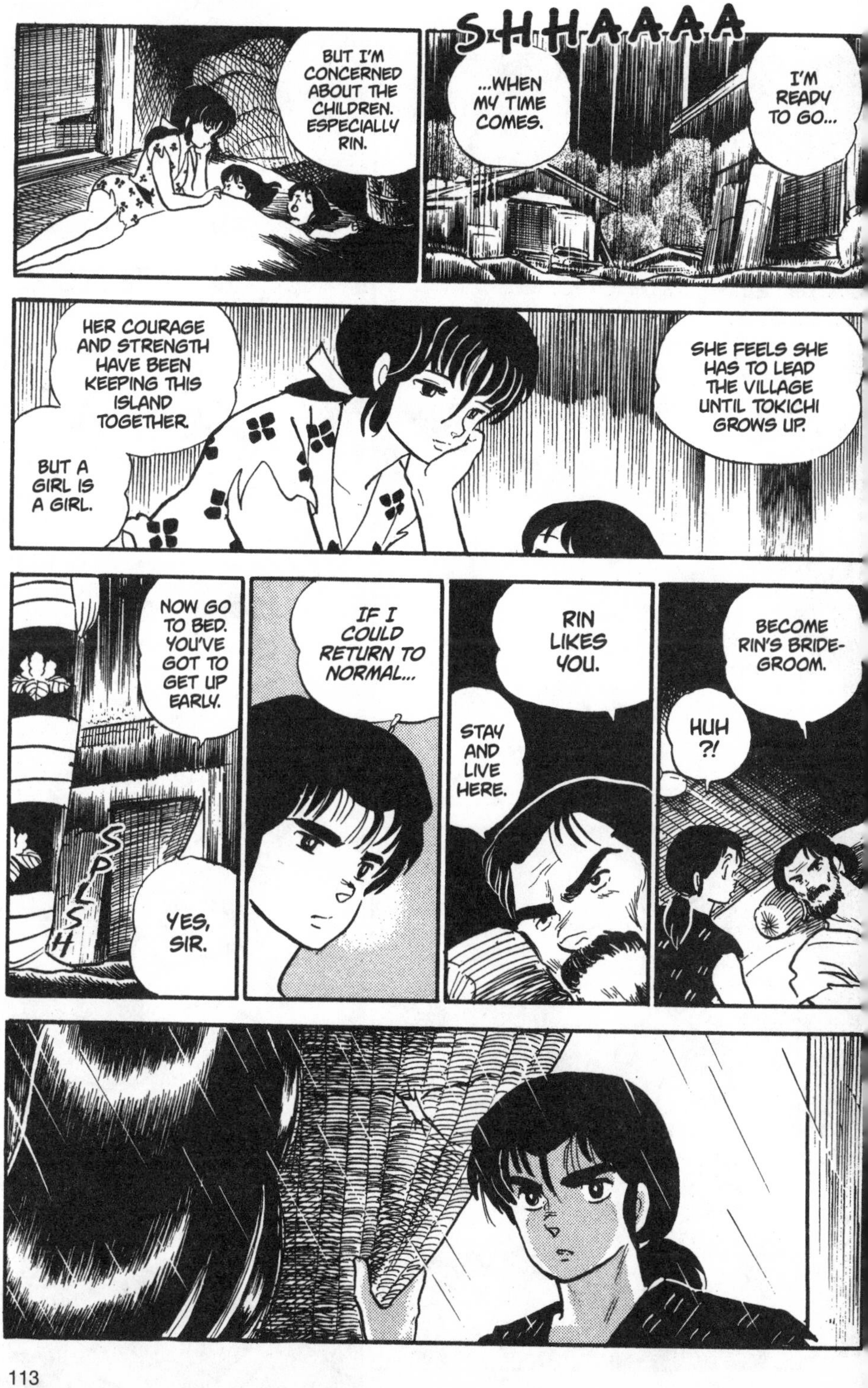
SHHAAAA
I'M READY TO GO...
...WHEN MY TIME COMES.
BUT I'M CONCERNED ABOUT THE CHILDREN. ESPECIALLY RIN.
SHE FEELS SHE HAS TO LEAD THE VILLAGE UNTIL TOKICHI GROWS UP.
HER COURAGE AND STRENGTH HAVE BEEN KEEPING THIS ISLAND TOGETHER.
BUT A GIRL IS A GIRL.
BECOME RIN'S BRIDE-GROOM.
HUH?!
RIN LIKES YOU.
STAY AND LIVE HERE.
IF I COULD RETURN TO NORMAL...
NOW GO TO BED. YOU'VE GOT TO GET UP EARLY.
SPLISH
YES, SIR.

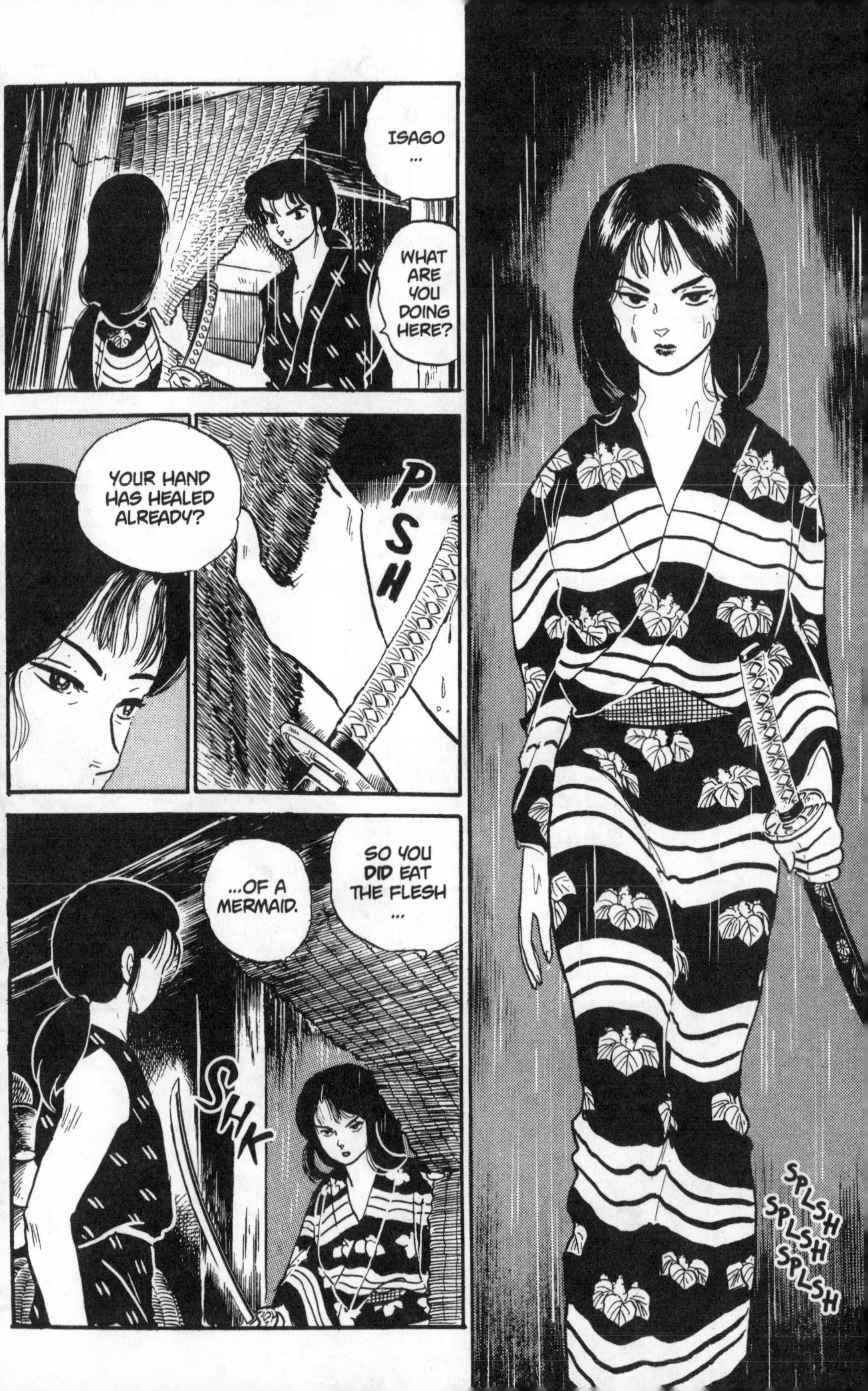
SPLSH SPLSH SPLSH
ISAGO ...
WHAT ARE YOU DOING HERE?
PSH
YOUR HAND HAS HEALED ALREADY?
SO YOU DID EAT THE FLESH ...
...OF A MERMAID.
SHK

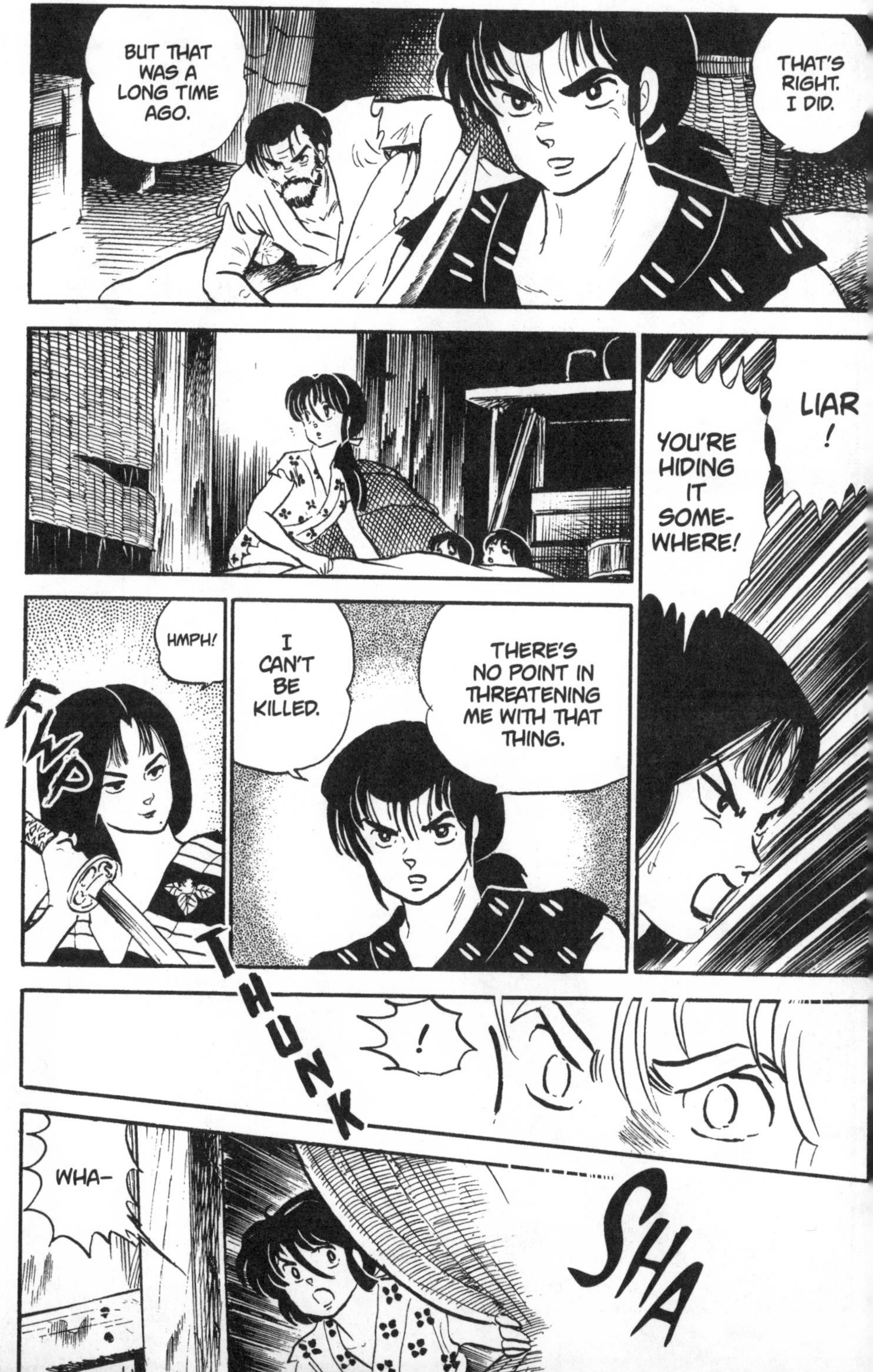
THAT'S RIGHT. I DID.
BUT THAT WAS A LONG TIME AGO.
LIAR!
YOU'RE HIDING IT SOMEWHERE!
THERE'S NO POINT IN THREATENING ME WITH THAT THING.
I CAN'T BE KILLED.
HMPH!
FWP
THUNK
!
SHA
WHA-

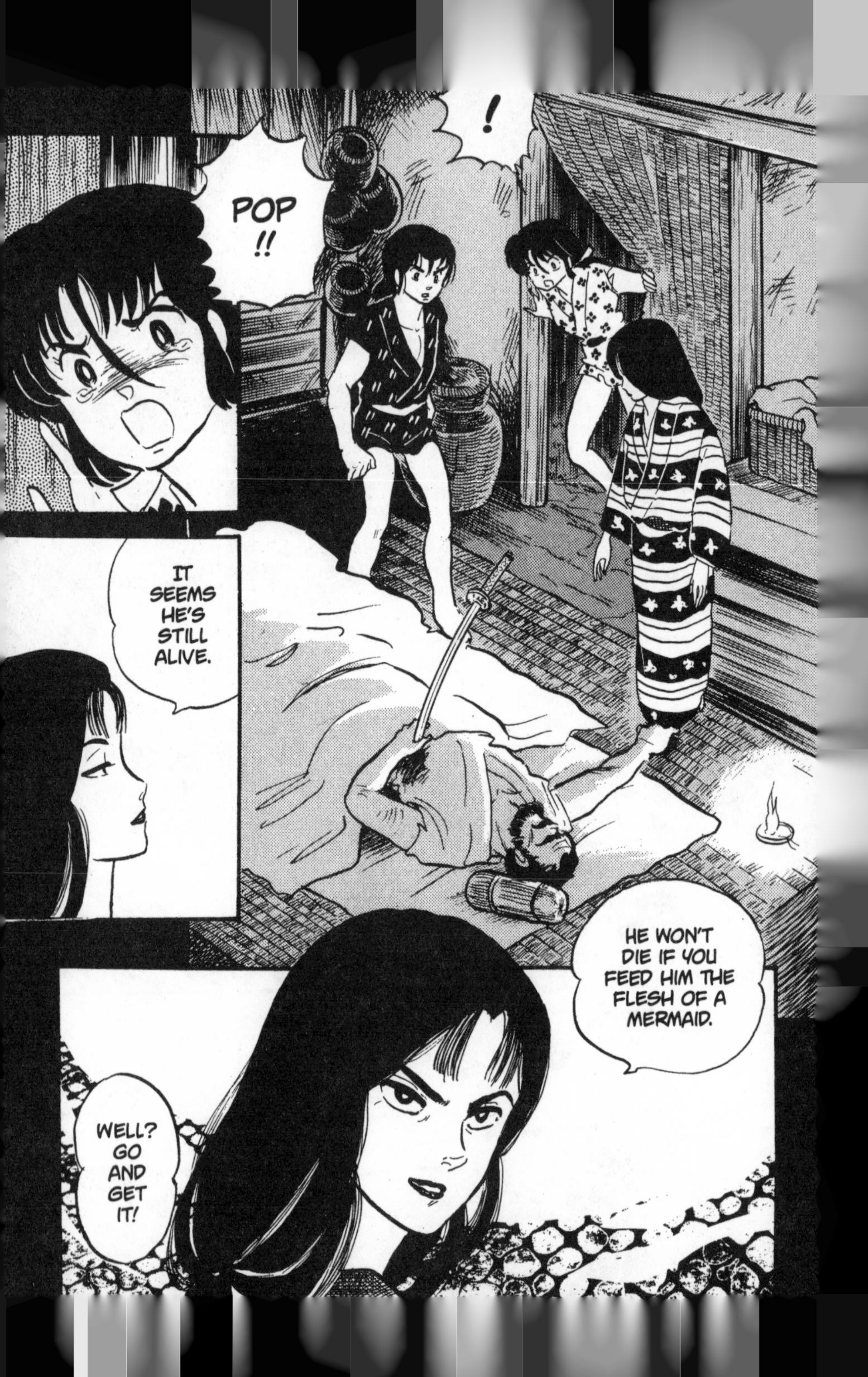
!
POP !!
IT SEEMS HE'S STILL ALIVE.
HE WON'T DIE IF YOU FEED HIM THE FLESH OF A MERMAID.
WELL? GO AND GET IT!

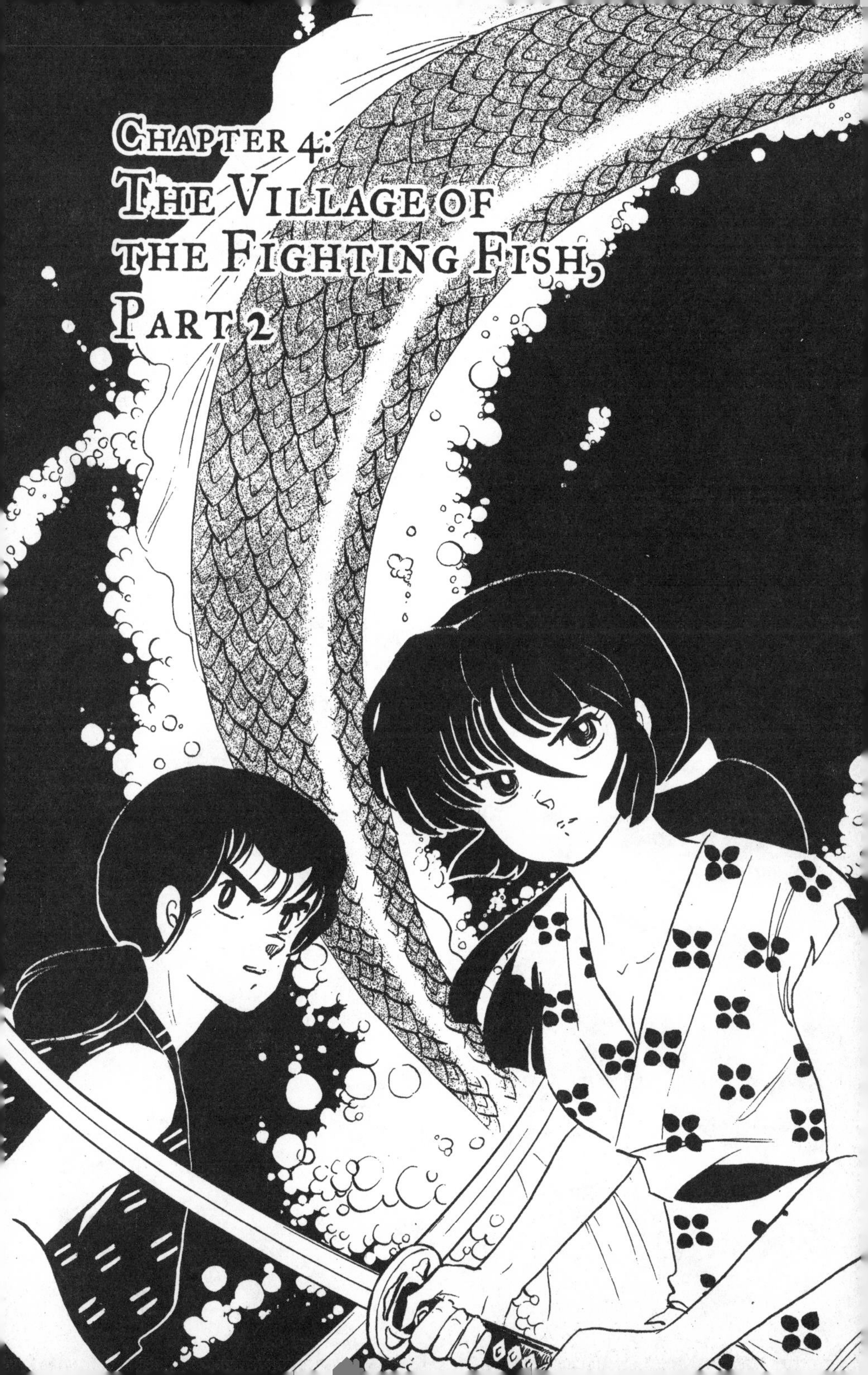
Chapter 4:
The Village of
the Fighting Fish,
Part 2

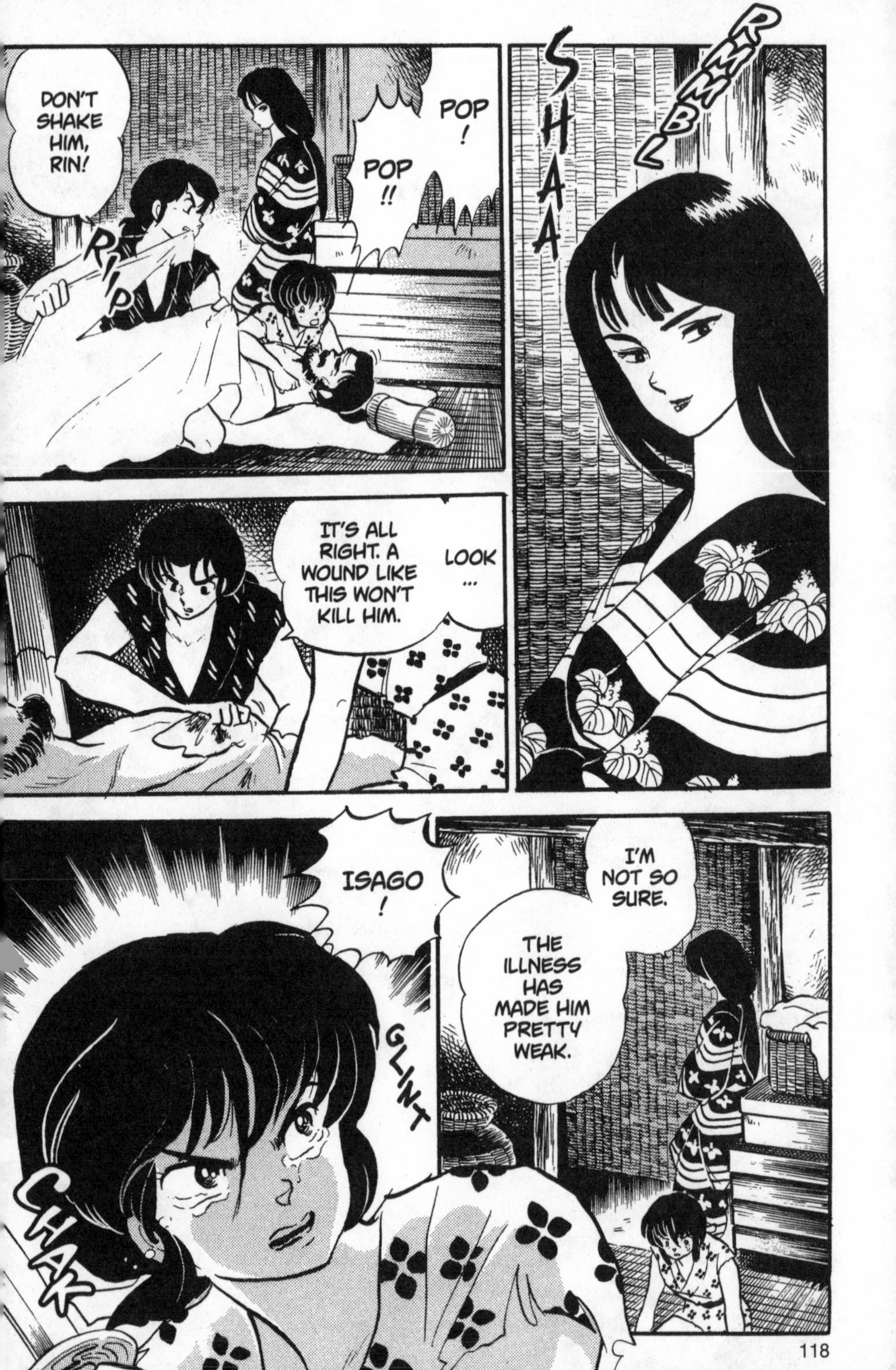
RMMBL
SHAA
DON'T SHAKE HIM, RIN!
POP!
POP!!
RIIP
IT'S ALL RIGHT. A WOUND LIKE THIS WON'T KILL HIM.
LOOK...
I'M NOT SO SURE.
THE ILLNESS HAS MADE HIM PRETTY WEAK.
ISAGO!
GLINT
CHAK

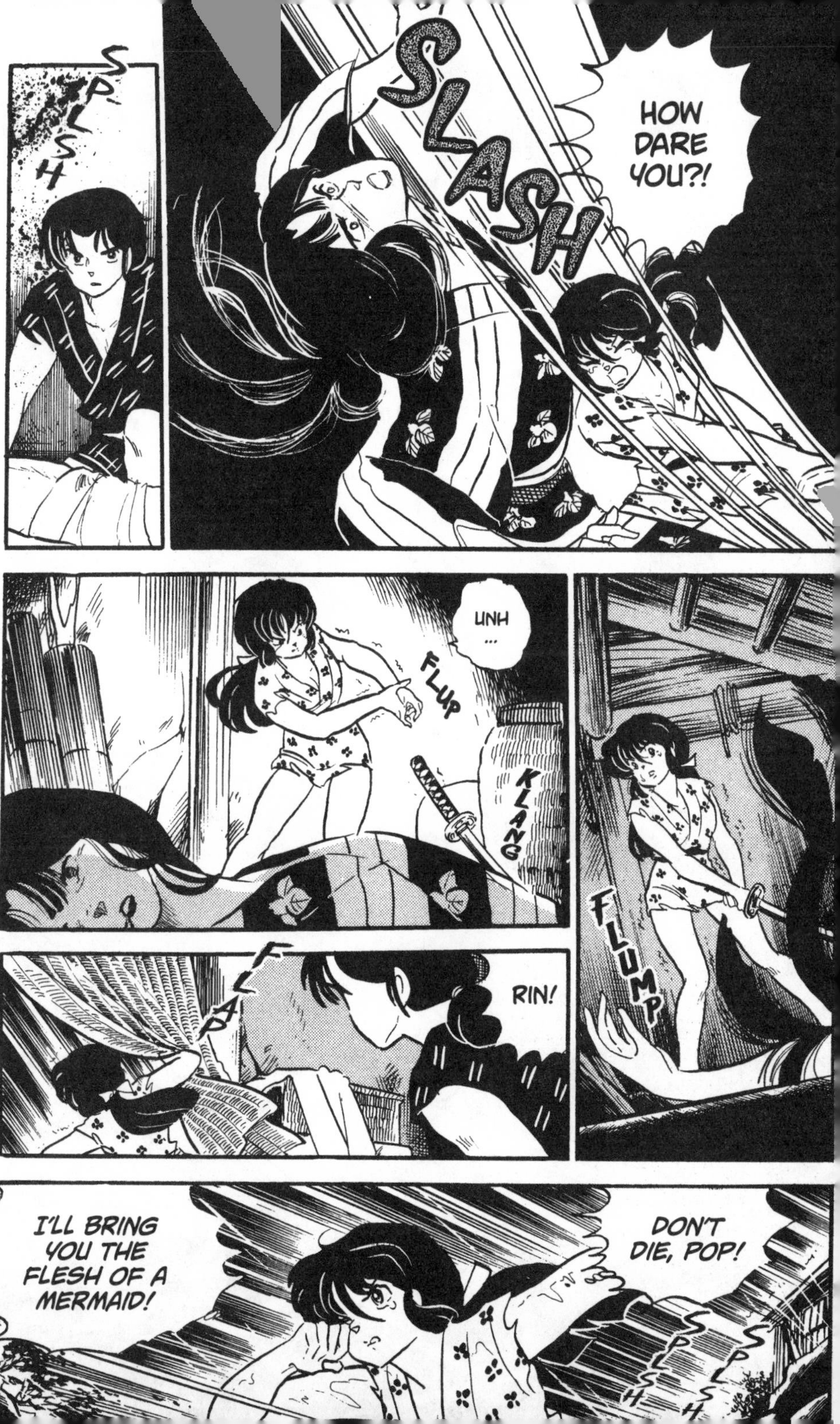
HOW DARE YOU?!
SLASH
SPLSH
FLUMP
UNH ...
FLUP
KLANG
RIN!
FLAP
DON'T DIE, POP!
I'LL BRING YOU THE FLESH OF A MERMAID!
SPLSH

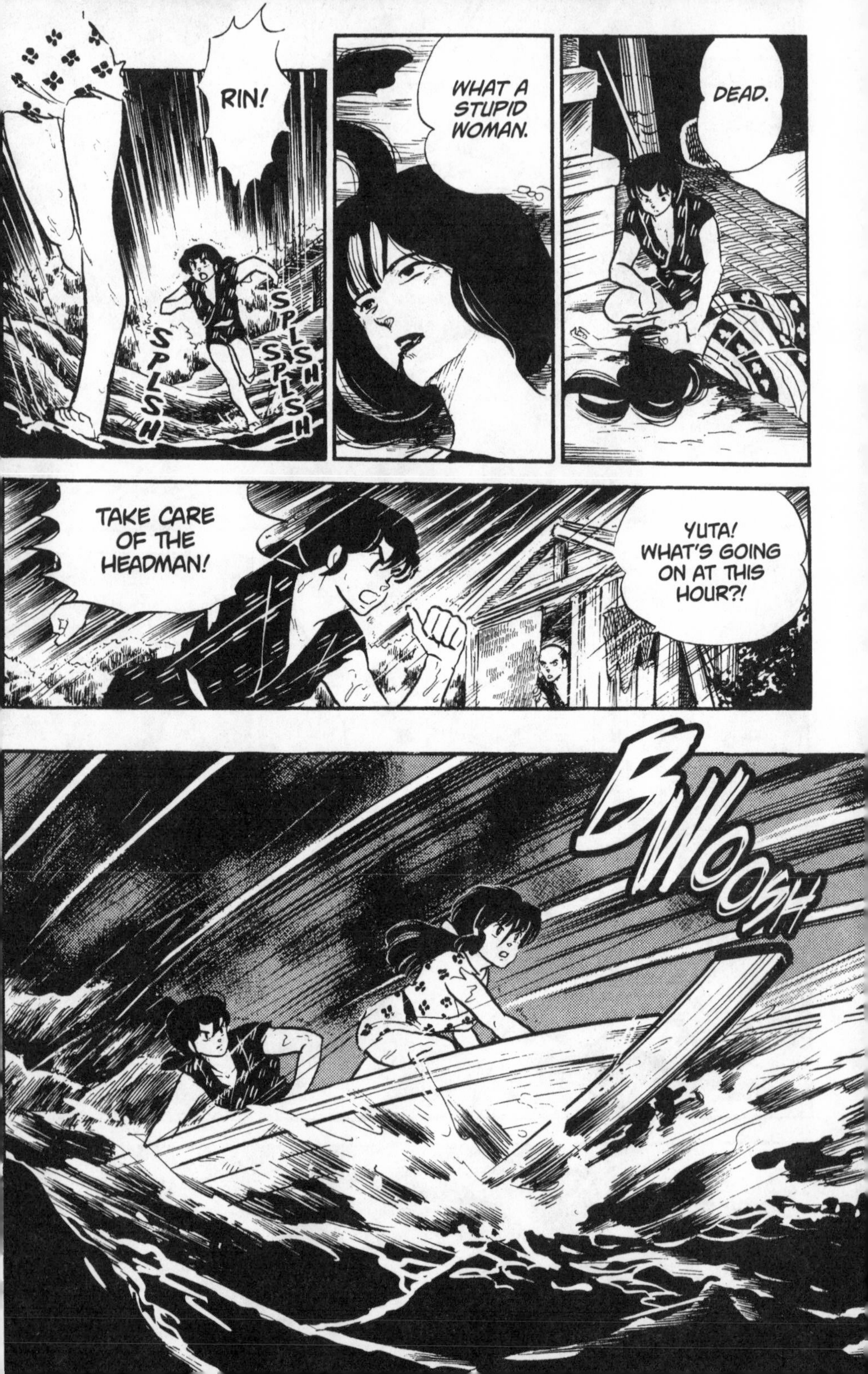
DEAD.
WHAT A STUPID WOMAN.
RIN!
SPLSH
SPLSH
SPLSH
YUTA! WHAT'S GOING ON AT THIS HOUR?!
TAKE CARE OF THE HEADMAN!
BWOOSH

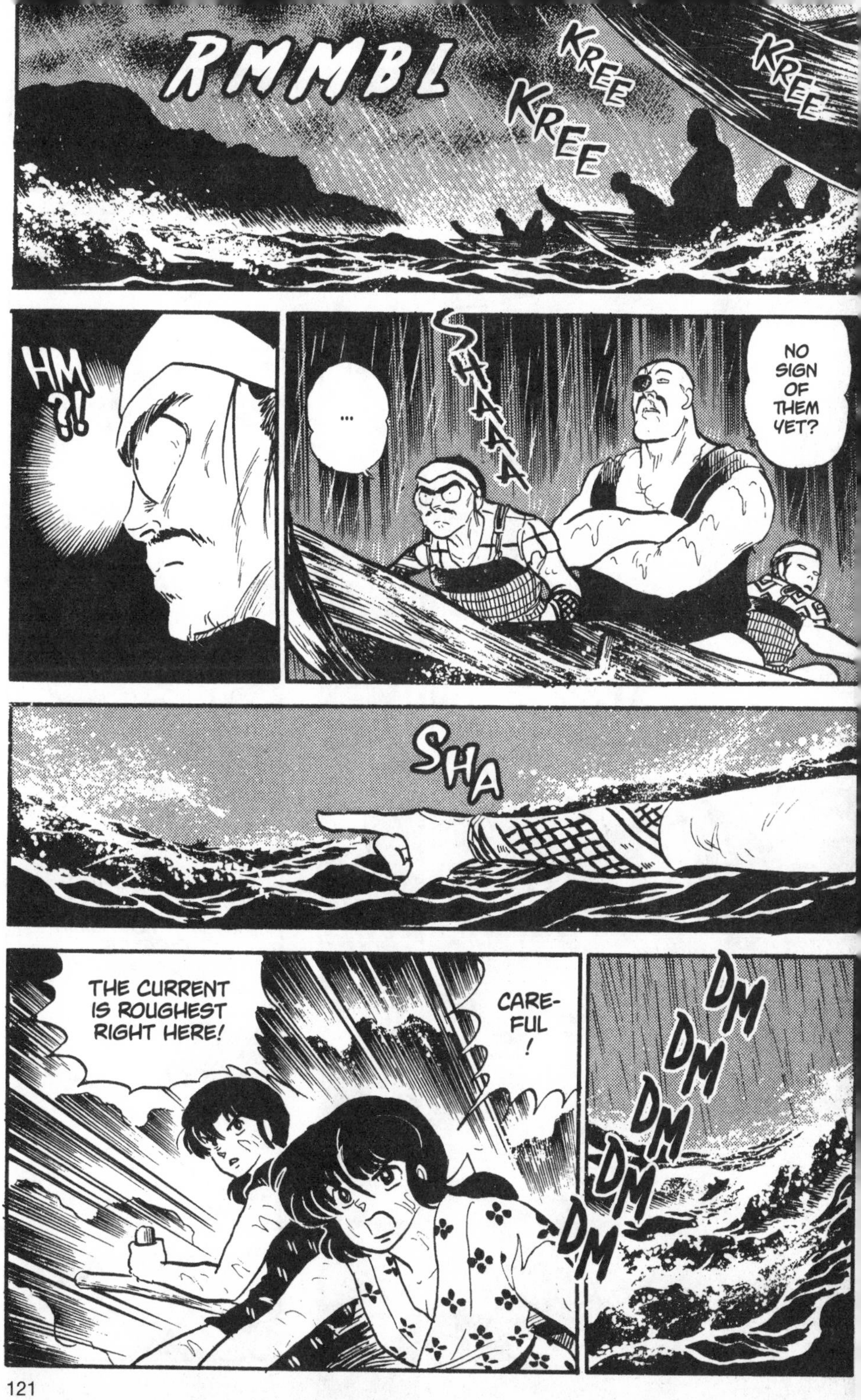

KREE
KREE
KREE
RMMBL
NO SIGN OF THEM YET?
SHAAAA
...
HM ?!
SHA
DM DM DM DM DM DM
CARE-FUL!
THE CURRENT IS ROUGHEST RIGHT HERE!

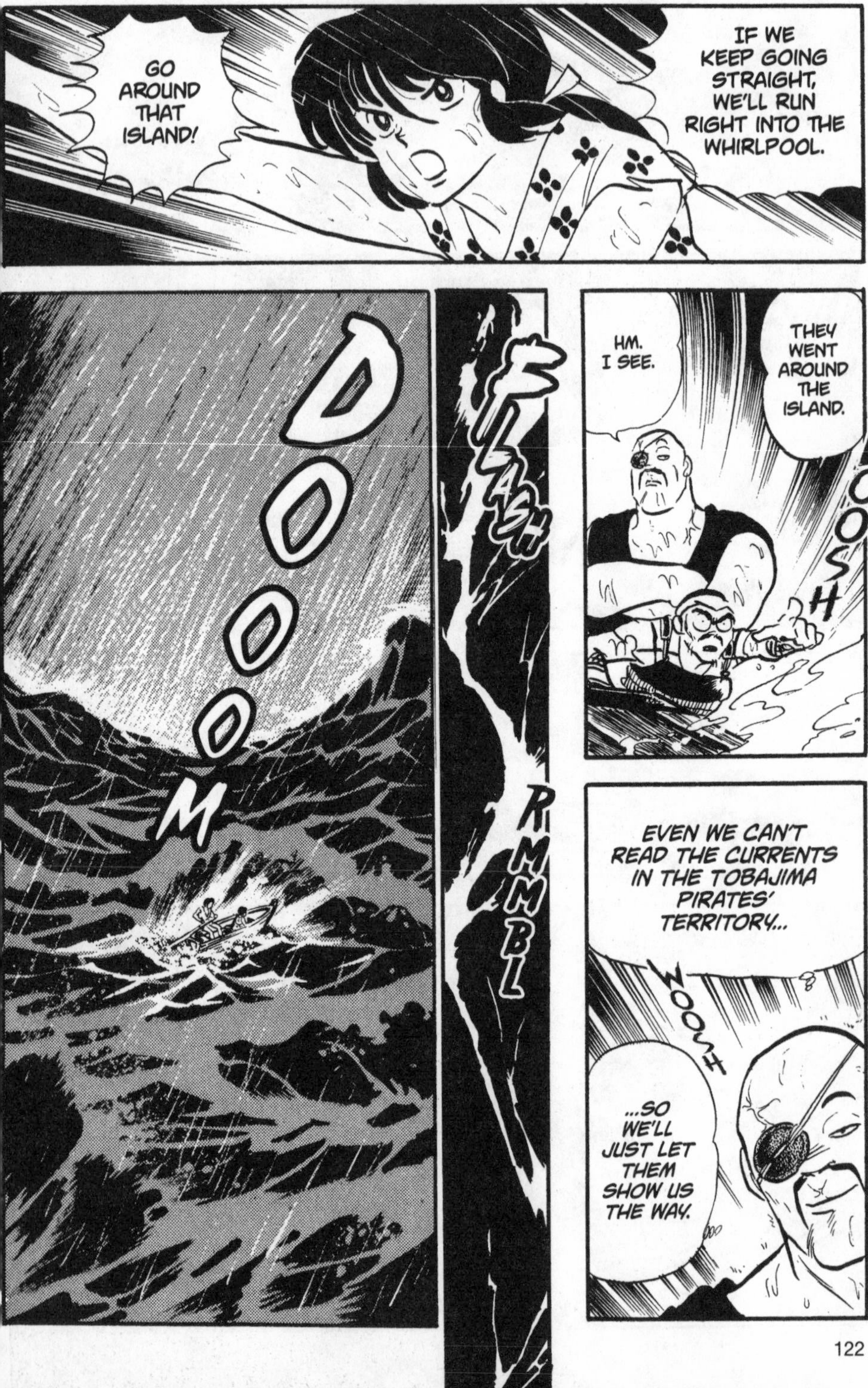
IF WE KEEP GOING STRAIGHT, WE'LL RUN RIGHT INTO THE WHIRLPOOL.
GO AROUND THAT ISLAND!
THEY WENT AROUND THE ISLAND.
HM. I SEE.
BOOOSH
EVEN WE CAN'T READ THE CURRENTS IN THE TOBAJIMA PIRATES' TERRITORY...
WOOSH
...SO WE'LL JUST LET THEM SHOW US THE WAY.
FLASH
RMMMBL
DOOOOOM

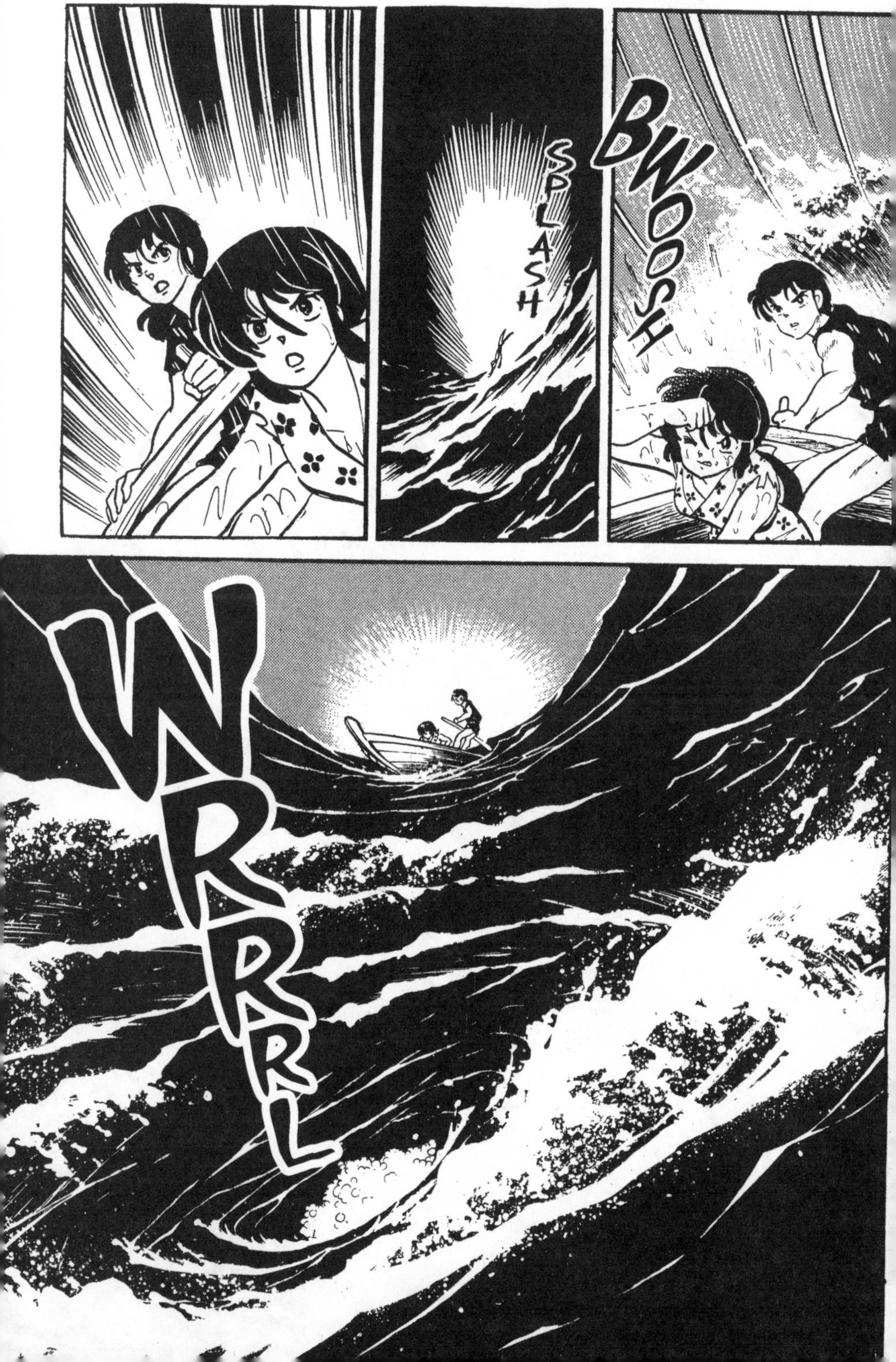
BWOOSH
SPLASH
WRRRL

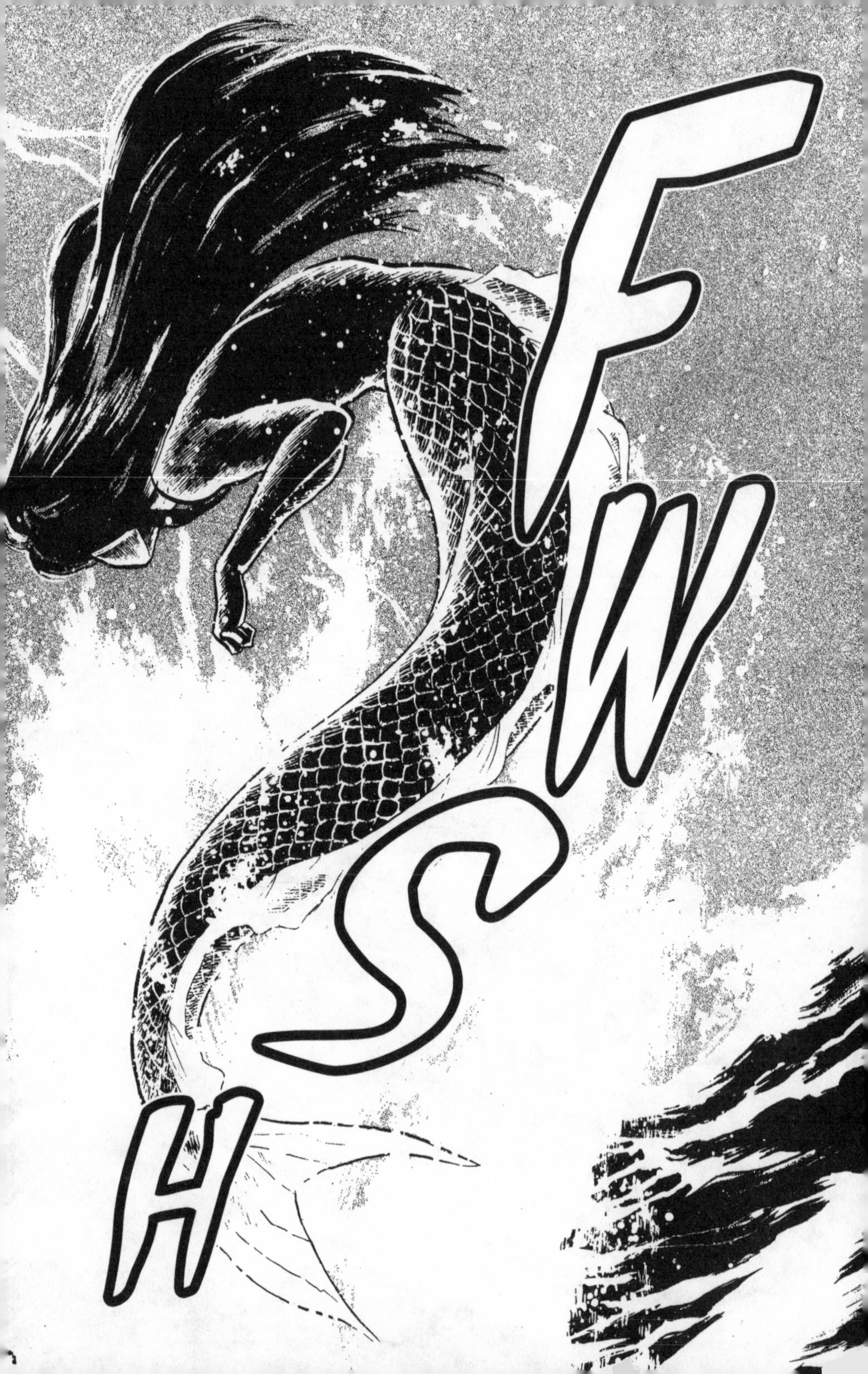
FWSH

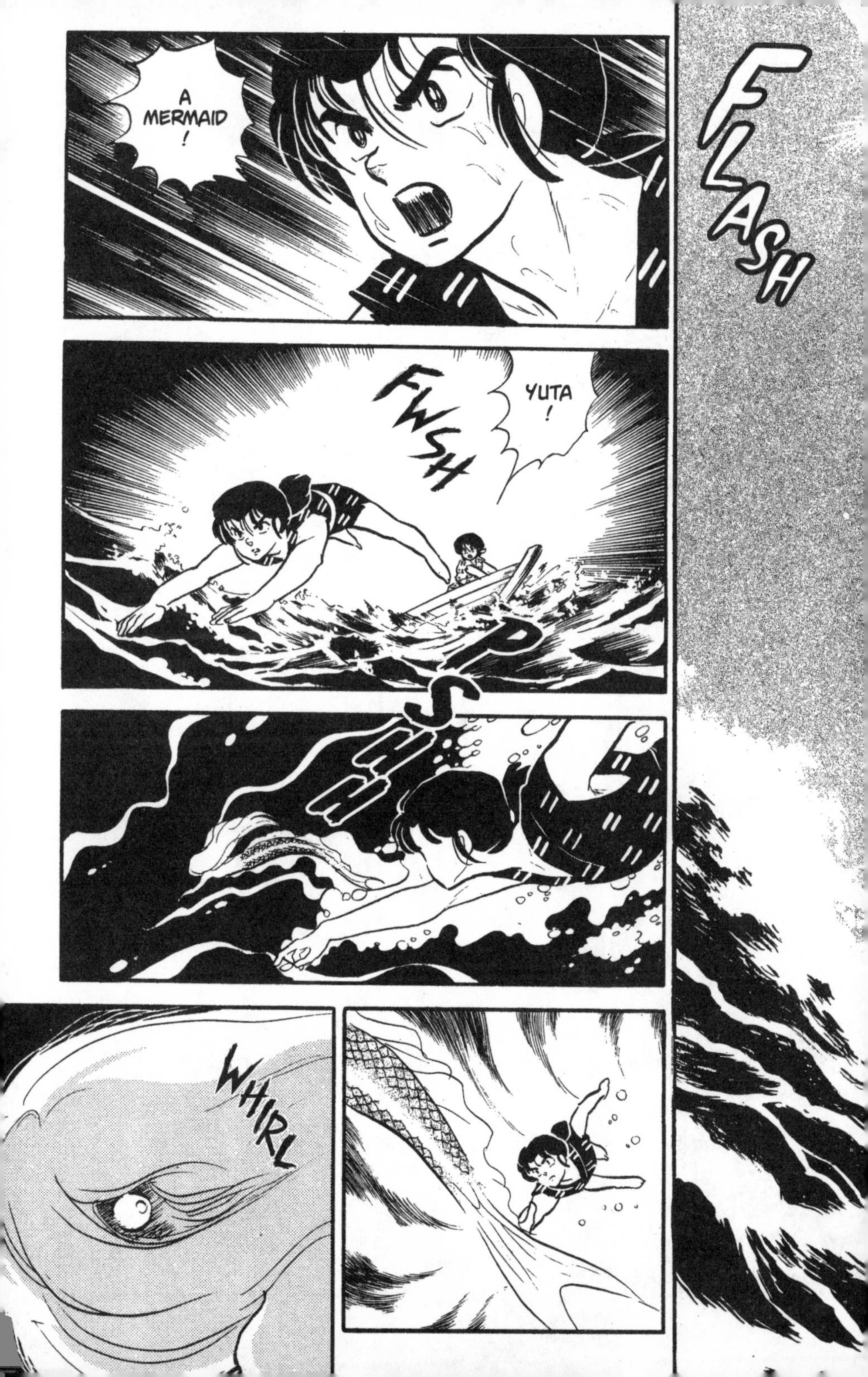
FLASH
A MERMAID!
FWSH
YUTA!
SPLSHH
WHIRL

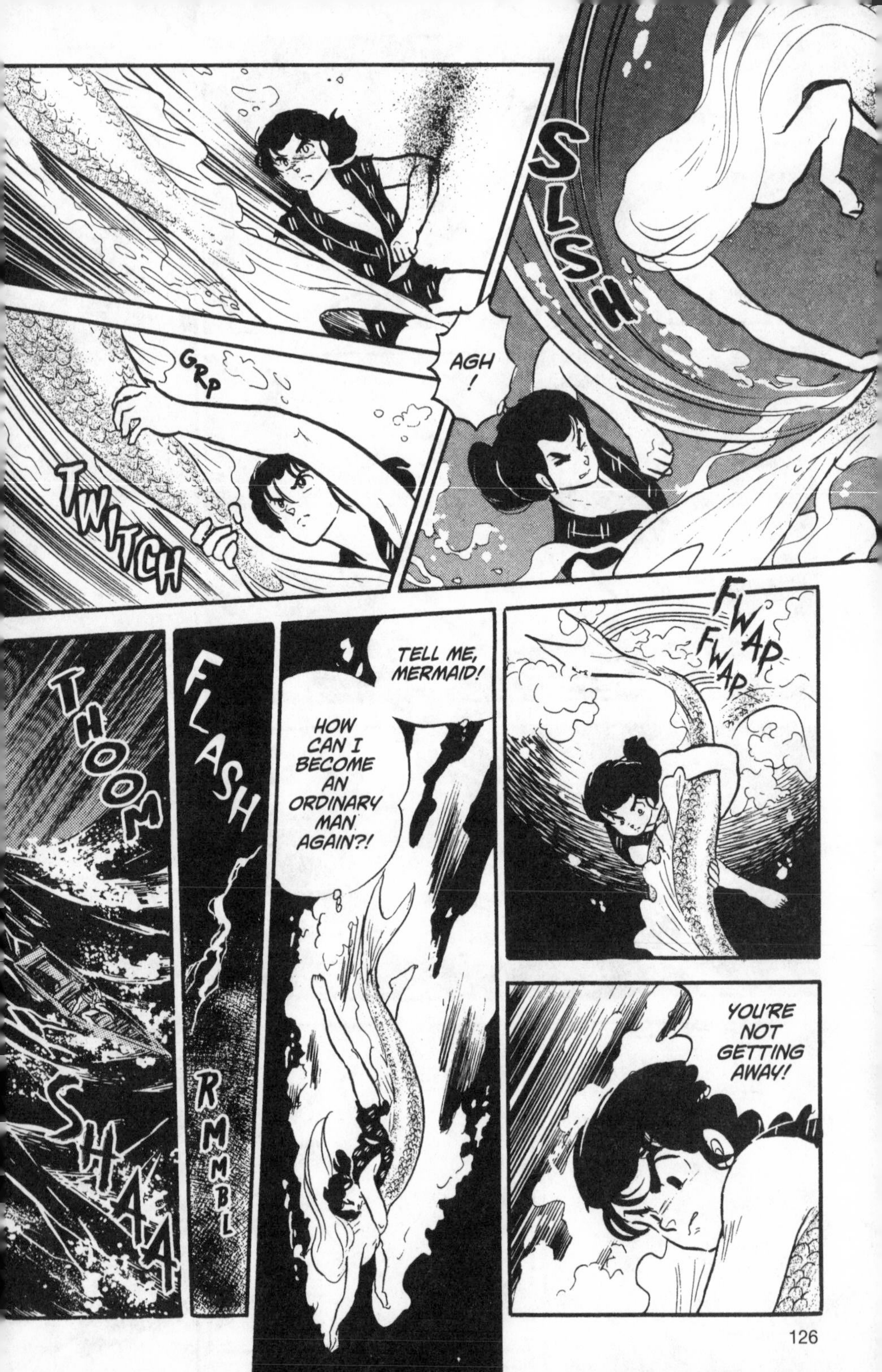
SLSH
AGH!
GRP
TWITCH
FWAP FWAP
YOU'RE NOT GETTING AWAY!
TELL ME, MERMAID!
HOW CAN I BECOME AN ORDINARY MAN AGAIN?!
FLASH
RMMBL
THOOM
SHAAA

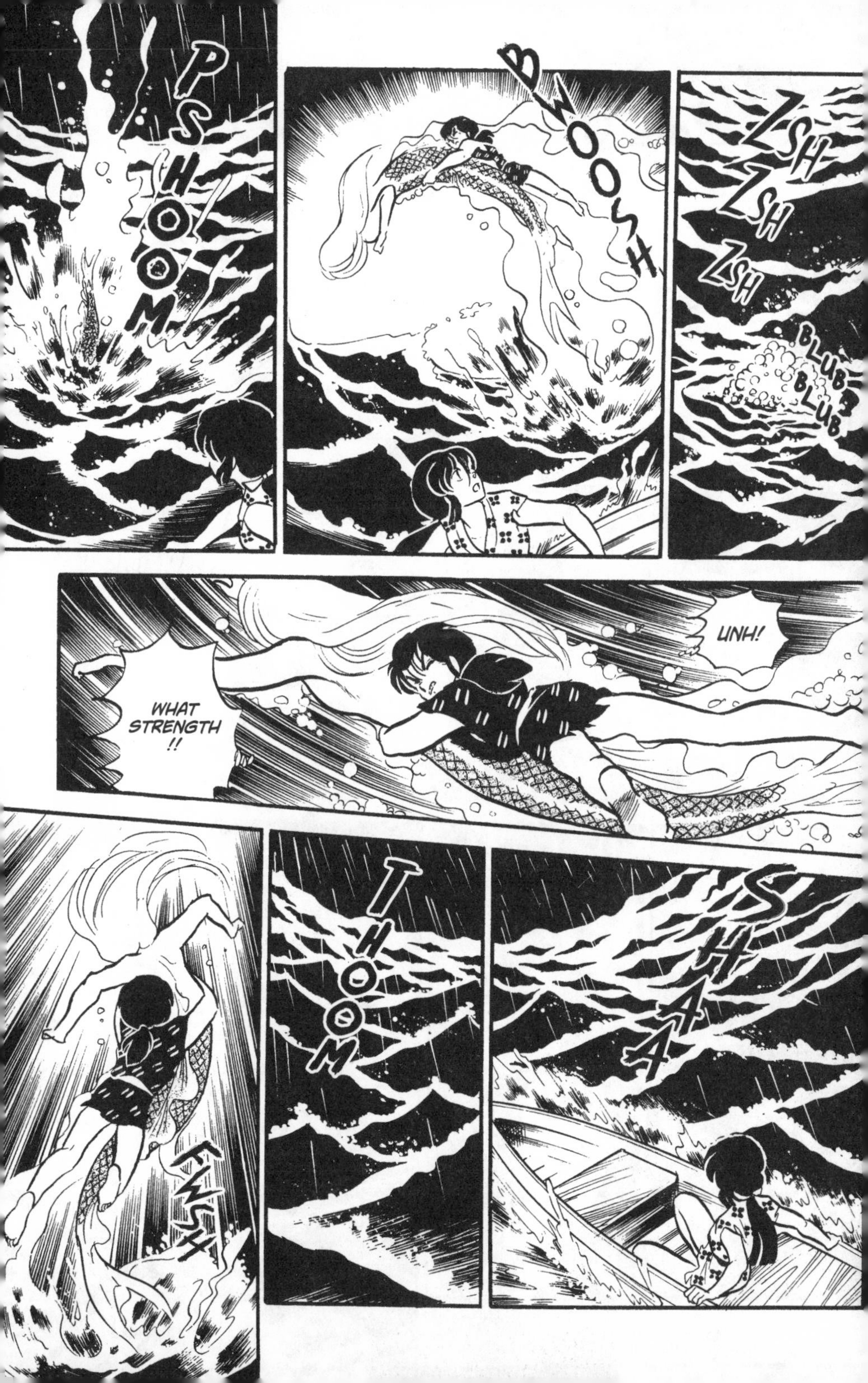
ZSH ZSH ZSH
BLUB BLUB
BWOOSH
PSHOOM
UNH!
WHAT STRENGTH !!
SHAAA
THOOM
FWSH

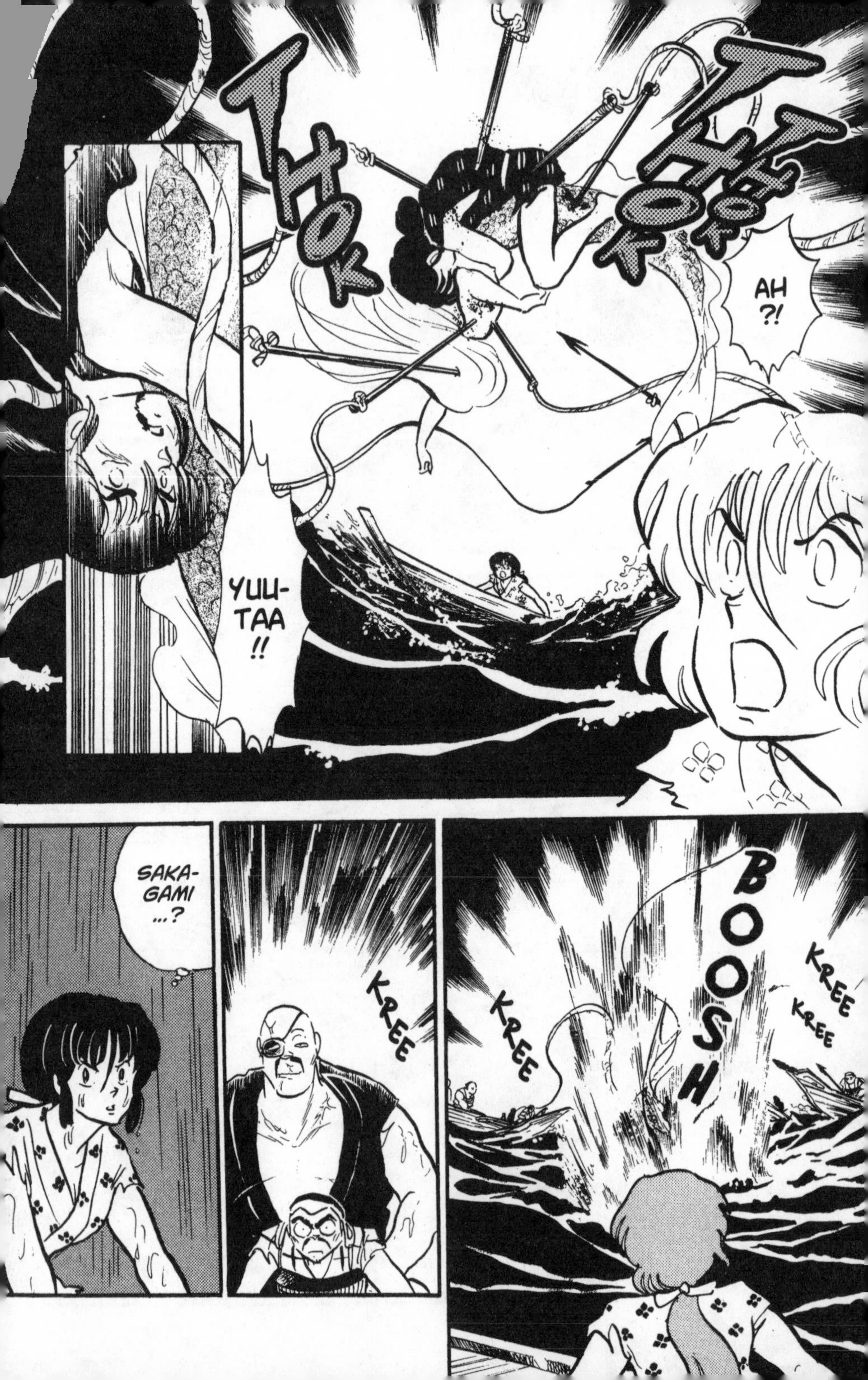
THOK
AH ?!
THOK
YUU-TAA !!
BOOSH
KREE
KREE
KREE
KREE
SAKA-GAMI ...?

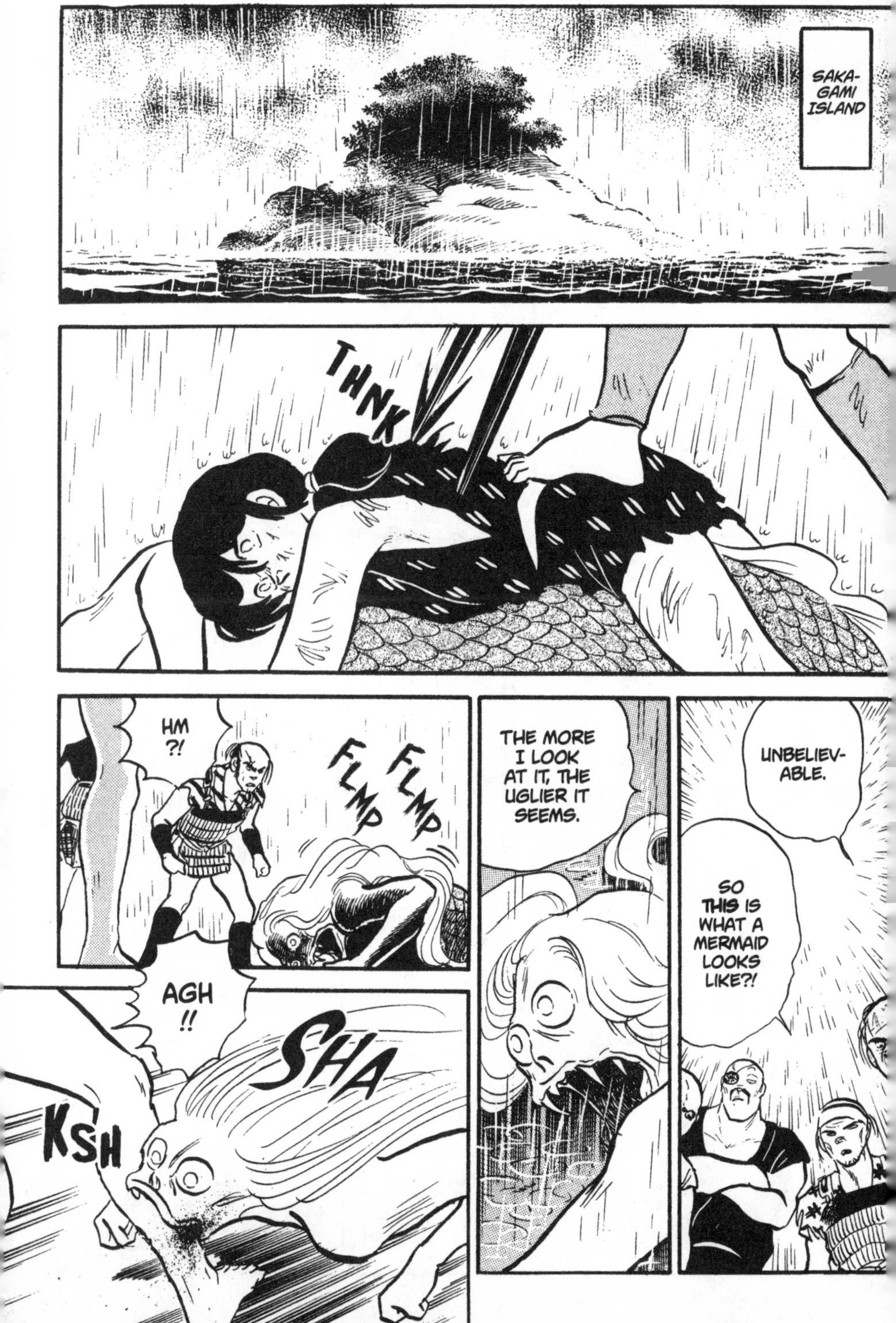
SAKA-GAMI ISLAND
THNK
UNBELIEV-ABLE.
SO THIS IS WHAT A MERMAID LOOKS LIKE?!
THE MORE I LOOK AT IT, THE UGLIER IT SEEMS.
HM ?!
FLMP FLMP
AGH !!
SHA
KSH

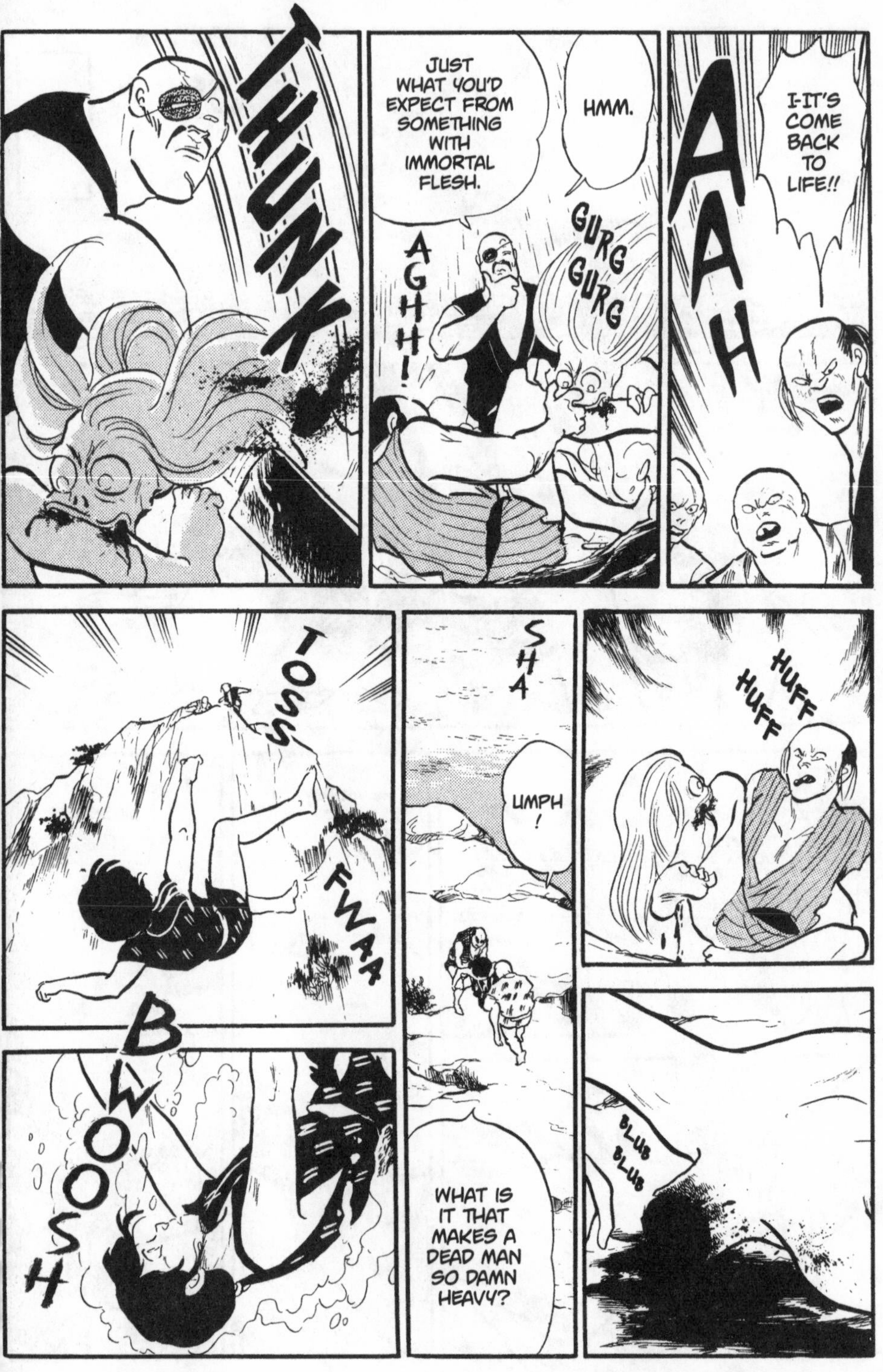
AAH
I-IT'S COME BACK TO LIFE!!
HMM.
JUST WHAT YOU'D EXPECT FROM SOMETHING WITH IMMORTAL FLESH.
GURG GURG
AGHH!
THUNK
HUFF HUFF
BLUB BLUB
SHA
UMPH!
WHAT IS IT THAT MAKES A DEAD MAN SO DAMN HEAVY?
TOSS
FWAA
BWOOSH

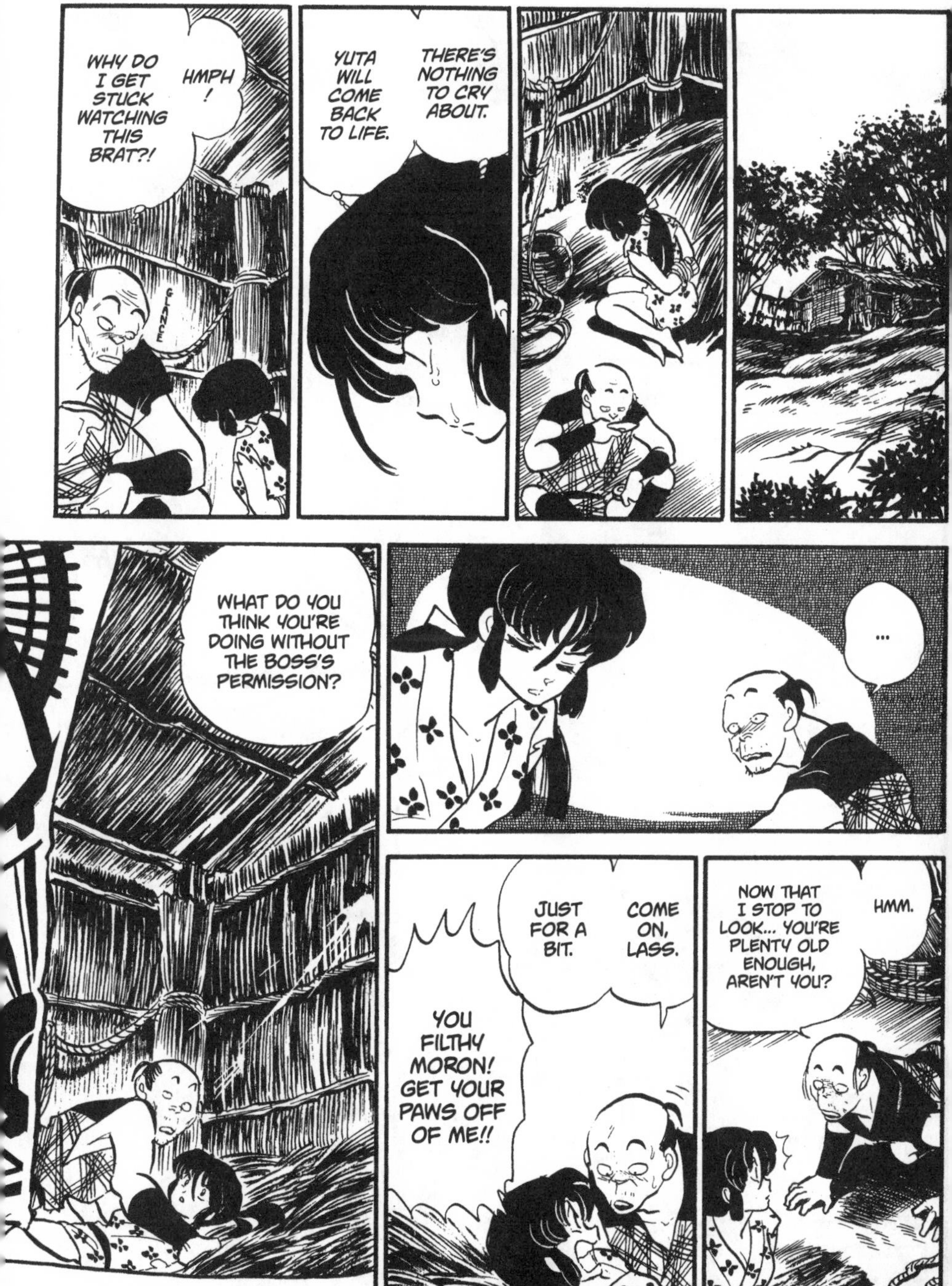
THERE'S NOTHING TO CRY ABOUT.
YUTA WILL COME BACK TO LIFE.
HMPH!
WHY DO I GET STUCK WATCHING THIS BRAT?!
GLANCE
...
HMM.
NOW THAT I STOP TO LOOK... YOU'RE PLENTY OLD ENOUGH, AREN'T YOU?
COME ON, LASS.
JUST FOR A BIT.
YOU FILTHY MORON! GET YOUR PAWS OFF OF ME!!
WHAT DO YOU THINK YOU'RE DOING WITHOUT THE BOSS'S PERMISSION?

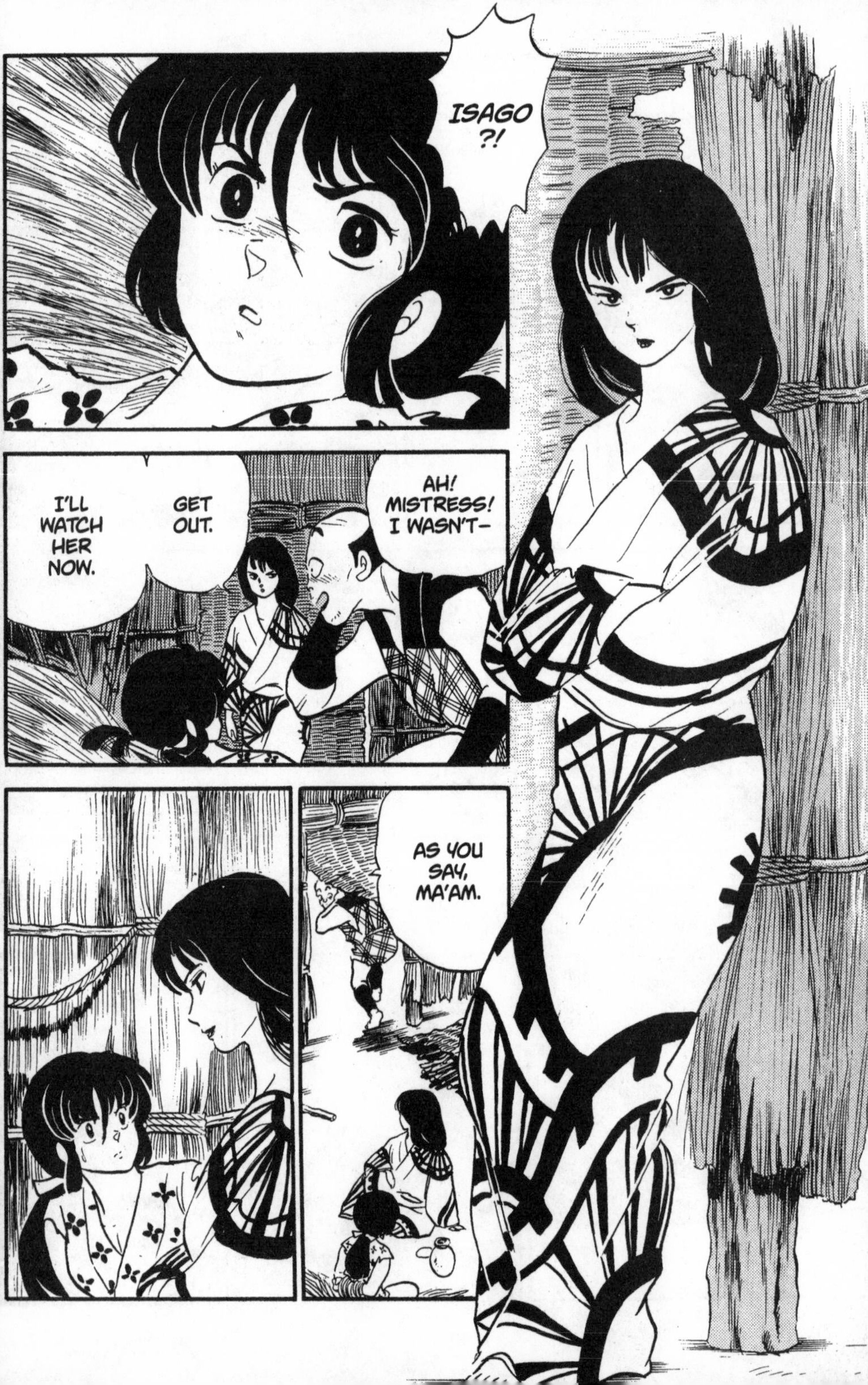
ISAGO ?!
AH! MISTRESS! I WASN'T–
GET OUT.
I'LL WATCH HER NOW.
AS YOU SAY, MA'AM.

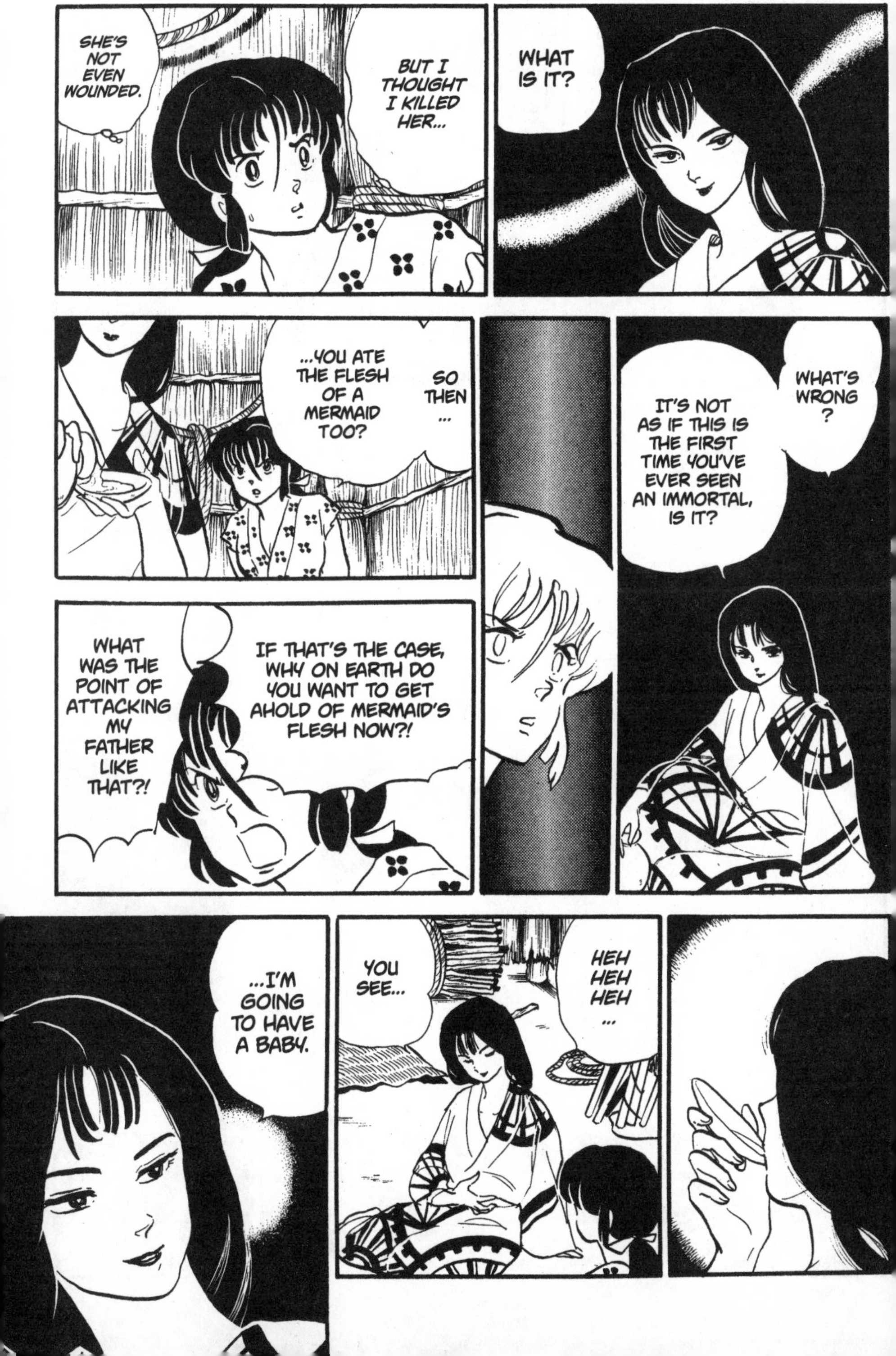
WHAT IS IT?
BUT I THOUGHT I KILLED HER...
SHE'S NOT EVEN WOUNDED.
WHAT'S WRONG?
IT'S NOT AS IF THIS IS THE FIRST TIME YOU'VE EVER SEEN AN IMMORTAL, IS IT?
SO THEN ...
...YOU ATE THE FLESH OF A MERMAID TOO?
IF THAT'S THE CASE, WHY ON EARTH DO YOU WANT TO GET AHOLD OF MERMAID'S FLESH NOW?!
WHAT WAS THE POINT OF ATTACKING MY FATHER LIKE THAT?!
HEH HEH HEH ...
YOU SEE...
...I'M GOING TO HAVE A BABY.

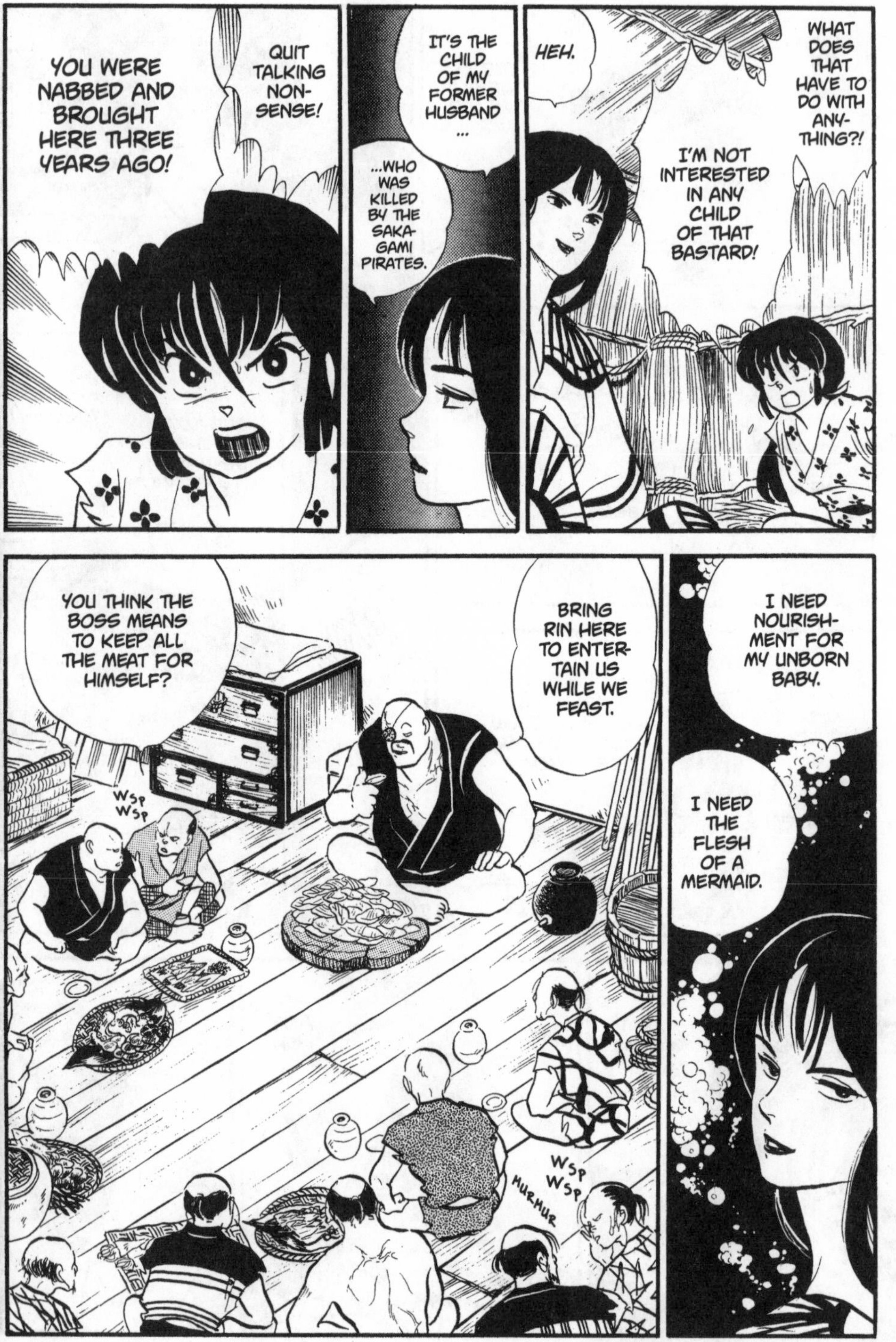
WHAT DOES THAT HAVE TO DO WITH ANY-THING?!
I'M NOT INTERESTED IN ANY CHILD OF THAT BASTARD!
HEH.
IT'S THE CHILD OF MY FORMER HUSBAND ...
...WHO WAS KILLED BY THE SAKA-GAMI PIRATES.
QUIT TALKING NON-SENSE!
YOU WERE NABBED AND BROUGHT HERE THREE YEARS AGO!
I NEED NOURISH-MENT FOR MY UNBORN BABY.
I NEED THE FLESH OF A MERMAID.
BRING RIN HERE TO ENTER-TAIN US WHILE WE FEAST.
YOU THINK THE BOSS MEANS TO KEEP ALL THE MEAT FOR HIMSELF?
WSP WSP
WSP WSP
MURMUR

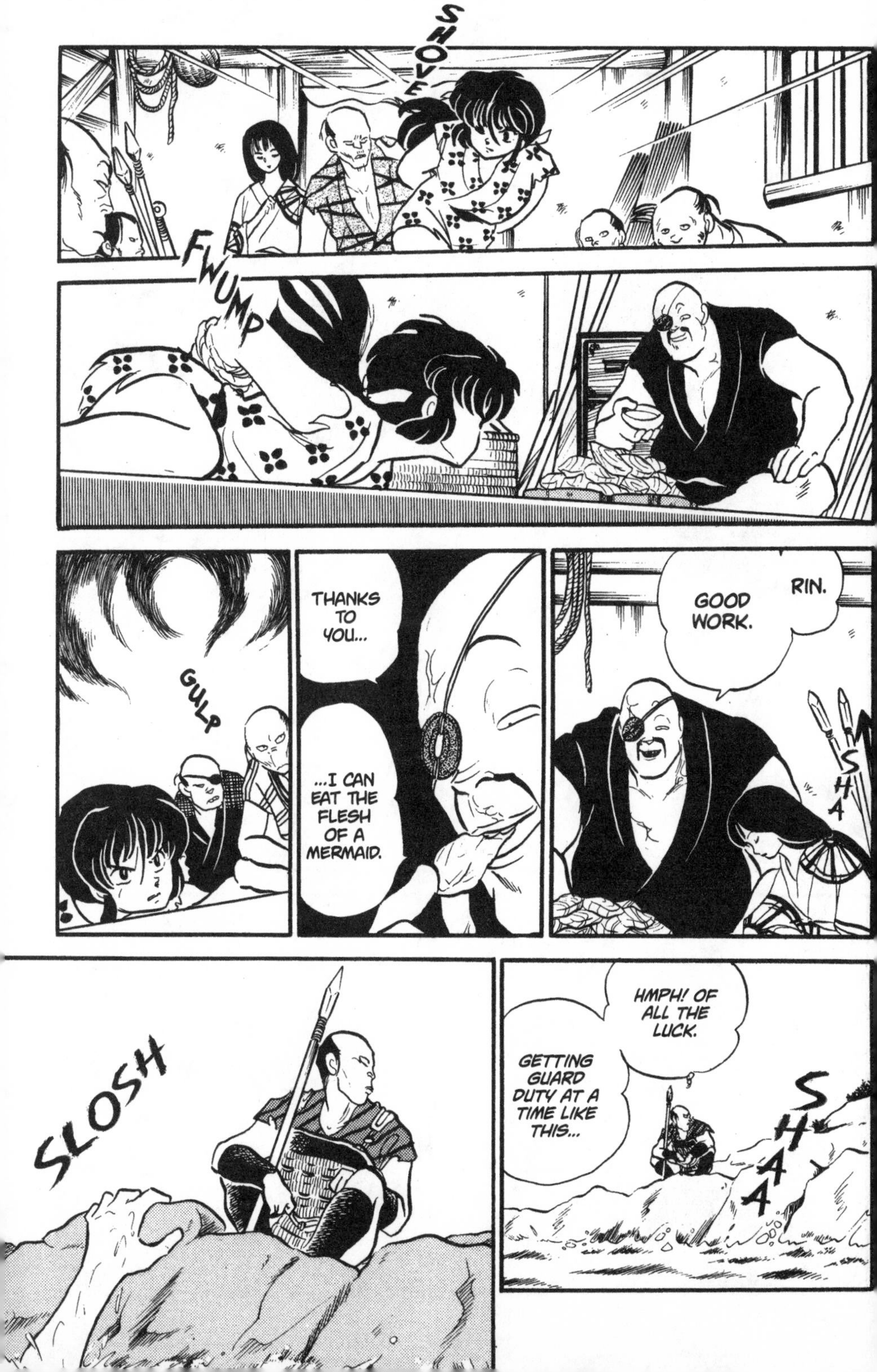
SHOVE
FWUMP
RIN.
GOOD WORK.
SHA
THANKS TO YOU...
...I CAN EAT THE FLESH OF A MERMAID.
GULP
HMPH! OF ALL THE LUCK.
GETTING GUARD DUTY AT A TIME LIKE THIS...
SHAAA
SLOSH

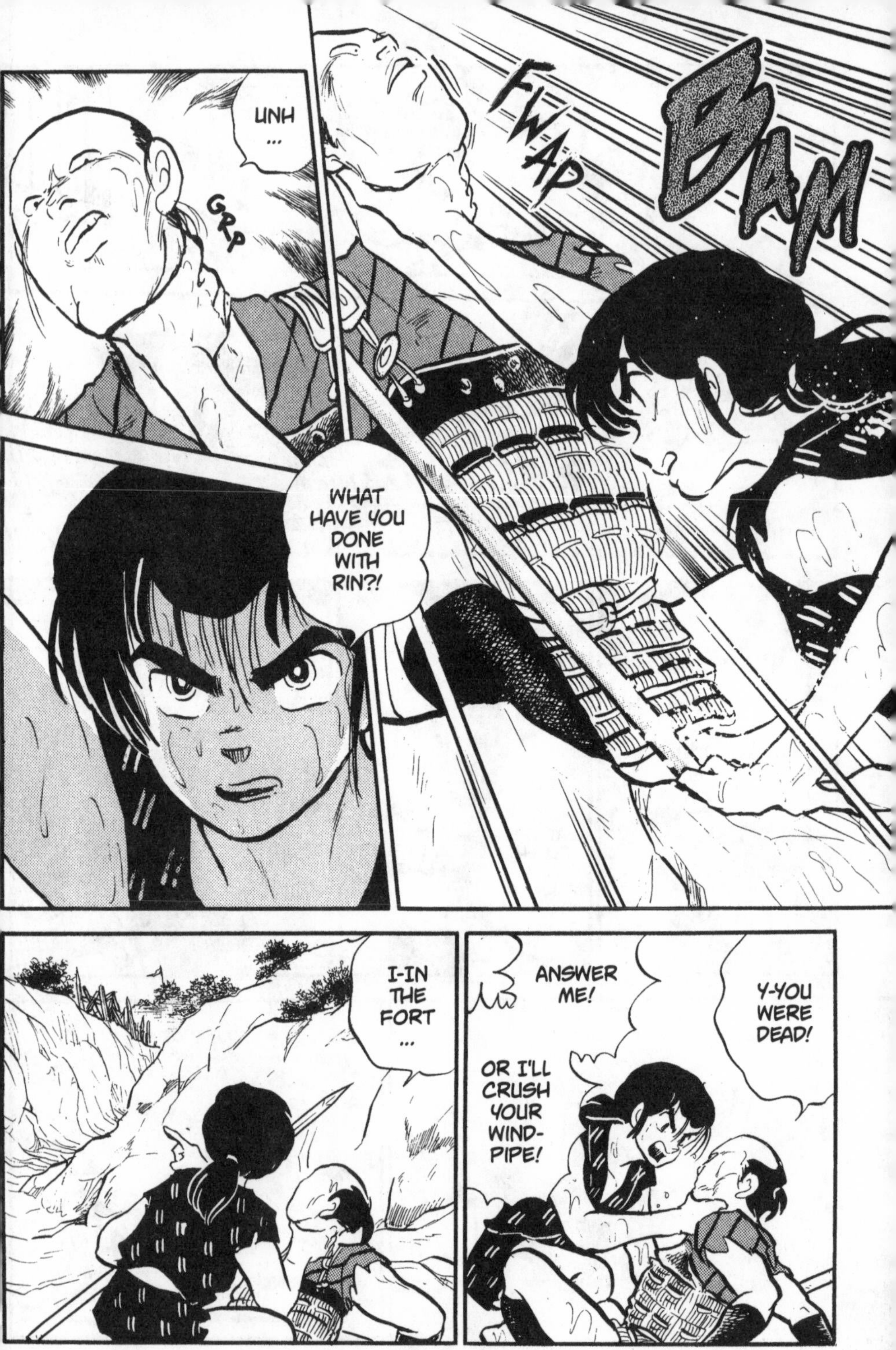
BAM
FWAP
UNH ...
GRP
WHAT HAVE YOU DONE WITH RIN?!
ANSWER ME!
OR I'LL CRUSH YOUR WIND-PIPE!
Y-YOU WERE DEAD!
I-IN THE FORT ...

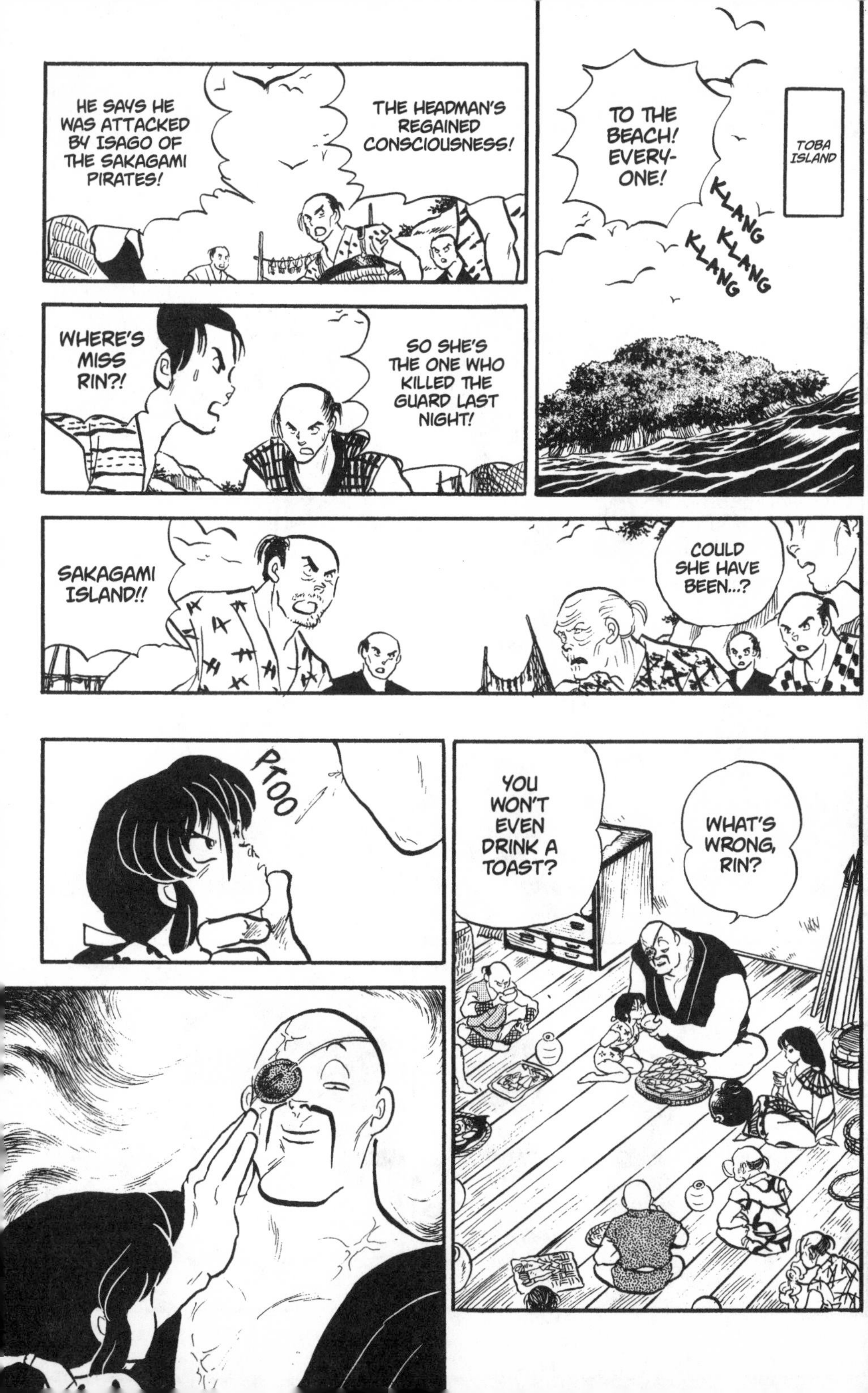
TOBA ISLAND
TO THE BEACH! EVERY-ONE!
KLANG KLANG KLANG
THE HEADMAN'S REGAINED CONSCIOUSNESS!
HE SAYS HE WAS ATTACKED BY ISAGO OF THE SAKAGAMI PIRATES!
SO SHE'S THE ONE WHO KILLED THE GUARD LAST NIGHT!
WHERE'S MISS RIN?!
COULD SHE HAVE BEEN...?
SAKAGAMI ISLAND!!
WHAT'S WRONG, RIN?
YOU WON'T EVEN DRINK A TOAST?
PTOO

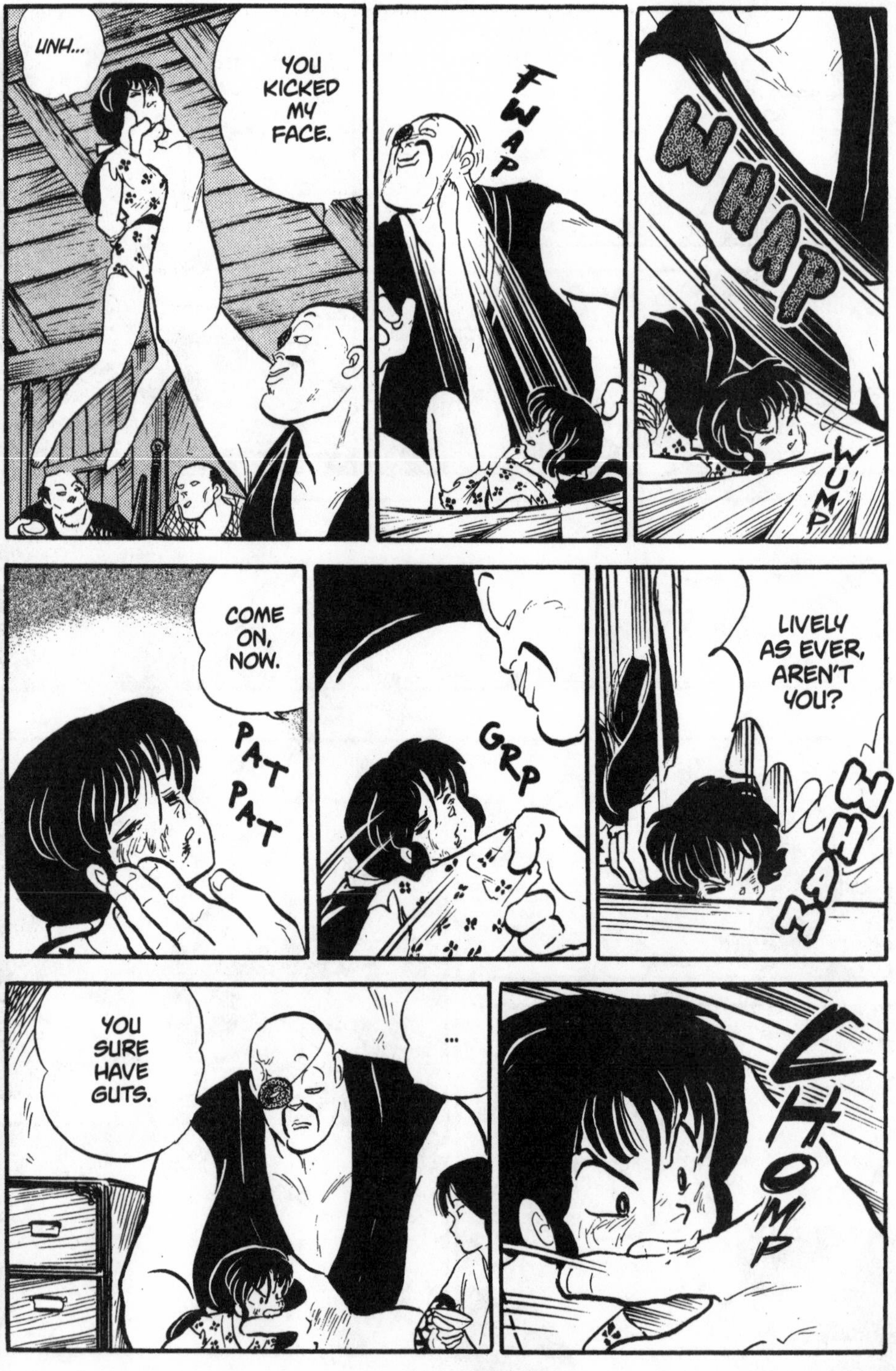
WHAP
WUMP
FWAP
YOU KICKED MY FACE.
UNH...
LIVELY AS EVER, AREN'T YOU?
WHAM
GRP
COME ON, NOW.
PAT PAT
CHOMP
...
YOU SURE HAVE GUTS.

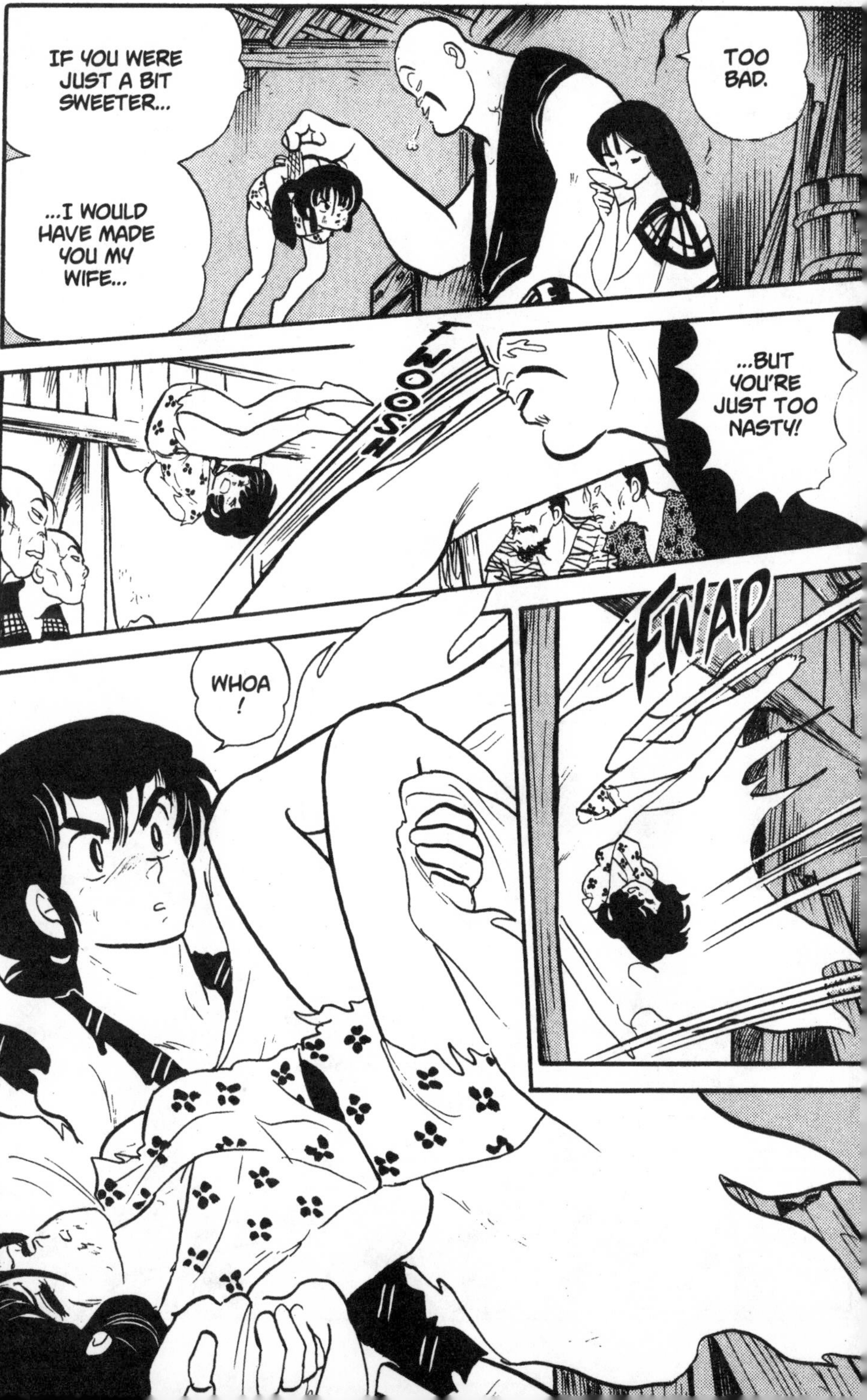
TOO BAD.
IF YOU WERE JUST A BIT SWEETER...
...I WOULD HAVE MADE YOU MY WIFE...
...BUT YOU'RE JUST TOO NASTY!
FWOOSH
FWAP
WHOA!

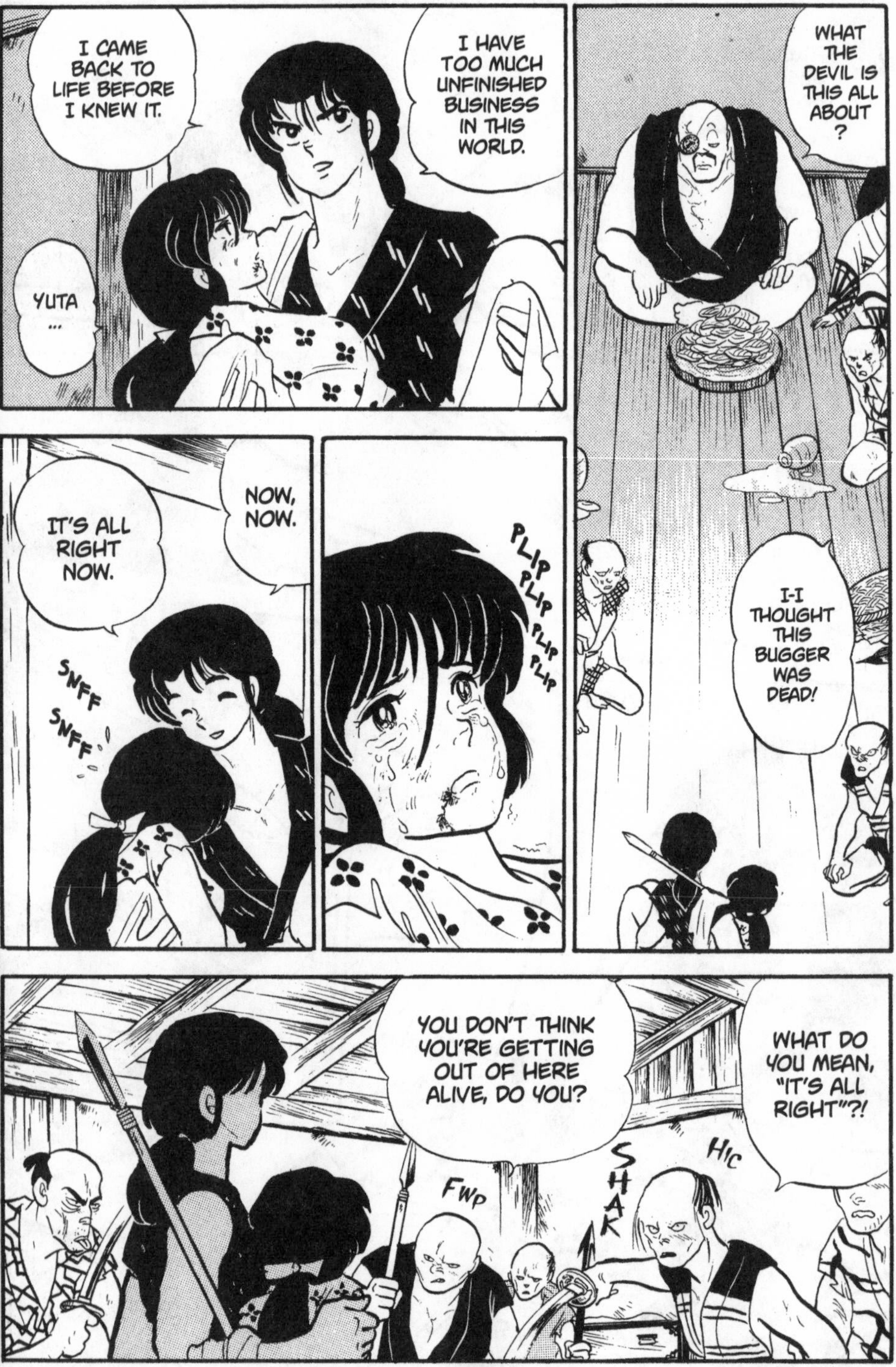
WHAT THE DEVIL IS THIS ALL ABOUT ?
I-I THOUGHT THIS BUGGER WAS DEAD!
I HAVE TOO MUCH UNFINISHED BUSINESS IN THIS WORLD.
I CAME BACK TO LIFE BEFORE I KNEW IT.
YUTA ...
PLIP PLIP PLIP PLIP
NOW, NOW.
IT'S ALL RIGHT NOW.
SNFF SNFF
WHAT DO YOU MEAN, "IT'S ALL RIGHT"?!
HIC
YOU DON'T THINK YOU'RE GETTING OUT OF HERE ALIVE, DO YOU?
SHAK
FWP

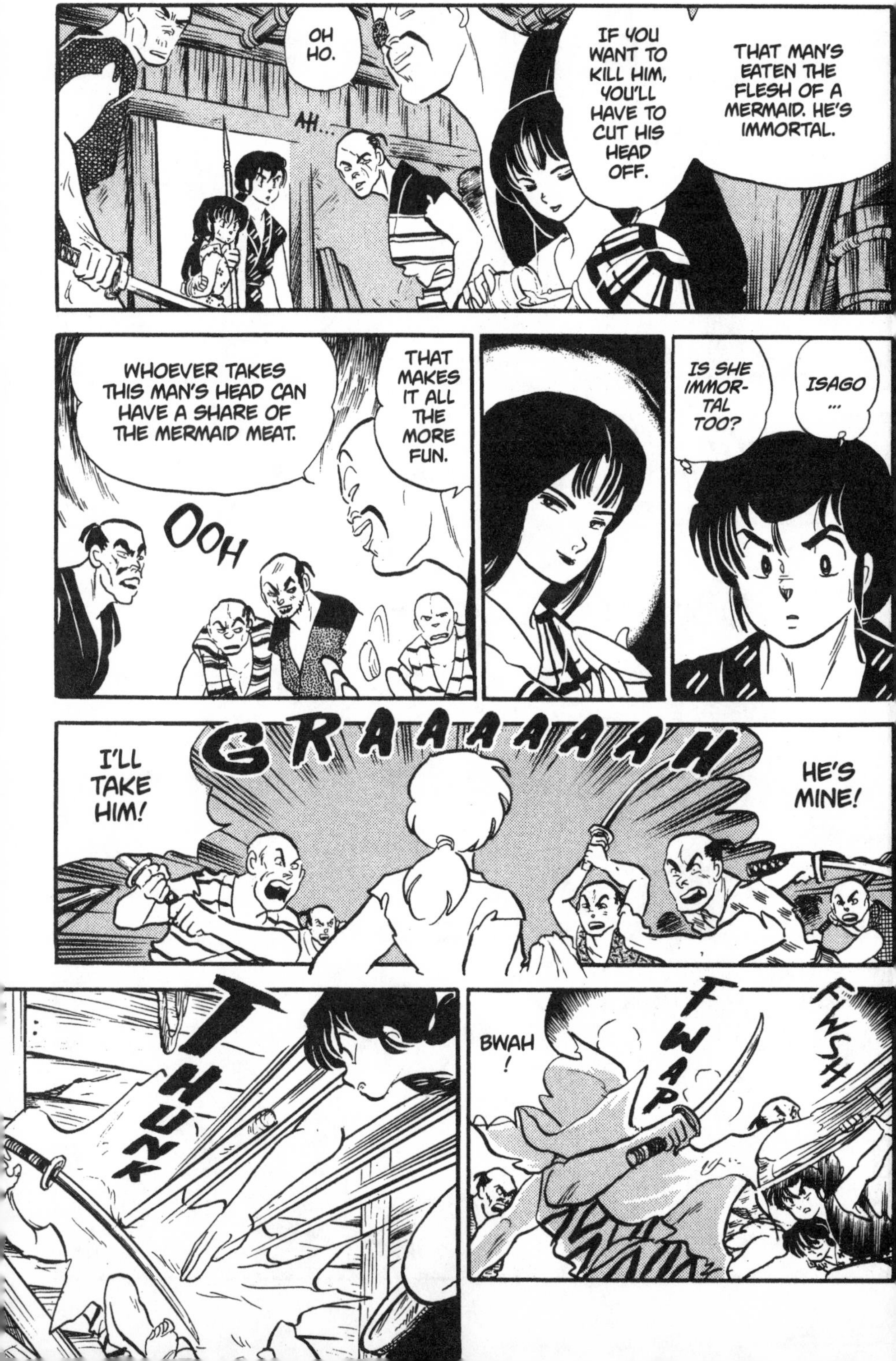
THAT MAN'S EATEN THE FLESH OF A MERMAID. HE'S IMMORTAL.
IF YOU WANT TO KILL HIM, YOU'LL HAVE TO CUT HIS HEAD OFF.
OH HO.
AH...
ISAGO ...
IS SHE IMMORTAL TOO?
THAT MAKES IT ALL THE MORE FUN.
WHOEVER TAKES THIS MAN'S HEAD CAN HAVE A SHARE OF THE MERMAID MEAT.
OOH
HE'S MINE!
GRAAAAAAAH
I'LL TAKE HIM!
FWSH
TWAP
BWAH!
THUNK

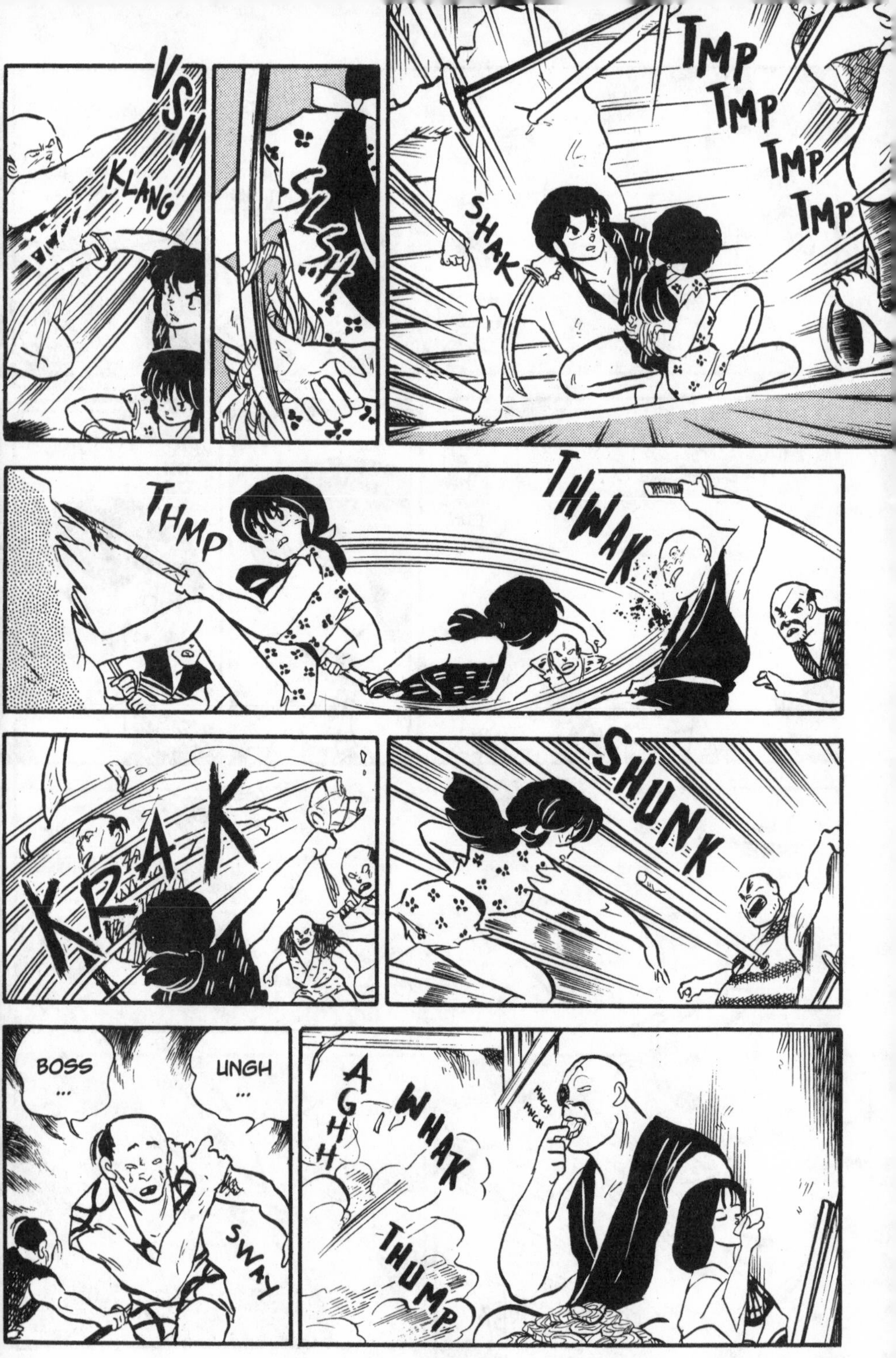
TMP
TMP
TMP
TMP
SHAK
SLSH...
VSH
KLANG
THWAK
THMP
SHUNK
KRAK
AGHH
WHAK
THUMP
MNCH MNCH
UNGH ...
BOSS ...
SWAY

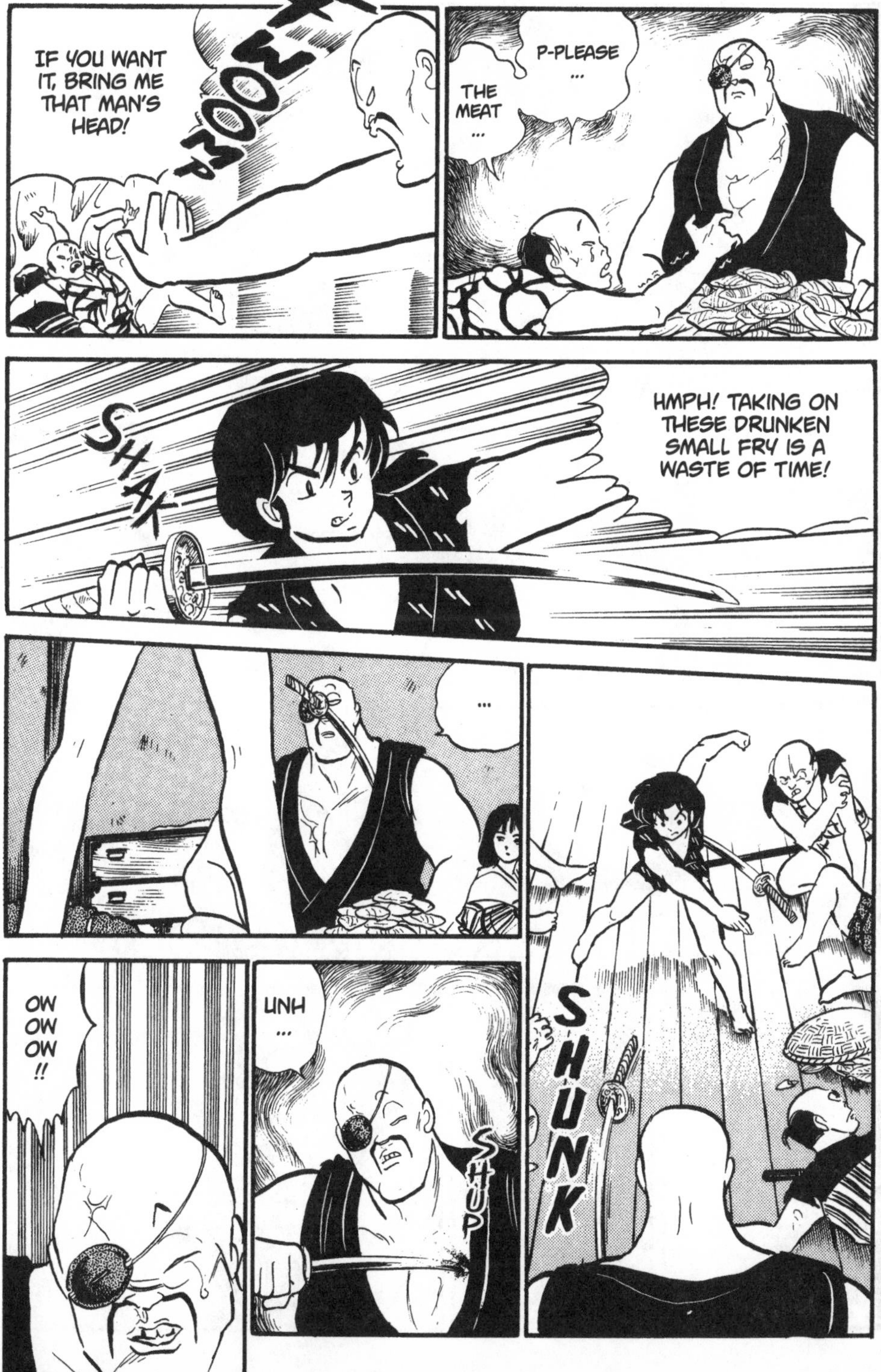
P-PLEASE ...
THE MEAT ...
TWOOMP
IF YOU WANT IT, BRING ME THAT MAN'S HEAD!
HMPH! TAKING ON THESE DRUNKEN SMALL FRY IS A WASTE OF TIME!
SHAK
SHUNK
...
UNH ...
SHUP
OW OW OW !!

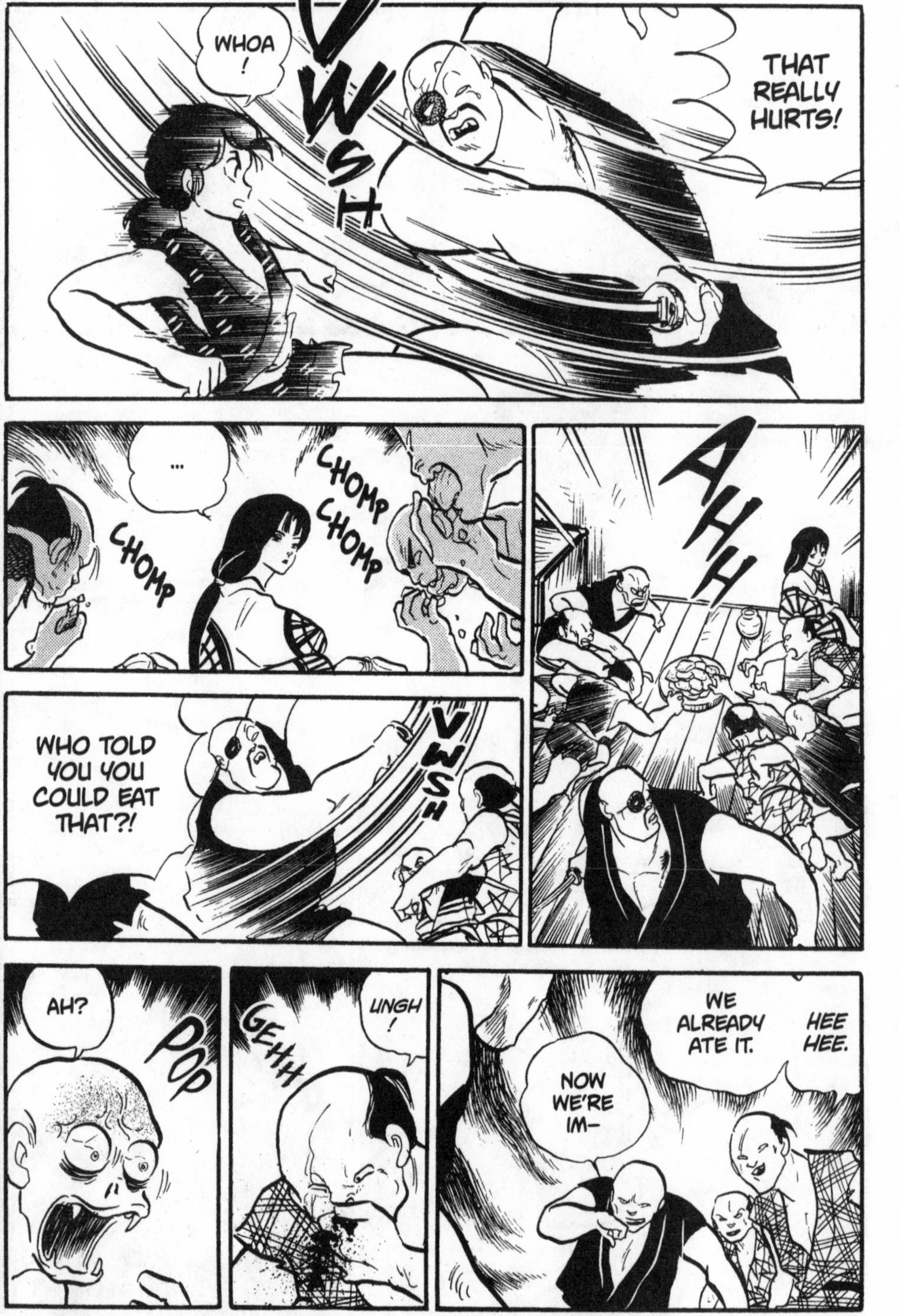
THAT REALLY HURTS!
VWSH
WHOA!
AHH
CHOMP CHOMP
...
CHOMP
VWSH
WHO TOLD YOU YOU COULD EAT THAT?!
HEE HEE.
WE ALREADY ATE IT.
NOW WE'RE IM-
UNGH!
GEHHH
POP
AH?

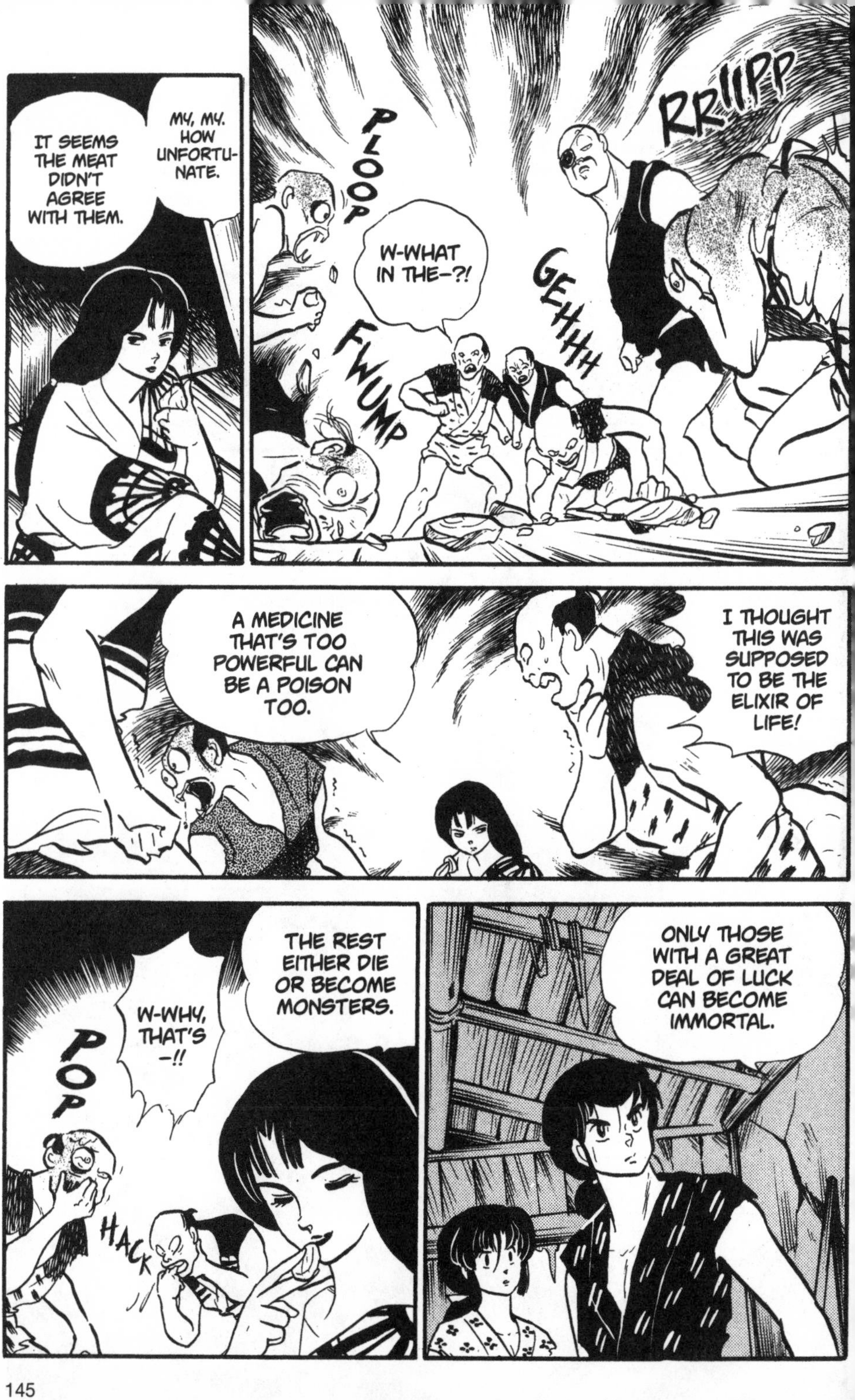
RRIIPP
GEHHHH
W-WHAT IN THE-?!
PLOOP
FWUMP
MY, MY. HOW UNFORTUNATE.
IT SEEMS THE MEAT DIDN'T AGREE WITH THEM.
I THOUGHT THIS WAS SUPPOSED TO BE THE ELIXIR OF LIFE!
A MEDICINE THAT'S TOO POWERFUL CAN BE A POISON TOO.
ONLY THOSE WITH A GREAT DEAL OF LUCK CAN BECOME IMMORTAL.
THE REST EITHER DIE OR BECOME MONSTERS.
W-WHY, THAT'S-!!
POP
HACK

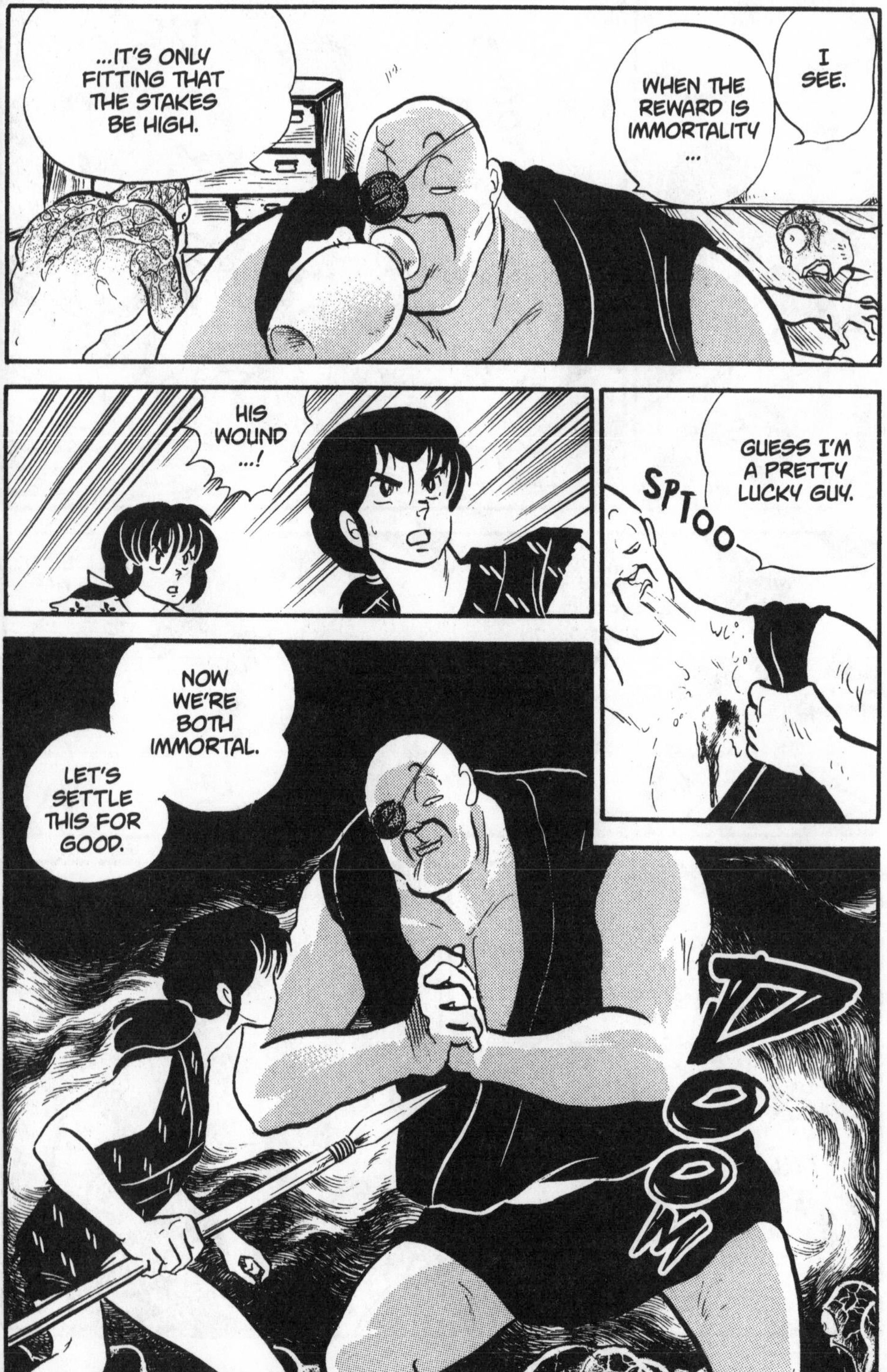
I SEE.
WHEN THE REWARD IS IMMORTALITY ...
...IT'S ONLY FITTING THAT THE STAKES BE HIGH.
GUESS I'M A PRETTY LUCKY GUY.
SPTOO
HIS WOUND ...!
NOW WE'RE BOTH IMMORTAL.
LET'S SETTLE THIS FOR GOOD.
DOOOM

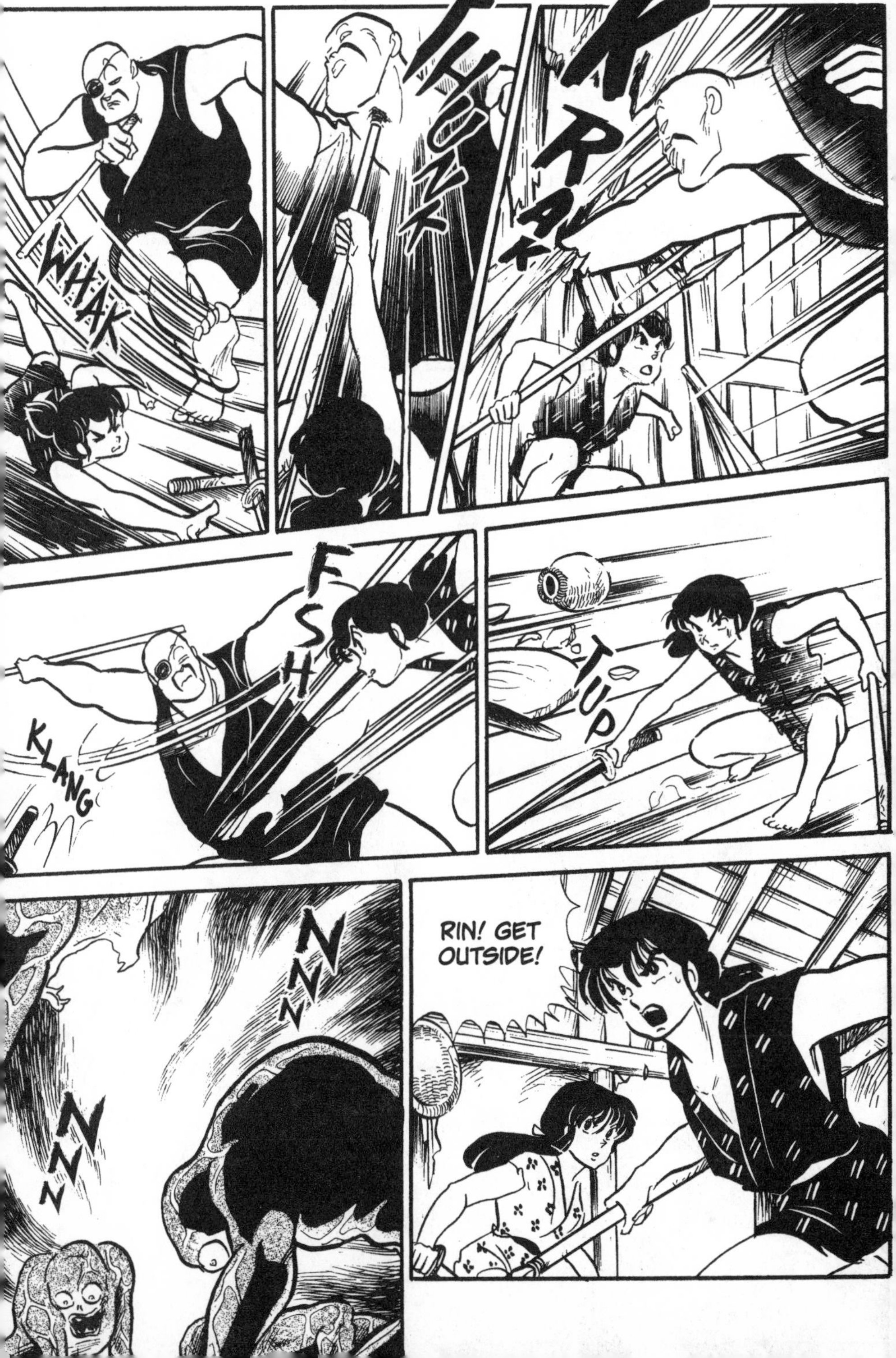
KRAK
THUNK
WHAK
TUP
FSH
KLANG
RIN! GET OUTSIDE!
NNN
NNN

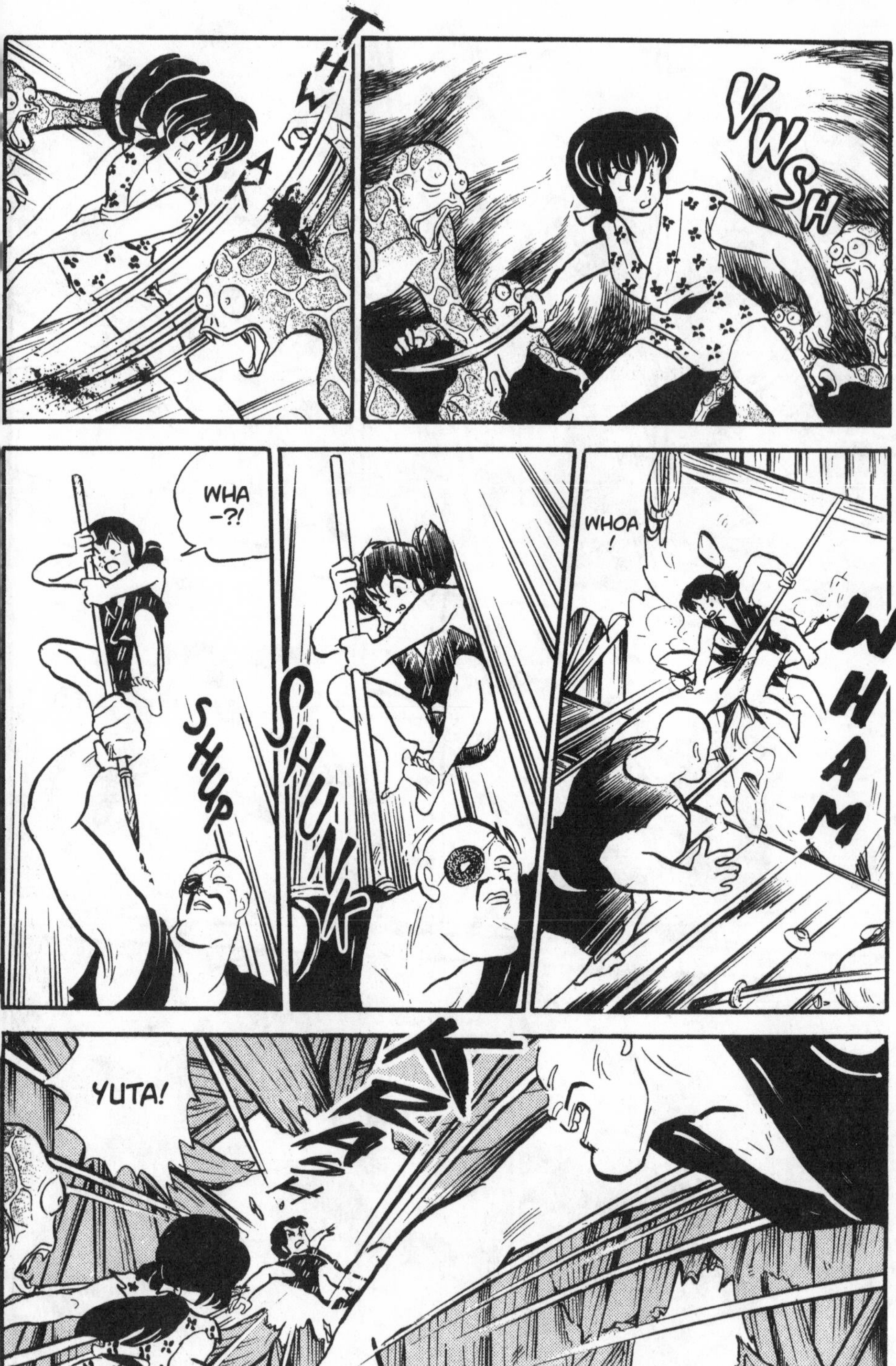
VWSH
THWAK
WHOA!
WHAM
SHUNK
WHA-?!
SHUP
KRASH
YUTA!

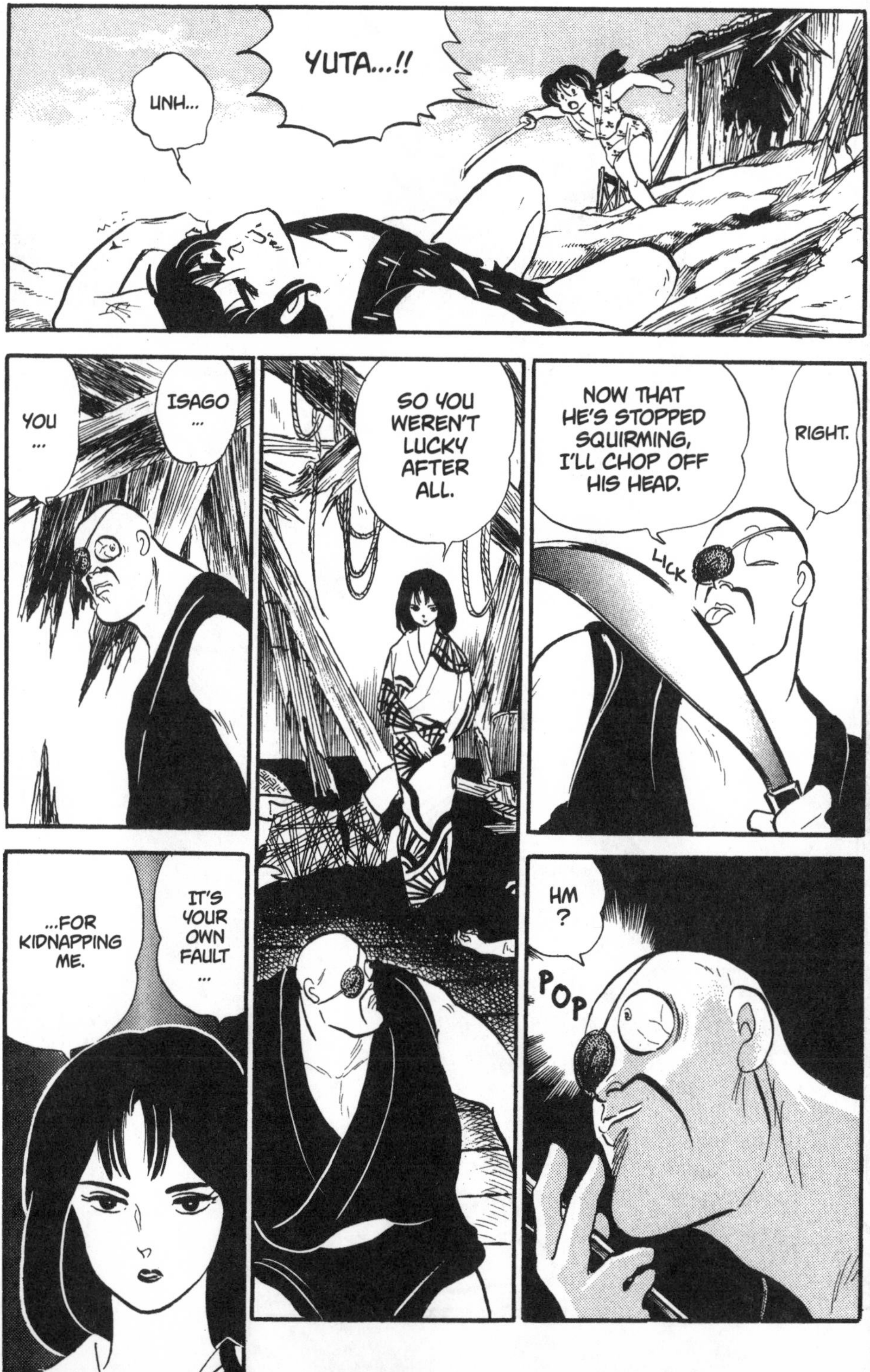
YUTA...!!
UNH...
RIGHT.
NOW THAT HE'S STOPPED SQUIRMING, I'LL CHOP OFF HIS HEAD.
LICK
SO YOU WEREN'T LUCKY AFTER ALL.
ISAGO ...
YOU ...
HM ?
POP
IT'S YOUR OWN FAULT ...
...FOR KIDNAPPING ME.

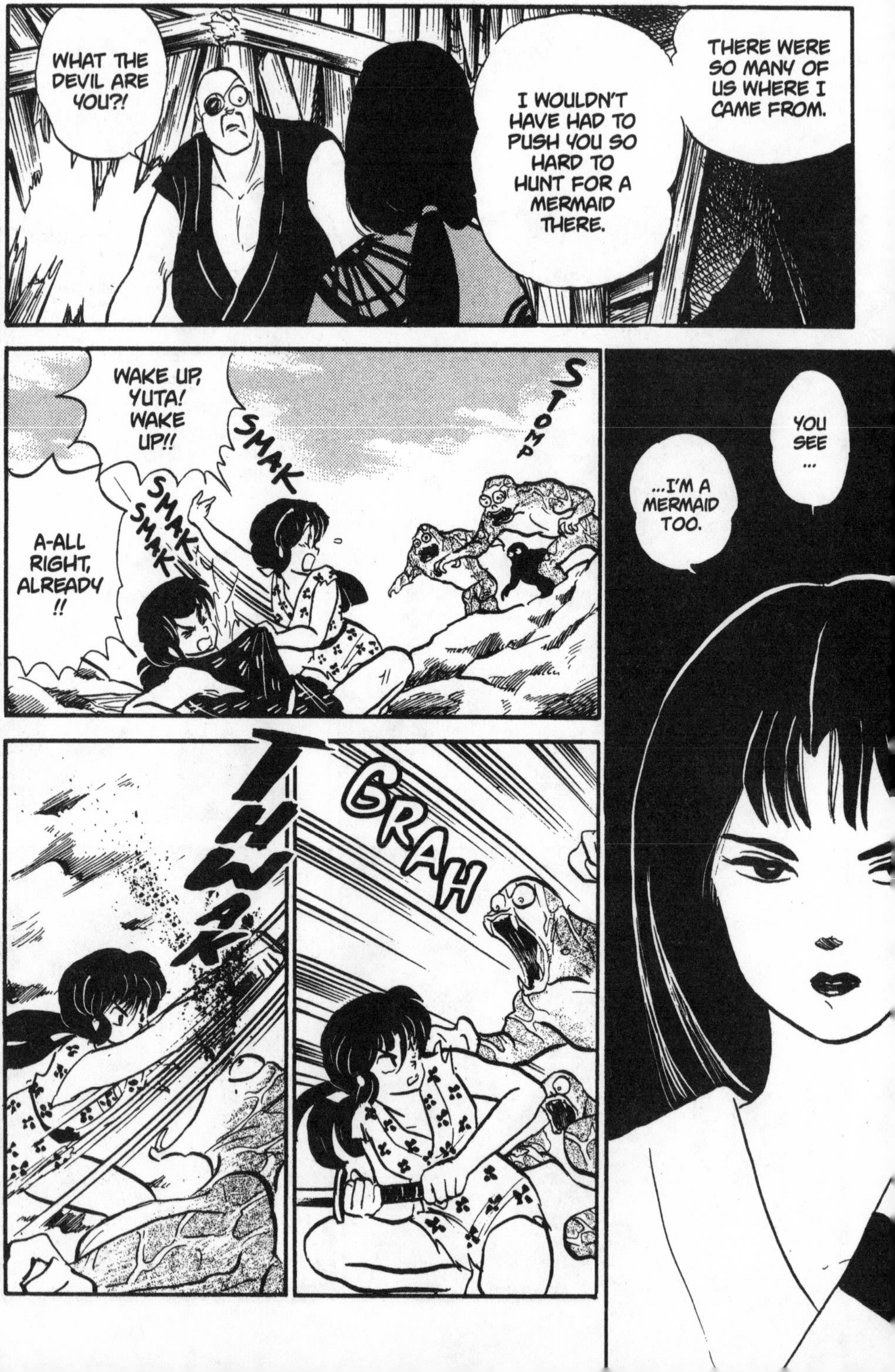
THERE WERE SO MANY OF US WHERE I CAME FROM.
I WOULDN'T HAVE HAD TO PUSH YOU SO HARD TO HUNT FOR A MERMAID THERE.
WHAT THE DEVIL ARE YOU?!
YOU SEE ...
...I'M A MERMAID TOO.
STOMP
SMAK
WAKE UP, YUTA! WAKE UP!!
SMAK SMAK
A-ALL RIGHT, ALREADY !!
GRAH
THWAK

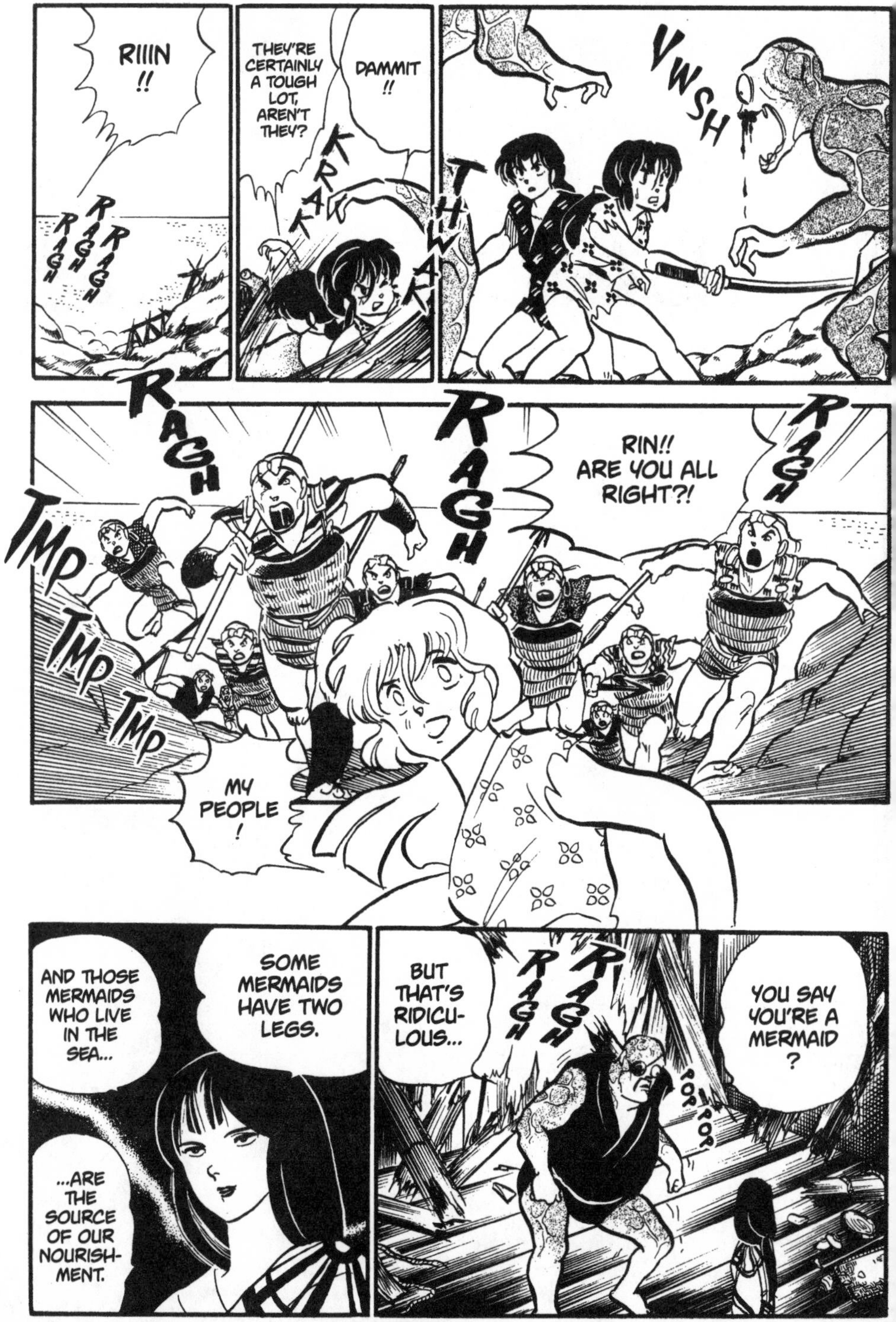
VWSH
THWAK
DAMMIT!!
THEY'RE CERTAINLY A TOUGH LOT, AREN'T THEY?
KRAK
RIIIN!!
RAGH RAGH RAGH RAGH
RAGH
RIN!! ARE YOU ALL RIGHT?!
RAGH
RAGH
TMP TMP TMP
MY PEOPLE!
YOU SAY YOU'RE A MERMAID?
BUT THAT'S RIDICULOUS...
RAGH RAGH
POP POP
SOME MERMAIDS HAVE TWO LEGS.
AND THOSE MERMAIDS WHO LIVE IN THE SEA...
...ARE THE SOURCE OF OUR NOURISHMENT.

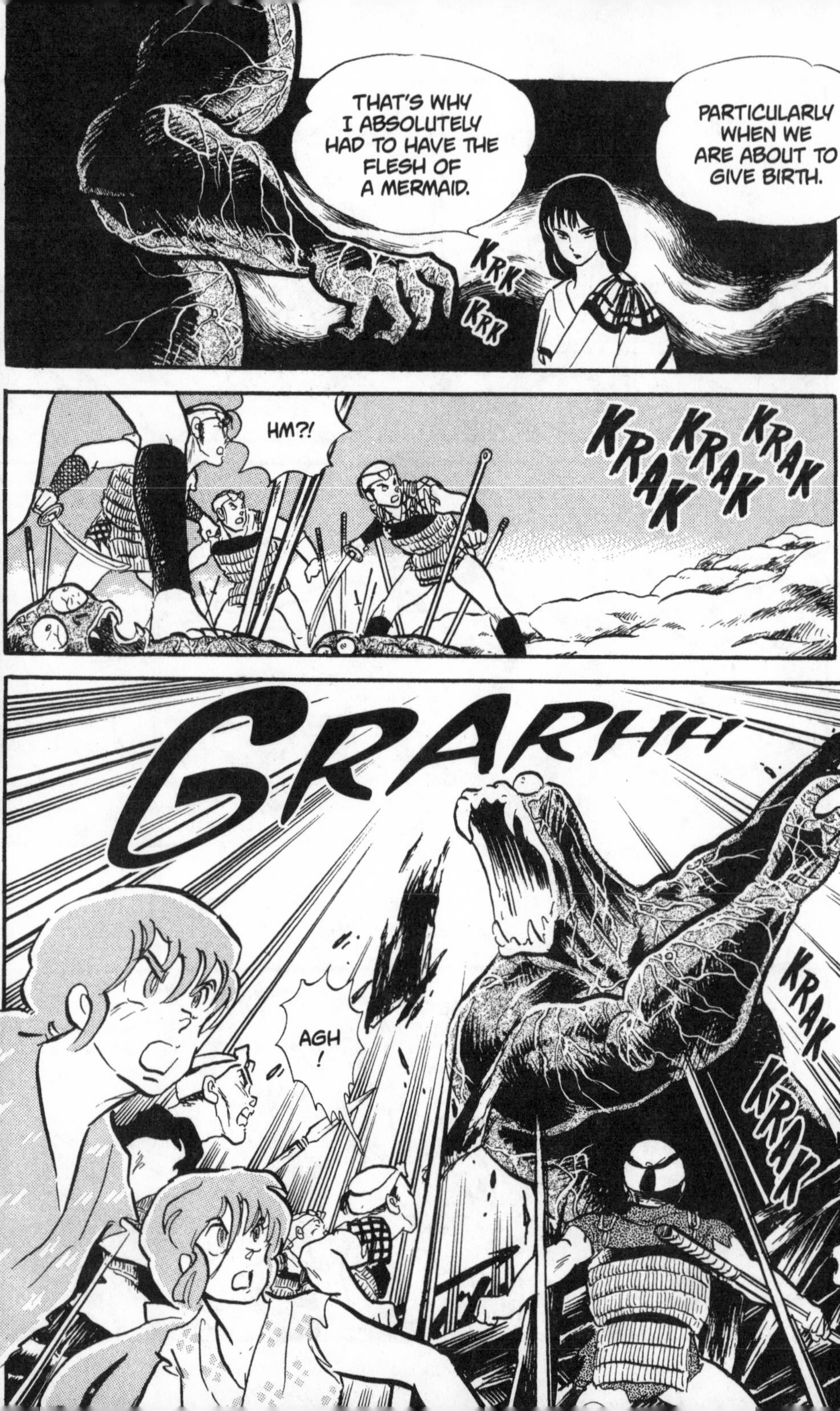
PARTICULARLY WHEN WE ARE ABOUT TO GIVE BIRTH.
THAT'S WHY I ABSOLUTELY HAD TO HAVE THE FLESH OF A MERMAID.
KRK KRK
KRAK KRAK KRAK
HM?!
GRARHH
KRAK KRAK KRAK
AGH!

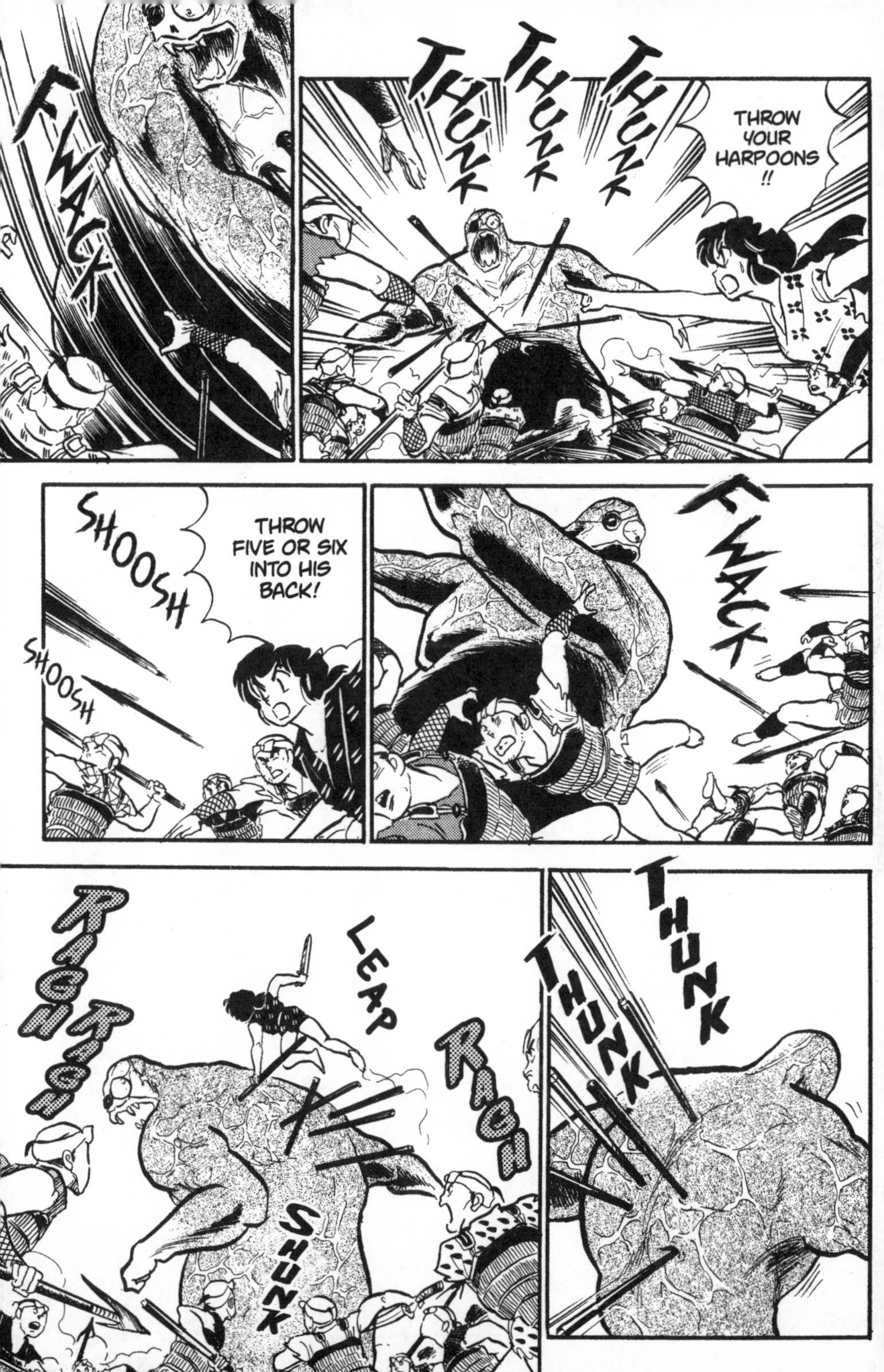
THUNK
THUNK
THUNK
THROW YOUR HARPOONS !!
FWACK
FWACK
SHOOSH
THROW FIVE OR SIX INTO HIS BACK!
SHOOSH
THUNK
THUNK
RAGH
LEAP
SHUNK
RAGH
RAGH

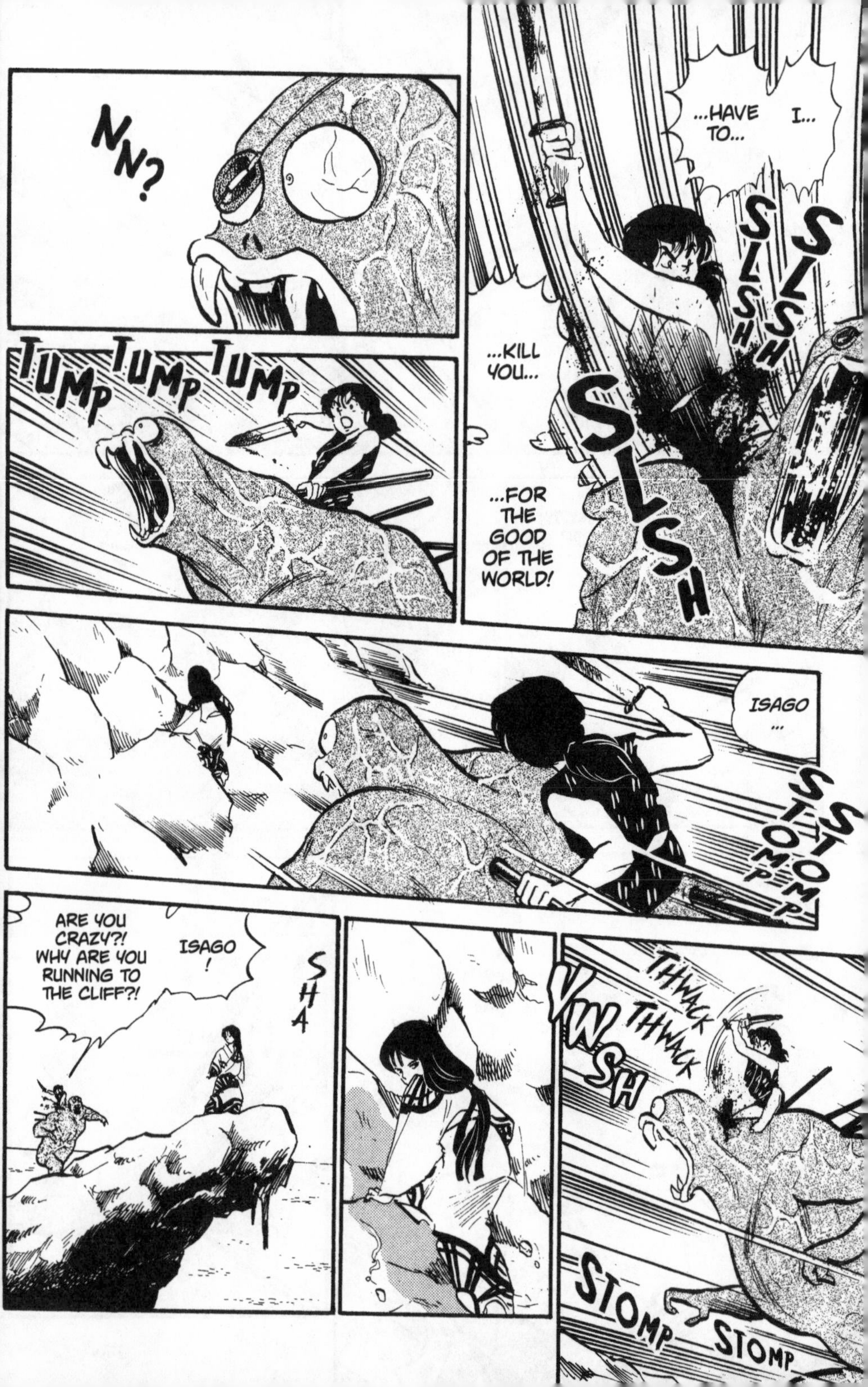
I...
...HAVE TO...
SLSH SLSH
...KILL YOU...
SLSH
...FOR THE GOOD OF THE WORLD!
NN?
TUMP TUMP TUMP
ISAGO ...
STOMP STOMP
THWACK THWACK
VWSH
STOMP STOMP
ISAGO!
ARE YOU CRAZY?! WHY ARE YOU RUNNING TO THE CLIFF?!
SHA

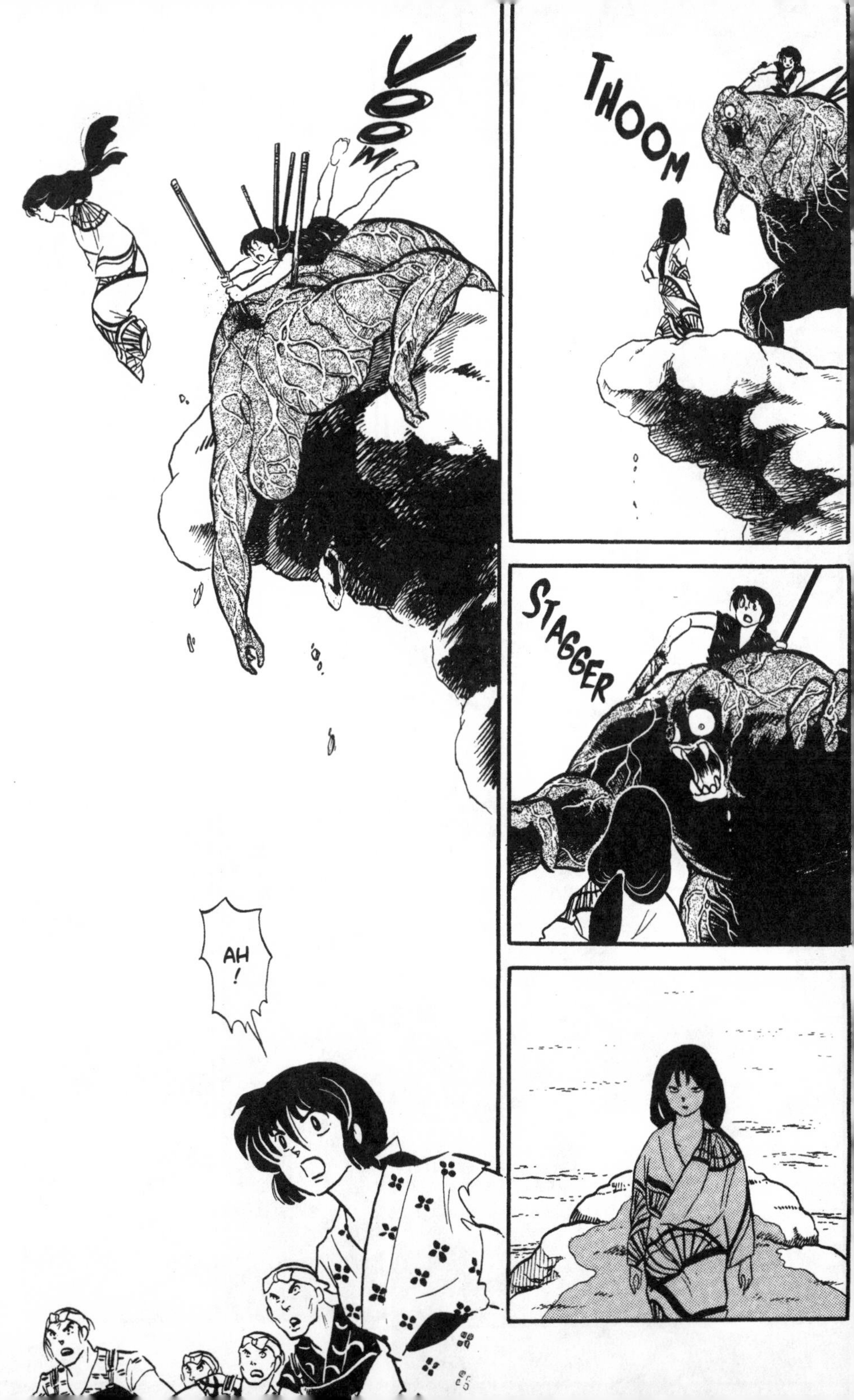
THOOM
STAGGER
VOOM
AH!

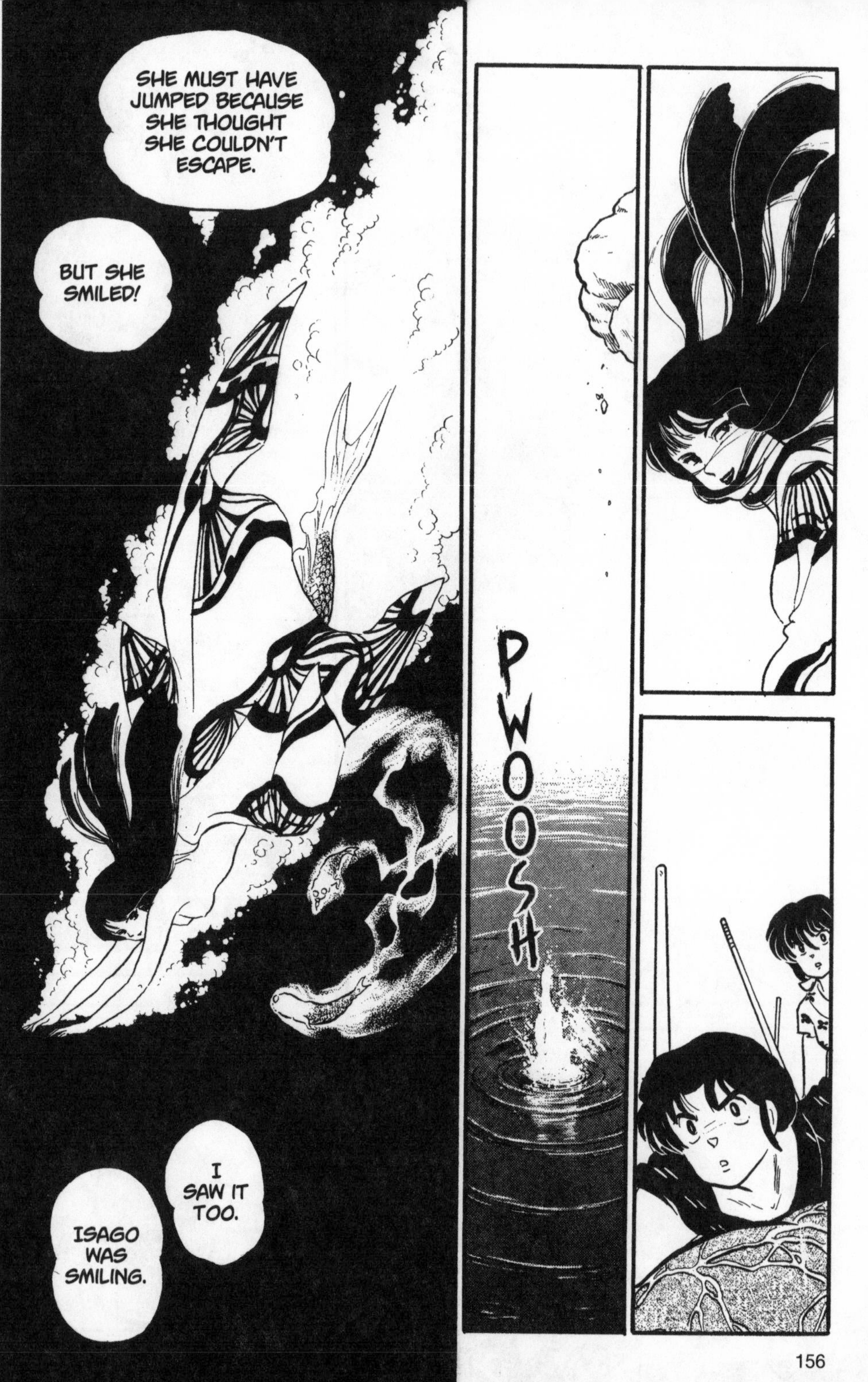
PWOOSH
SHE MUST HAVE JUMPED BECAUSE SHE THOUGHT SHE COULDN'T ESCAPE.
BUT SHE SMILED!
I SAW IT TOO.
ISAGO WAS SMILING.

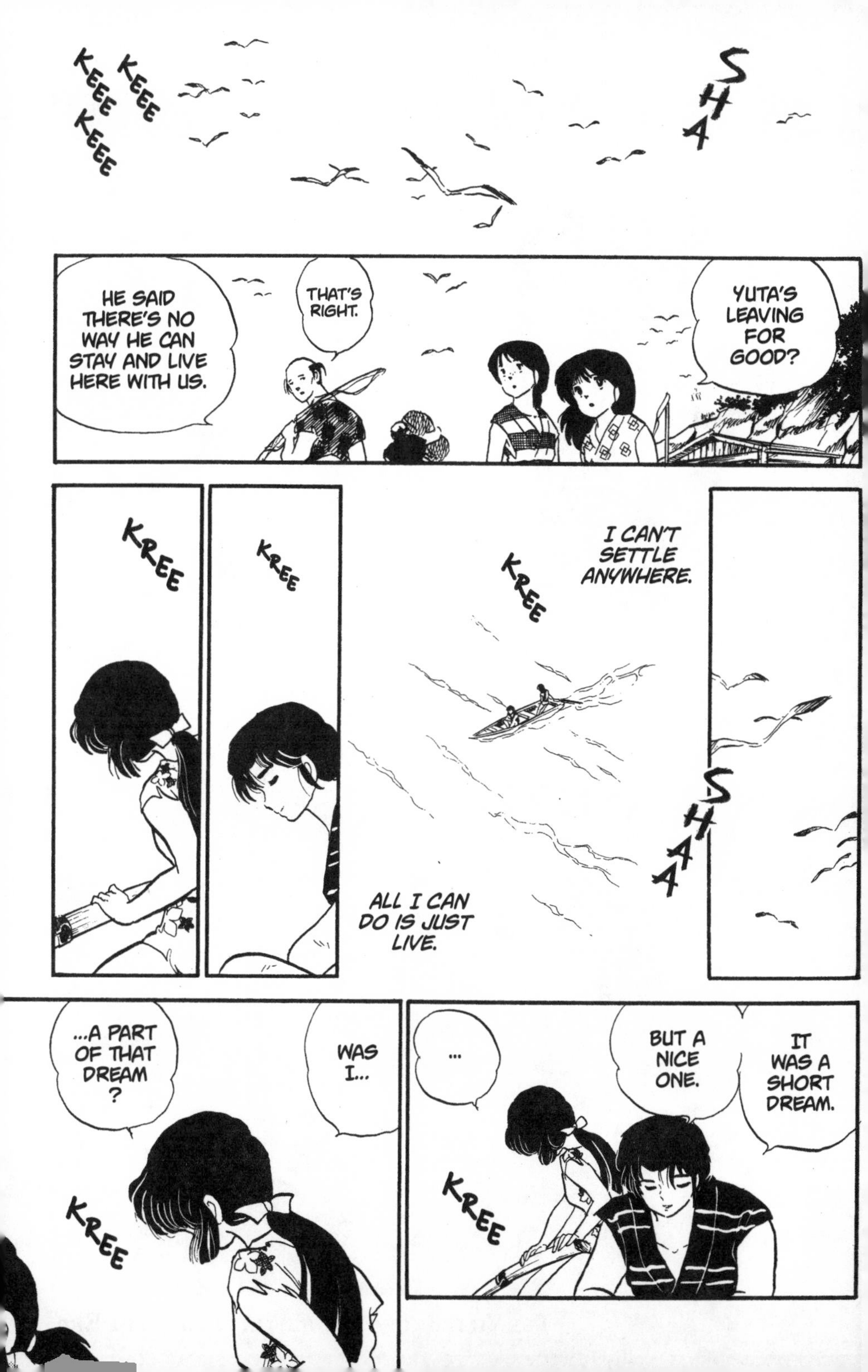
SHA
KEEE
KEEE
KEEE
YUTA'S LEAVING FOR GOOD?
THAT'S RIGHT.
HE SAID THERE'S NO WAY HE CAN STAY AND LIVE HERE WITH US.
SHAAA
I CAN'T SETTLE ANYWHERE.
KREE
ALL I CAN DO IS JUST LIVE.
KREE
KREE
IT WAS A SHORT DREAM.
BUT A NICE ONE.
...
KREE
WAS I...
...A PART OF THAT DREAM ?
KREE

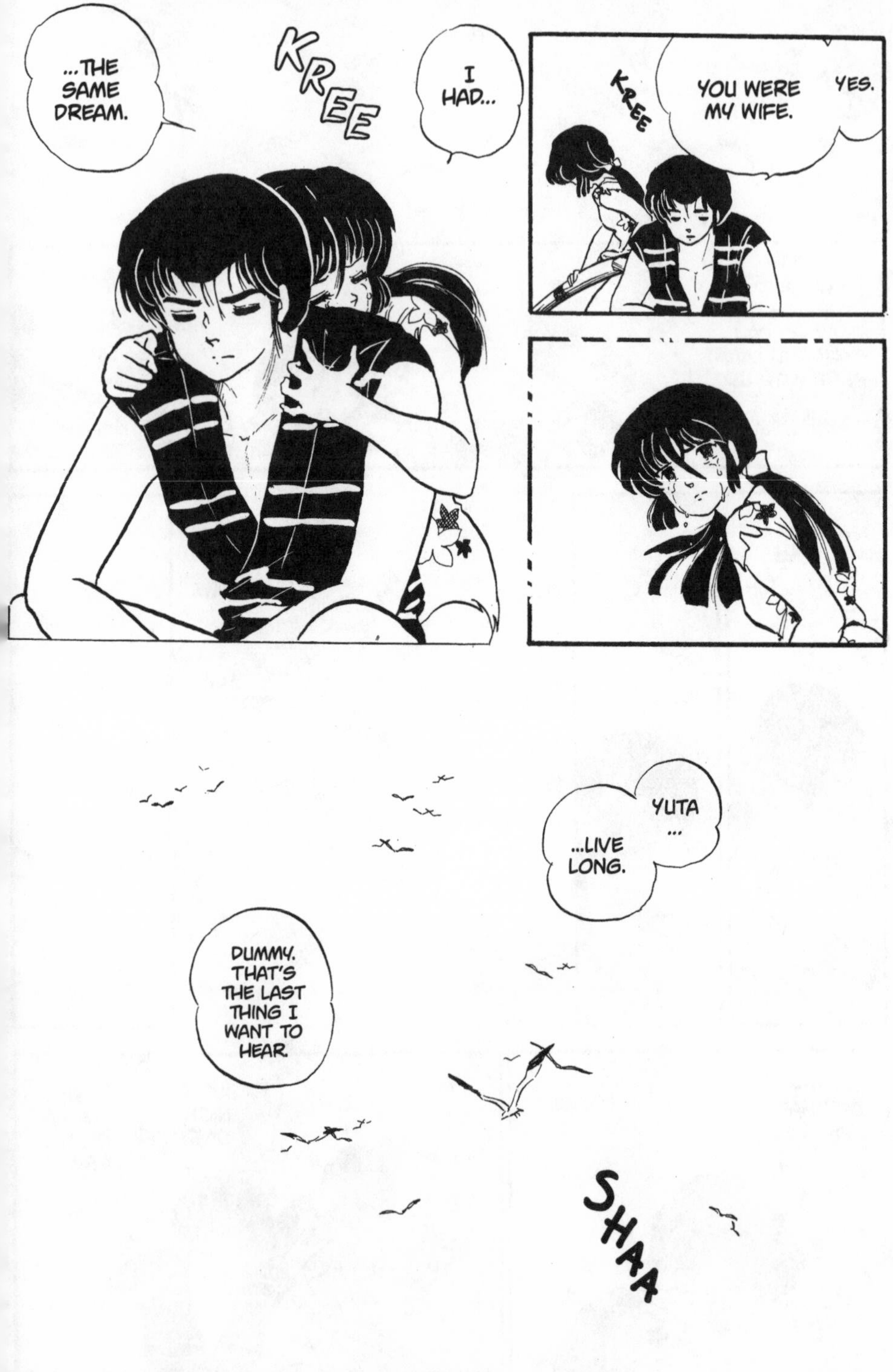
I HAD...
...THE SAME DREAM.
KREE
YES.
YOU WERE MY WIFE.
KREE
YUTA ...
...LIVE LONG.
DUMMY. THAT'S THE LAST THING I WANT TO HEAR.
SHAA

THE VILLAGE OF THE FIGHTING FISH / THE END

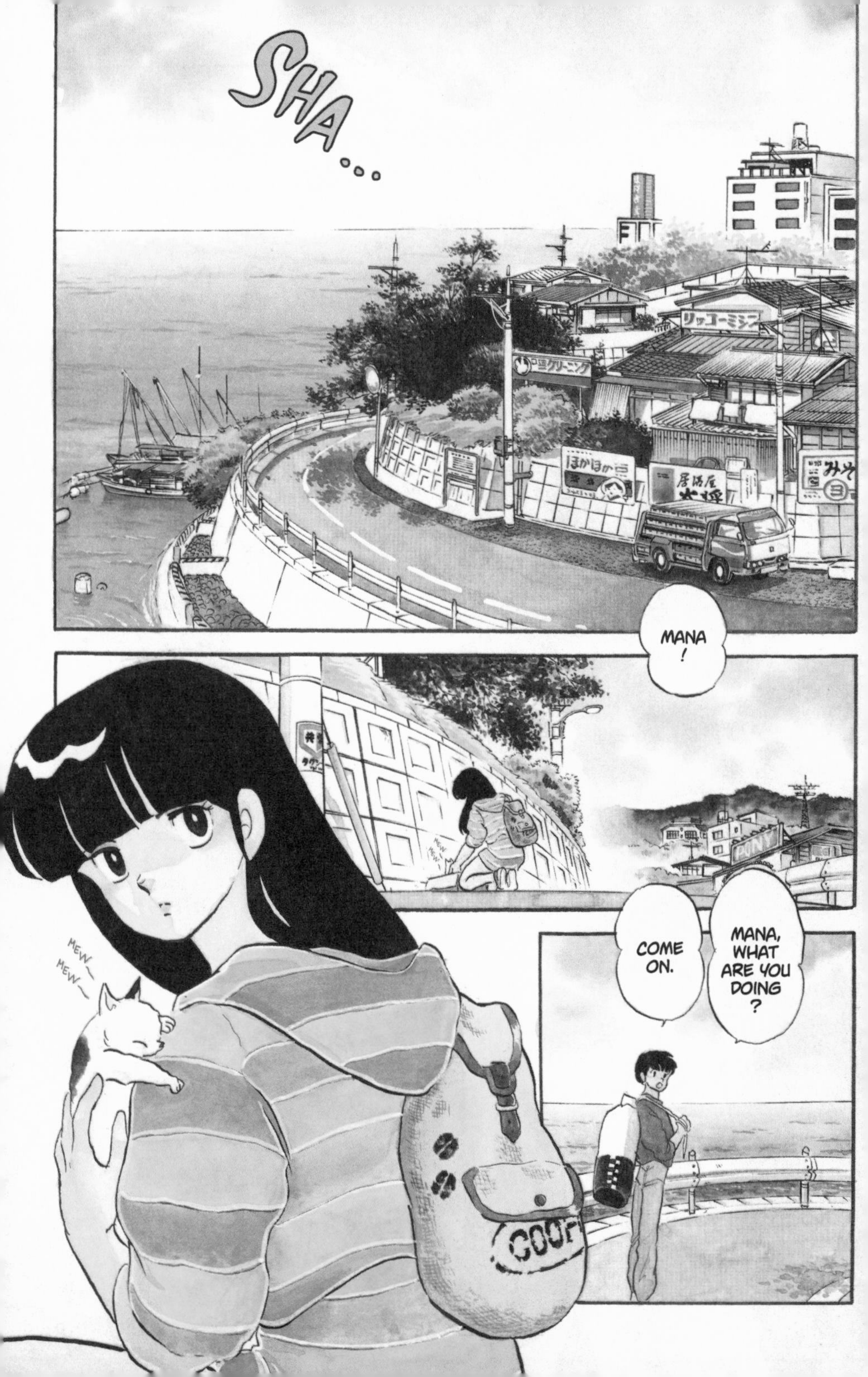
SHA...
MANA!
MEW MEW
MANA!
MANA, WHAT ARE YOU DOING?
COME ON.
MEW~ MEW~

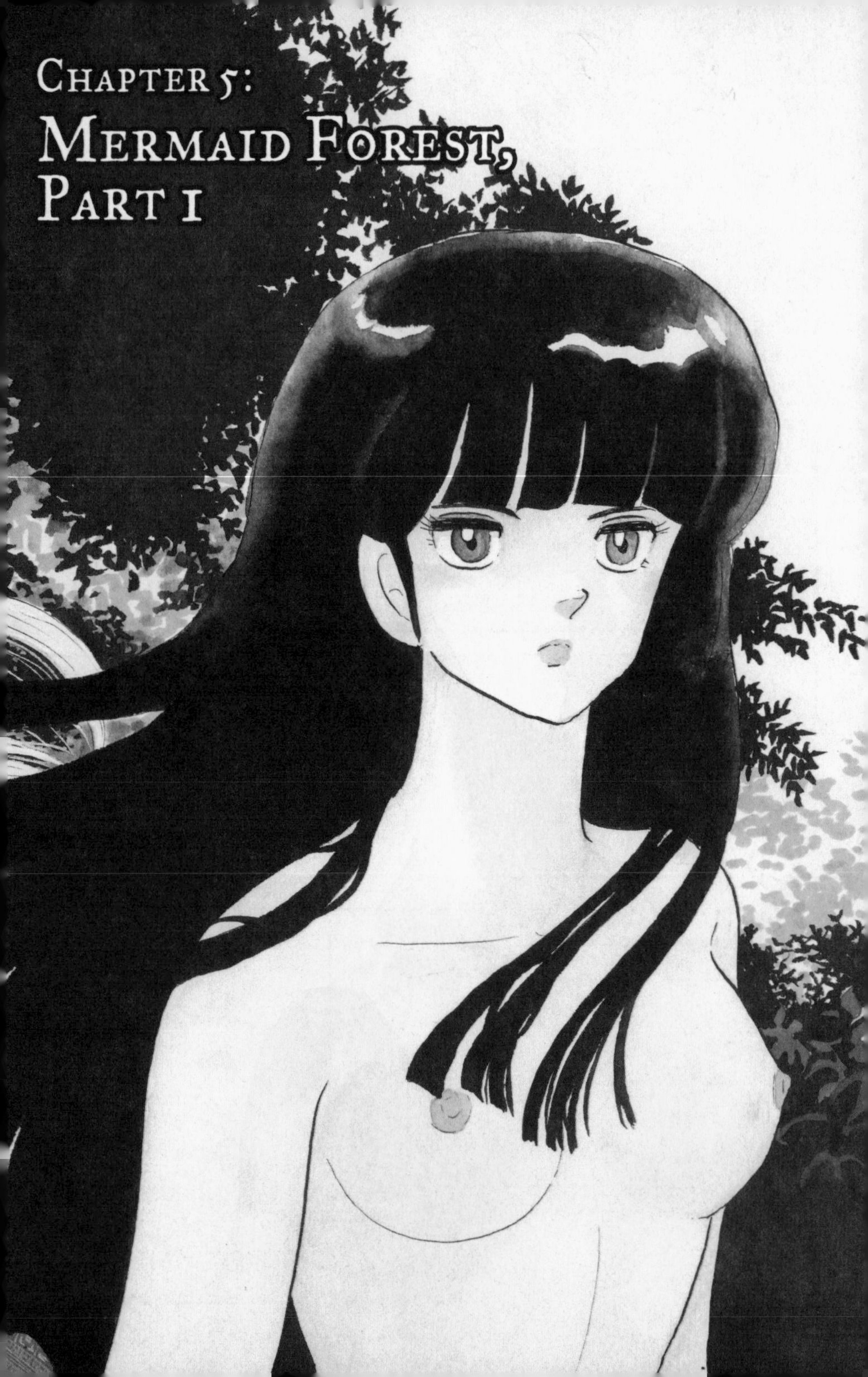
Chapter 5:
Mermaid Forest,
Part 1

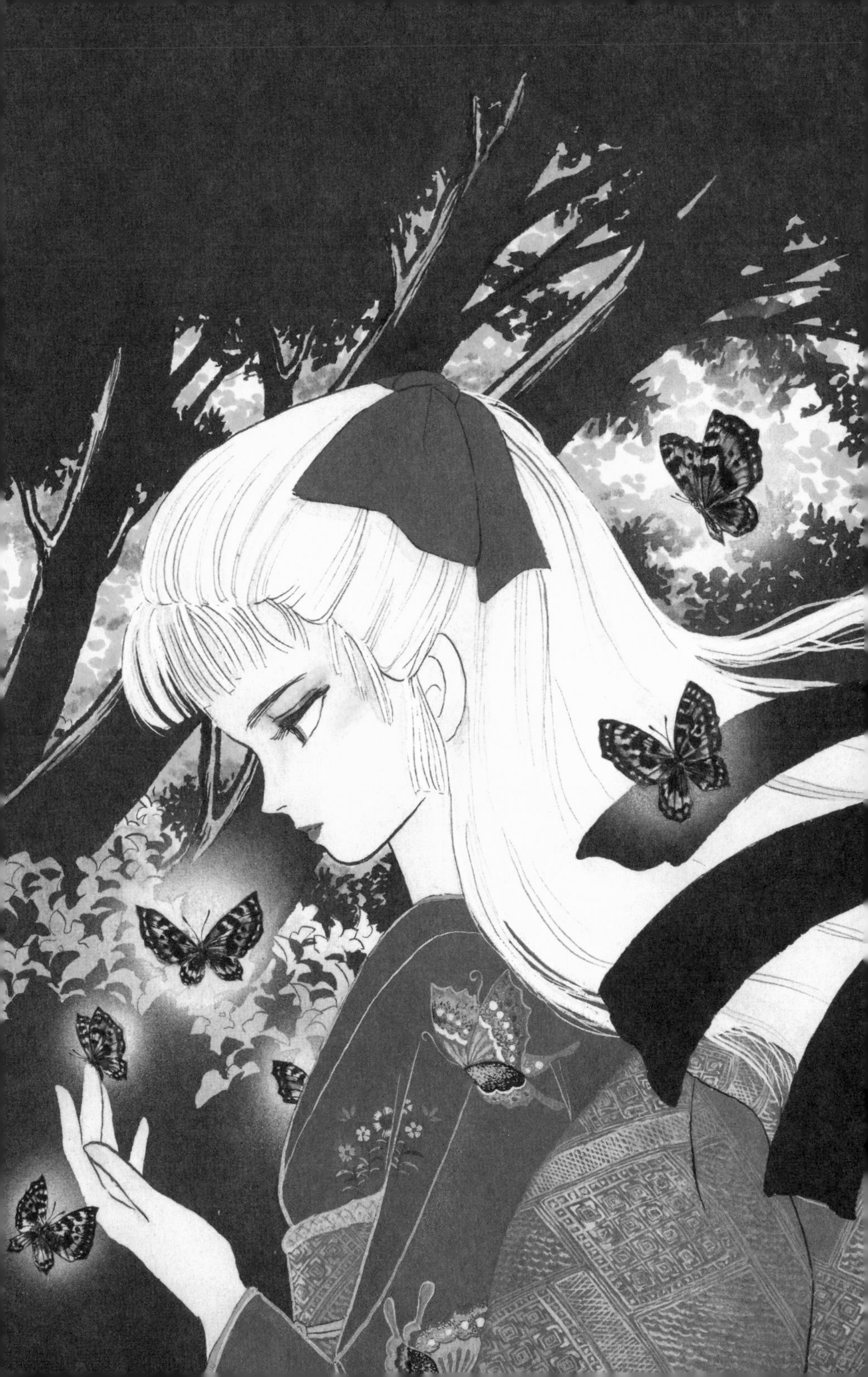

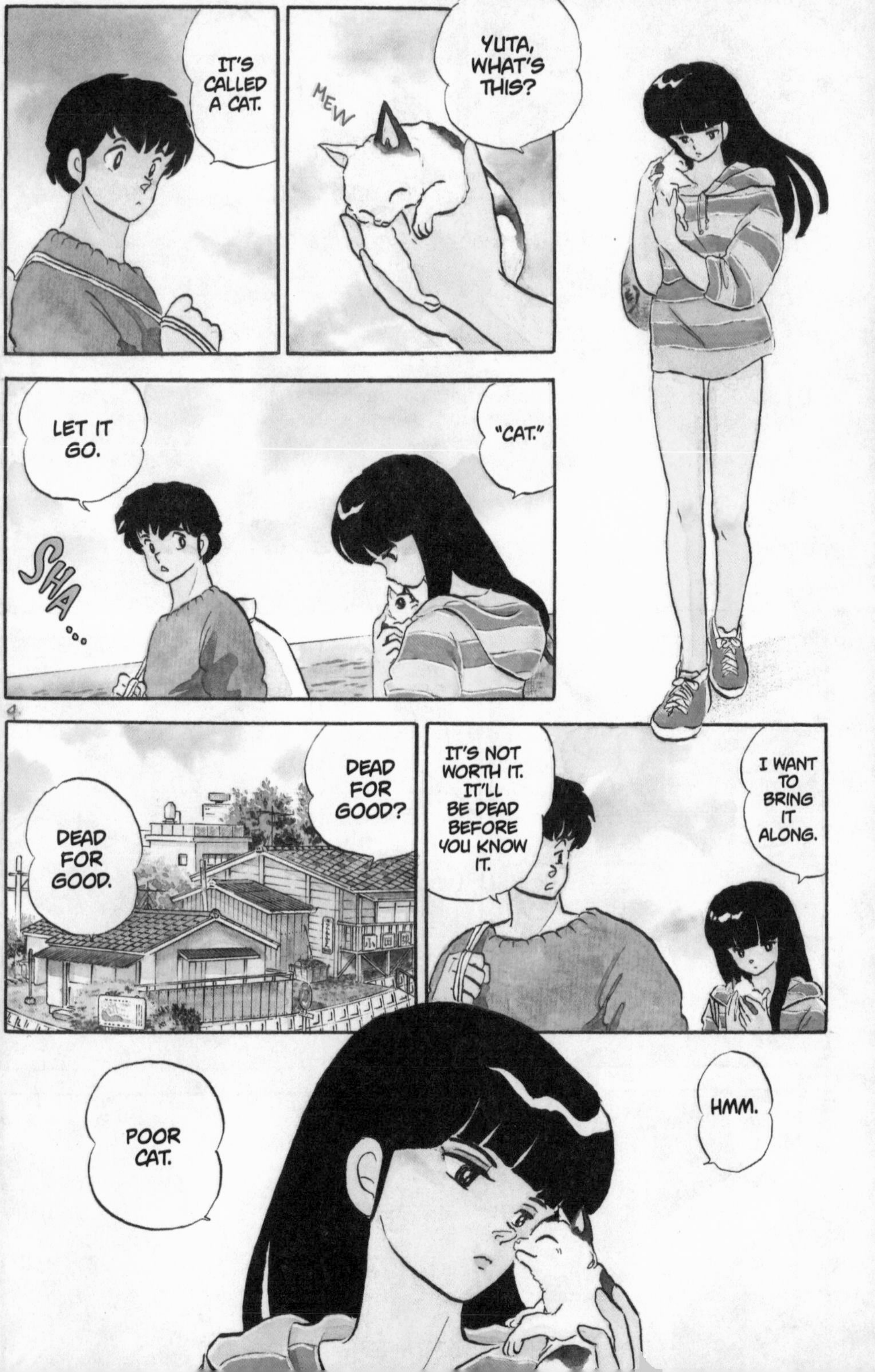
YUTA, WHAT'S THIS?
MEW
IT'S CALLED A CAT.
"CAT."
LET IT GO.
SHA...
I WANT TO BRING IT ALONG.
IT'S NOT WORTH IT. IT'LL BE DEAD BEFORE YOU KNOW IT.
DEAD FOR GOOD?
DEAD FOR GOOD.
HMM.
POOR CAT.

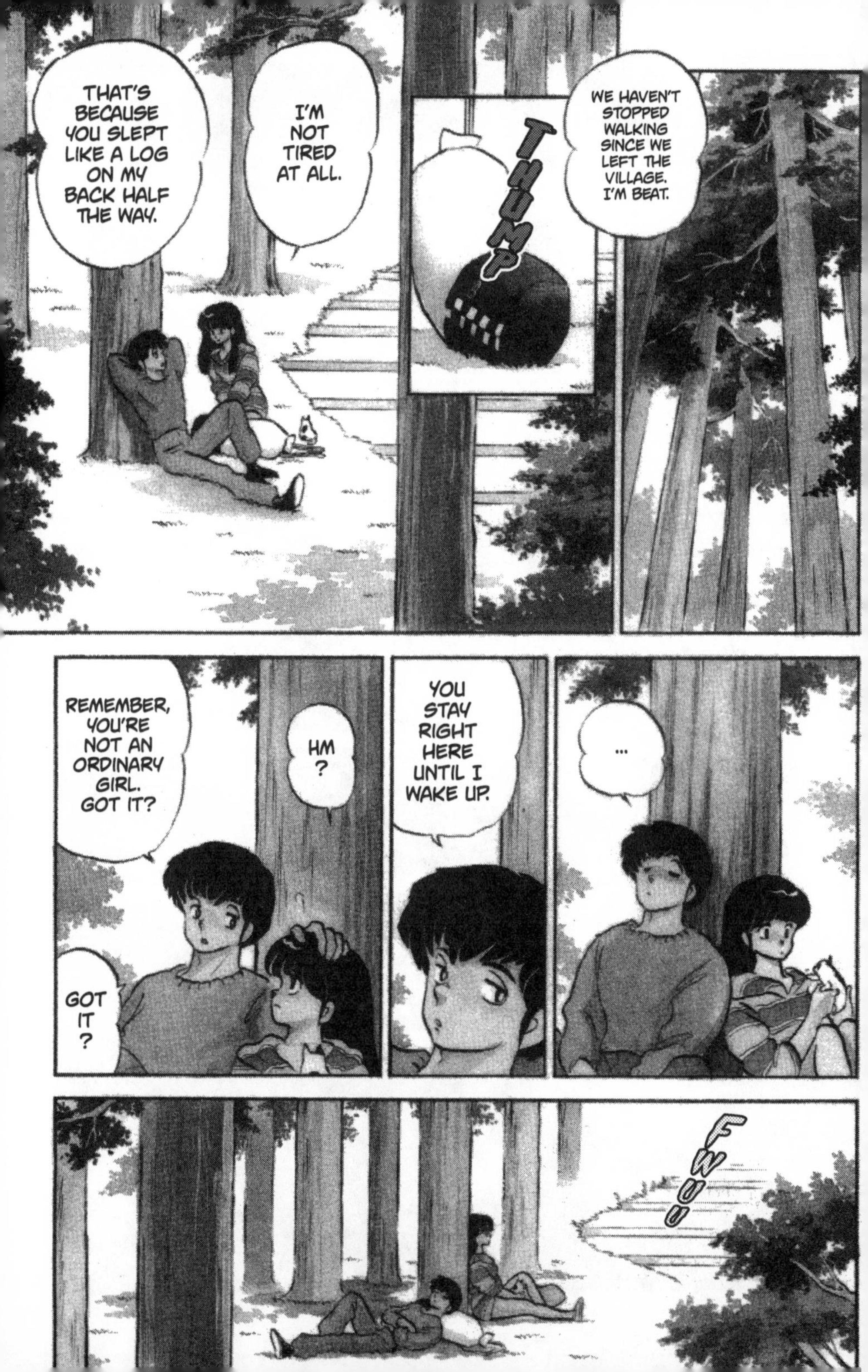
WE HAVEN'T STOPPED WALKING SINCE WE LEFT THE VILLAGE. I'M BEAT.
THUMP
I'M NOT TIRED AT ALL.
THAT'S BECAUSE YOU SLEPT LIKE A LOG ON MY BACK HALF THE WAY.
...
YOU STAY RIGHT HERE UNTIL I WAKE UP.
REMEMBER, YOU'RE NOT AN ORDINARY GIRL. GOT IT?
HM?
GOT IT?
FWUU

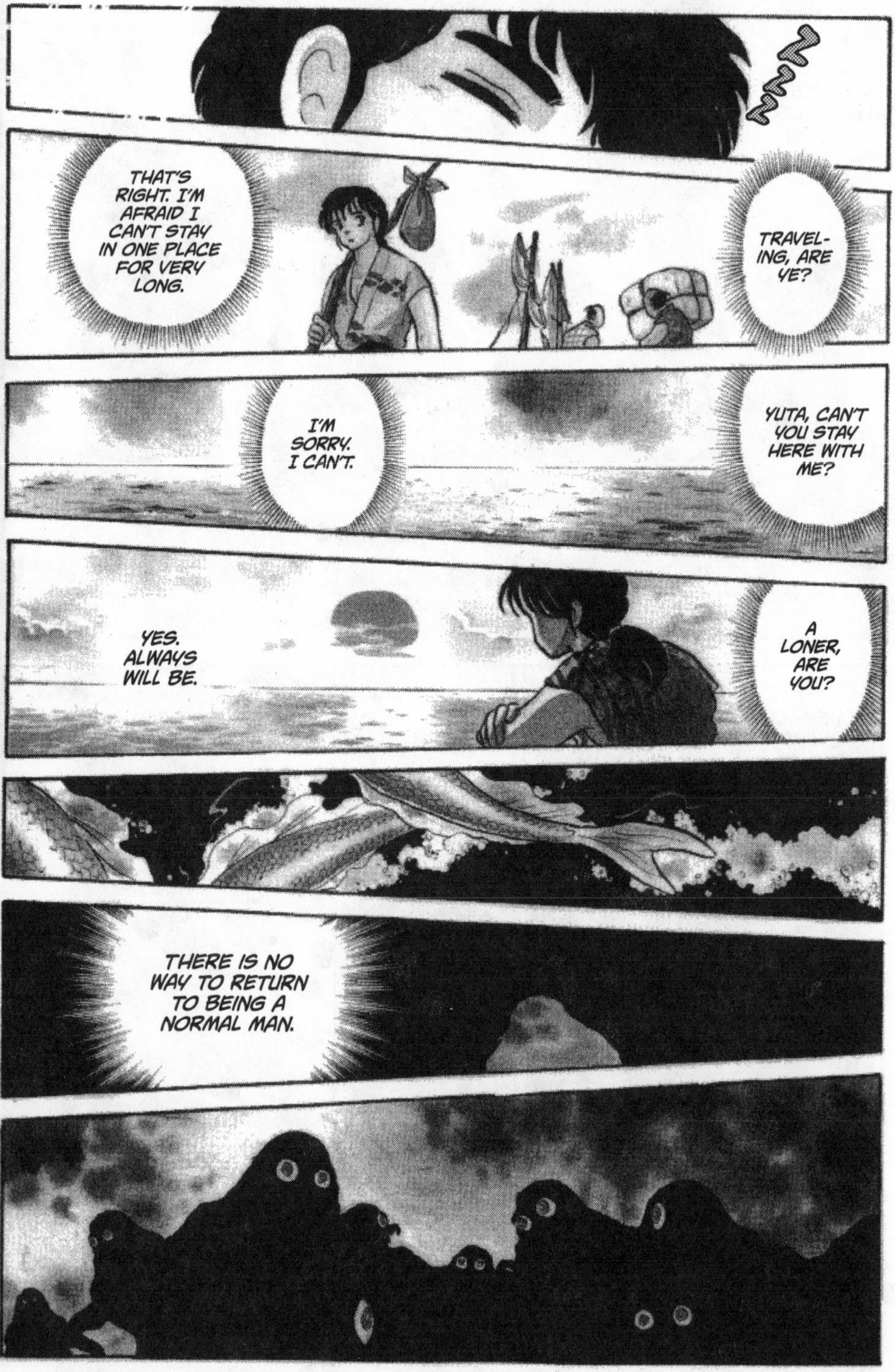
ZZZ
TRAVEL-ING, ARE YE?
THAT'S RIGHT. I'M AFRAID I CAN'T STAY IN ONE PLACE FOR VERY LONG.
YUTA, CAN'T YOU STAY HERE WITH ME?
I'M SORRY. I CAN'T.
A LONER, ARE YOU?
YES. ALWAYS WILL BE.
THERE IS NO WAY TO RETURN TO BEING A NORMAL MAN.

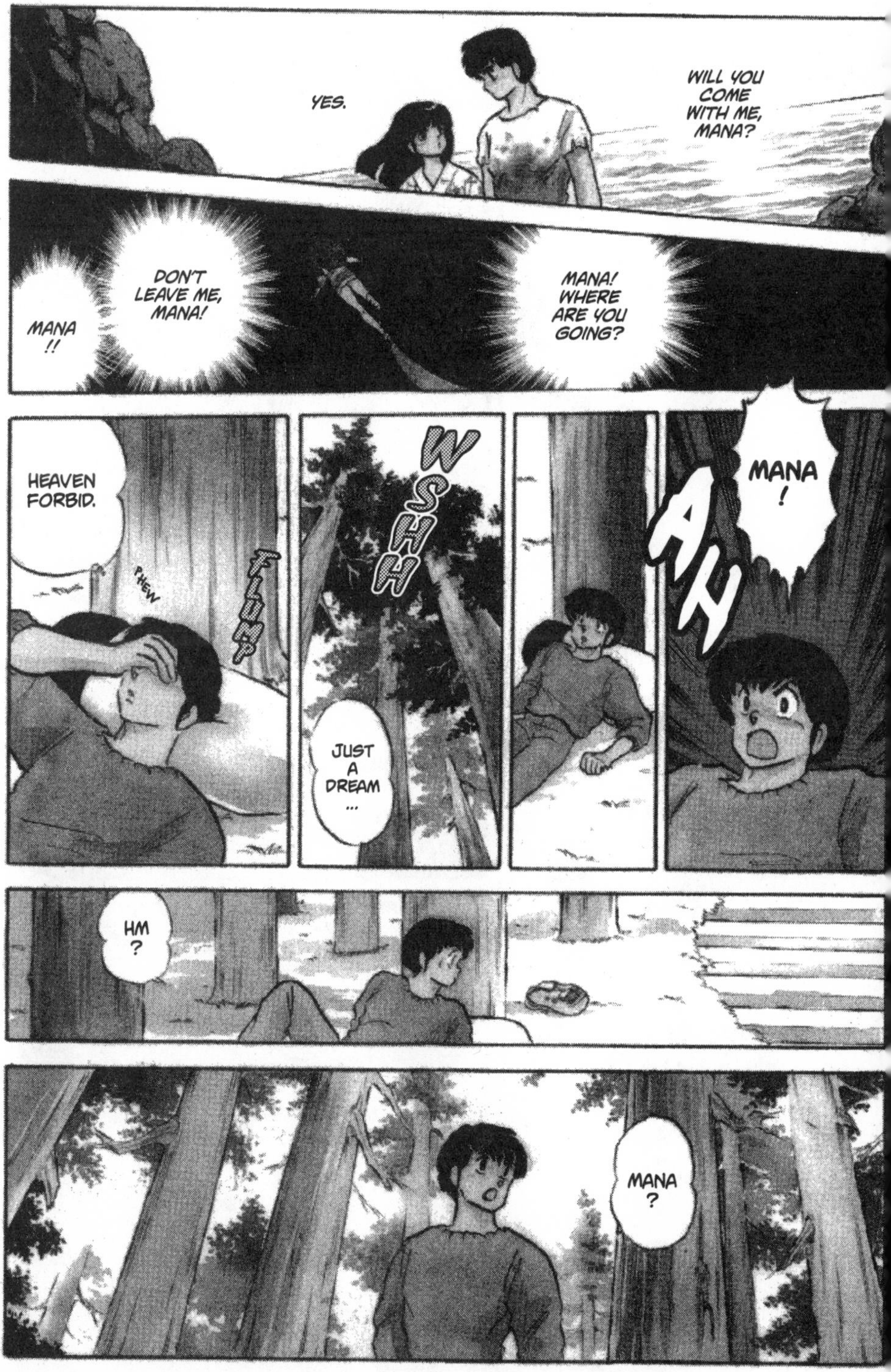
WILL YOU COME WITH ME, MANA?
YES.
MANA! WHERE ARE YOU GOING?
DON'T LEAVE ME, MANA!
MANA !!
MANA !
AH
WSHH
JUST A DREAM ...
HEAVEN FORBID.
FLUMP
PHEW
HM ?
MANA ?

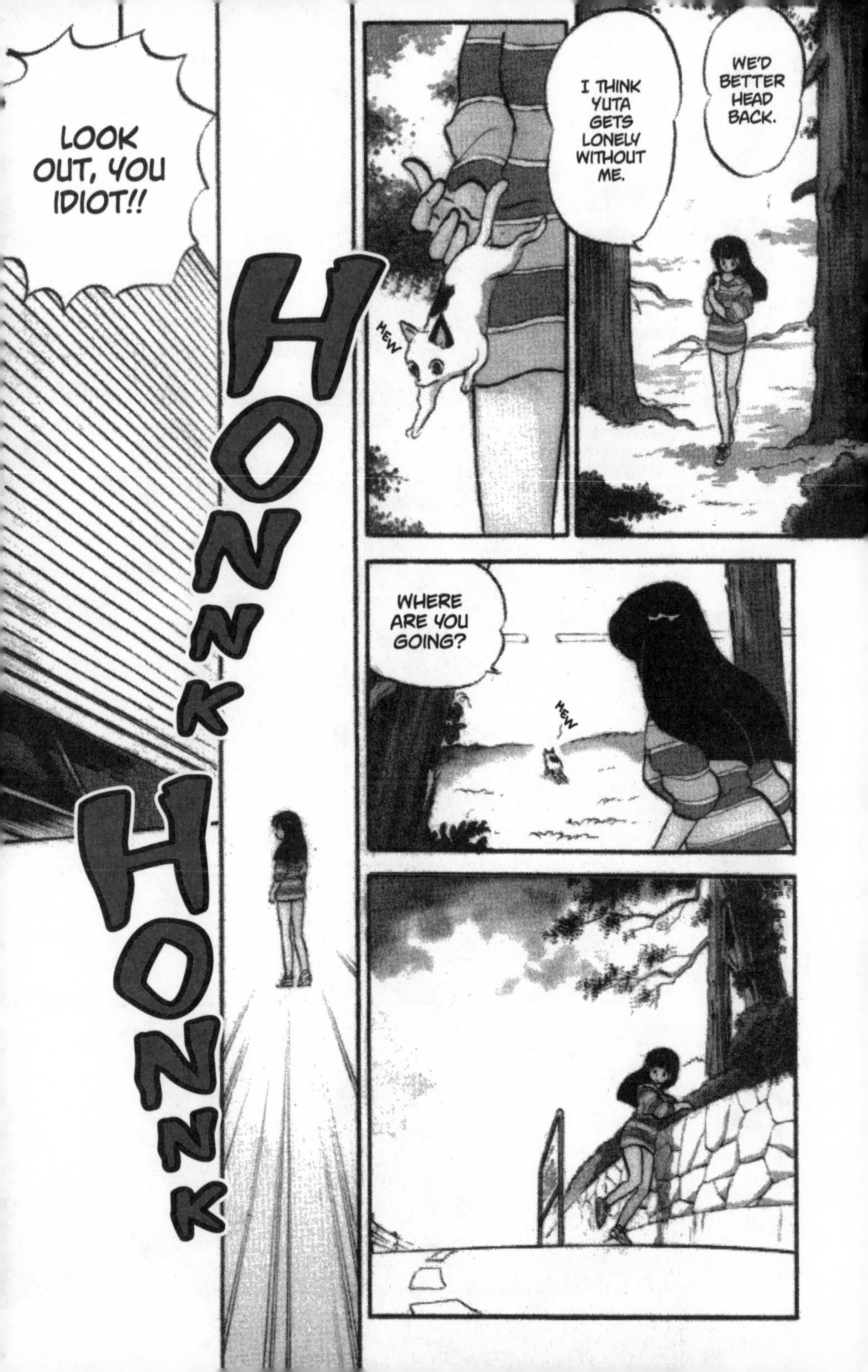
WE'D BETTER HEAD BACK.
I THINK YUTA GETS LONELY WITHOUT ME.
MEW
WHERE ARE YOU GOING?
MEW
HONNK HONNK
LOOK OUT, YOU IDIOT!!

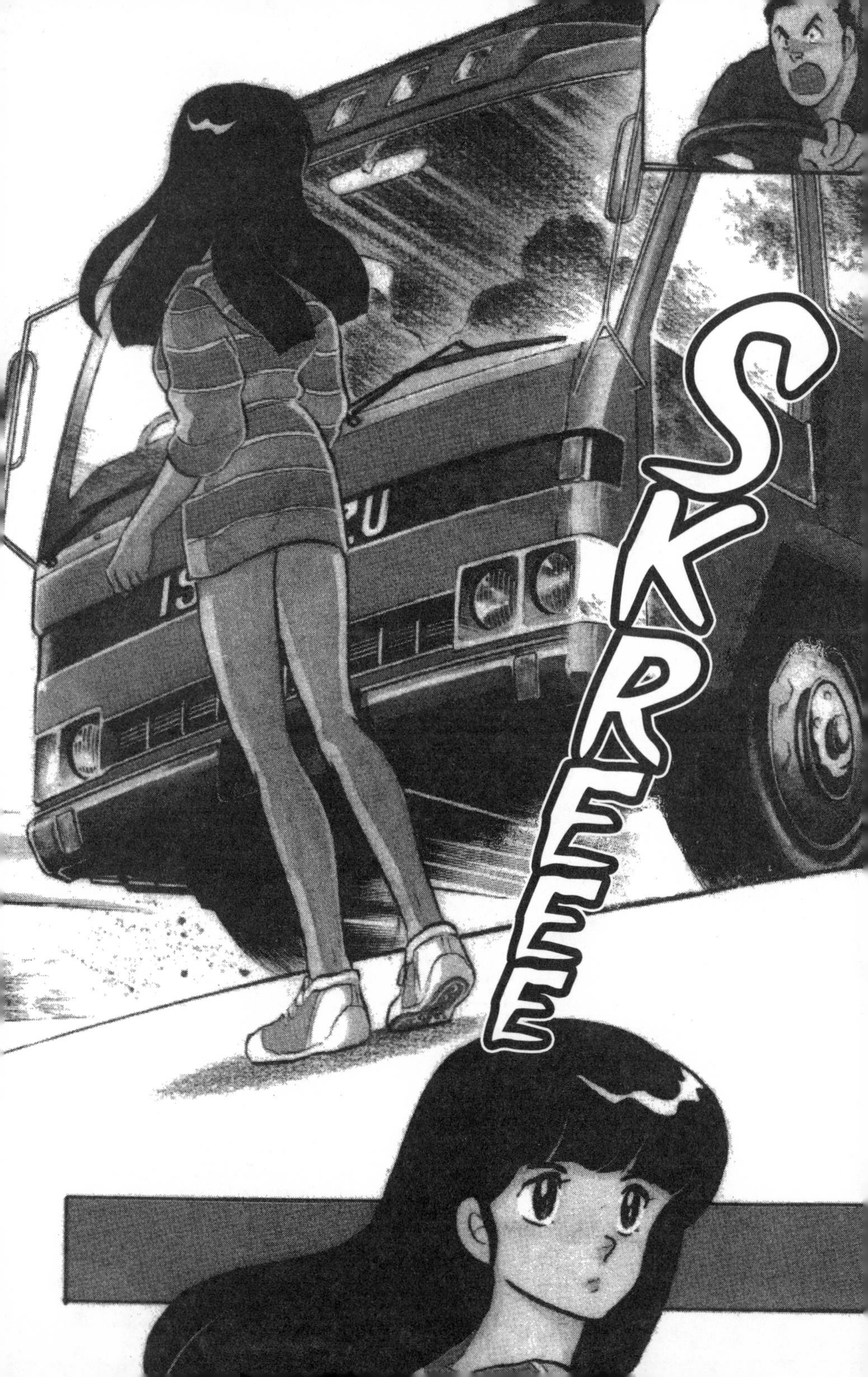
SKREEE

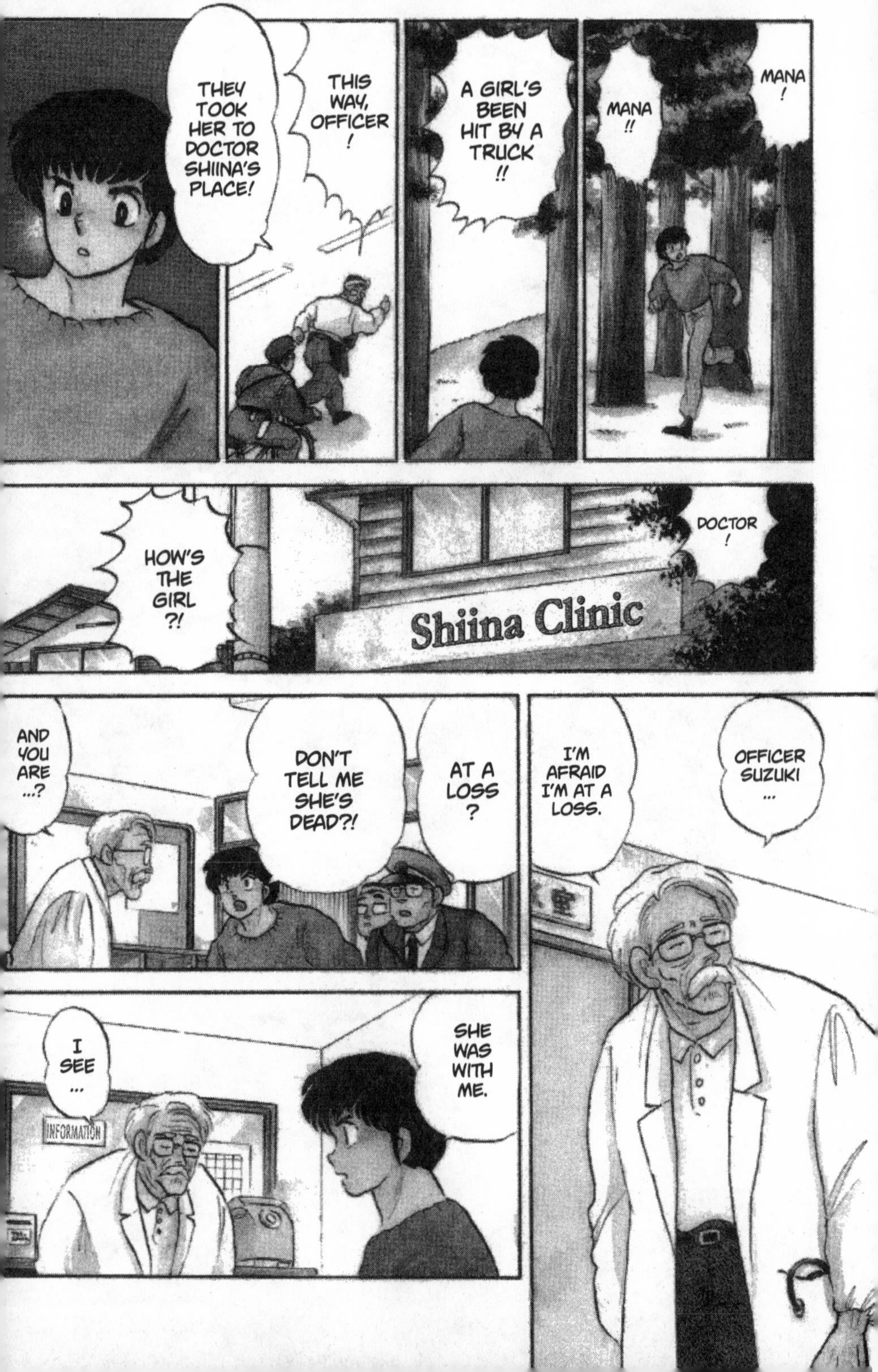
MANA!
MANA!!
A GIRL'S BEEN HIT BY A TRUCK!!
THIS WAY, OFFICER!
THEY TOOK HER TO DOCTOR SHIINA'S PLACE!
DOCTOR!
Shiina Clinic
HOW'S THE GIRL?!
OFFICER SUZUKI...
I'M AFRAID I'M AT A LOSS.
AT A LOSS?
DON'T TELL ME SHE'S DEAD?!
AND YOU ARE...?
SHE WAS WITH ME.
I SEE...
INFORMATION

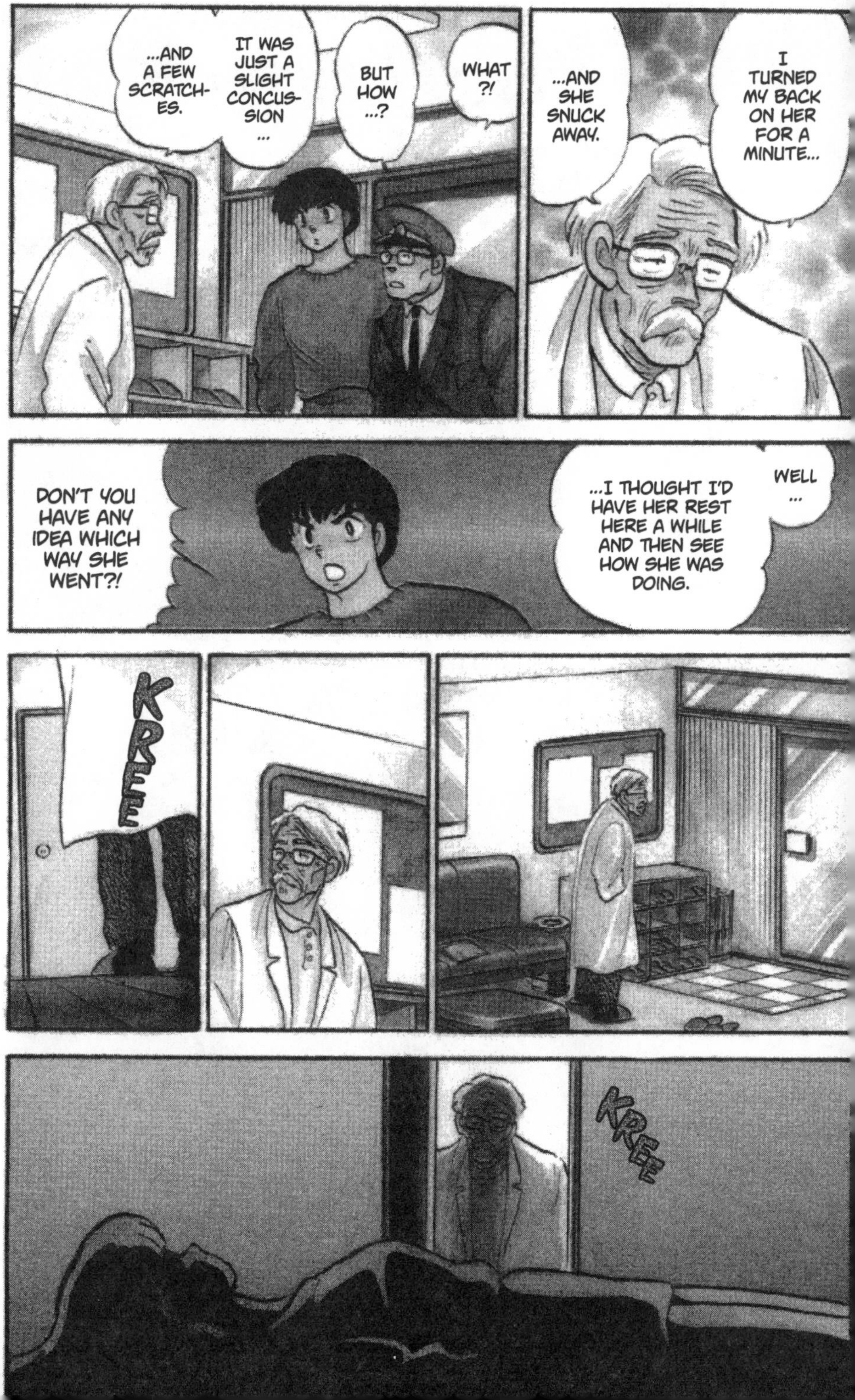
I TURNED MY BACK ON HER FOR A MINUTE...
...AND SHE SNUCK AWAY.
WHAT?!
BUT HOW ...?
IT WAS JUST A SLIGHT CONCUSSION ...
...AND A FEW SCRATCHES.
WELL ...
...I THOUGHT I'D HAVE HER REST HERE A WHILE AND THEN SEE HOW SHE WAS DOING.
DON'T YOU HAVE ANY IDEA WHICH WAY SHE WENT?!
KREE
KREE

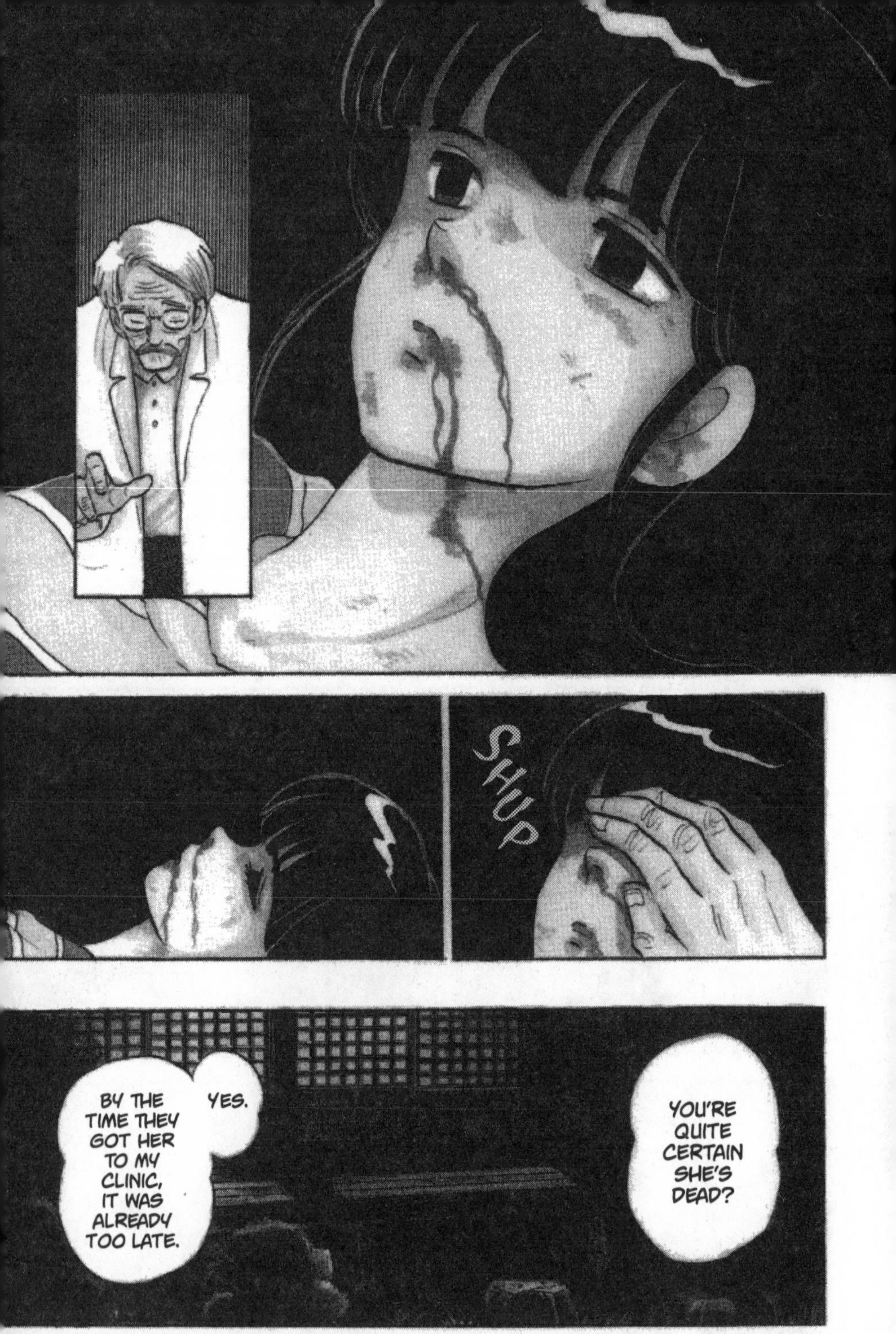
SHUP
YOU'RE QUITE CERTAIN SHE'S DEAD?
YES.
BY THE TIME THEY GOT HER TO MY CLINIC, IT WAS ALREADY TOO LATE.

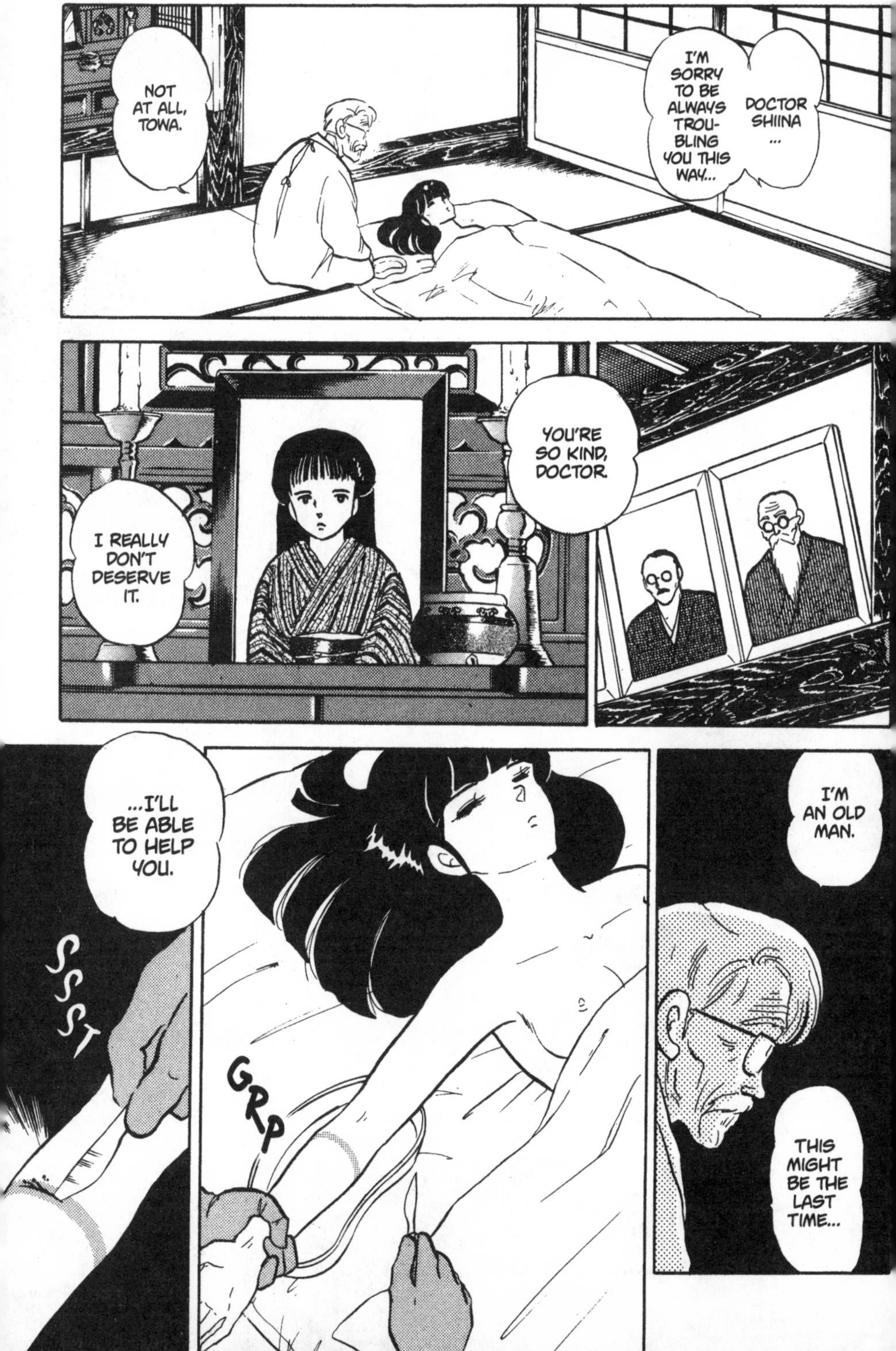
DOCTOR SHIINA ...
I'M SORRY TO BE ALWAYS TROU-BLING YOU THIS WAY...
NOT AT ALL, TOWA.
YOU'RE SO KIND, DOCTOR.
I REALLY DON'T DESERVE IT.
I'M AN OLD MAN.
THIS MIGHT BE THE LAST TIME...
...I'LL BE ABLE TO HELP YOU.
GRP
SSST

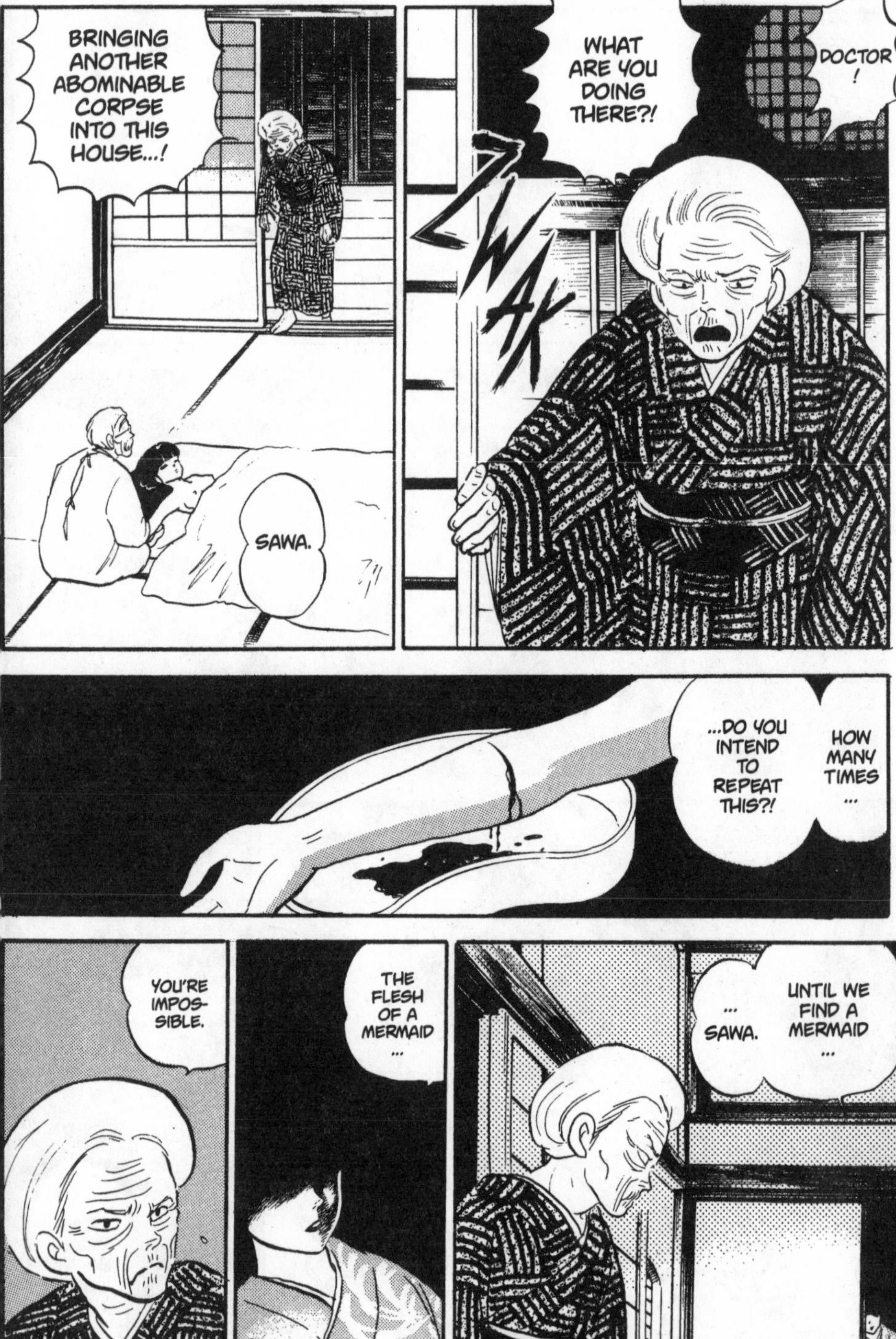
DOCTOR!
WHAT ARE YOU DOING THERE?!
ZWAK
BRINGING ANOTHER ABOMINABLE CORPSE INTO THIS HOUSE...!
SAWA.
HOW MANY TIMES...
...DO YOU INTEND TO REPEAT THIS?!
UNTIL WE FIND A MERMAID...
...SAWA.
THE FLESH OF A MERMAID...
YOU'RE IMPOS-SIBLE.

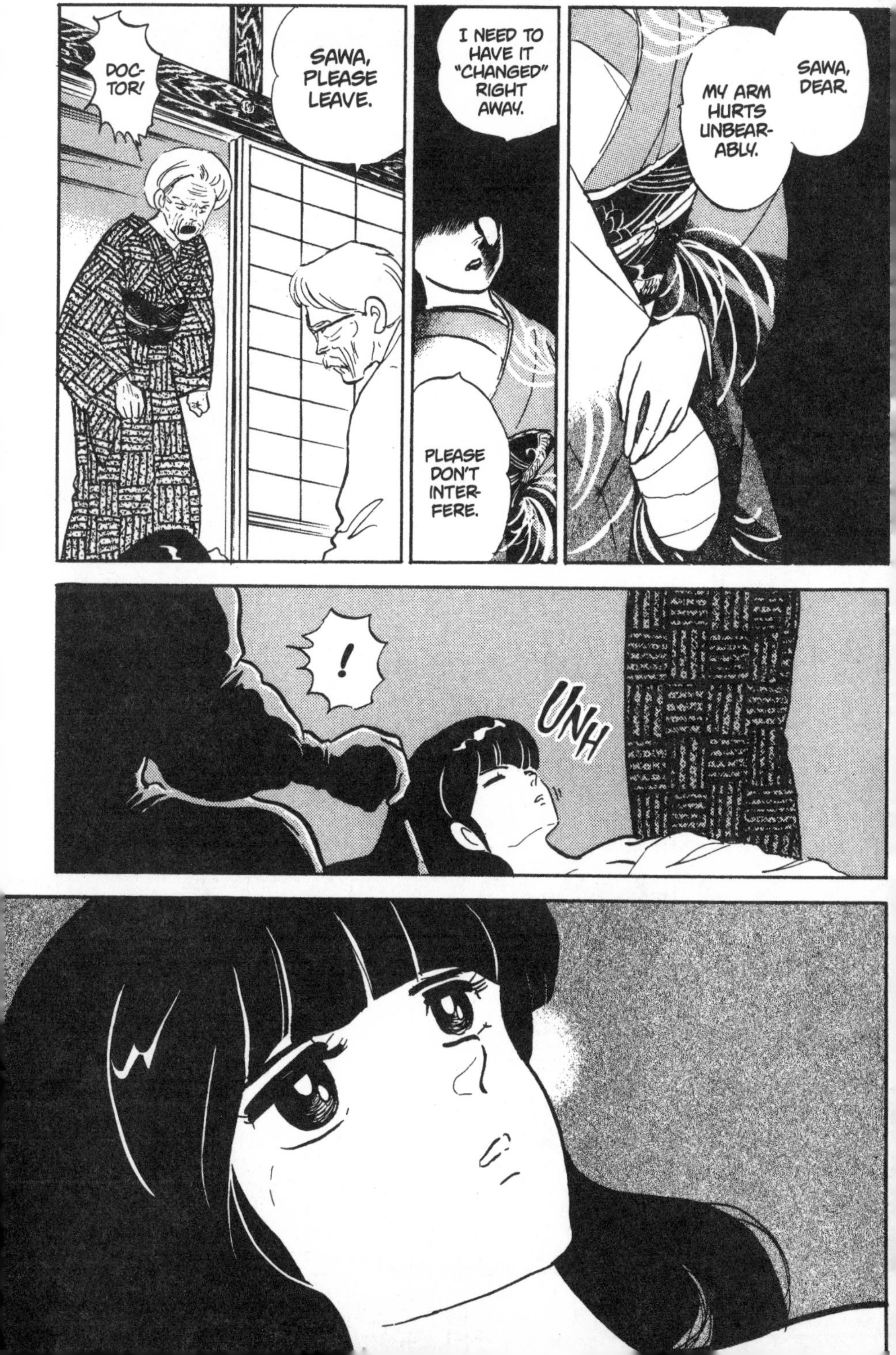
SAWA, DEAR.
MY ARM HURTS UNBEARABLY.
I NEED TO HAVE IT "CHANGED" RIGHT AWAY.
PLEASE DON'T INTERFERE.
SAWA, PLEASE LEAVE.
DOC-TOR!
!
UNH

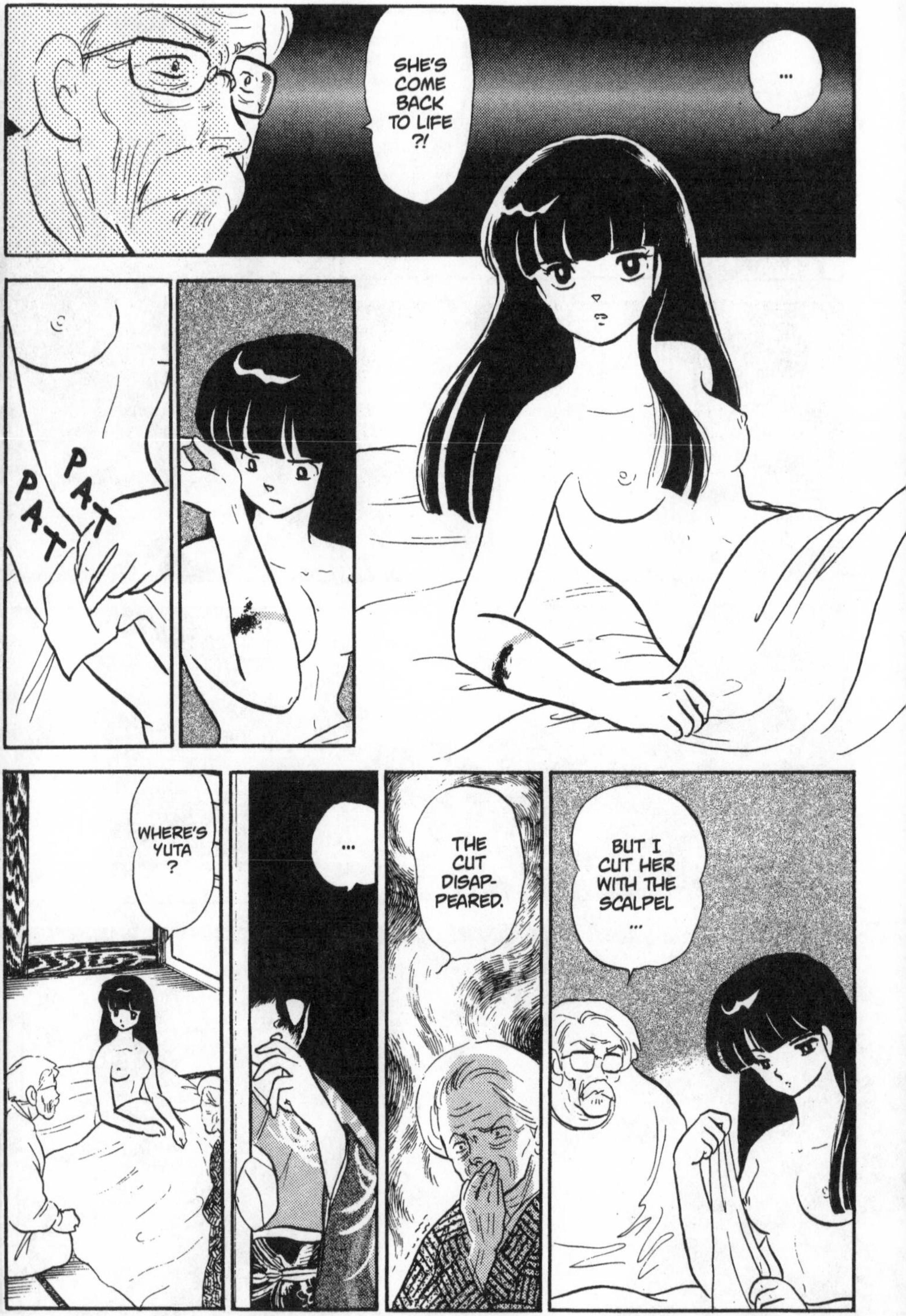
...
SHE'S COME BACK TO LIFE ?!
PAT PAT
BUT I CUT HER WITH THE SCALPEL ...
THE CUT DISAP-PEARED.
...
WHERE'S YUTA ?

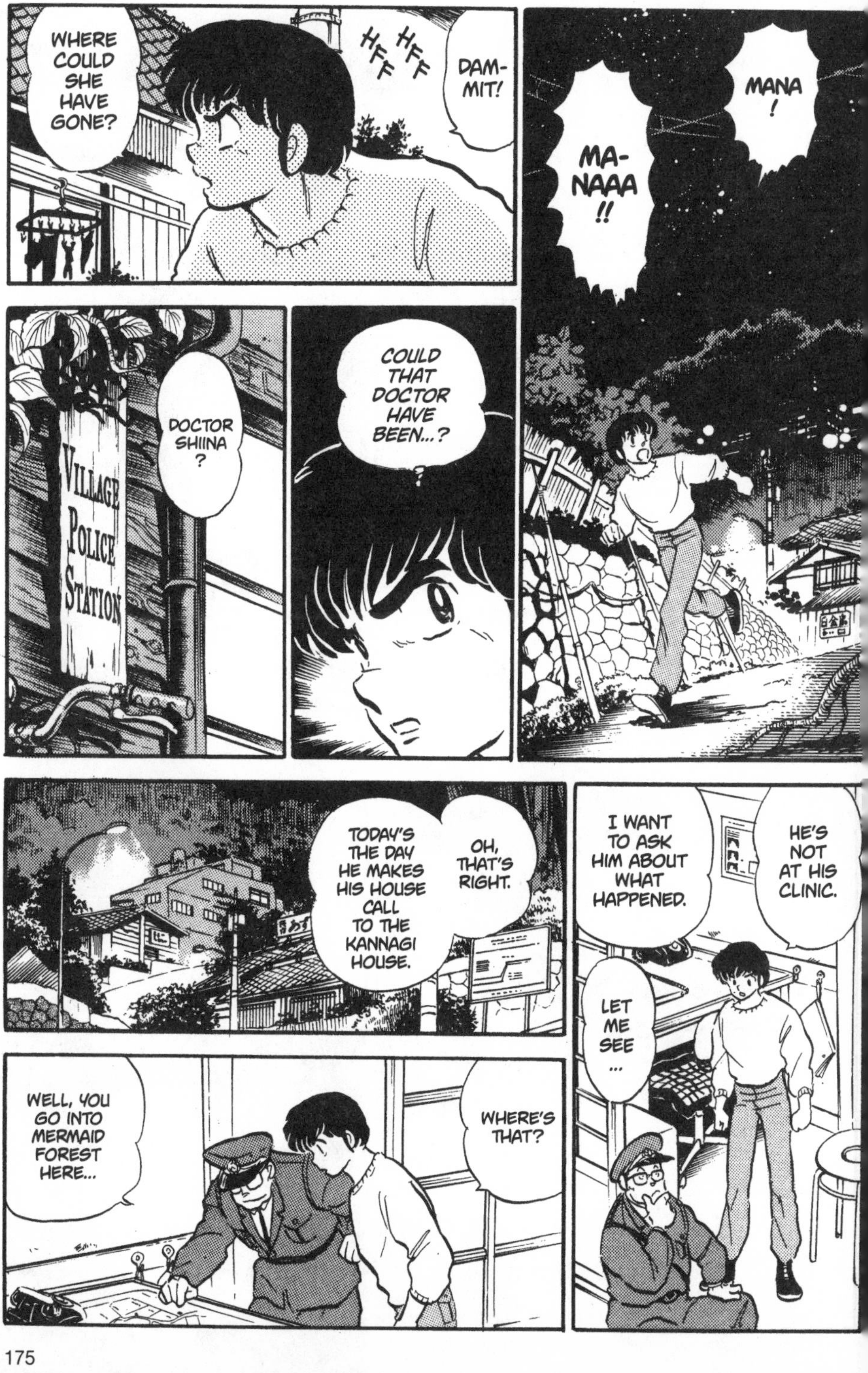
MANA!
MA-NAAA!!
HFF HFF
DAM-MIT!
WHERE COULD SHE HAVE GONE?
COULD THAT DOCTOR HAVE BEEN...?
DOCTOR SHIINA?
VILLAGE POLICE STATION
HE'S NOT AT HIS CLINIC.
I WANT TO ASK HIM ABOUT WHAT HAPPENED.
LET ME SEE...
OH, THAT'S RIGHT.
TODAY'S THE DAY HE MAKES HIS HOUSE CALL TO THE KANNAGI HOUSE.
WHERE'S THAT?
WELL, YOU GO INTO MERMAID FOREST HERE...

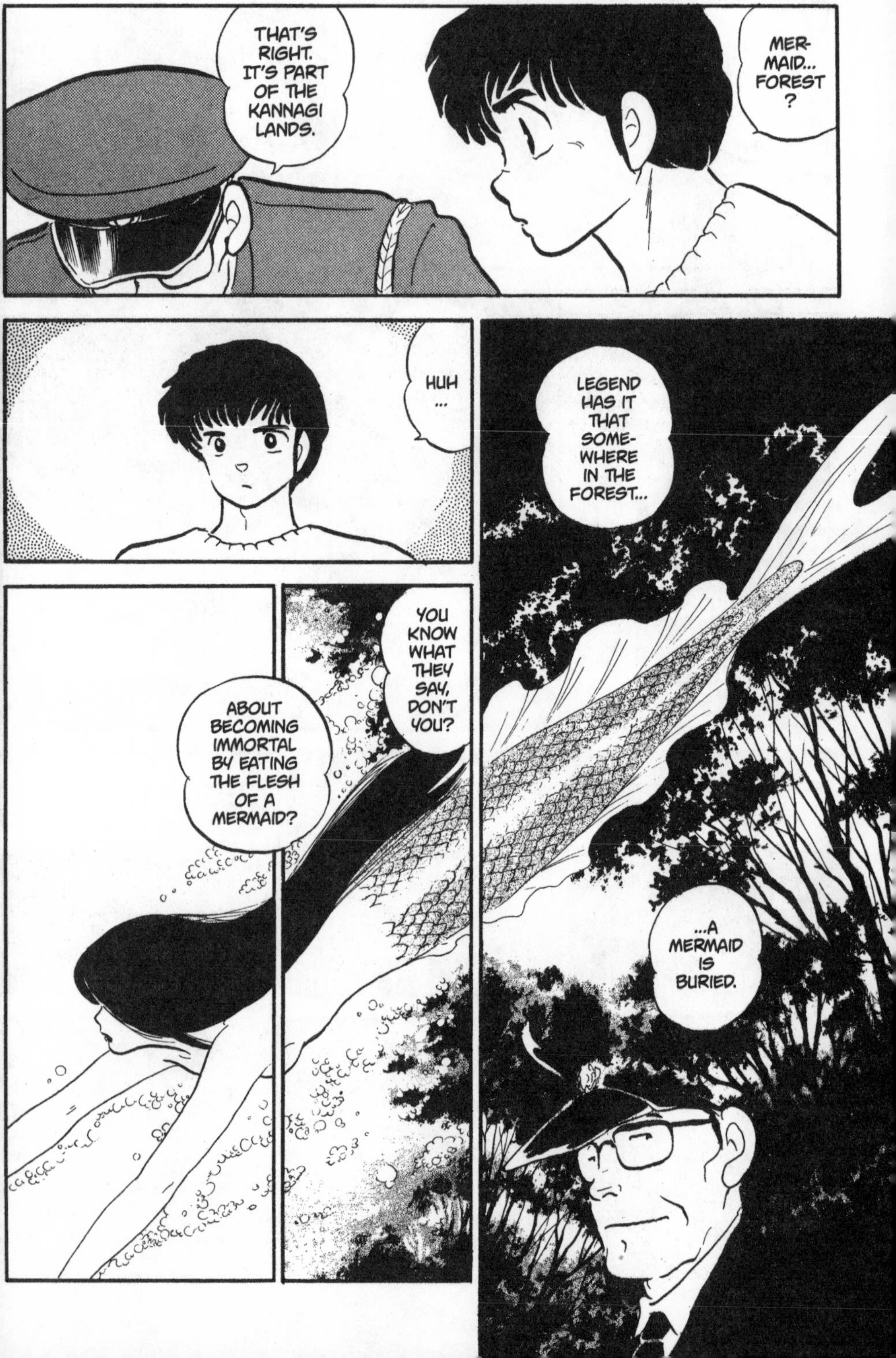
MER-MAID... FOREST?
THAT'S RIGHT. IT'S PART OF THE KANNAGI LANDS.
HUH...
LEGEND HAS IT THAT SOME-WHERE IN THE FOREST...
...A MERMAID IS BURIED.
YOU KNOW WHAT THEY SAY, DON'T YOU?
ABOUT BECOMING IMMORTAL BY EATING THE FLESH OF A MERMAID?

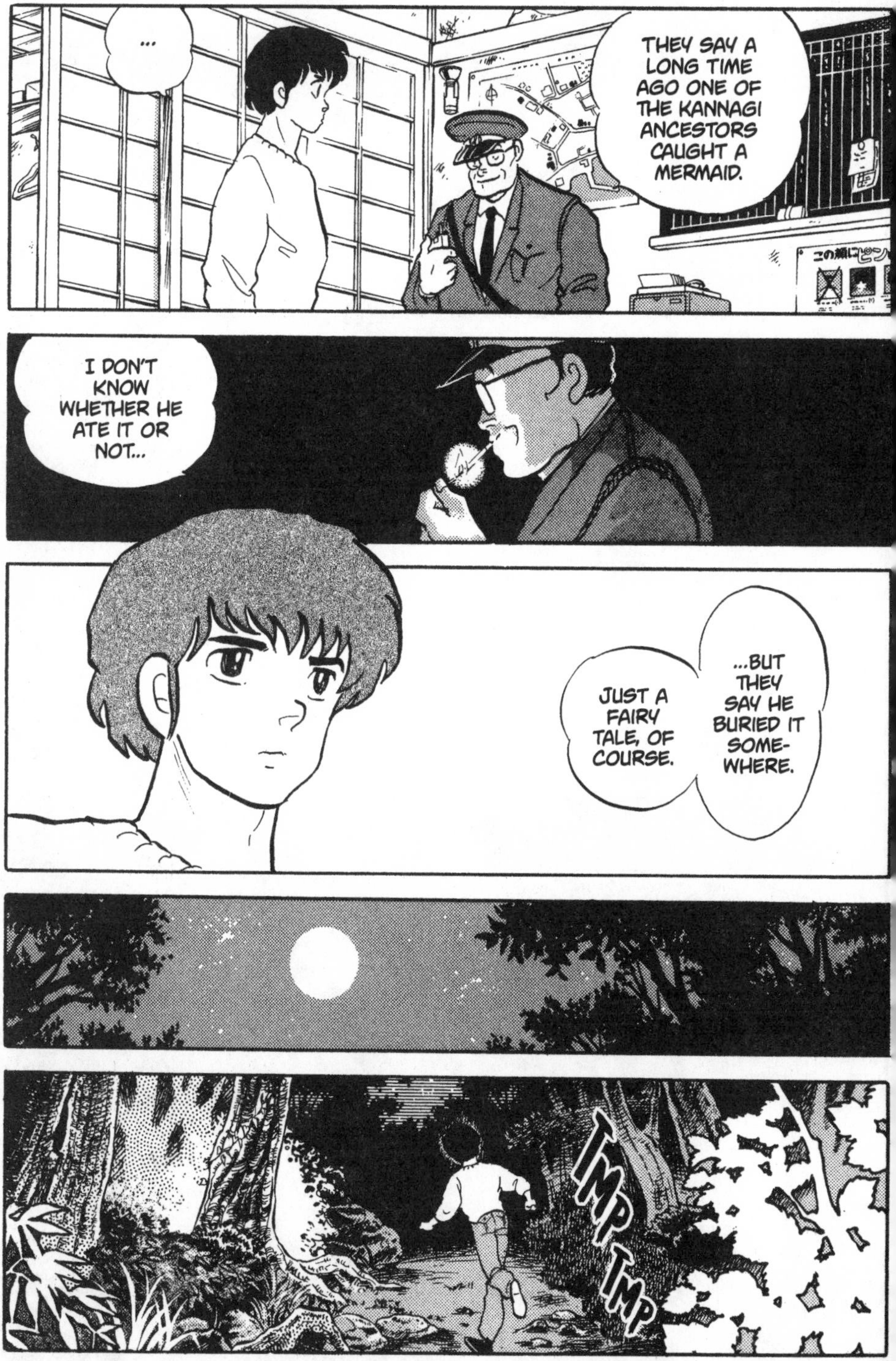
THEY SAY A LONG TIME AGO ONE OF THE KANNAGI ANCESTORS CAUGHT A MERMAID.
...
I DON'T KNOW WHETHER HE ATE IT OR NOT...
...BUT THEY SAY HE BURIED IT SOME-WHERE.
JUST A FAIRY TALE, OF COURSE.
TMP TMP

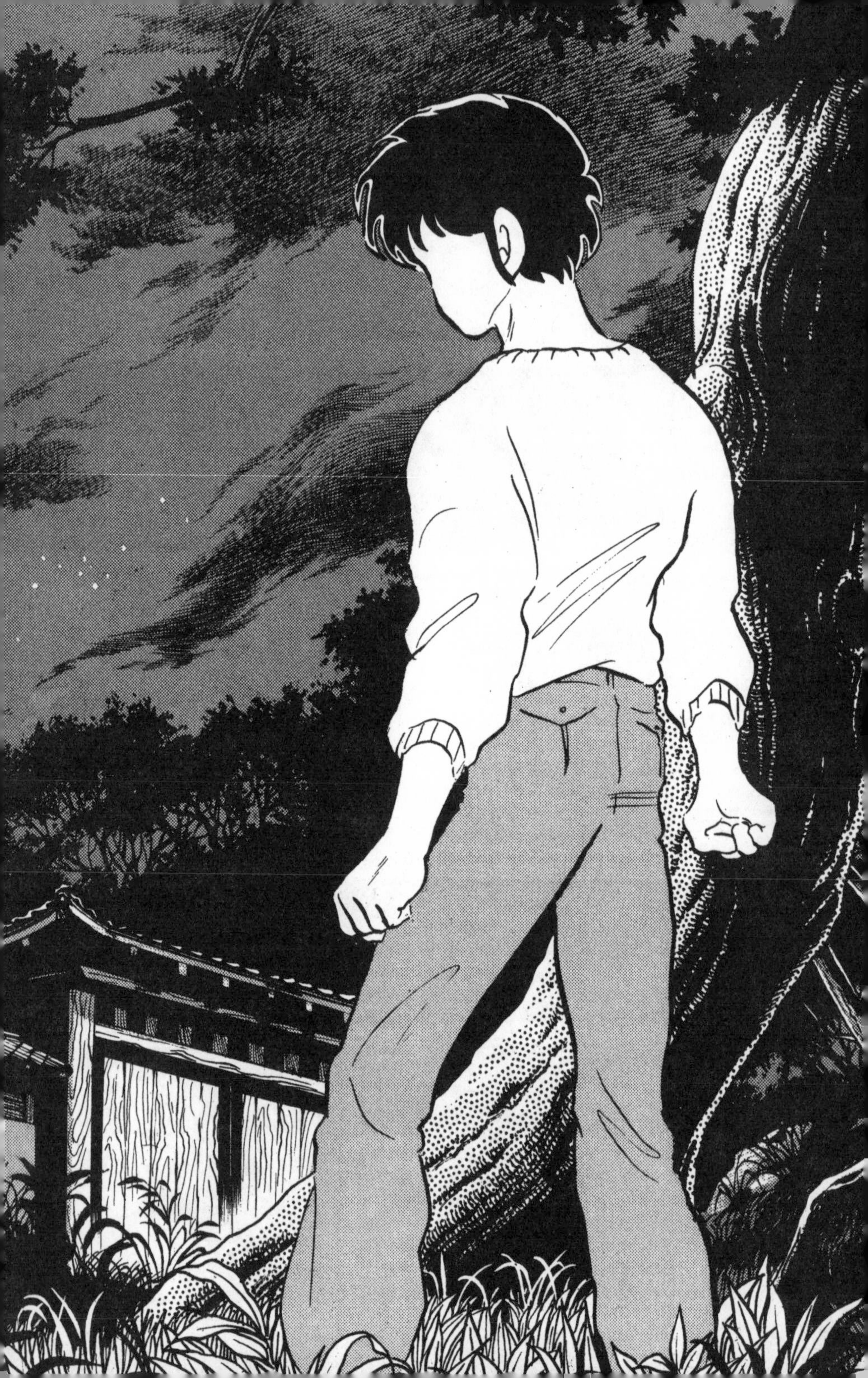

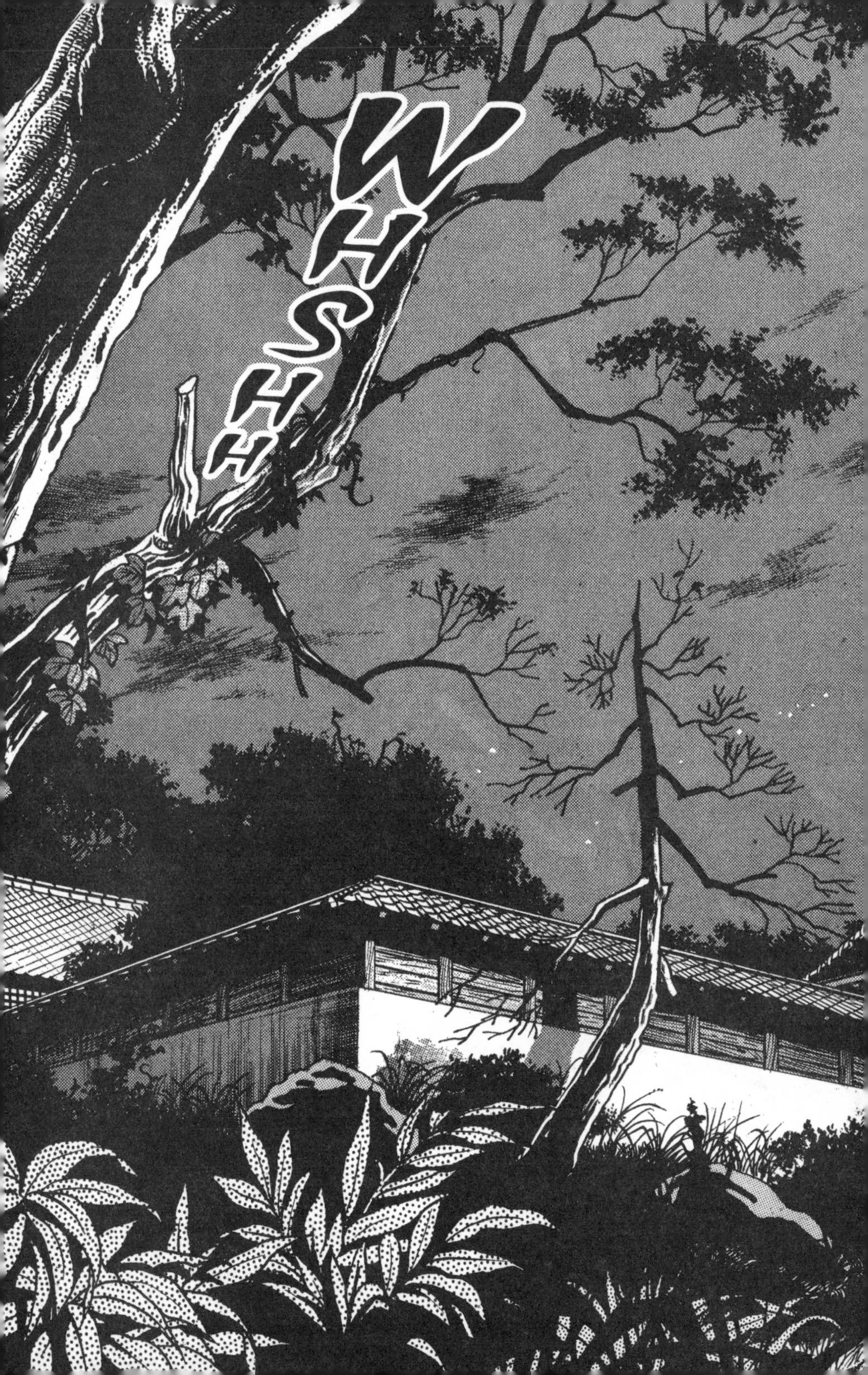
WHSHH

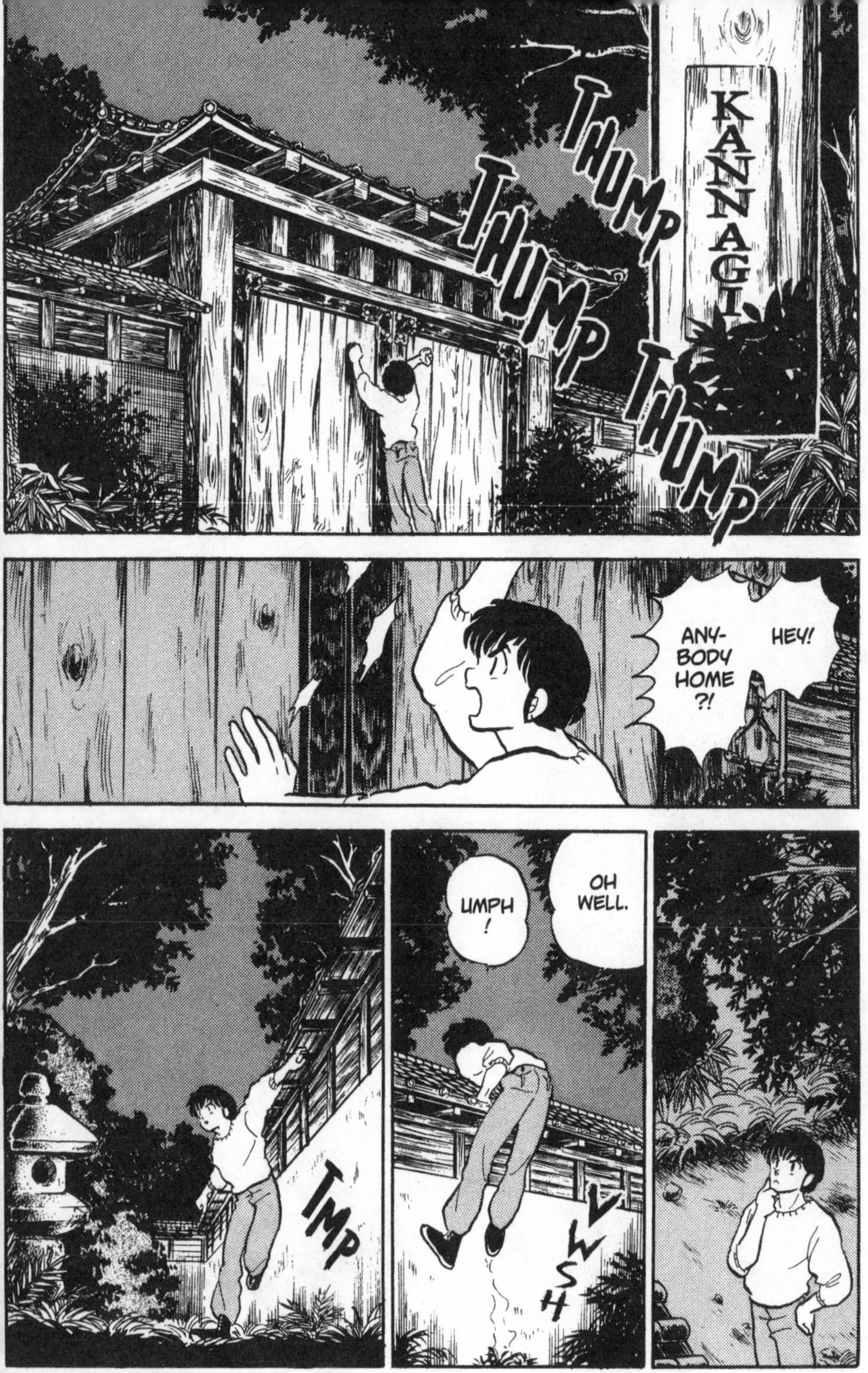
KANNAGI
THUMP THUMP
THUMP THUMP
HEY!
ANY-BODY HOME ?!
OH WELL.
UMPH !
VWSH
TMP

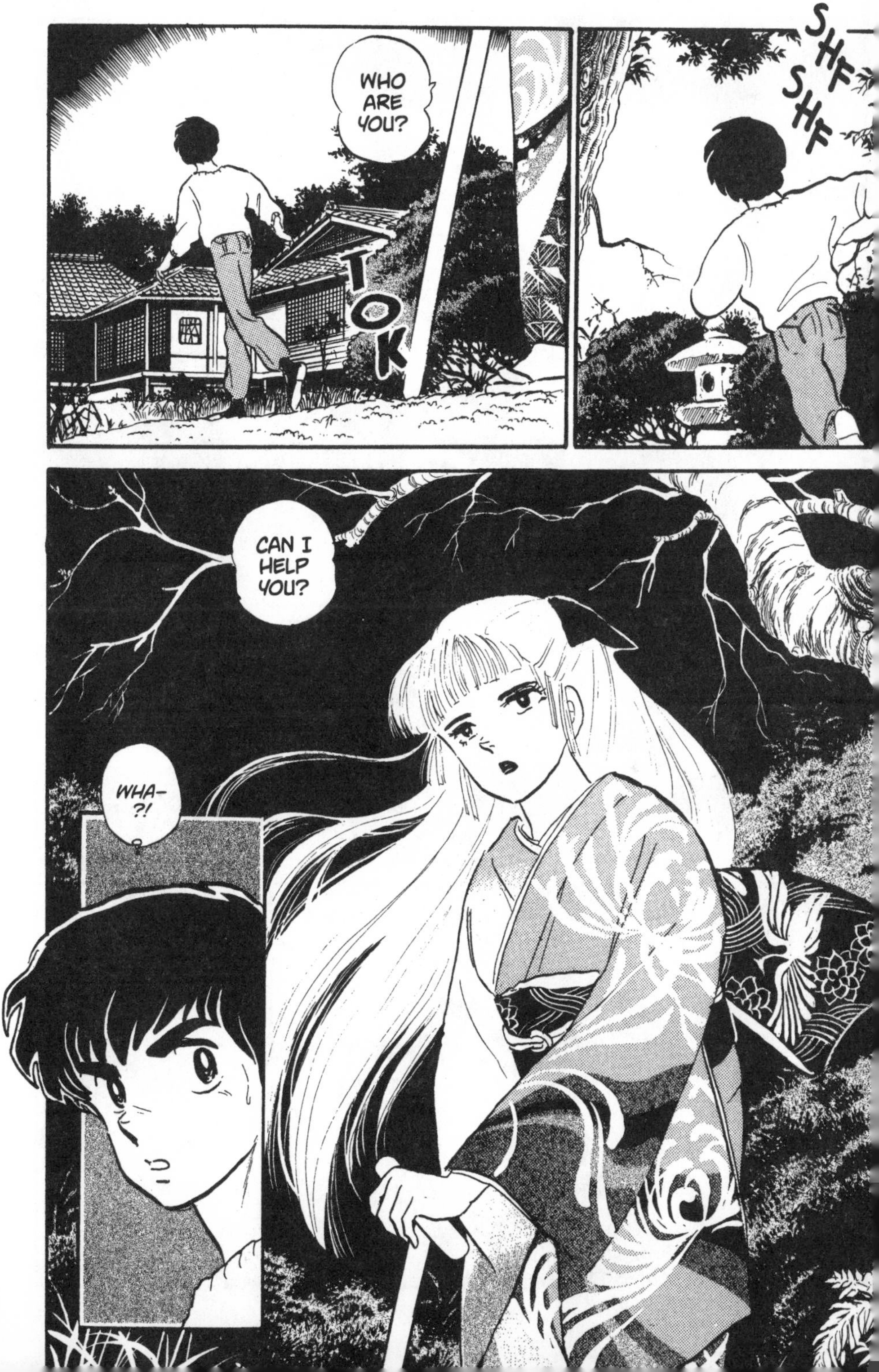
SHF
SHF
SHF
WHO ARE YOU?
TOK
CAN I HELP YOU?
WHA-?!

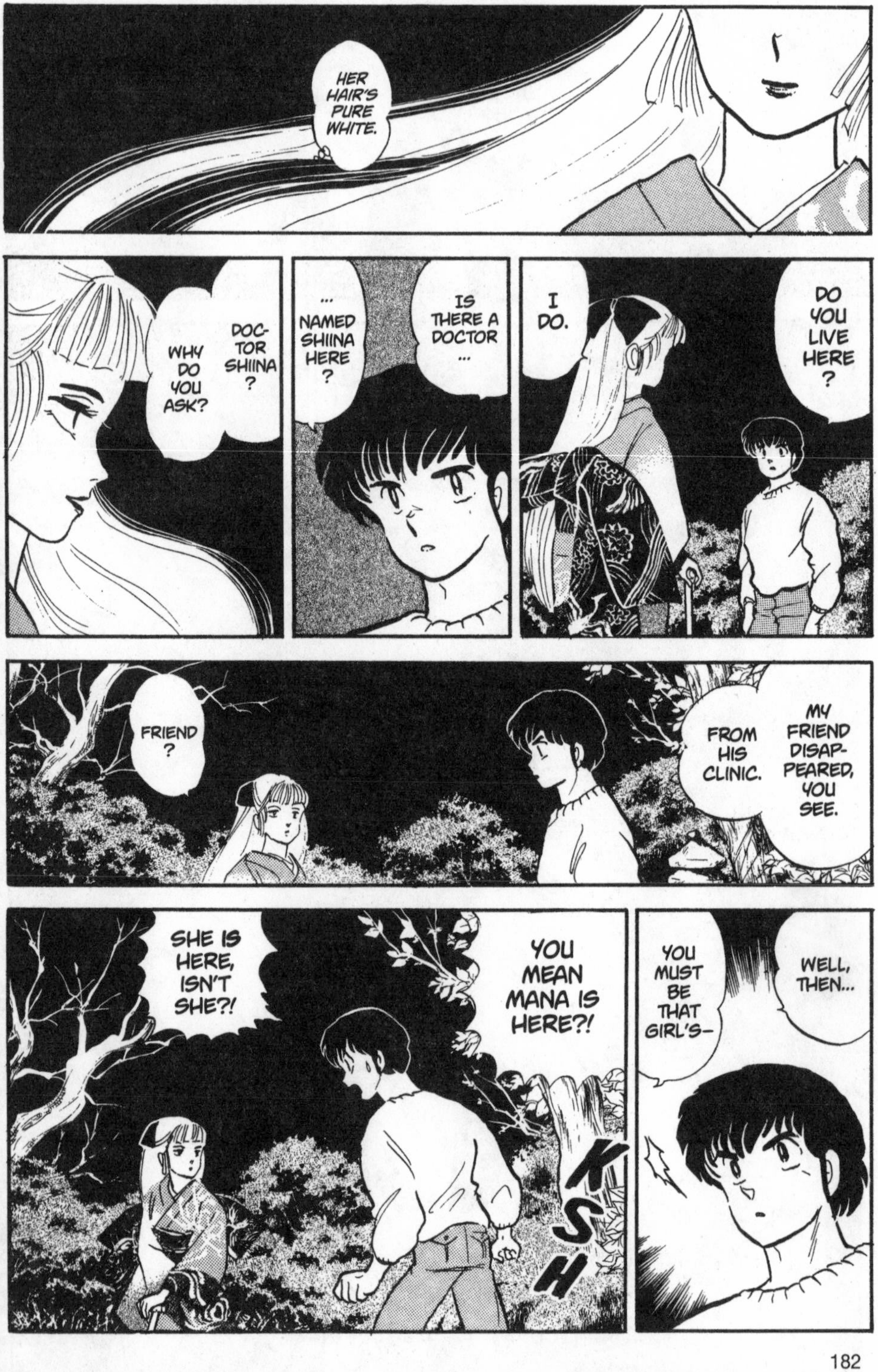
HER HAIR'S PURE WHITE.
DO YOU LIVE HERE?
I DO.
IS THERE A DOCTOR ...
... NAMED SHIINA HERE?
DOCTOR SHIINA?
WHY DO YOU ASK?
MY FRIEND DISAPPEARED, YOU SEE.
FROM HIS CLINIC.
FRIEND?
WELL, THEN...
YOU MUST BE THAT GIRL'S-
YOU MEAN MANA IS HERE?!
SHE IS HERE, ISN'T SHE?!
KSSH

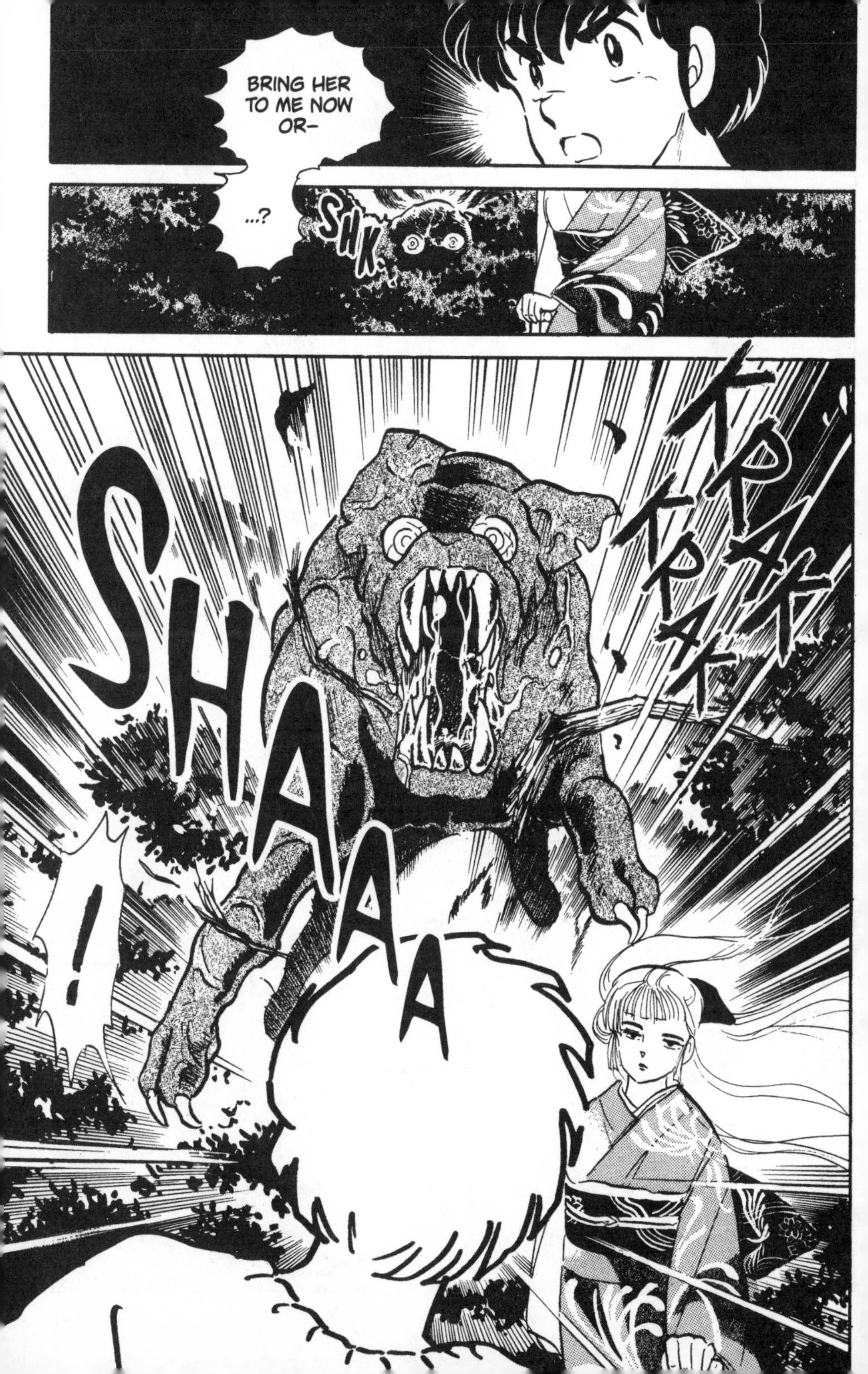
BRING HER TO ME NOW OR–
...?
SHK
KRAK KRAK
SHAAAA
!

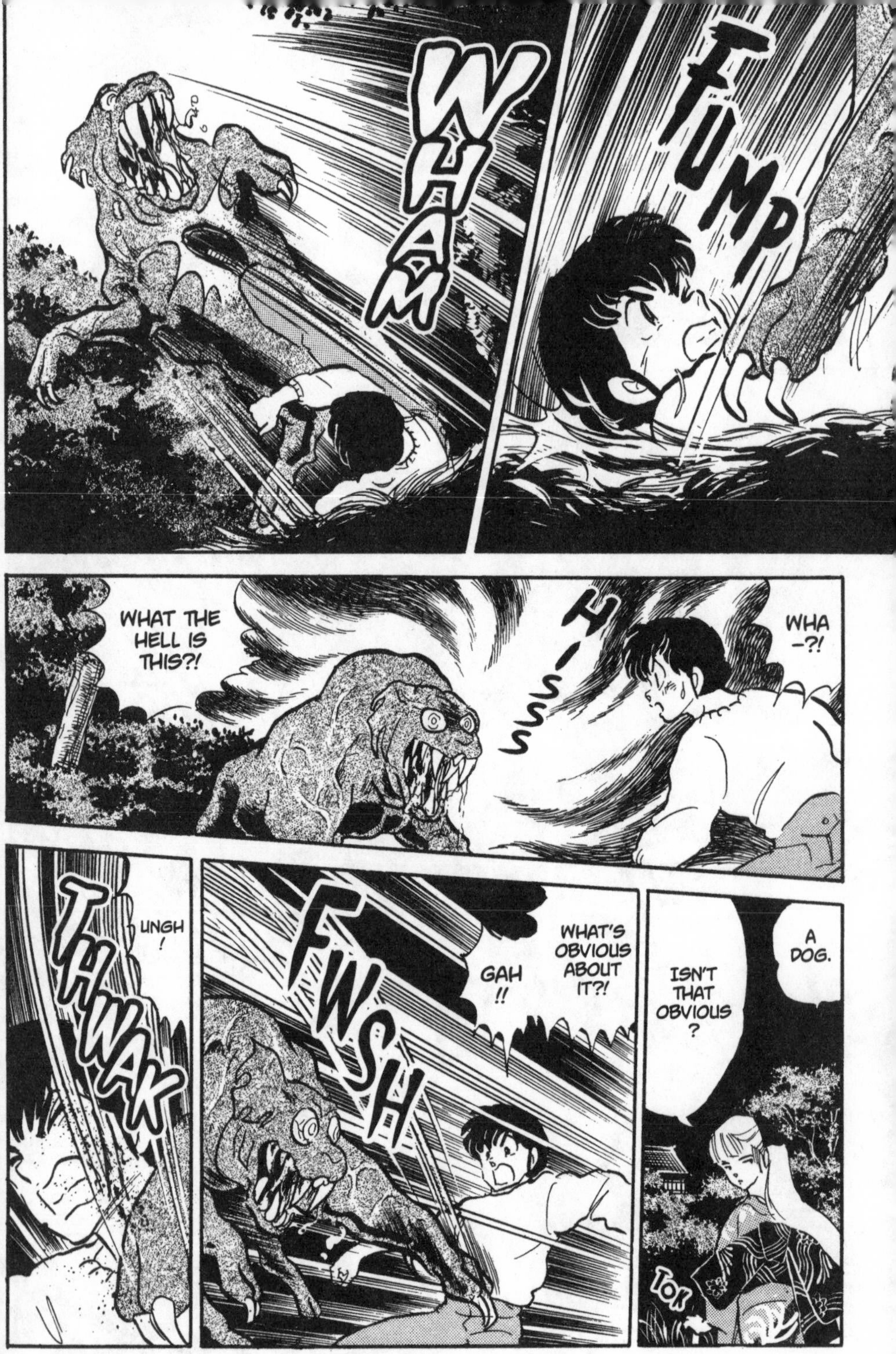
FUMP
WHAM
WHA—?!
HISSS
WHAT THE HELL IS THIS?!
A DOG.
ISN'T THAT OBVIOUS?
TOK
WHAT'S OBVIOUS ABOUT IT?!
GAH!!
FWSH
UNGH!
THWAK

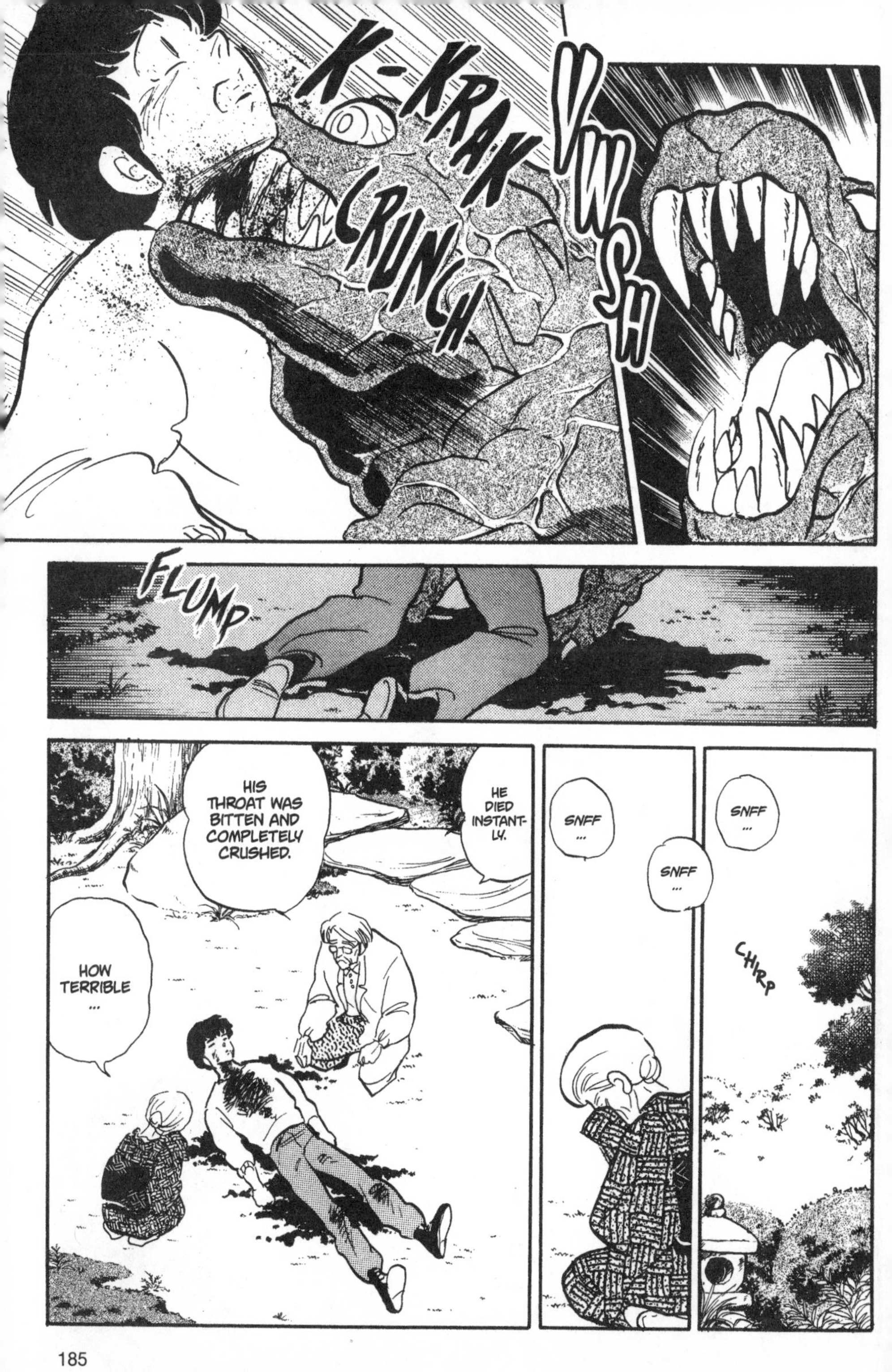
VWSH
K-KRAK CRUNCH
FLUMP
SNFF ...
SNFF ...
CHIRP
SNFF ...
HE DIED INSTANT-LY.
HIS THROAT WAS BITTEN AND COMPLETELY CRUSHED.
HOW TERRIBLE ...

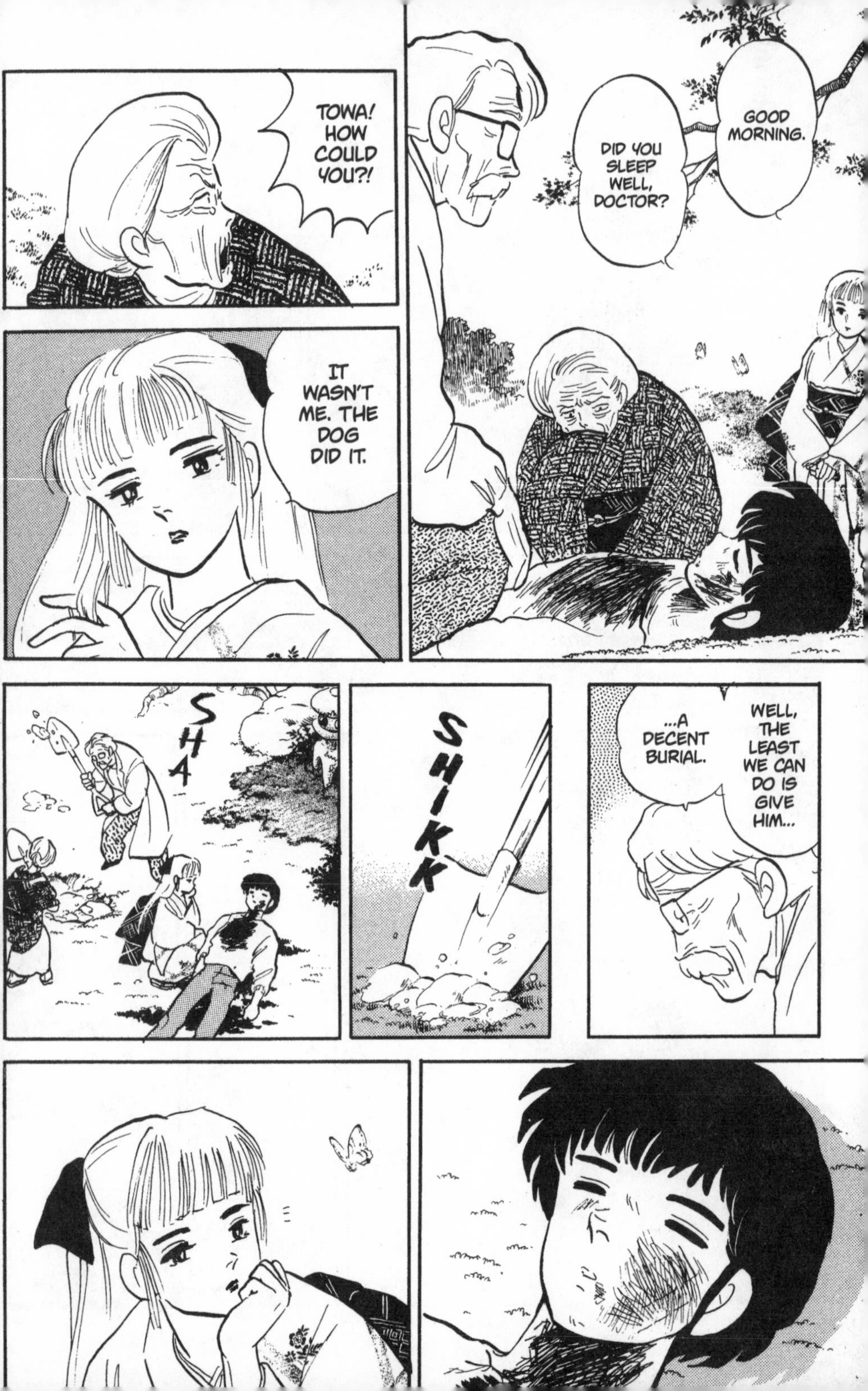
GOOD MORNING.
DID YOU SLEEP WELL, DOCTOR?
TOWA! HOW COULD YOU?!
IT WASN'T ME. THE DOG DID IT.
WELL, THE LEAST WE CAN DO IS GIVE HIM...
...A DECENT BURIAL.
SHIKK
SHA

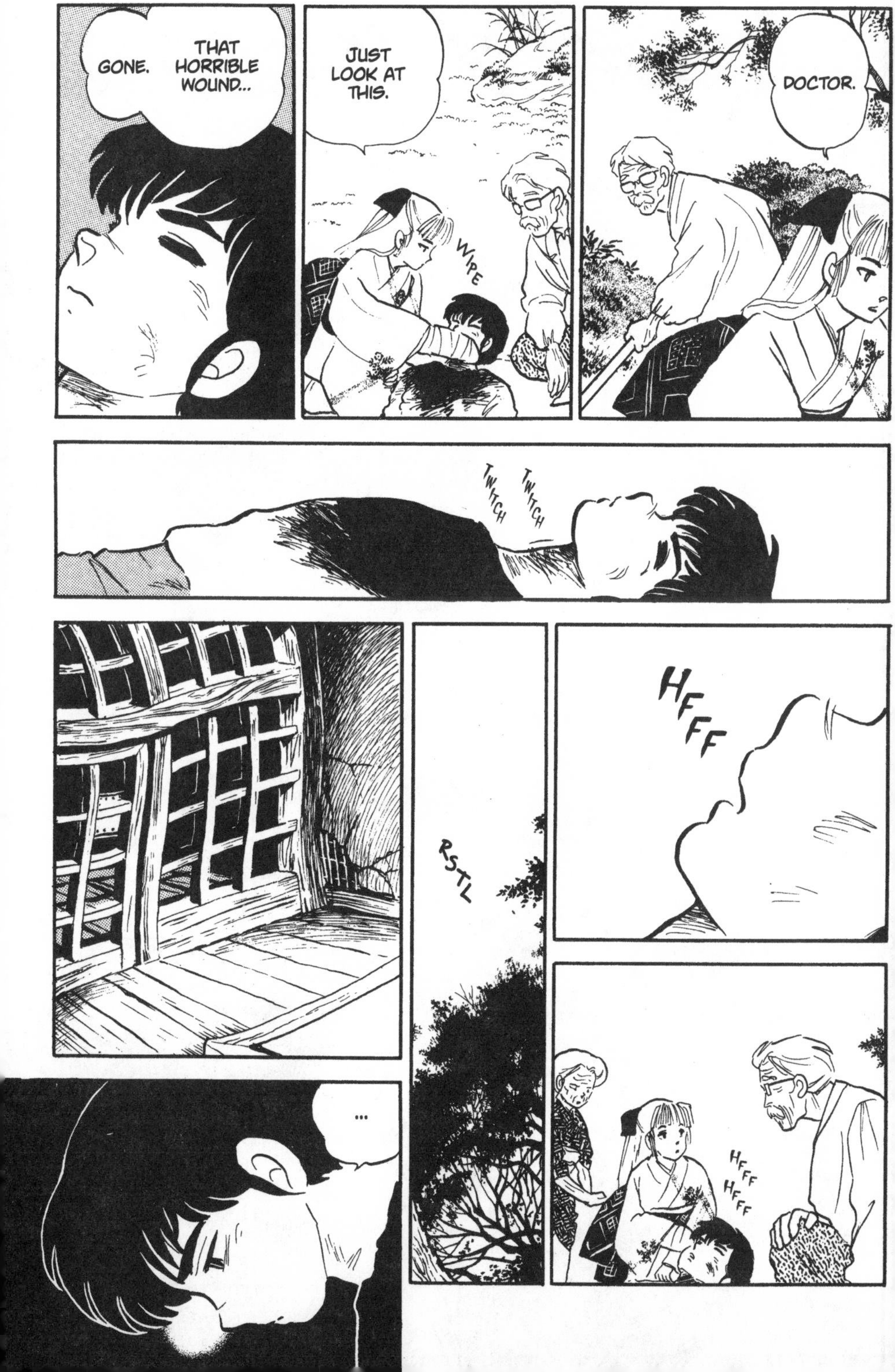
DOCTOR.
JUST LOOK AT THIS.
WIPE
THAT HORRIBLE WOUND... GONE.
TWITCH
TWITCH
HFFF
HFFF HFFF
RSTL
...

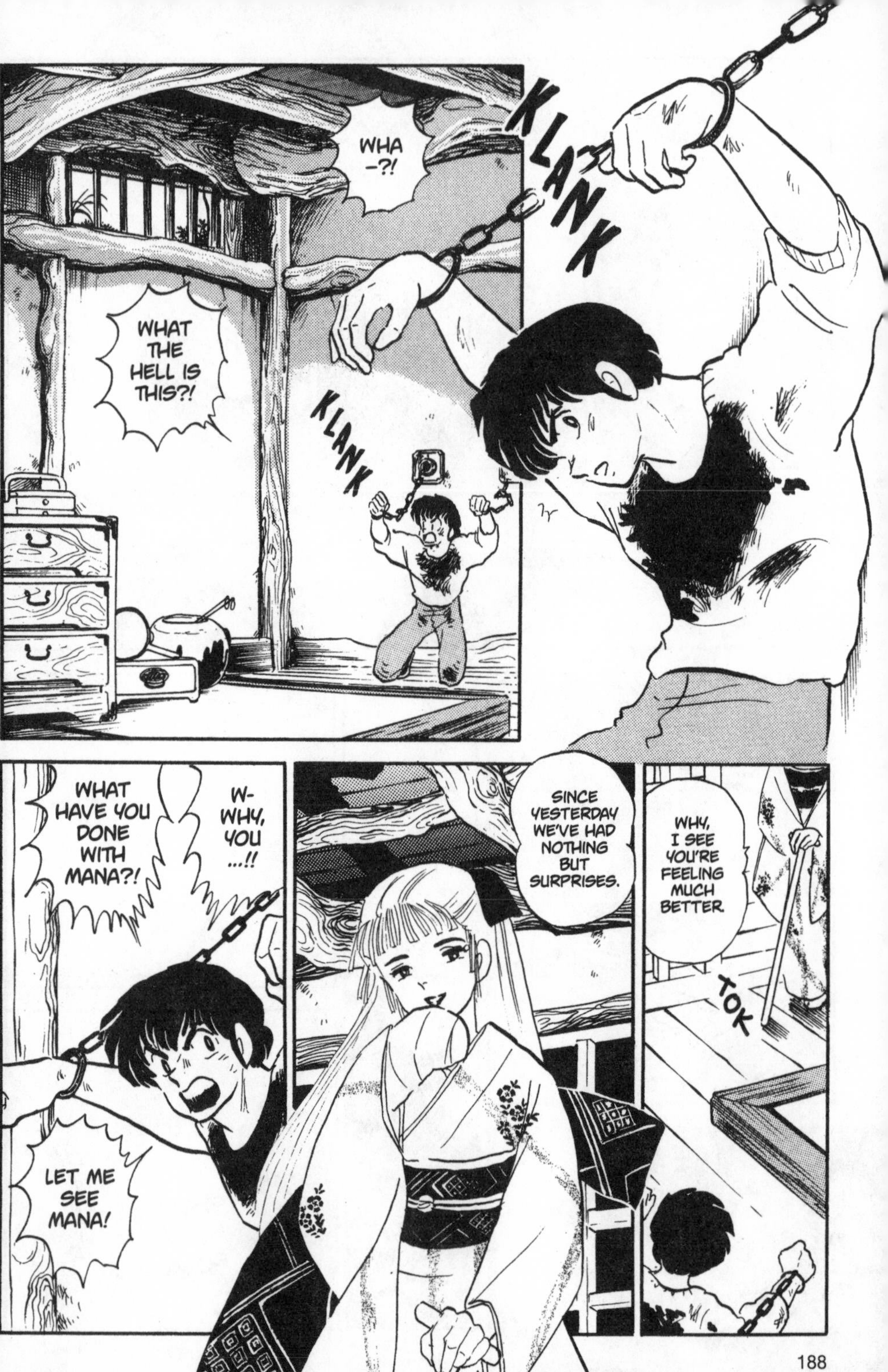
KLANK
WHA –?!
KLANK
WHAT THE HELL IS THIS?!
WHY, I SEE YOU'RE FEELING MUCH BETTER.
TOK
SINCE YESTERDAY WE'VE HAD NOTHING BUT SURPRISES.
W-WHY, YOU ...!!
WHAT HAVE YOU DONE WITH MANA?!
LET ME SEE MANA!

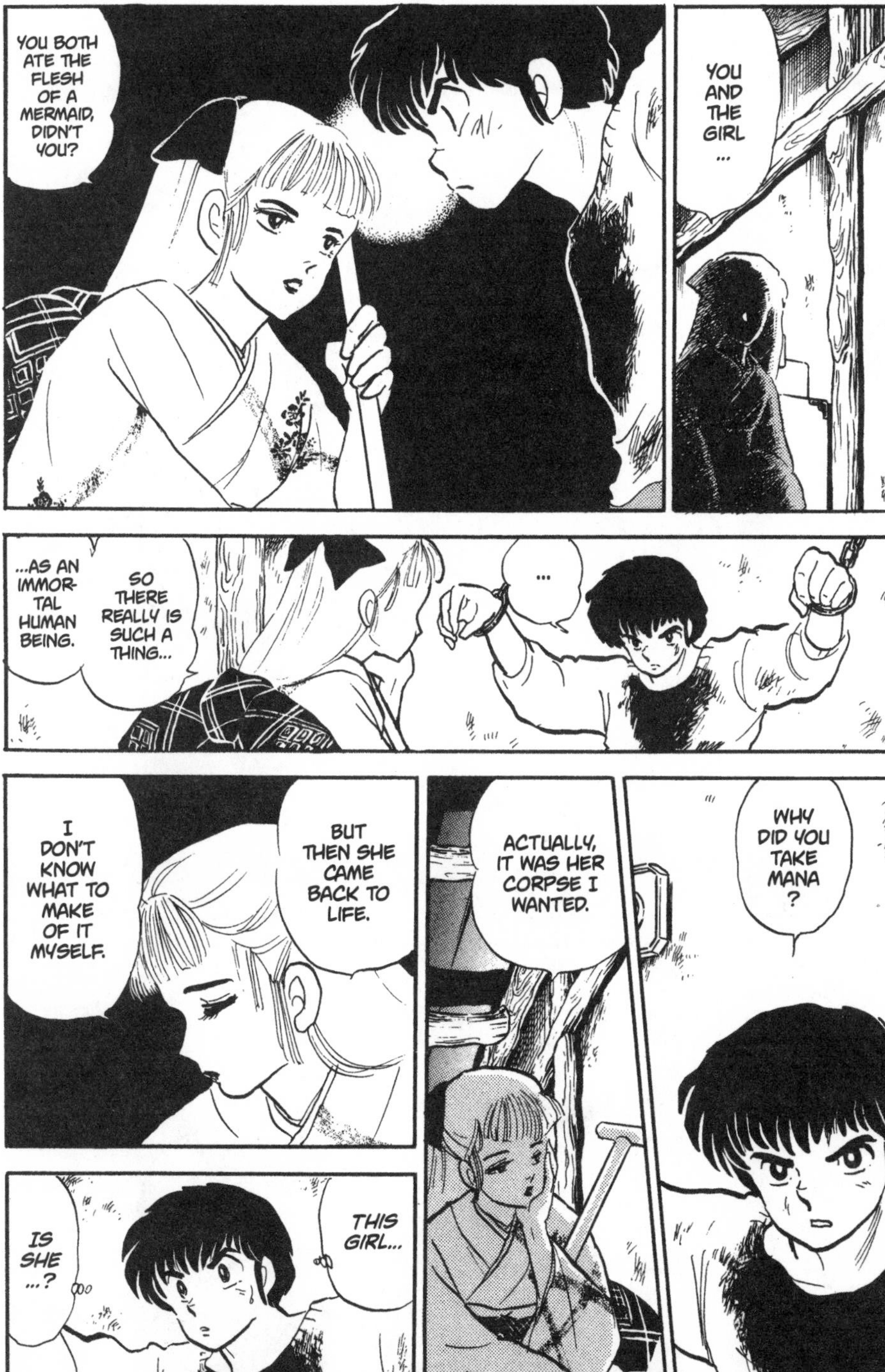
YOU AND THE GIRL ...
YOU BOTH ATE THE FLESH OF A MERMAID, DIDN'T YOU?
...
SO THERE REALLY IS SUCH A THING...
...AS AN IMMORTAL HUMAN BEING.
WHY DID YOU TAKE MANA?
ACTUALLY, IT WAS HER CORPSE I WANTED.
BUT THEN SHE CAME BACK TO LIFE.
I DON'T KNOW WHAT TO MAKE OF IT MYSELF.
THIS GIRL...
IS SHE ...?

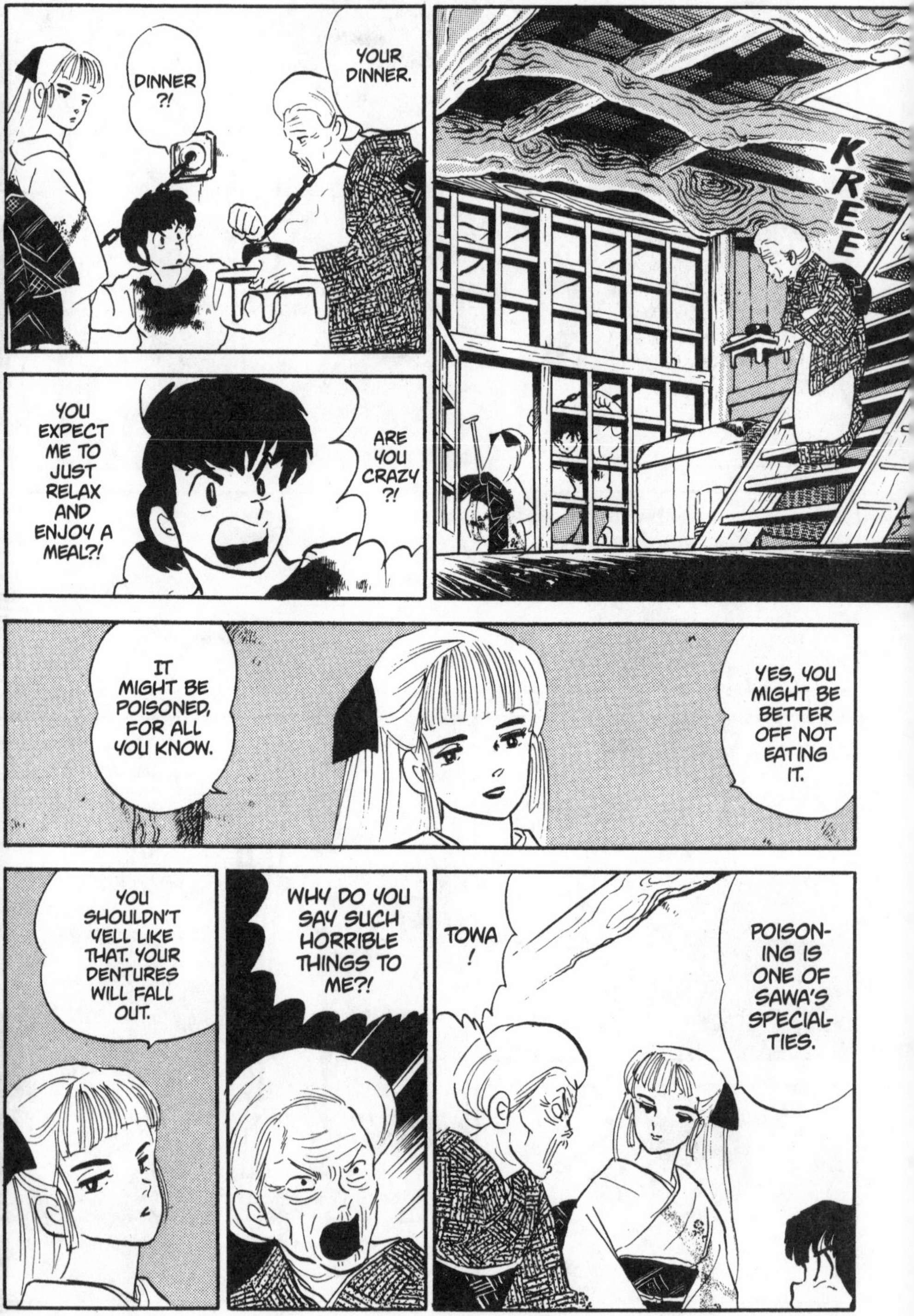
KREE
YOUR DINNER.
DINNER ?!
ARE YOU CRAZY ?!
YOU EXPECT ME TO JUST RELAX AND ENJOY A MEAL?!
YES, YOU MIGHT BE BETTER OFF NOT EATING IT.
IT MIGHT BE POISONED, FOR ALL YOU KNOW.
POISON-ING IS ONE OF SAWA'S SPECIAL-TIES.
TOWA !
WHY DO YOU SAY SUCH HORRIBLE THINGS TO ME?!
YOU SHOULDN'T YELL LIKE THAT. YOUR DENTURES WILL FALL OUT.

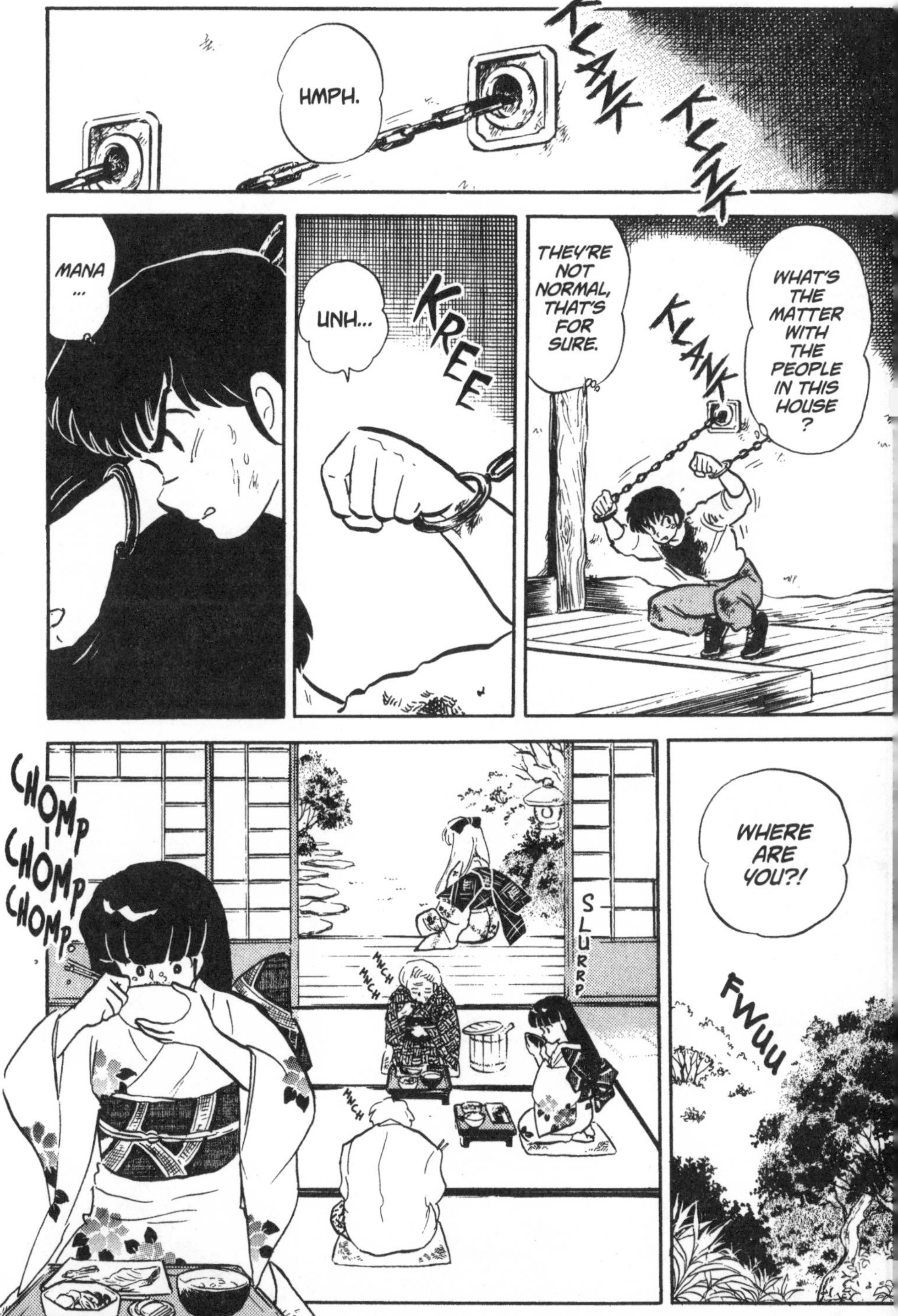
KLANK
KLINK
HMPH.
WHAT'S THE MATTER WITH THE PEOPLE IN THIS HOUSE?
KLANK
THEY'RE NOT NORMAL, THAT'S FOR SURE.
KREE
UNH...
MANA...
WHERE ARE YOU?!
FWUU
SLURRP
MNCH MNCH
MNCH
CHOMP CHOMP CHOMP

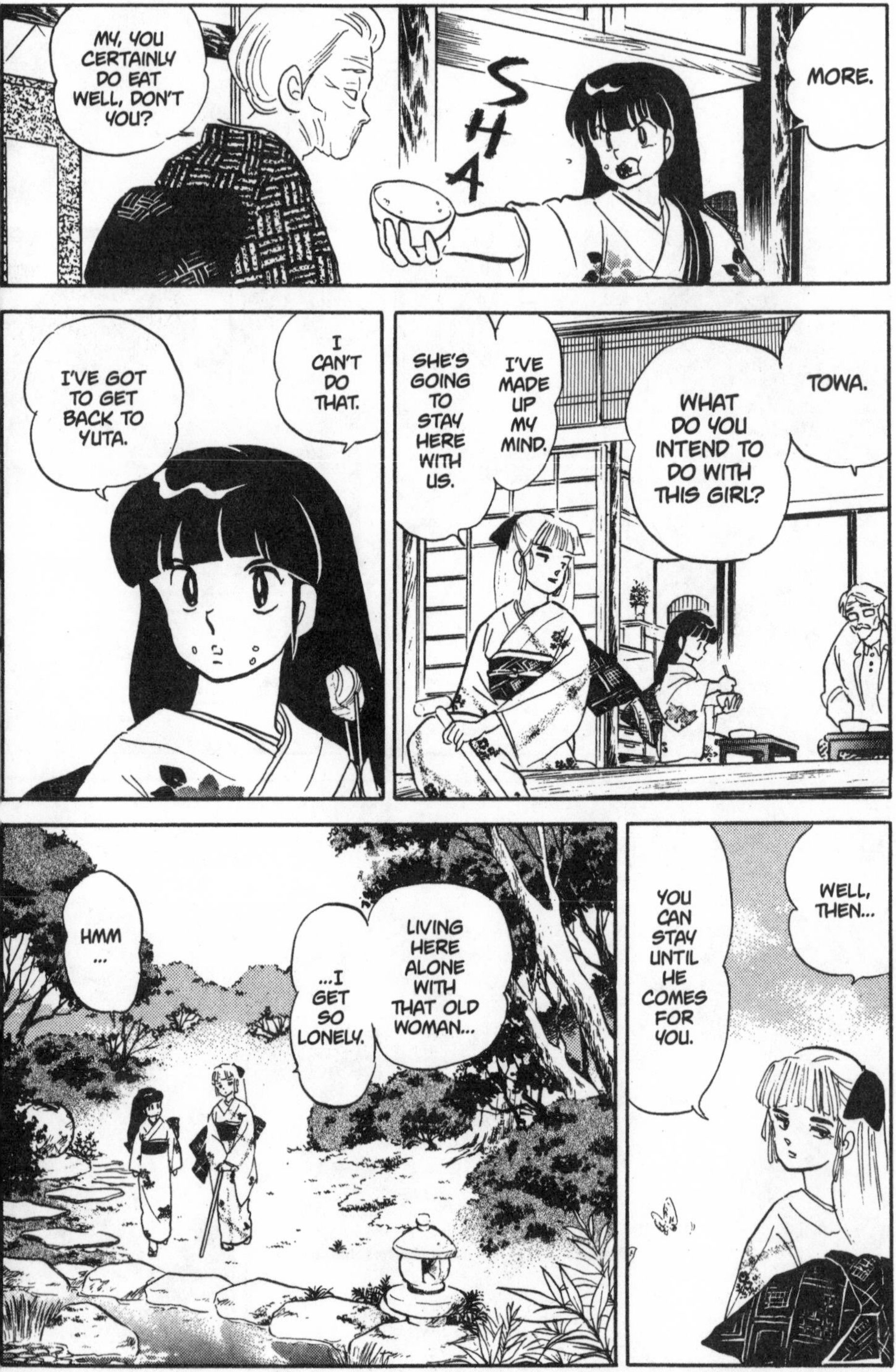
MORE.
SHA
MY, YOU CERTAINLY DO EAT WELL, DON'T YOU?
TOWA.
WHAT DO YOU INTEND TO DO WITH THIS GIRL?
I'VE MADE UP MY MIND.
SHE'S GOING TO STAY HERE WITH US.
I CAN'T DO THAT.
I'VE GOT TO GET BACK TO YUTA.
WELL, THEN...
YOU CAN STAY UNTIL HE COMES FOR YOU.
LIVING HERE ALONE WITH THAT OLD WOMAN...
...I GET SO LONELY.
HMM...

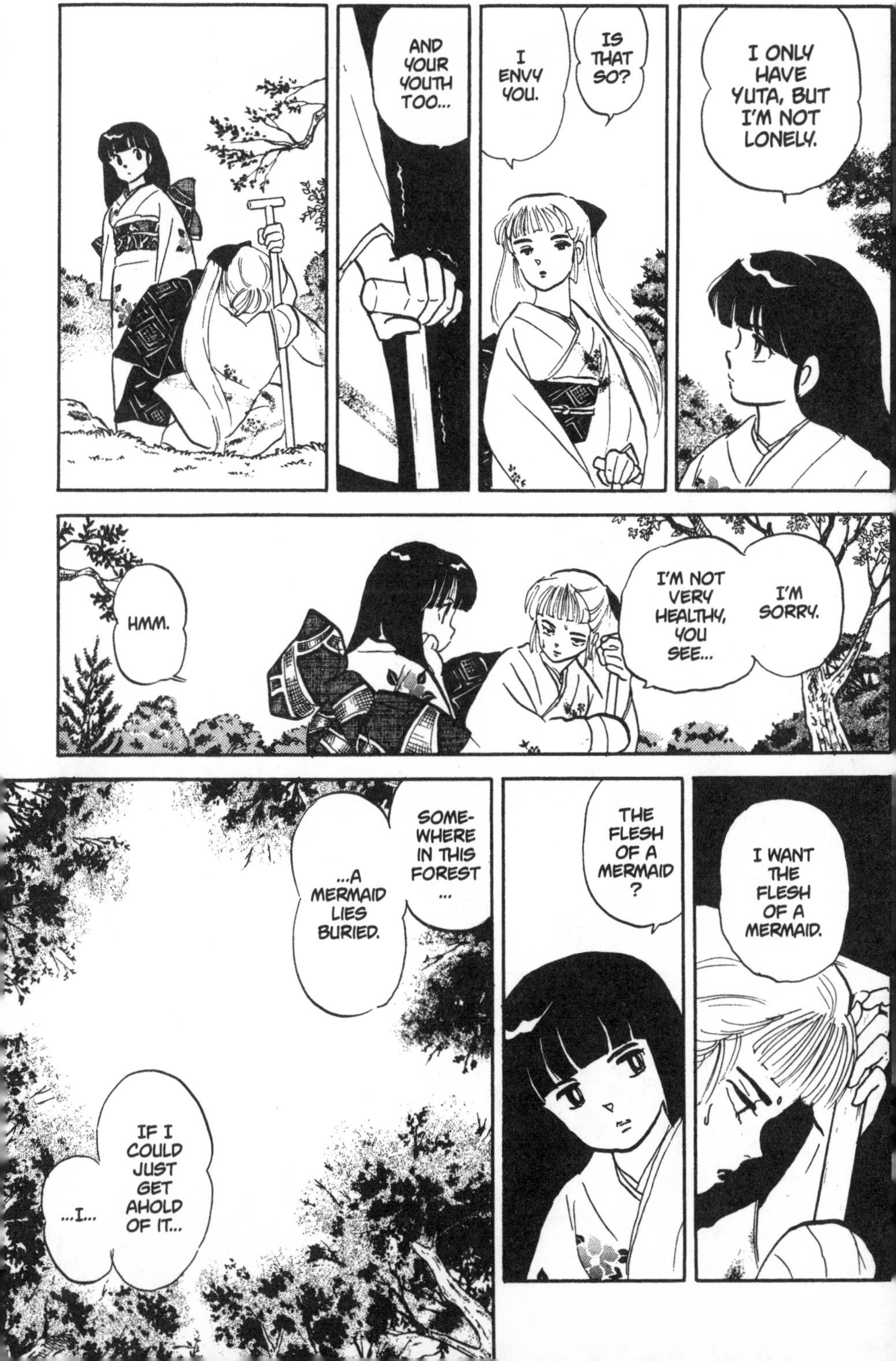
I ONLY HAVE YUTA, BUT I'M NOT LONELY.
IS THAT SO?
I ENVY YOU.
AND YOUR YOUTH TOO...
I'M SORRY.
I'M NOT VERY HEALTHY, YOU SEE...
HMM.
I WANT THE FLESH OF A MERMAID.
THE FLESH OF A MERMAID?
SOME-WHERE IN THIS FOREST...
...A MERMAID LIES BURIED.
IF I COULD JUST GET AHOLD OF IT...
...I...

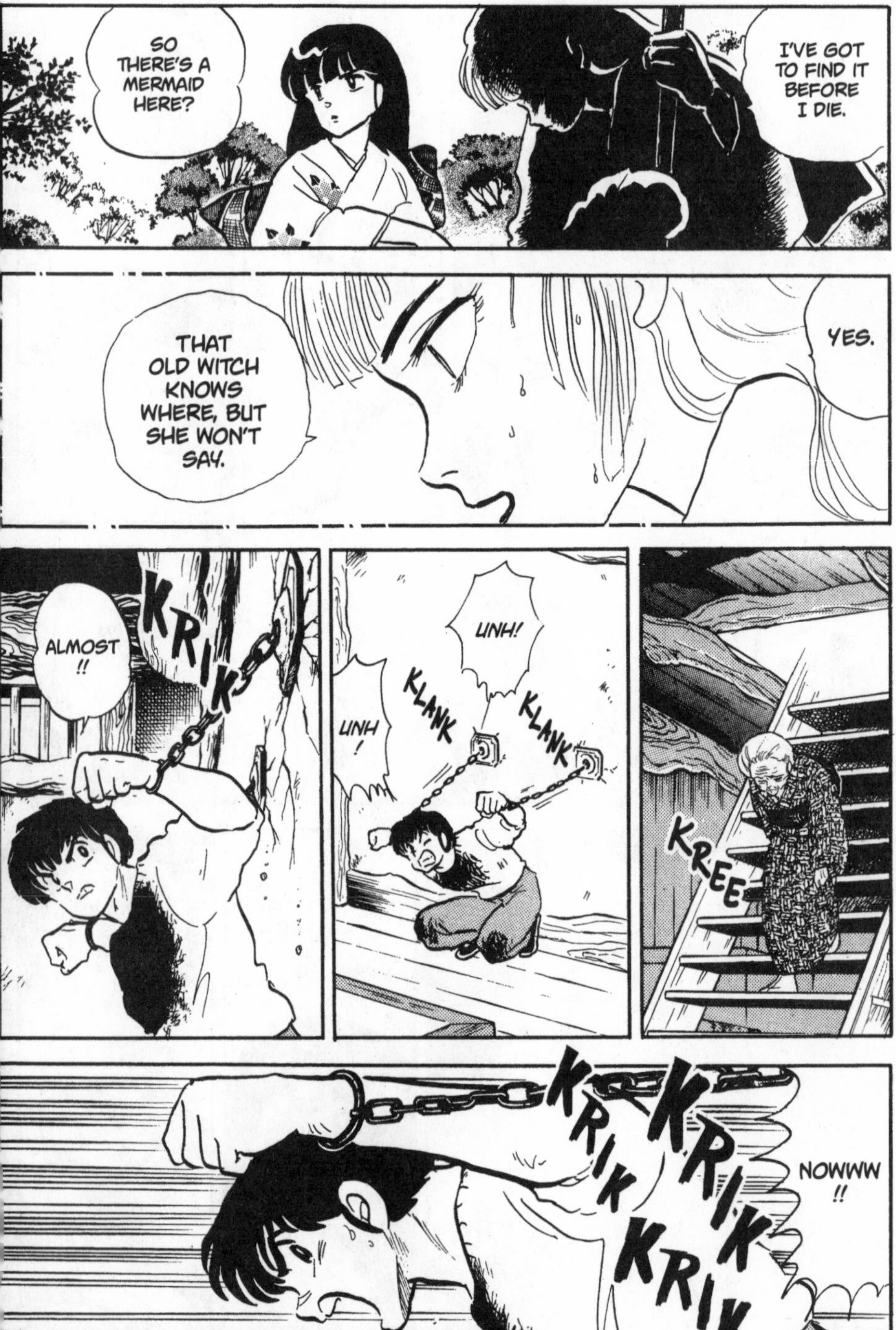
I'VE GOT TO FIND IT BEFORE I DIE.
SO THERE'S A MERMAID HERE?
YES.
THAT OLD WITCH KNOWS WHERE, BUT SHE WON'T SAY.
KREE
UNH!
KLANK
KLANK
UNH!
KRIK
ALMOST!!
NOWWW!!
KRIK KRIK KRIK

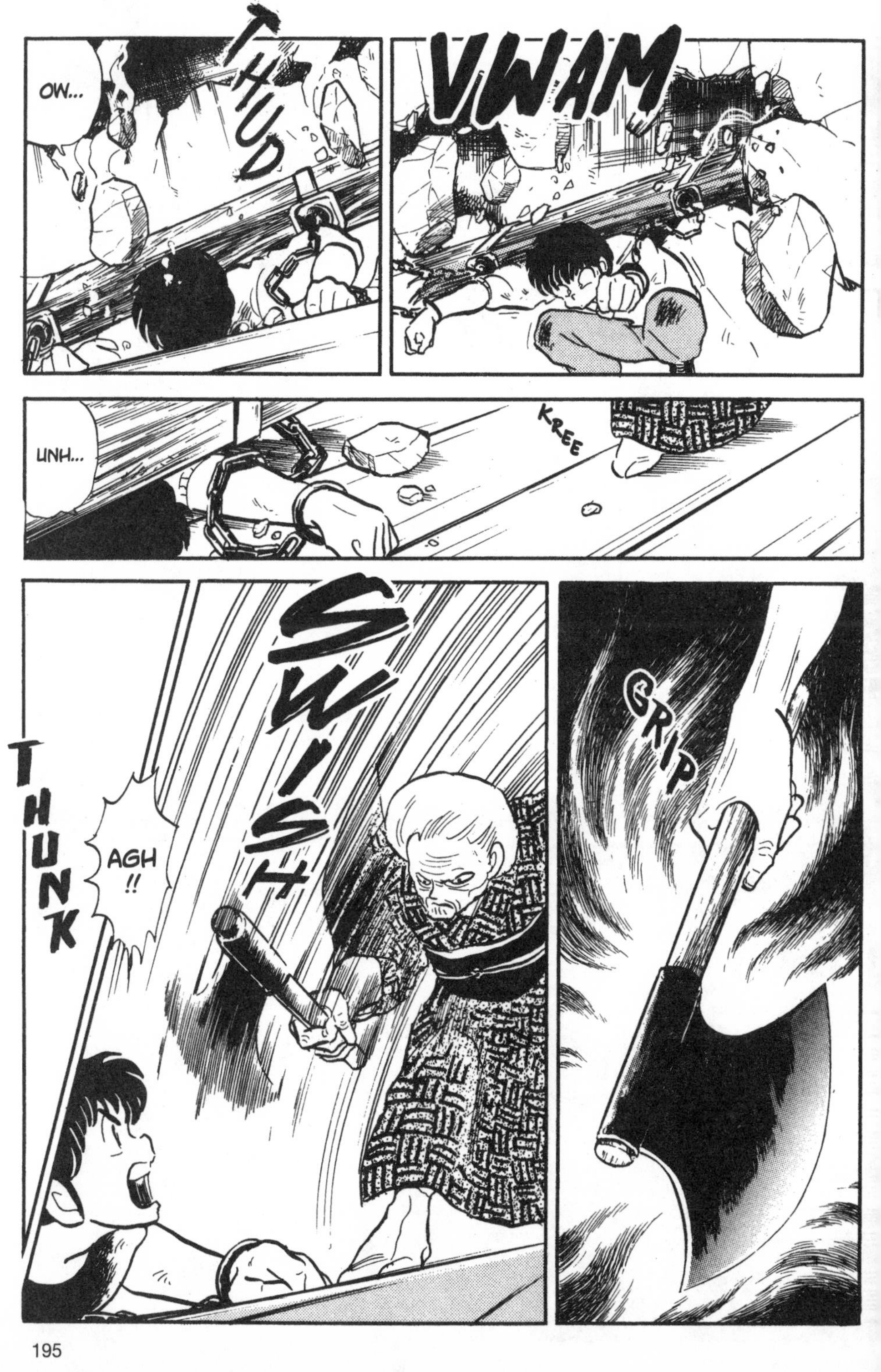
VWAM
THUD
OW...
KREE
UNH...
GRIP
SWISH
AGH!!
THUNK

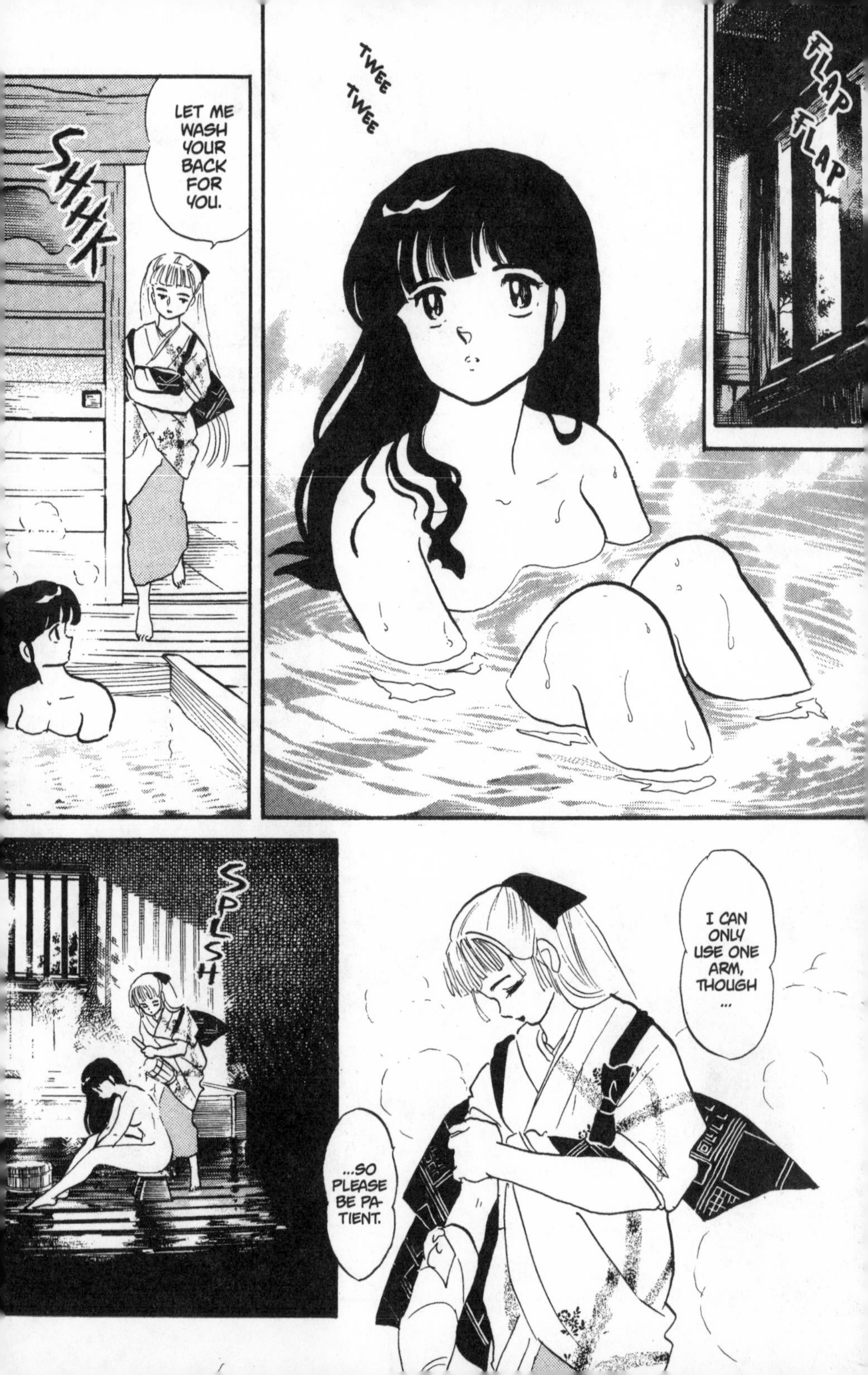
FLAP FLAP
TWEE TWEE
SHHK
LET ME WASH YOUR BACK FOR YOU.
I CAN ONLY USE ONE ARM, THOUGH ...
...SO PLEASE BE PATIENT.
SPLSH

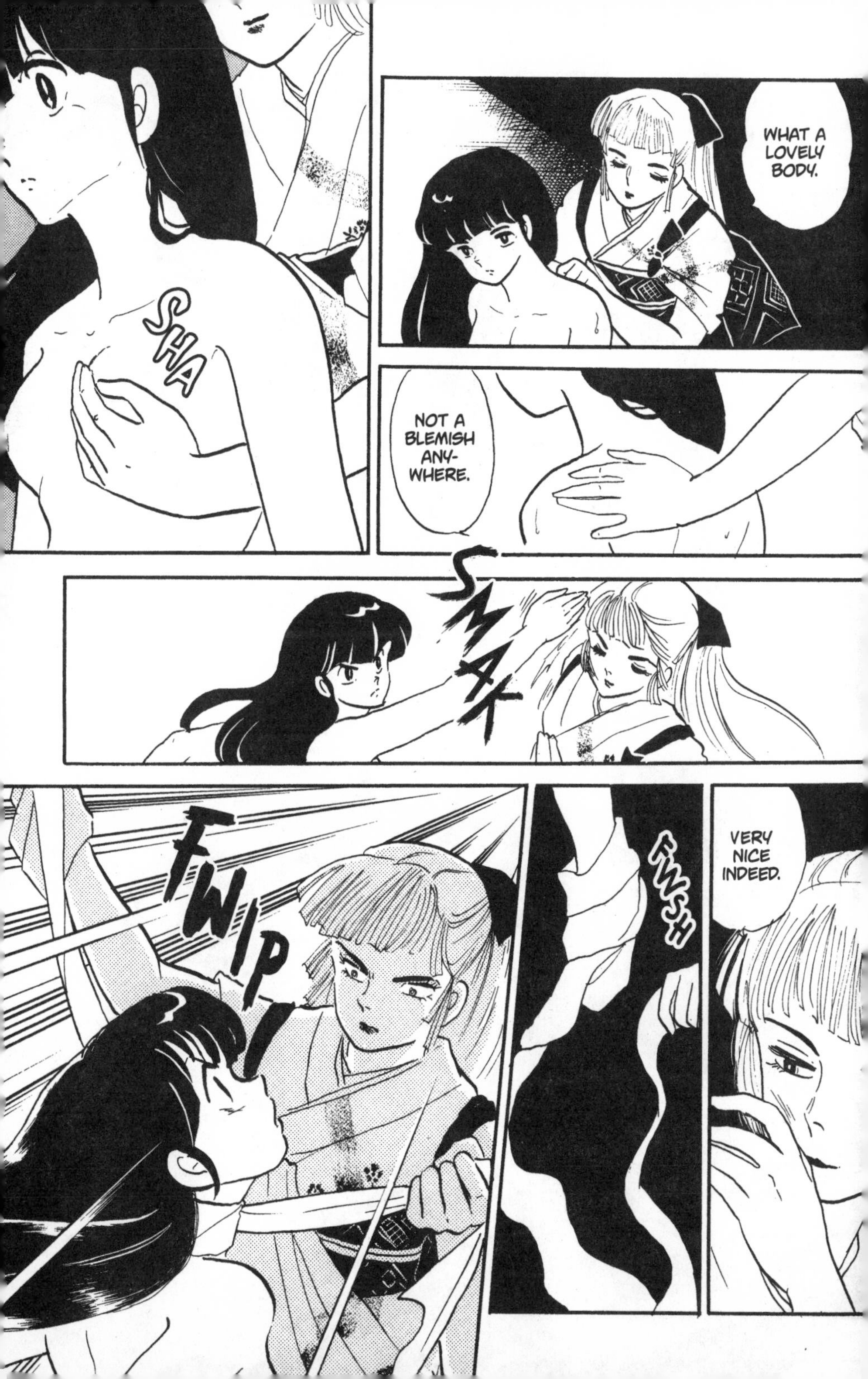
WHAT A LOVELY BODY.
NOT A BLEMISH ANY-WHERE.
SHA
SMAK
VERY NICE INDEED.
FWSH
FWIP

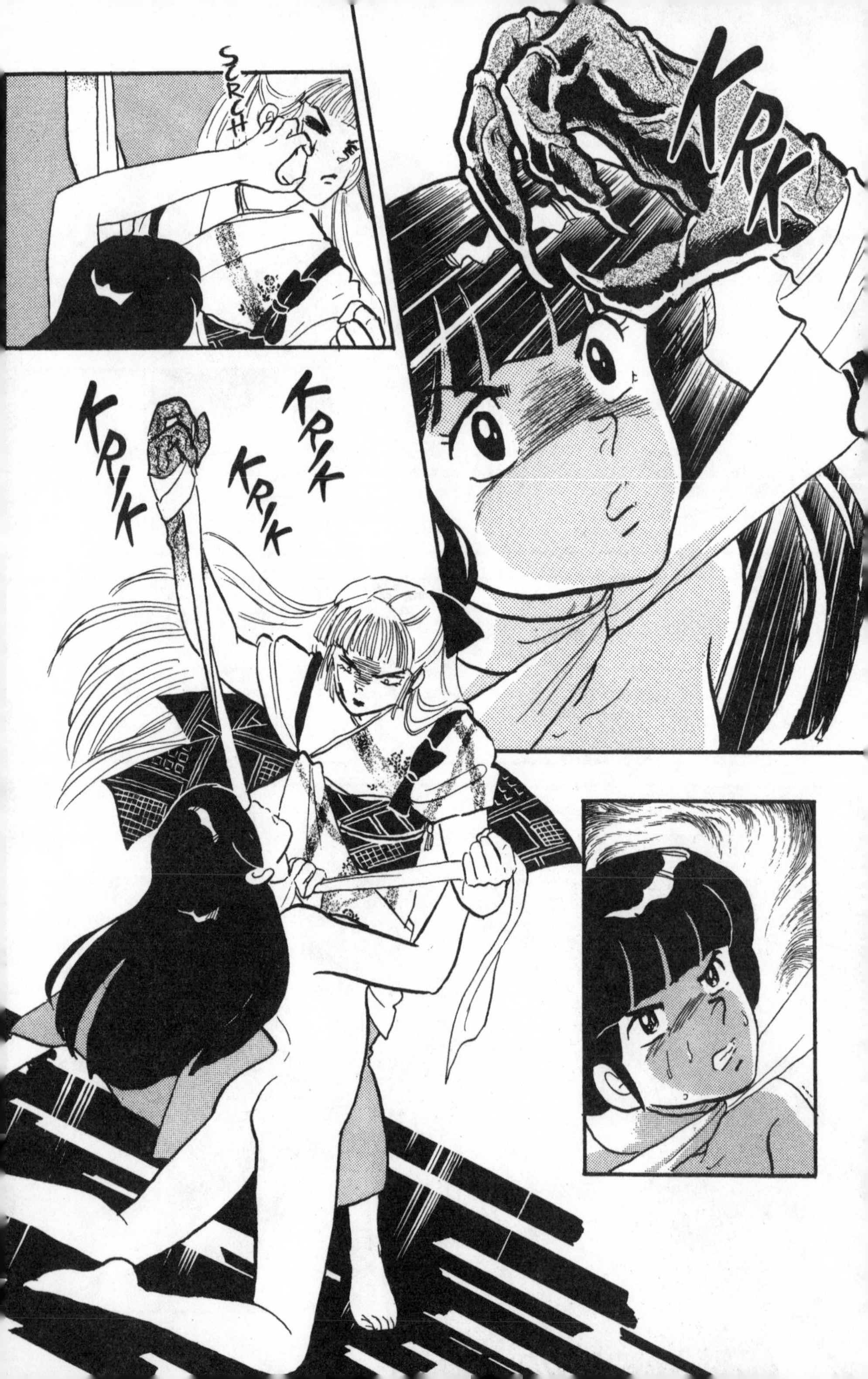
KRK
SCRCH
KRIK
KRIK
KRIK

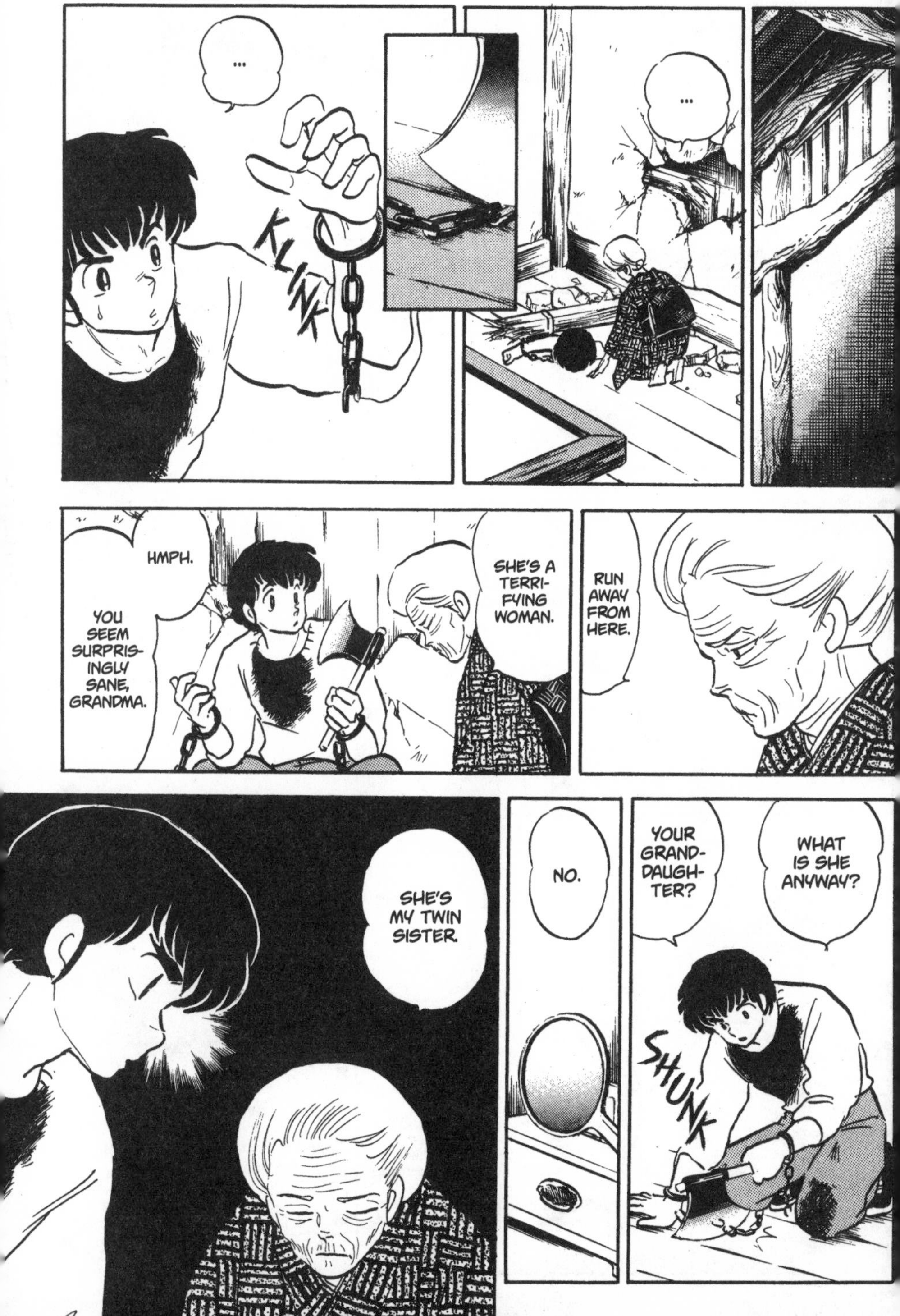
...
...
KLINK
RUN AWAY FROM HERE.
SHE'S A TERRI-FYING WOMAN.
HMPH.
YOU SEEM SURPRIS-INGLY SANE, GRANDMA.
WHAT IS SHE ANYWAY?
YOUR GRAND-DAUGH-TER?
SHUNK
NO.
SHE'S MY TWIN SISTER.

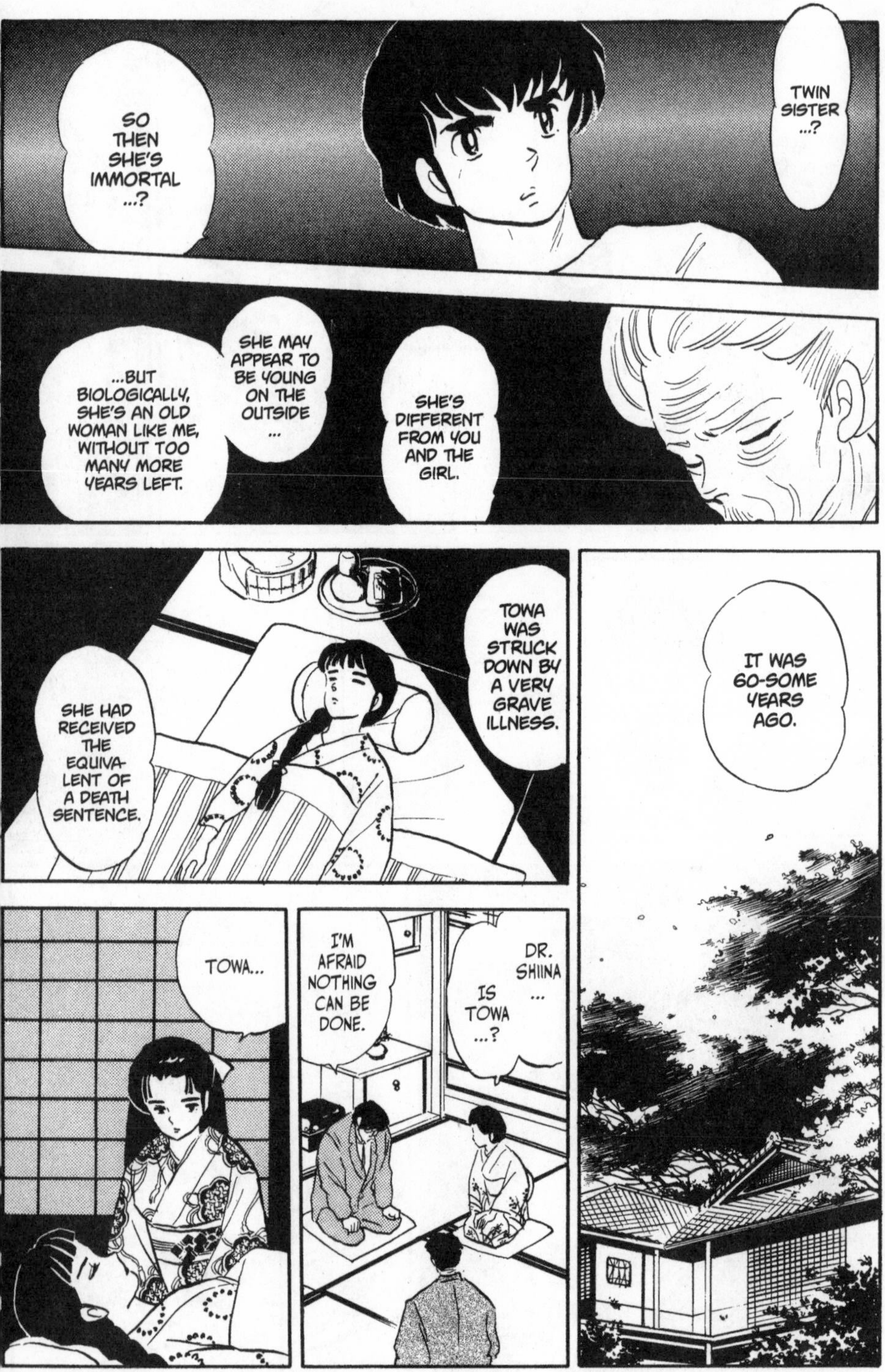
TWIN SISTER ...?
SO THEN SHE'S IMMORTAL ...?
SHE'S DIFFERENT FROM YOU AND THE GIRL.
SHE MAY APPEAR TO BE YOUNG ON THE OUTSIDE ...
...BUT BIOLOGICALLY, SHE'S AN OLD WOMAN LIKE ME, WITHOUT TOO MANY MORE YEARS LEFT.
IT WAS 60-SOME YEARS AGO.
TOWA WAS STRUCK DOWN BY A VERY GRAVE ILLNESS.
SHE HAD RECEIVED THE EQUIVA-LENT OF A DEATH SENTENCE.
DR. SHIINA ...
IS TOWA ...?
I'M AFRAID NOTHING CAN BE DONE.
TOWA...

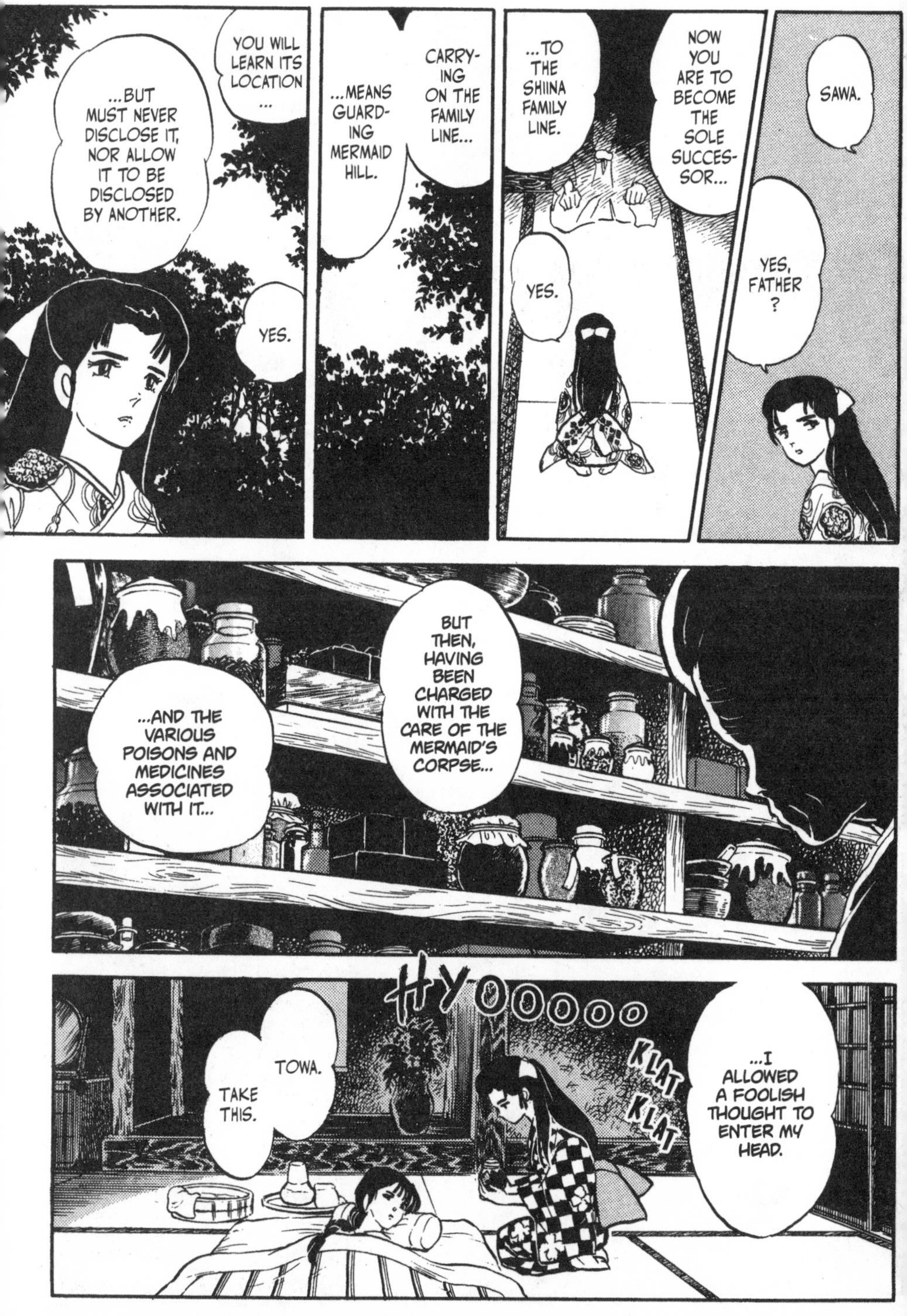
SAWA.
YES, FATHER ?
NOW YOU ARE TO BECOME THE SOLE SUCCES-SOR...
...TO THE SHIINA FAMILY LINE.
YES.
CARRY-ING ON THE FAMILY LINE...
...MEANS GUARD-ING MERMAID HILL.
YOU WILL LEARN ITS LOCATION ...
...BUT MUST NEVER DISCLOSE IT, NOR ALLOW IT TO BE DISCLOSED BY ANOTHER.
YES.
BUT THEN, HAVING BEEN CHARGED WITH THE CARE OF THE MERMAID'S CORPSE...
...AND THE VARIOUS POISONS AND MEDICINES ASSOCIATED WITH IT...
HYOOOOO
...I ALLOWED A FOOLISH THOUGHT TO ENTER MY HEAD.
KLAT KLAT
TOWA.
TAKE THIS.

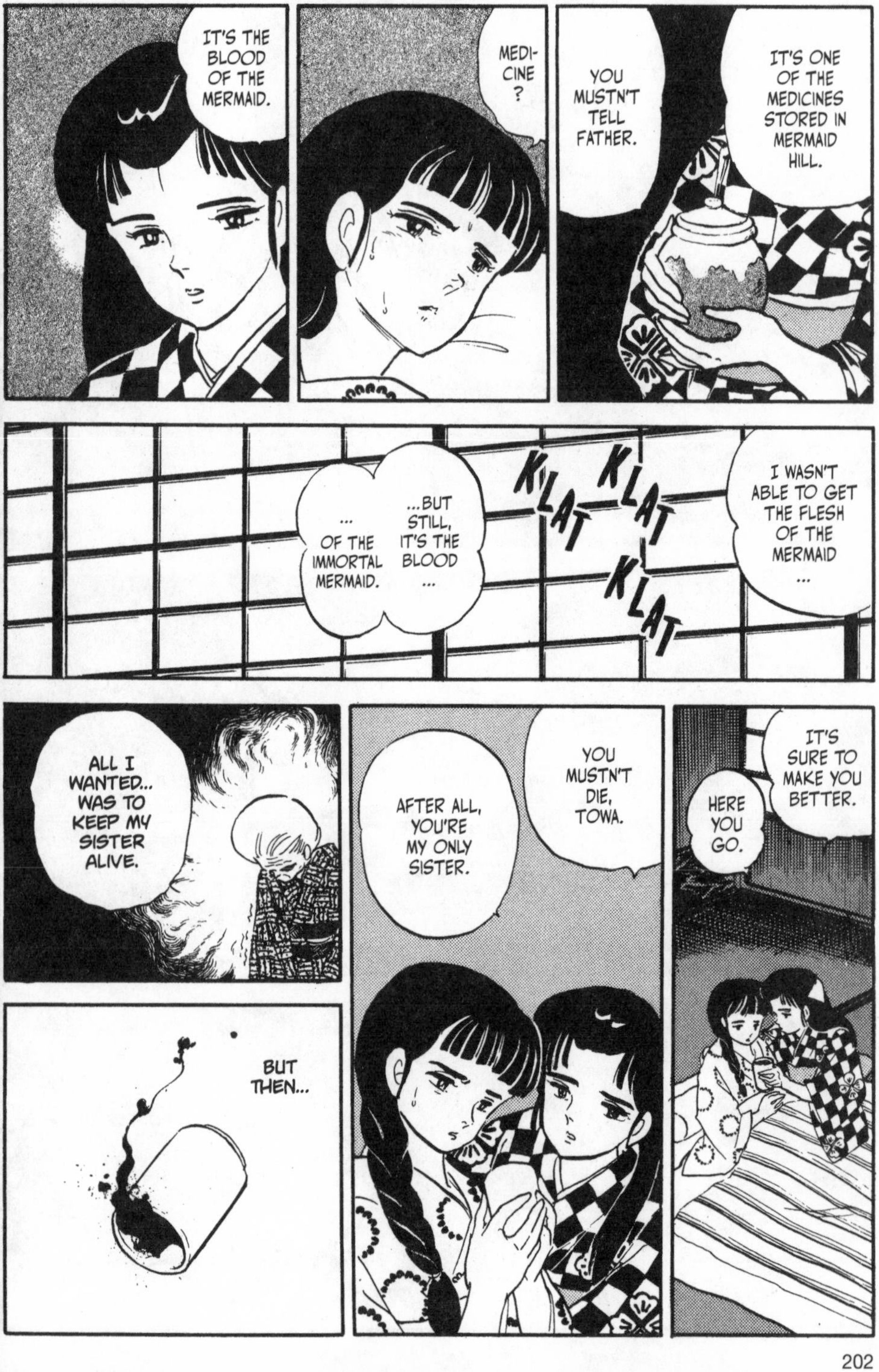
IT'S ONE OF THE MEDICINES STORED IN MERMAID HILL.
YOU MUSTN'T TELL FATHER.
MEDICINE?
IT'S THE BLOOD OF THE MERMAID.
I WASN'T ABLE TO GET THE FLESH OF THE MERMAID ...
KLAT KLAT
KLAT KLAT
...BUT STILL, IT'S THE BLOOD ...
... OF THE IMMORTAL MERMAID.
IT'S SURE TO MAKE YOU BETTER.
HERE YOU GO.
YOU MUSTN'T DIE, TOWA.
AFTER ALL, YOU'RE MY ONLY SISTER.
ALL I WANTED... WAS TO KEEP MY SISTER ALIVE.
BUT THEN...

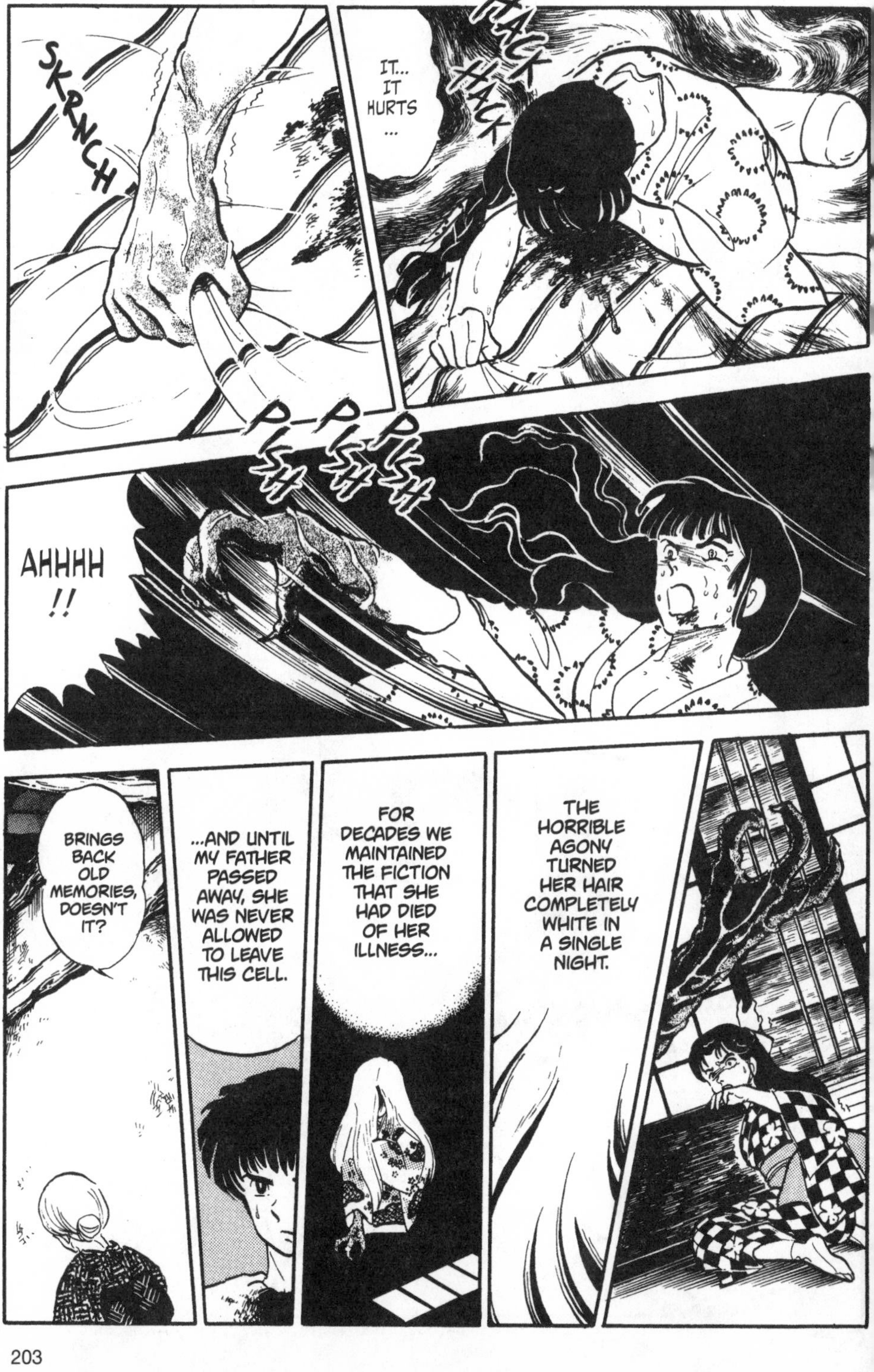
HACK HACK
IT... IT HURTS ...
SKRNCH
PISH PISH PISH
AHHHH !!
THE HORRIBLE AGONY TURNED HER HAIR COMPLETELY WHITE IN A SINGLE NIGHT.
FOR DECADES WE MAINTAINED THE FICTION THAT SHE HAD DIED OF HER ILLNESS...
...AND UNTIL MY FATHER PASSED AWAY, SHE WAS NEVER ALLOWED TO LEAVE THIS CELL.
BRINGS BACK OLD MEMORIES, DOESN'T IT?

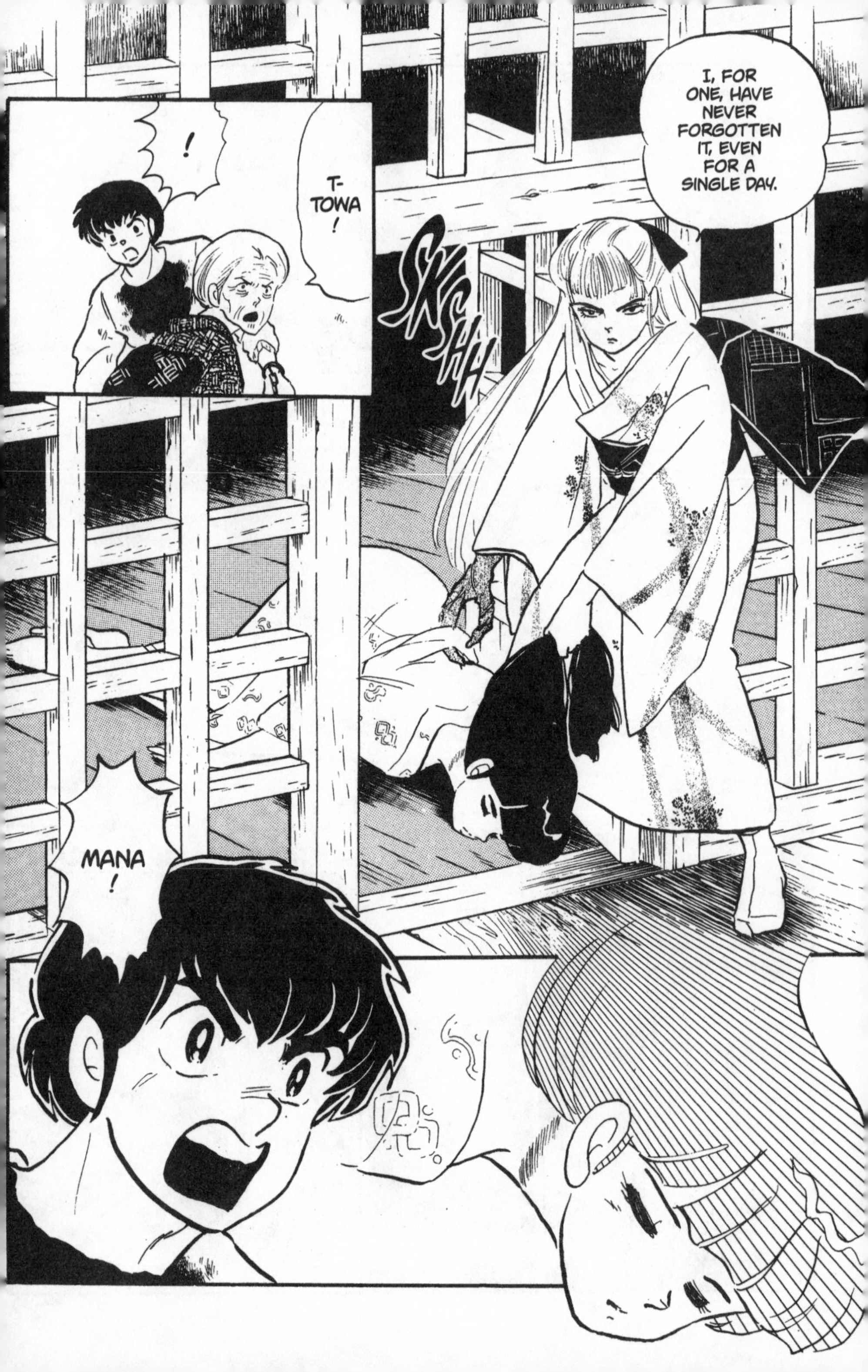
I, FOR ONE, HAVE NEVER FORGOTTEN IT, EVEN FOR A SINGLE DAY.
SKSHH
T-TOWA!
!
MANA!

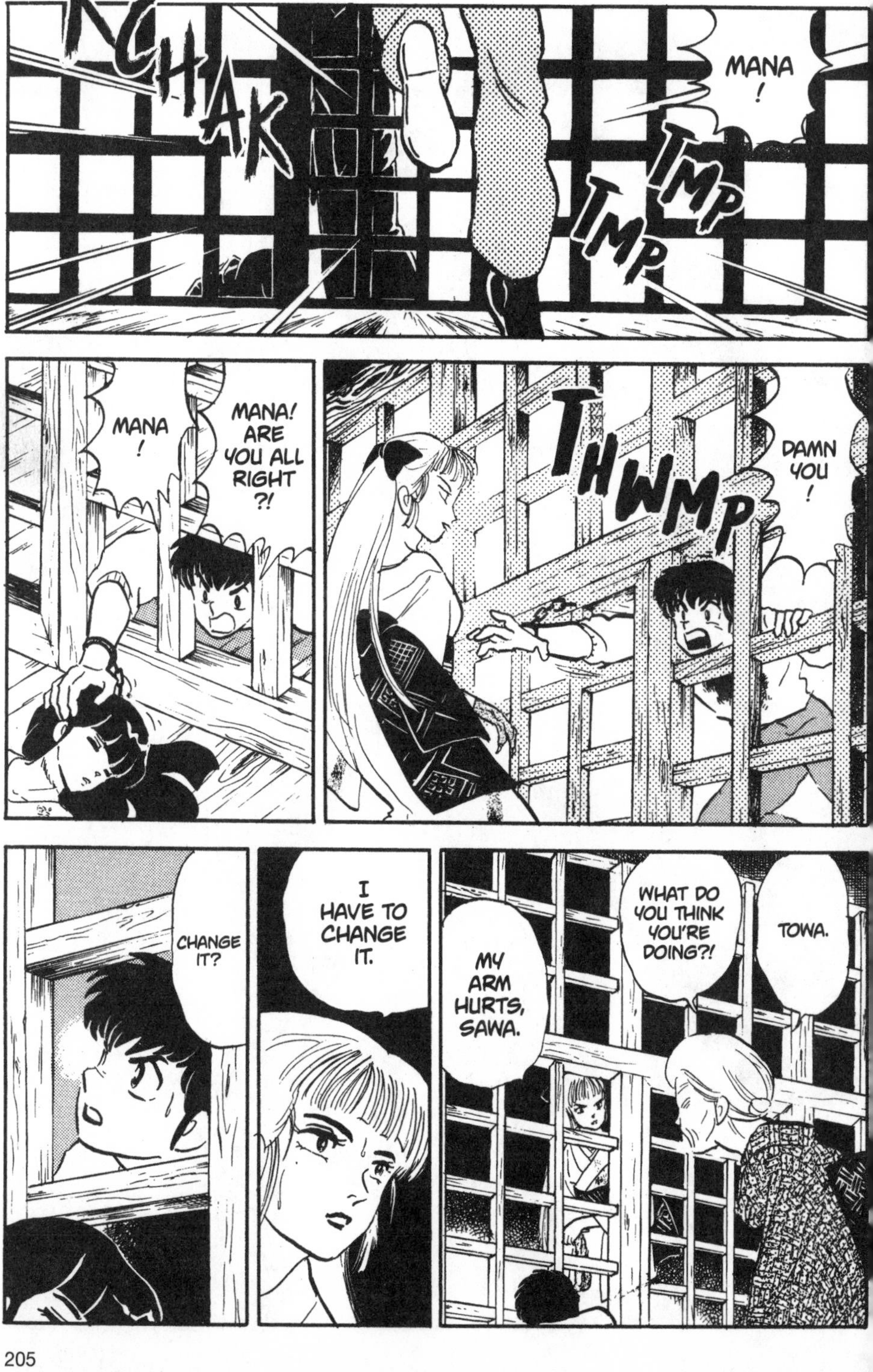
MANA!
KCHAK
TMP TMP
DAMN YOU!
THWMP
MANA! ARE YOU ALL RIGHT?!
MANA!
TOWA.
WHAT DO YOU THINK YOU'RE DOING?!
MY ARM HURTS, SAWA.
I HAVE TO CHANGE IT.
CHANGE IT?

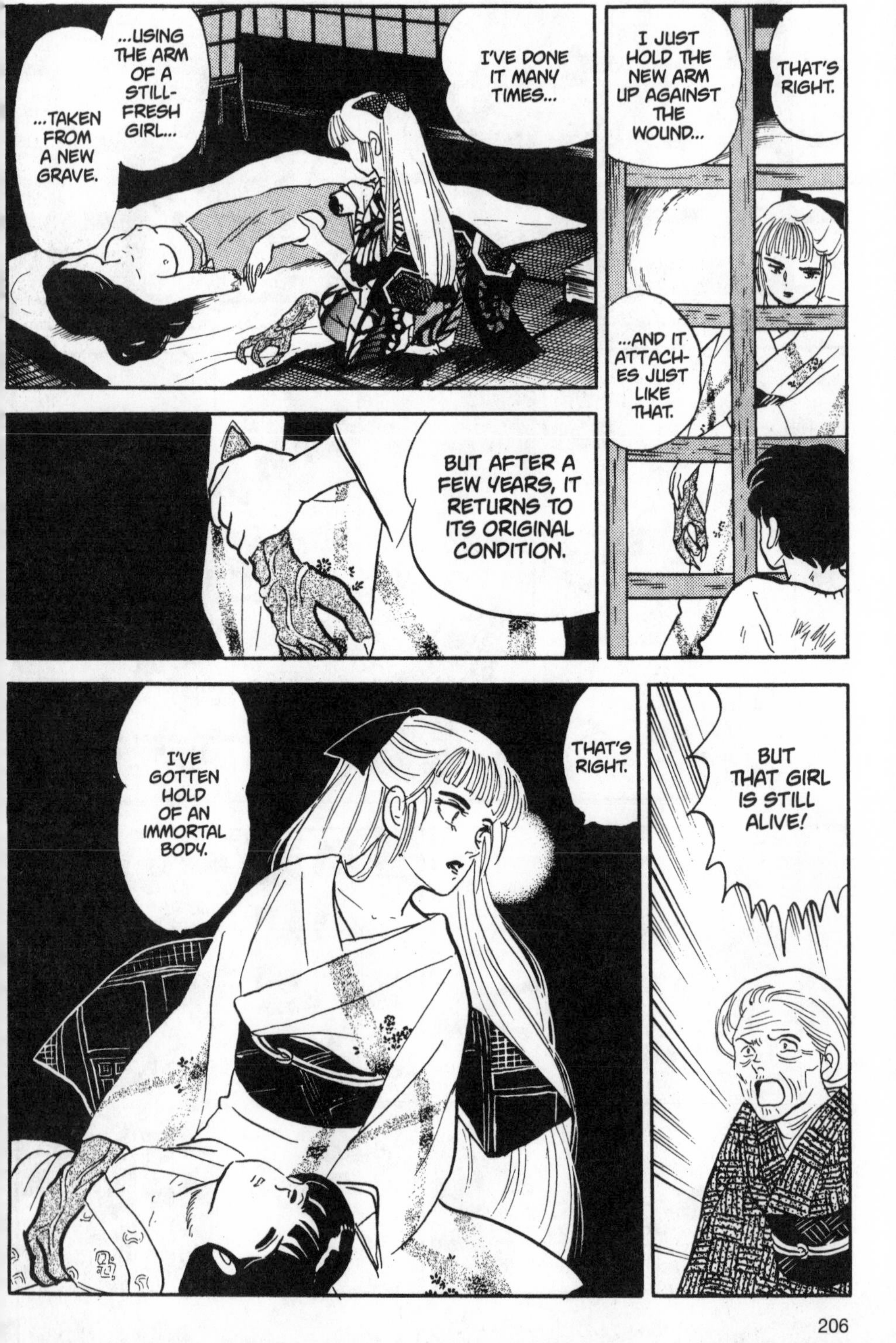
THAT'S RIGHT.
I JUST HOLD THE NEW ARM UP AGAINST THE WOUND...
...AND IT ATTACHES JUST LIKE THAT.
I'VE DONE IT MANY TIMES...
...USING THE ARM OF A STILL-FRESH GIRL...
...TAKEN FROM A NEW GRAVE.
BUT AFTER A FEW YEARS, IT RETURNS TO ITS ORIGINAL CONDITION.
BUT THAT GIRL IS STILL ALIVE!
THAT'S RIGHT.
I'VE GOTTEN HOLD OF AN IMMORTAL BODY.

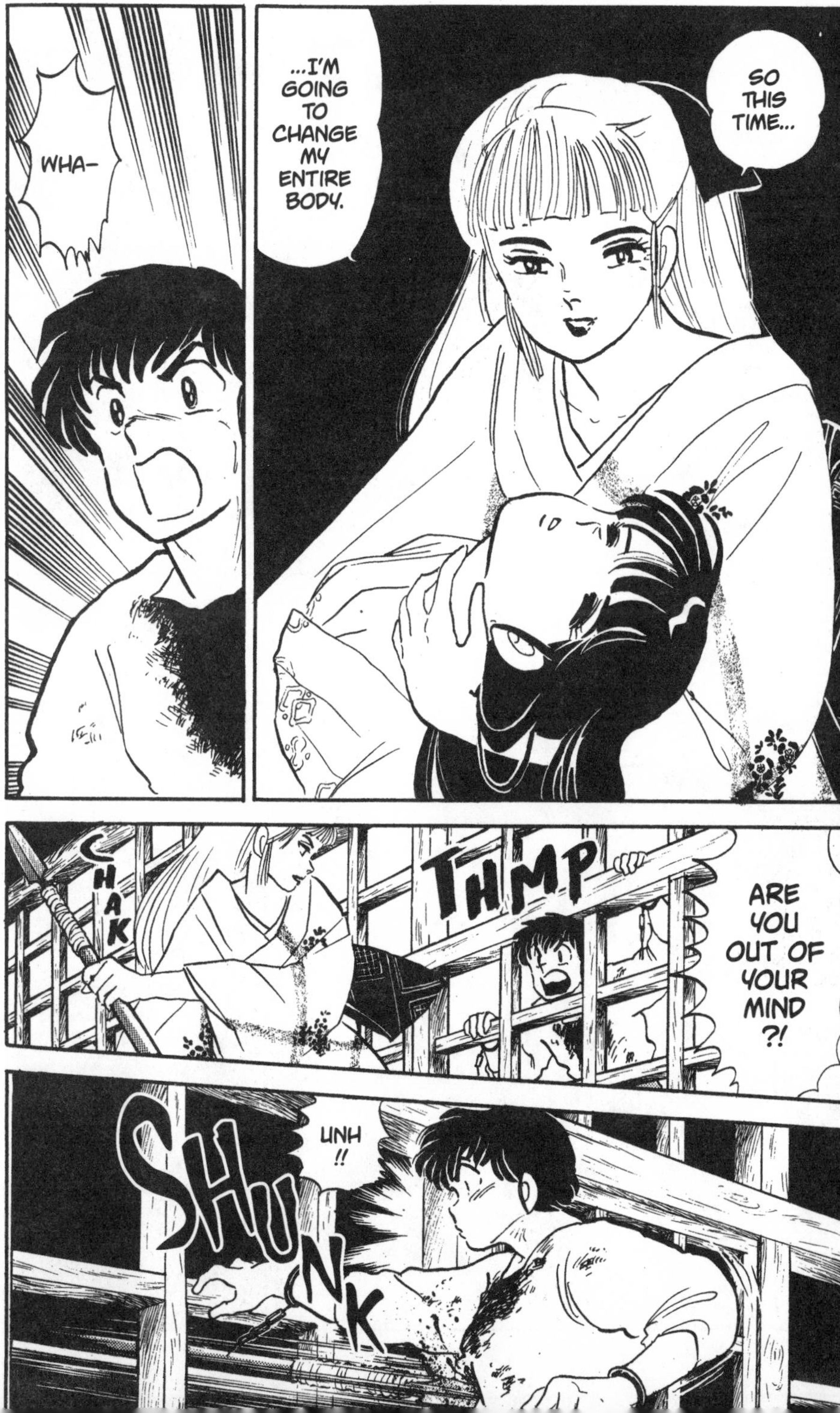
SO THIS TIME...
...I'M GOING TO CHANGE MY ENTIRE BODY.
WHA-
ARE YOU OUT OF YOUR MIND ?!
THMP
CHAK
UNH !!
SHUNK

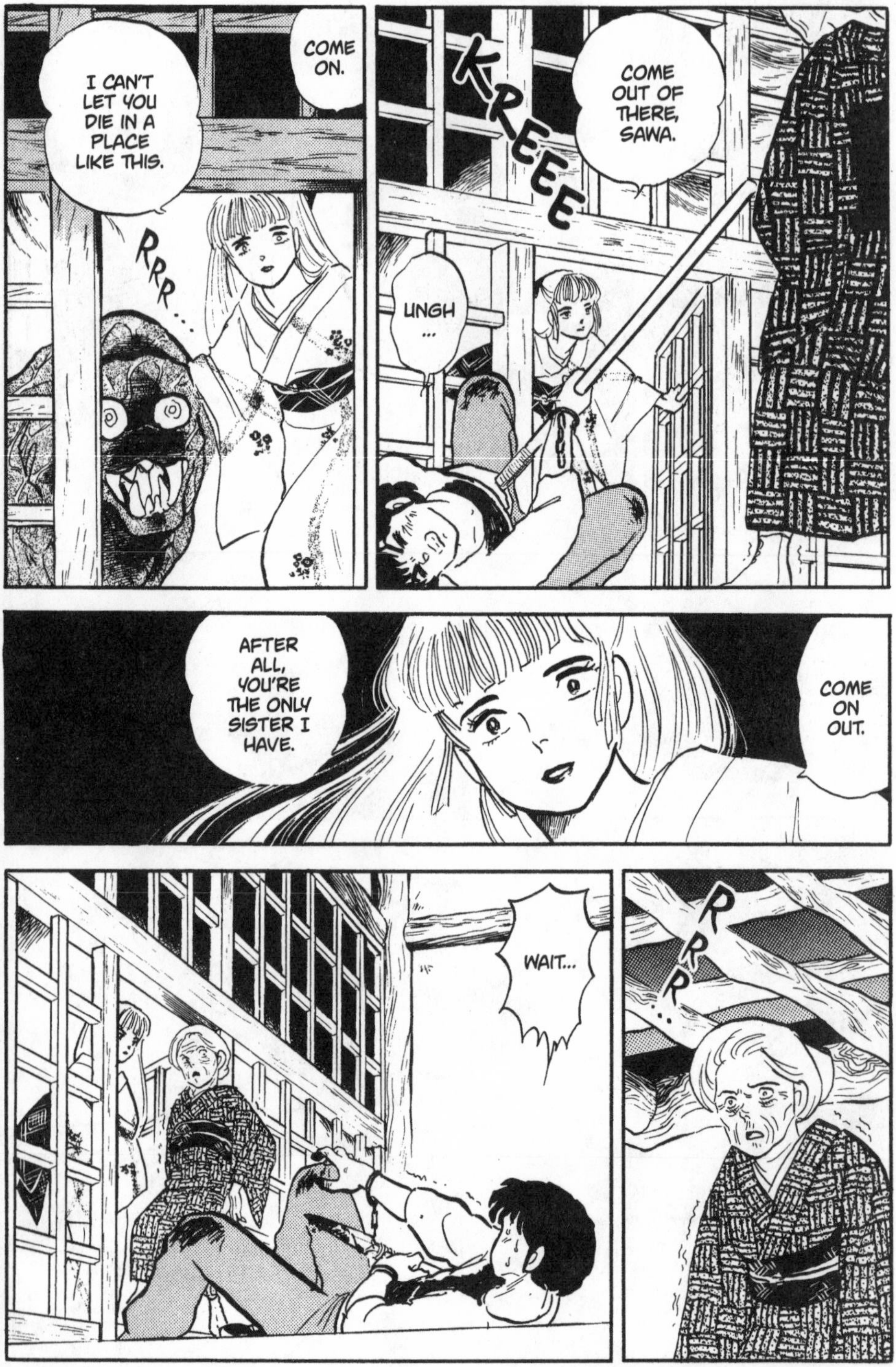
COME OUT OF THERE, SAWA.
KREEEE
UNGH...
COME ON.
I CAN'T LET YOU DIE IN A PLACE LIKE THIS.
RRR...
COME ON OUT.
AFTER ALL, YOU'RE THE ONLY SISTER I HAVE.
RRR...
WAIT...

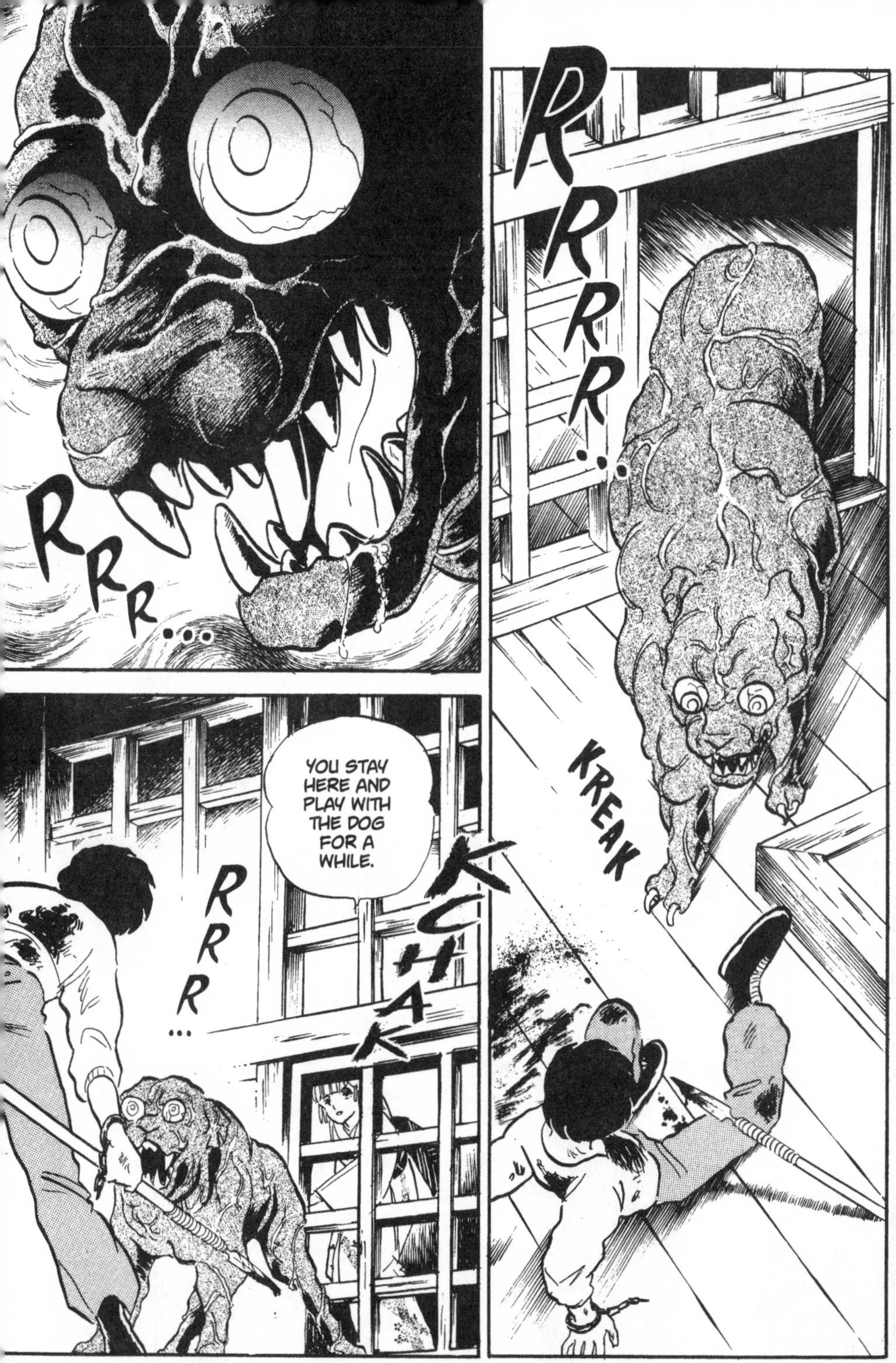
RRRRR...
KREAK
RRR...
YOU STAY HERE AND PLAY WITH THE DOG FOR A WHILE.
RRRR...
KCHAK

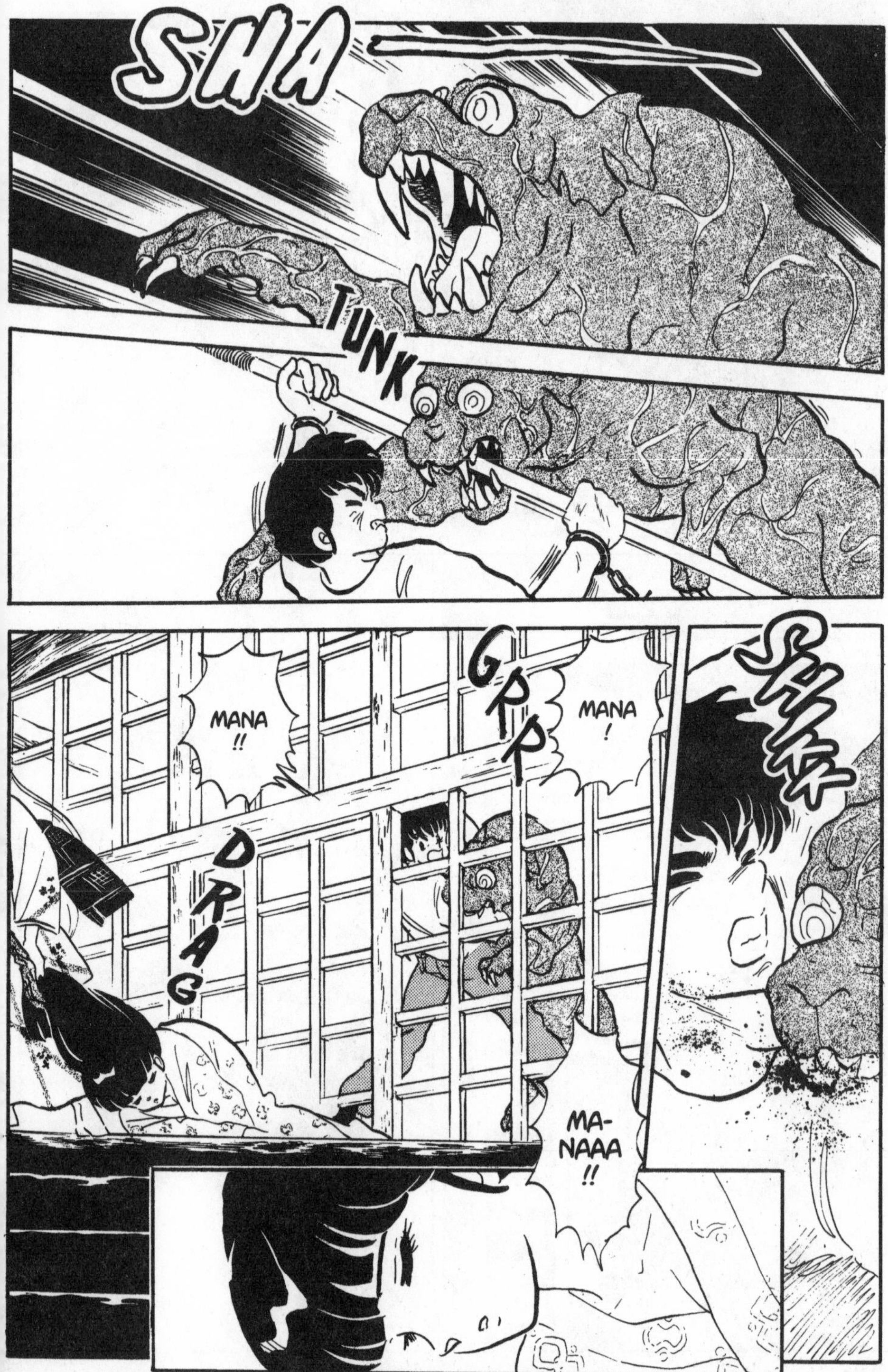
SHA
TUNK
SHIKK
MANA !
GRR
MANA !!
DRAG
MA-NAAA !!

Chapter 6: Mermaid Forest, Part 2

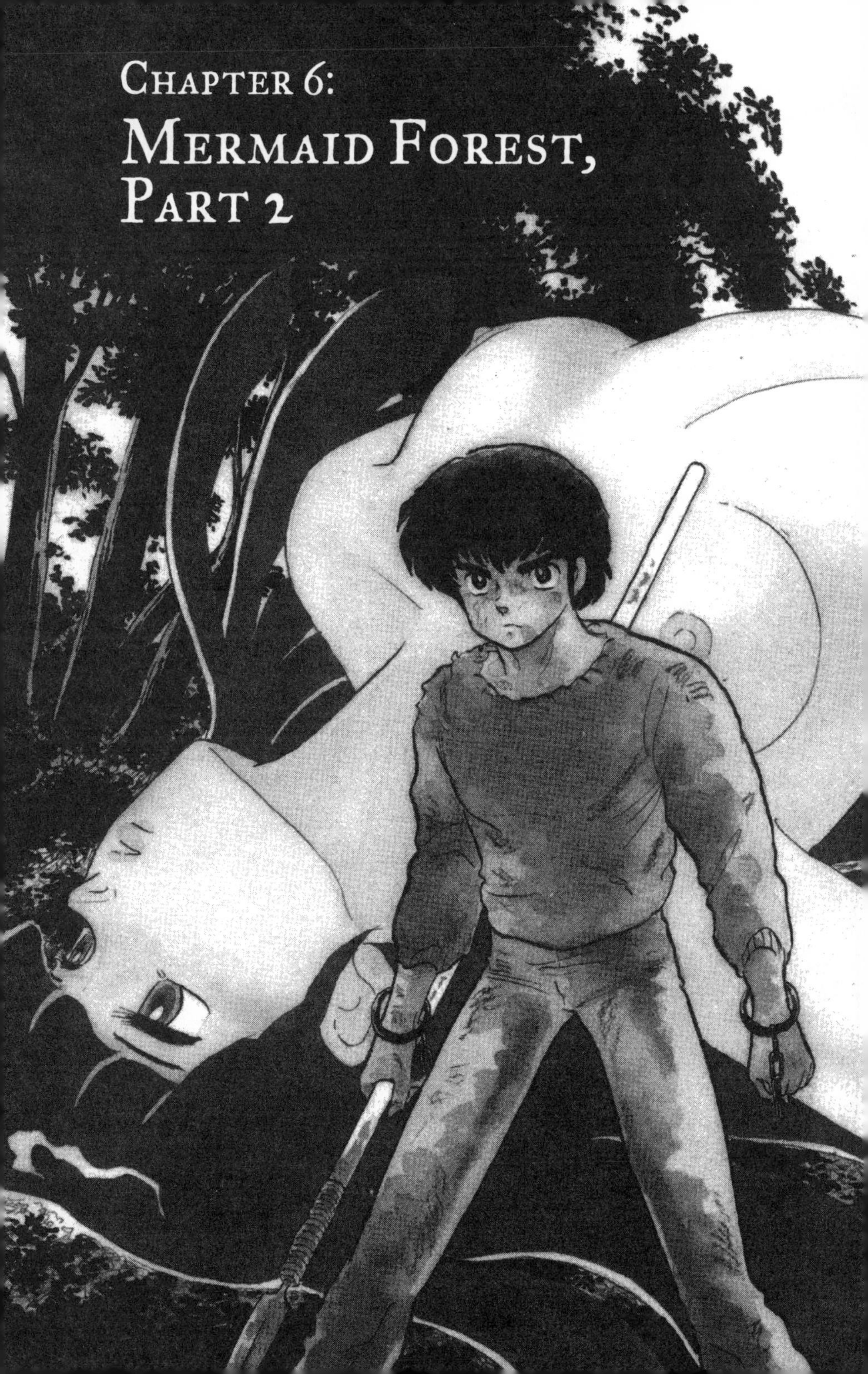

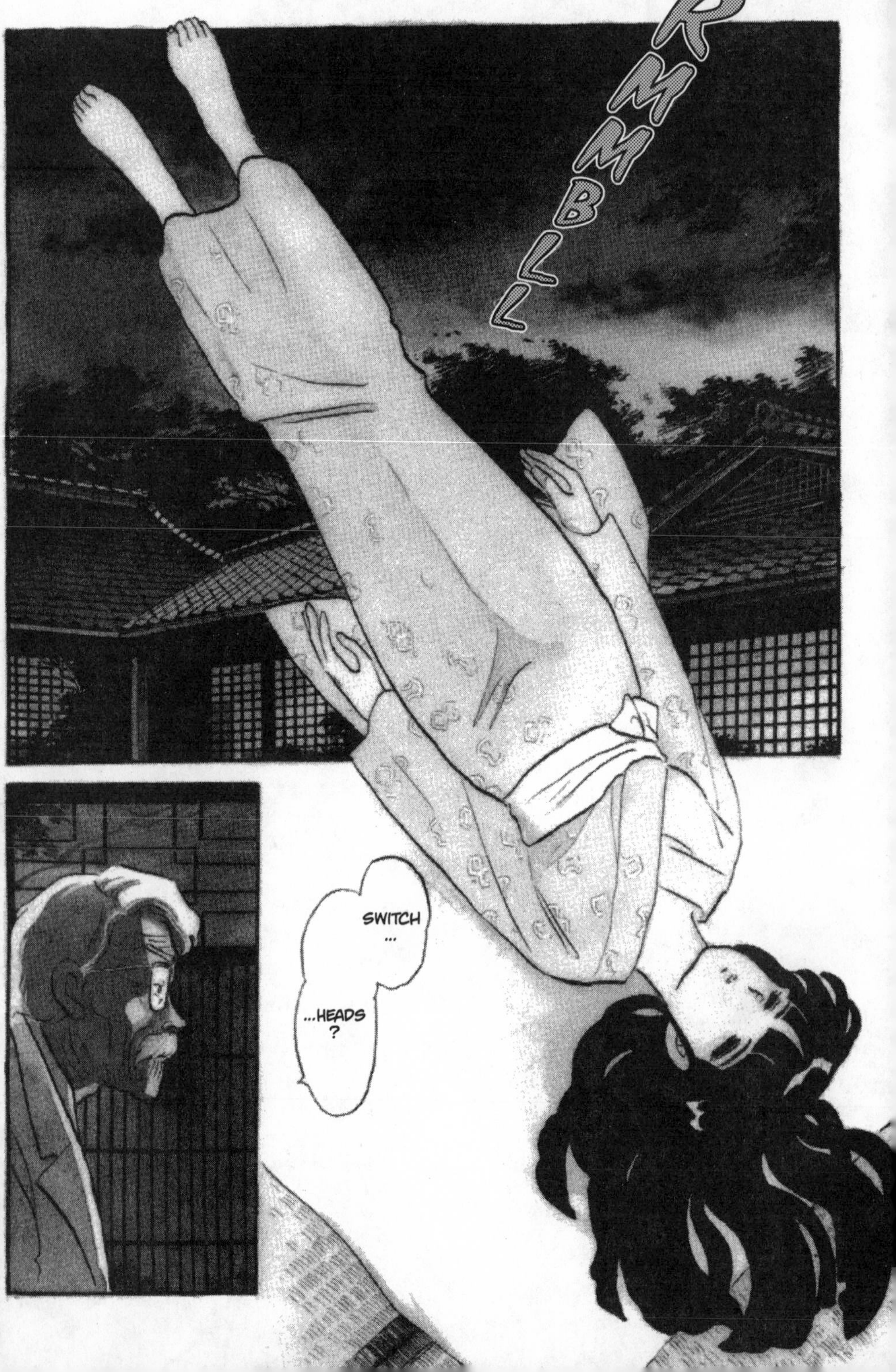
RMMBLL
SWITCH ...
...HEADS ?

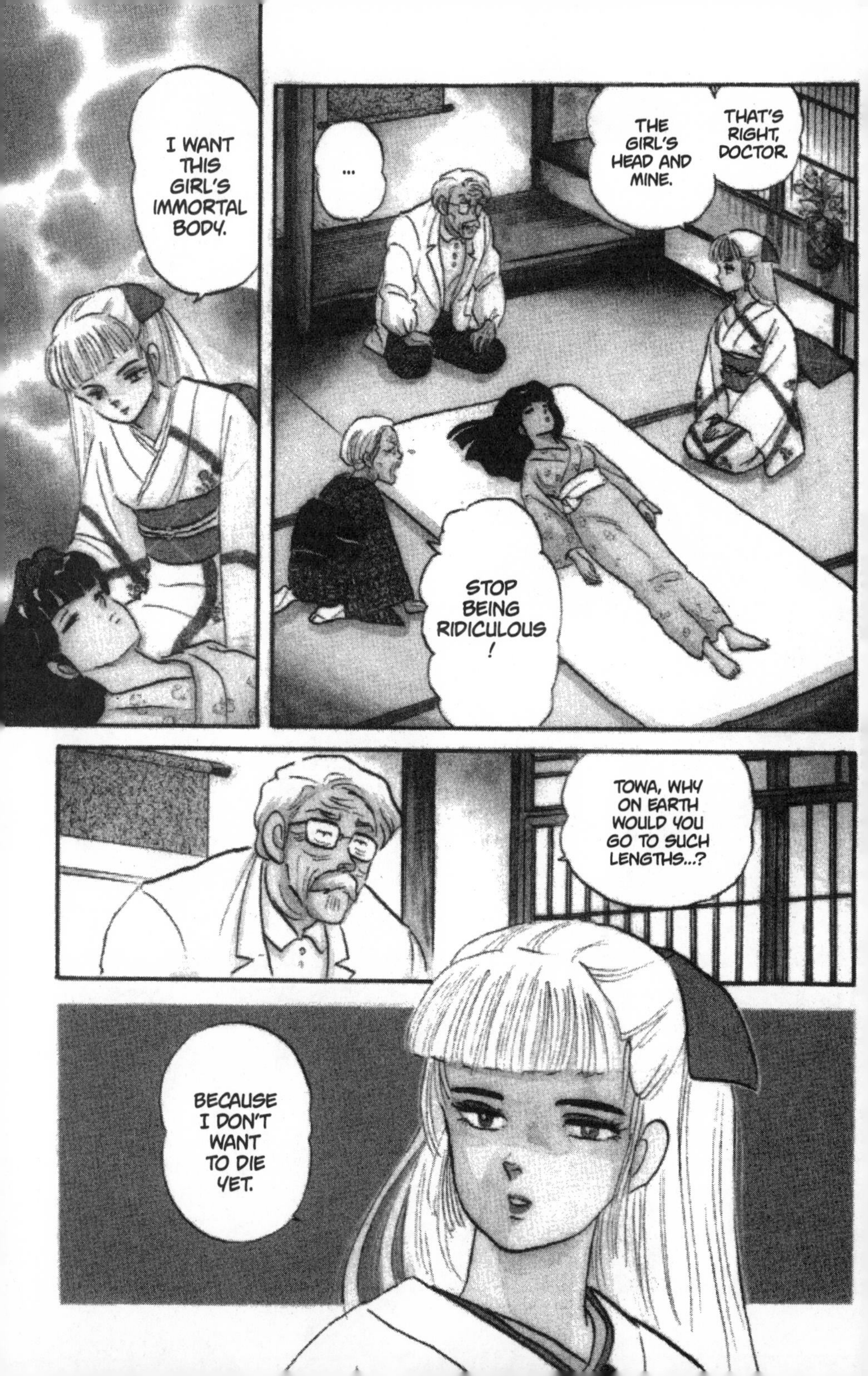
THE GIRL'S HEAD AND MINE.
THAT'S RIGHT, DOCTOR.
...
STOP BEING RIDICULOUS!
I WANT THIS GIRL'S IMMORTAL BODY.
TOWA, WHY ON EARTH WOULD YOU GO TO SUCH LENGTHS...?
BECAUSE I DON'T WANT TO DIE YET.

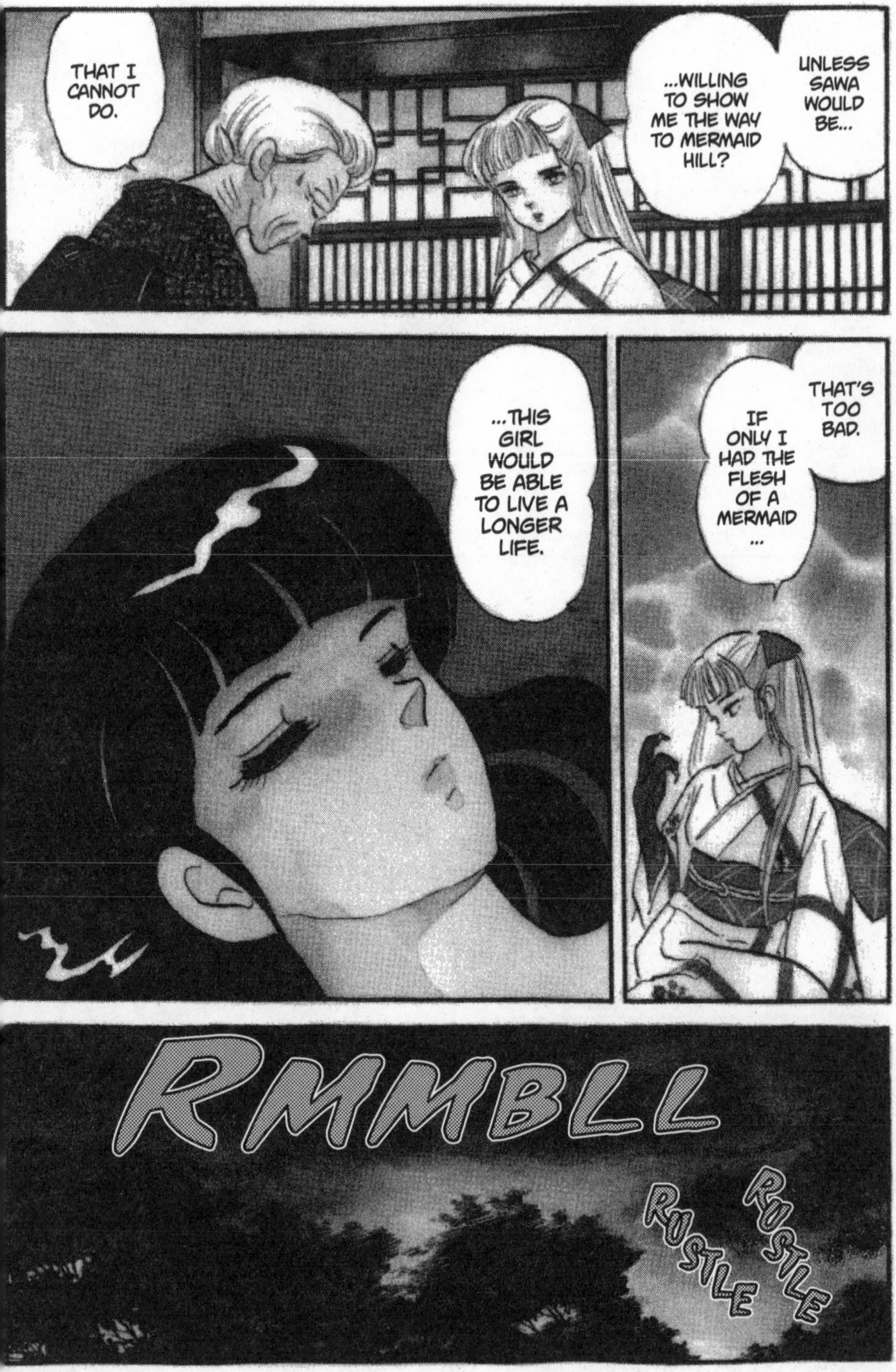
UNLESS SAWA WOULD BE...
...WILLING TO SHOW ME THE WAY TO MERMAID HILL?
THAT I CANNOT DO.
THAT'S TOO BAD.
IF ONLY I HAD THE FLESH OF A MERMAID ...
...THIS GIRL WOULD BE ABLE TO LIVE A LONGER LIFE.
RMMBLL
RUSTLE RUSTLE

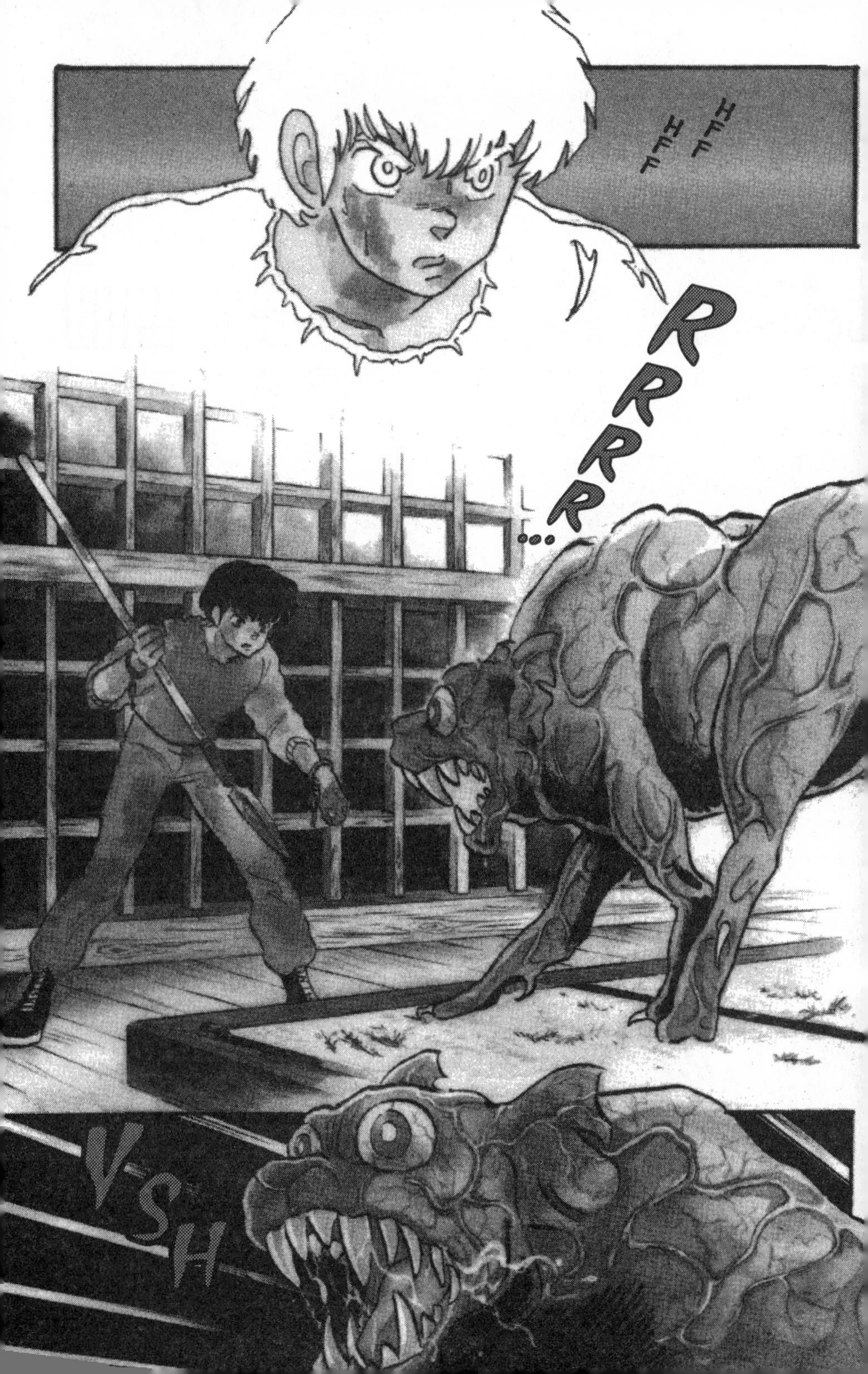
HFF
HFF
RRRRR...
VSH

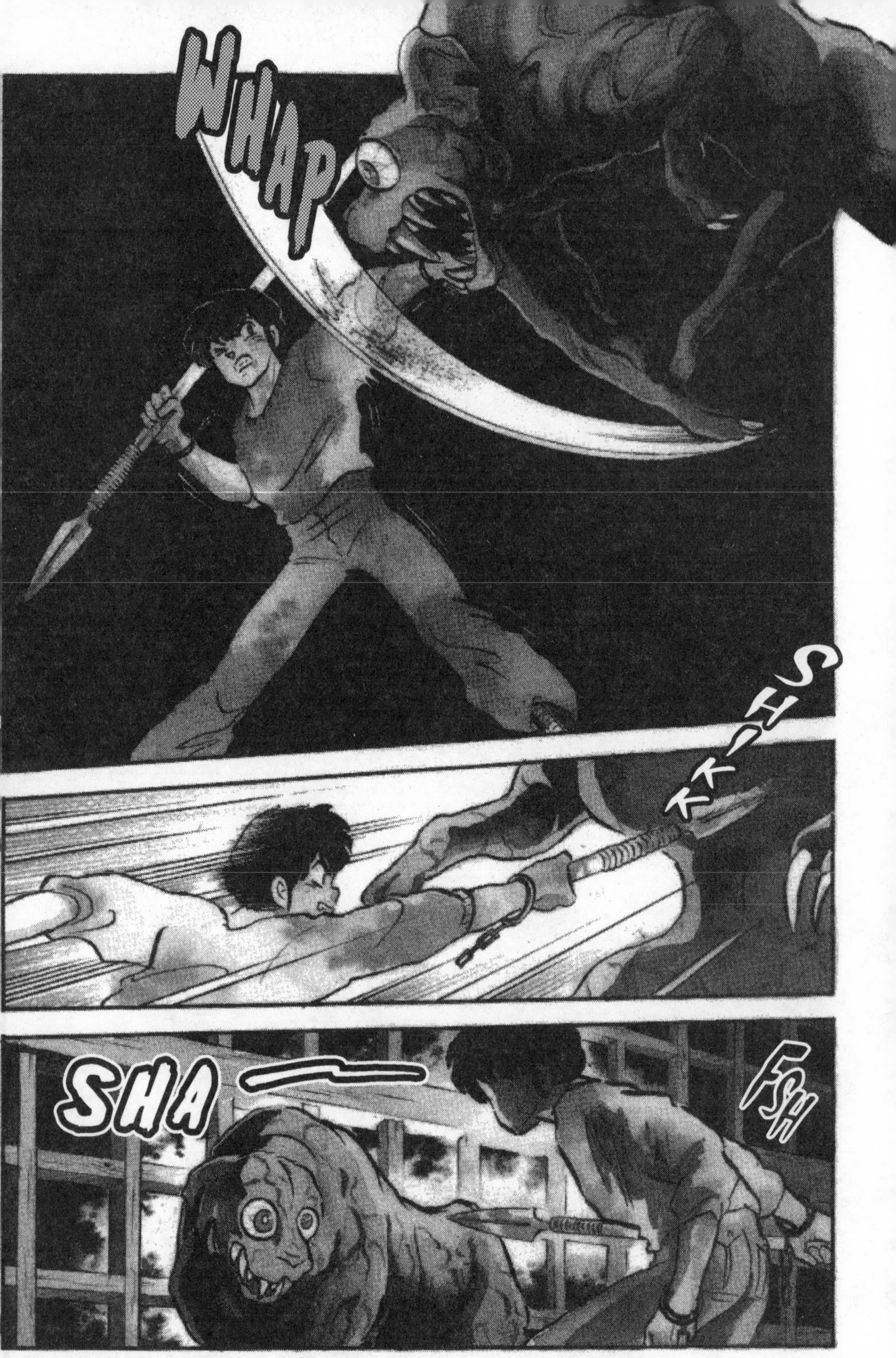
WHAP
SHIKK
FSH
SHA

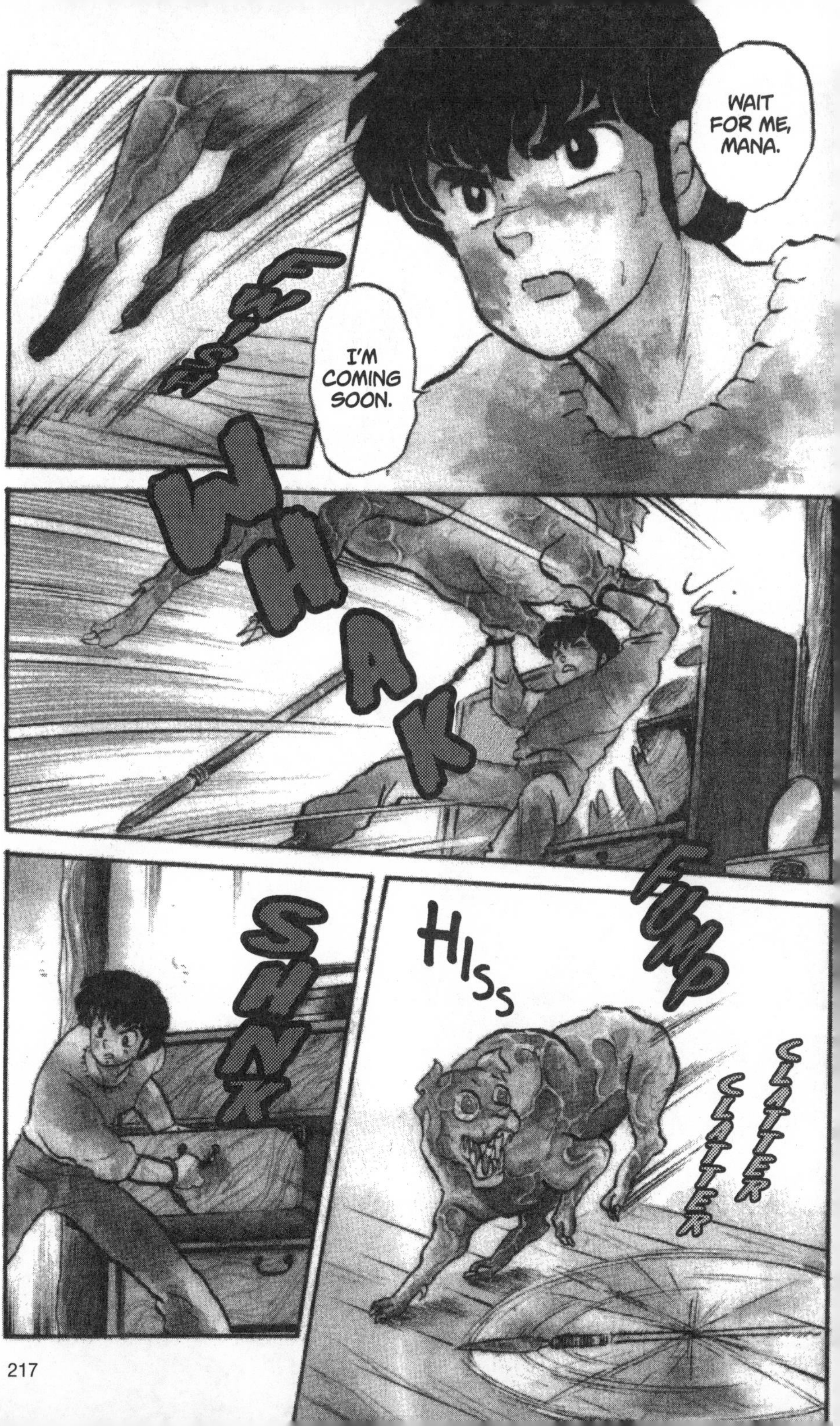
WAIT FOR ME, MANA.
I'M COMING SOON.
FWISH
WHAK
FUMP
HISS
CLATTER CLATTER
SHNK

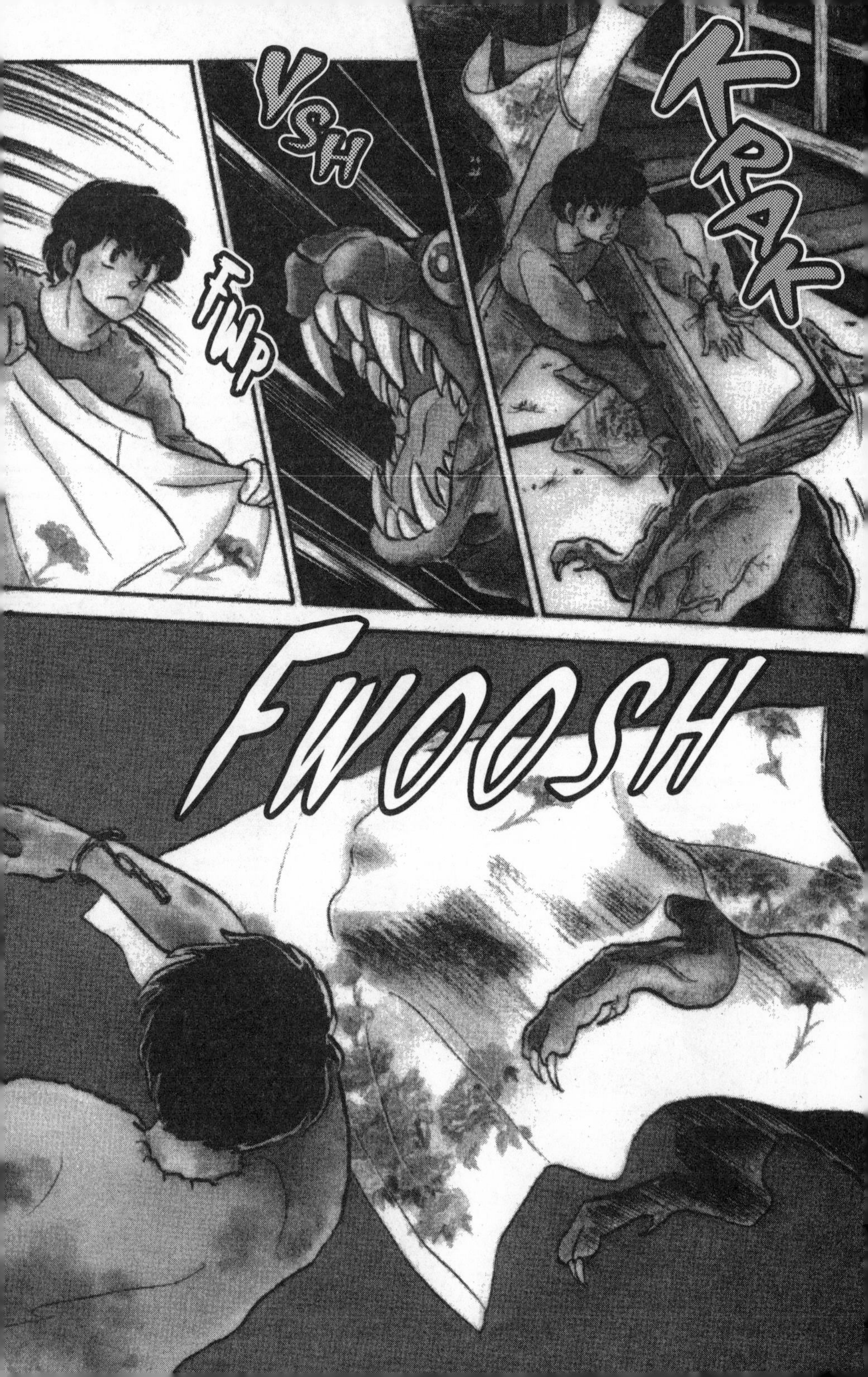
KRAK
VSH
FWP
FWOOSH

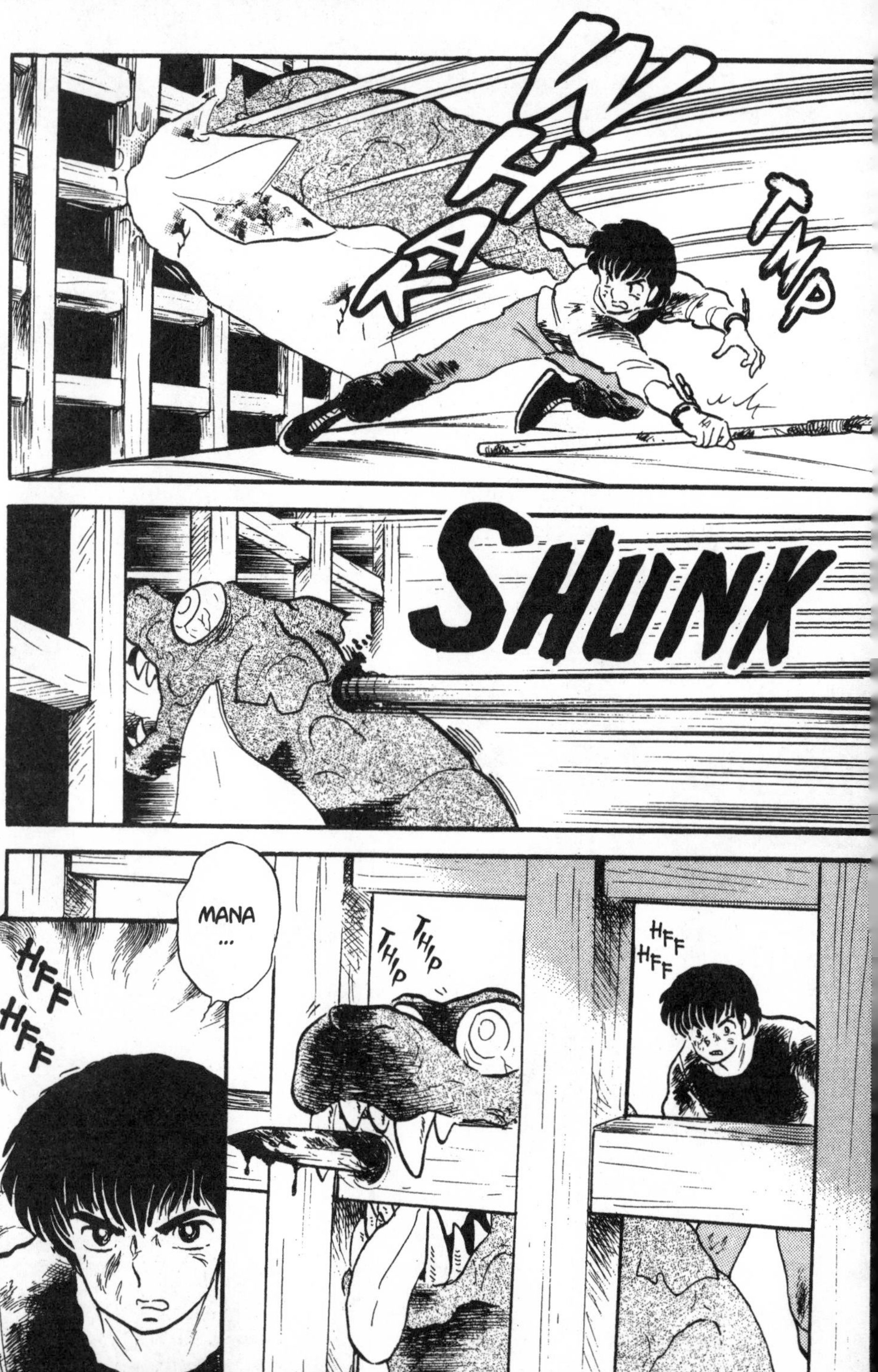
WHAKA
TMP
SHUNK
HFF HFF
THIP THIP
MANA ...
HFF HFF

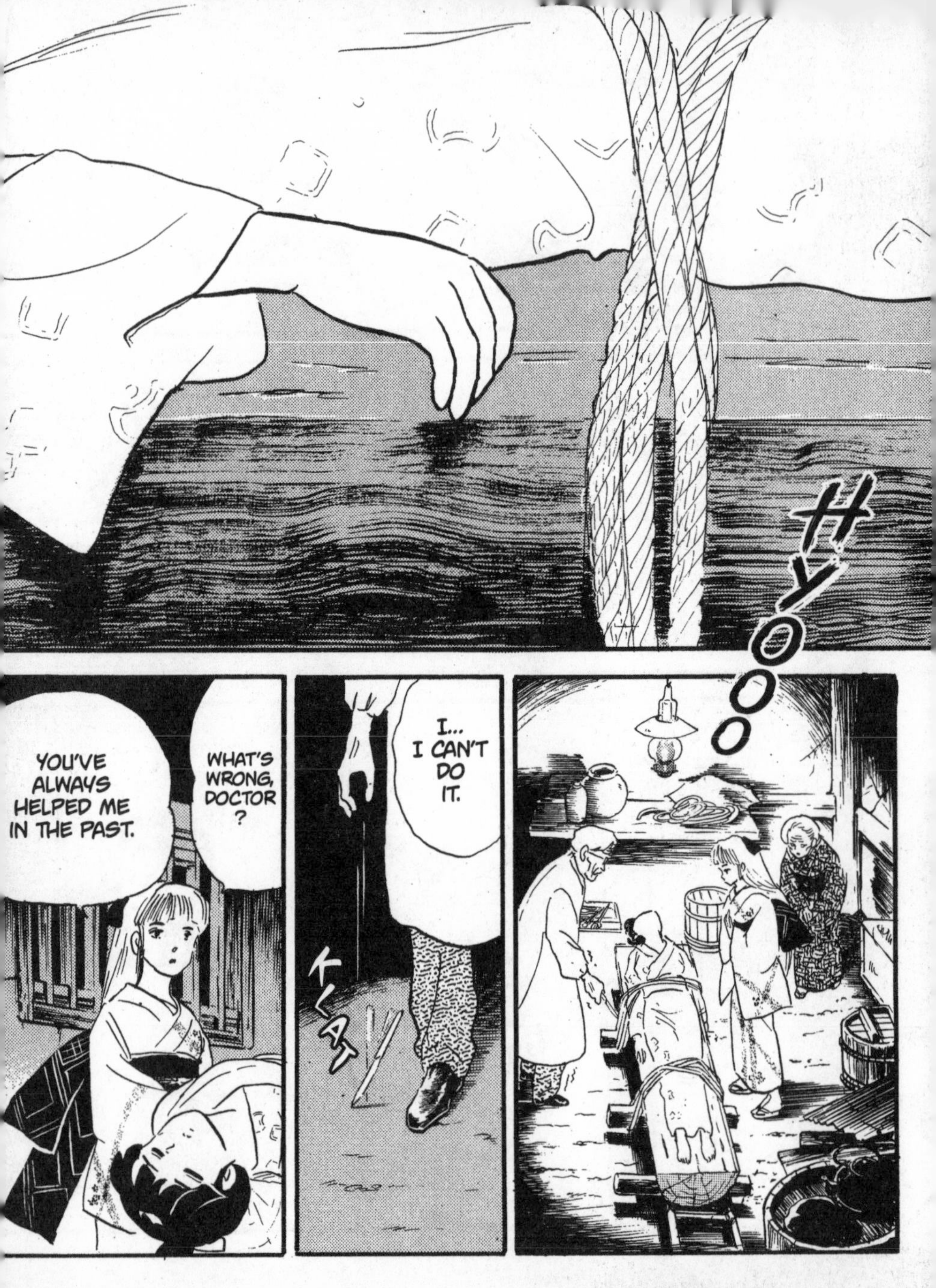
HYOOOO
I... I CAN'T DO IT.
KLAT
WHAT'S WRONG, DOCTOR?
YOU'VE ALWAYS HELPED ME IN THE PAST.

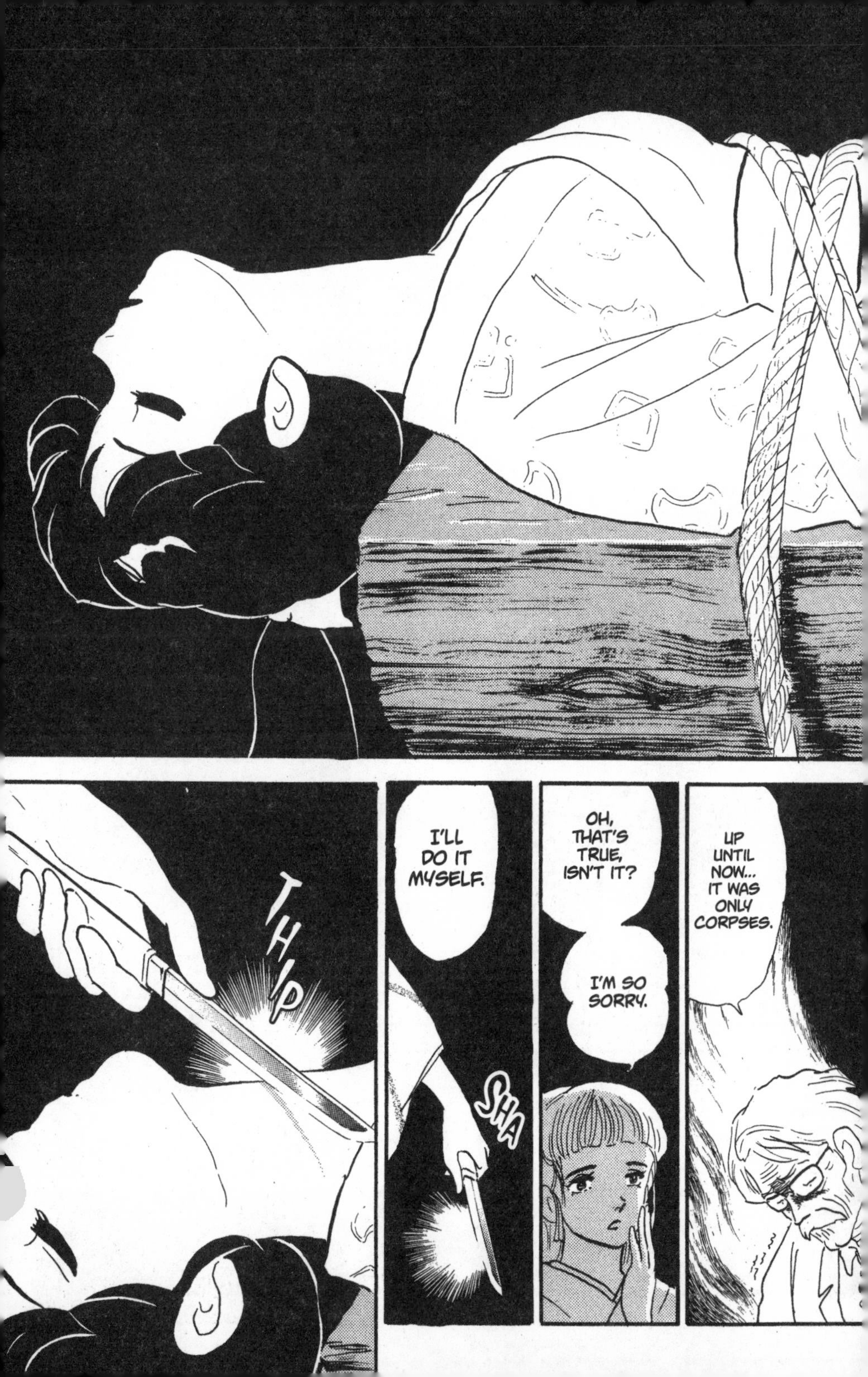
UP UNTIL NOW... IT WAS ONLY CORPSES.
OH, THAT'S TRUE, ISN'T IT?
I'M SO SORRY.
I'LL DO IT MYSELF.
SHA
THIP

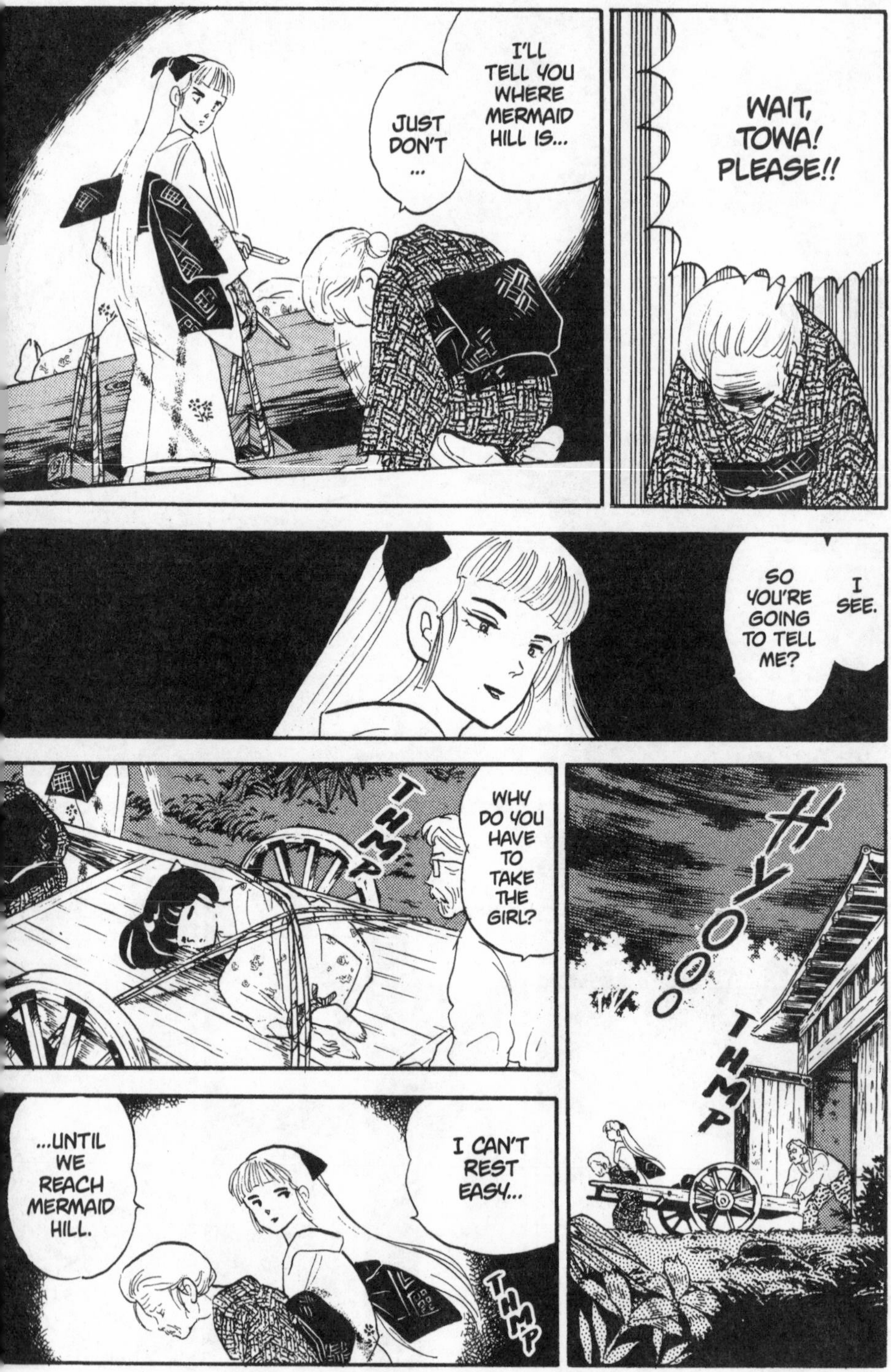
WAIT, TOWA! PLEASE!!
I'LL TELL YOU WHERE MERMAID HILL IS...
JUST DON'T ...
I SEE.
SO YOU'RE GOING TO TELL ME?
HYOOOO
THMP
THMP
WHY DO YOU HAVE TO TAKE THE GIRL?
I CAN'T REST EASY...
...UNTIL WE REACH MERMAID HILL.
THMP

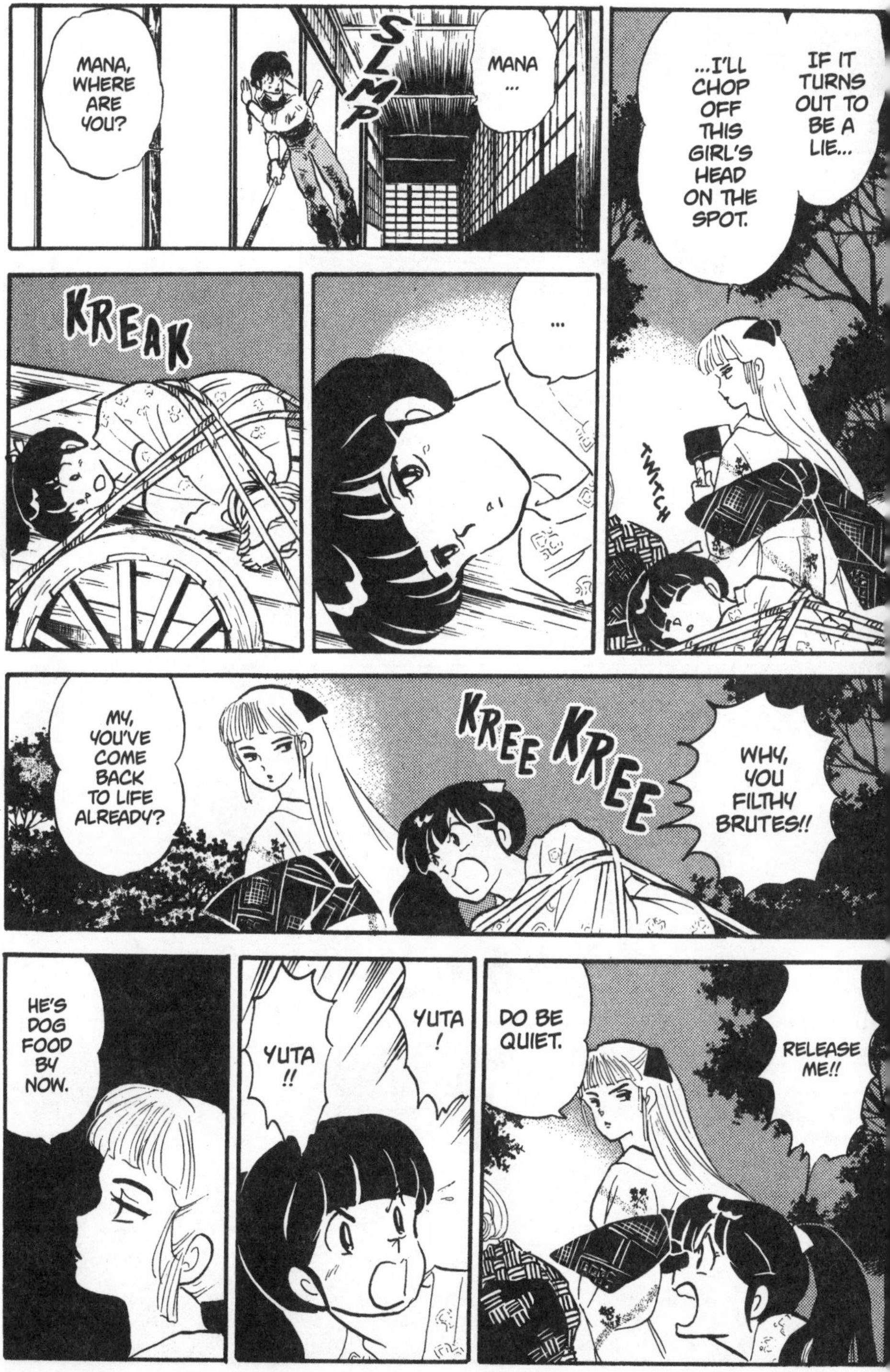
IF IT TURNS OUT TO BE A LIE...
...I'LL CHOP OFF THIS GIRL'S HEAD ON THE SPOT.
TWITCH
MANA ...
SLMP
MANA, WHERE ARE YOU?
...
KREAK
WHY, YOU FILTHY BRUTES!!
KREE KREE
MY, YOU'VE COME BACK TO LIFE ALREADY?
RELEASE ME!!
DO BE QUIET.
YUTA !
YUTA !!
HE'S DOG FOOD BY NOW.

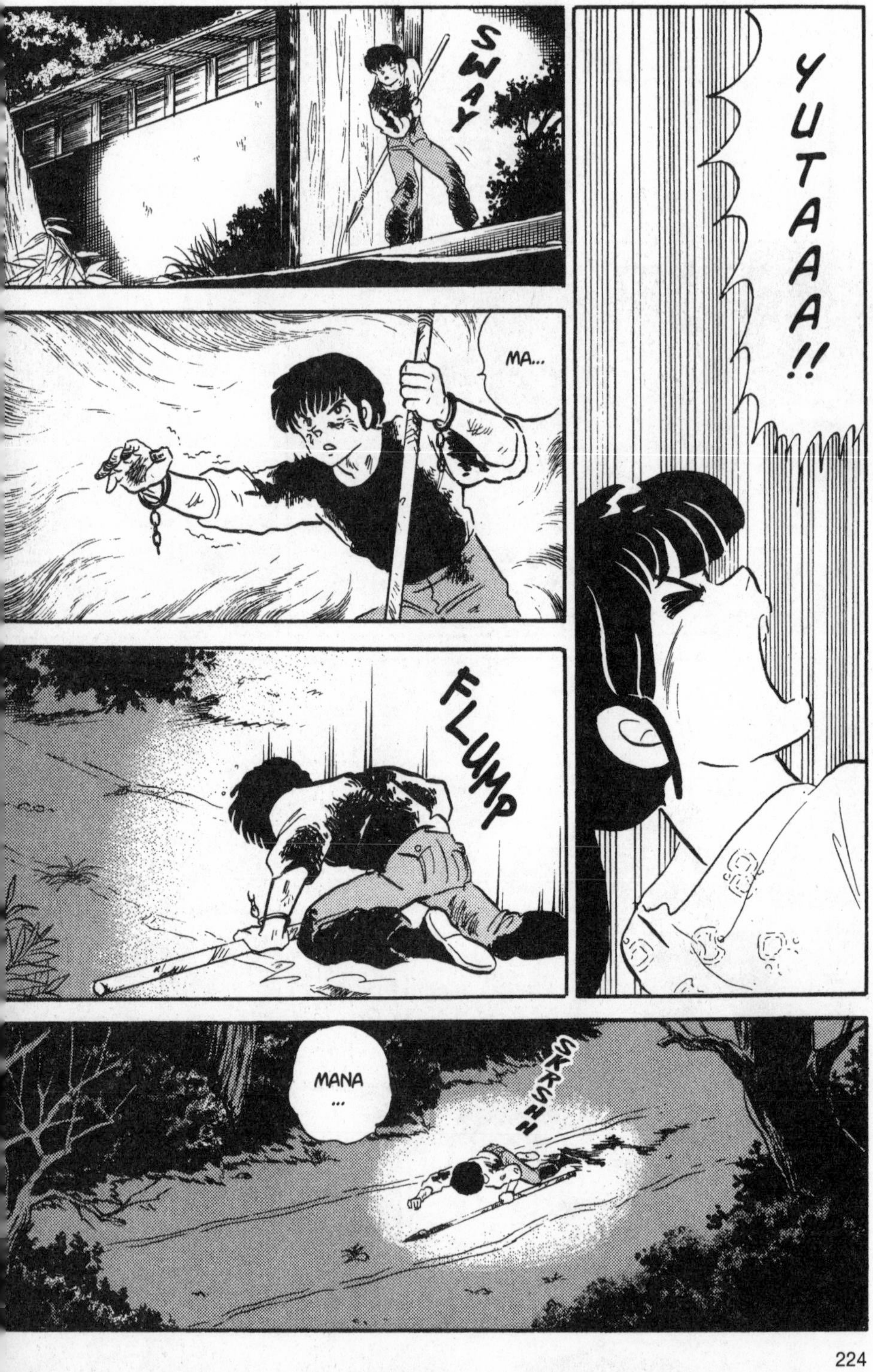
YUTAAAA!!
SWAY
MA...
FLUMP
MANA ...
SKRSHH

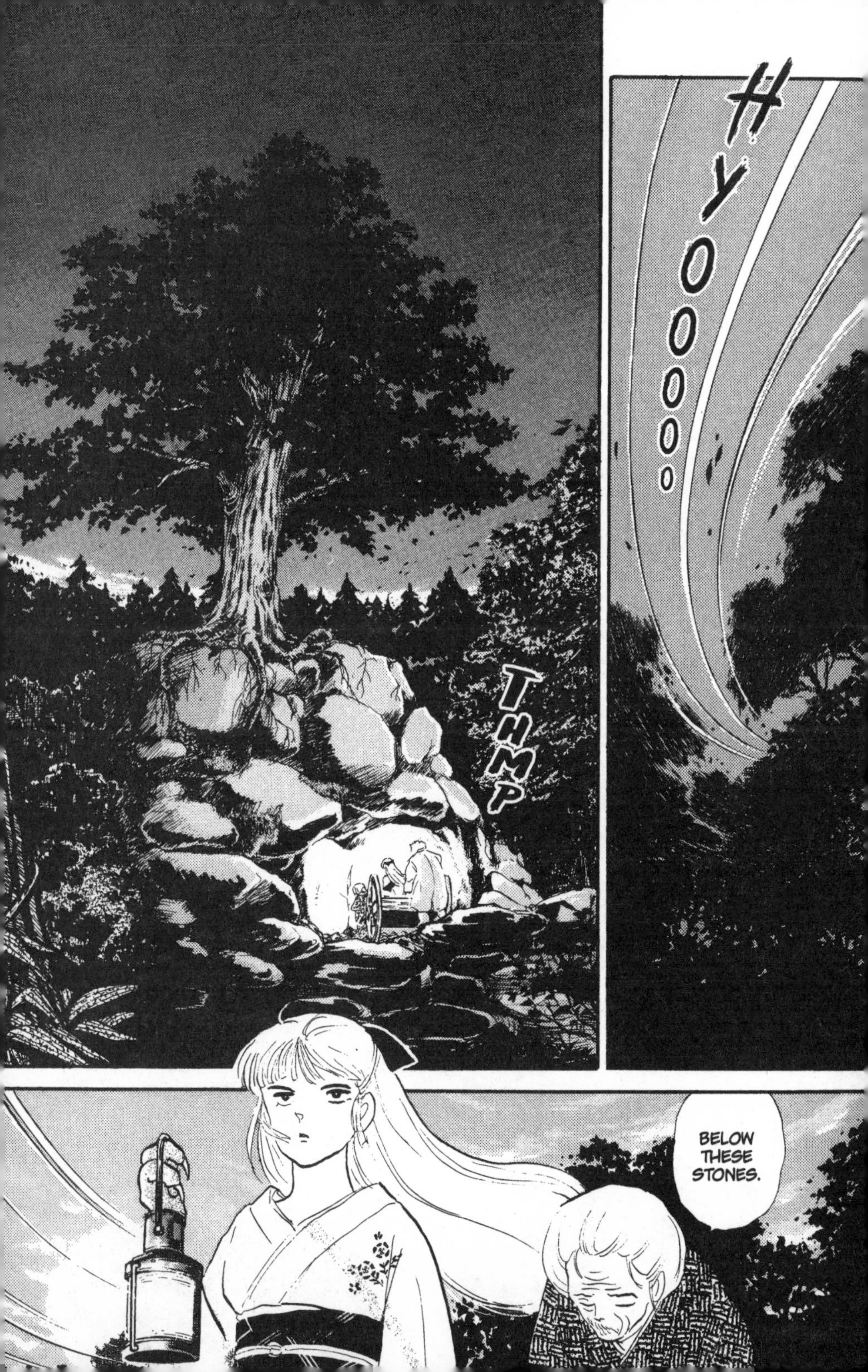
HYOOOOOO
THUMP
BELOW THESE STONES.

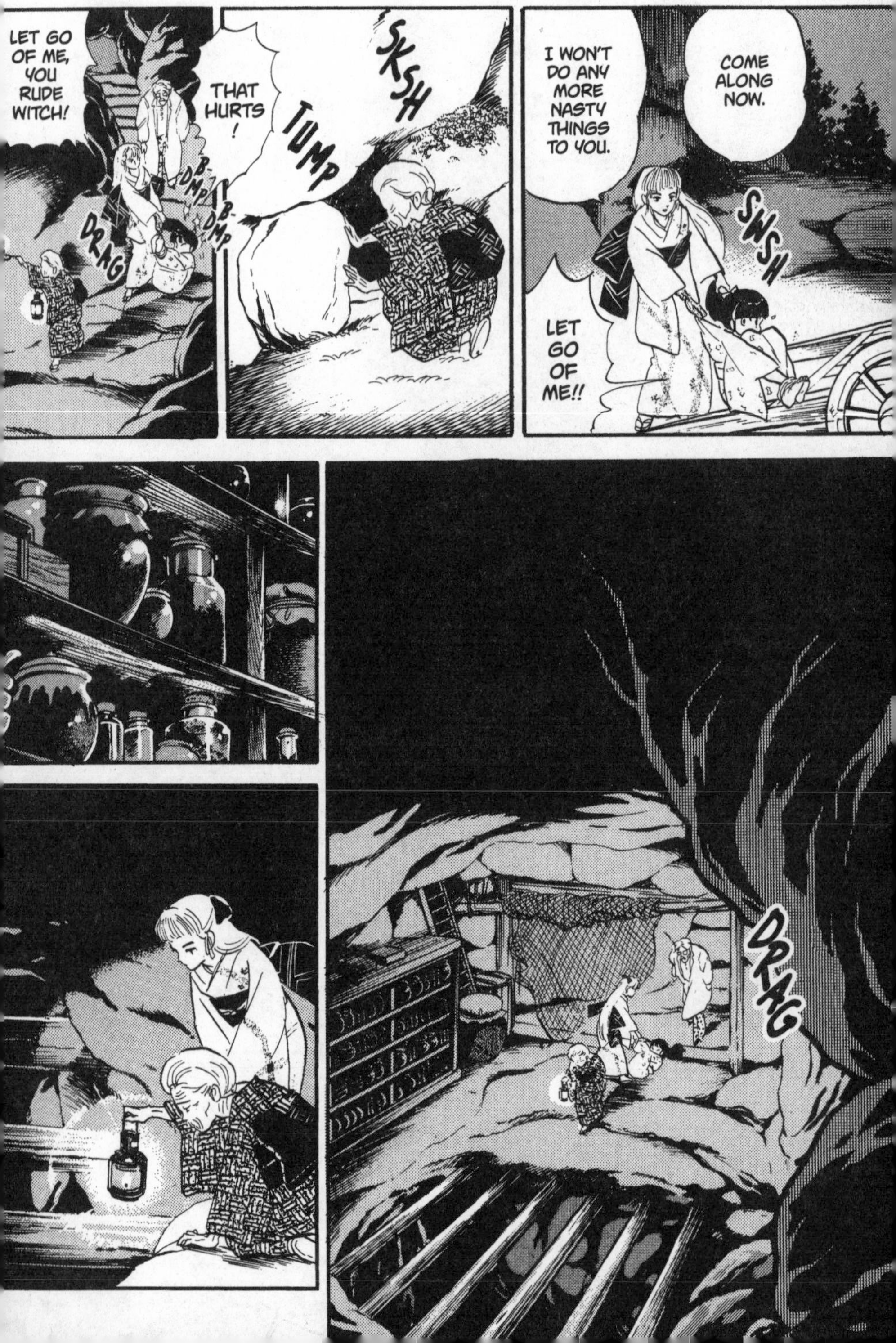
COME ALONG NOW.
I WON'T DO ANY MORE NASTY THINGS TO YOU.
SWSH
LET GO OF ME!!
SKSH
TUMP
THAT HURTS!
LET GO OF ME, YOU RUDE WITCH!
B-DMP
B-DMP
DRAG
DRAG

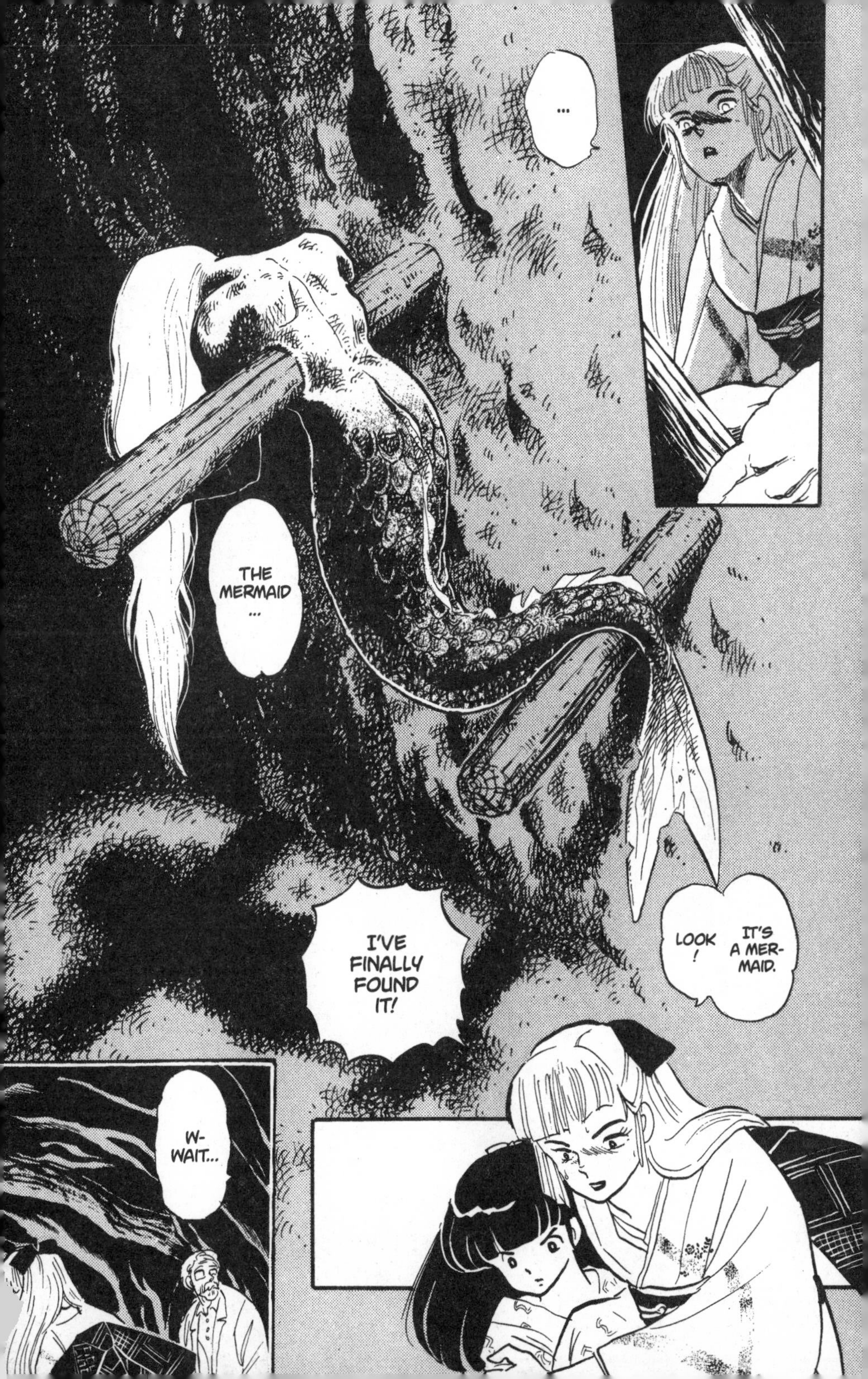
...
THE MERMAID ...
LOOK! IT'S A MERMAID.
I'VE FINALLY FOUND IT!
W-WAIT...

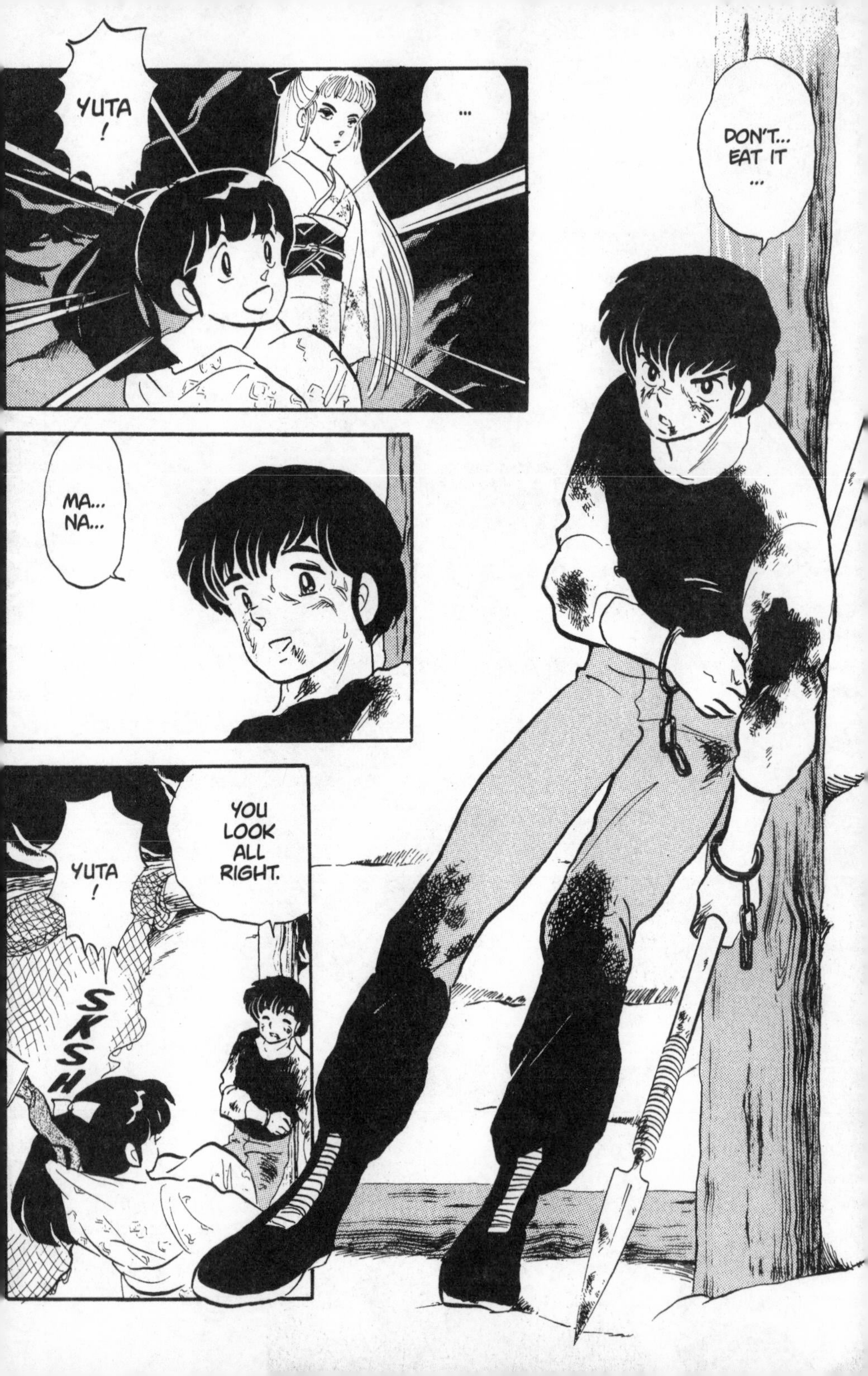
YUTA !
...
MA... NA...
YUTA !
YOU LOOK ALL RIGHT.
SKSH
DON'T... EAT IT ...

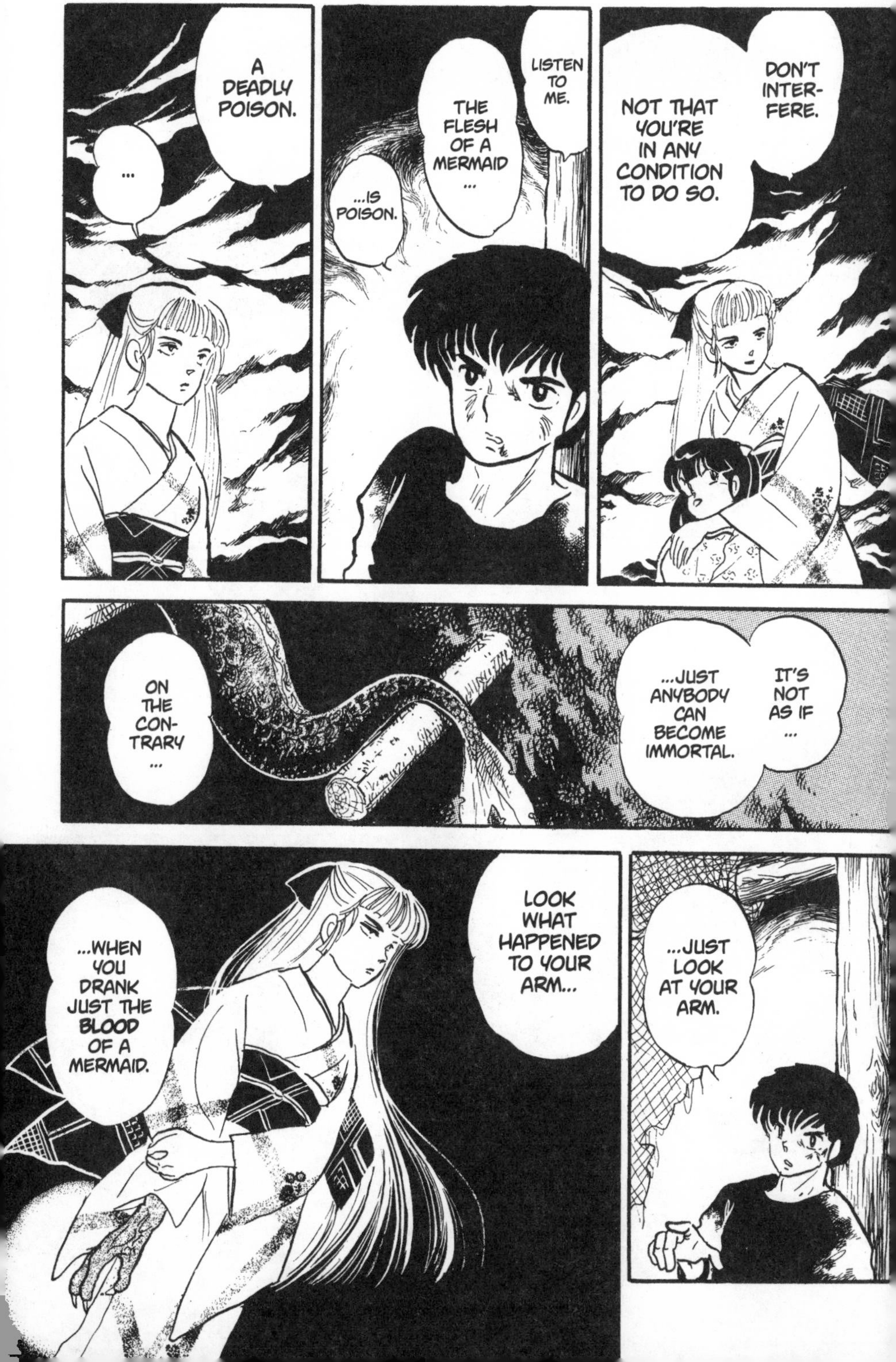
DON'T INTERFERE.
NOT THAT YOU'RE IN ANY CONDITION TO DO SO.
LISTEN TO ME.
THE FLESH OF A MERMAID...
...IS POISON.
A DEADLY POISON.
...
IT'S NOT AS IF...
...JUST ANYBODY CAN BECOME IMMORTAL.
ON THE CONTRARY...
...JUST LOOK AT YOUR ARM.
LOOK WHAT HAPPENED TO YOUR ARM...
...WHEN YOU DRANK JUST THE BLOOD OF A MERMAID.

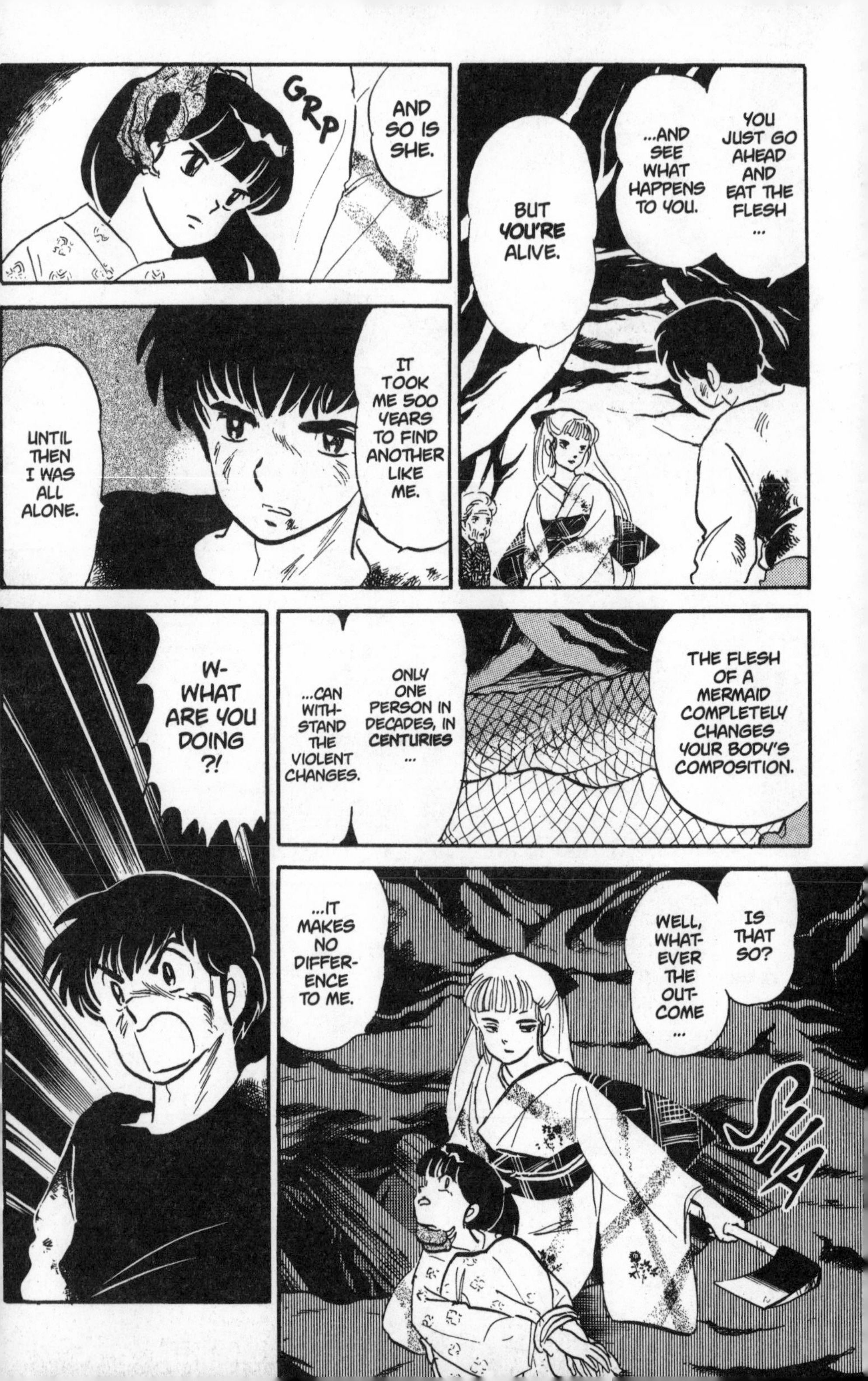
YOU JUST GO AHEAD AND EAT THE FLESH ...
...AND SEE WHAT HAPPENS TO YOU.
BUT **YOU'RE** ALIVE.
GRP
AND SO IS SHE.
IT TOOK ME 500 YEARS TO FIND ANOTHER LIKE ME.
UNTIL THEN I WAS ALL ALONE.
THE FLESH OF A MERMAID COMPLETELY CHANGES YOUR BODY'S COMPOSITION.
ONLY ONE PERSON IN DECADES, IN **CENTURIES** ...
...CAN WITH-STAND THE VIOLENT CHANGES.
IS THAT SO?
WELL, WHAT-EVER THE OUT-COME ...
...IT MAKES NO DIFFER-ENCE TO ME.
SHA
W-WHAT ARE YOU DOING ?!

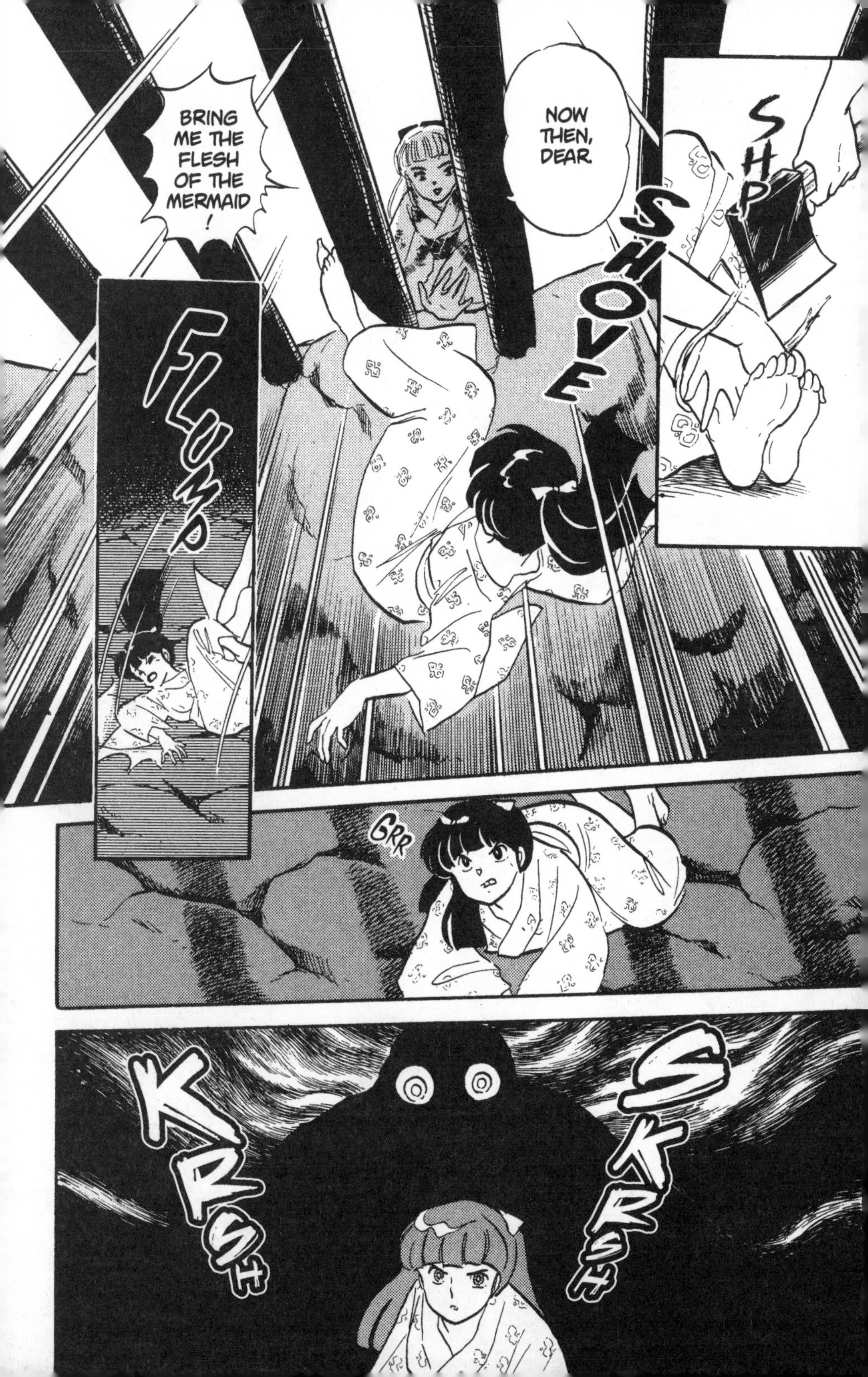
SHP
SHOVE
NOW THEN, DEAR.
BRING ME THE FLESH OF THE MERMAID!
FLUMP
GRR
SKRSH
KRSH

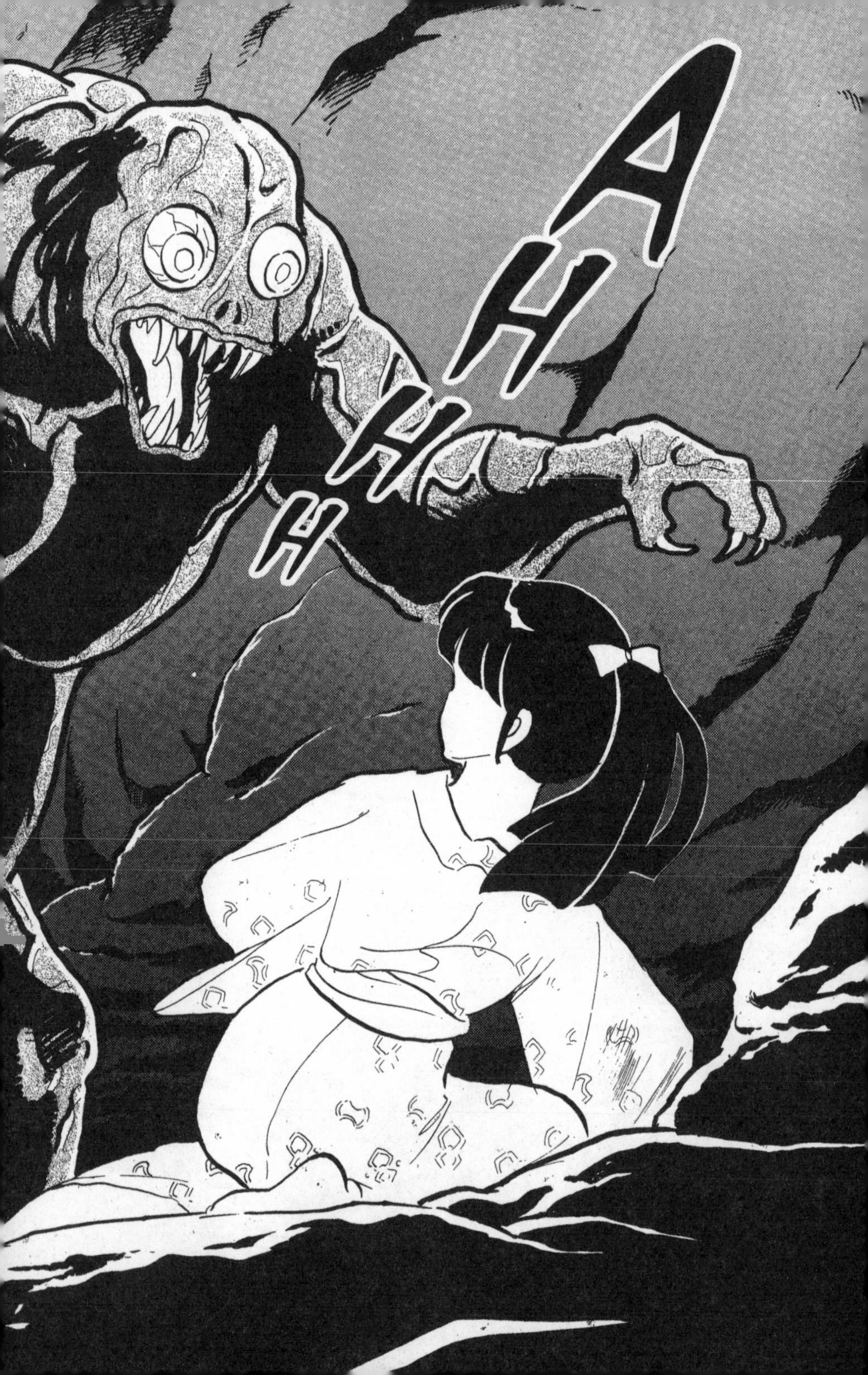
AHHHH

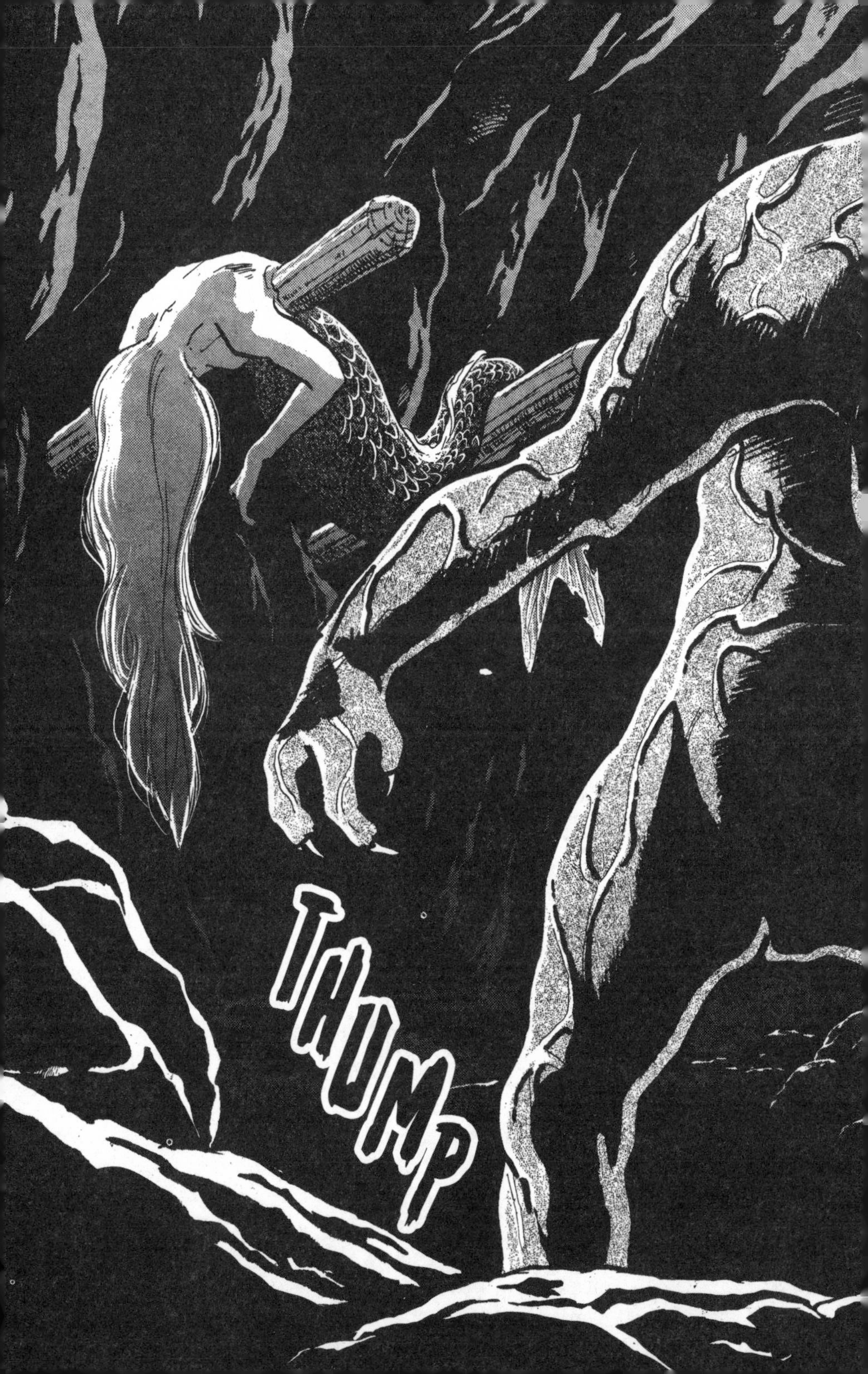
THUMP

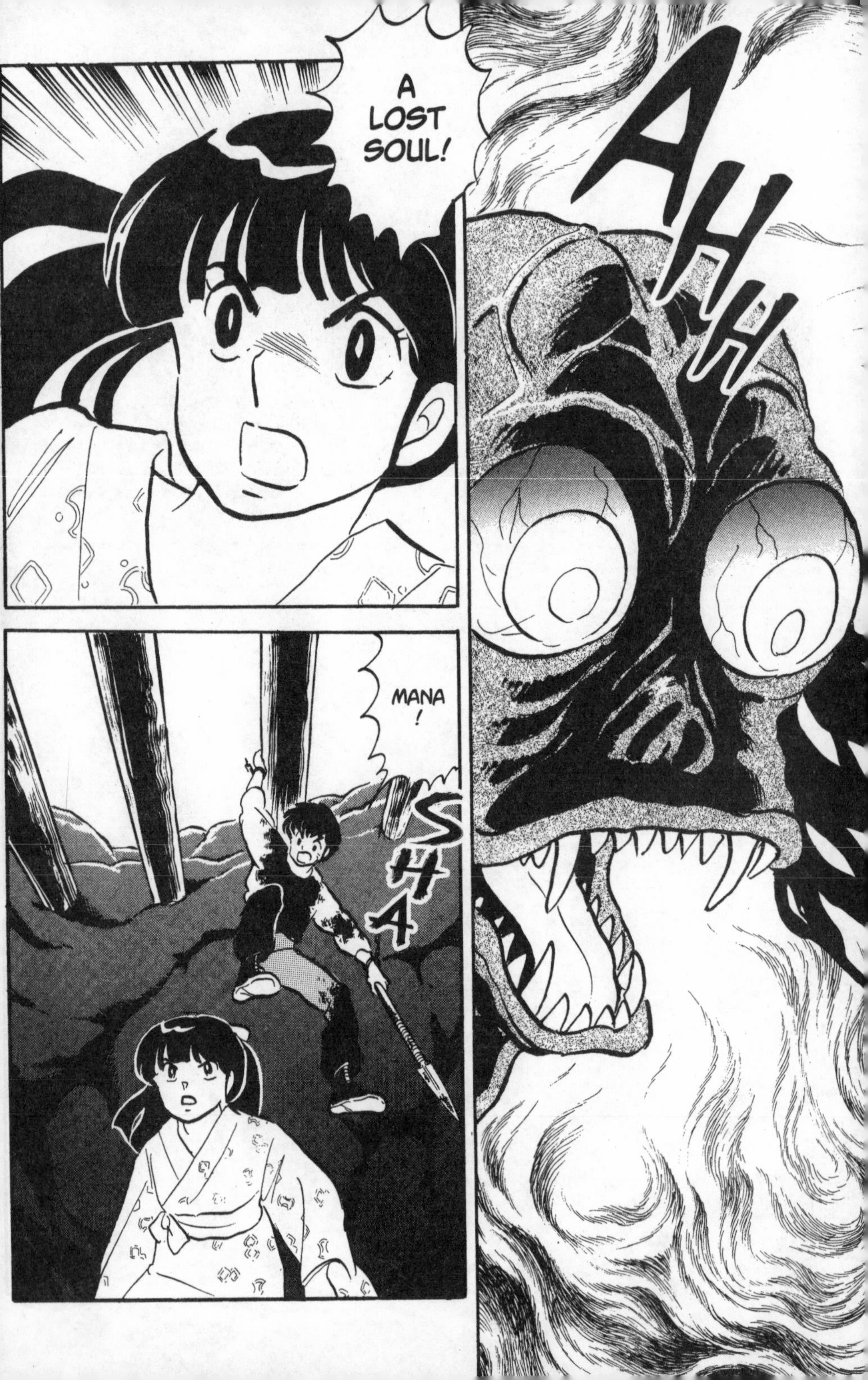
AHHH
A LOST SOUL!
MANA!
SHA

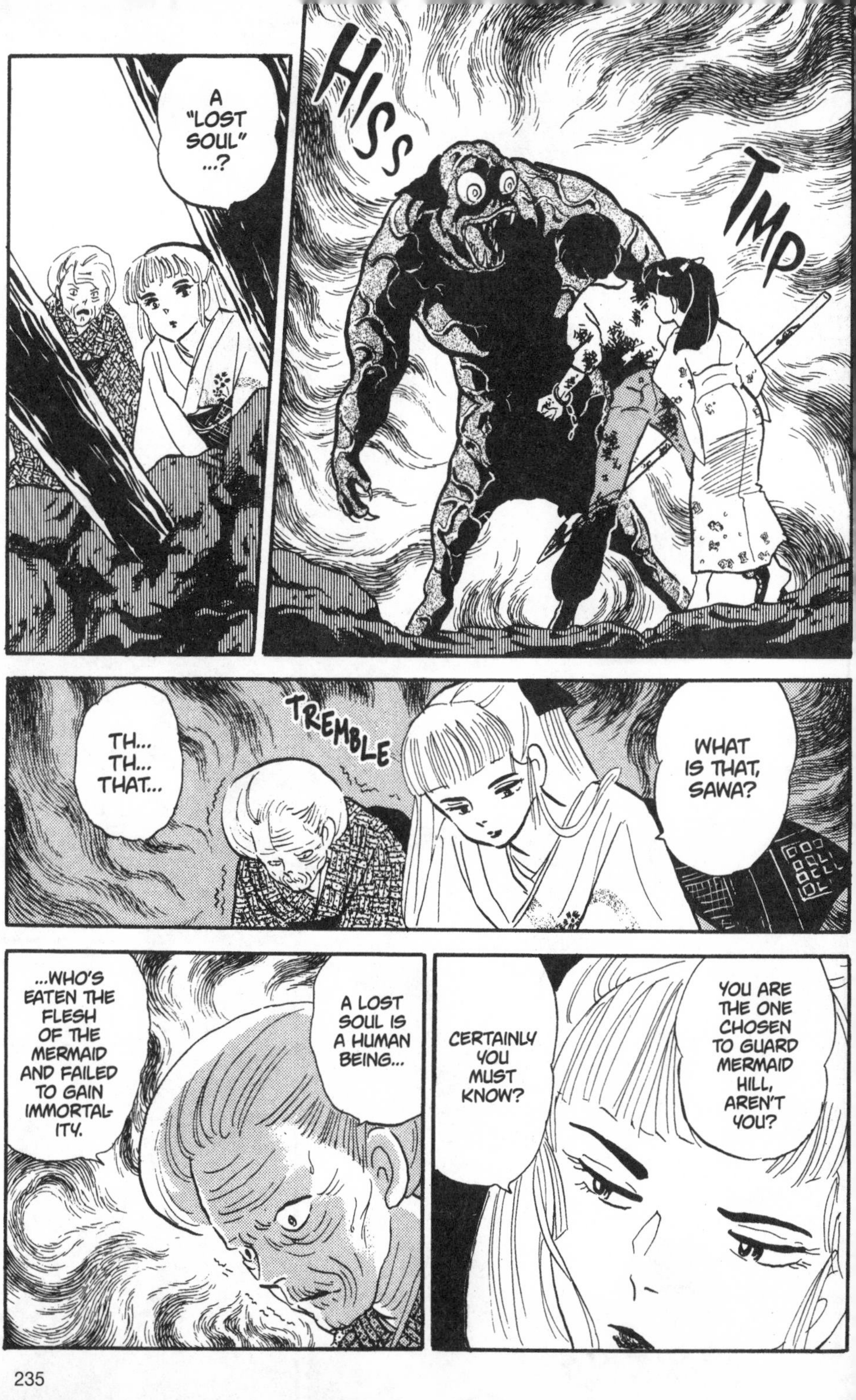
HISS
TMP
A "LOST SOUL" ...?
WHAT IS THAT, SAWA?
TREMBLE
TH... TH... THAT...
YOU ARE THE ONE CHOSEN TO GUARD MERMAID HILL, AREN'T YOU?
CERTAINLY YOU MUST KNOW?
A LOST SOUL IS A HUMAN BEING...
...WHO'S EATEN THE FLESH OF THE MERMAID AND FAILED TO GAIN IMMORTAL-ITY.

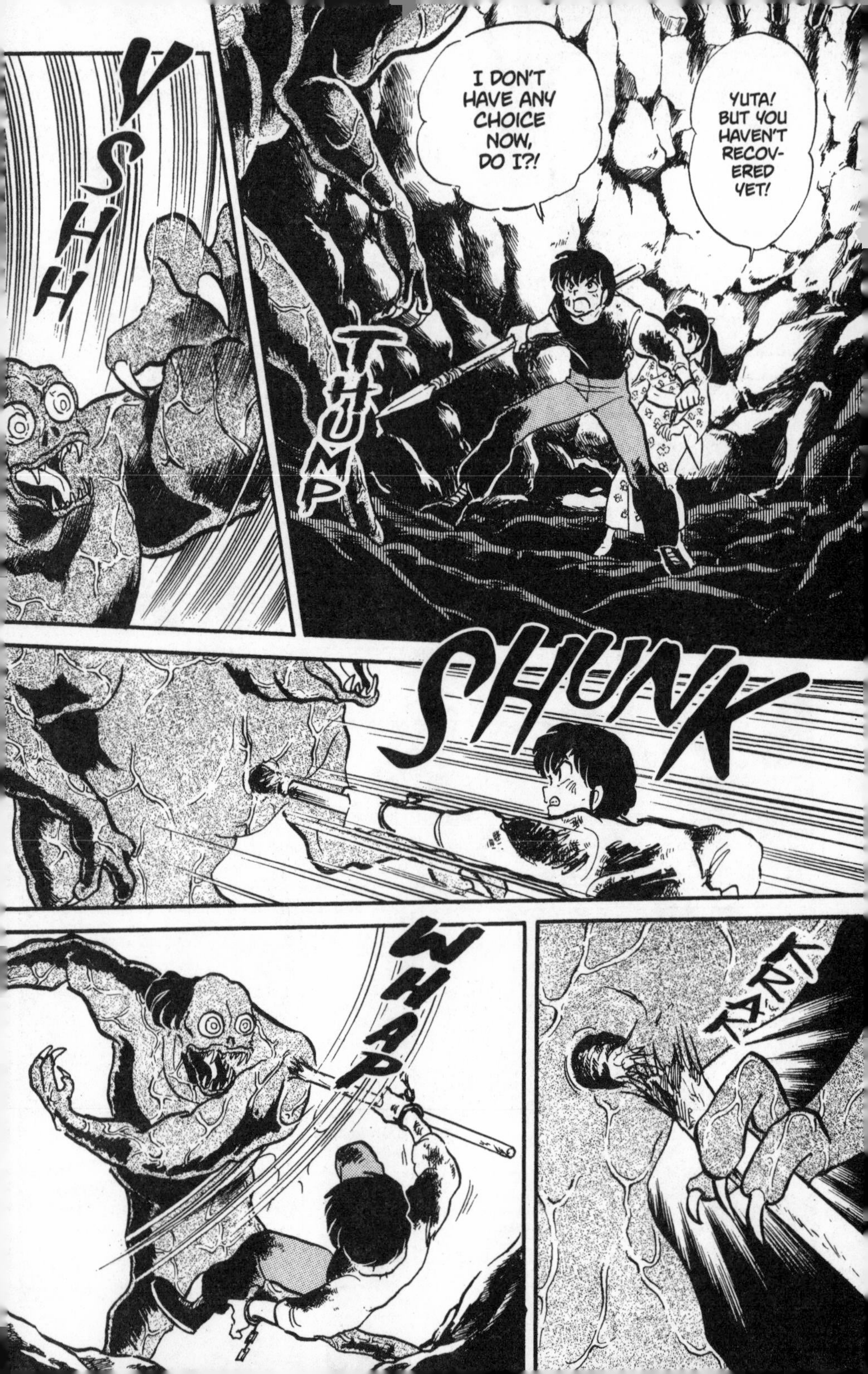
YUTA! BUT YOU HAVEN'T RECOV-ERED YET!
I DON'T HAVE ANY CHOICE NOW, DO I?!
THUMP
VSHH
SHUNK
TANT
WHAP

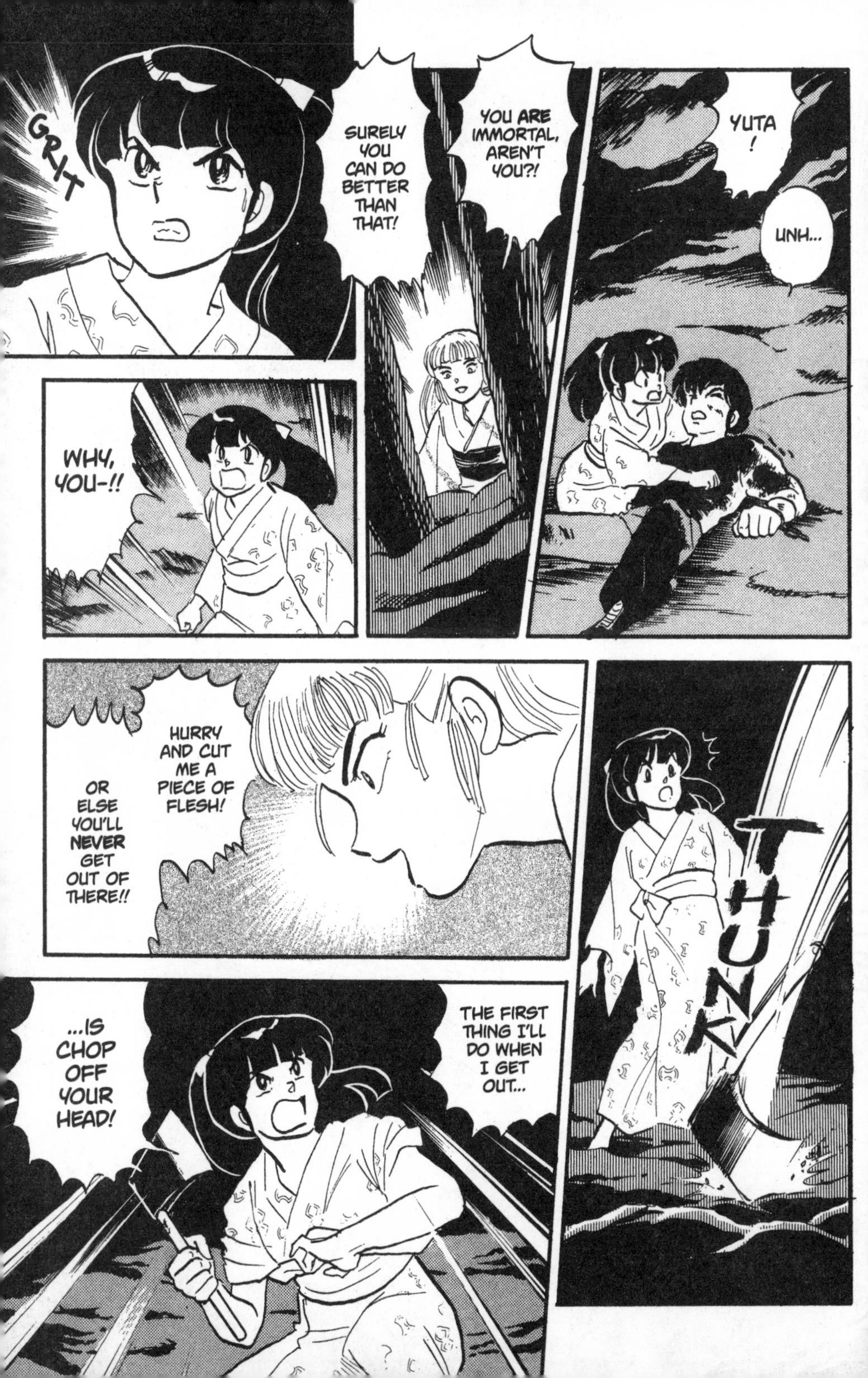
YUTA!
UNH...
YOU ARE IMMORTAL, AREN'T YOU?!
SURELY YOU CAN DO BETTER THAN THAT!
GRIT
WHY, YOU-!!
THUNK
HURRY AND CUT ME A PIECE OF FLESH!
OR ELSE YOU'LL NEVER GET OUT OF THERE!!
THE FIRST THING I'LL DO WHEN I GET OUT...
...IS CHOP OFF YOUR HEAD!

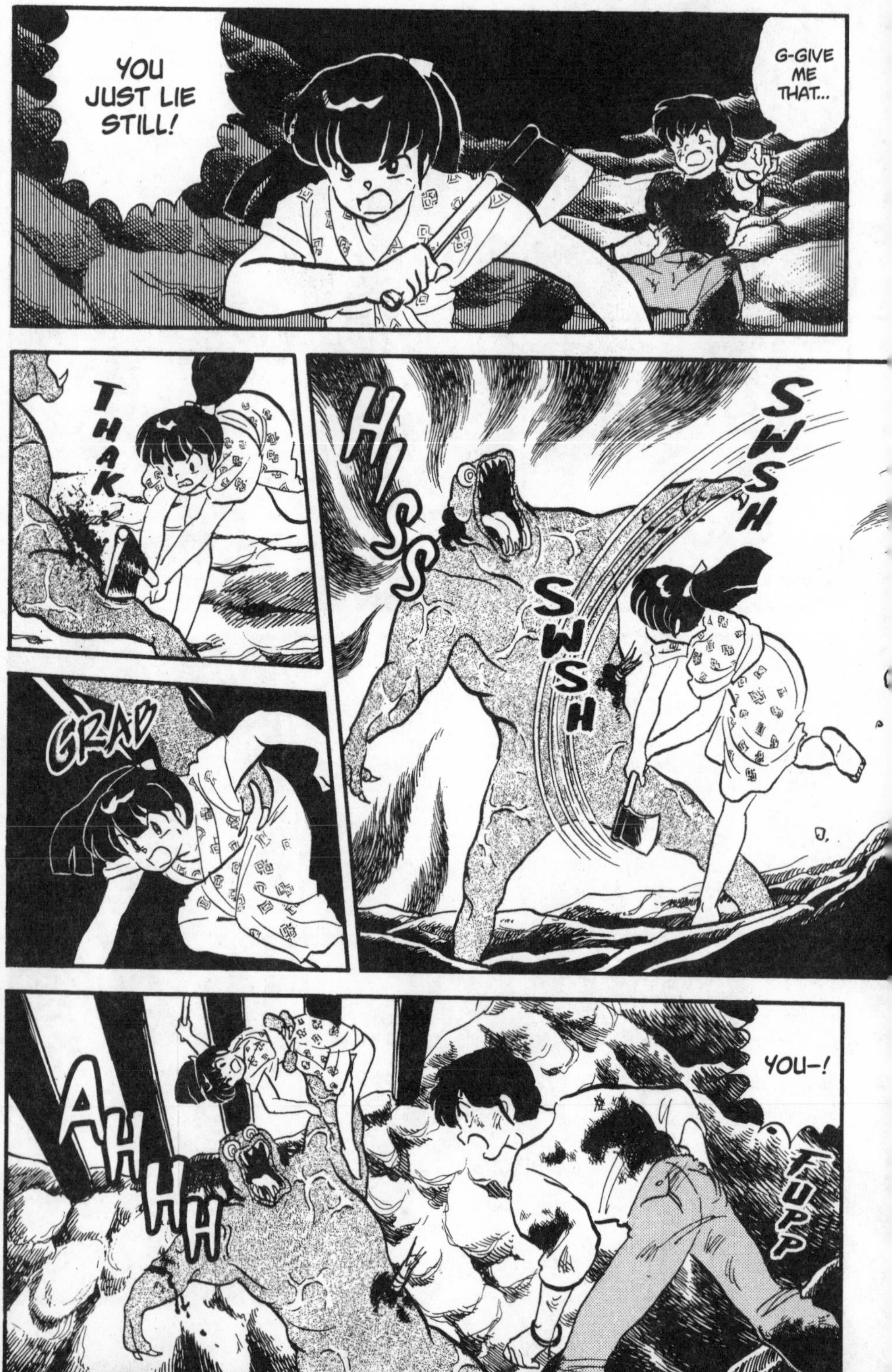
G-GIVE ME THAT...
YOU JUST LIE STILL!
SWSH
HISS
SWSH
THAK
GRAB
YOU-!
FWUPP
AHHHH

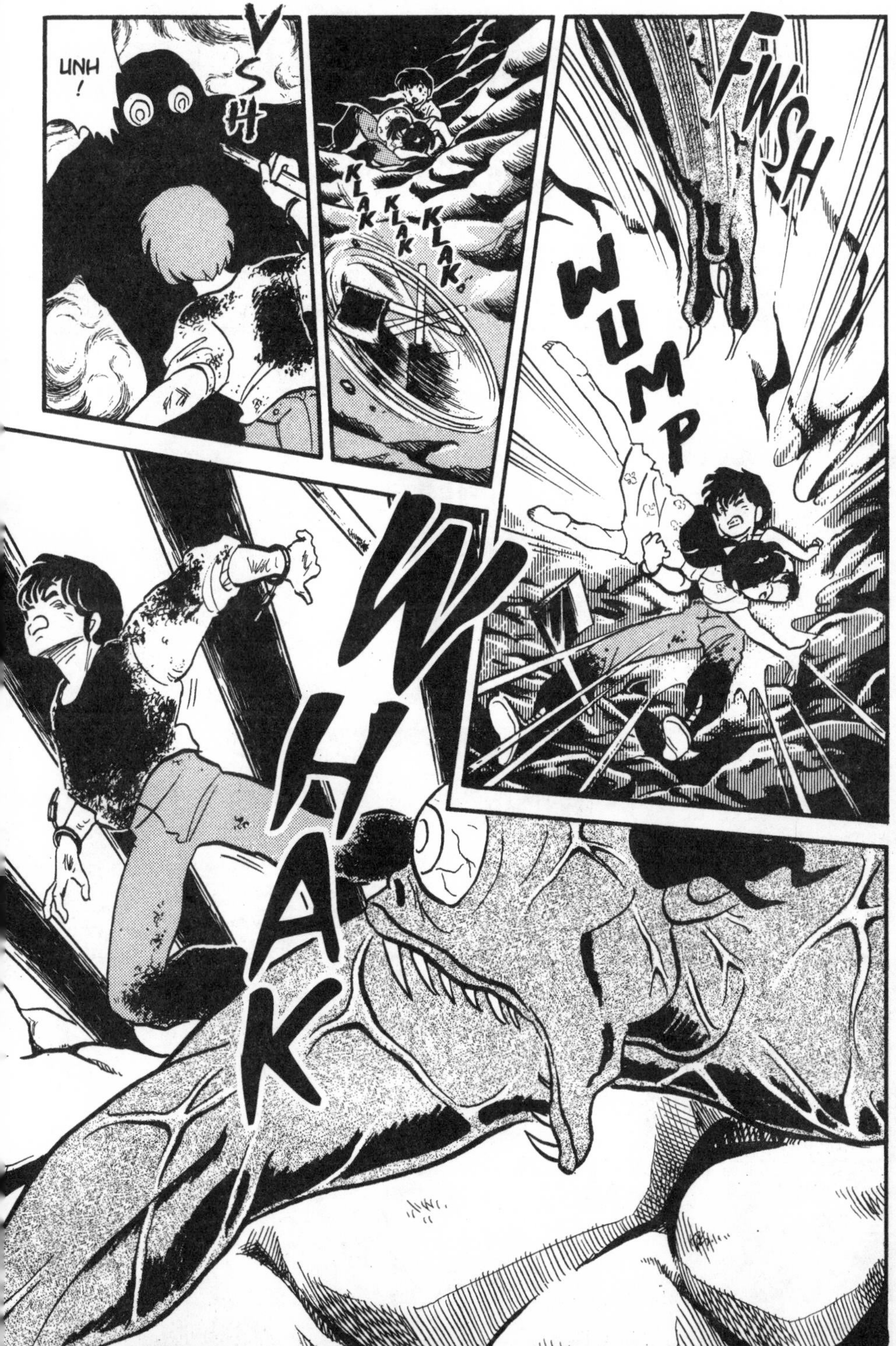
FWSH
WUMP
KLAK KLAK KLAK
VSH
UNH!
WHAK

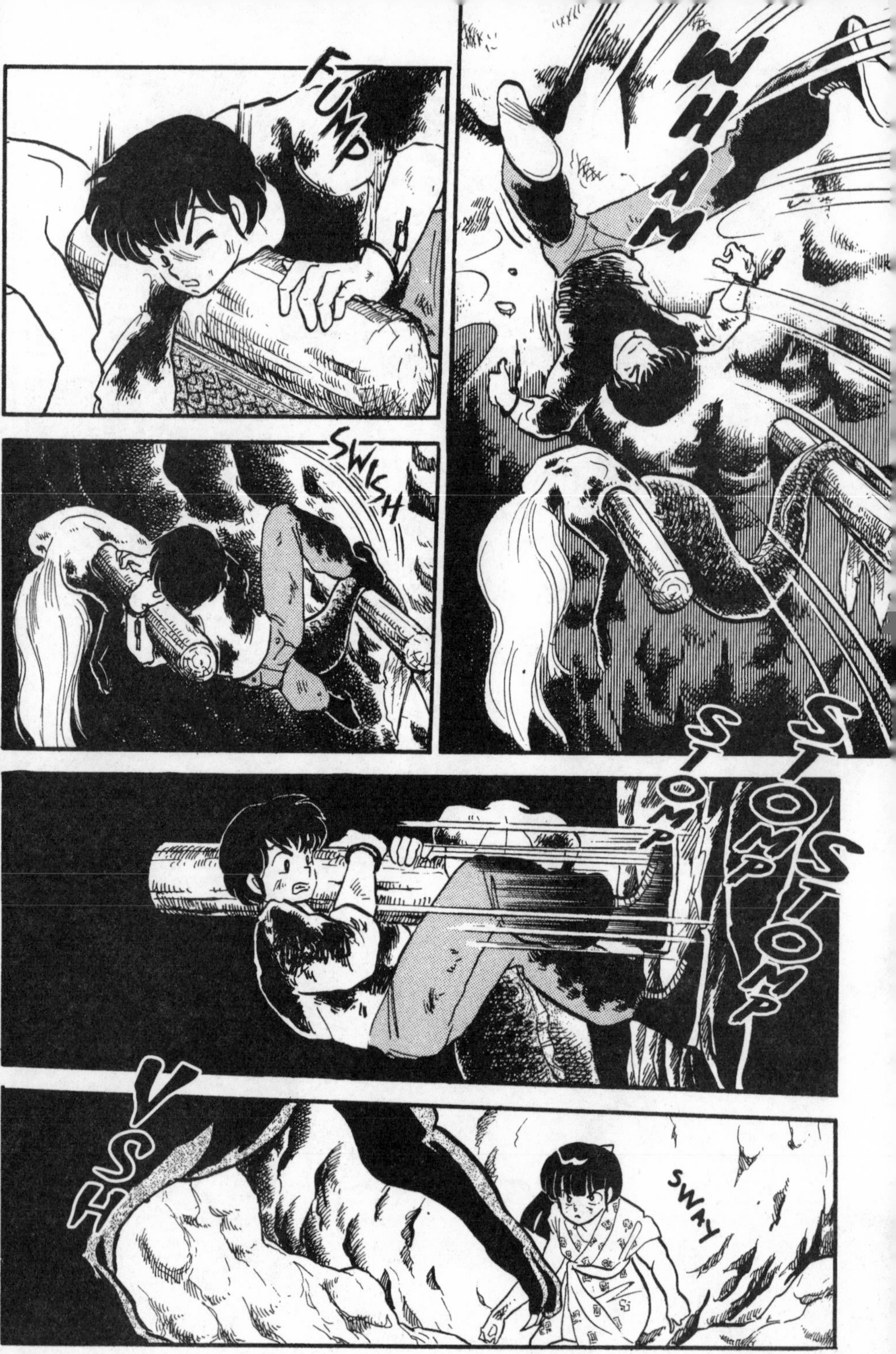
WHAM
FUMP
SWISH
STOMP STOMP
STOMP STOMP
VSSH
SWAY

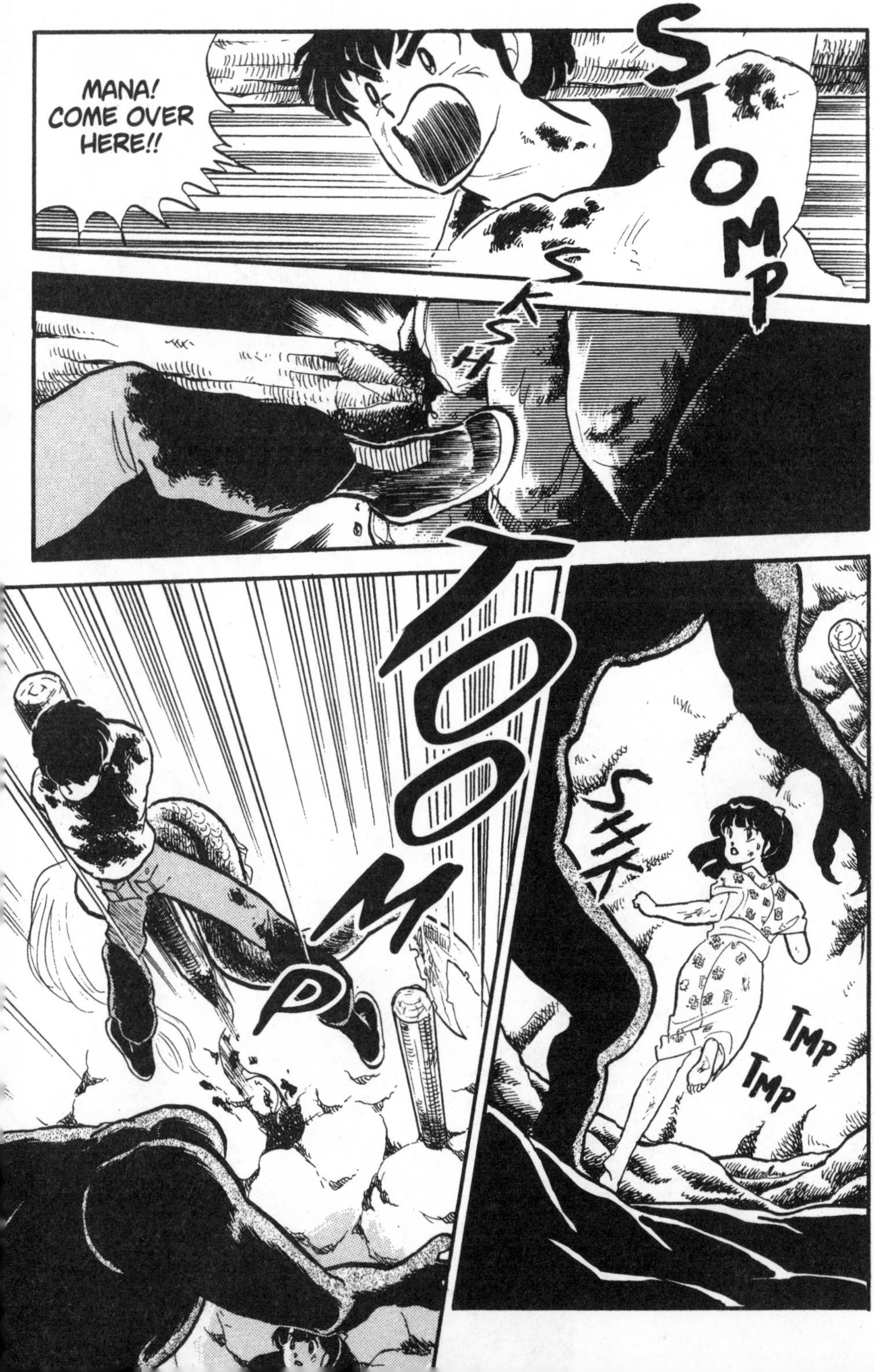
MANA! COME OVER HERE!!
STOMP
SKSH
STOMP
SHK
TMP TMP

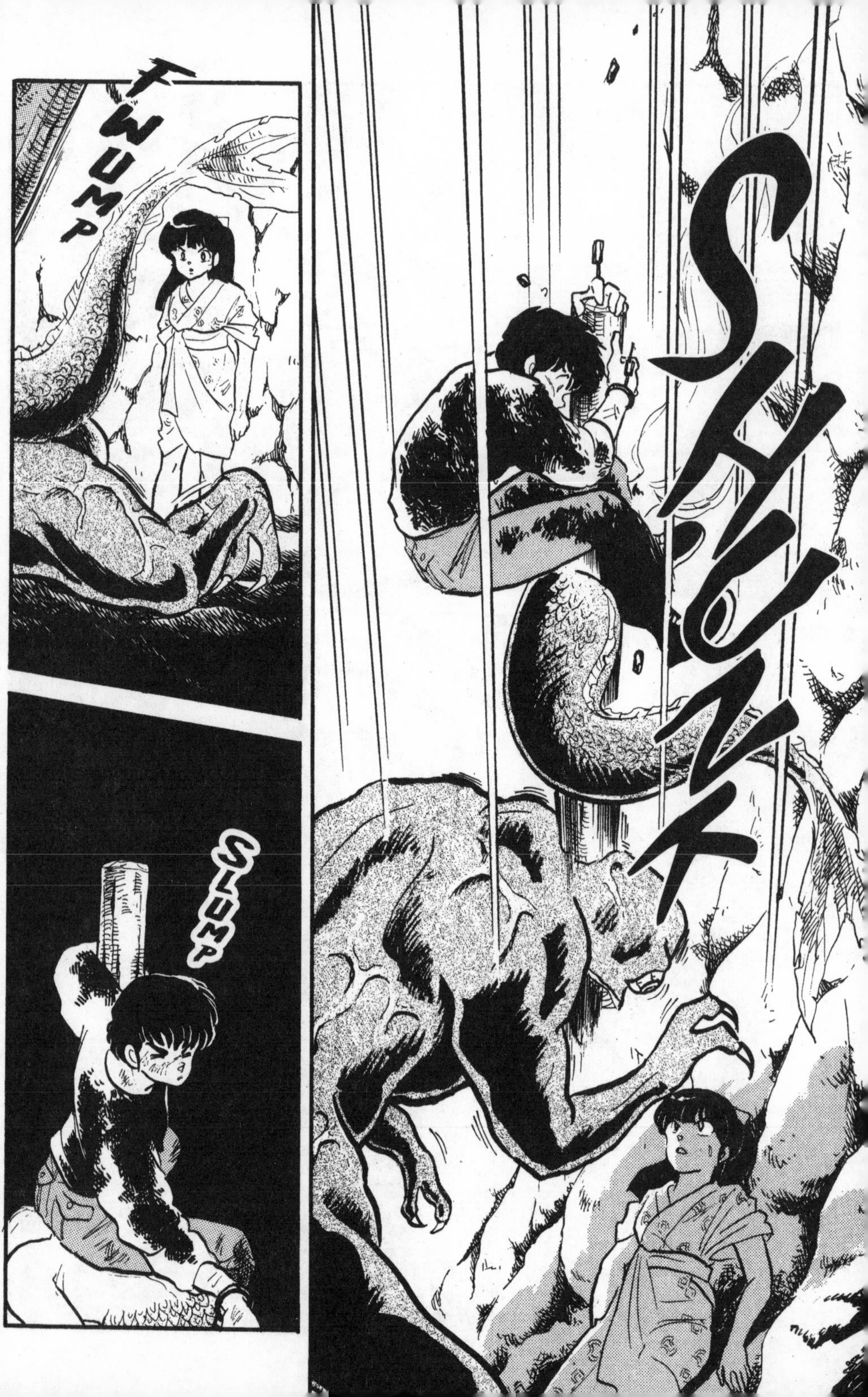
SHUNK
FWUMP
SLUMP

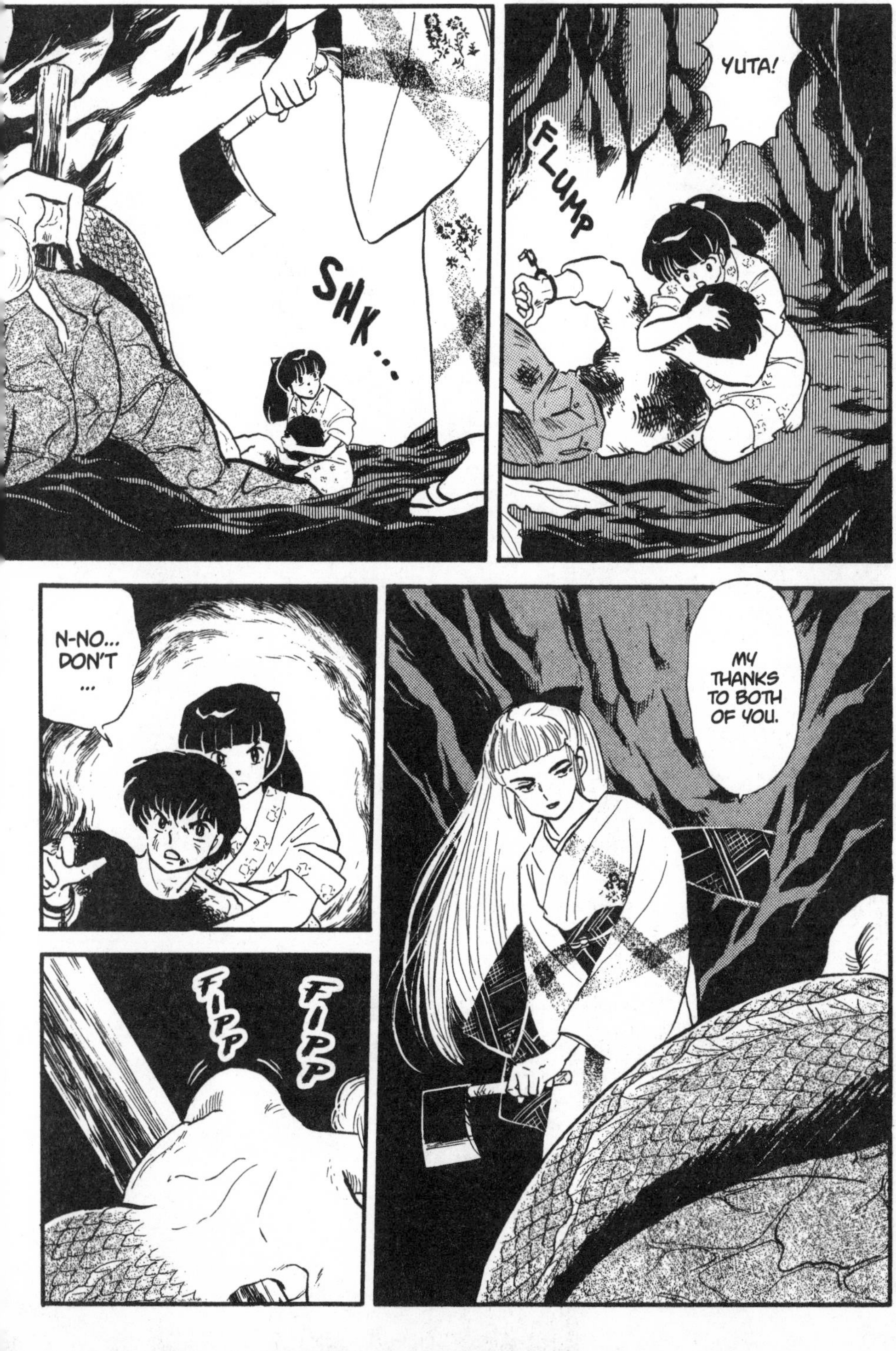
YUTA!
FLUMP
SHK...
MY THANKS TO BOTH OF YOU.
N-NO... DON'T ...
FIPP
FIPP

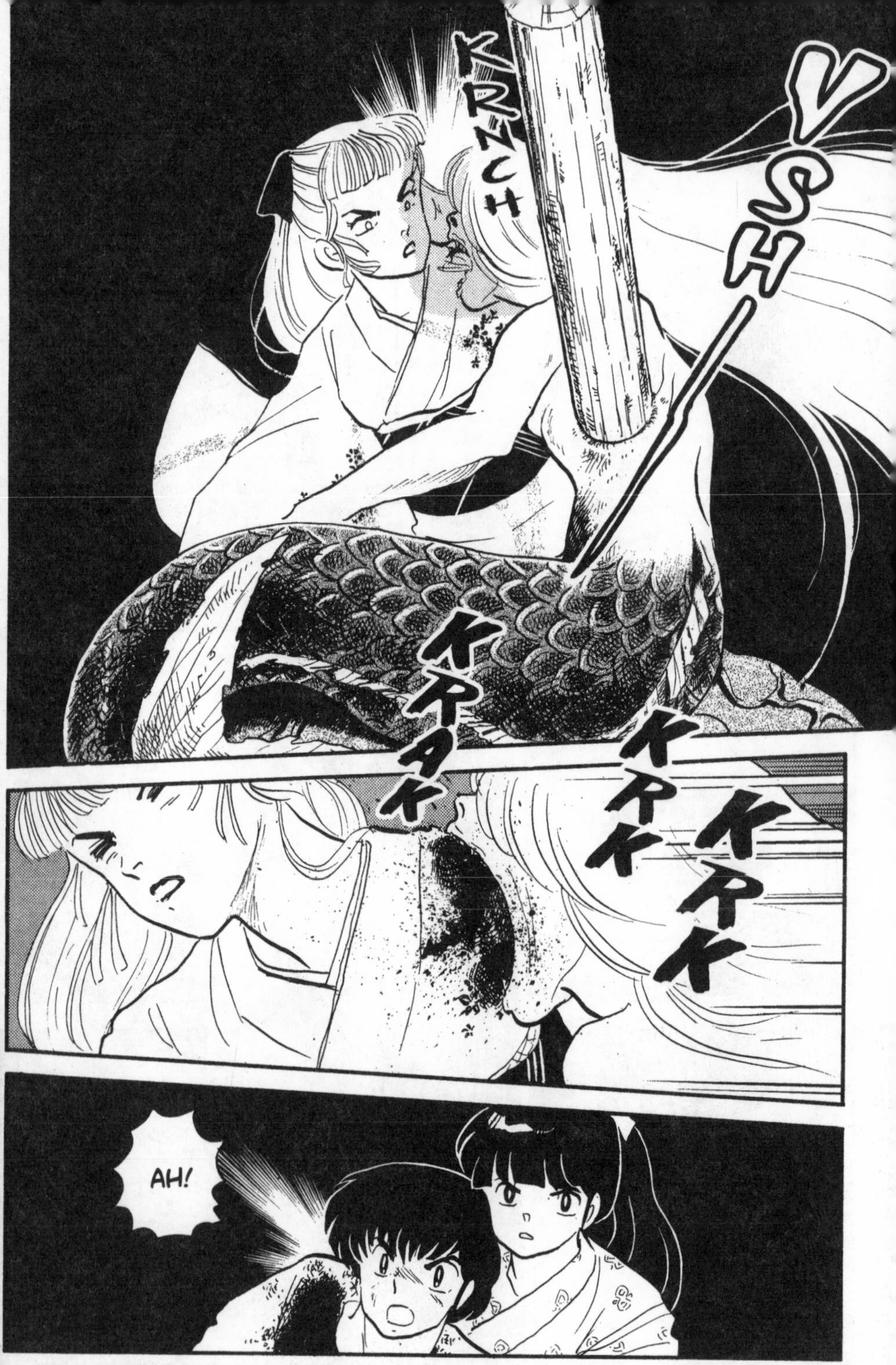
VSH
KRNCH
KRAK
KRK
KRK
AH!

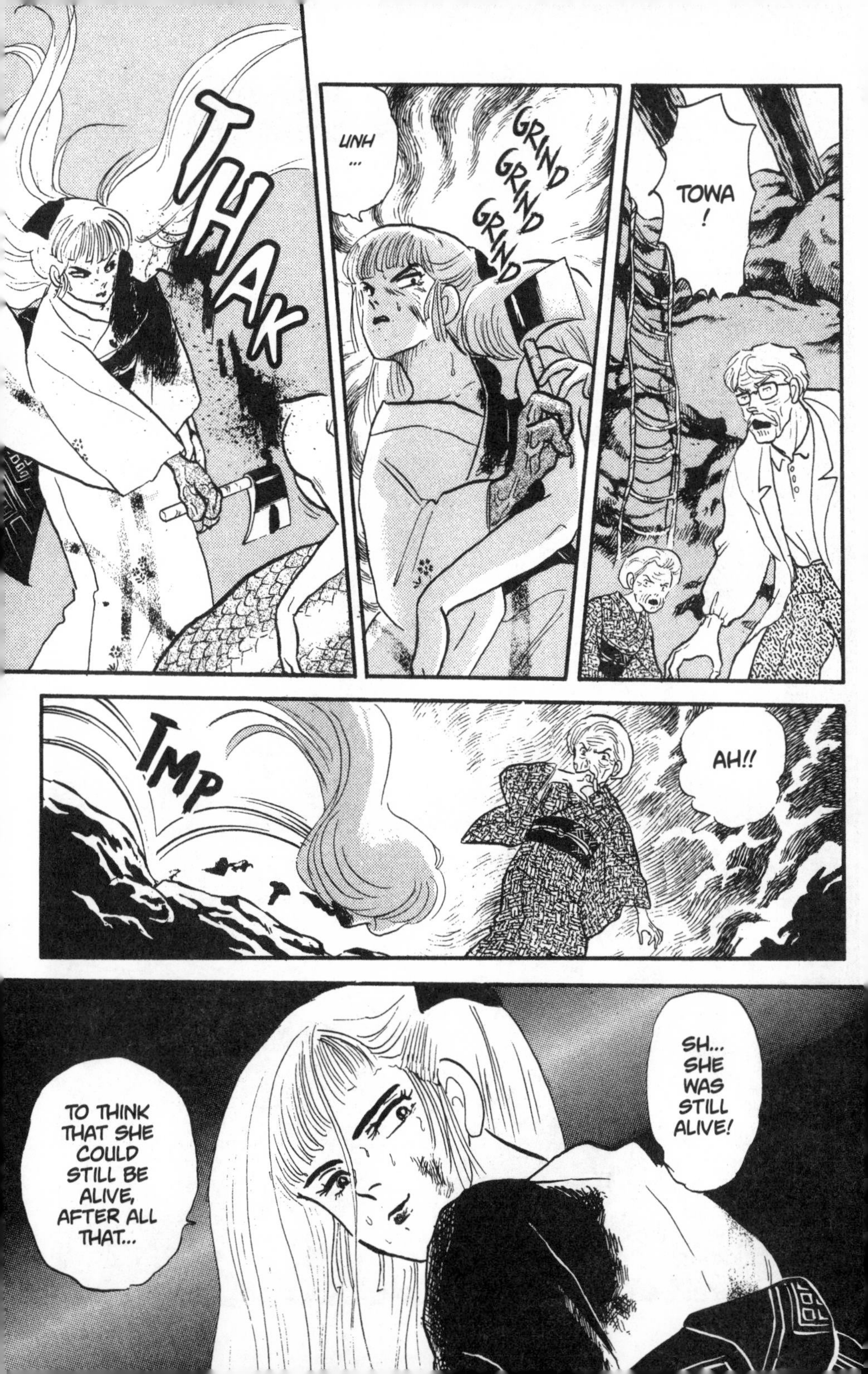
TOWA!
UNH...
GRIND GRIND GRIND
THAK
AH!!
TMP
SH... SHE WAS STILL ALIVE!
TO THINK THAT SHE COULD STILL BE ALIVE, AFTER ALL THAT...

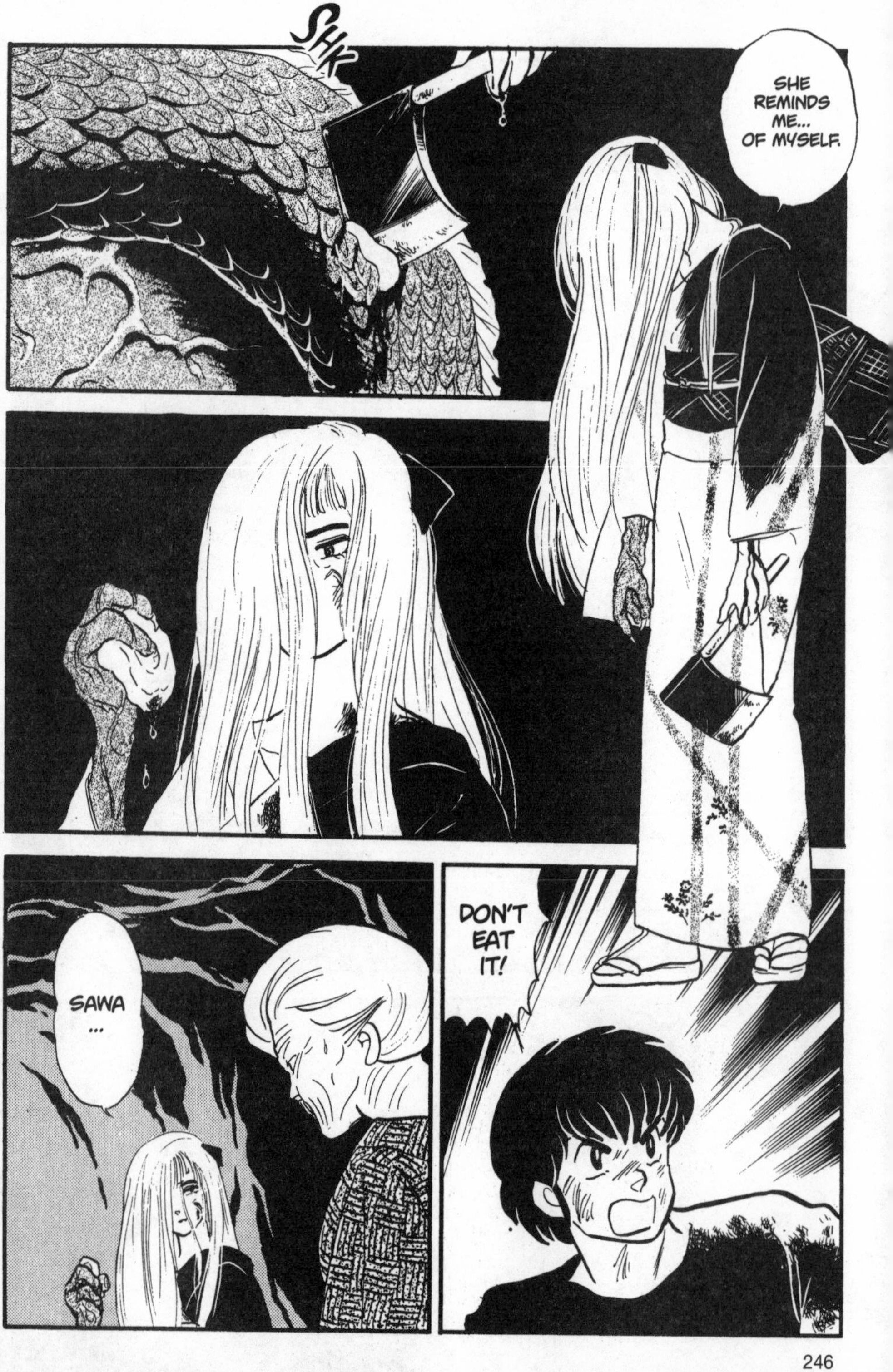
SHE REMINDS ME... OF MYSELF.
SHK
DON'T EAT IT!
SAWA ...

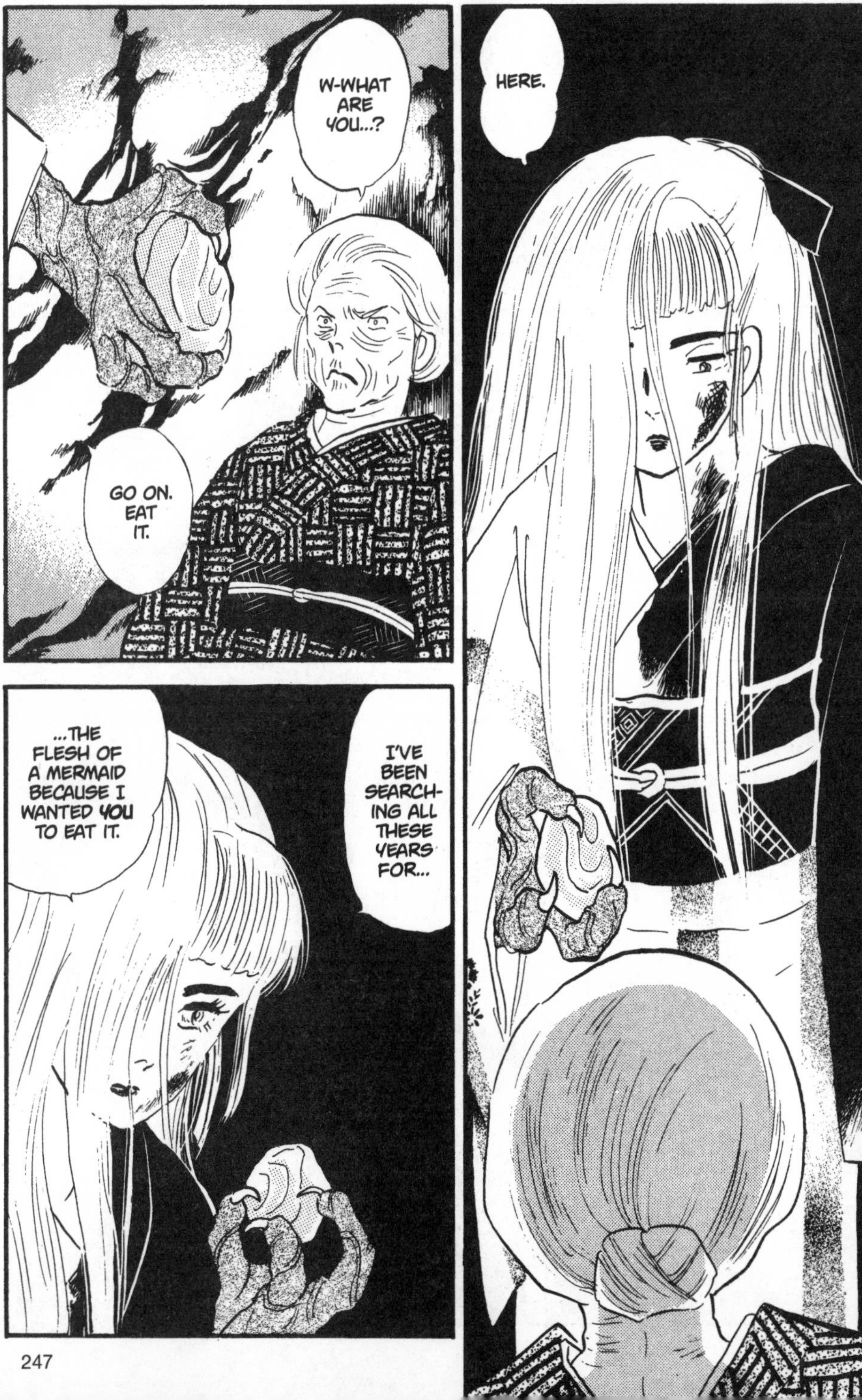
HERE.
W-WHAT ARE YOU...?
GO ON. EAT IT.
I'VE BEEN SEARCHING ALL THESE YEARS FOR...
...THE FLESH OF A MERMAID BECAUSE I WANTED YOU TO EAT IT.

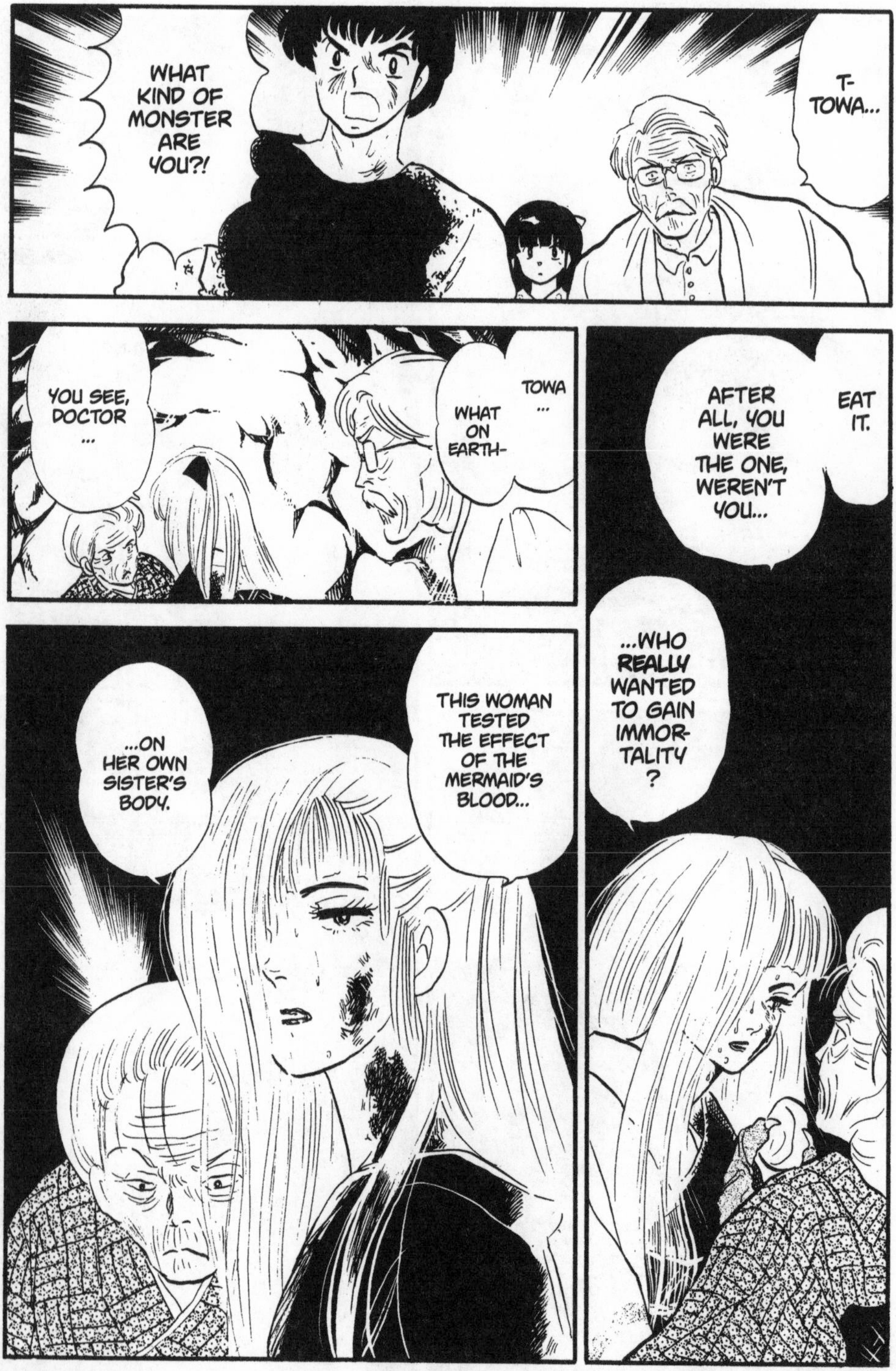
T-TOWA...
WHAT KIND OF MONSTER ARE YOU?!
TOWA... WHAT ON EARTH-
YOU SEE, DOCTOR...
THIS WOMAN TESTED THE EFFECT OF THE MERMAID'S BLOOD...
...ON HER OWN SISTER'S BODY.
EAT IT.
AFTER ALL, YOU WERE THE ONE, WEREN'T YOU...
...WHO REALLY WANTED TO GAIN IMMORTALITY?

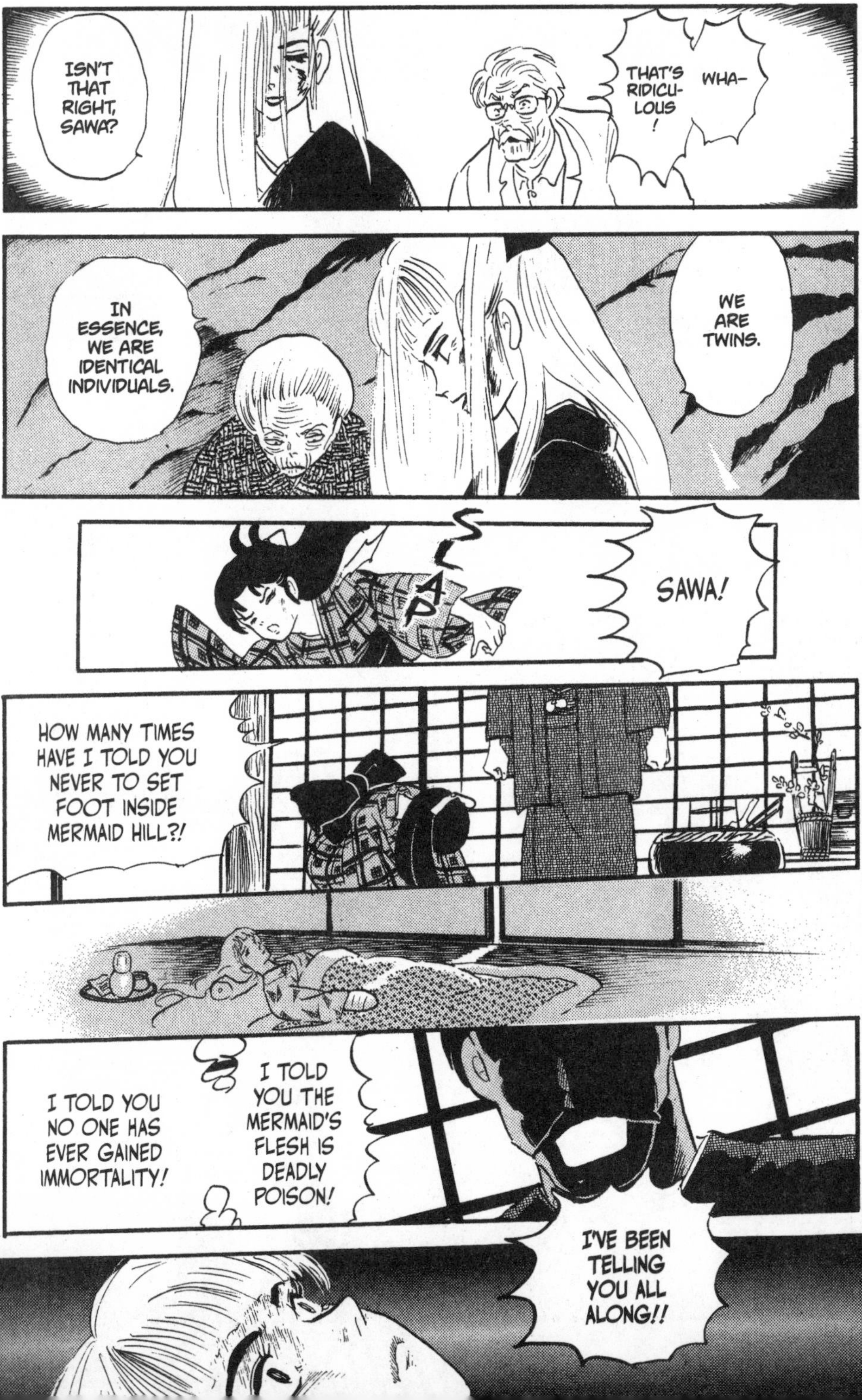
WHA-
THAT'S RIDICULOUS!
ISN'T THAT RIGHT, SAWA?
WE ARE TWINS.
IN ESSENCE, WE ARE IDENTICAL INDIVIDUALS.
SAWA!
SLAP
HOW MANY TIMES HAVE I TOLD YOU NEVER TO SET FOOT INSIDE MERMAID HILL?!
I TOLD YOU THE MERMAID'S FLESH IS DEADLY POISON!
I TOLD YOU NO ONE HAS EVER GAINED IMMORTALITY!
I'VE BEEN TELLING YOU ALL ALONG!!

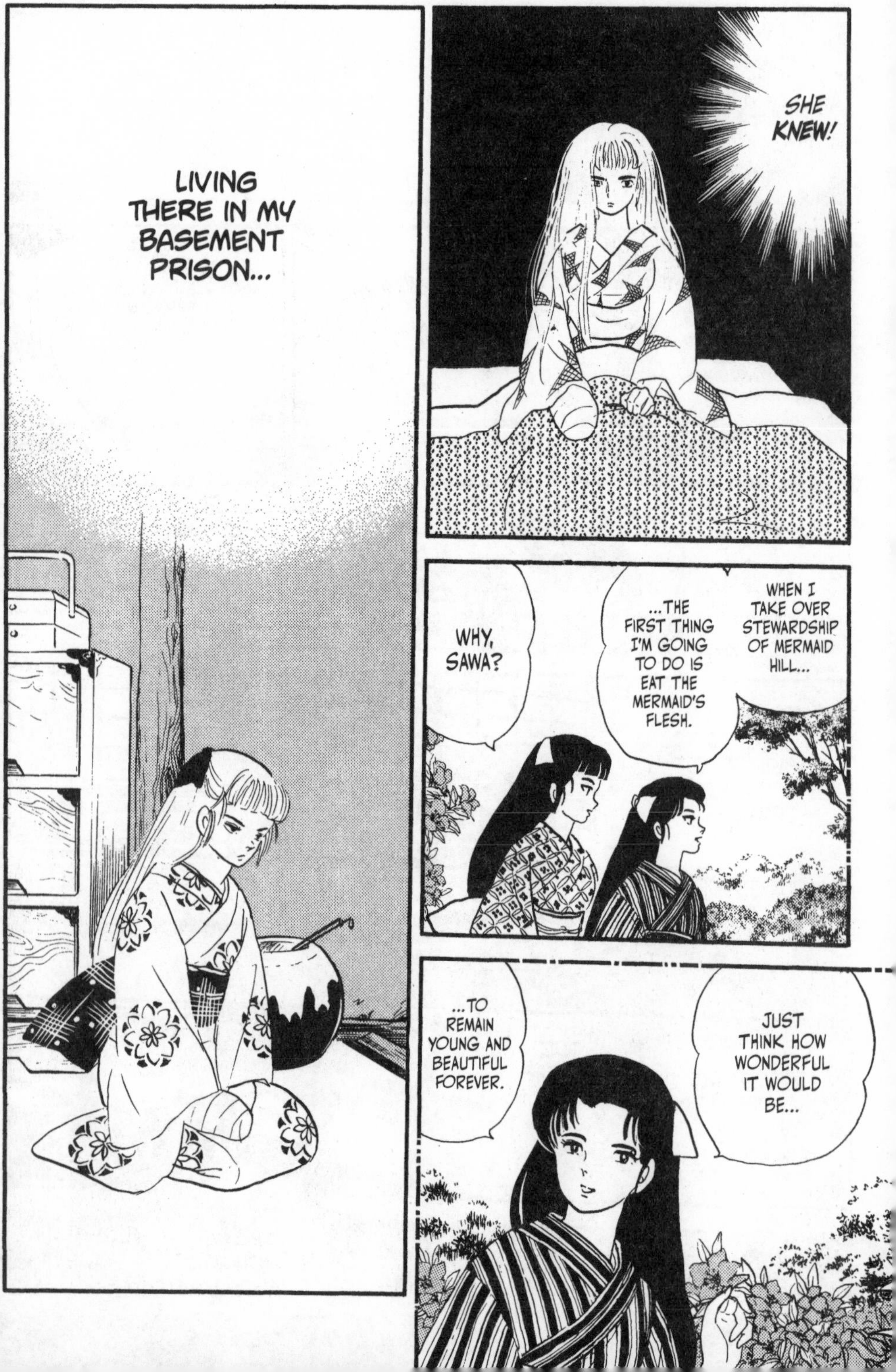
SHE KNEW!
WHEN I TAKE OVER STEWARDSHIP OF MERMAID HILL...
...THE FIRST THING I'M GOING TO DO IS EAT THE MERMAID'S FLESH.
WHY, SAWA?
JUST THINK HOW WONDERFUL IT WOULD BE...
...TO REMAIN YOUNG AND BEAUTIFUL FOREVER.
LIVING THERE IN MY BASEMENT PRISON...

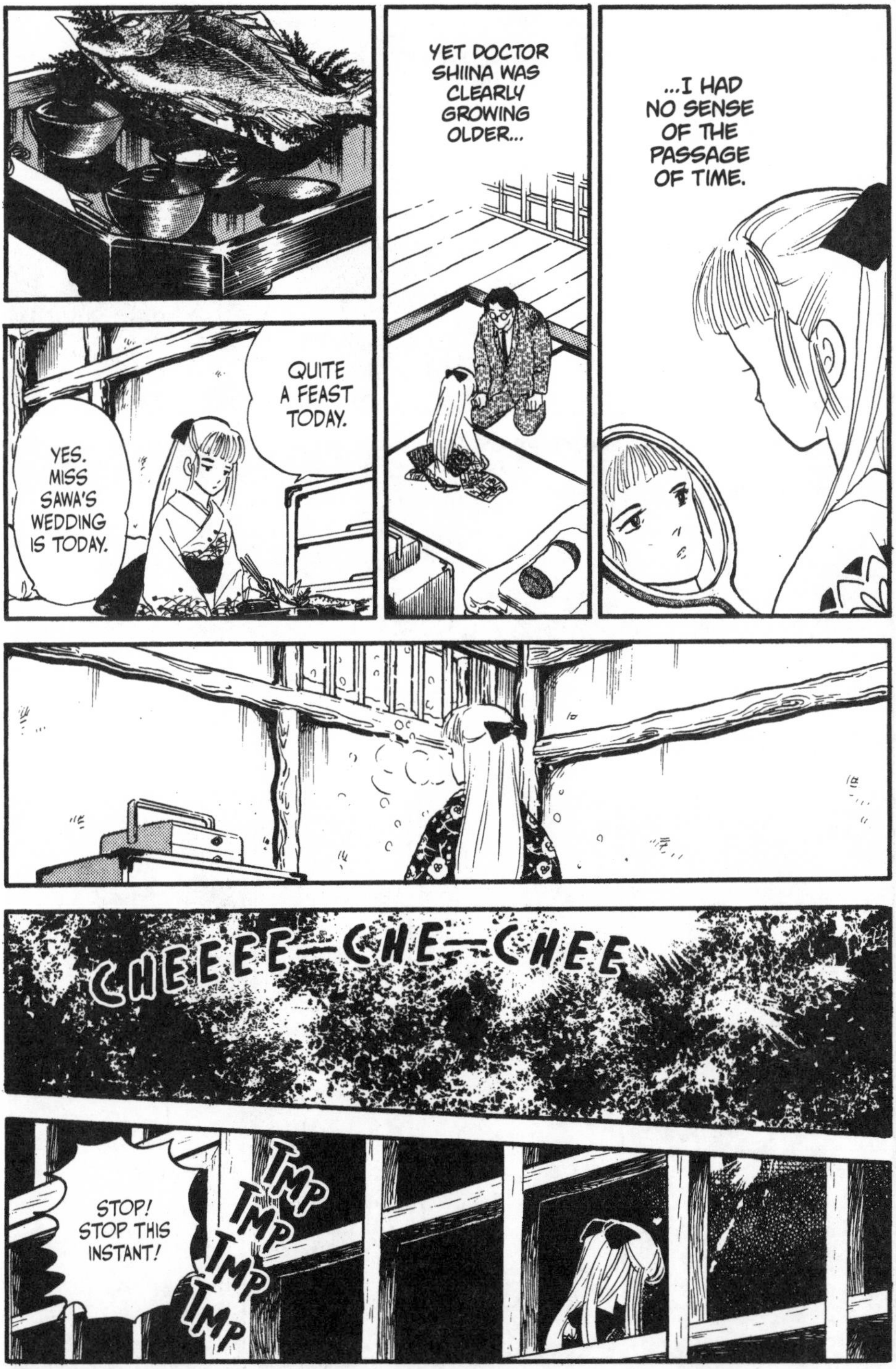
...I HAD NO SENSE OF THE PASSAGE OF TIME.
YET DOCTOR SHIINA WAS CLEARLY GROWING OLDER...
QUITE A FEAST TODAY.
YES. MISS SAWA'S WEDDING IS TODAY.
CHEEEE-CHE-CHEE
TMP TMP TMP TMP
STOP! STOP THIS INSTANT!

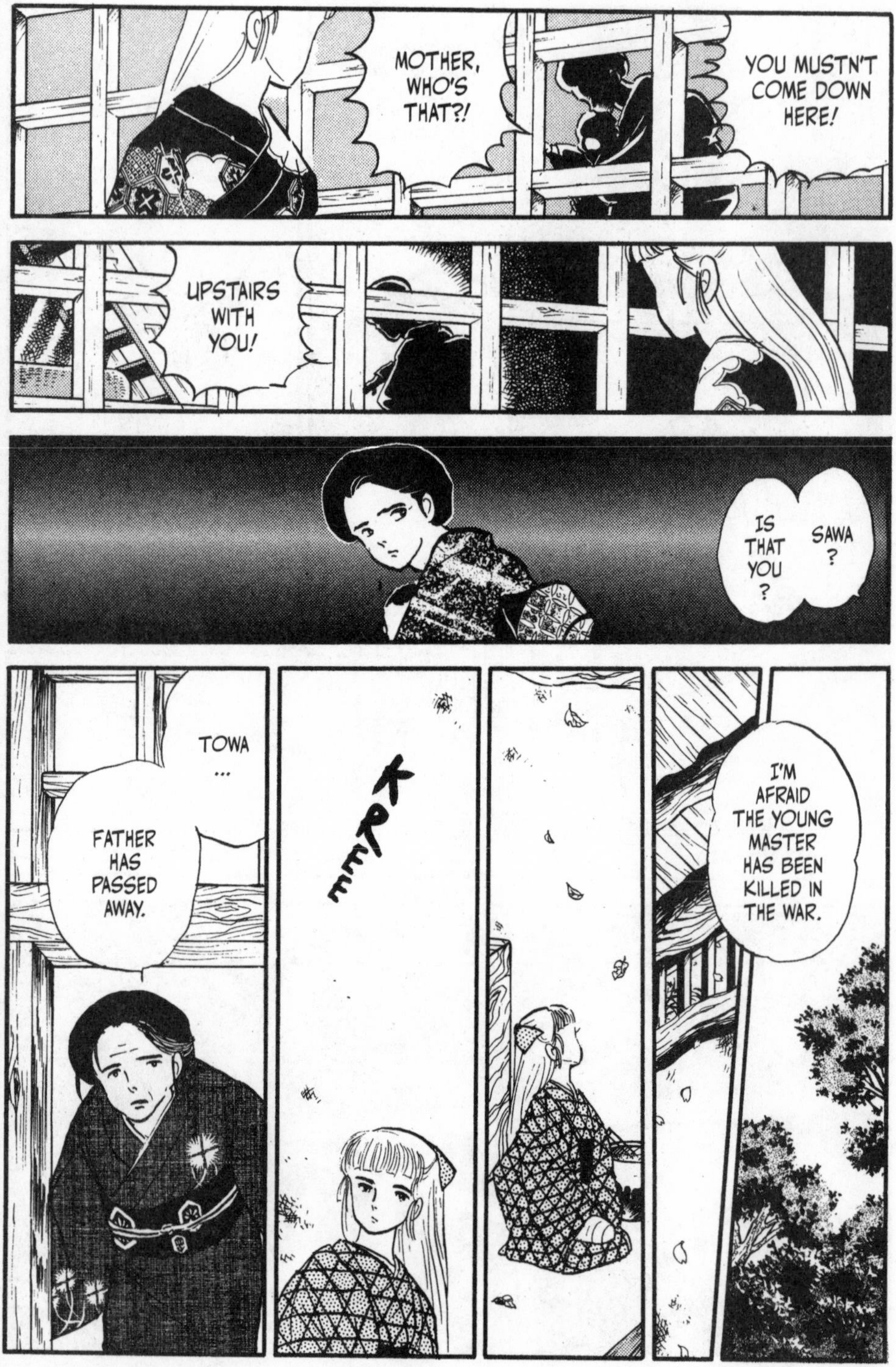
YOU MUSTN'T COME DOWN HERE!
MOTHER, WHO'S THAT?!
UPSTAIRS WITH YOU!
SAWA?
IS THAT YOU?
I'M AFRAID THE YOUNG MASTER HAS BEEN KILLED IN THE WAR.
KREEE
TOWA...
FATHER HAS PASSED AWAY.

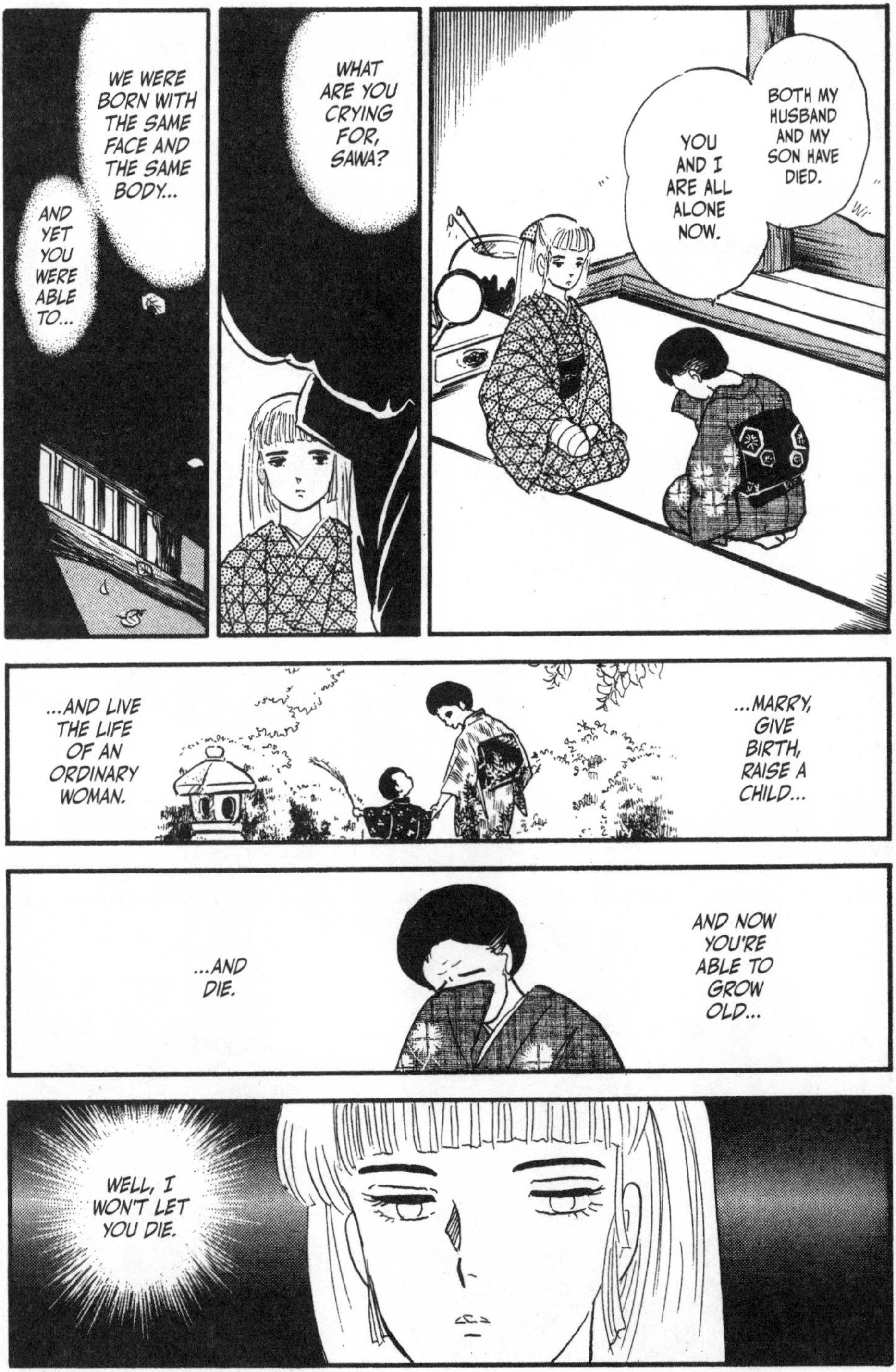
BOTH MY HUSBAND AND MY SON HAVE DIED.
YOU AND I ARE ALL ALONE NOW.
WHAT ARE YOU CRYING FOR, SAWA?
WE WERE BORN WITH THE SAME FACE AND THE SAME BODY...
AND YET YOU WERE ABLE TO...
...MARRY, GIVE BIRTH, RAISE A CHILD...
...AND LIVE THE LIFE OF AN ORDINARY WOMAN.
AND NOW YOU'RE ABLE TO GROW OLD...
...AND DIE.
WELL, I WON'T LET YOU DIE.

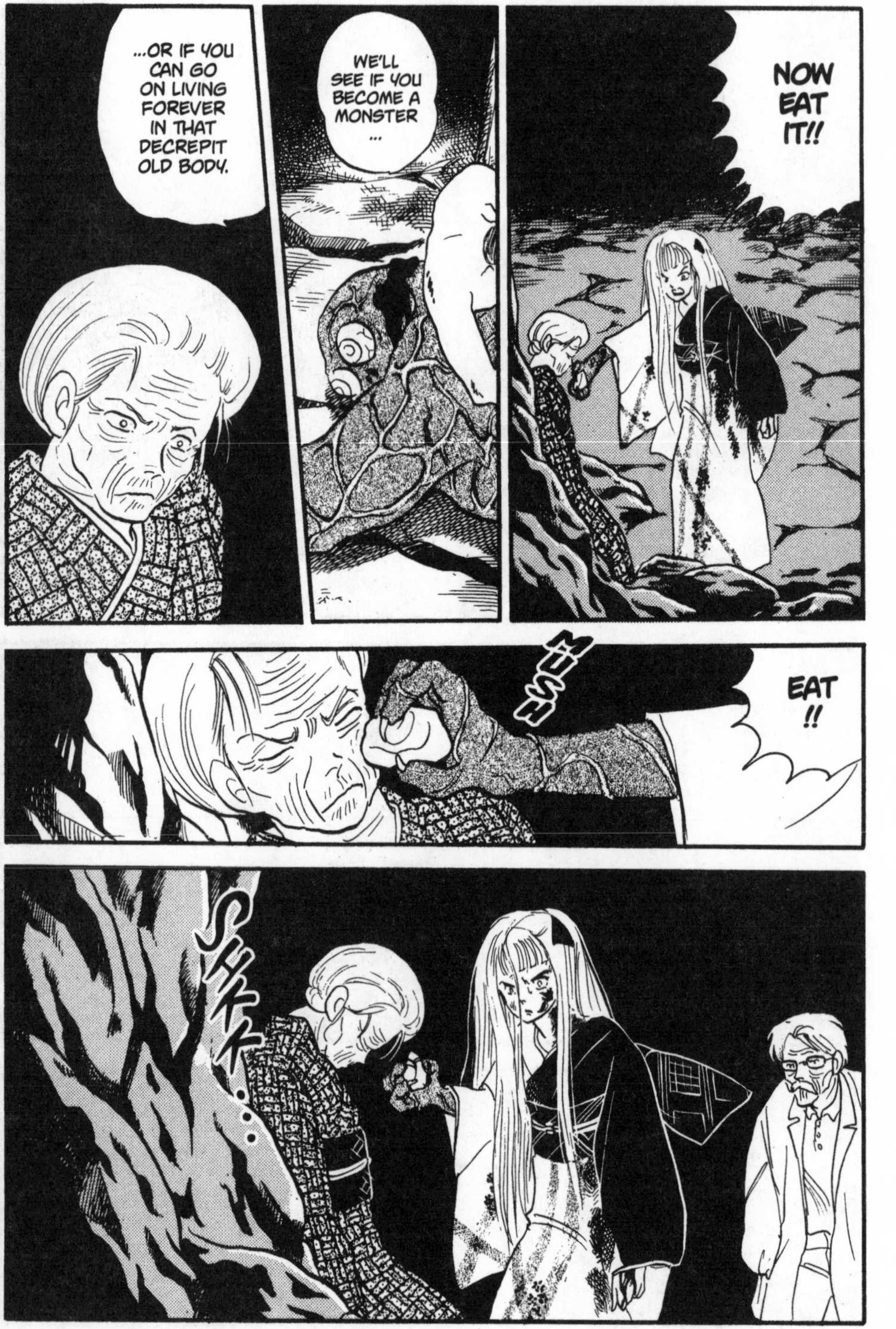
NOW EAT IT!!
WE'LL SEE IF YOU BECOME A MONSTER ...
...OR IF YOU CAN GO ON LIVING FOREVER IN THAT DECREPIT OLD BODY.
EAT !!
MUSH
SHKK...

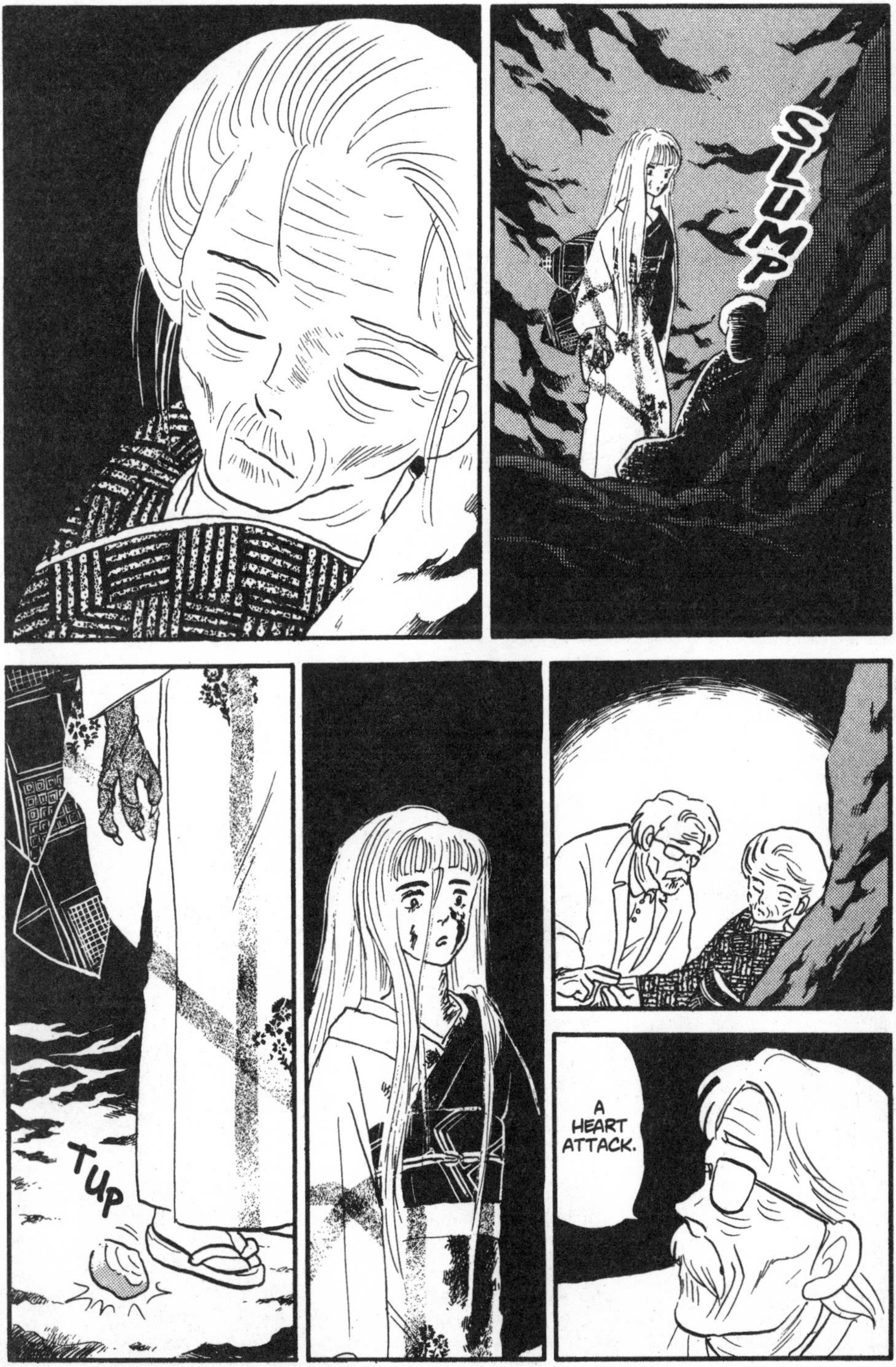
SLUMP
A HEART ATTACK.
TUP

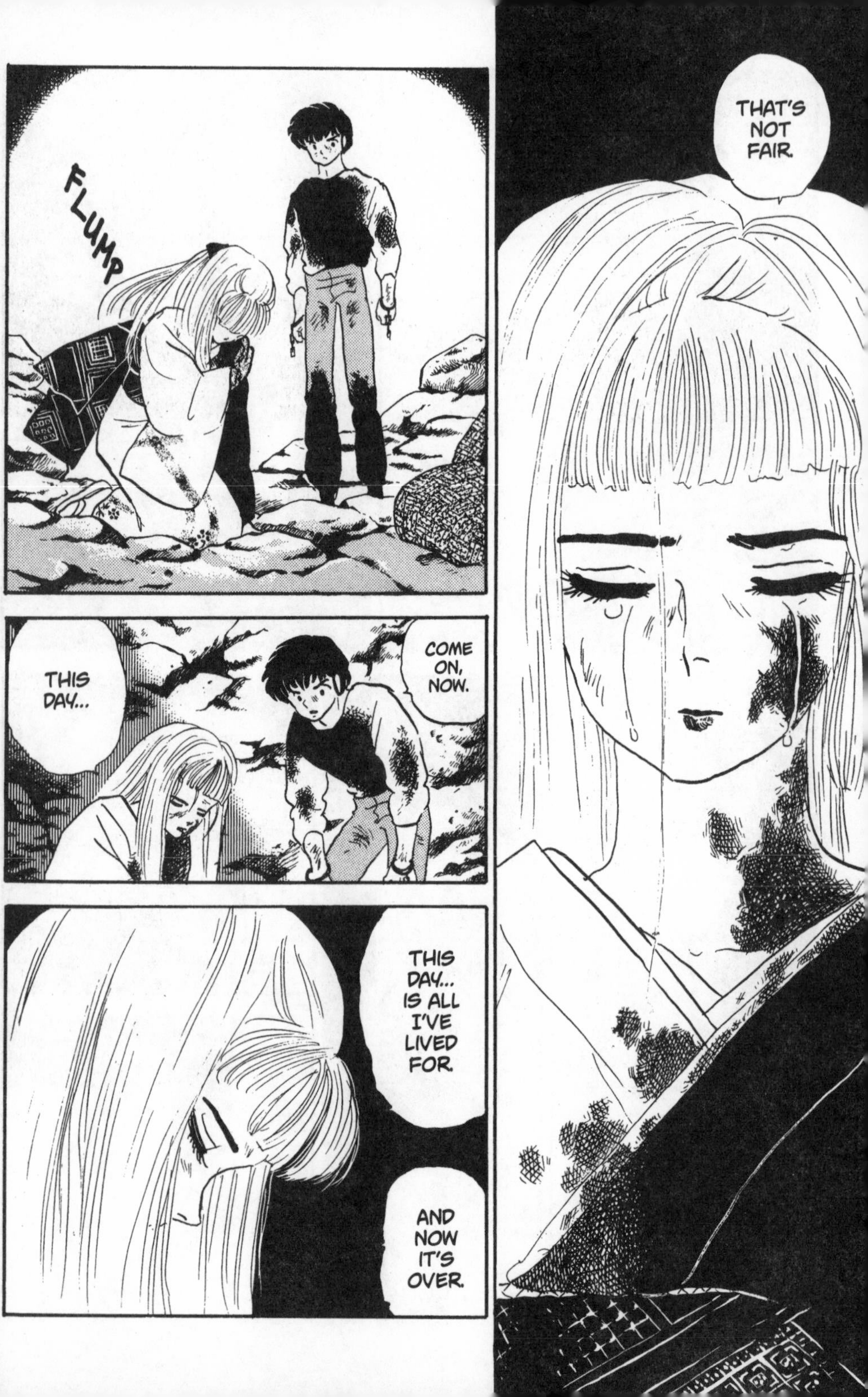
FLUMP
COME ON, NOW.
THIS DAY...
THIS DAY... IS ALL I'VE LIVED FOR.
AND NOW IT'S OVER.
THAT'S NOT FAIR.

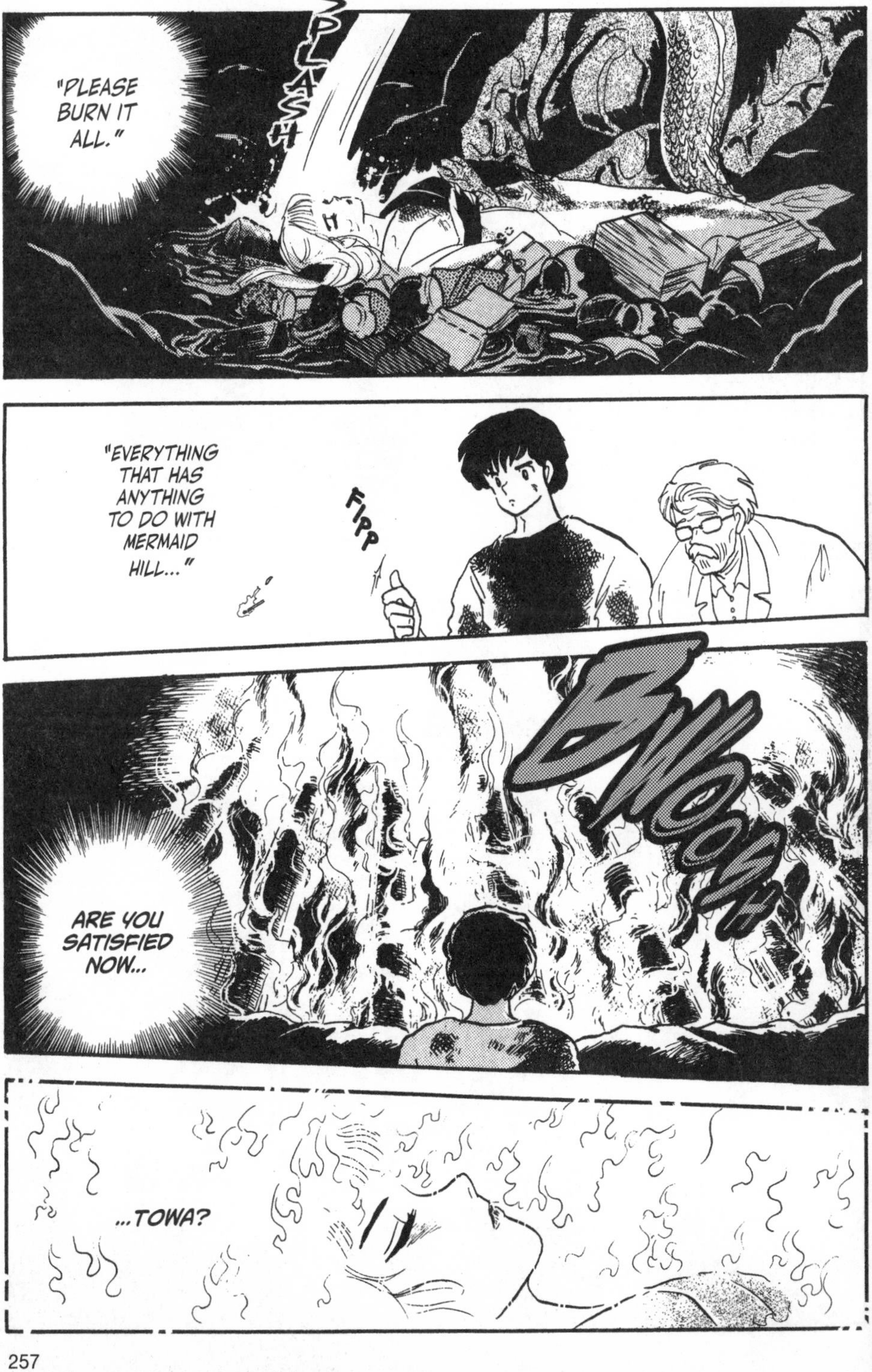
"PLEASE BURN IT ALL."
SPLASH
"EVERYTHING THAT HAS ANYTHING TO DO WITH MERMAID HILL..."
FIPP
ARE YOU SATISFIED NOW...
...TOWA?

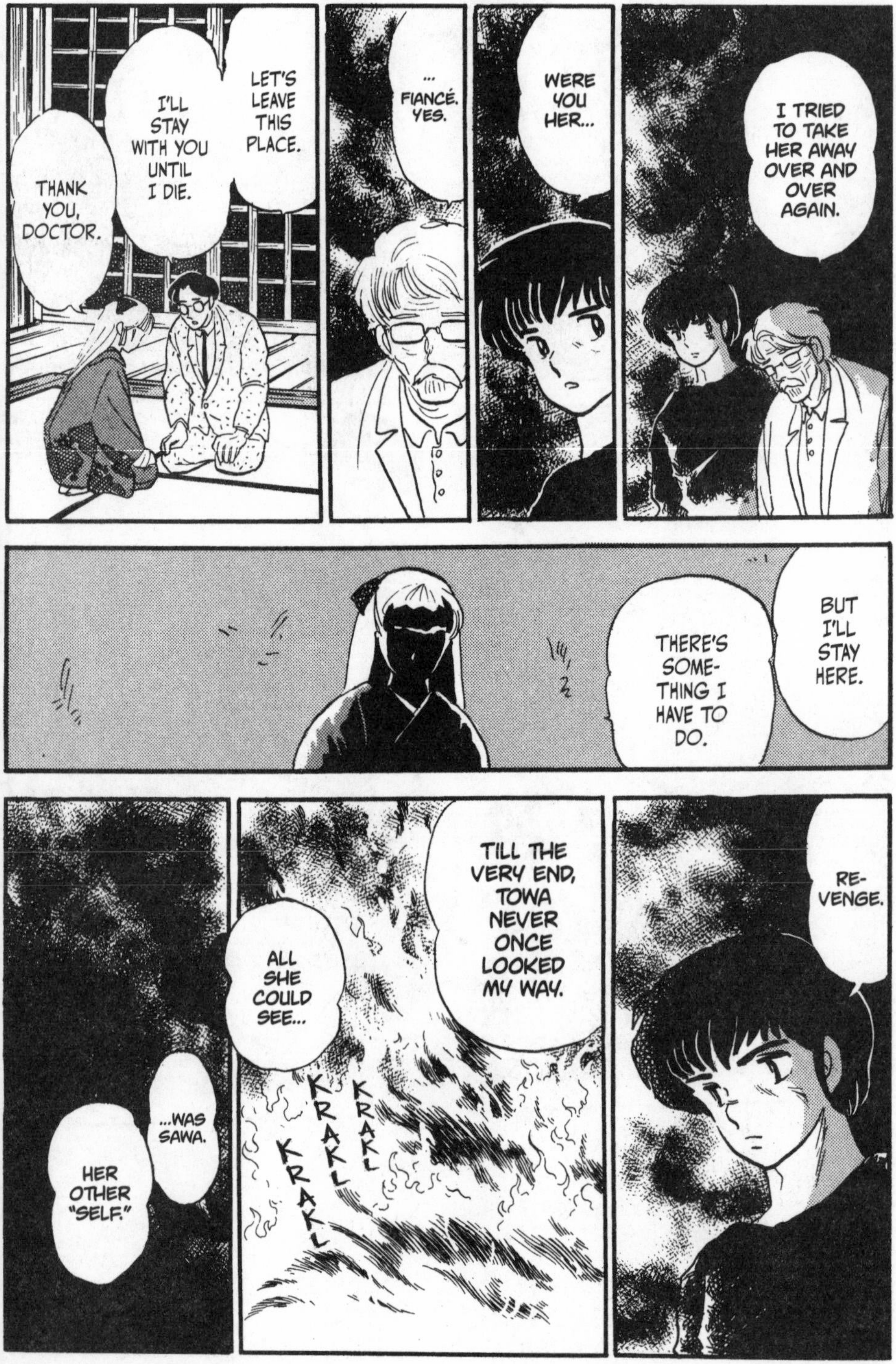

I TRIED TO TAKE HER AWAY OVER AND OVER AGAIN.
WERE YOU HER...
... FIANCÉ. YES.
LET'S LEAVE THIS PLACE.
I'LL STAY WITH YOU UNTIL I DIE.
THANK YOU, DOCTOR.
BUT I'LL STAY HERE.
THERE'S SOME- THING I HAVE TO DO.
RE- VENGE.
TILL THE VERY END, TOWA NEVER ONCE LOOKED MY WAY.
ALL SHE COULD SEE...
KRAKL KRAKL KRAKL
...WAS SAWA.
HER OTHER "SELF."

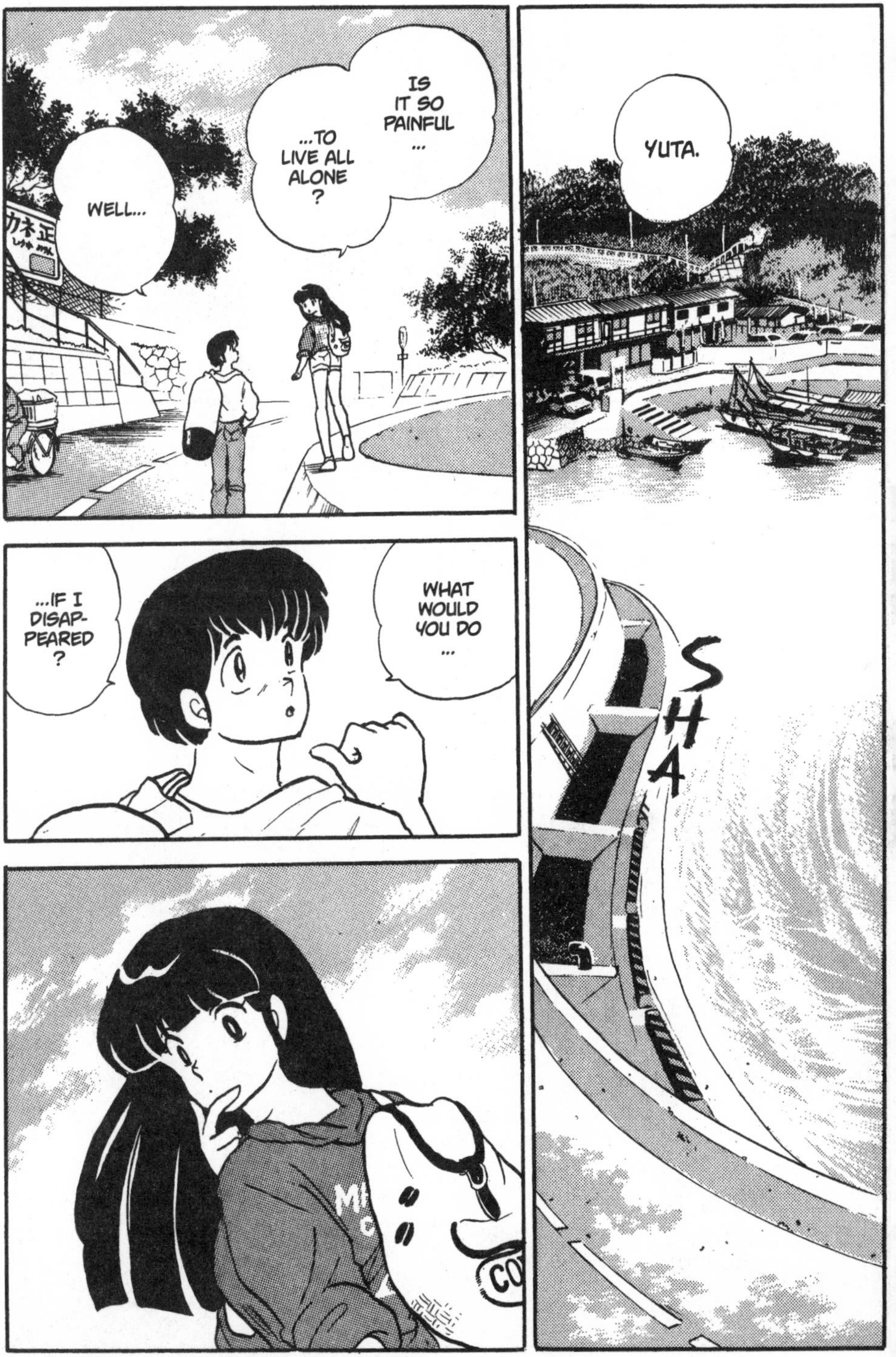
YUTA.
SHA
IS IT SO PAINFUL ...
...TO LIVE ALL ALONE ?
WELL...
WHAT WOULD YOU DO ...
...IF I DISAP-PEARED ?

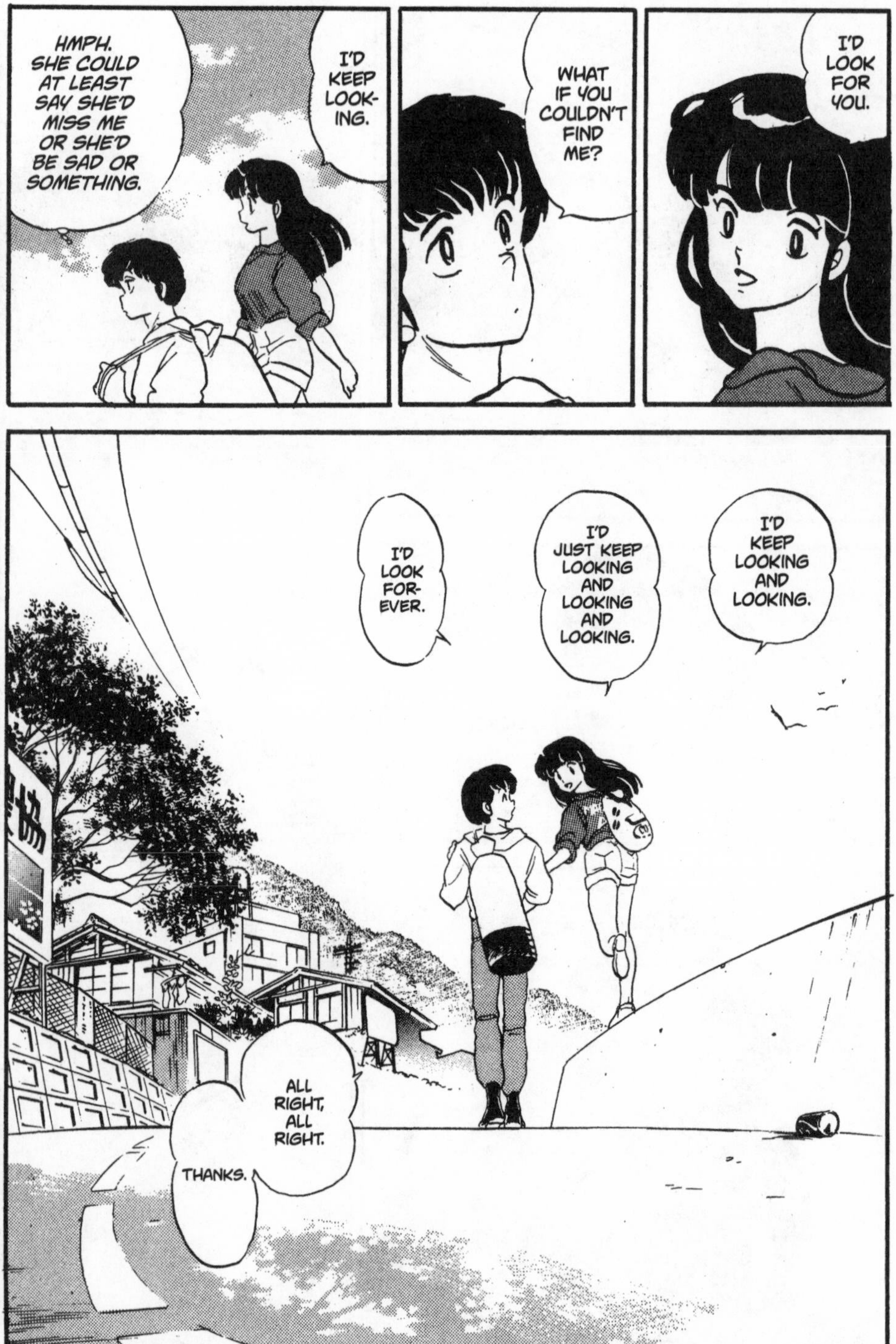
I'D LOOK FOR YOU.
WHAT IF YOU COULDN'T FIND ME?
I'D KEEP LOOK-ING.
HMPH. SHE COULD AT LEAST SAY SHE'D MISS ME OR SHE'D BE SAD OR SOMETHING.
I'D KEEP LOOKING AND LOOKING.
I'D JUST KEEP LOOKING AND LOOKING AND LOOKING.
I'D LOOK FOR-EVER.
ALL RIGHT, ALL RIGHT.
THANKS.

MERMAID FOREST / THE END

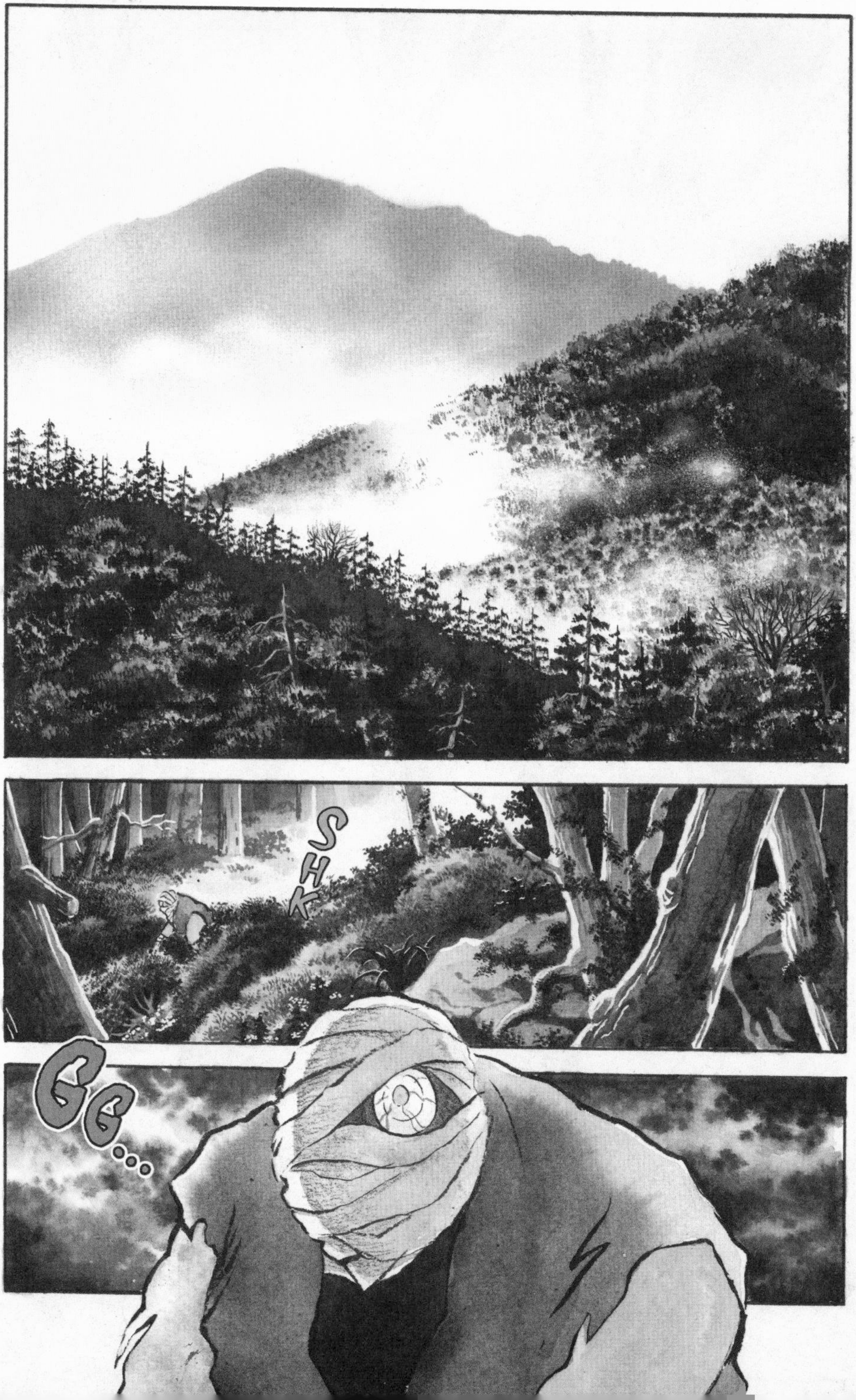
SHK
GG...

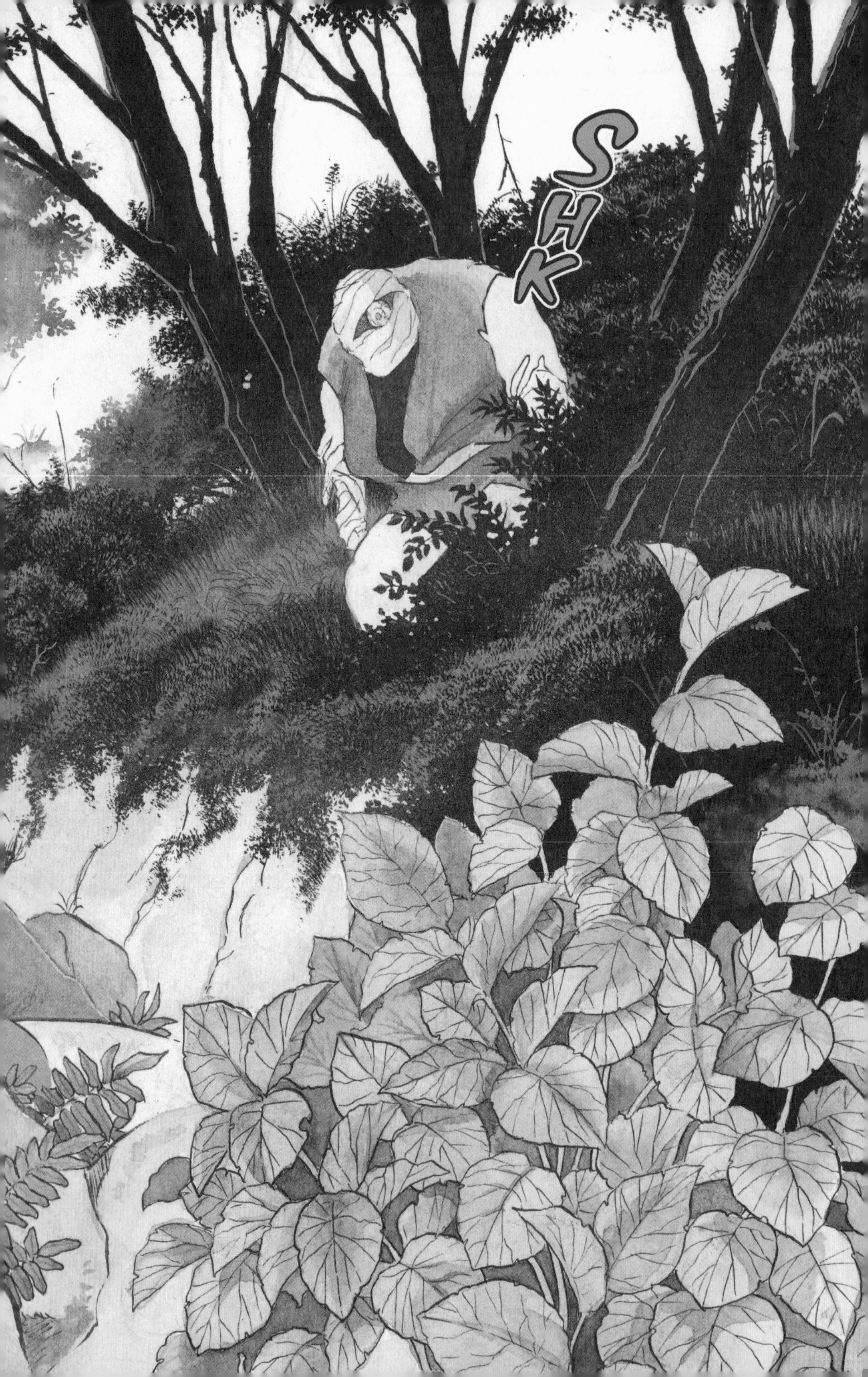
SHK

Chapter 7: Dream's End

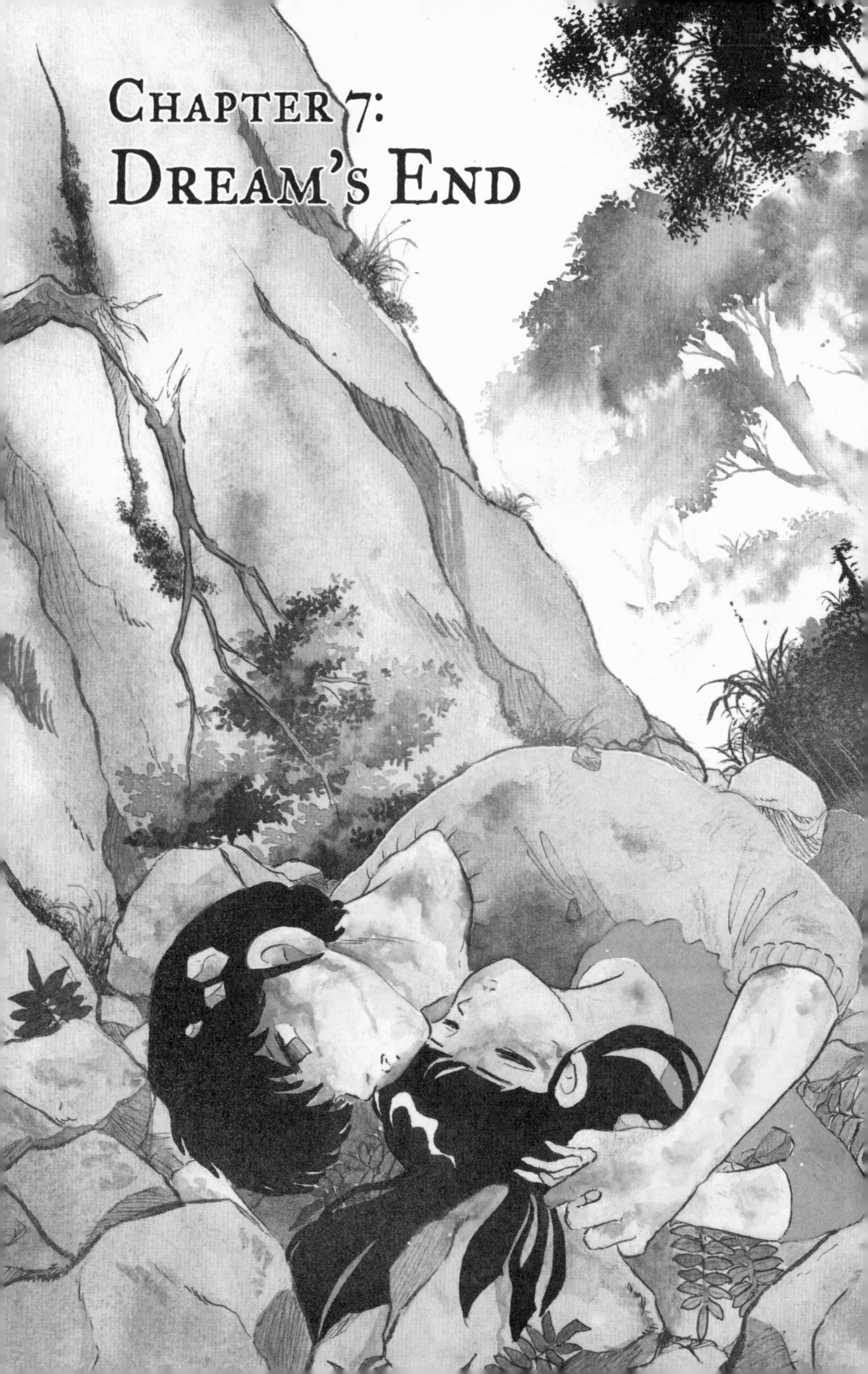

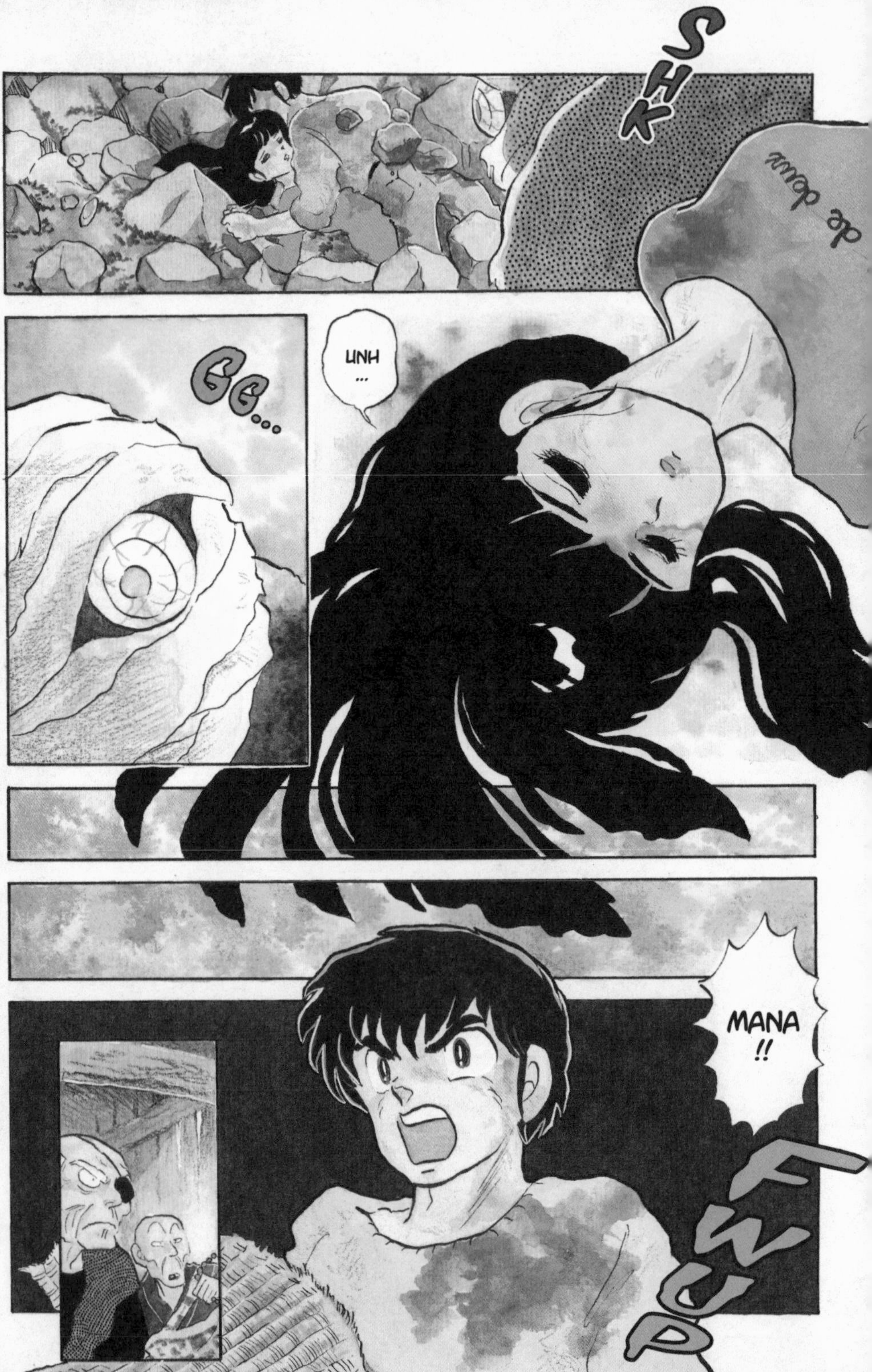
SHK
UNH ...
GG...
MANA !!
FWUP

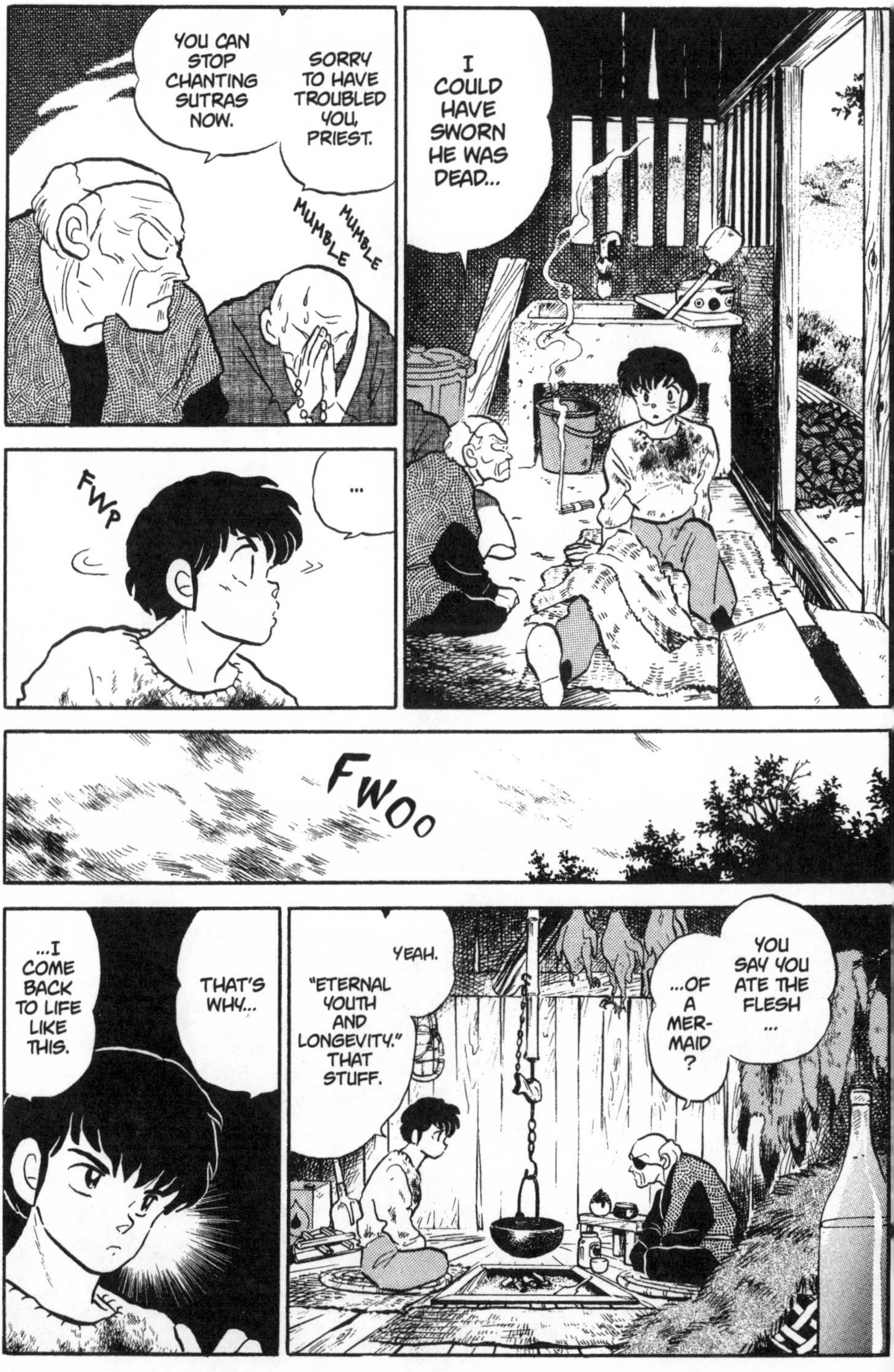
I COULD HAVE SWORN HE WAS DEAD...
SORRY TO HAVE TROUBLED YOU, PRIEST.
YOU CAN STOP CHANTING SUTRAS NOW.
MUMBLE MUMBLE
...
FWP
FWOO
YOU SAY YOU ATE THE FLESH ...
...OF A MER-MAID?
YEAH.
"ETERNAL YOUTH AND LONGEVITY." THAT STUFF.
THAT'S WHY...
...I COME BACK TO LIFE LIKE THIS.

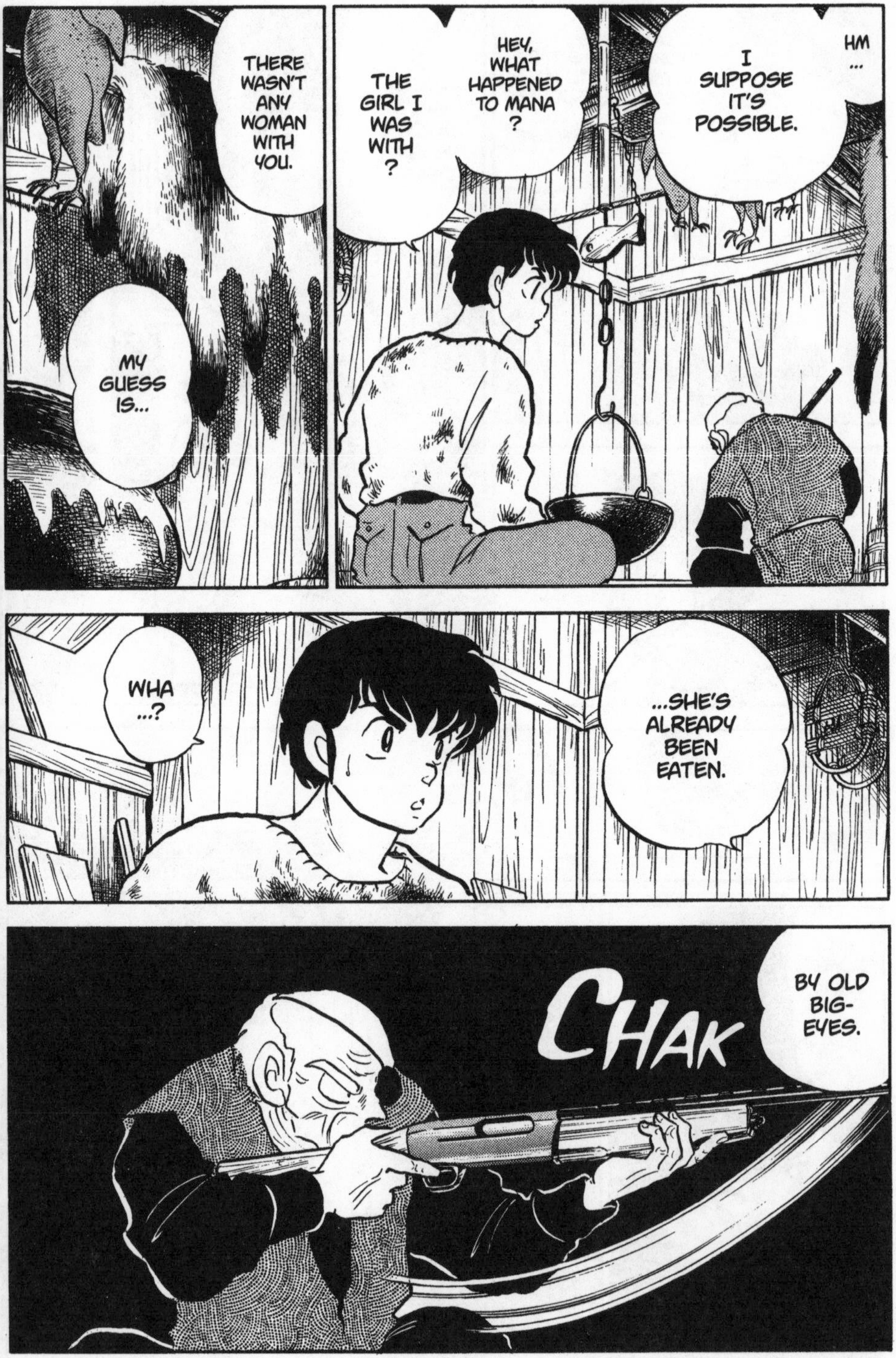
HM ...
I SUPPOSE IT'S POSSIBLE.
HEY, WHAT HAPPENED TO MANA?
THE GIRL I WAS WITH?
THERE WASN'T ANY WOMAN WITH YOU.
MY GUESS IS...
...SHE'S ALREADY BEEN EATEN.
WHA ...?
BY OLD BIG-EYES.
CHAK

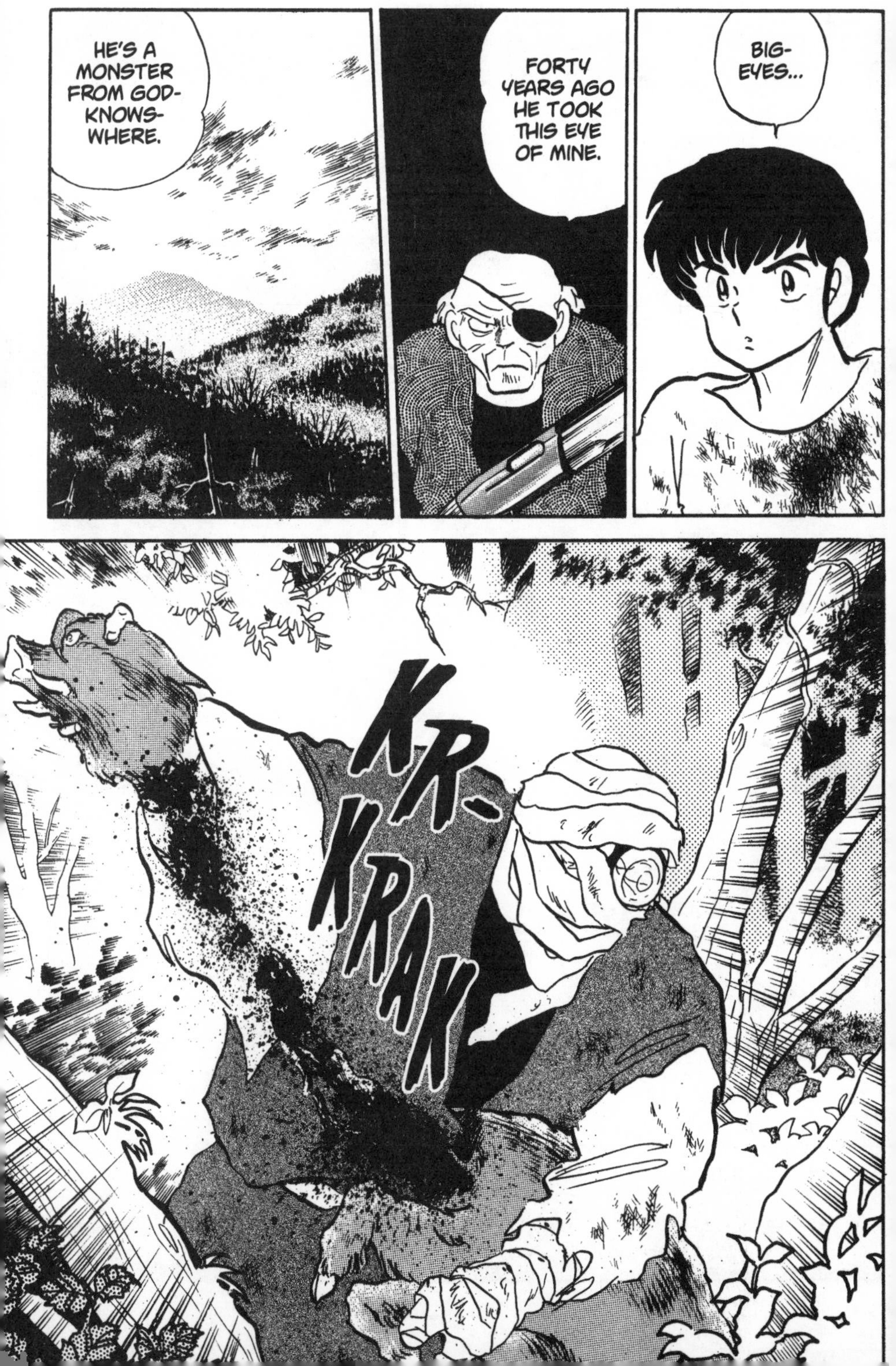
BIG-EYES...
FORTY YEARS AGO HE TOOK THIS EYE OF MINE.
HE'S A MONSTER FROM GOD-KNOWS-WHERE.
KR-KRAK

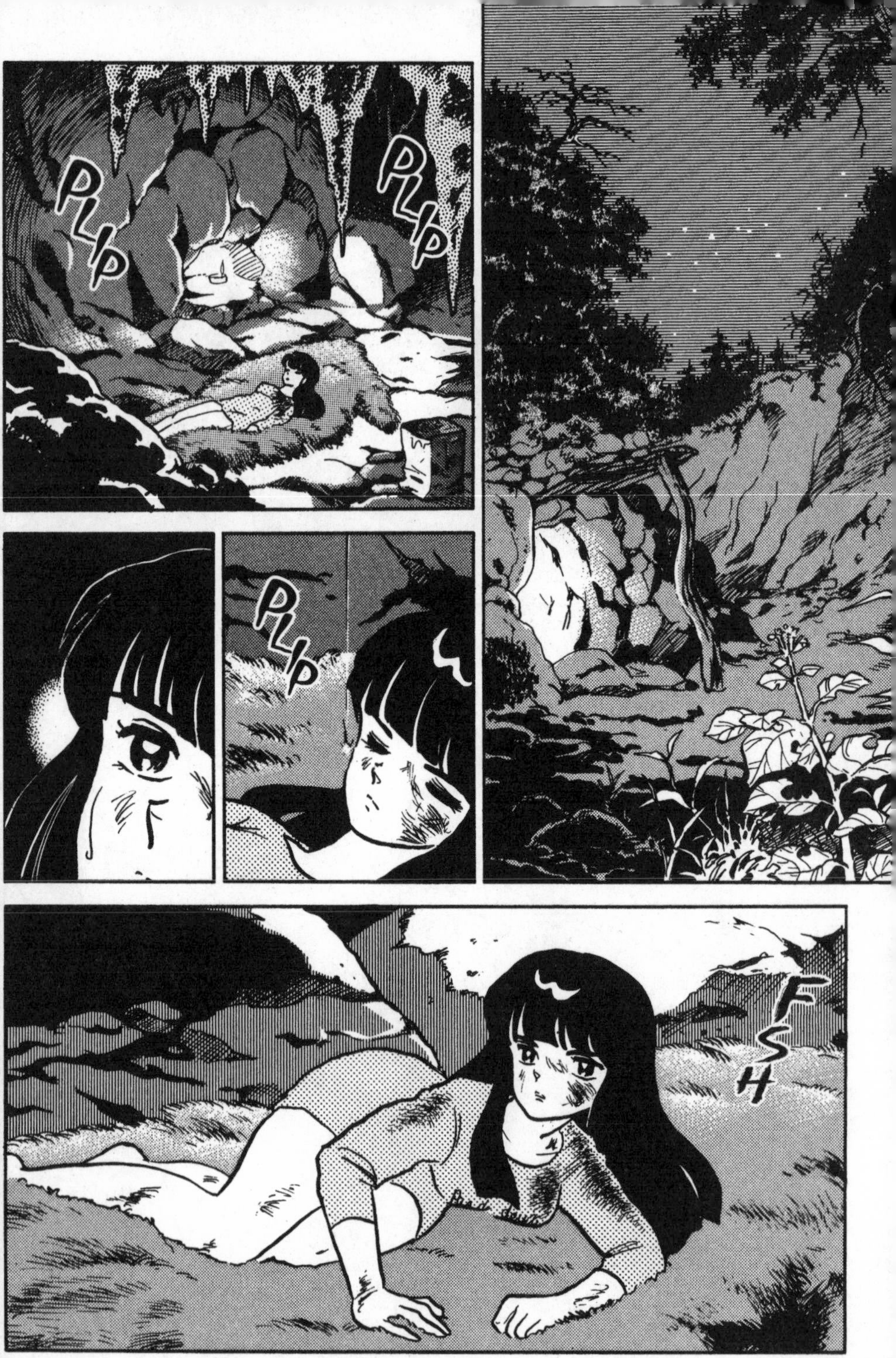
PLIP
PLIP
PLIP
FSH

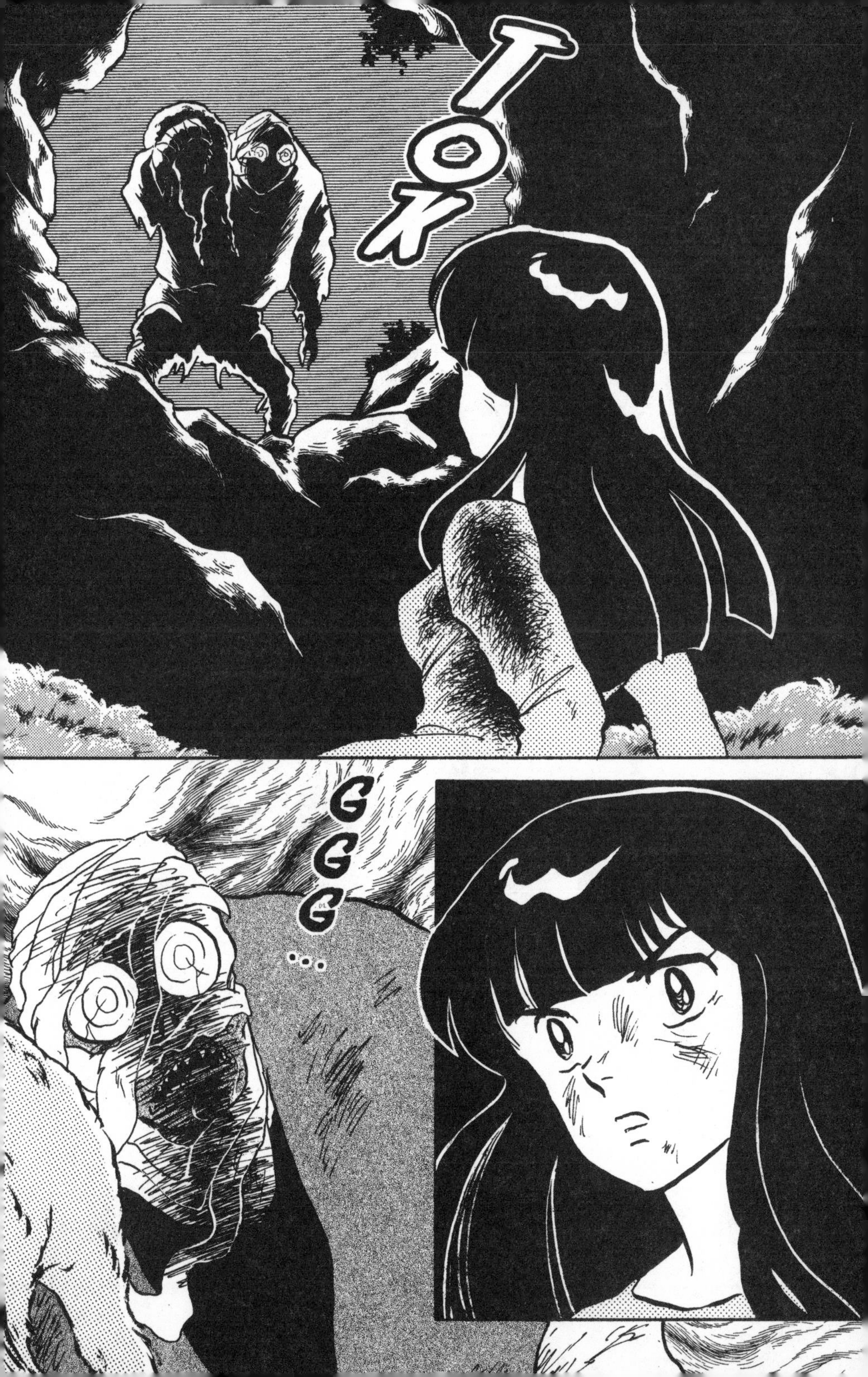
TOK
GGG
...

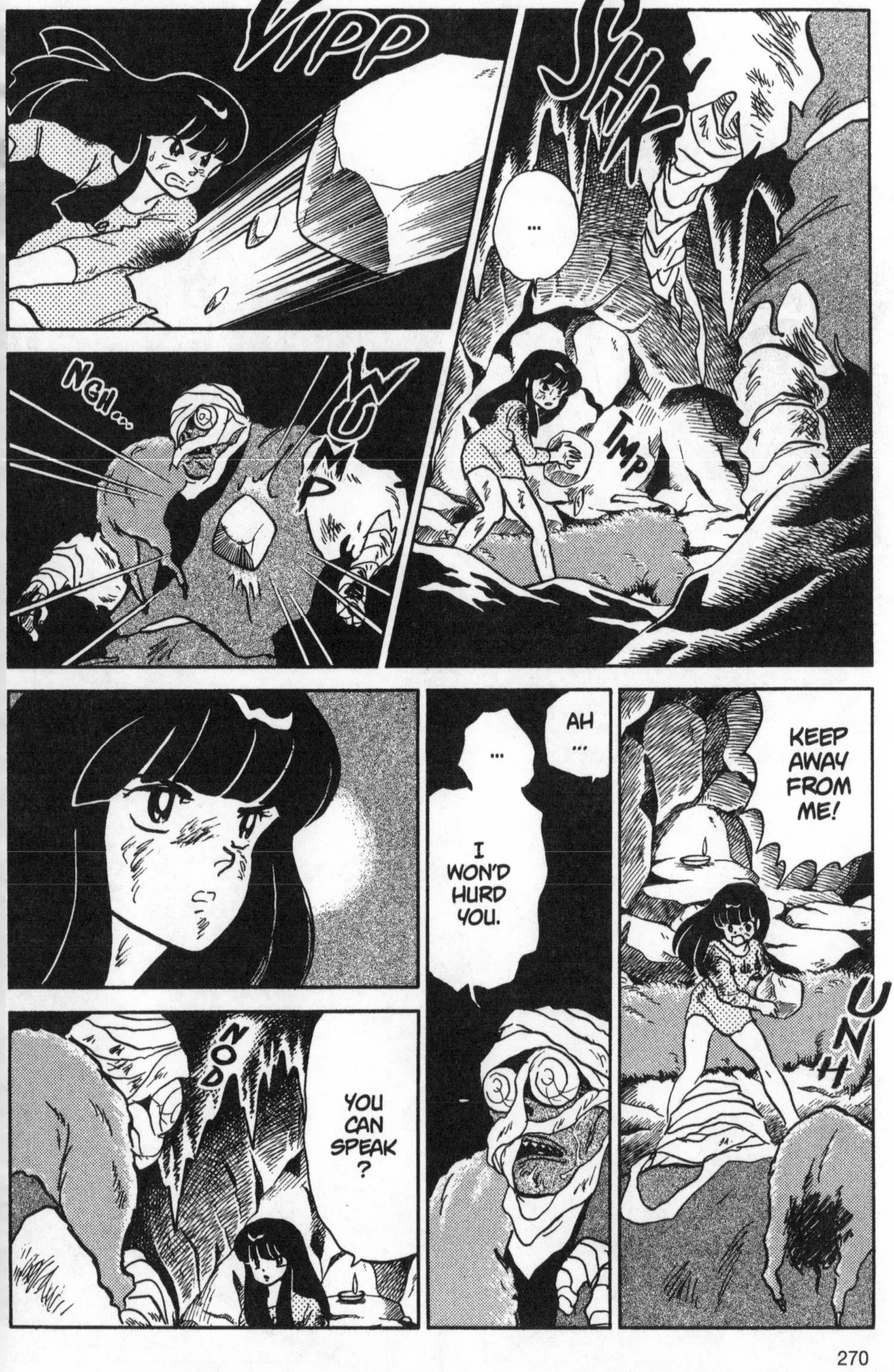
SHK
...
TMP
VIPP
WUMP
Neh...
KEEP AWAY FROM ME!
UNH
AH ...
...
I WON'D HURD YOU.
NOD
YOU CAN SPEAK ?

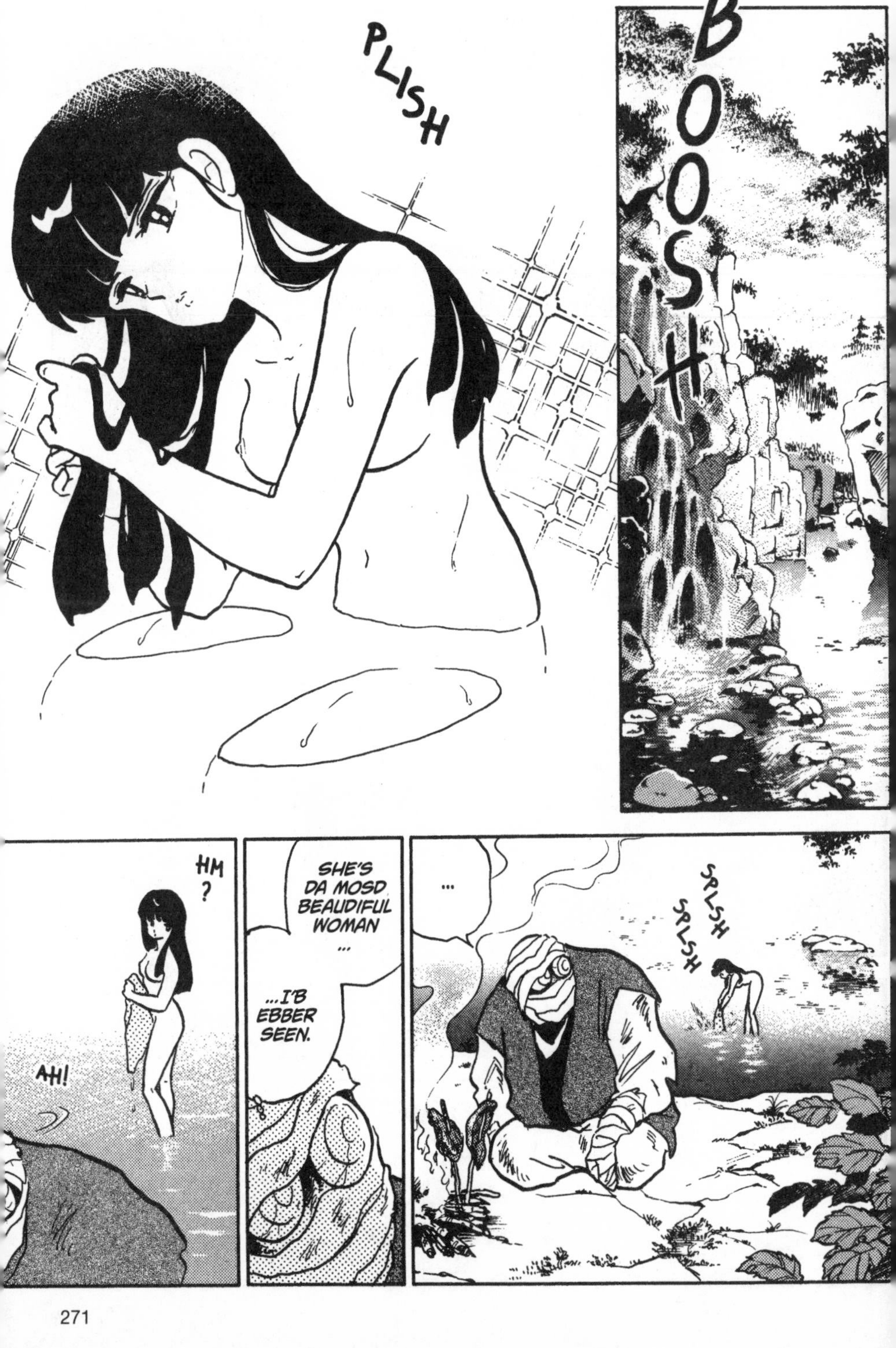
BOOOSH
PLISH
...
SRLSH SRLSH
SHE'S DA MOSD BEAUDIFUL WOMAN ...
...I'B EBBER SEEN.
HM ?
AH!

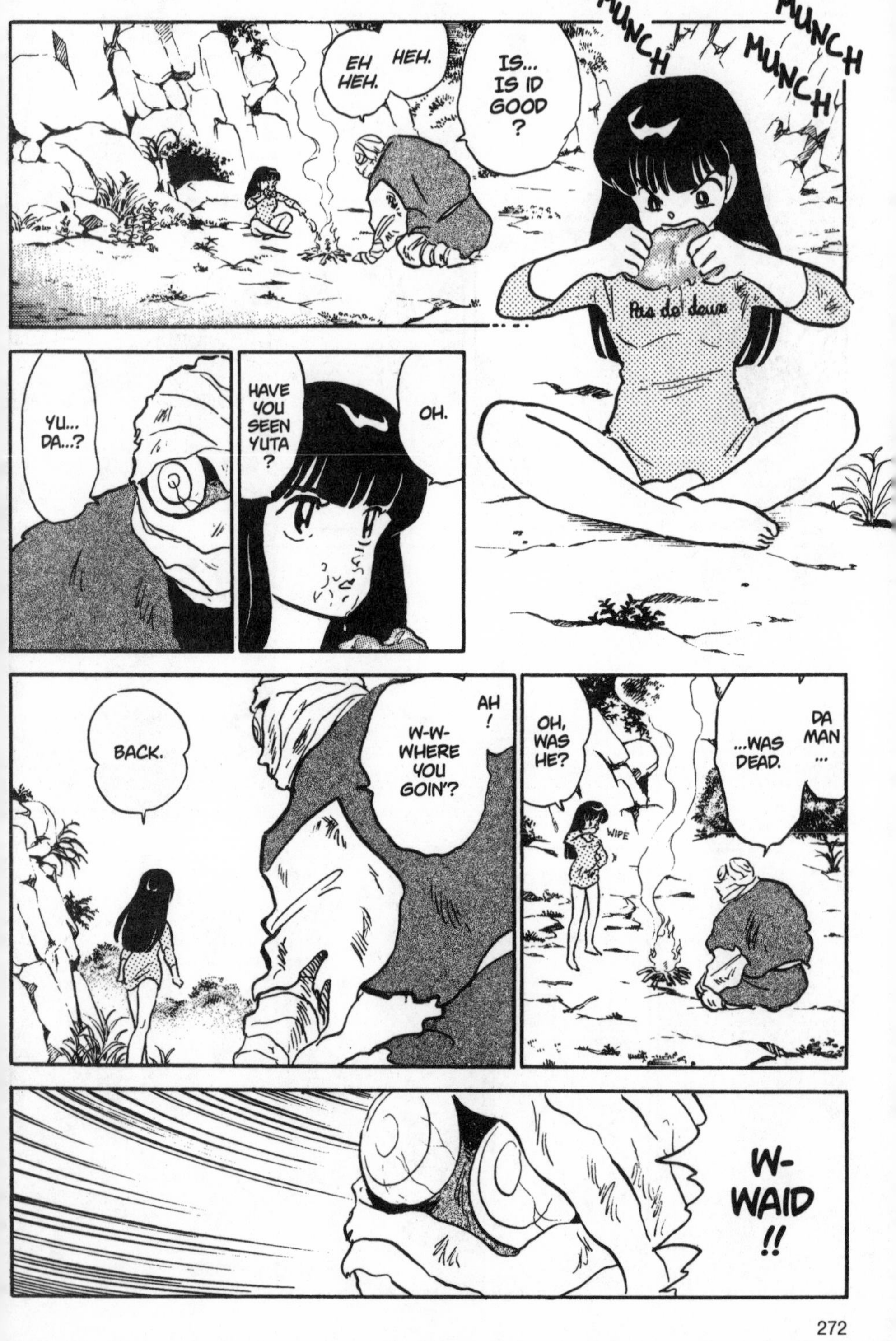
MUNCH MUNCH MUNCH
IS... IS ID GOOD?
HEH. EH HEH.
Pas de deux
OH.
HAVE YOU SEEN YUTA?
YU... DA...?
DA MAN...
...WAS DEAD.
OH, WAS HE?
WIPE
AH!
W-W-WHERE YOU GOIN'?
BACK.
W-WAID!!

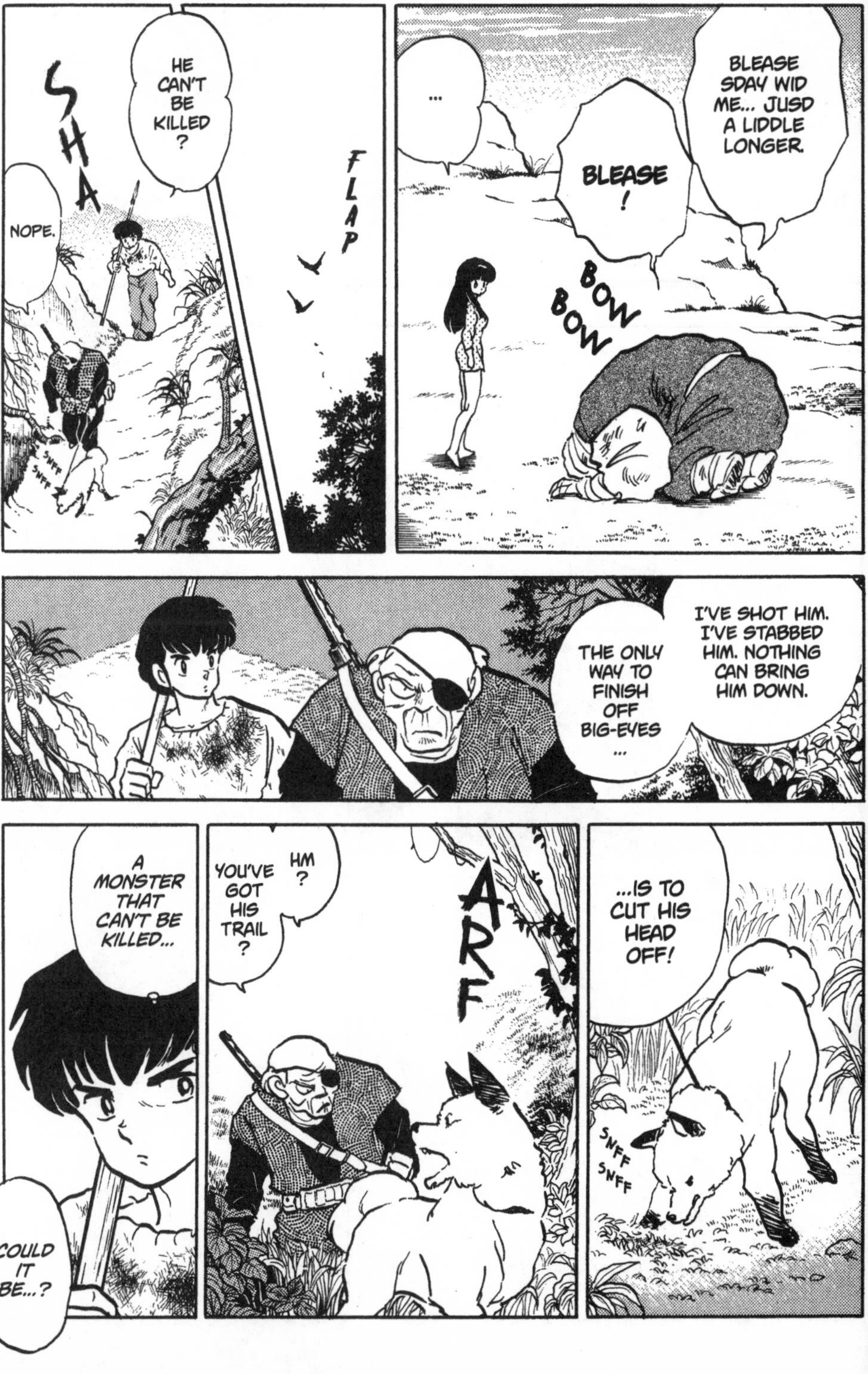
BLEASE SDAY WID ME... JUSD A LIDDLE LONGER.
BLEASE!
...
BOW BOW
HE CAN'T BE KILLED?
SHA
NOPE.
FLAP
SNFF SNFF
I'VE SHOT HIM. I'VE STABBED HIM. NOTHING CAN BRING HIM DOWN.
THE ONLY WAY TO FINISH OFF BIG-EYES...
...IS TO CUT HIS HEAD OFF!
SNFF SNFF
HM?
YOU'VE GOT HIS TRAIL?
ARF
A MONSTER THAT CAN'T BE KILLED...
COULD IT BE...?

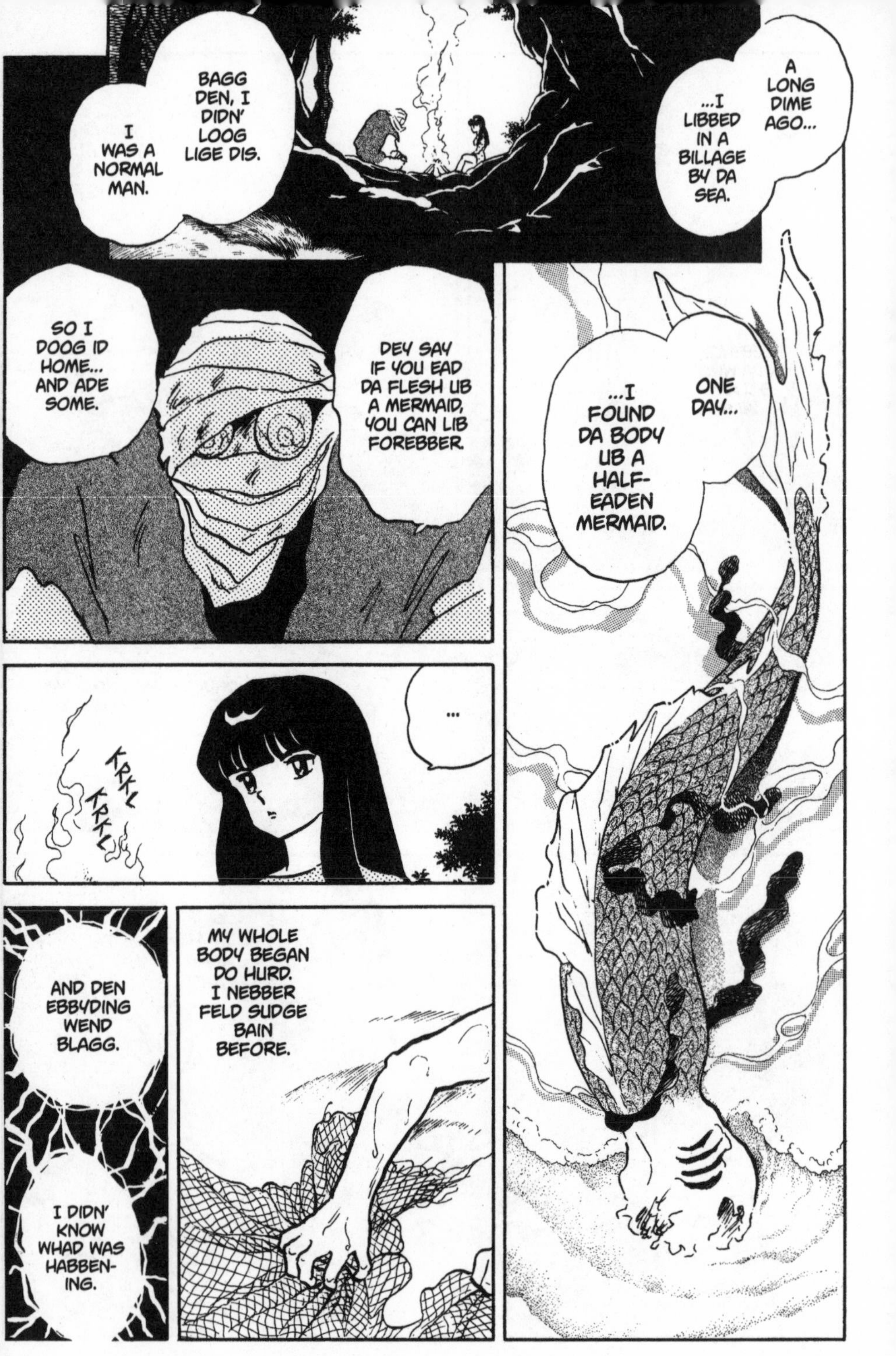
A LONG DIME AGO...
...I LIBBED IN A BILLAGE BY DA SEA.
BAGG DEN, I DIDN' LOOG LIGE DIS.
I WAS A NORMAL MAN.
ONE DAY...
...I FOUND DA BODY UB A HALF-EADEN MERMAID.
DEY SAY IF YOU EAD DA FLESH UB A MERMAID, YOU CAN LIB FOREBBER.
SO I DOOG ID HOME... AND ADE SOME.
...
KRKL KRKL
MY WHOLE BODY BEGAN DO HURD. I NEBBER FELD SUDGE BAIN BEFORE.
AND DEN EBBYDING WEND BLAGG.
I DIDN' KNOW WHAD WAS HABBEN-ING.

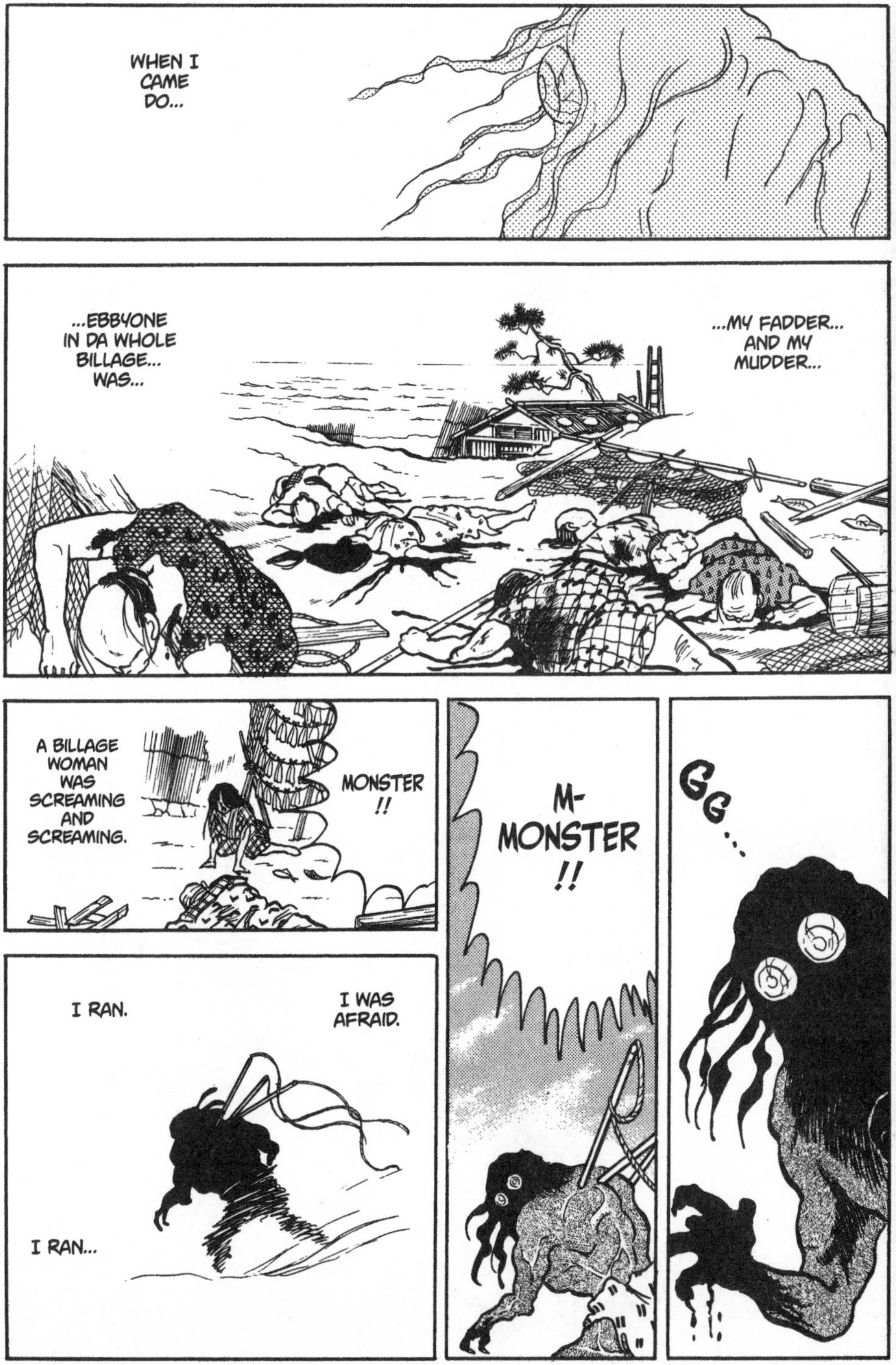

WHEN I CAME DO...
...EBBYONE IN DA WHOLE BILLAGE... WAS...
...MY FADDER... AND MY MUDDER...
A BILLAGE WOMAN WAS SCREAMING AND SCREAMING.
MONSTER !!
I RAN.
I WAS AFRAID.
I RAN...
M-MONSTER !!
GG...

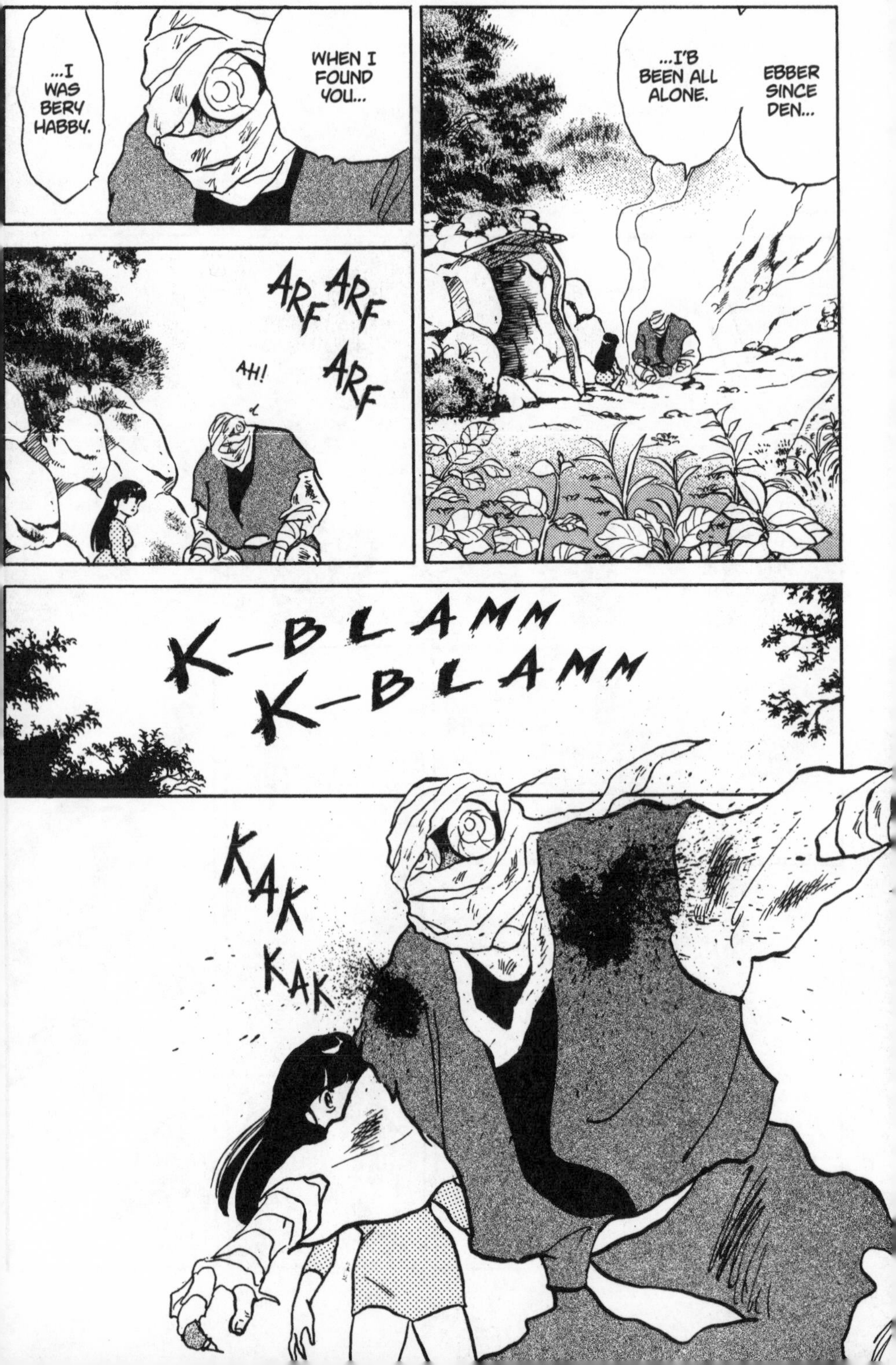
EBBER SINCE DEN...
...I'B BEEN ALL ALONE.
WHEN I FOUND YOU...
...I WAS BERY HABBY.
ARF ARF
ARF
AH!
K-BLAMM
K-BLAMM
KAK
KAK

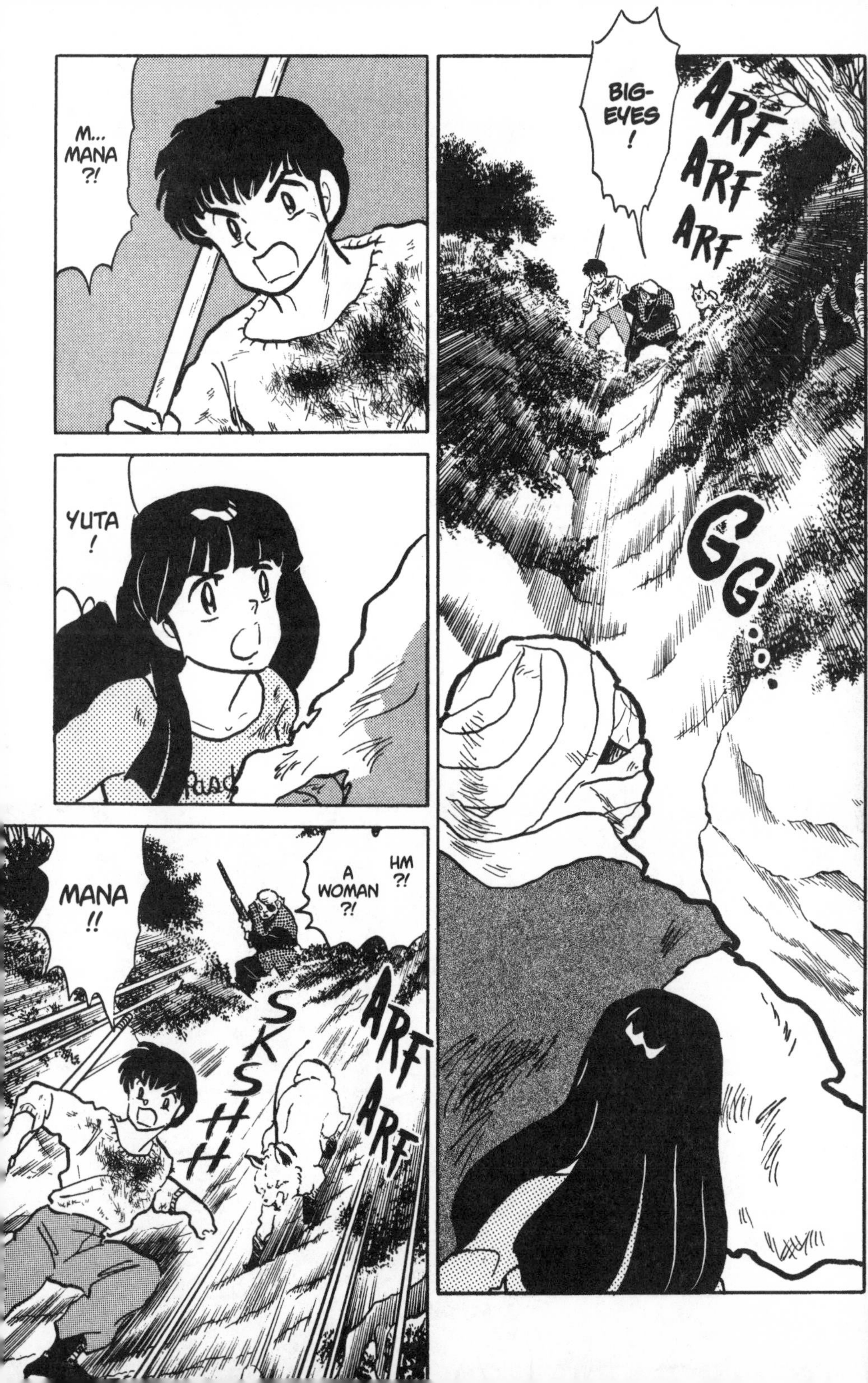
BIG-EYES!
ARF ARF ARF
GG...
M... MANA?!
YUTA!
HM?!
A WOMAN?!
MANA!!
SKSHH
ARF ARF

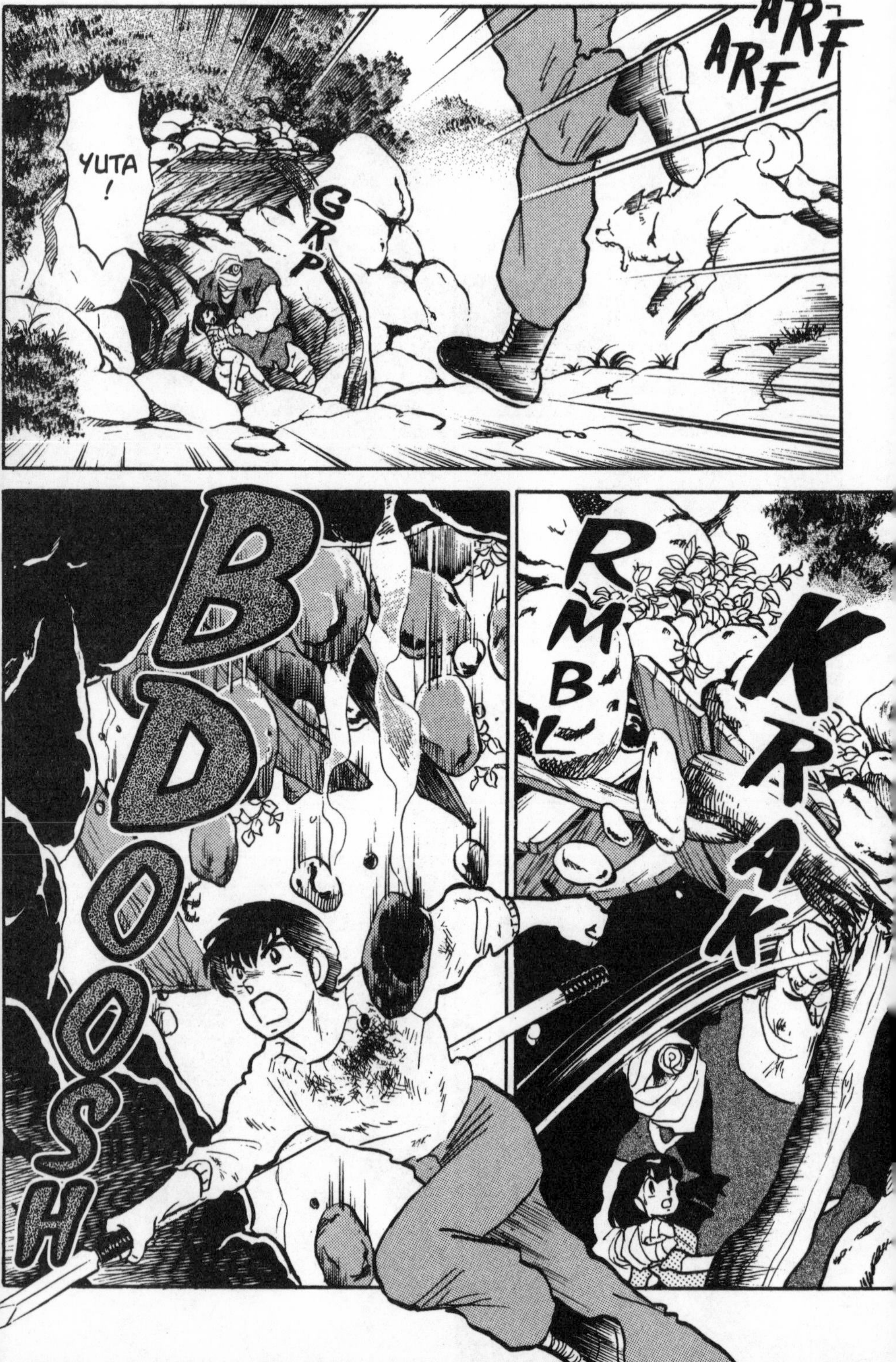
ARF
ARF
YUTA!
GRP
RMBL
KRAK
BDOOOSH

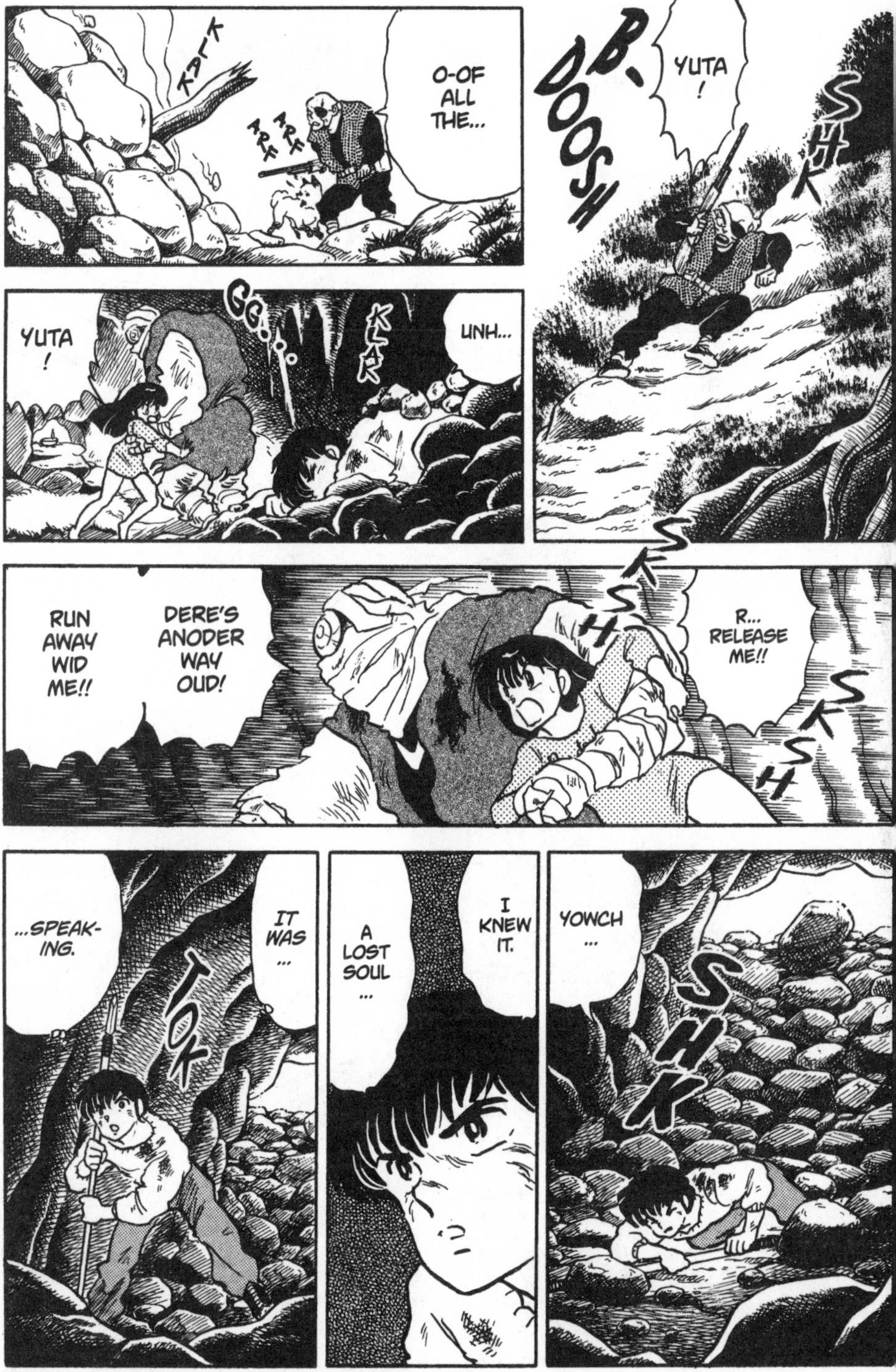
YUTA!
B-DOOSH
SHK
O-OF ALL THE...
ARF ARF
UNH...
KLAK
GG...
YUTA!
R... RELEASE ME!!
SKSH
SKSH
DERE'S ANODER WAY OUD!
RUN AWAY WID ME!!
YOWCH ...
SHK
I KNEW IT.
A LOST SOUL ...
IT WAS ...
...SPEAKING.
TOK

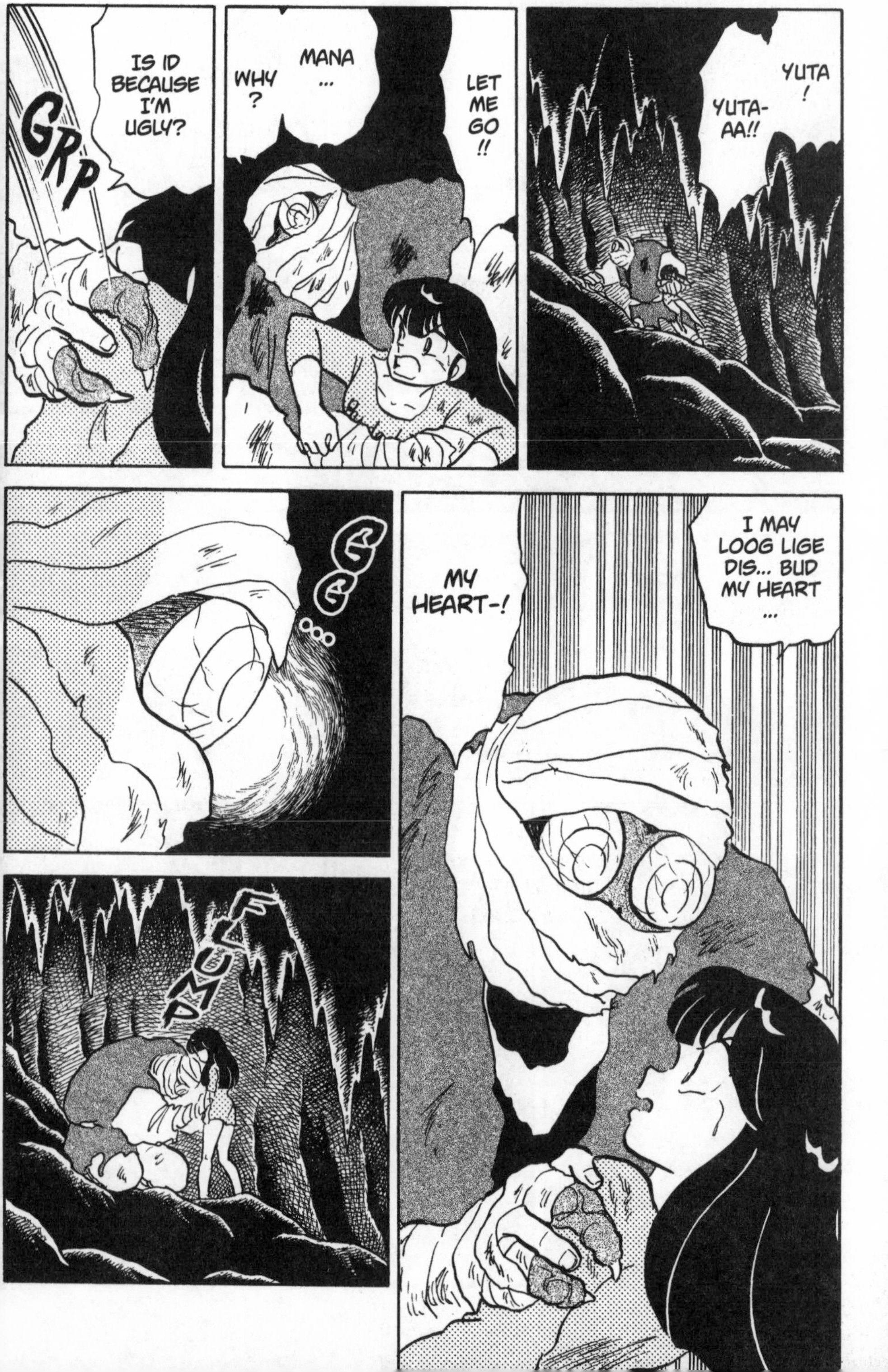
YUTA!
YUTA-AA!!
LET ME GO!!
MANA...
WHY?
IS ID BECAUSE I'M UGLY?
GRP
I MAY LOOG LIGE DIS... BUD MY HEART...
MY HEART-!
GEE ooo
FLUMP

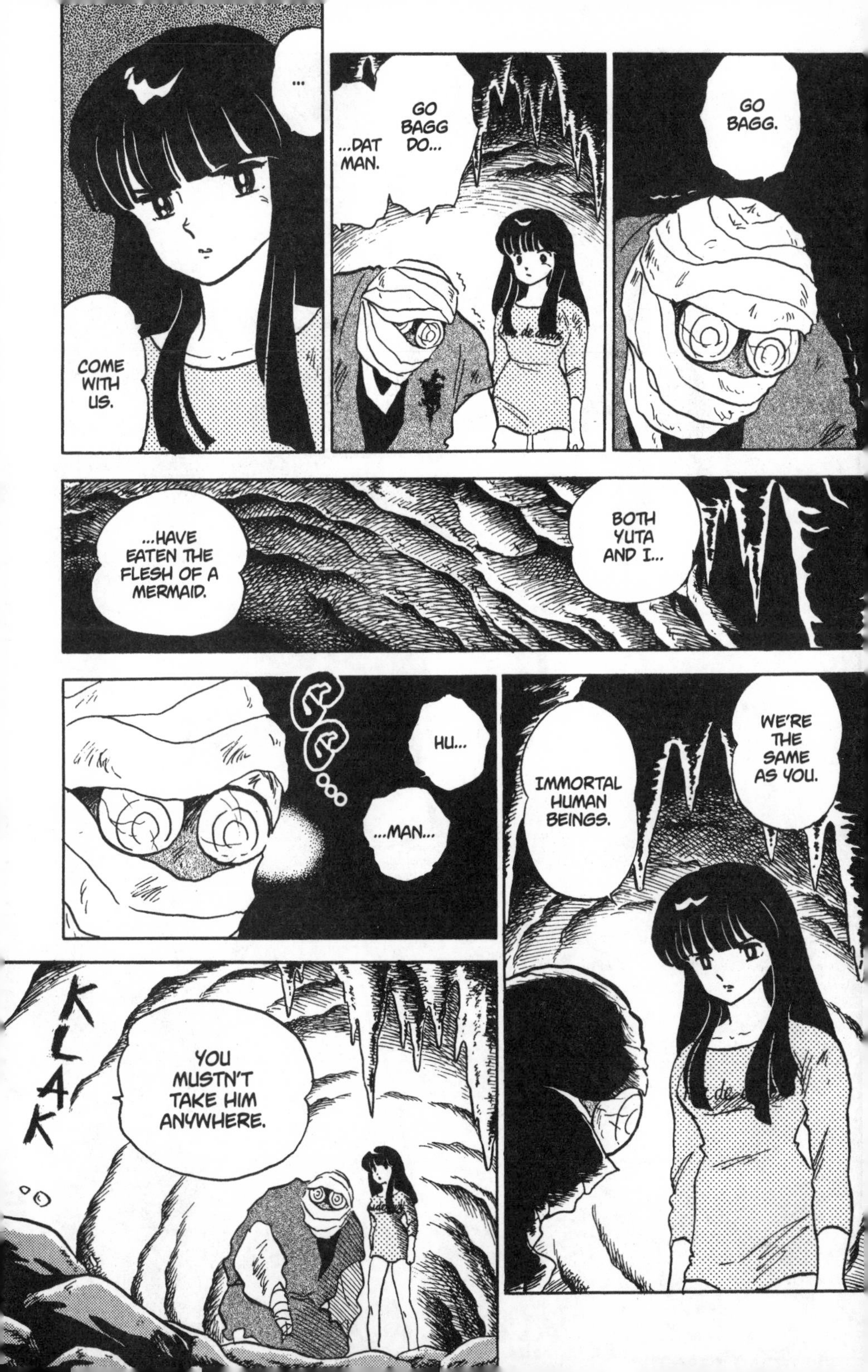
GO BAGG.
GO BAGG DO...
...DAT MAN.
...
COME WITH US.
BOTH YUTA AND I...
...HAVE EATEN THE FLESH OF A MERMAID.
WE'RE THE SAME AS YOU.
IMMORTAL HUMAN BEINGS.
HU...
...MAN...
YOU MUSTN'T TAKE HIM ANYWHERE.
KLAK

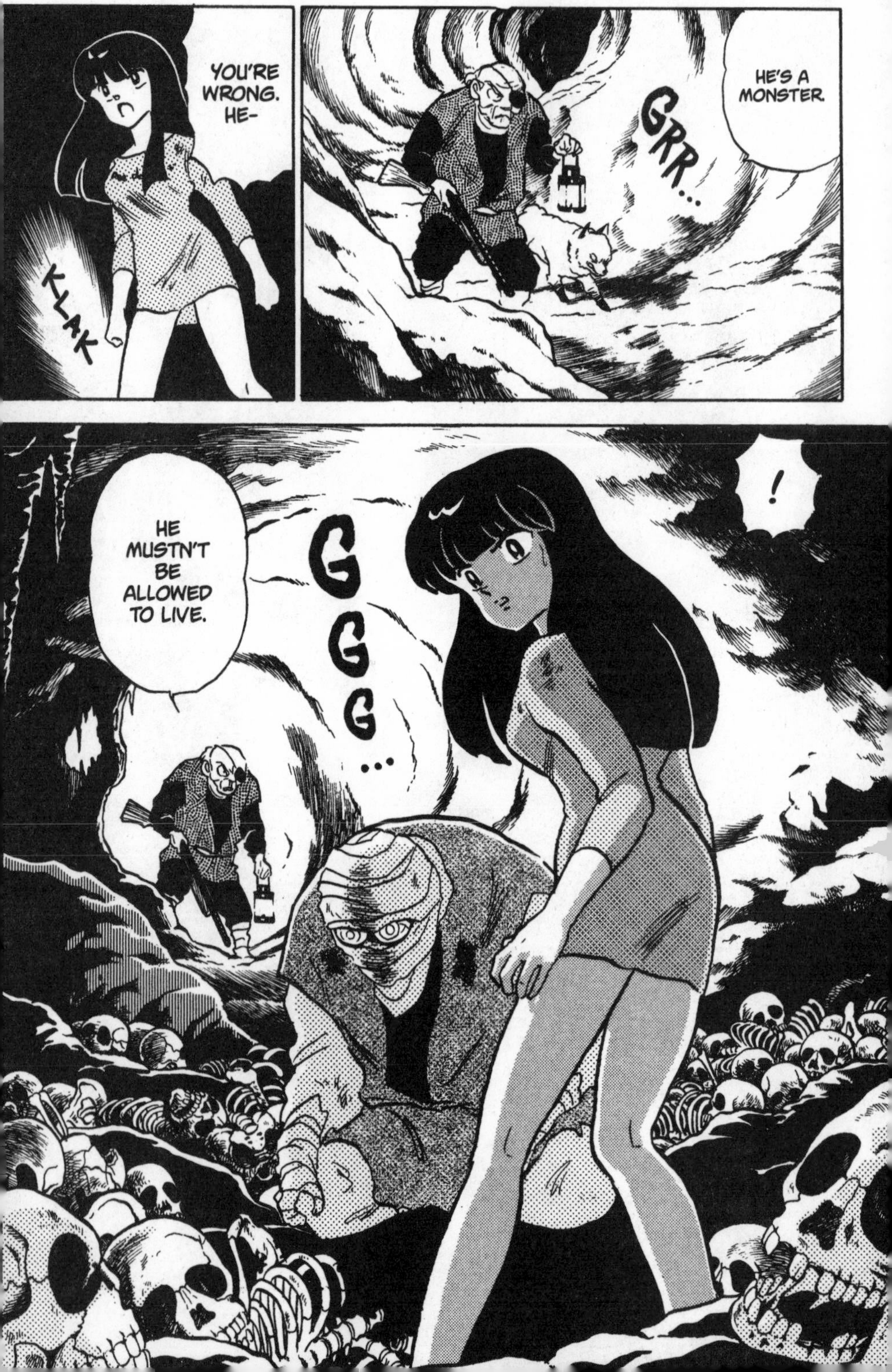
HE'S A MONSTER.
GRR...
YOU'RE WRONG. HE-
KLAK
!
GGG...
HE MUSTN'T BE ALLOWED TO LIVE.

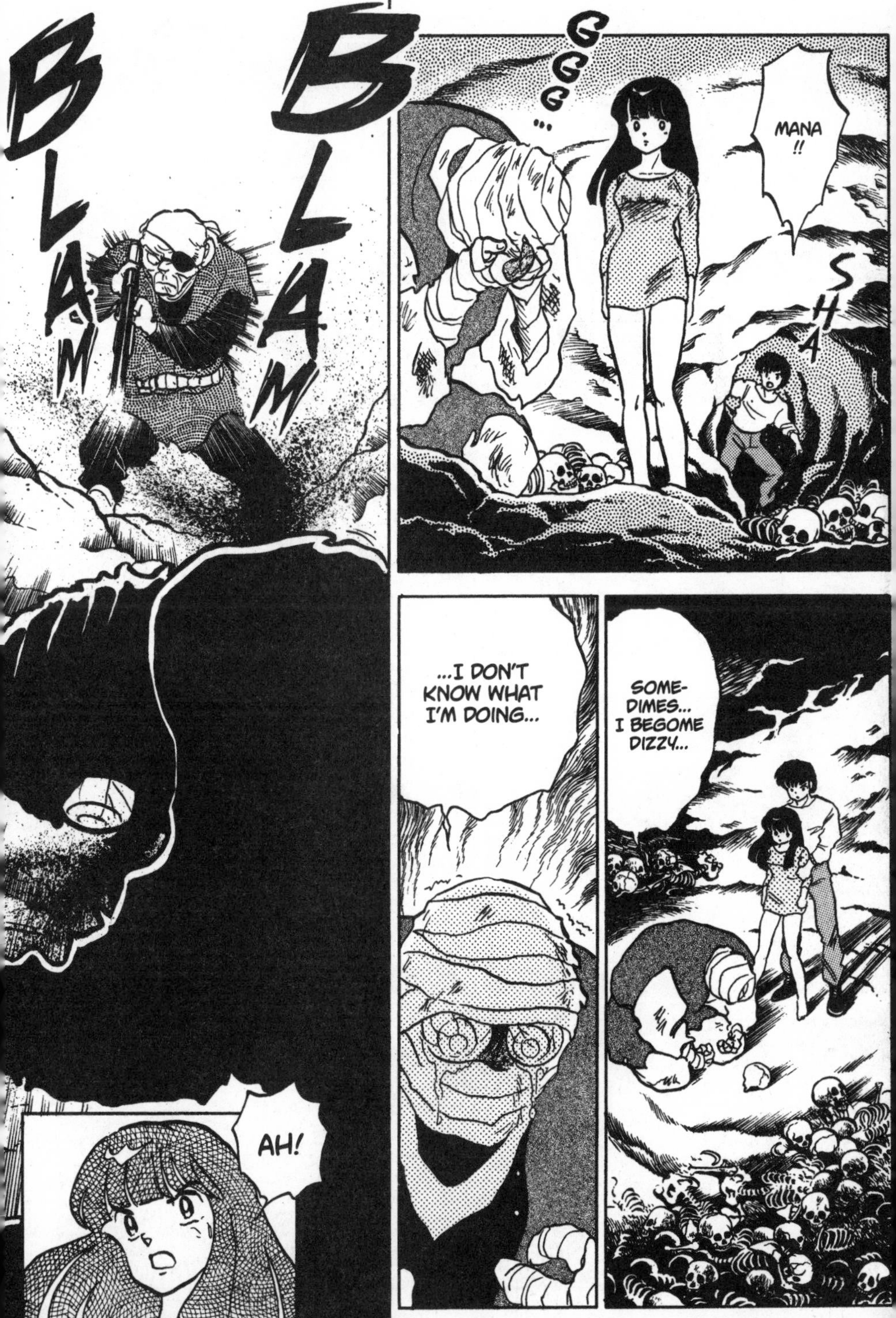
GGG...
MANA!!
SHA
SOME-DIMES... I BEGOME DIZZY...
...I DON'T KNOW WHAT I'M DOING...
BLAM
BLAM
AH!

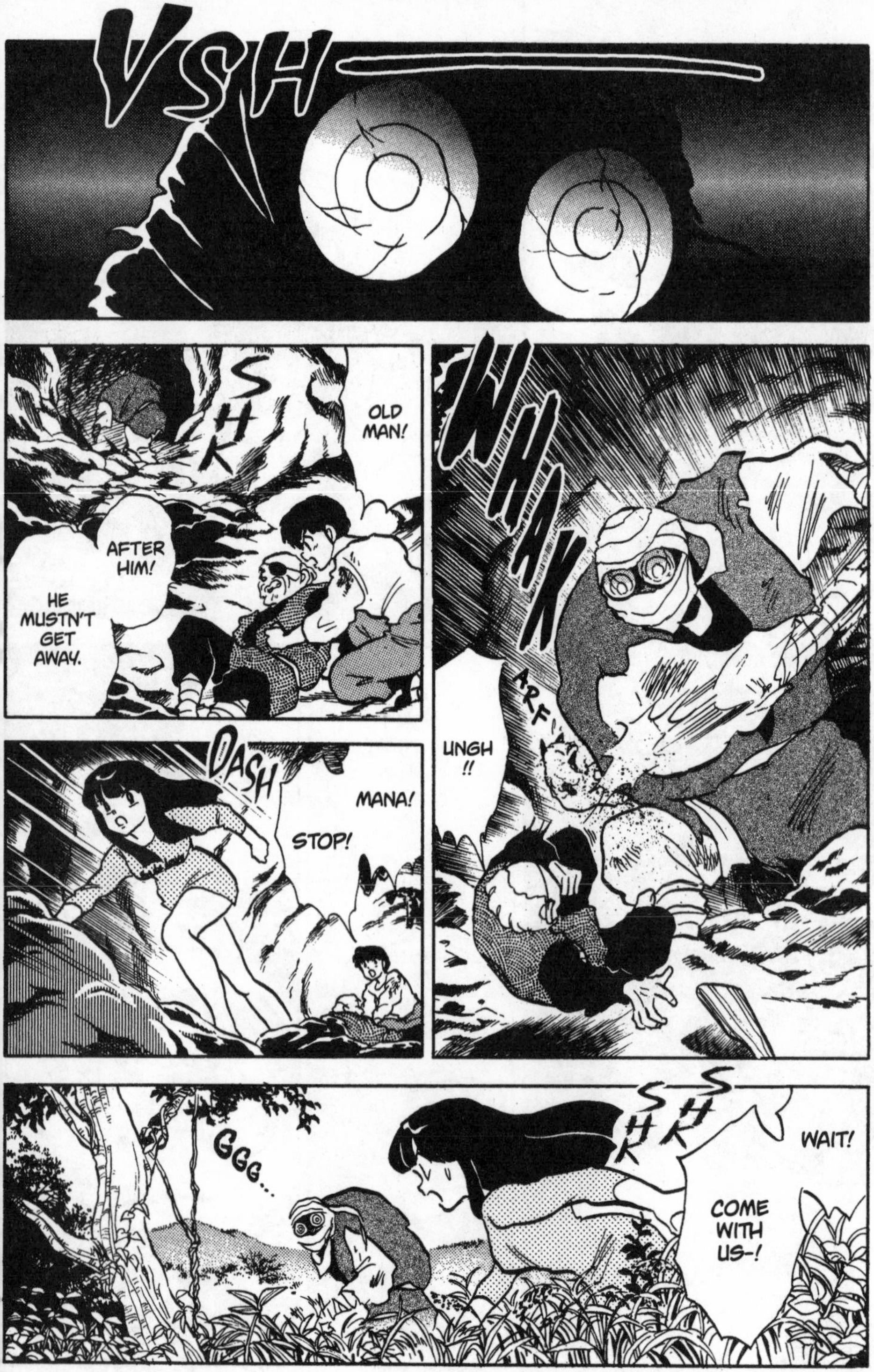
VSH
WHAK
ARF
UNGH!!
SHK
OLD MAN!
AFTER HIM!
HE MUSTN'T GET AWAY.
DASH
MANA!
STOP!
SHK
SHK
WAIT!
COME WITH US-!
GGG...

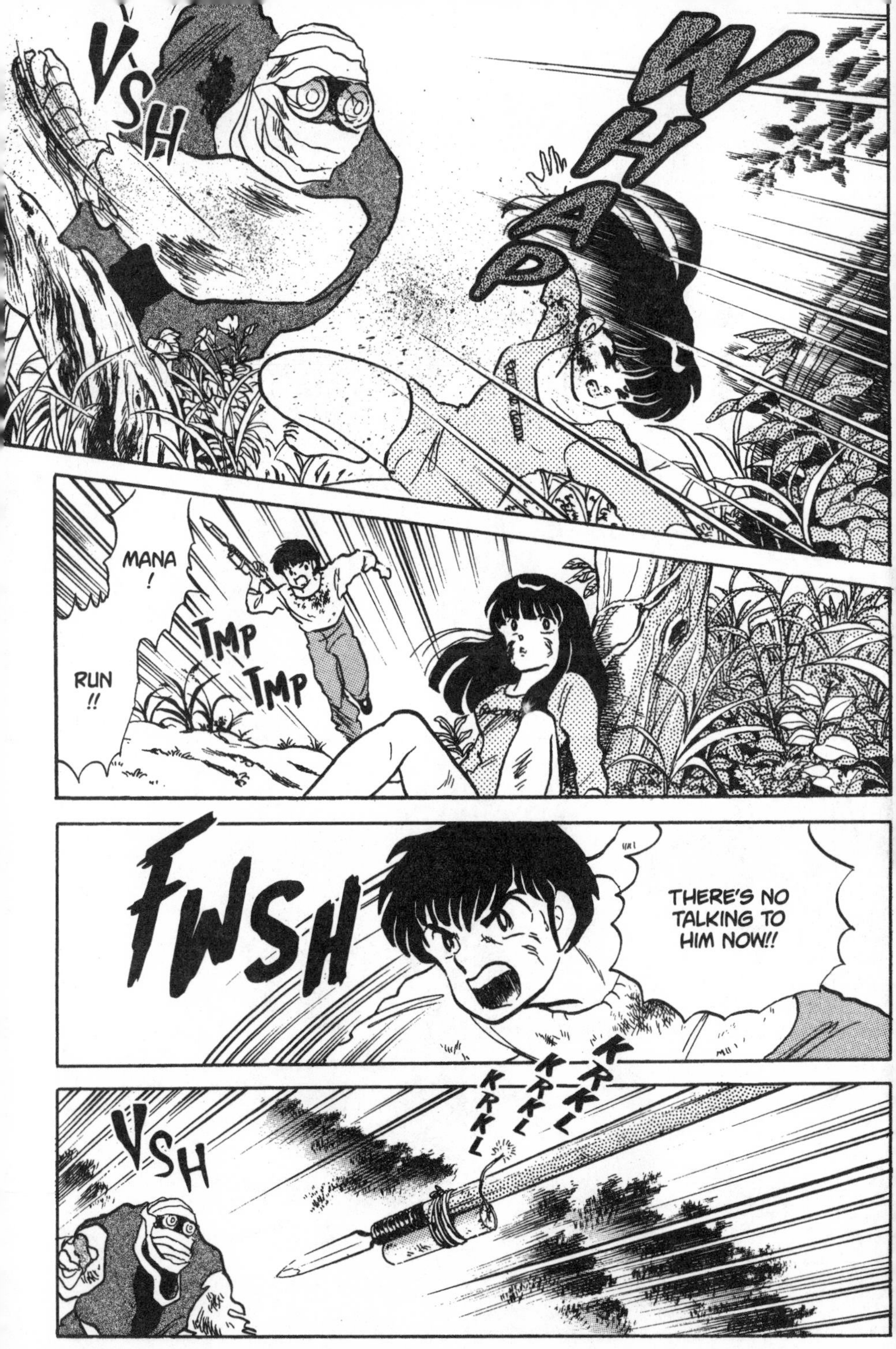
VSH
WHAP
MANA!
RUN!!
TMP TMP
FWSH
THERE'S NO TALKING TO HIM NOW!!
KRKL KRKL KRKL
VSH

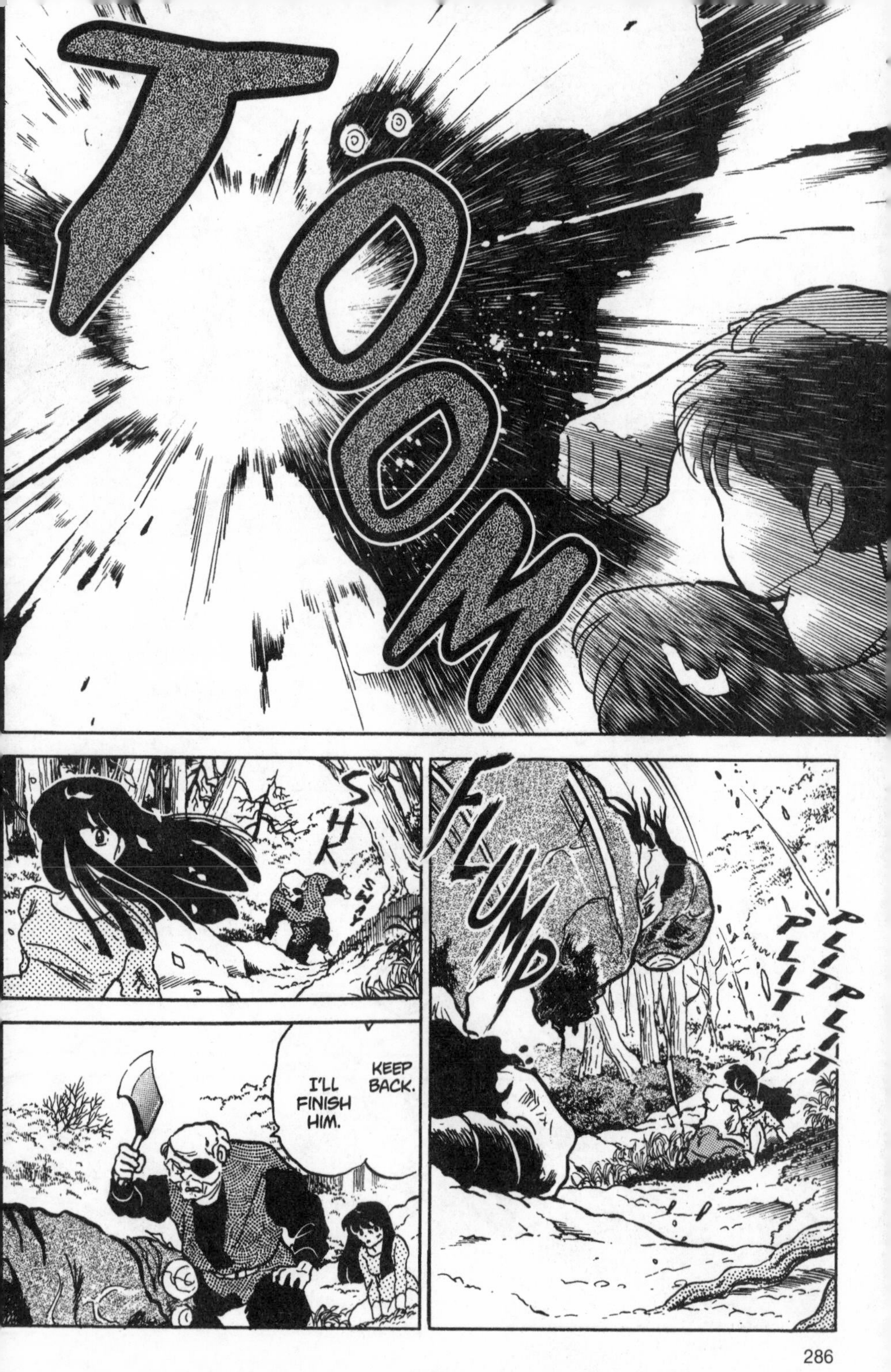
TOOM
FLUMP
PLIT PLIT
PLIT PLIT
SHK
SWAY
KEEP BACK.
I'LL FINISH HIM.

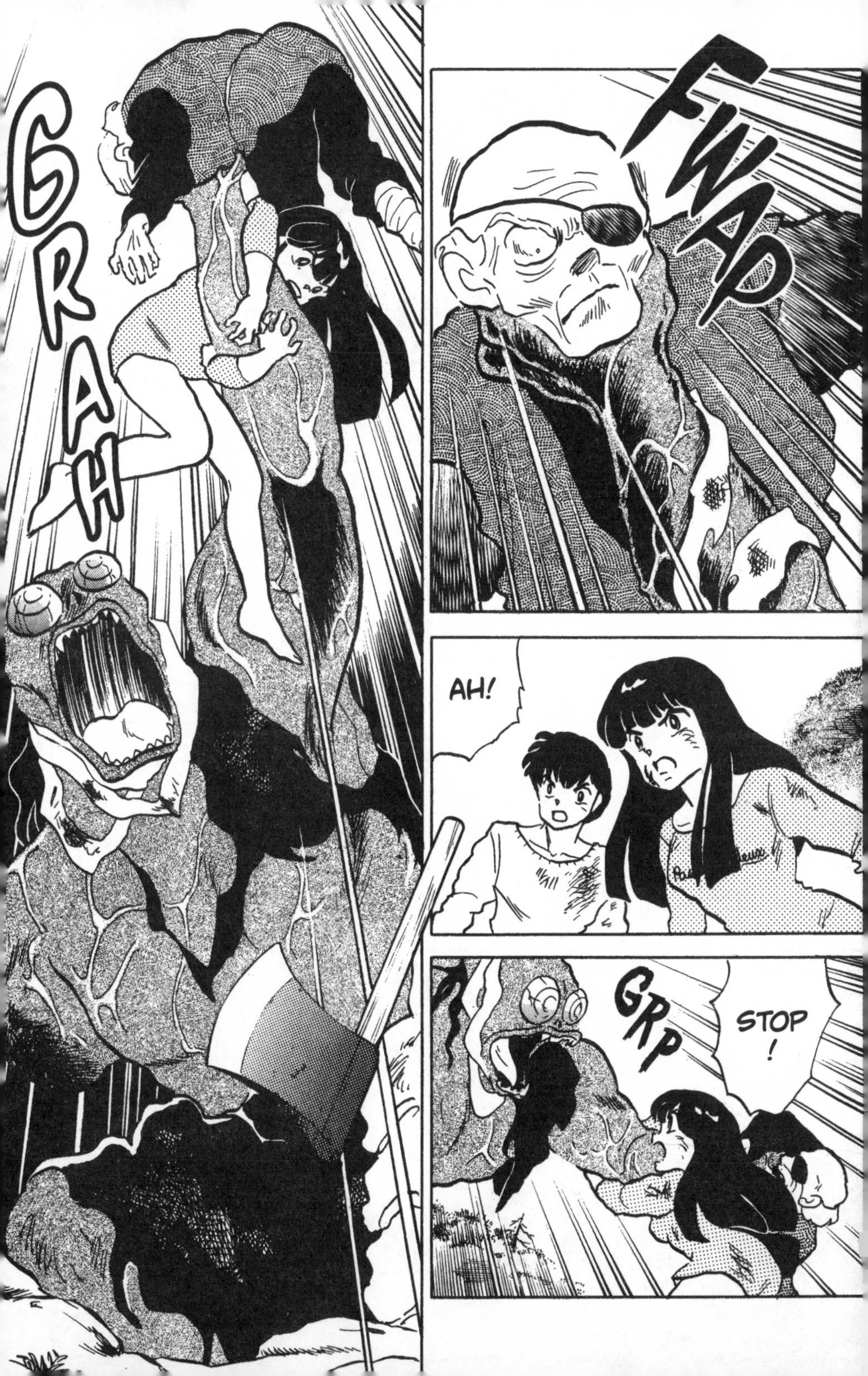
FWAP
AH!
GRP
STOP !
GRAH

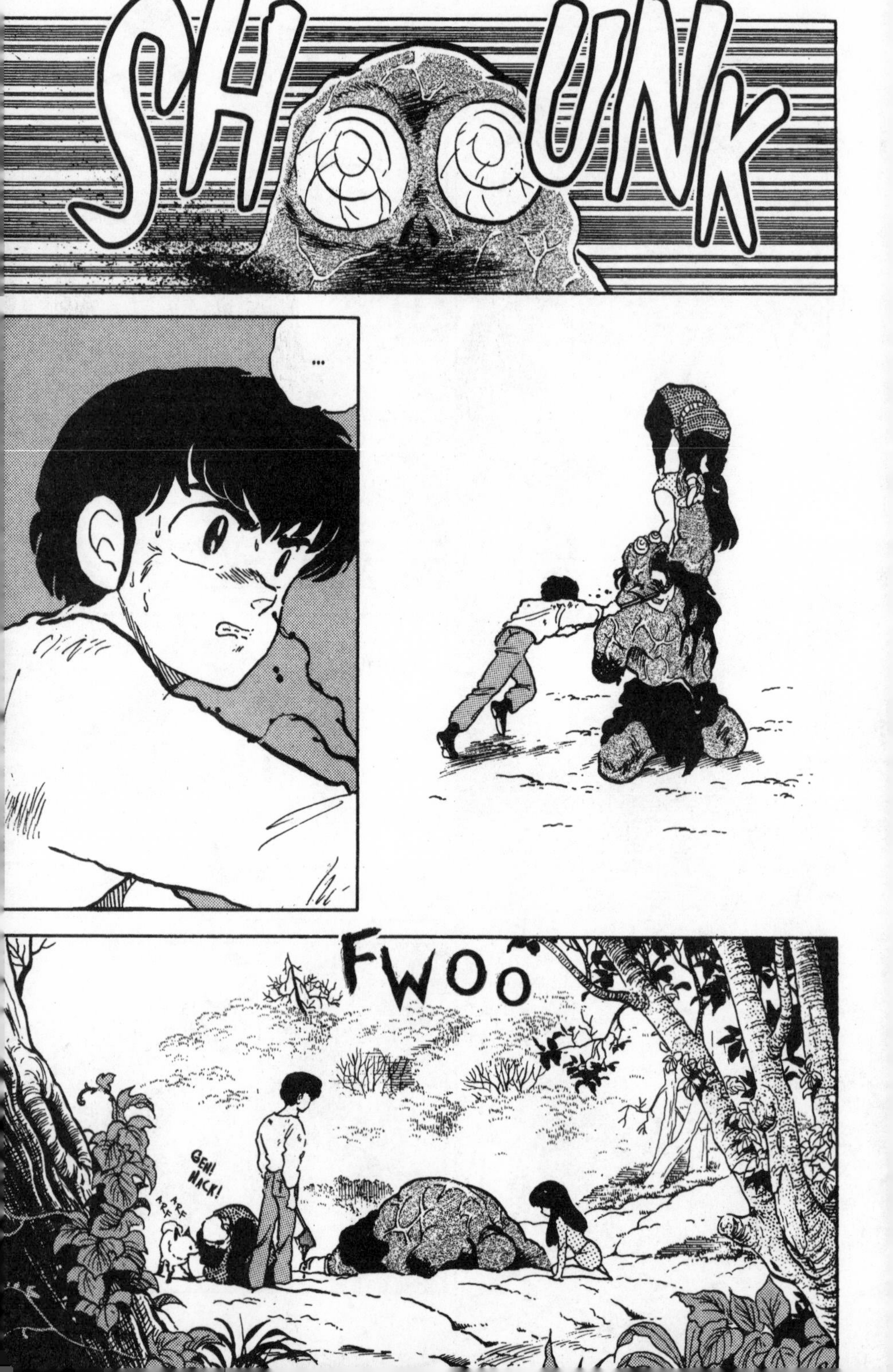
SH UNK
...
FWOO
GEH! HACK!
ARF ARF

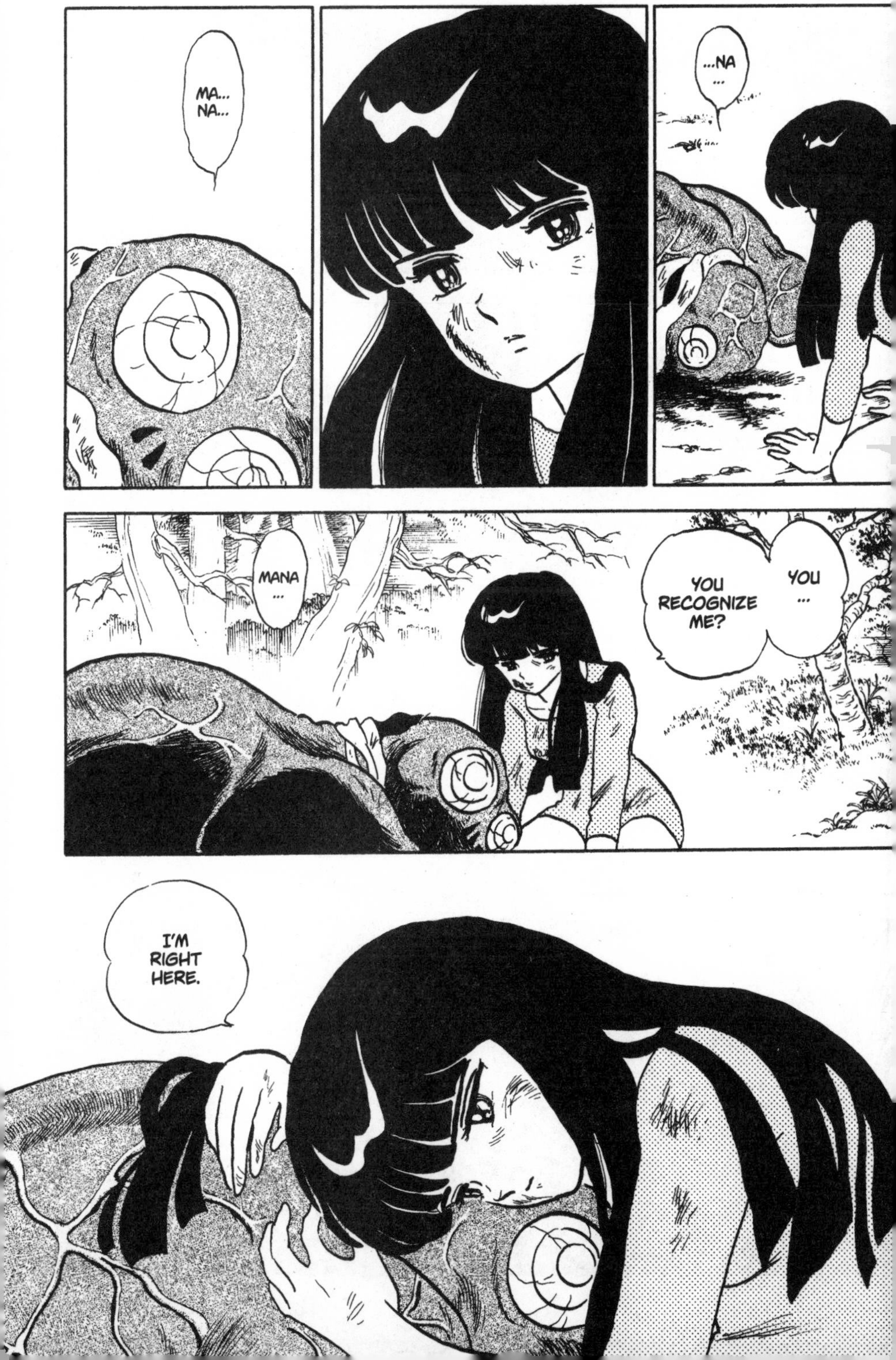
...NA ...
MA... NA...
YOU ...
YOU RECOGNIZE ME?
MANA ...
I'M RIGHT HERE.

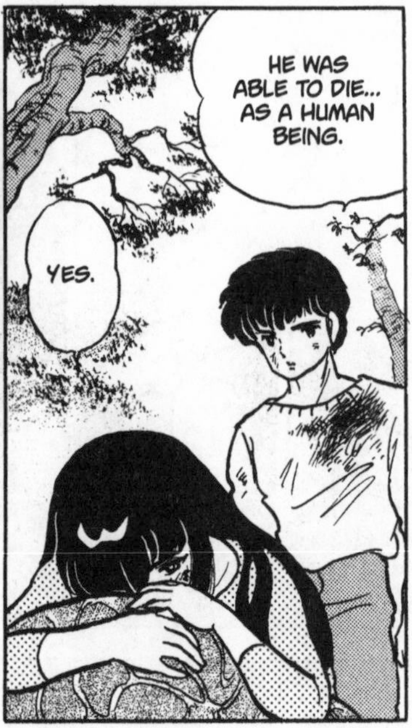
HE WAS ABLE TO DIE... AS A HUMAN BEING.
YES.
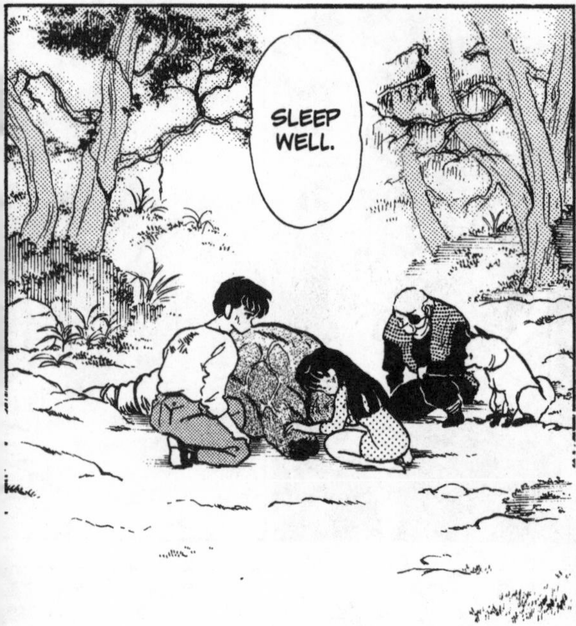
SLEEP WELL.
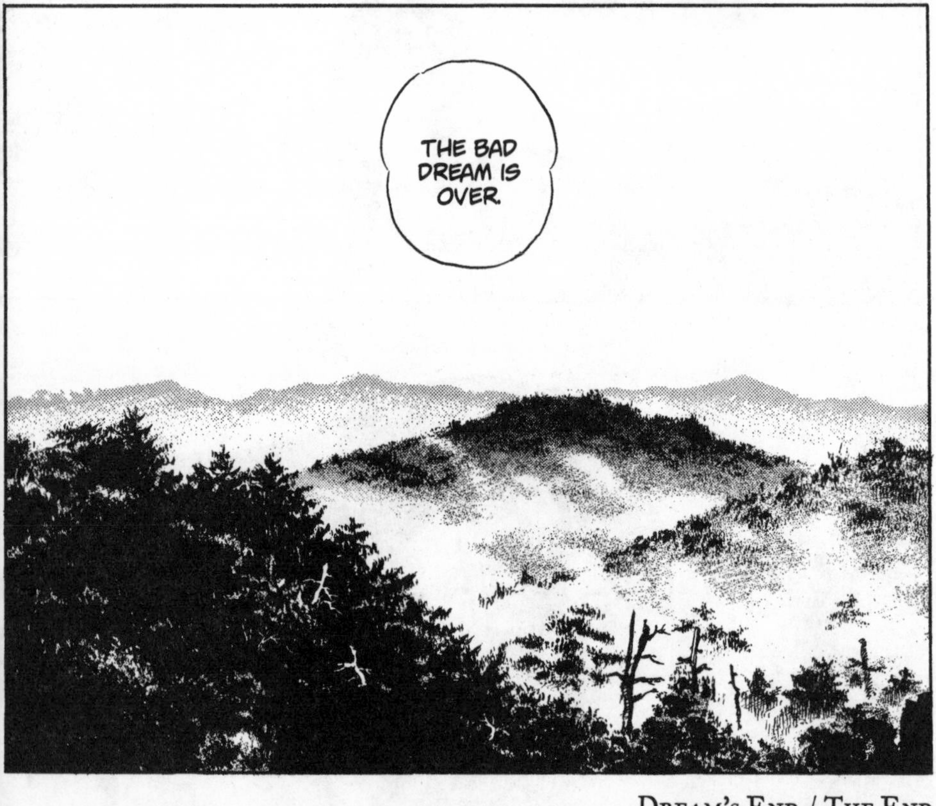
THE BAD DREAM IS OVER.

DREAM'S END / THE END

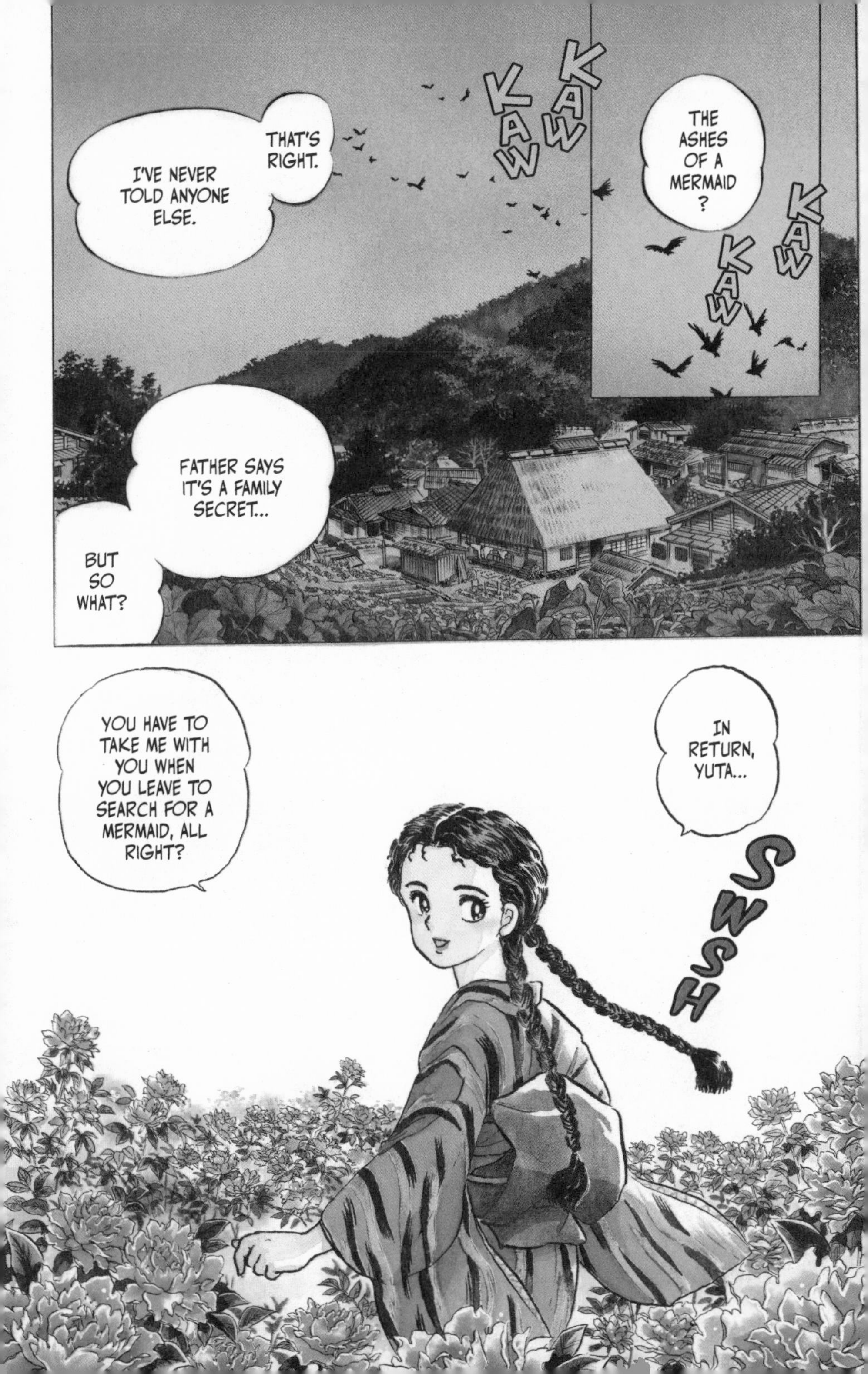
KAW KAW
THE ASHES OF A MERMAID?
KAW KAW
THAT'S RIGHT.
I'VE NEVER TOLD ANYONE ELSE.
FATHER SAYS IT'S A FAMILY SECRET...
BUT SO WHAT?
IN RETURN, YUTA...
SWSH
YOU HAVE TO TAKE ME WITH YOU WHEN YOU LEAVE TO SEARCH FOR A MERMAID, ALL RIGHT?

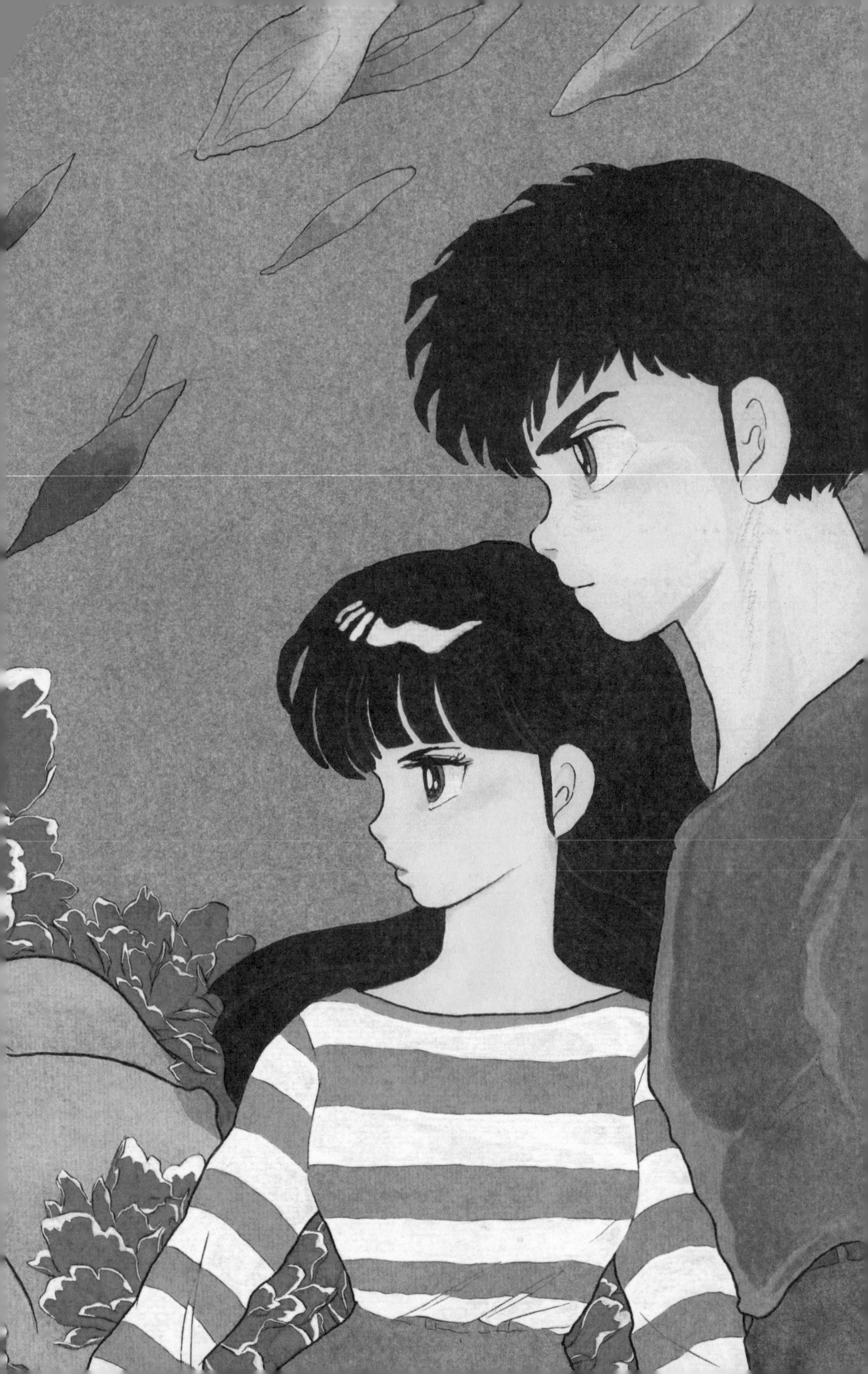

Chapter 8: Mermaid's Promise, Part 1

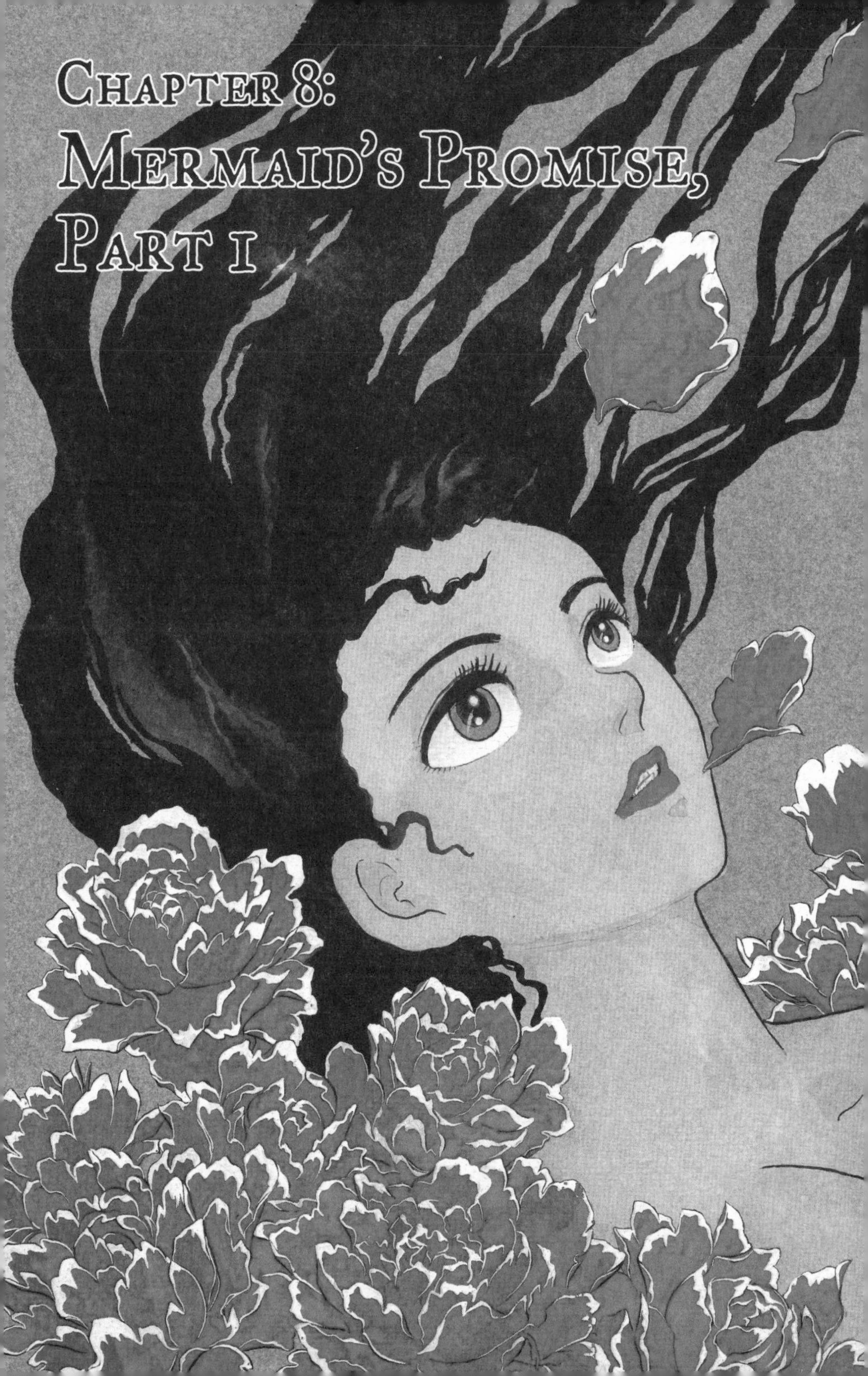

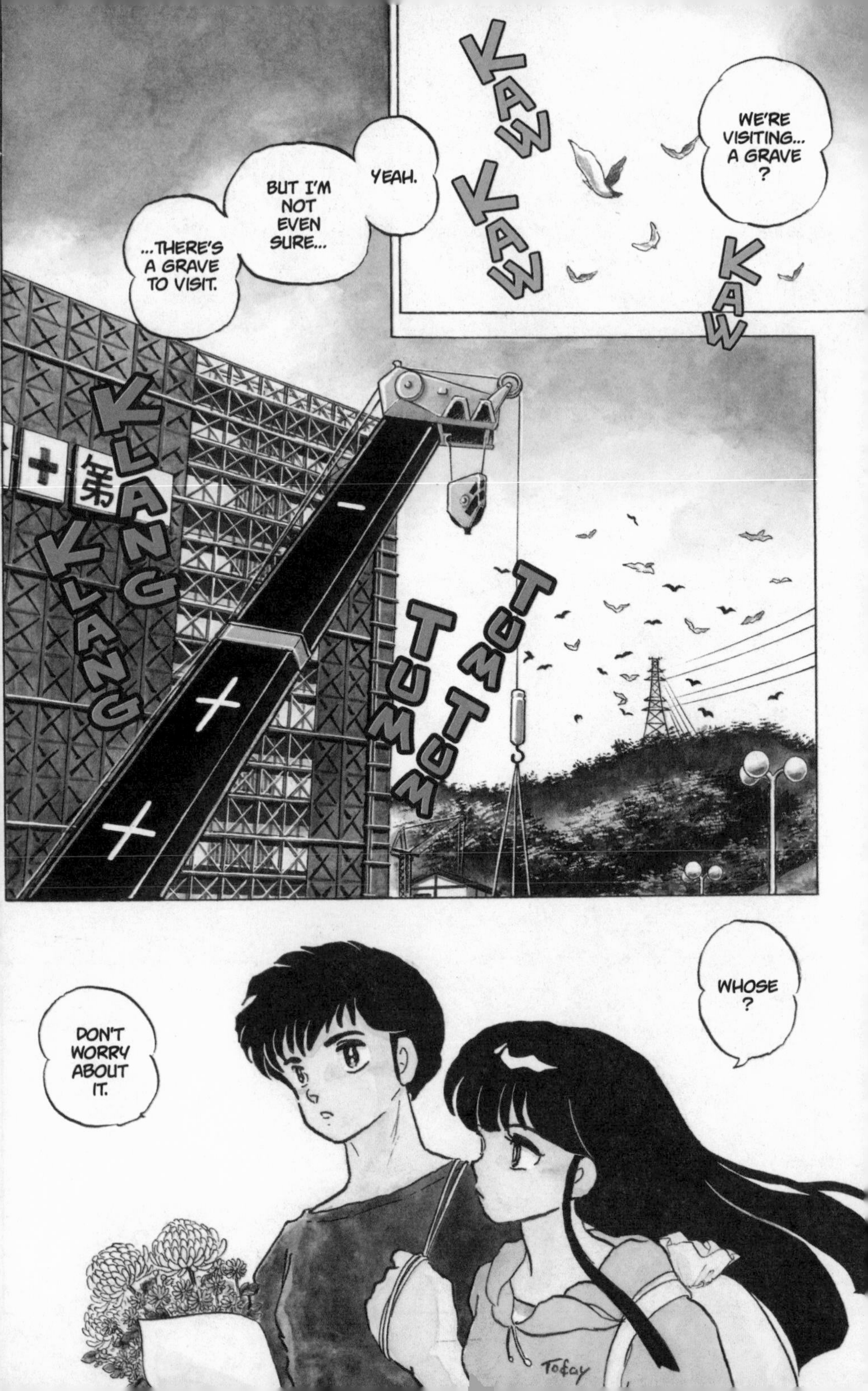
WE'RE VISITING... A GRAVE?
KAW KAW
KAW KAW
YEAH.
BUT I'M NOT EVEN SURE...
...THERE'S A GRAVE TO VISIT.
TUMTUM TUMTUM
KLANG KLANG
KLANG KLANG
WHOSE?
DON'T WORRY ABOUT IT.

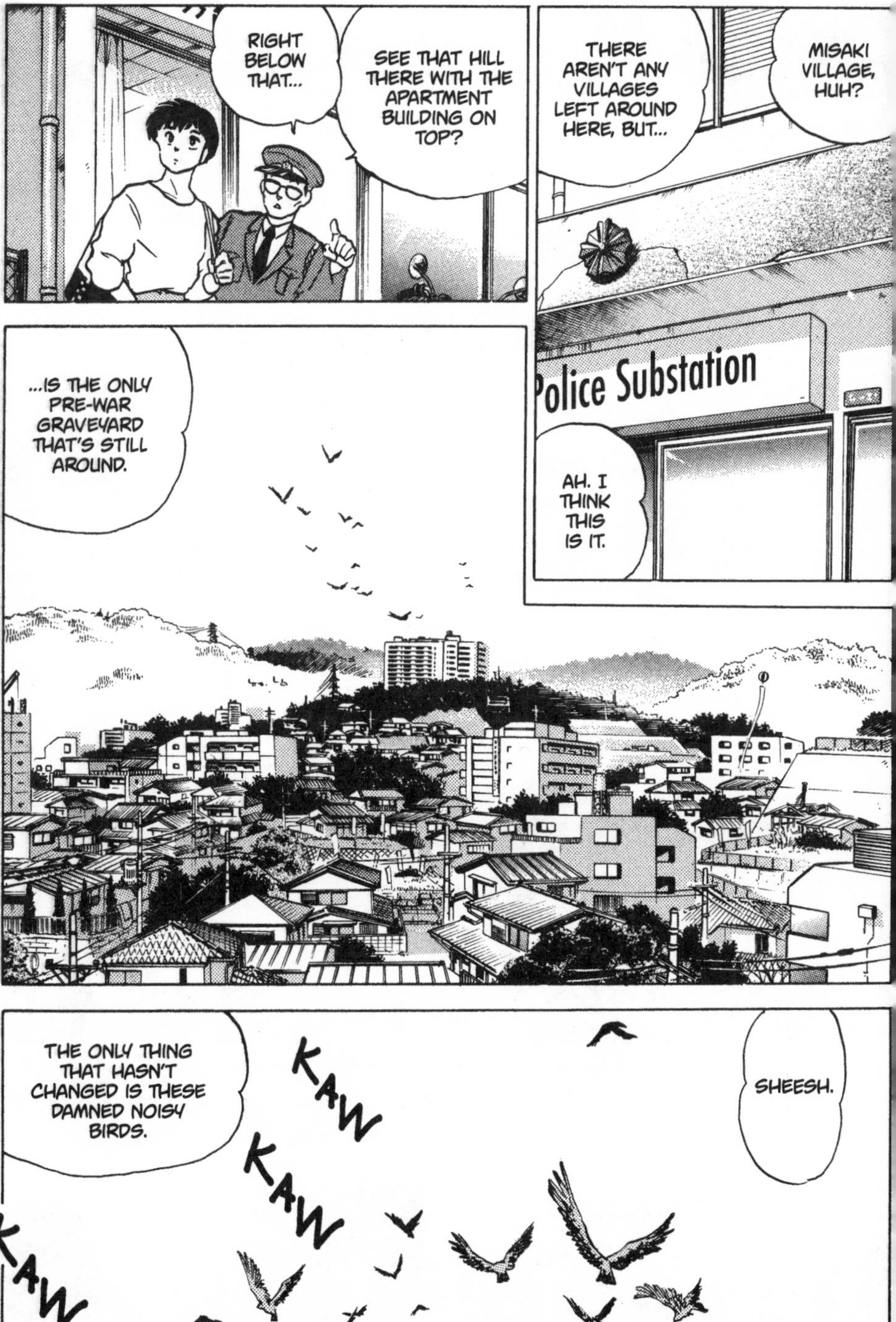

MISAKI VILLAGE, HUH?
THERE AREN'T ANY VILLAGES LEFT AROUND HERE, BUT...
Police Substation
AH. I THINK THIS IS IT.
SEE THAT HILL THERE WITH THE APARTMENT BUILDING ON TOP?
RIGHT BELOW THAT...
...IS THE ONLY PRE-WAR GRAVEYARD THAT'S STILL AROUND.
SHEESH.
THE ONLY THING THAT HASN'T CHANGED IS THESE DAMNED NOISY BIRDS.
KAW
KAW
KAW

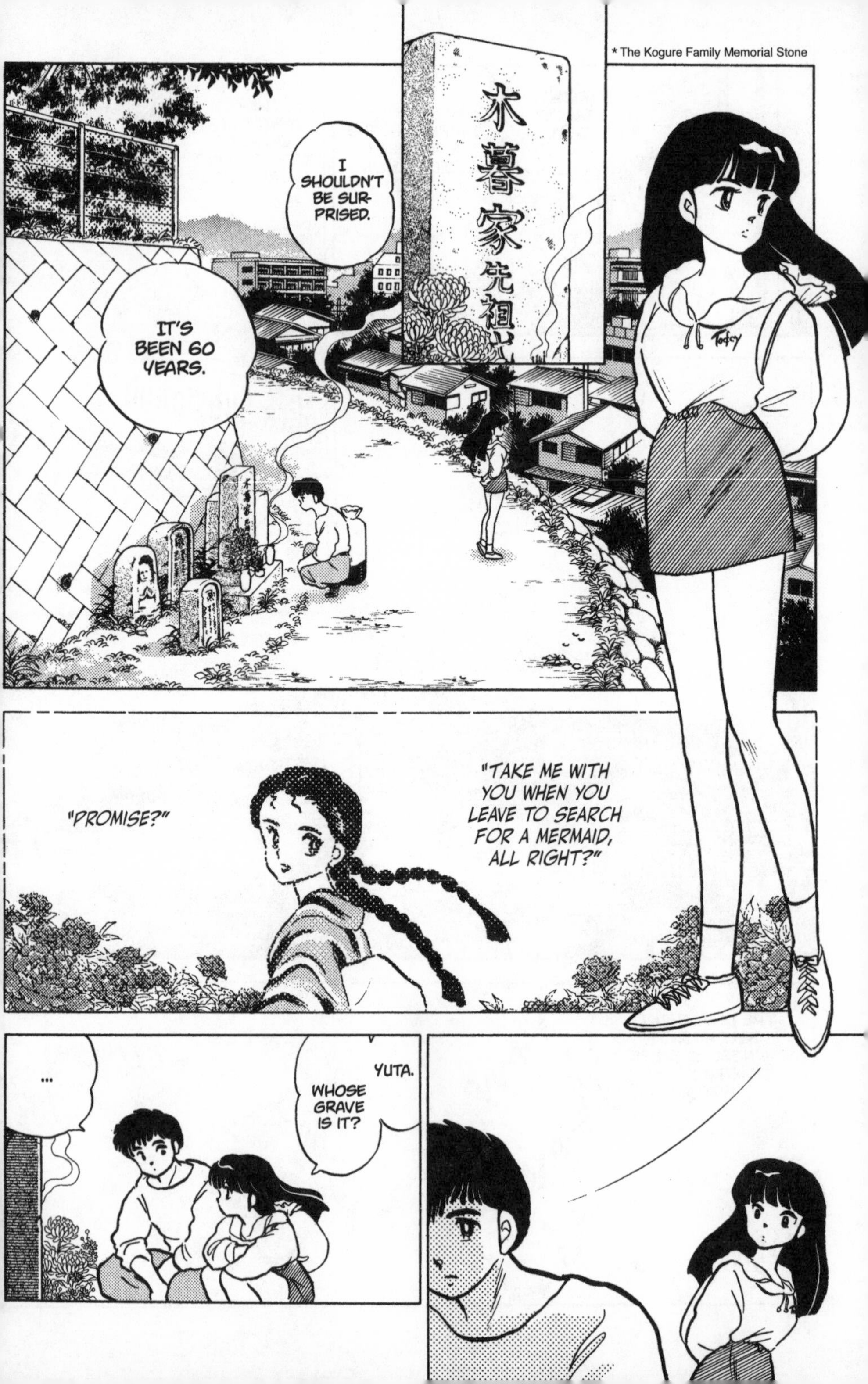
木暮家先祖
I SHOULDN'T BE SURPRISED.
IT'S BEEN 60 YEARS.
"TAKE ME WITH YOU WHEN YOU LEAVE TO SEARCH FOR A MERMAID, ALL RIGHT?"
"PROMISE?"
YUTA.
WHOSE GRAVE IS IT?
...
* The Kogure Family Memorial Stone

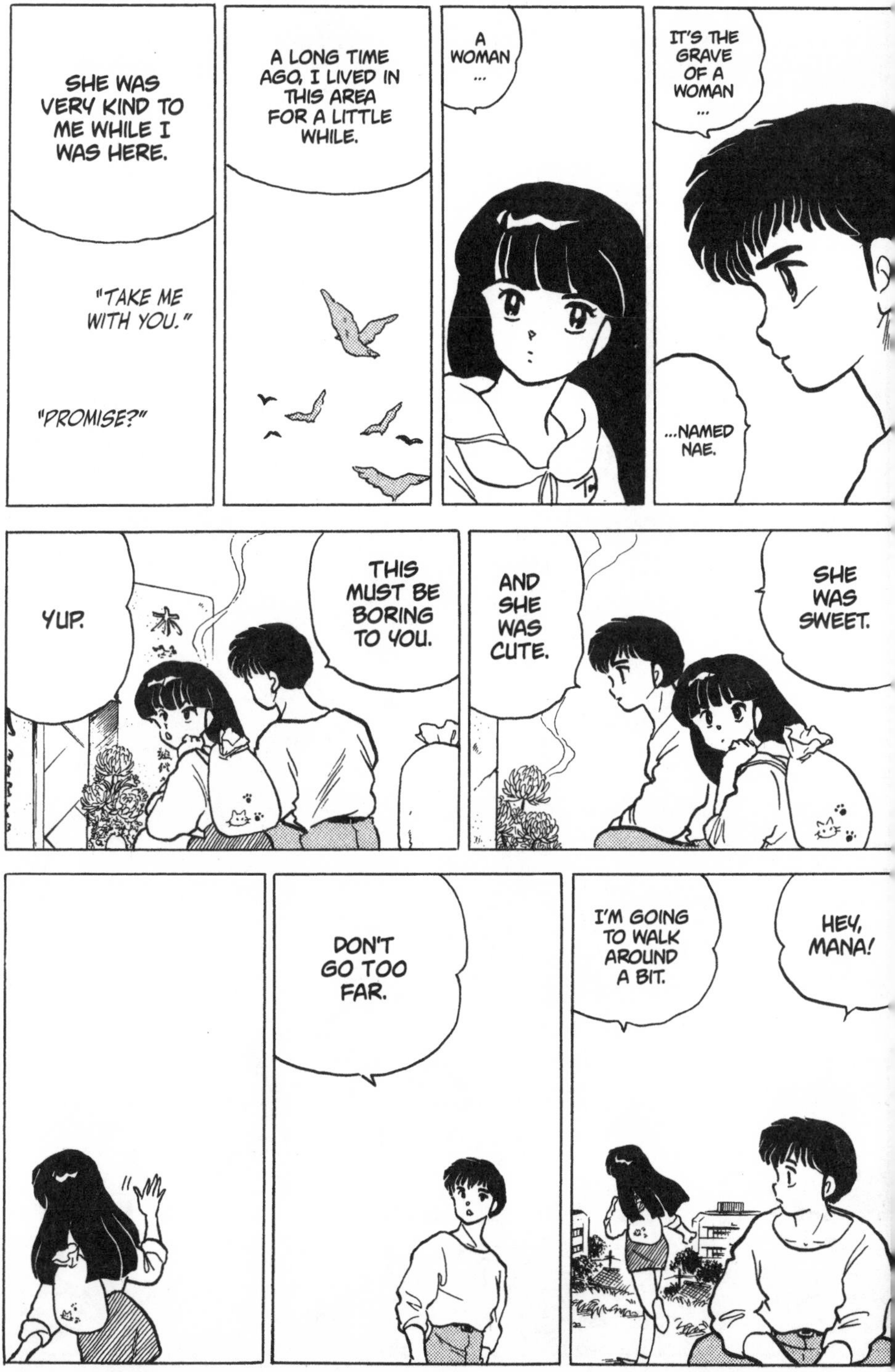
IT'S THE GRAVE OF A WOMAN ...
...NAMED NAE.
A WOMAN ...
A LONG TIME AGO, I LIVED IN THIS AREA FOR A LITTLE WHILE.
SHE WAS VERY KIND TO ME WHILE I WAS HERE.
"TAKE ME WITH YOU."
"PROMISE?"
SHE WAS SWEET.
AND SHE WAS CUTE.
THIS MUST BE BORING TO YOU.
YUP.
HEY, MANA!
I'M GOING TO WALK AROUND A BIT.
DON'T GO TOO FAR.

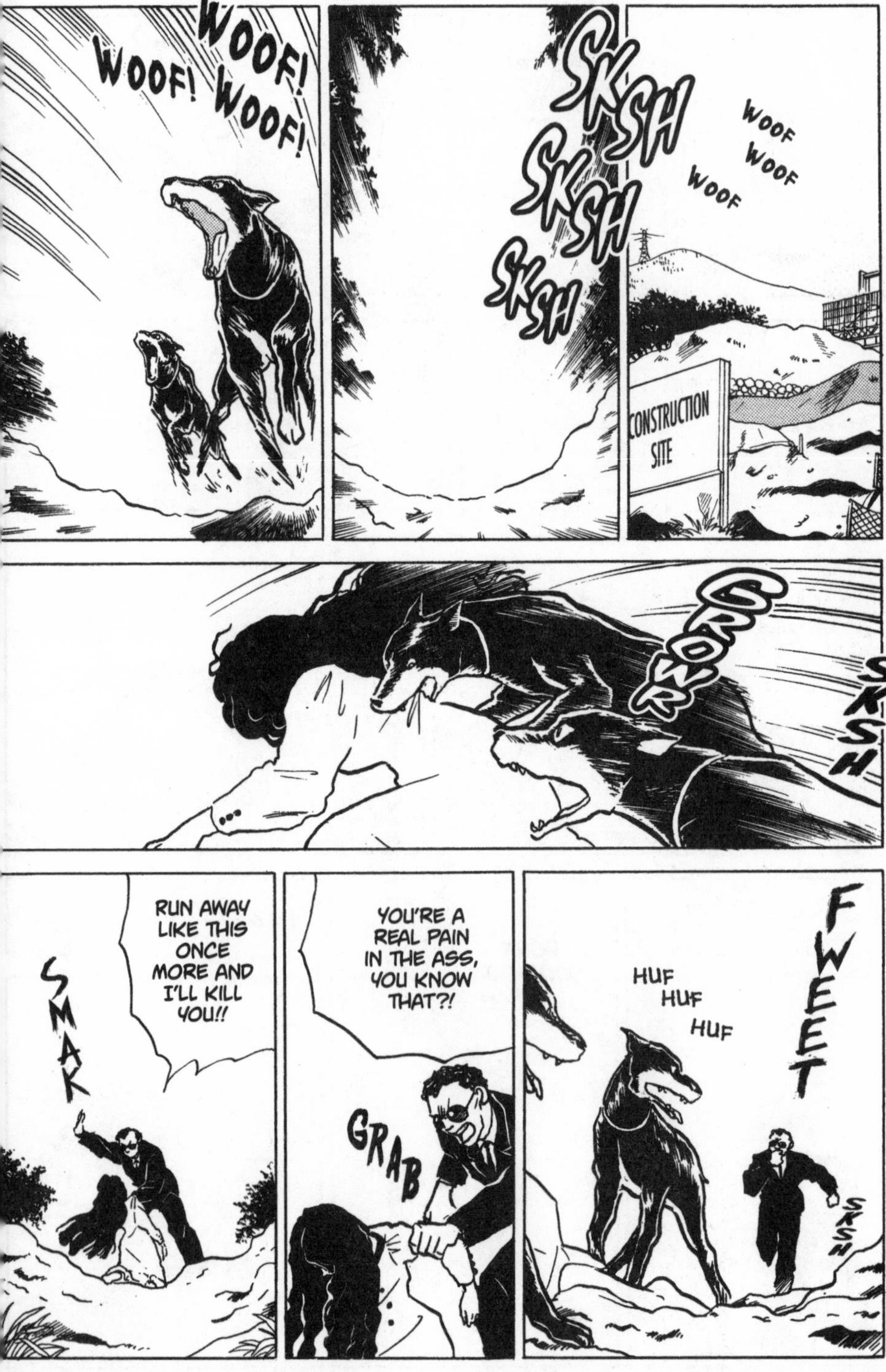
WOOF
WOOF
WOOF
CONSTRUCTION SITE
SKSH
SKSH
SKSH
WOOF!
WOOF! WOOF!
GROWR
SKSH
FWEET
HUF
HUF
HUF
SKSH
YOU'RE A REAL PAIN IN THE ASS, YOU KNOW THAT?!
GRAB
RUN AWAY LIKE THIS ONCE MORE AND I'LL KILL YOU!!
SMAK

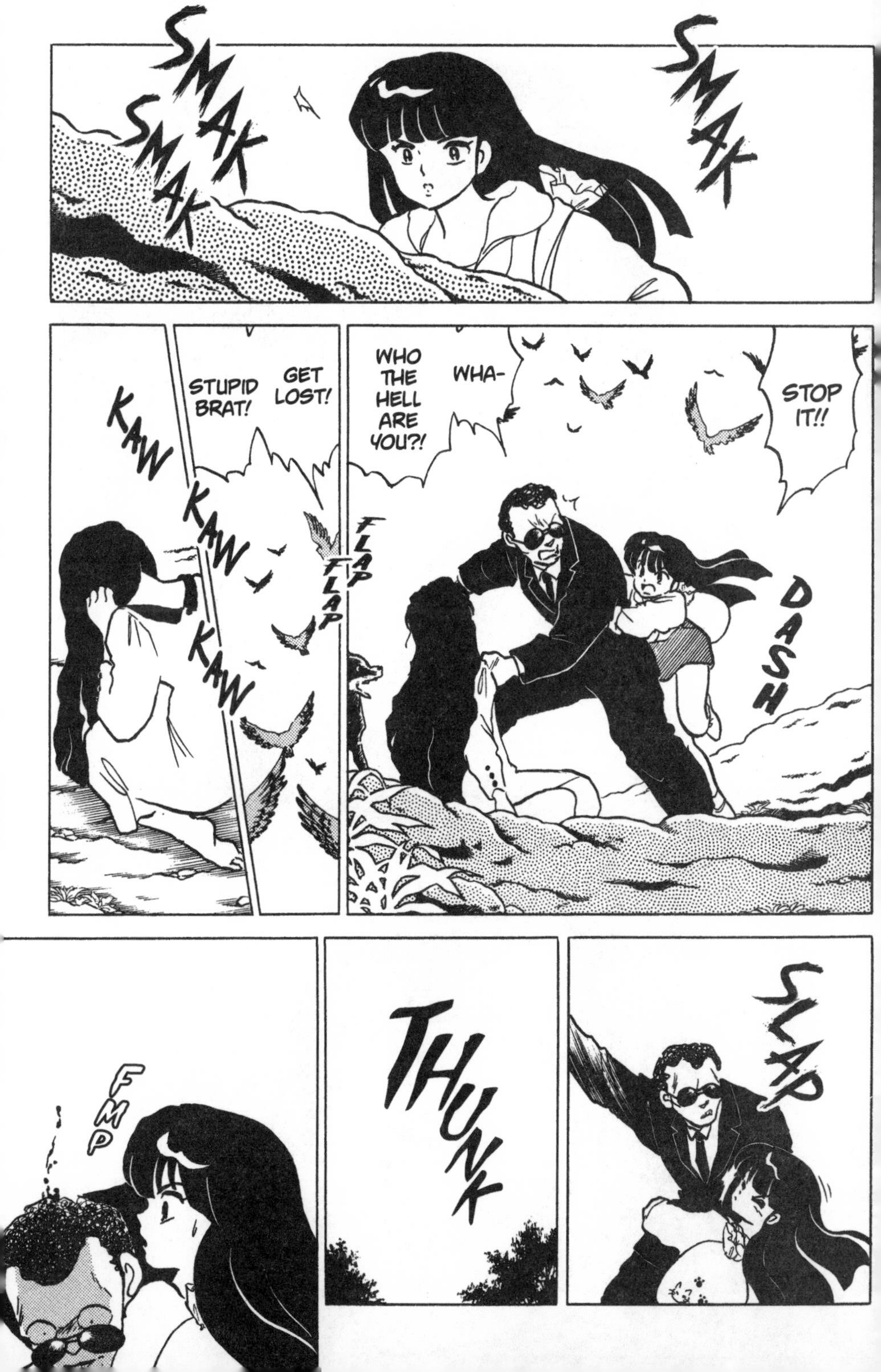
SMAK
SMAK
SMAK
STOP IT!!
WHA-
WHO THE HELL ARE YOU?!
DASH
GET LOST!
STUPID BRAT!
FLAP
FLAP
KAW
KAW
KAW
SLAP
THUNK
FMP

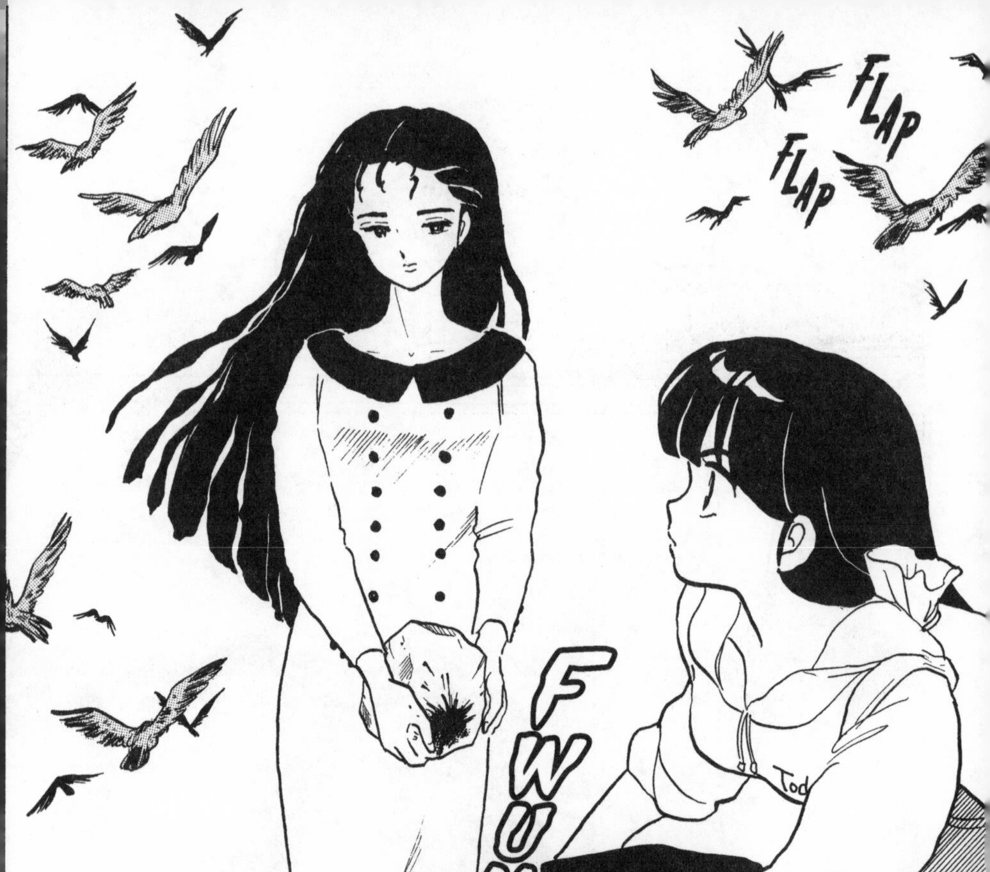
FLAP
FLAP
FWUMP
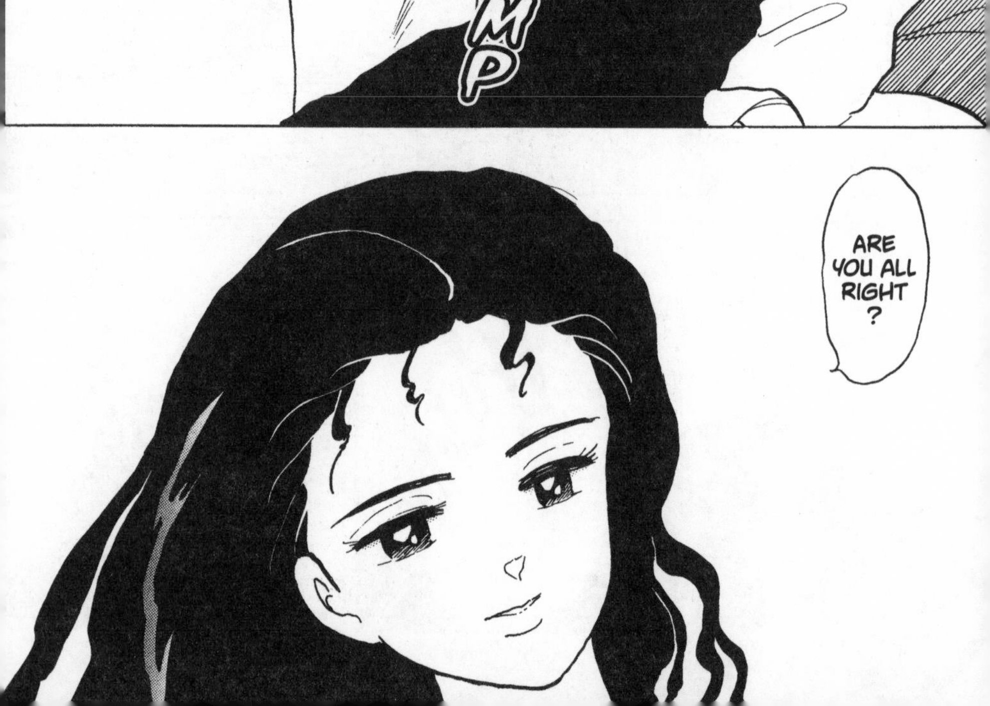
ARE YOU ALL RIGHT ?

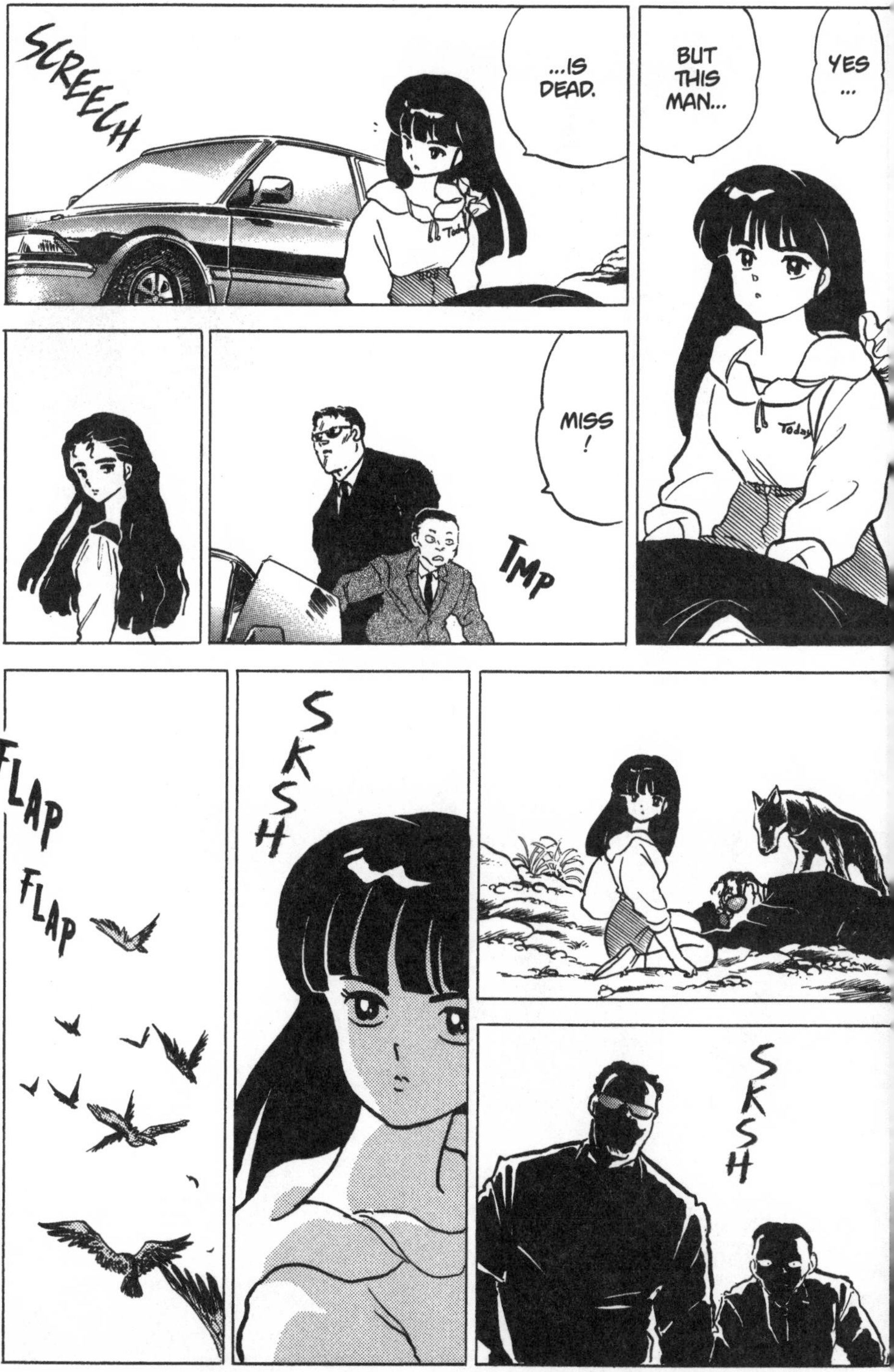
YES ...
BUT THIS MAN...
...IS DEAD.
SCREECH
MISS!
TMP
SKSH
SKSH
FLAP
FLAP

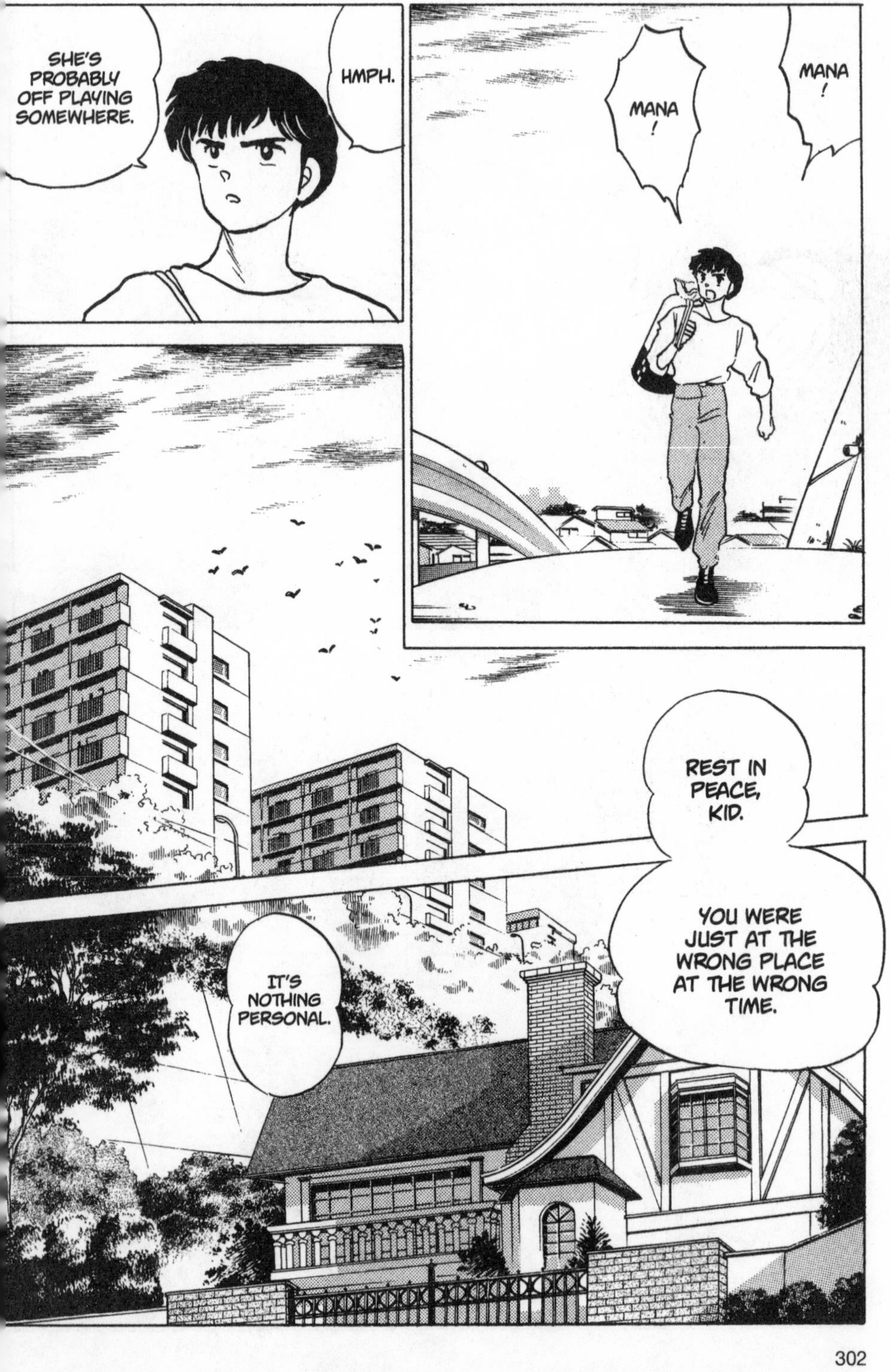
MANA!
MANA!
HMPH.
SHE'S PROBABLY OFF PLAYING SOMEWHERE.
REST IN PEACE, KID.
YOU WERE JUST AT THE WRONG PLACE AT THE WRONG TIME.
IT'S NOTHING PERSONAL.

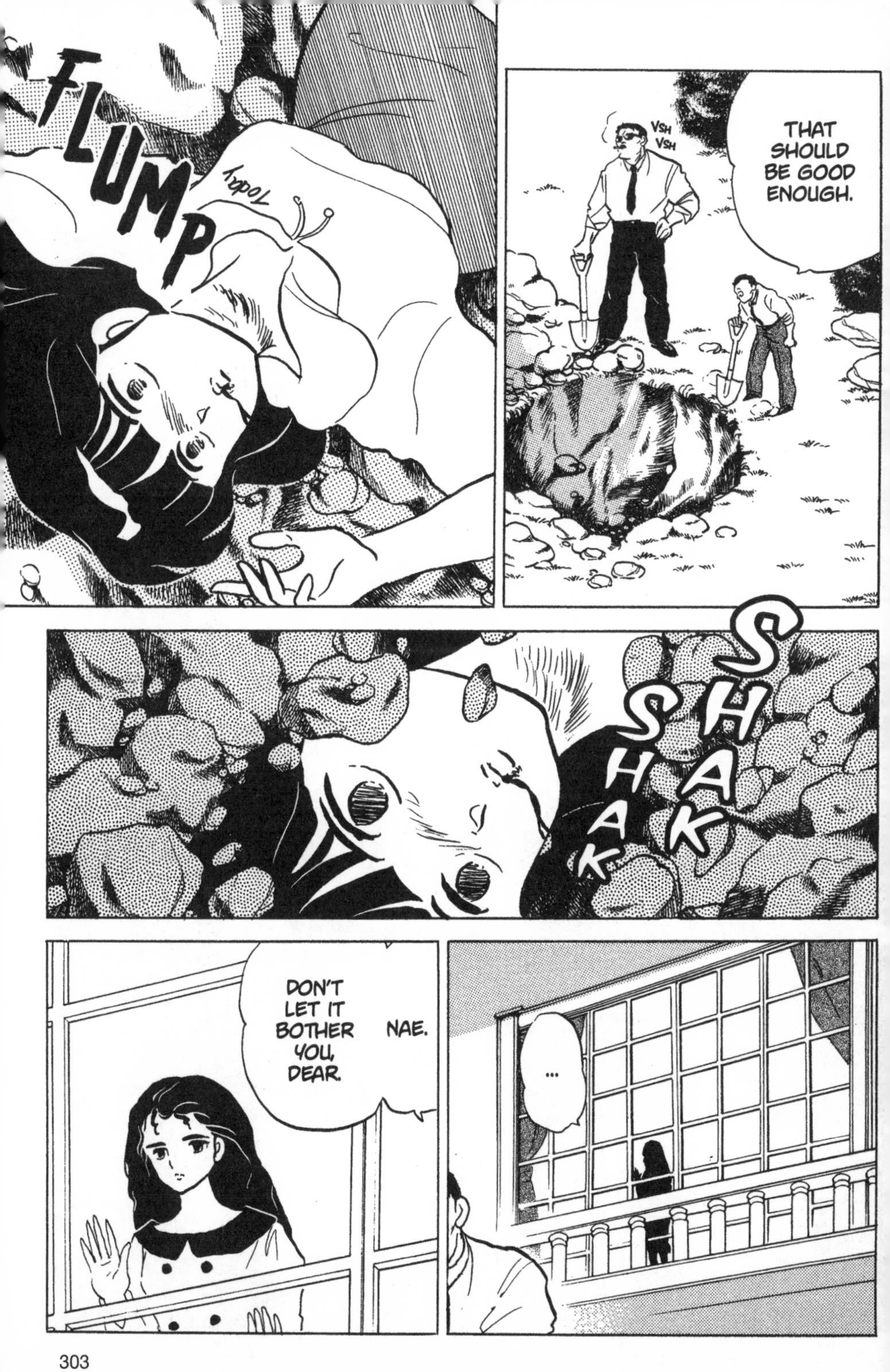
VSH VSH
THAT SHOULD BE GOOD ENOUGH.
FLUMP
Today
SHAK SHAK
...
DON'T LET IT BOTHER YOU, DEAR.
NAE.

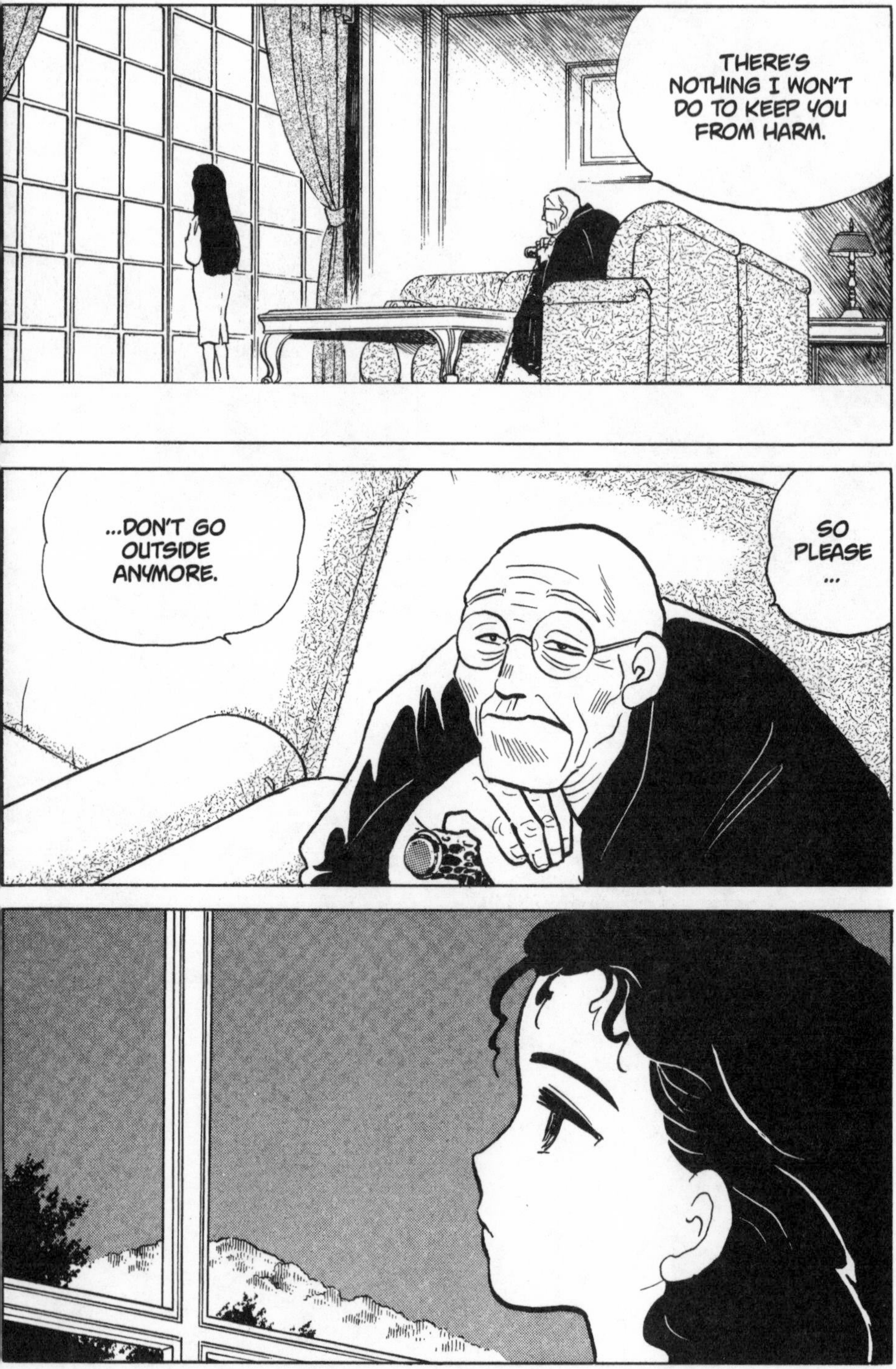
THERE'S NOTHING I WON'T DO TO KEEP YOU FROM HARM.
SO PLEASE ...
...DON'T GO OUTSIDE ANYMORE.

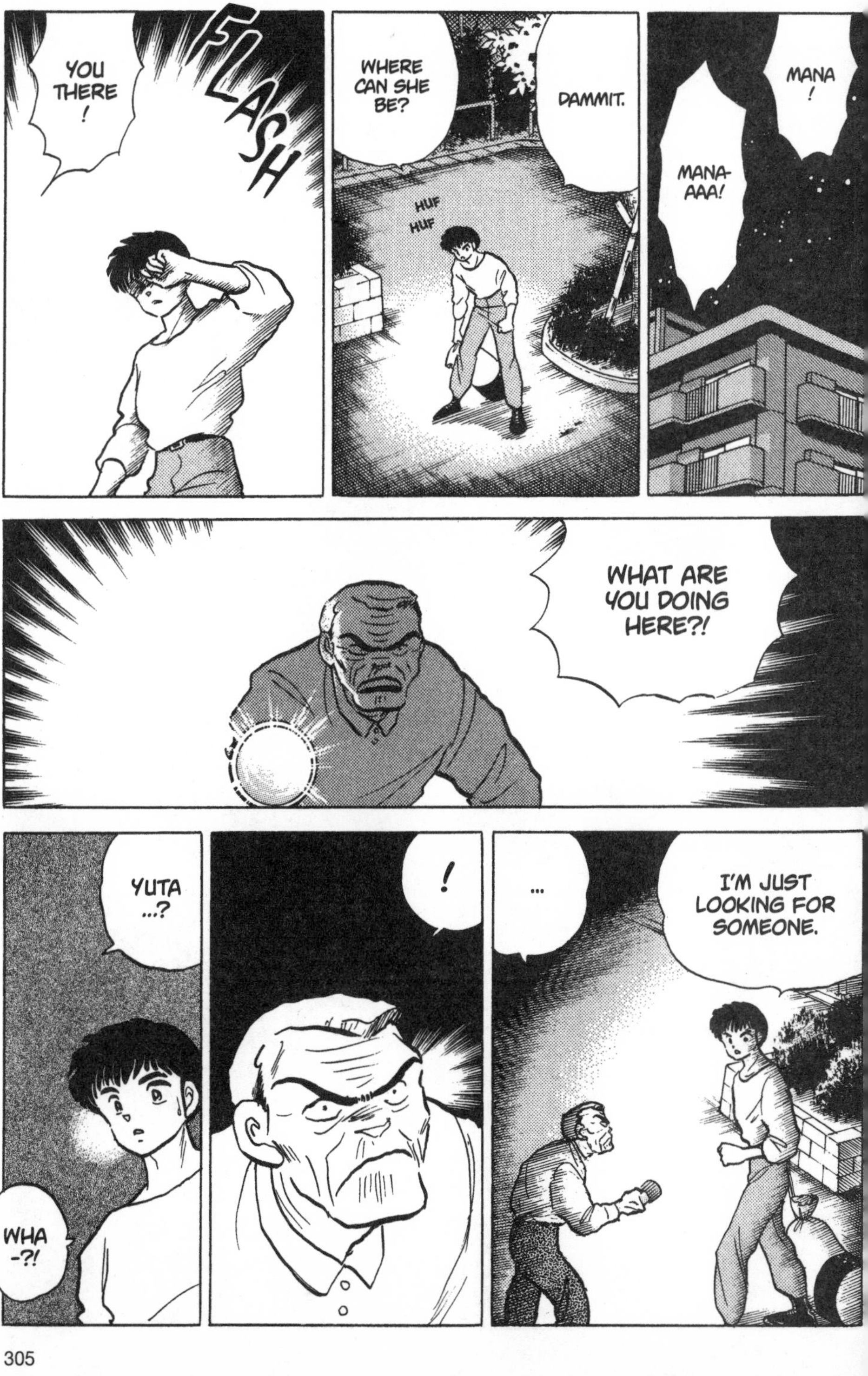
MANA!
MANA-AAA!
DAMMIT.
WHERE CAN SHE BE?
HUF HUF
FLASH
YOU THERE!
WHAT ARE YOU DOING HERE?!
I'M JUST LOOKING FOR SOMEONE.
...
!
YUTA ...?
WHA-?!

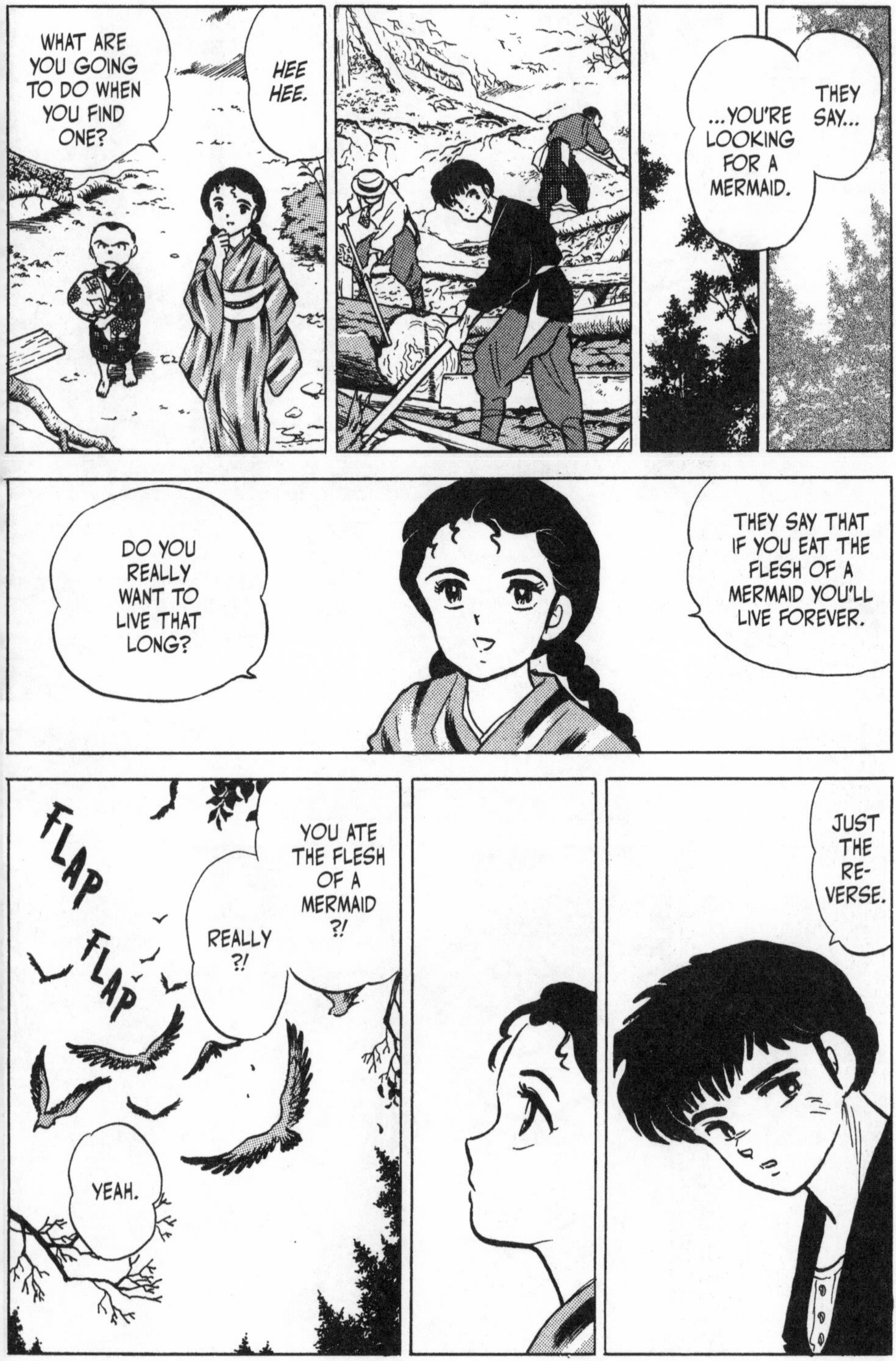
THEY SAY...
...YOU'RE LOOKING FOR A MERMAID.
HEE HEE.
WHAT ARE YOU GOING TO DO WHEN YOU FIND ONE?
THEY SAY THAT IF YOU EAT THE FLESH OF A MERMAID YOU'LL LIVE FOREVER.
DO YOU REALLY WANT TO LIVE THAT LONG?
JUST THE RE-VERSE.
YOU ATE THE FLESH OF A MERMAID ?!
REALLY ?!
FLAP
FLAP
FLAP
YEAH.

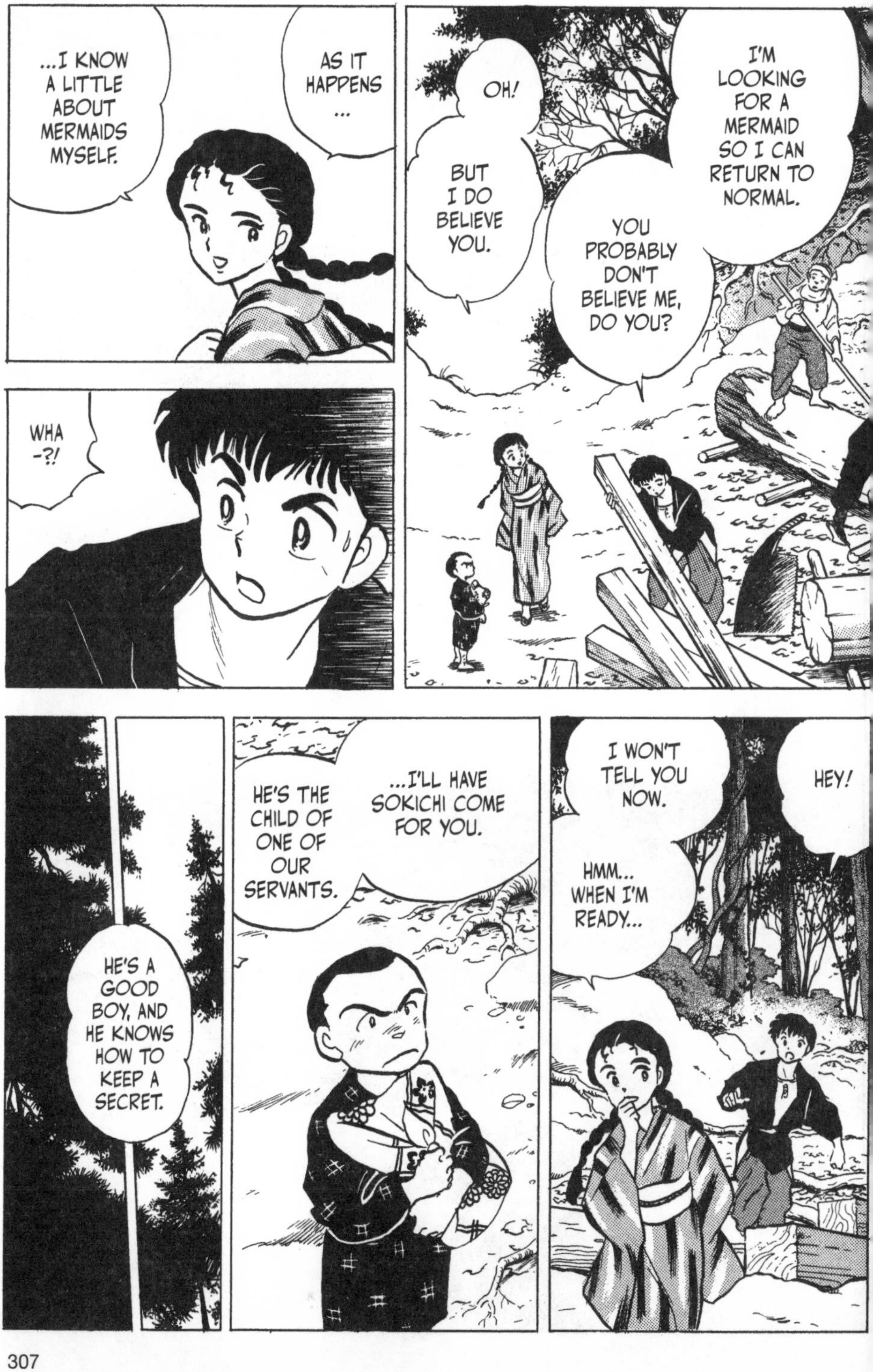
I'M LOOKING FOR A MERMAID SO I CAN RETURN TO NORMAL.
YOU PROBABLY DON'T BELIEVE ME, DO YOU?
OH!
BUT I DO BELIEVE YOU.
AS IT HAPPENS ...
...I KNOW A LITTLE ABOUT MERMAIDS MYSELF.
WHA -?!
HEY!
I WON'T TELL YOU NOW.
HMM... WHEN I'M READY...
...I'LL HAVE SOKICHI COME FOR YOU.
HE'S THE CHILD OF ONE OF OUR SERVANTS.
HE'S A GOOD BOY, AND HE KNOWS HOW TO KEEP A SECRET.

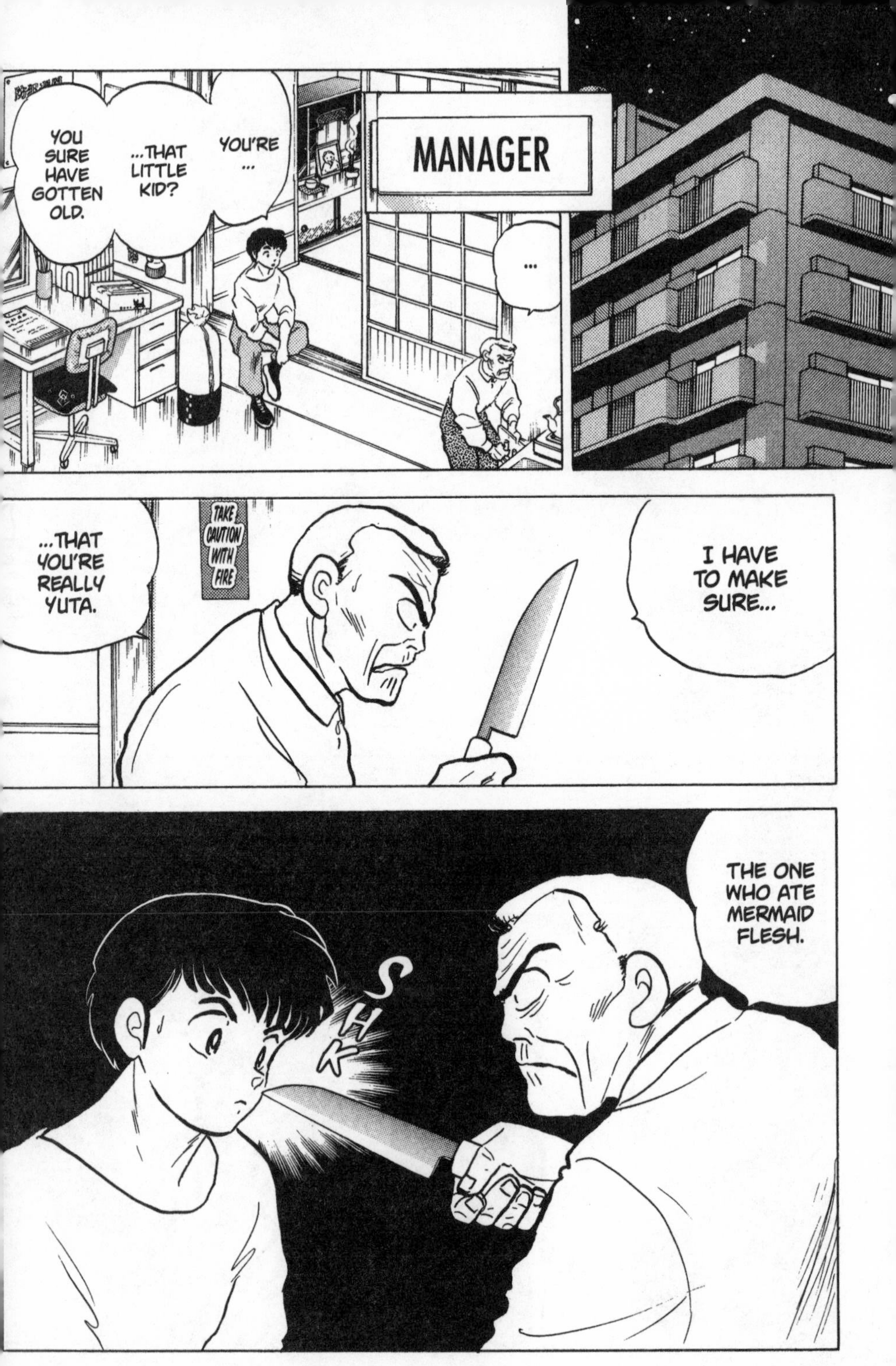
MANAGER
...
YOU'RE ...
...THAT LITTLE KID?
YOU SURE HAVE GOTTEN OLD.
I HAVE TO MAKE SURE...
TAKE CAUTION WITH FIRE
...THAT YOU'RE REALLY YUTA.
THE ONE WHO ATE MERMAID FLESH.
SHK

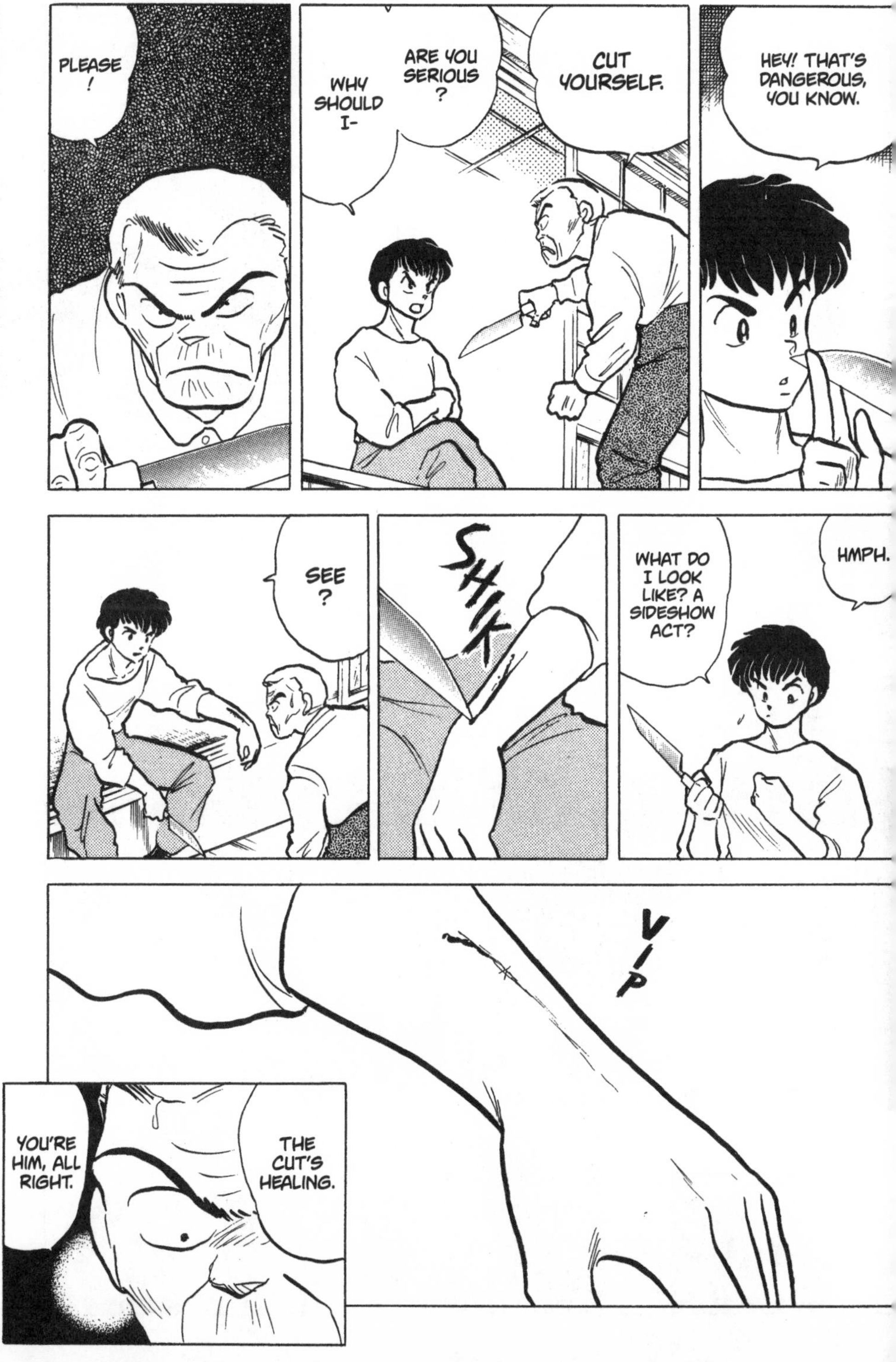
HEY! THAT'S DANGEROUS, YOU KNOW.
CUT YOURSELF.
ARE YOU SERIOUS?
WHY SHOULD I-
PLEASE!
HMPH.
WHAT DO I LOOK LIKE? A SIDESHOW ACT?
SHIK
SEE?
VIP
THE CUT'S HEALING.
YOU'RE HIM, ALL RIGHT.

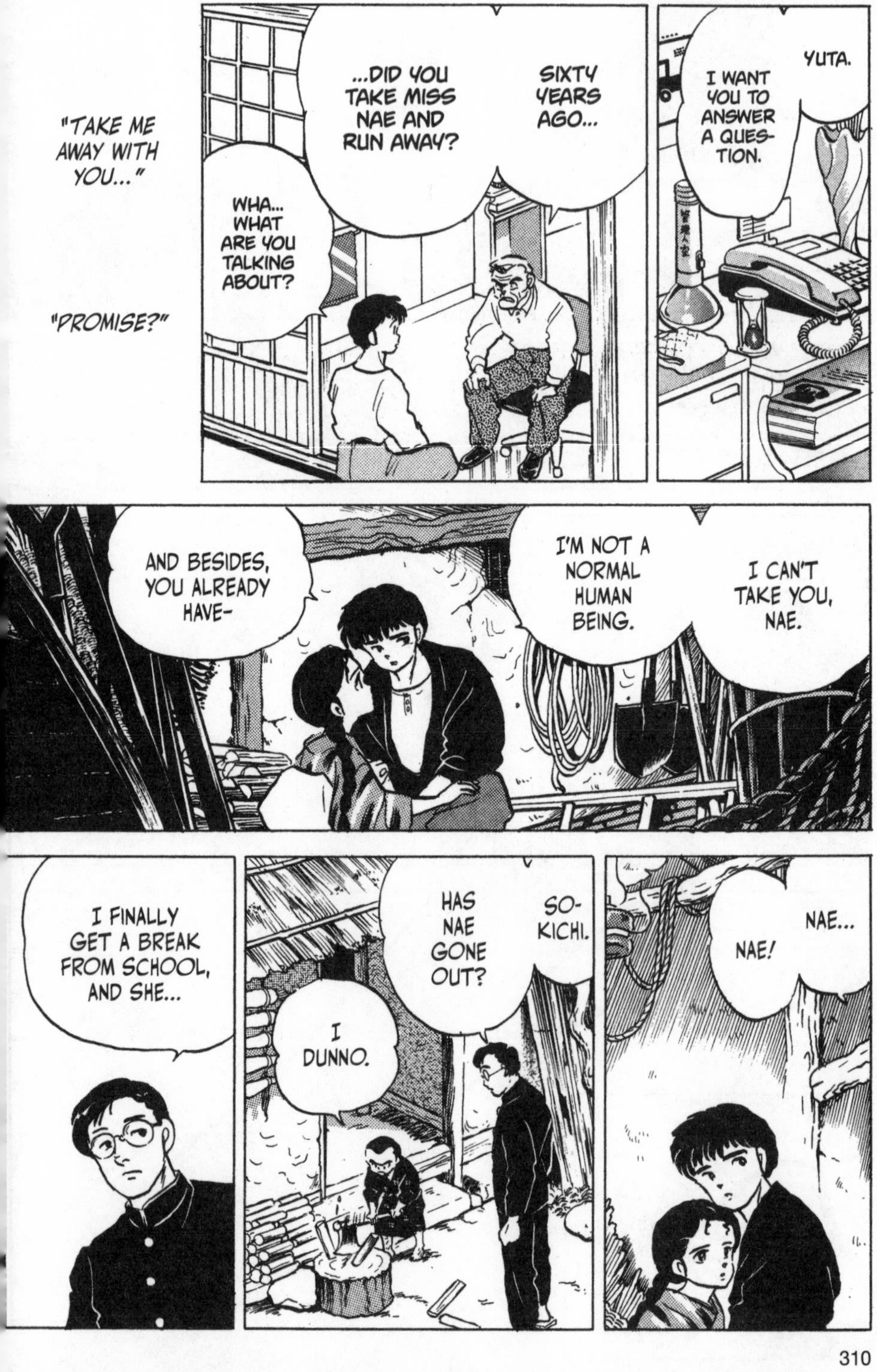
YUTA.
I WANT YOU TO ANSWER A QUES-TION.
SIXTY YEARS AGO...
...DID YOU TAKE MISS NAE AND RUN AWAY?
WHA... WHAT ARE YOU TALKING ABOUT?
"TAKE ME AWAY WITH YOU..."
"PROMISE?"
I CAN'T TAKE YOU, NAE.
I'M NOT A NORMAL HUMAN BEING.
AND BESIDES, YOU ALREADY HAVE-
NAE...
NAE!
SO-KICHI.
HAS NAE GONE OUT?
I DUNNO.
I FINALLY GET A BREAK FROM SCHOOL, AND SHE...

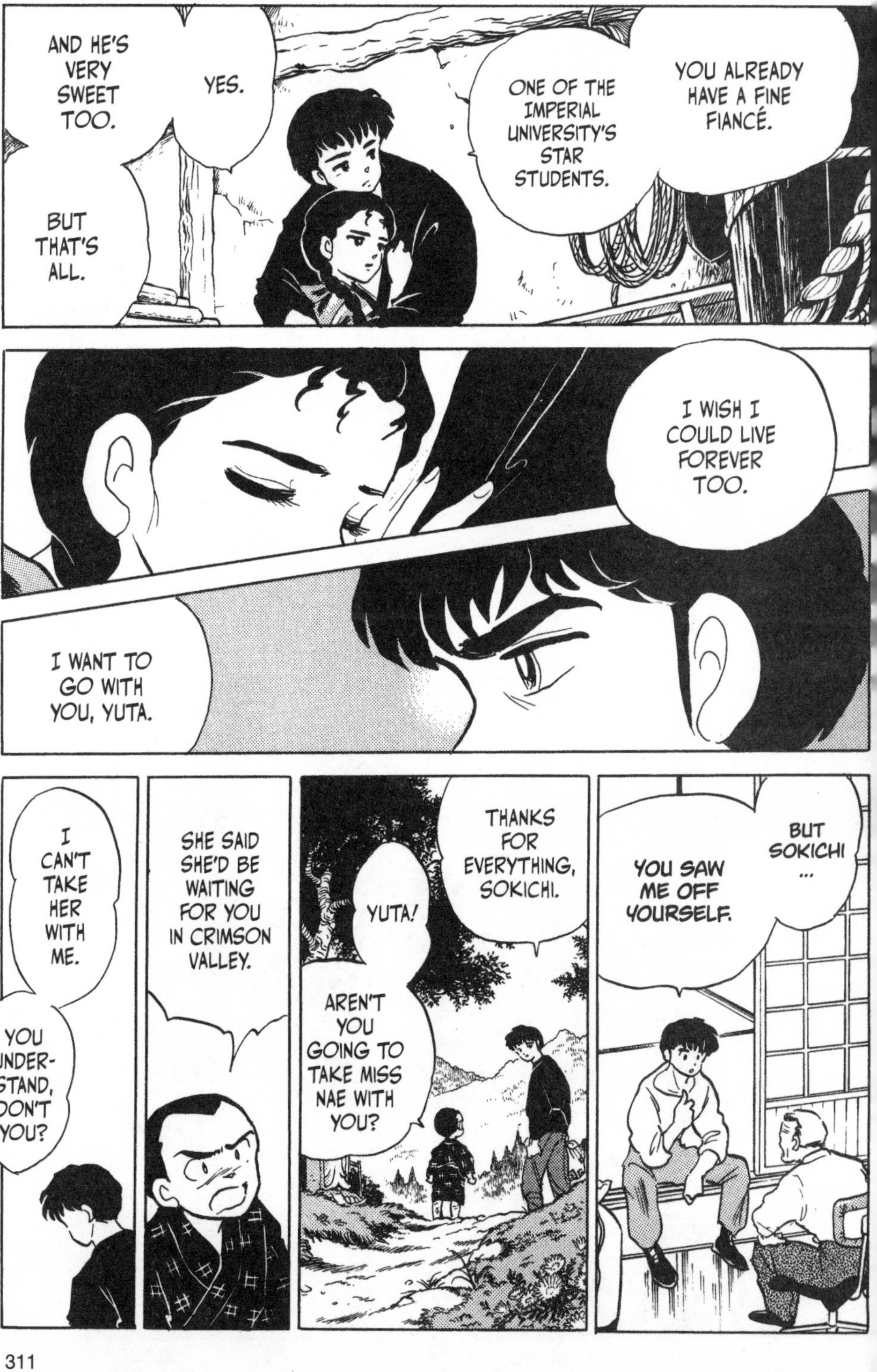
YOU ALREADY HAVE A FINE FIANCÉ.
ONE OF THE IMPERIAL UNIVERSITY'S STAR STUDENTS.
YES.
AND HE'S VERY SWEET TOO.
BUT THAT'S ALL.
I WISH I COULD LIVE FOREVER TOO.
I WANT TO GO WITH YOU, YUTA.
BUT SOKICHI ...
YOU SAW ME OFF YOURSELF.
THANKS FOR EVERYTHING, SOKICHI.
YUTA!
AREN'T YOU GOING TO TAKE MISS NAE WITH YOU?
SHE SAID SHE'D BE WAITING FOR YOU IN CRIMSON VALLEY.
I CAN'T TAKE HER WITH ME.
YOU UNDER-STAND, DON'T YOU?

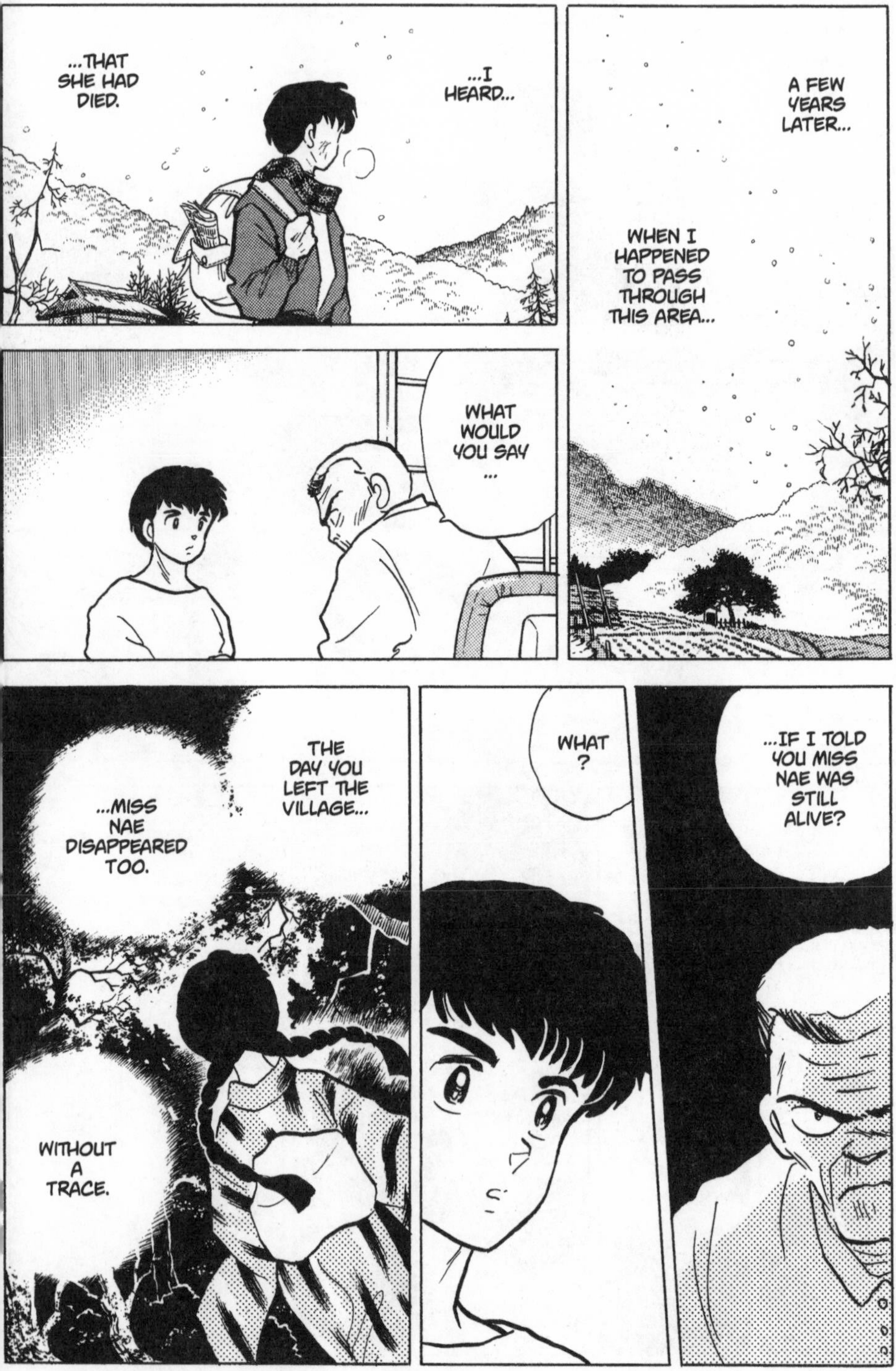
A FEW YEARS LATER...
WHEN I HAPPENED TO PASS THROUGH THIS AREA...
...I HEARD...
...THAT SHE HAD DIED.
WHAT WOULD YOU SAY ...
...IF I TOLD YOU MISS NAE WAS STILL ALIVE?
WHAT ?
THE DAY YOU LEFT THE VILLAGE...
...MISS NAE DISAPPEARED TOO.
WITHOUT A TRACE.

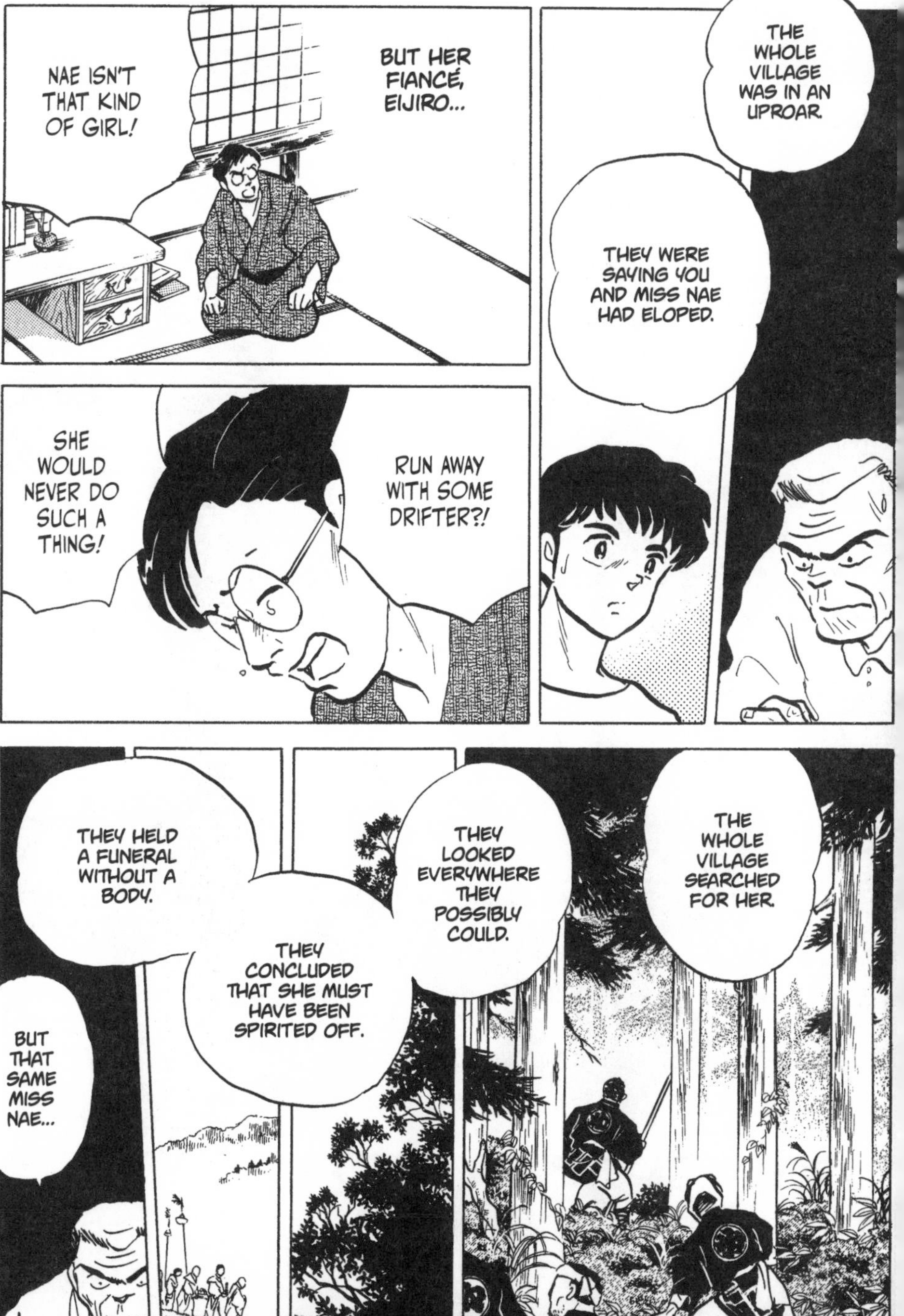
THE WHOLE VILLAGE WAS IN AN UPROAR.
THEY WERE SAYING YOU AND MISS NAE HAD ELOPED.
BUT HER FIANCÉ, EIJIRO...
NAE ISN'T THAT KIND OF GIRL!
RUN AWAY WITH SOME DRIFTER?!
SHE WOULD NEVER DO SUCH A THING!
THE WHOLE VILLAGE SEARCHED FOR HER.
THEY LOOKED EVERYWHERE THEY POSSIBLY COULD.
THEY CONCLUDED THAT SHE MUST HAVE BEEN SPIRITED OFF.
THEY HELD A FUNERAL WITHOUT A BODY.
BUT THAT SAME MISS NAE...

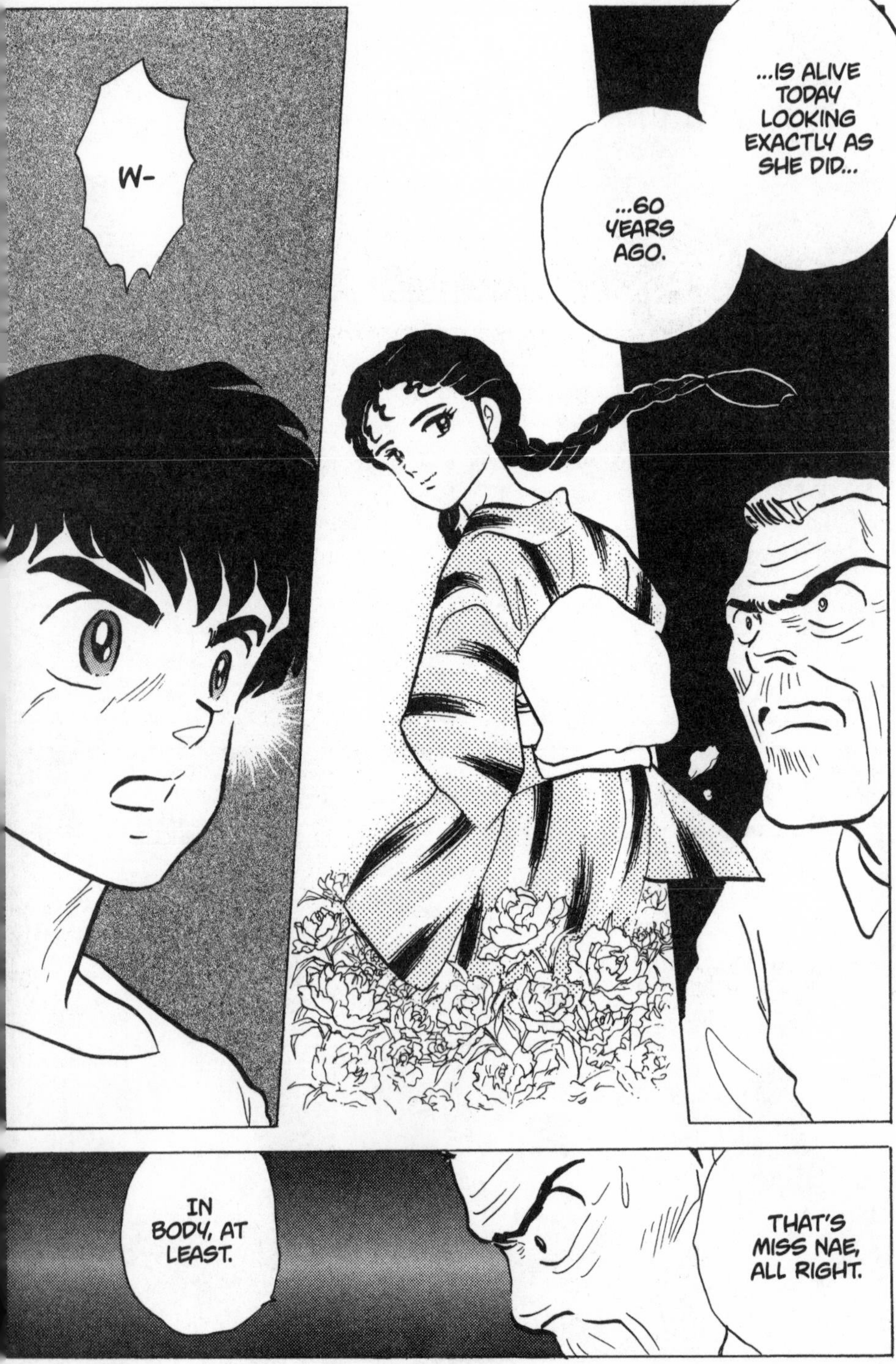
...IS ALIVE TODAY LOOKING EXACTLY AS SHE DID...
...60 YEARS AGO.
W-
THAT'S MISS NAE, ALL RIGHT.
IN BODY, AT LEAST.

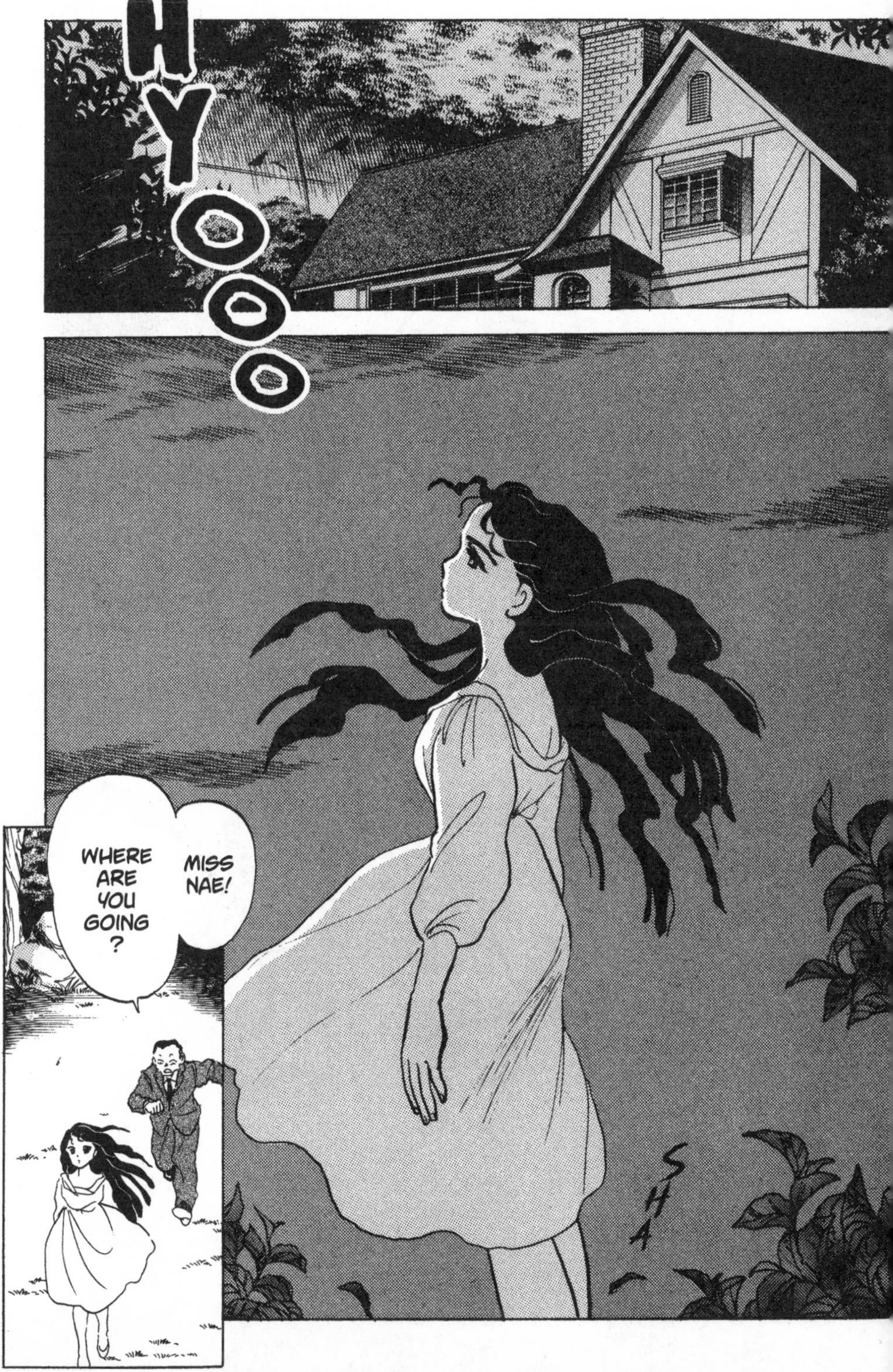
HYOOO
SHA
MISS NAE!
WHERE ARE YOU GOING?

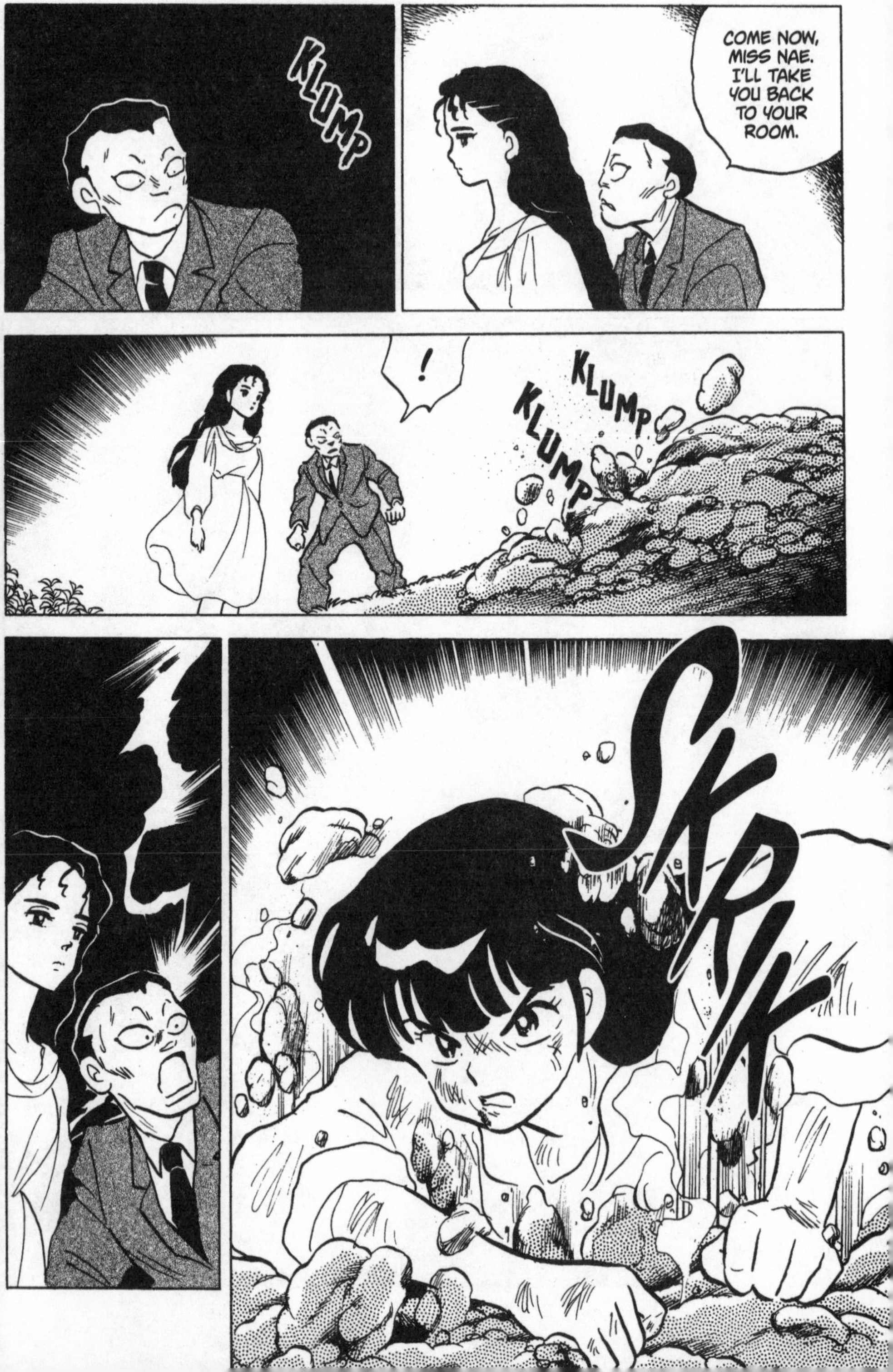
COME NOW, MISS NAE. I'LL TAKE YOU BACK TO YOUR ROOM.
KLUMP
KLUMP
KLUMP
KLUMP
!
SKRIK

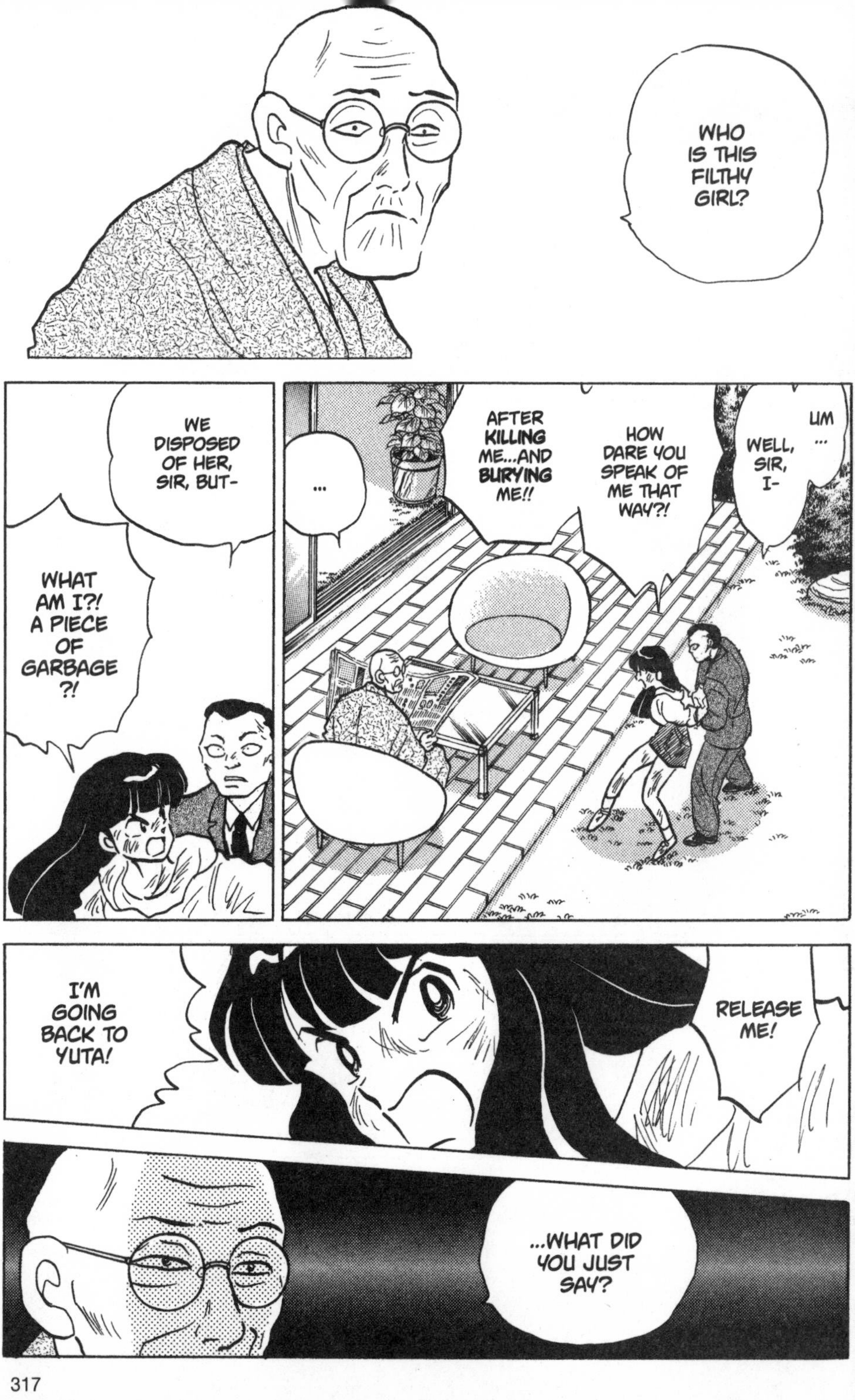
WHO IS THIS FILTHY GIRL?
UM ...
WELL, SIR, I-
HOW DARE YOU SPEAK OF ME THAT WAY?!
AFTER KILLING ME...AND BURYING ME!!
...
WE DISPOSED OF HER, SIR, BUT-
WHAT AM I?! A PIECE OF GARBAGE?!
RELEASE ME!
I'M GOING BACK TO YUTA!
...WHAT DID YOU JUST SAY?

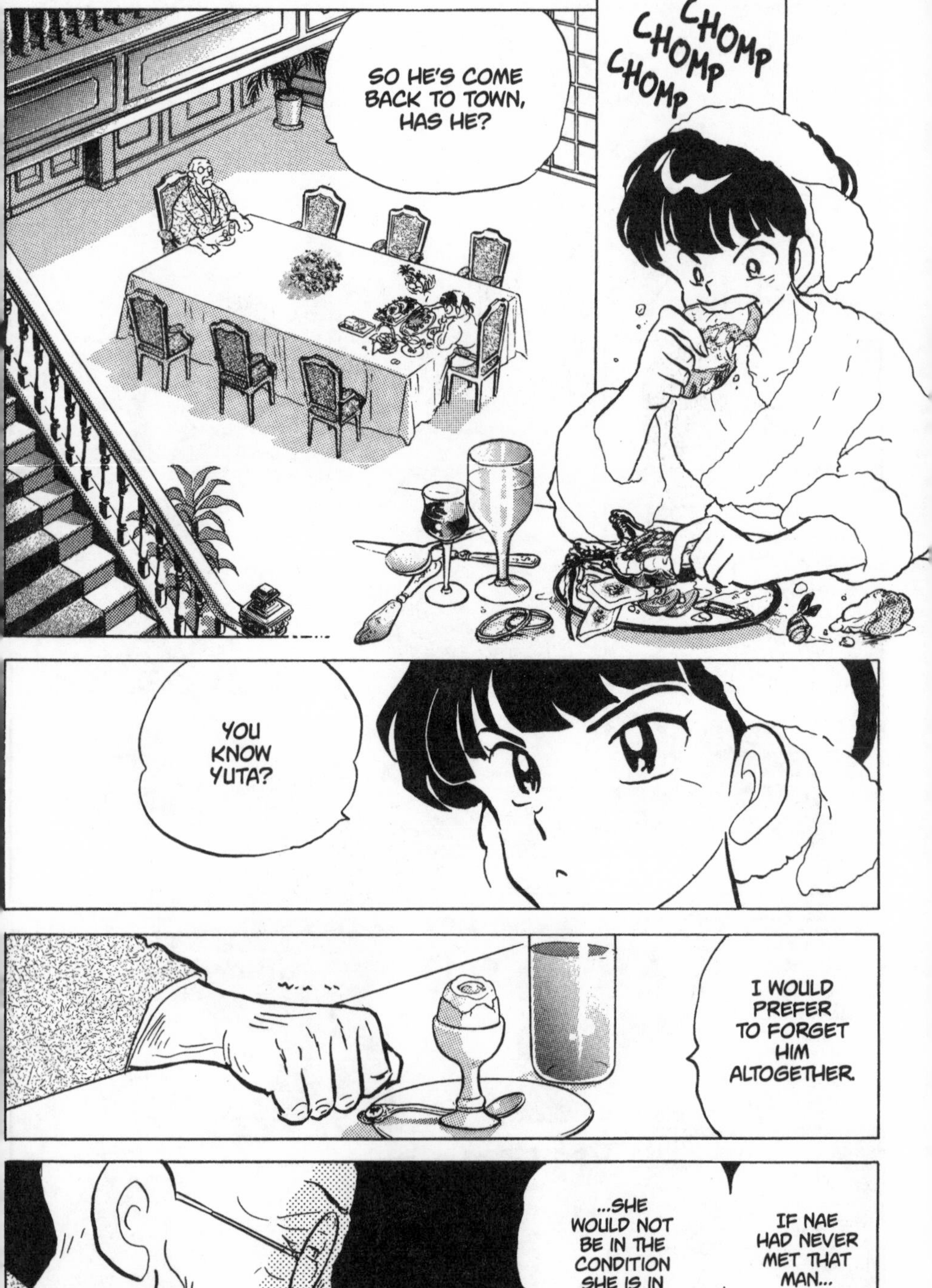
CHOMP CHOMP CHOMP
SO HE'S COME BACK TO TOWN, HAS HE?
YOU KNOW YUTA?
I WOULD PREFER TO FORGET HIM ALTOGETHER.
IF NAE HAD NEVER MET THAT MAN...
...SHE WOULD NOT BE IN THE CONDITION SHE IS IN TODAY.

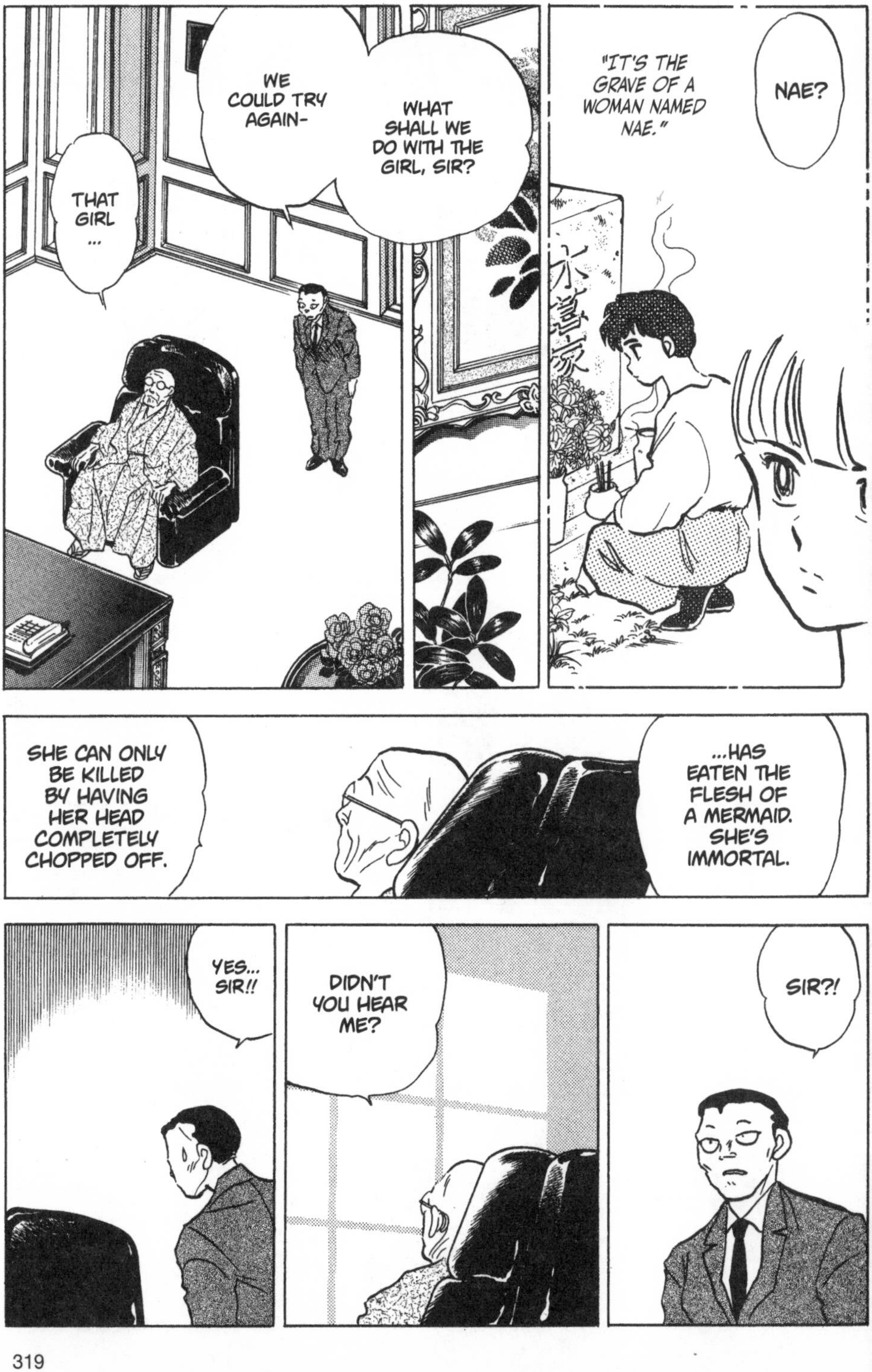
"IT'S THE GRAVE OF A WOMAN NAMED NAE."
NAE?
WHAT SHALL WE DO WITH THE GIRL, SIR?
WE COULD TRY AGAIN-
THAT GIRL ...
...HAS EATEN THE FLESH OF A MERMAID. SHE'S IMMORTAL.
SHE CAN ONLY BE KILLED BY HAVING HER HEAD COMPLETELY CHOPPED OFF.
SIR?!
DIDN'T YOU HEAR ME?
YES... SIR!!

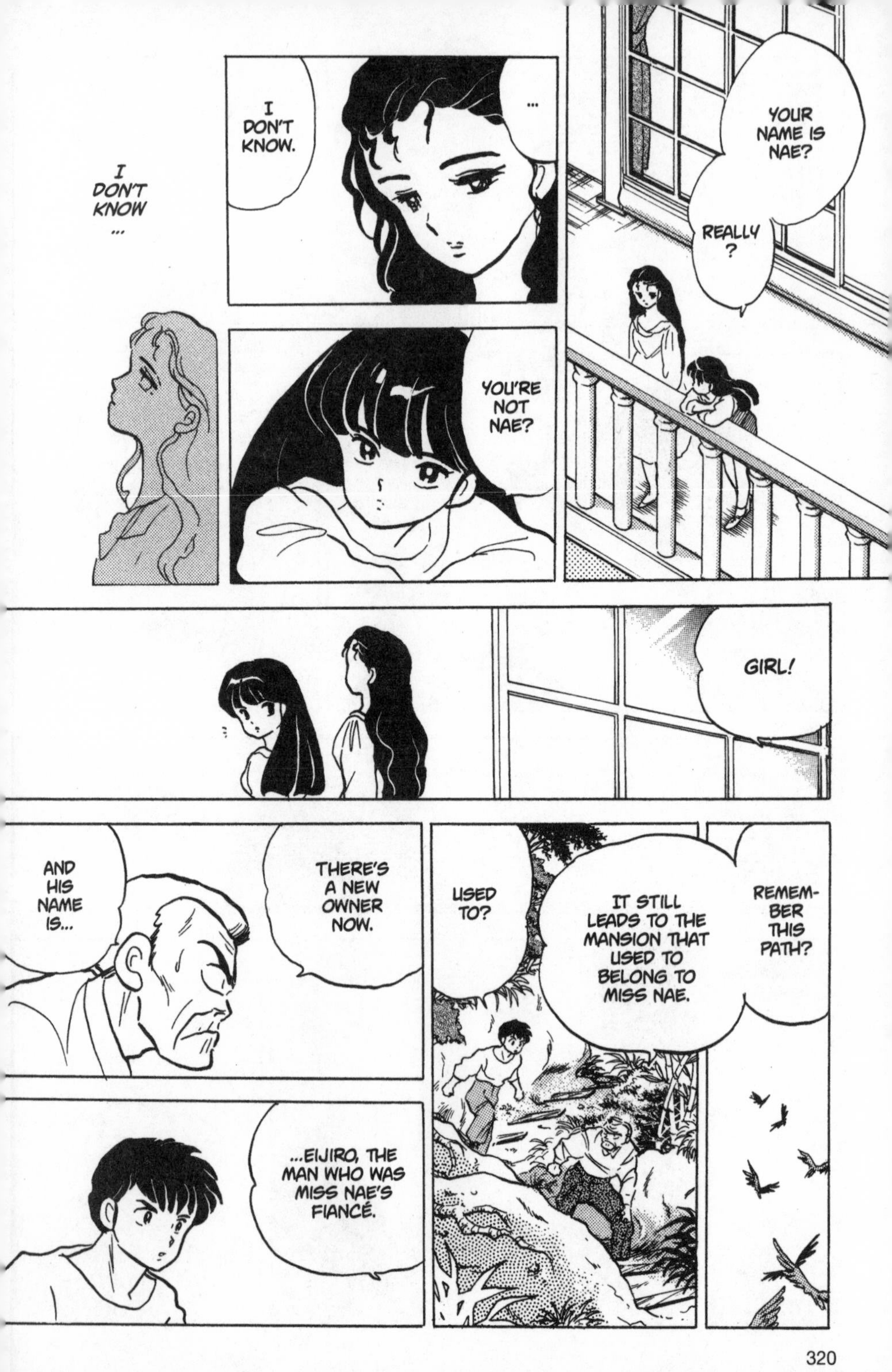
YOUR NAME IS NAE?
REALLY?
...
I DON'T KNOW.
YOU'RE NOT NAE?
I DON'T KNOW ...
GIRL!
REMEM-BER THIS PATH?
IT STILL LEADS TO THE MANSION THAT USED TO BELONG TO MISS NAE.
USED TO?
THERE'S A NEW OWNER NOW.
AND HIS NAME IS...
...EIJIRO, THE MAN WHO WAS MISS NAE'S FIANCÉ.

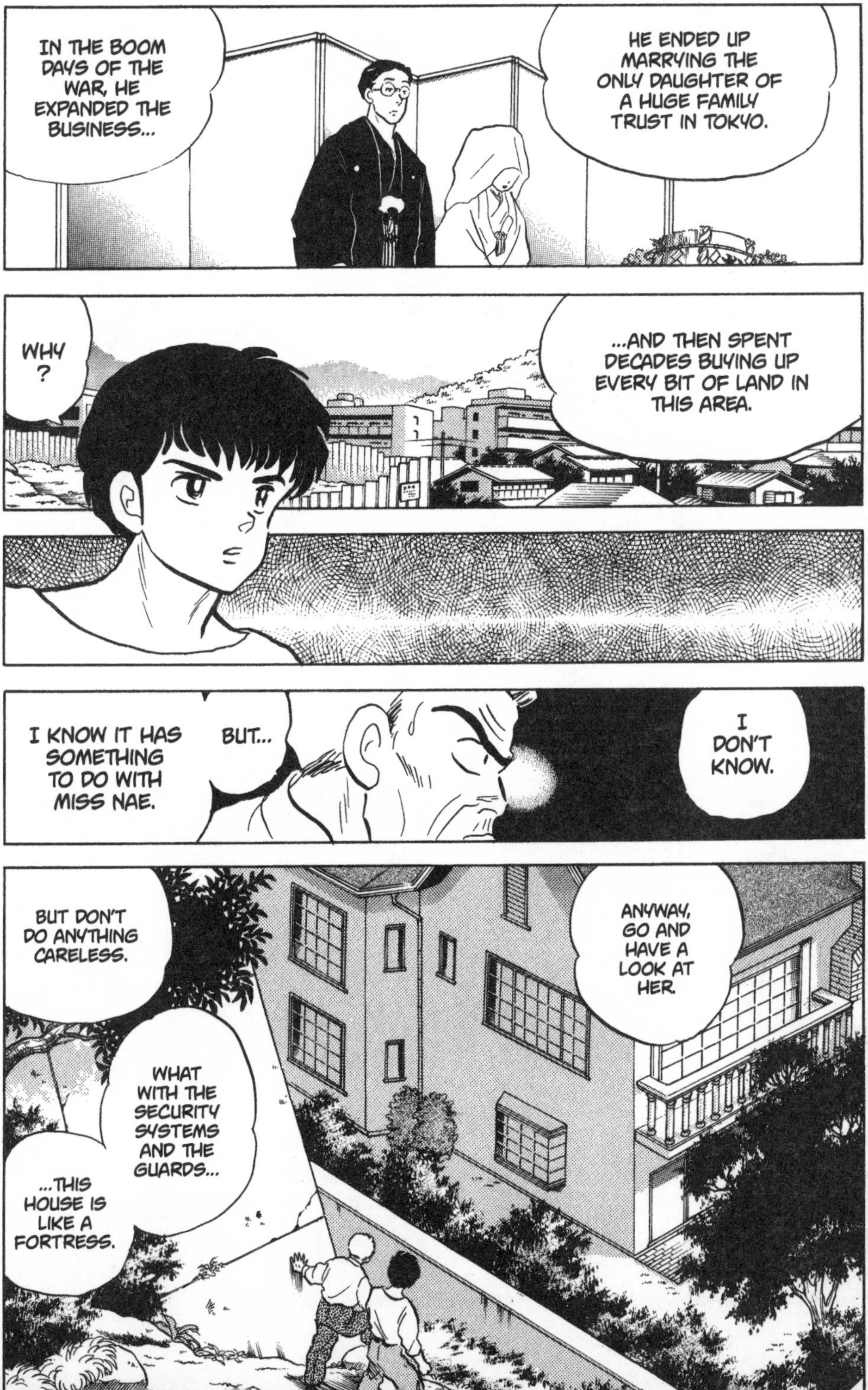
HE ENDED UP MARRYING THE ONLY DAUGHTER OF A HUGE FAMILY TRUST IN TOKYO.
IN THE BOOM DAYS OF THE WAR, HE EXPANDED THE BUSINESS...
...AND THEN SPENT DECADES BUYING UP EVERY BIT OF LAND IN THIS AREA.
WHY?
I DON'T KNOW.
BUT...
I KNOW IT HAS SOMETHING TO DO WITH MISS NAE.
ANYWAY, GO AND HAVE A LOOK AT HER.
BUT DON'T DO ANYTHING CARELESS.
WHAT WITH THE SECURITY SYSTEMS AND THE GUARDS...
...THIS HOUSE IS LIKE A FORTRESS.

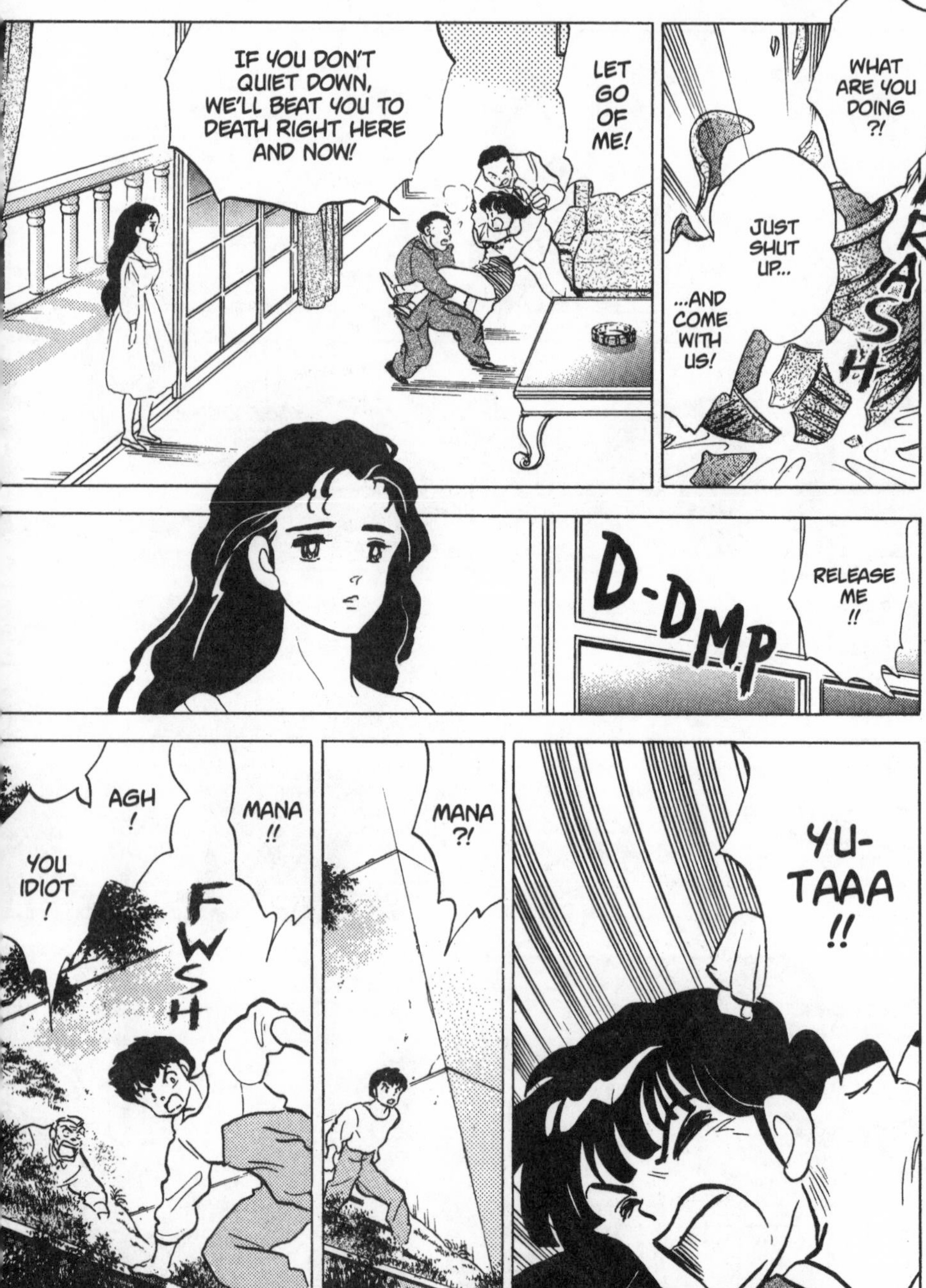
WHAT ARE YOU DOING ?!
KRASH
JUST SHUT UP...
...AND COME WITH US!
LET GO OF ME!
IF YOU DON'T QUIET DOWN, WE'LL BEAT YOU TO DEATH RIGHT HERE AND NOW!
RELEASE ME !!
D-DMP
YU-TAAA !!
MANA ?!
MANA !!
FWSH
AGH !
YOU IDIOT !

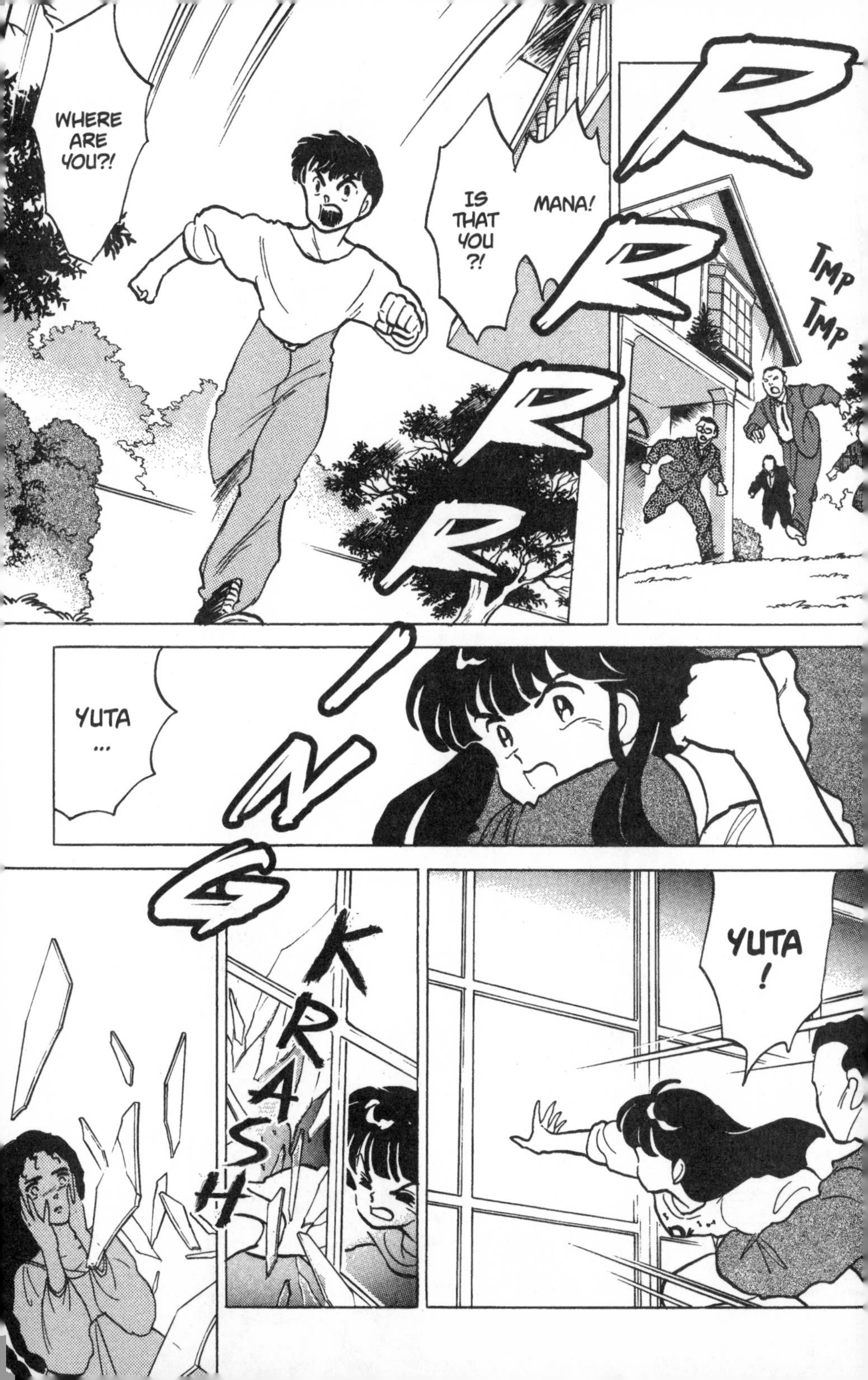
TMP TMP
MANA! IS THAT YOU?!
WHERE ARE YOU?!
RRRRING
YUTA ...
YUTA!
KRASH

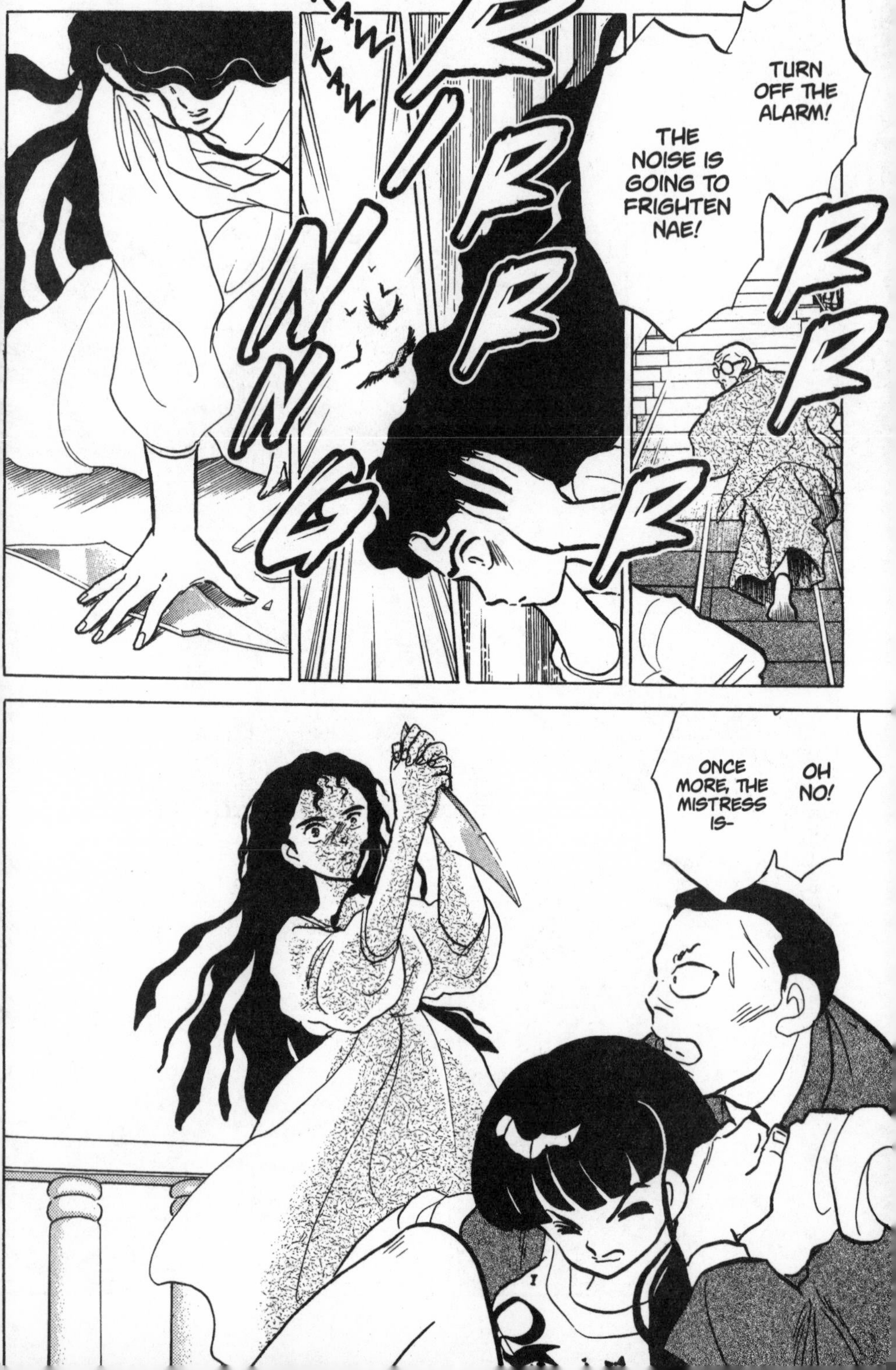
TURN OFF THE ALARM!
THE NOISE IS GOING TO FRIGHTEN NAE!
RRRR
RRRINNG
KAW KAW KAW
OH NO!
ONCE MORE, THE MISTRESS IS-

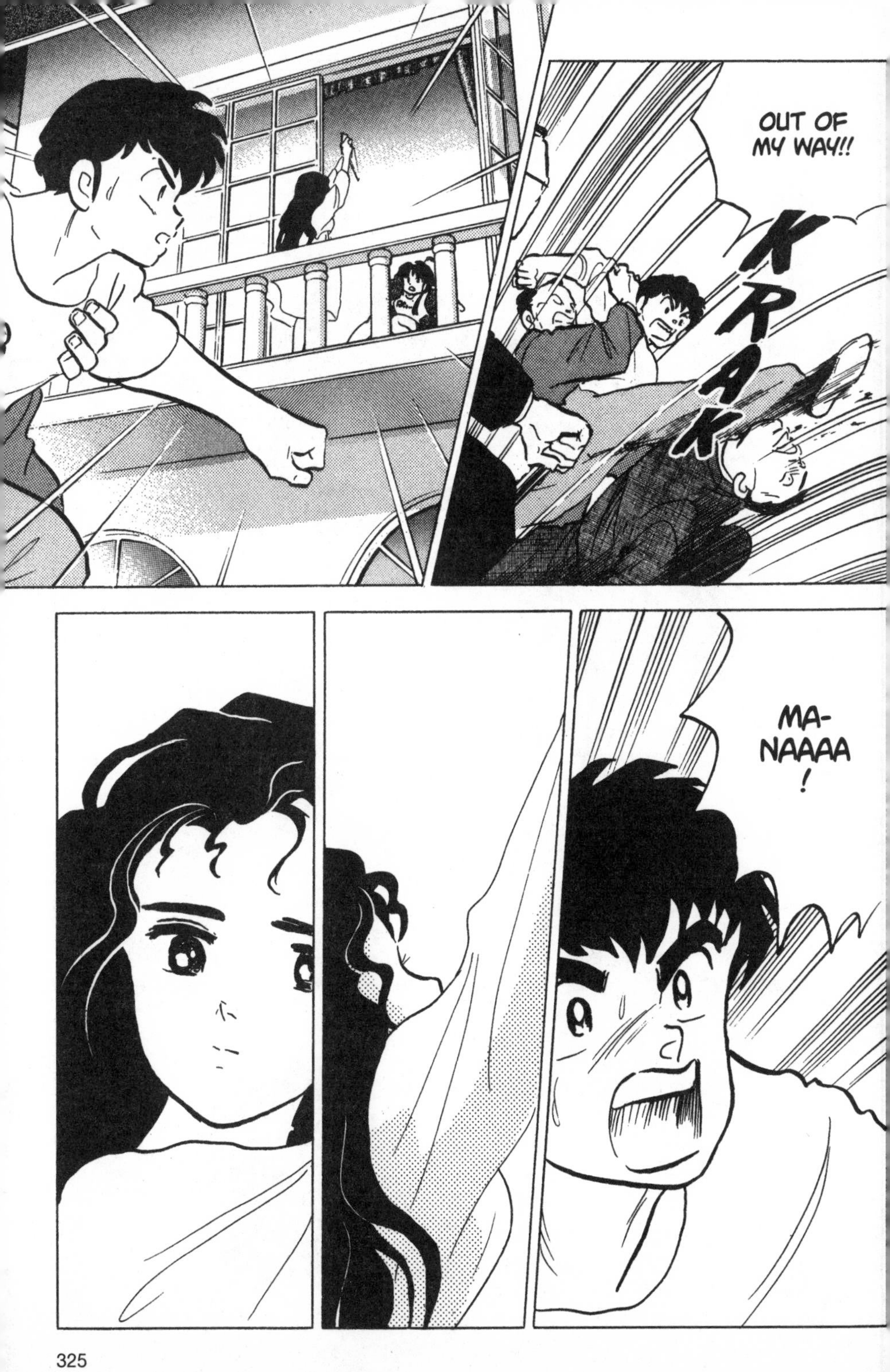
OUT OF MY WAY!!
KRAK
MA-NAAAA!

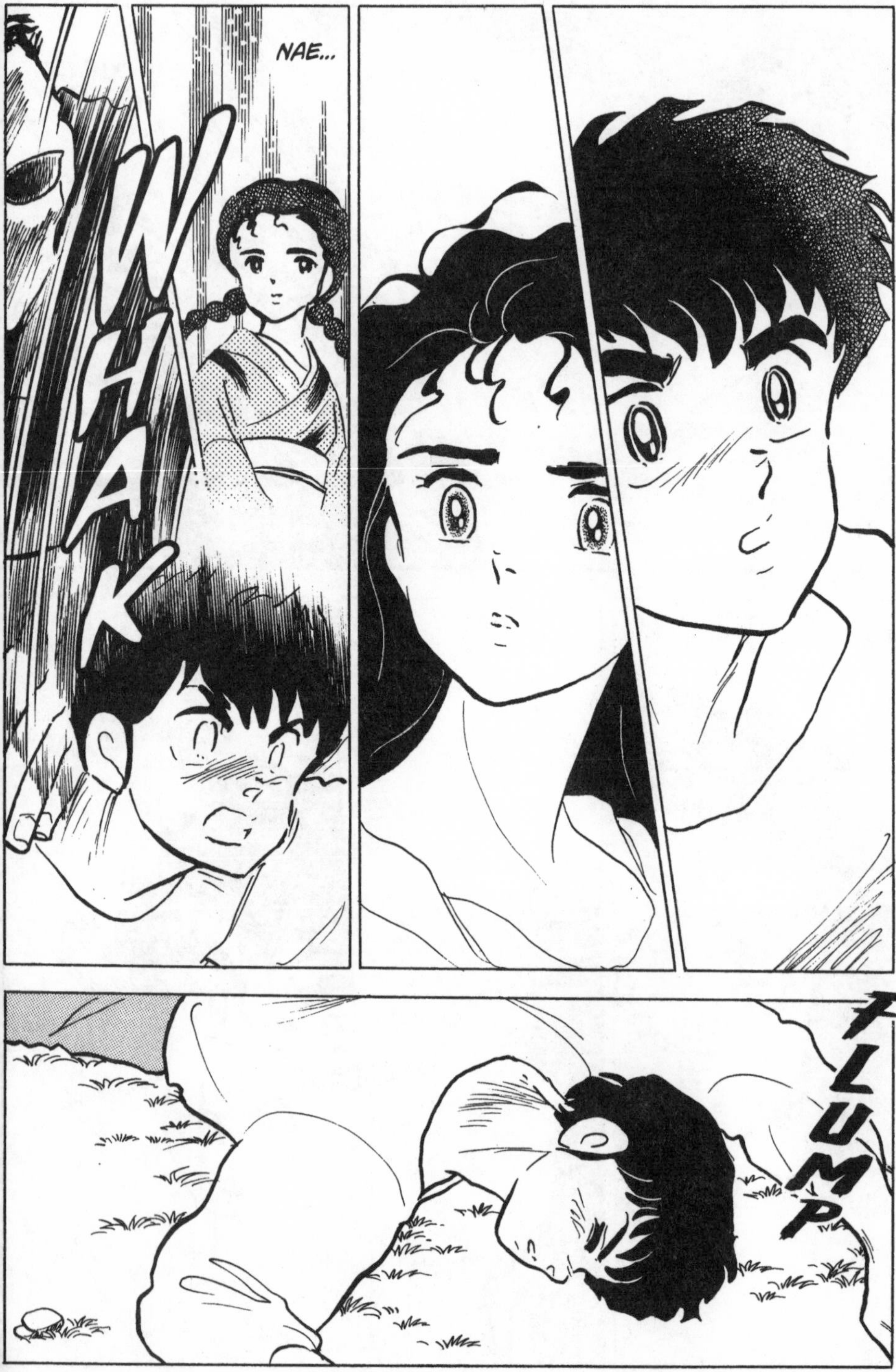
NAE...
WHAK
FLUMP

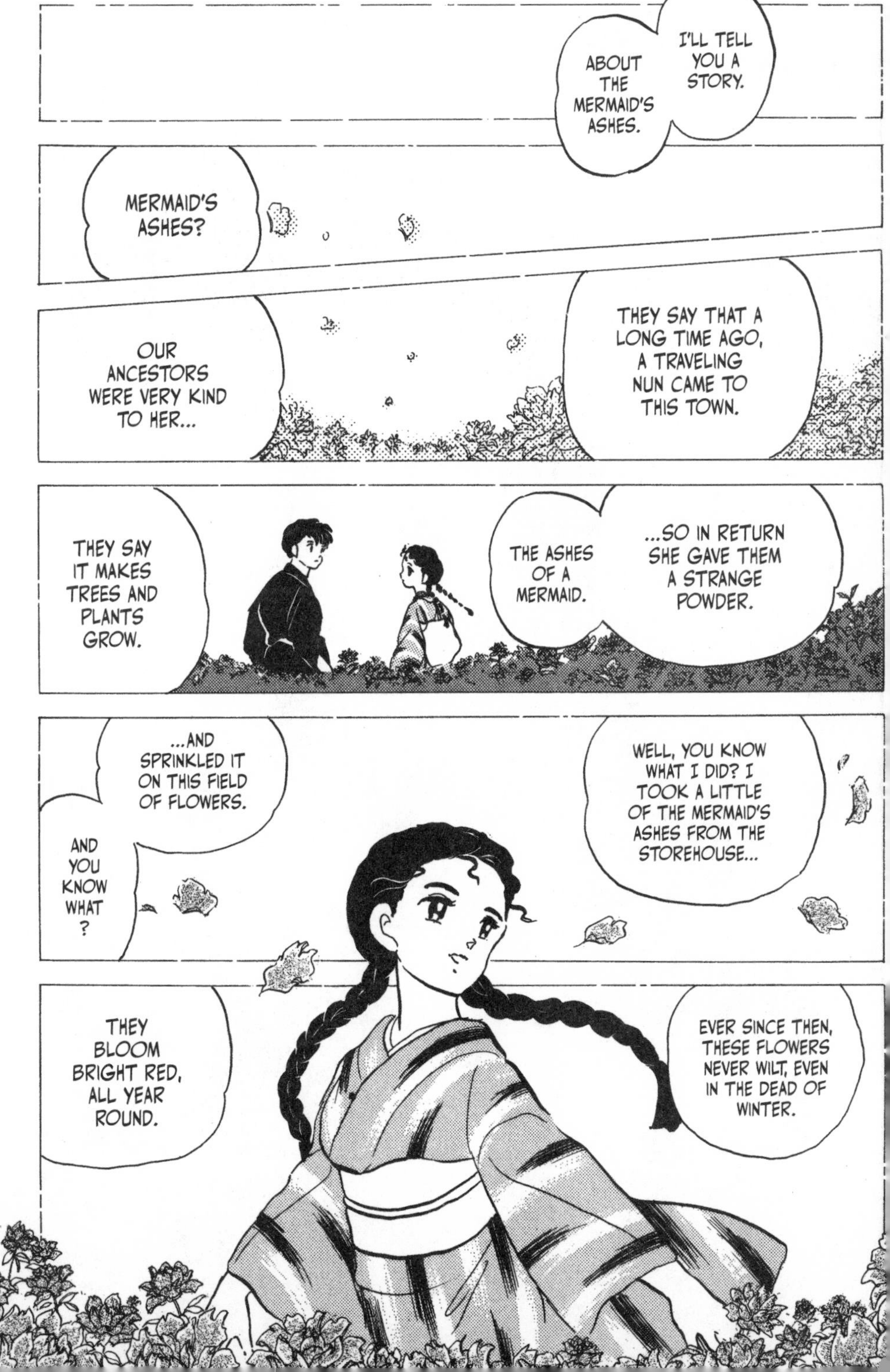
I'LL TELL YOU A STORY.
ABOUT THE MERMAID'S ASHES.
MERMAID'S ASHES?
THEY SAY THAT A LONG TIME AGO, A TRAVELING NUN CAME TO THIS TOWN.
OUR ANCESTORS WERE VERY KIND TO HER...
...SO IN RETURN SHE GAVE THEM A STRANGE POWDER.
THE ASHES OF A MERMAID.
THEY SAY IT MAKES TREES AND PLANTS GROW.
WELL, YOU KNOW WHAT I DID? I TOOK A LITTLE OF THE MERMAID'S ASHES FROM THE STOREHOUSE...
...AND SPRINKLED IT ON THIS FIELD OF FLOWERS.
AND YOU KNOW WHAT?
EVER SINCE THEN, THESE FLOWERS NEVER WILT, EVEN IN THE DEAD OF WINTER.
THEY BLOOM BRIGHT RED, ALL YEAR ROUND.

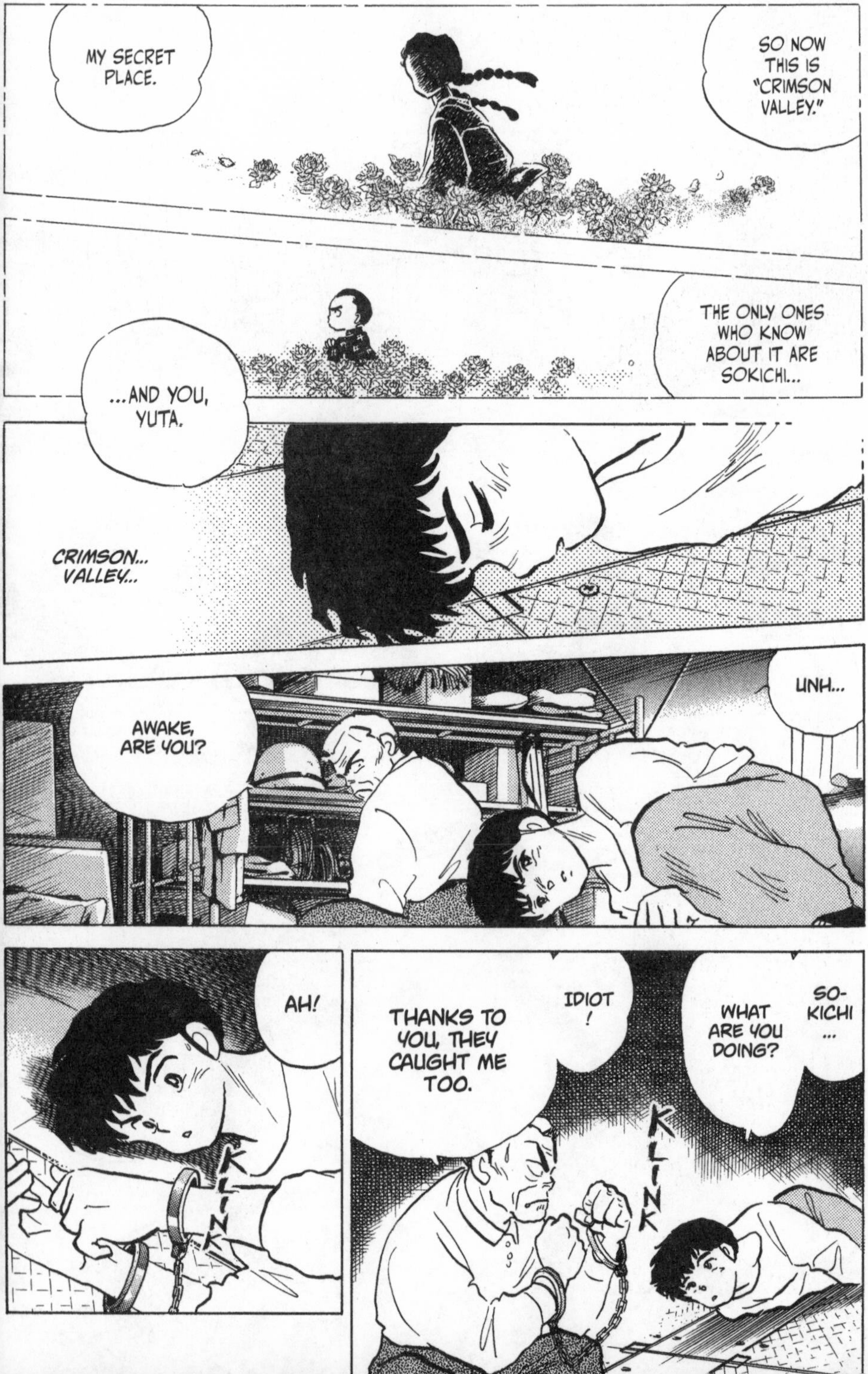
SO NOW THIS IS "CRIMSON VALLEY."
MY SECRET PLACE.
THE ONLY ONES WHO KNOW ABOUT IT ARE SOKICHI...
...AND YOU, YUTA.
CRIMSON... VALLEY...
UNH...
AWAKE, ARE YOU?
SO-KICHI...
WHAT ARE YOU DOING?
IDIOT!
THANKS TO YOU, THEY CAUGHT ME TOO.
KLINK
AH!
KLINK

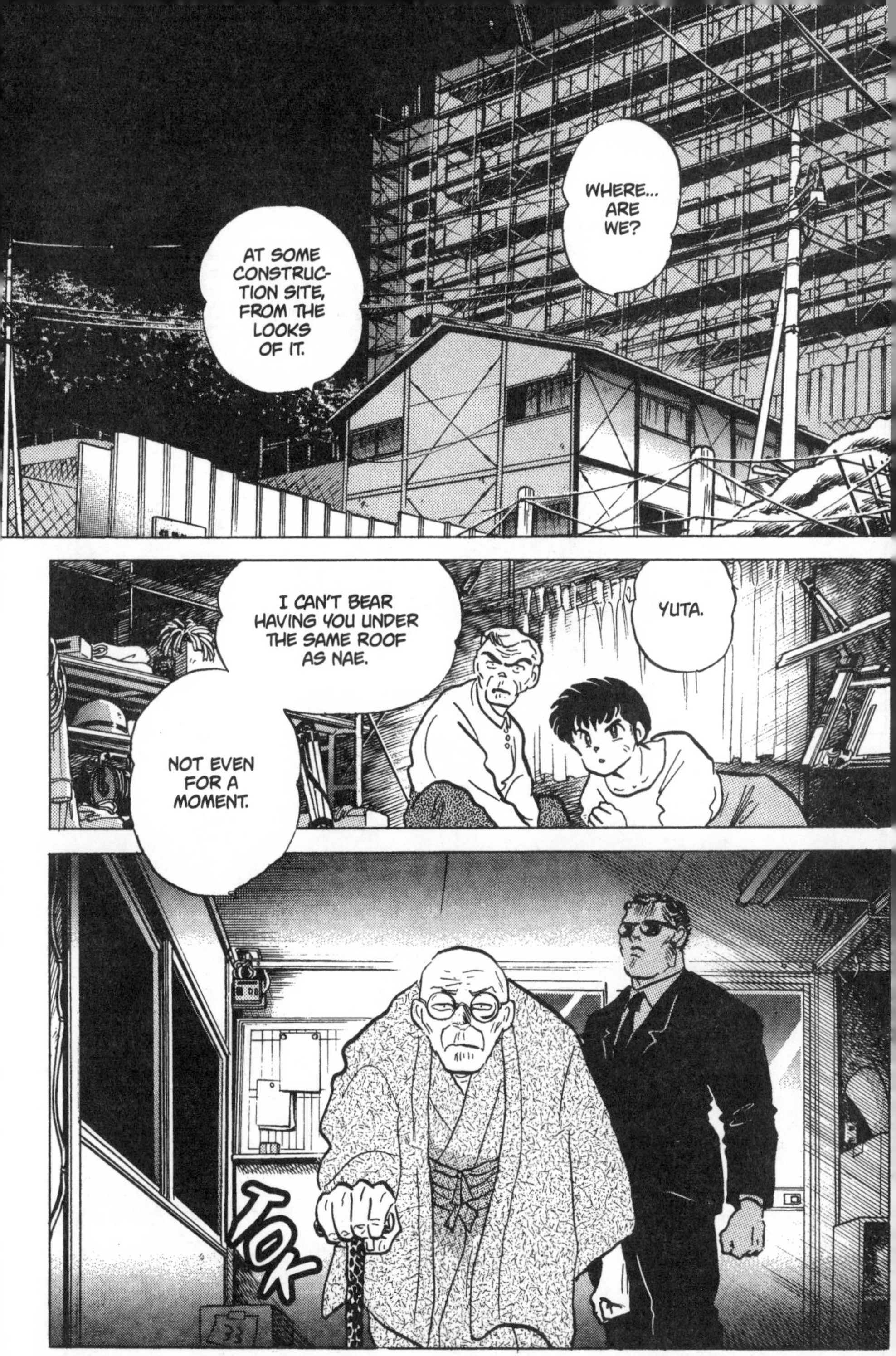
WHERE... ARE WE?
AT SOME CONSTRUCTION SITE, FROM THE LOOKS OF IT.
YUTA.
I CAN'T BEAR HAVING YOU UNDER THE SAME ROOF AS NAE.
NOT EVEN FOR A MOMENT.
TOK

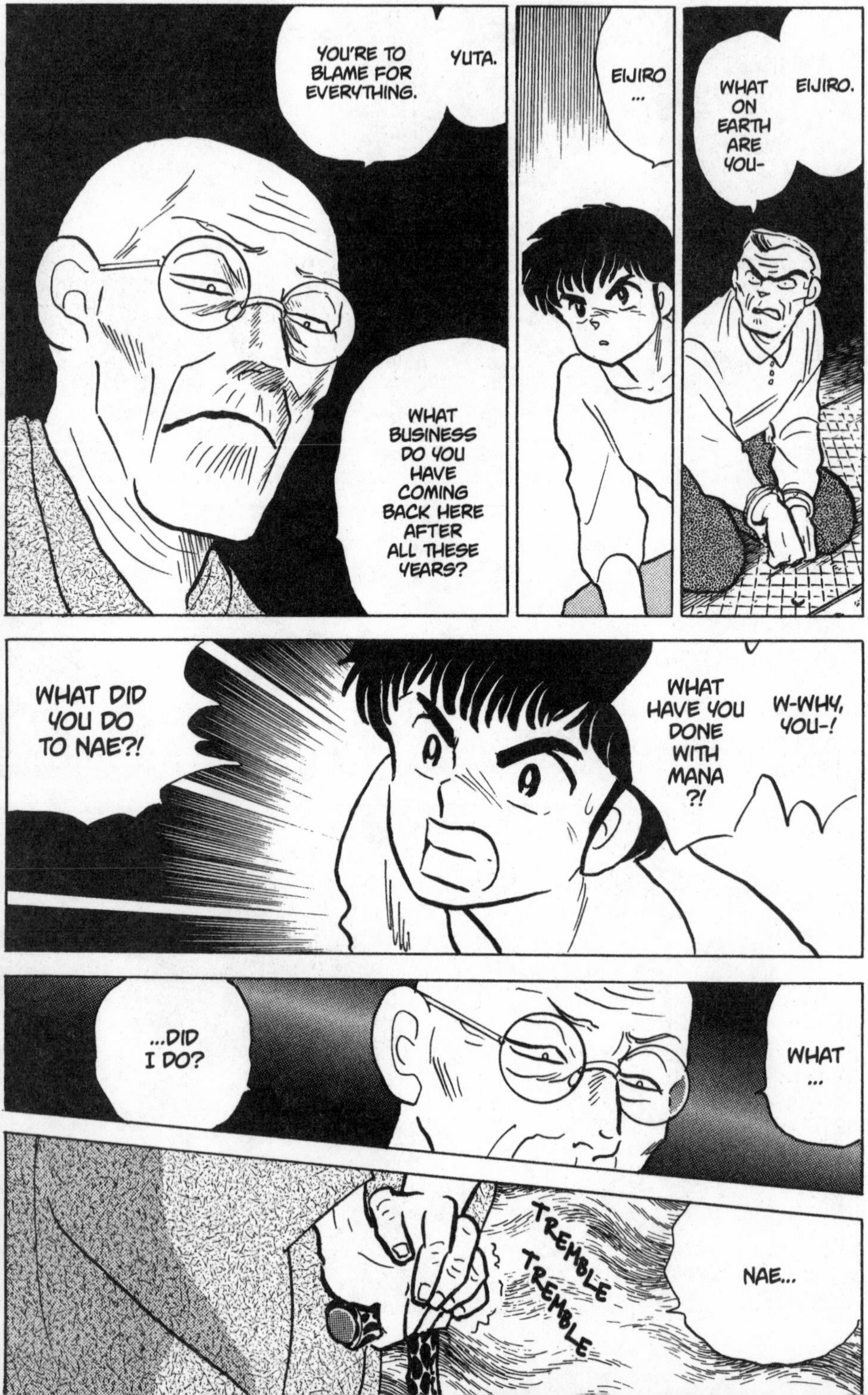
EIJIRO.
WHAT ON EARTH ARE YOU-
EIJIRO ...
YUTA.
YOU'RE TO BLAME FOR EVERYTHING.
WHAT BUSINESS DO YOU HAVE COMING BACK HERE AFTER ALL THESE YEARS?
W-WHY, YOU-!
WHAT HAVE YOU DONE WITH MANA ?!
WHAT DID YOU DO TO NAE?!
WHAT ...
...DID I DO?
NAE...
TREMBLE
TREMBLE

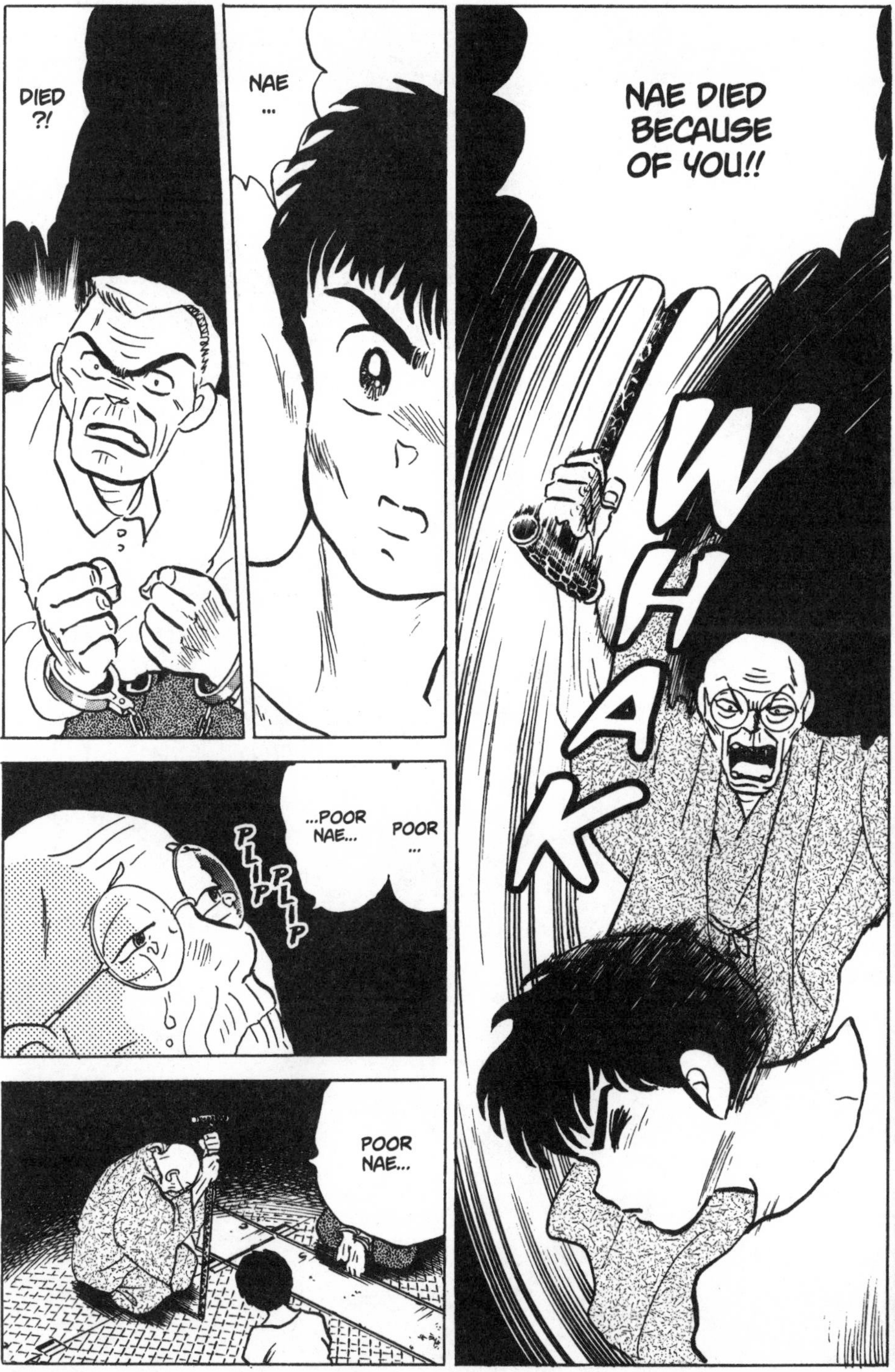
NAE DIED BECAUSE OF YOU!!
WHAK
NAE ...
DIED ?!
POOR ...
...POOR NAE...
PLIP PLIP
POOR NAE...

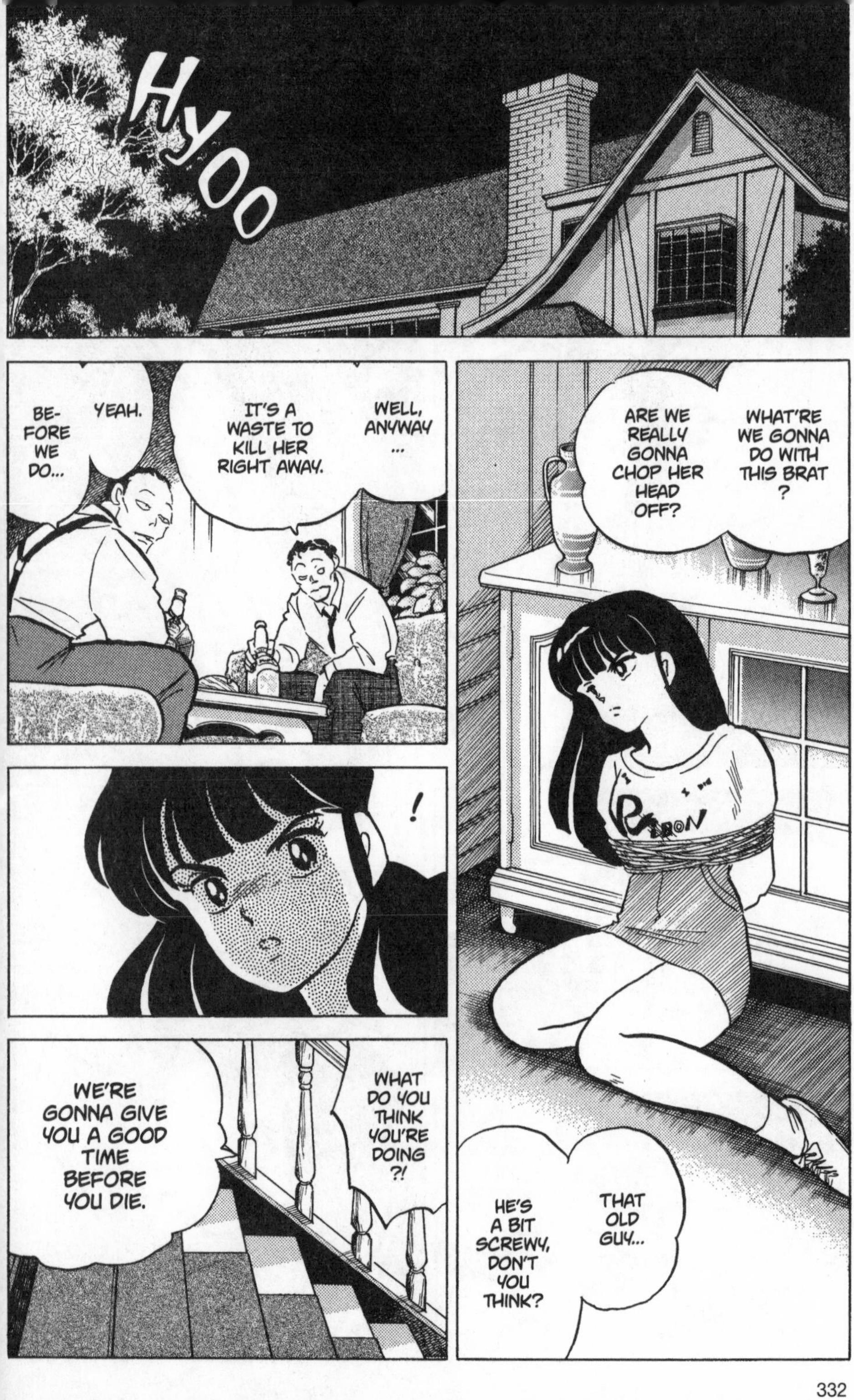
HyOO
WHAT'RE WE GONNA DO WITH THIS BRAT ?
ARE WE REALLY GONNA CHOP HER HEAD OFF?
THAT OLD GUY...
HE'S A BIT SCREWY, DON'T YOU THINK?
WELL, ANYWAY ...
IT'S A WASTE TO KILL HER RIGHT AWAY.
YEAH.
BE-FORE WE DO...
!
WHAT DO YOU THINK YOU'RE DOING ?!
WE'RE GONNA GIVE YOU A GOOD TIME BEFORE YOU DIE.

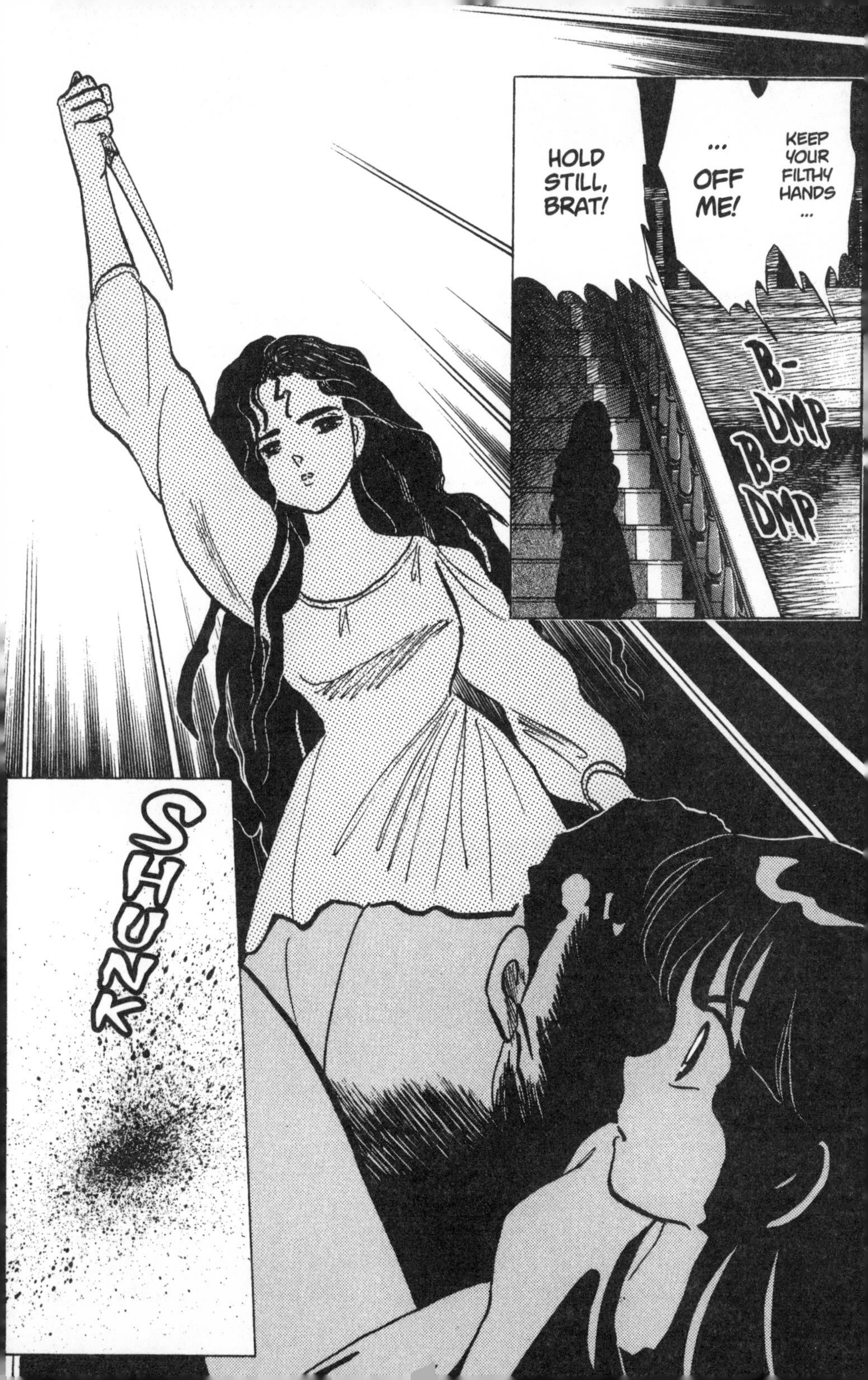
KEEP YOUR FILTHY HANDS ...
... OFF ME!
HOLD STILL, BRAT!
B-DMP B-DMP
SHUNK

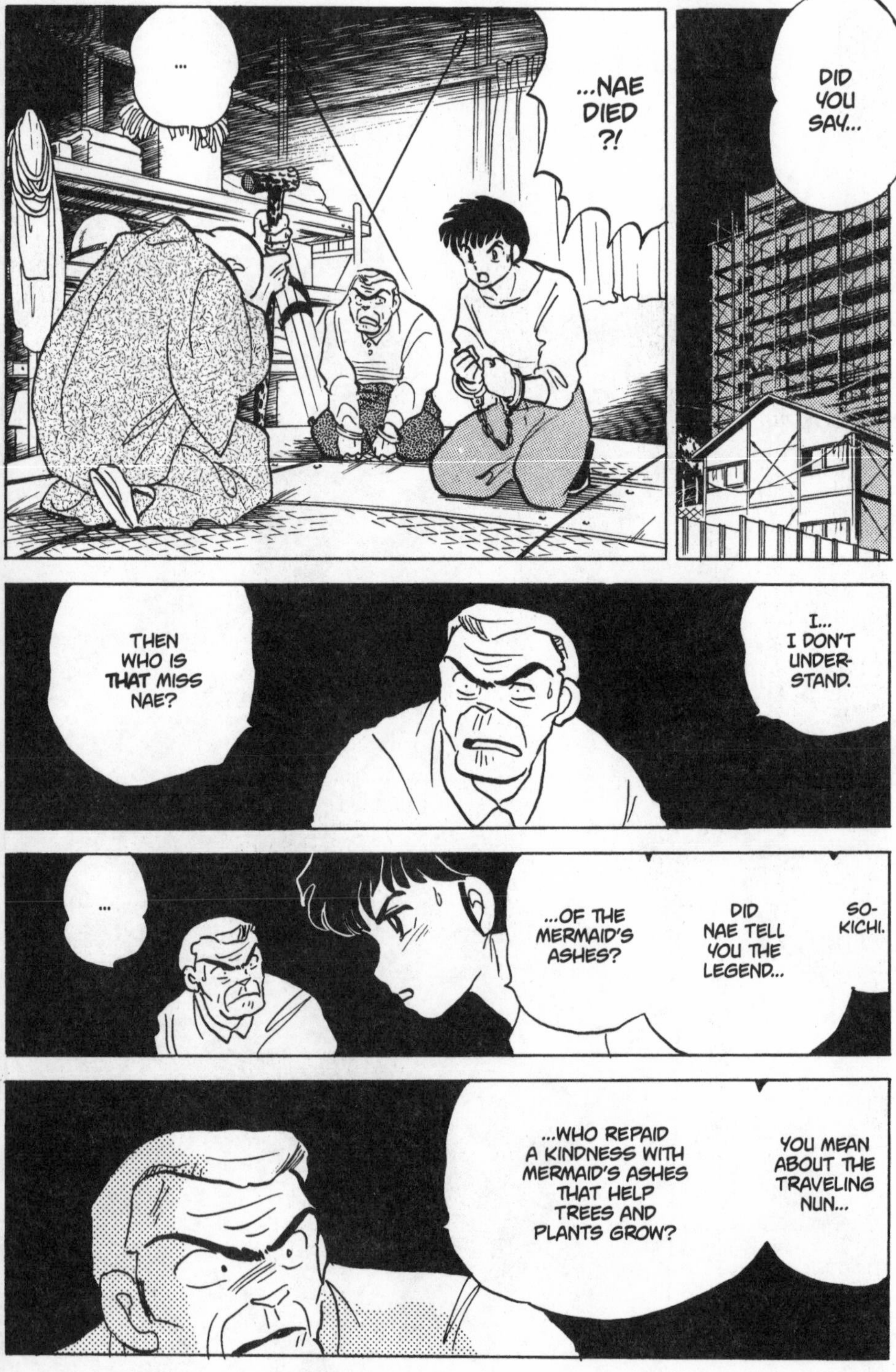
DID YOU SAY...
...NAE DIED?!
...
I... I DON'T UNDER-STAND.
THEN WHO IS THAT MISS NAE?
SO-KICHI.
DID NAE TELL YOU THE LEGEND...
...OF THE MERMAID'S ASHES?
...
YOU MEAN ABOUT THE TRAVELING NUN...
...WHO REPAID A KINDNESS WITH MERMAID'S ASHES THAT HELP TREES AND PLANTS GROW?

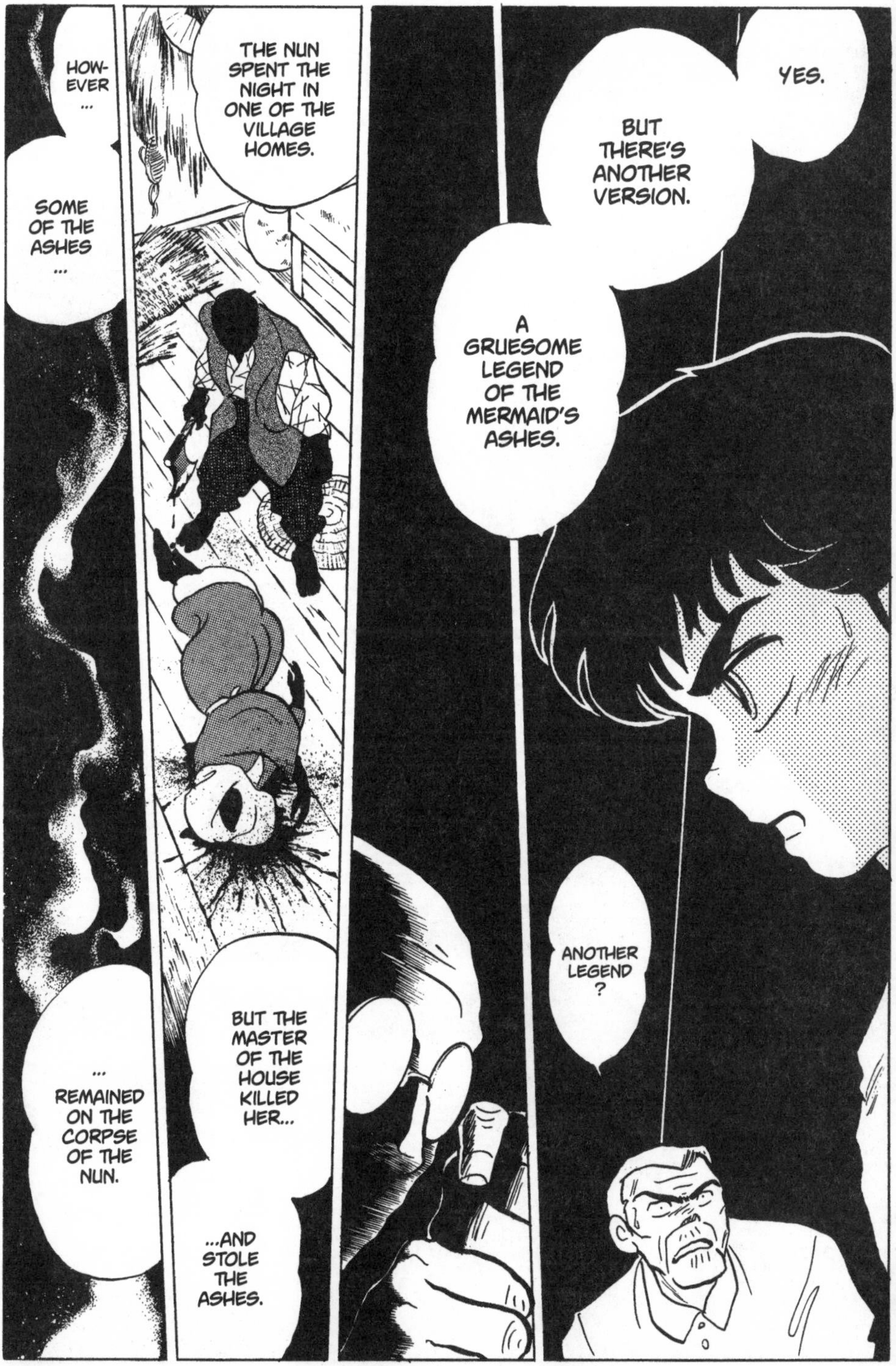
YES.
BUT THERE'S ANOTHER VERSION.
A GRUESOME LEGEND OF THE MERMAID'S ASHES.
ANOTHER LEGEND?
THE NUN SPENT THE NIGHT IN ONE OF THE VILLAGE HOMES.
BUT THE MASTER OF THE HOUSE KILLED HER...
...AND STOLE THE ASHES.
HOW-EVER...
SOME OF THE ASHES...
...REMAINED ON THE CORPSE OF THE NUN.

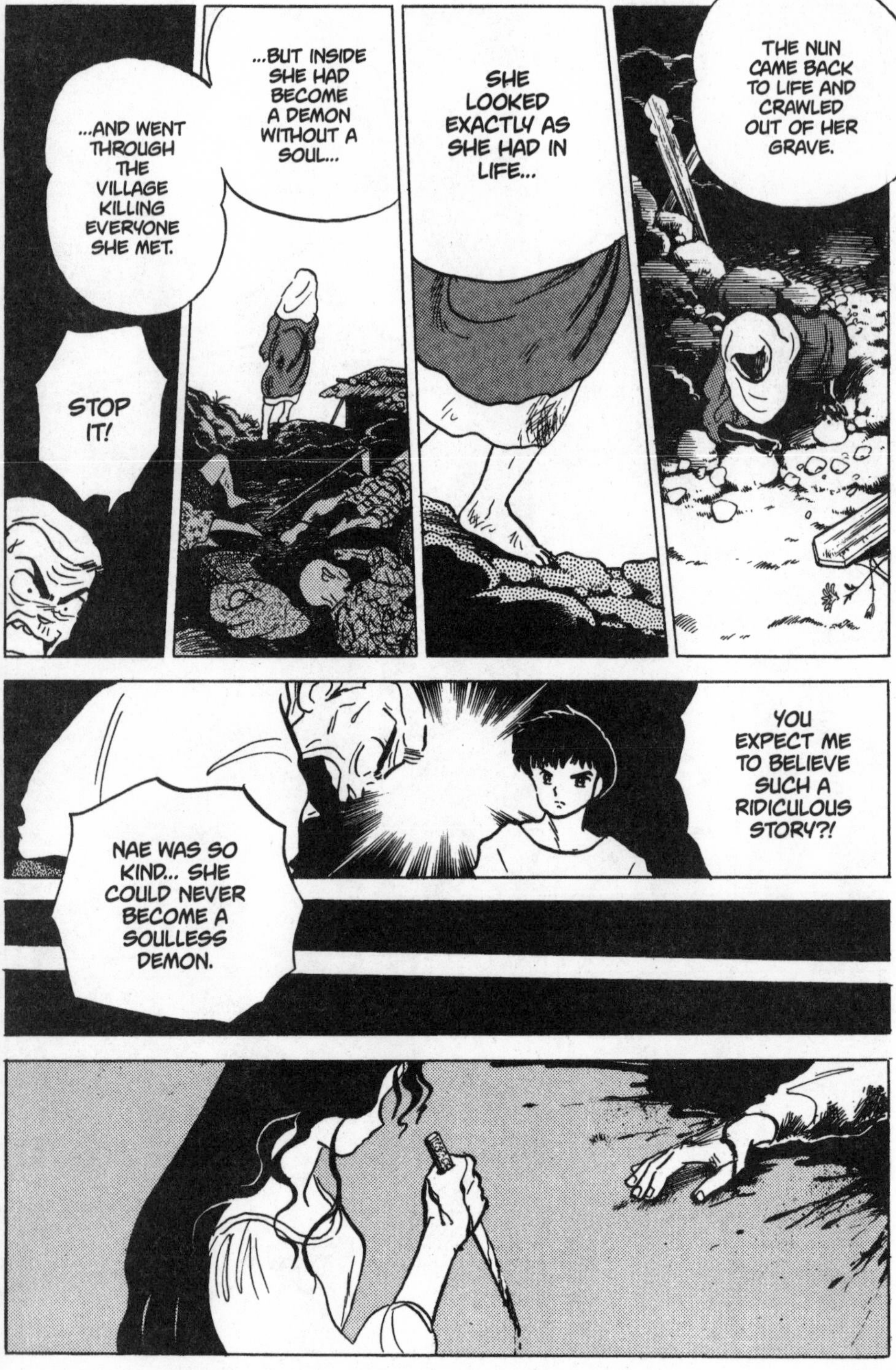
THE NUN CAME BACK TO LIFE AND CRAWLED OUT OF HER GRAVE.
SHE LOOKED EXACTLY AS SHE HAD IN LIFE...
...BUT INSIDE SHE HAD BECOME A DEMON WITHOUT A SOUL...
...AND WENT THROUGH THE VILLAGE KILLING EVERYONE SHE MET.
STOP IT!
YOU EXPECT ME TO BELIEVE SUCH A RIDICULOUS STORY?!
NAE WAS SO KIND... SHE COULD NEVER BECOME A SOULLESS DEMON.

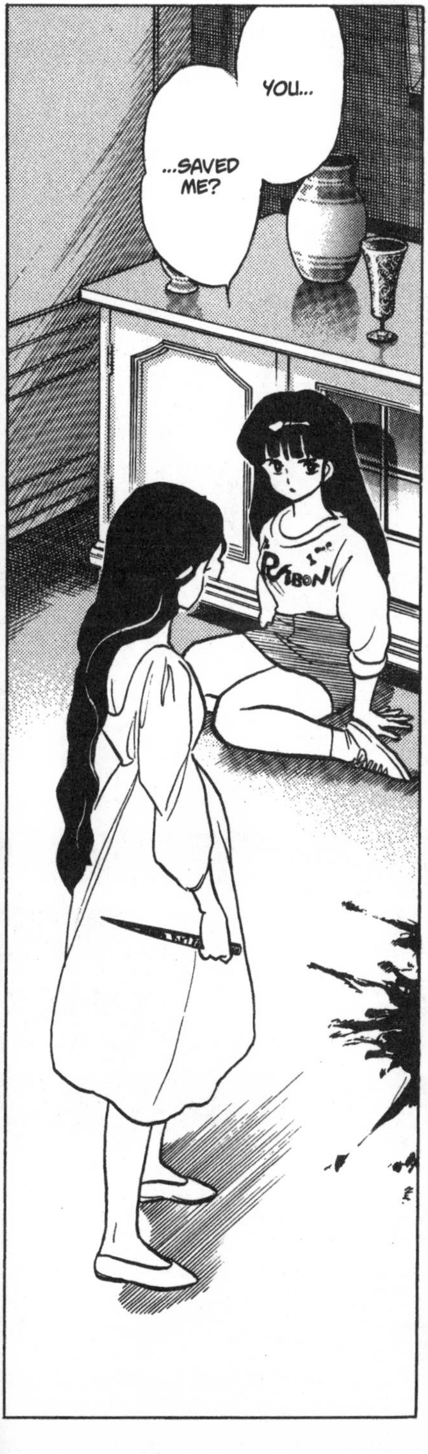
YOU...
...SAVED ME?

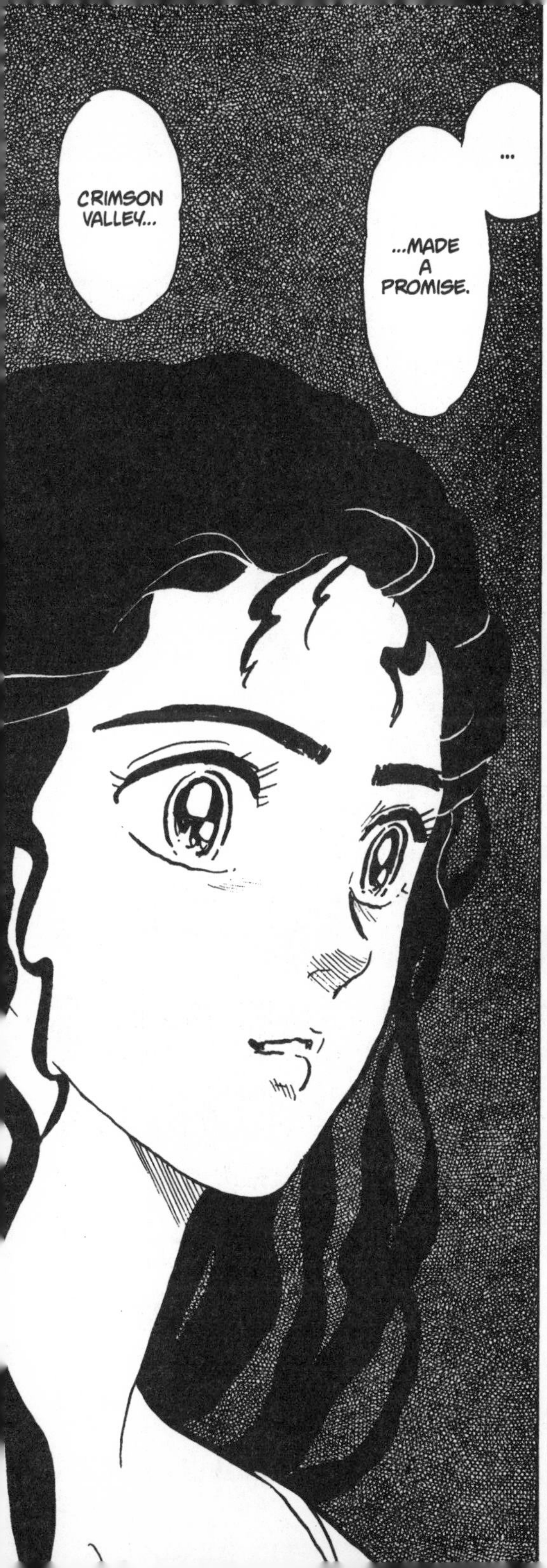
...
...MADE A PROMISE.
CRIMSON VALLEY...

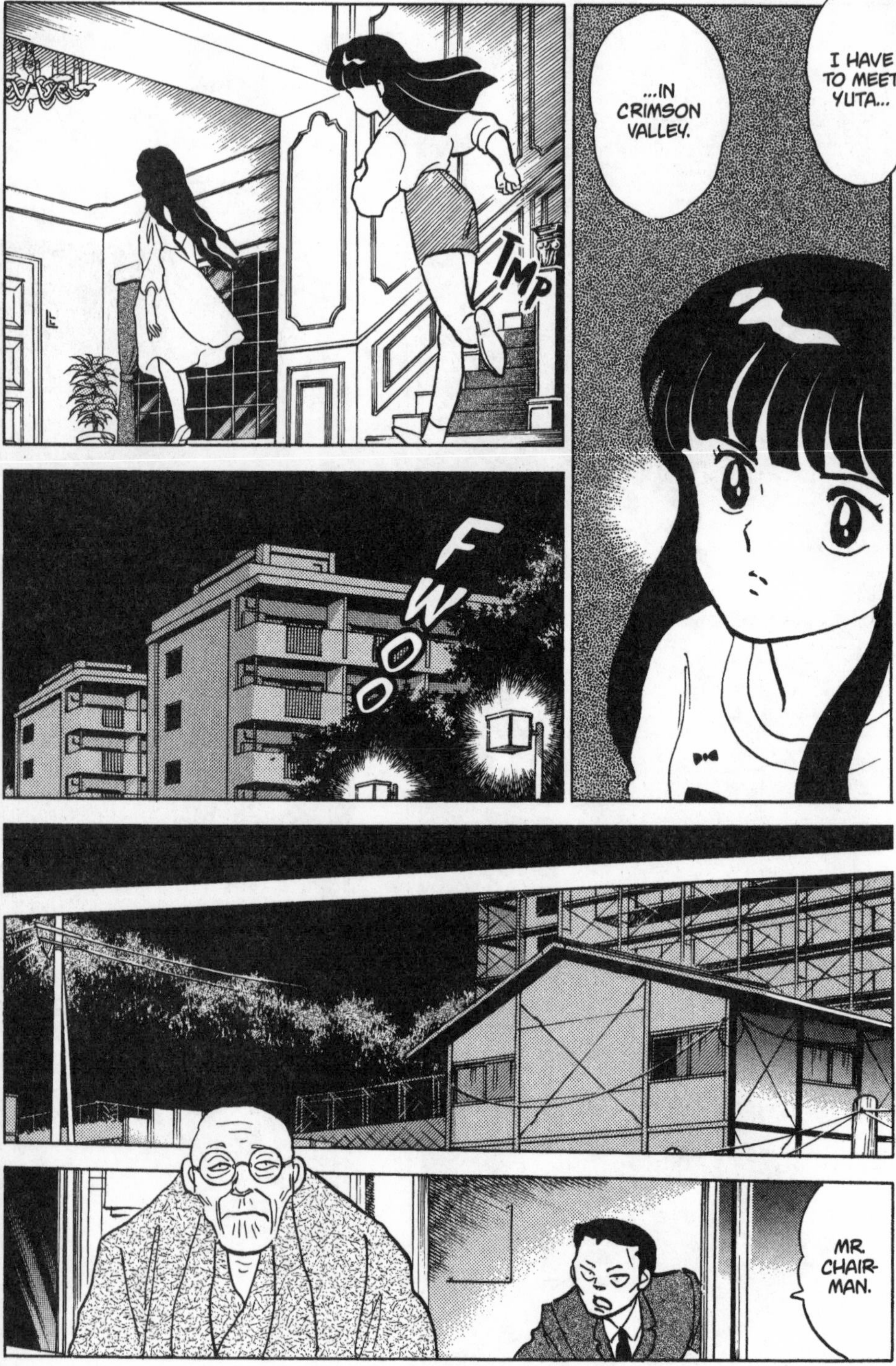
I HAVE TO MEET YUTA...
...IN CRIMSON VALLEY.
TMP
FWOOO
MR. CHAIR-MAN.

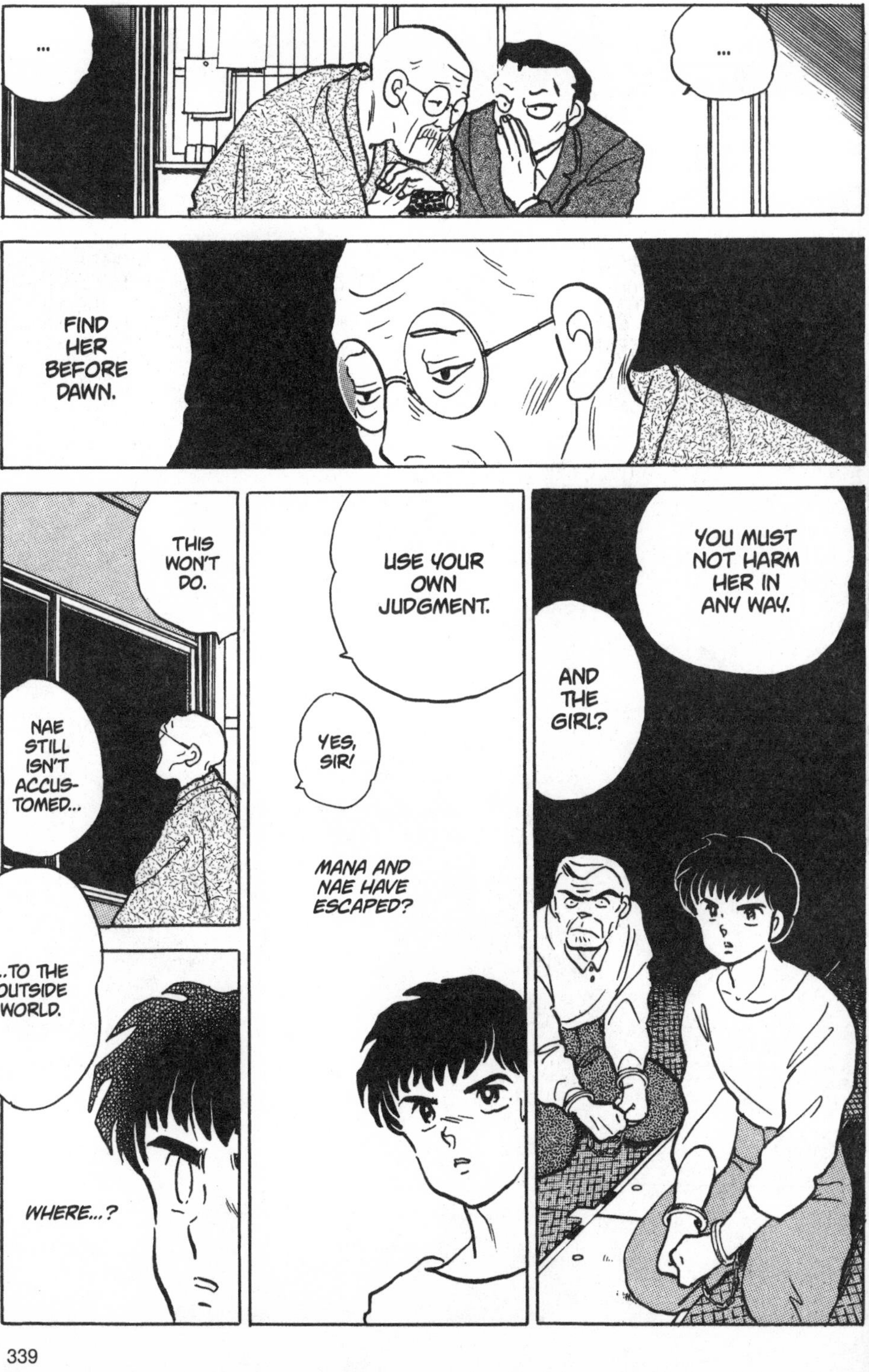
...
...
FIND HER BEFORE DAWN.
YOU MUST NOT HARM HER IN ANY WAY.
AND THE GIRL?
USE YOUR OWN JUDGMENT.
YES, SIR!
MANA AND NAE HAVE ESCAPED?
THIS WON'T DO.
NAE STILL ISN'T ACCUS-TOMED...
...TO THE OUTSIDE WORLD.
WHERE...?

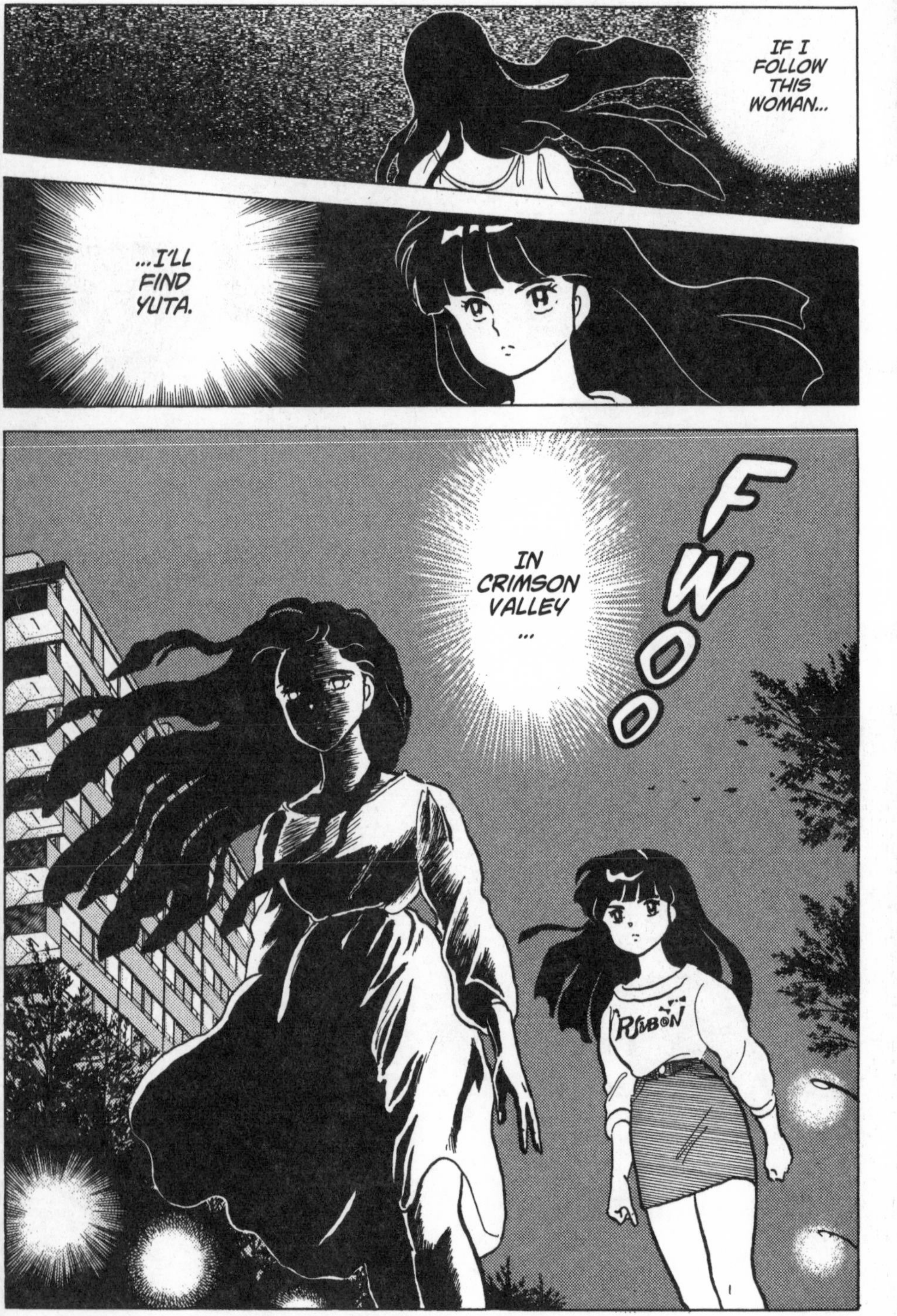
IF I FOLLOW THIS WOMAN...
...I'LL FIND YUTA.
FWOOO
IN CRIMSON VALLEY ...

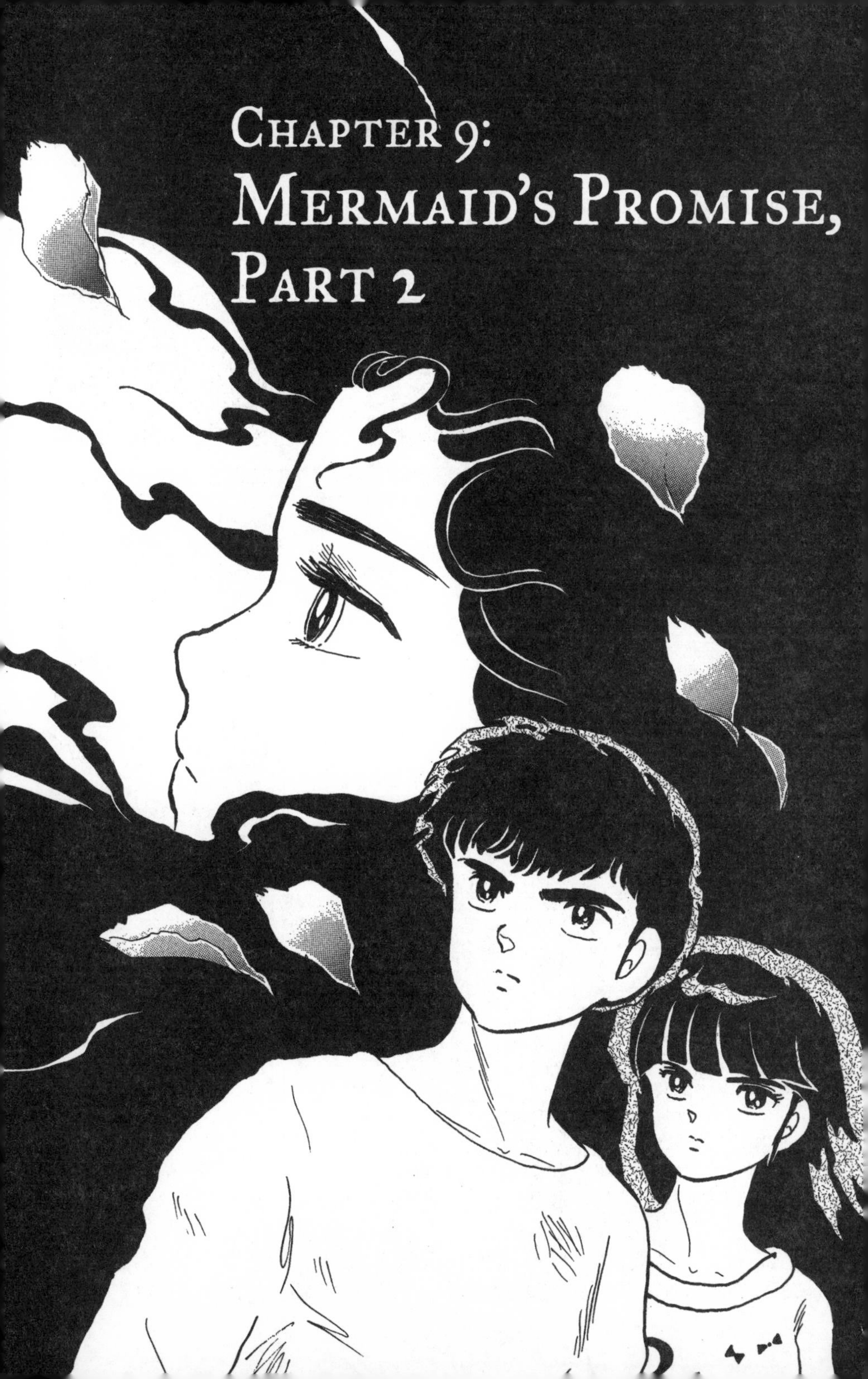
Chapter 9:
Mermaid's Promise, Part 2

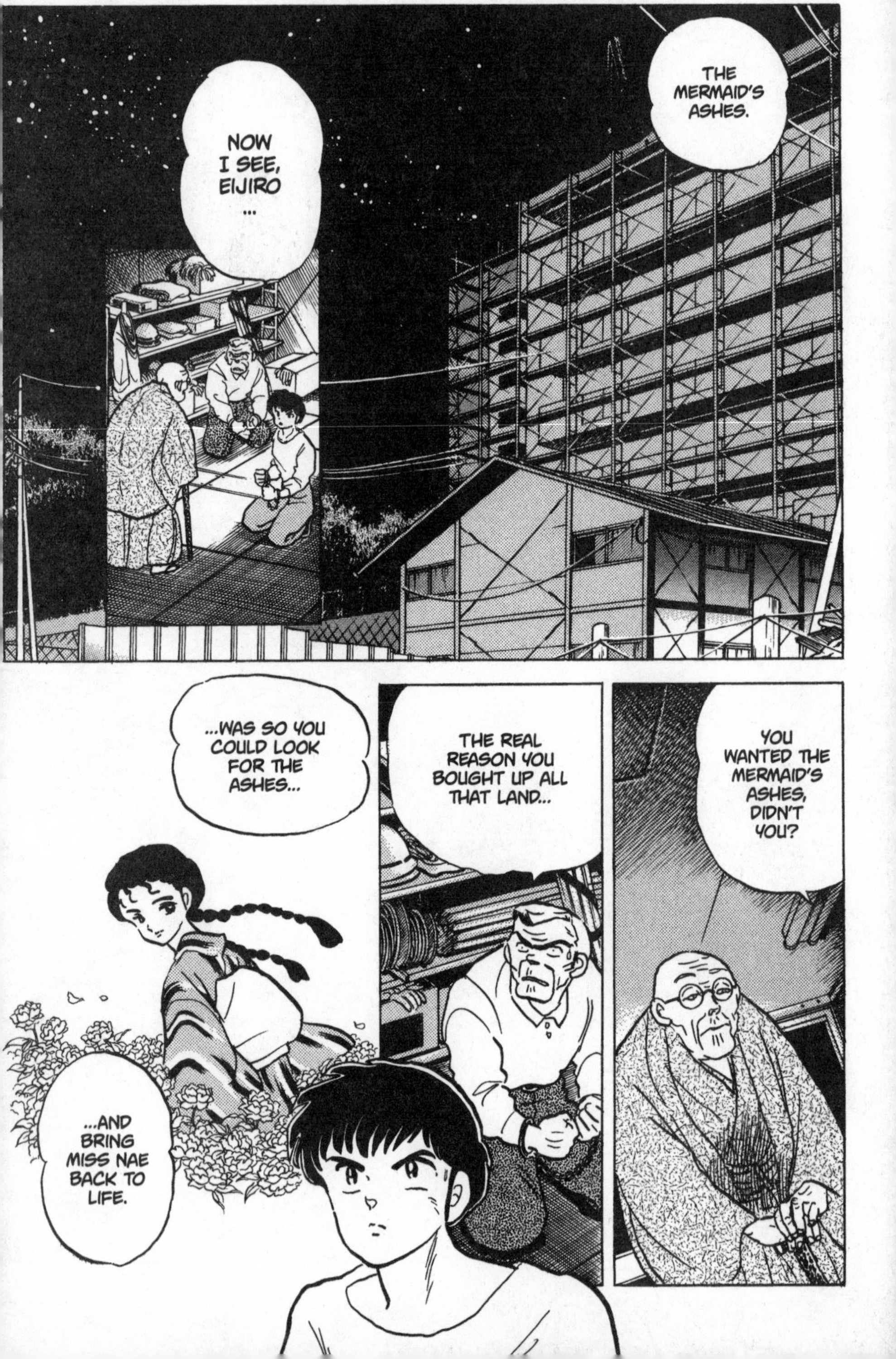
THE MERMAID'S ASHES.
NOW I SEE, EIJIRO ...
YOU WANTED THE MERMAID'S ASHES, DIDN'T YOU?
THE REAL REASON YOU BOUGHT UP ALL THAT LAND...
...WAS SO YOU COULD LOOK FOR THE ASHES...
...AND BRING MISS NAE BACK TO LIFE.

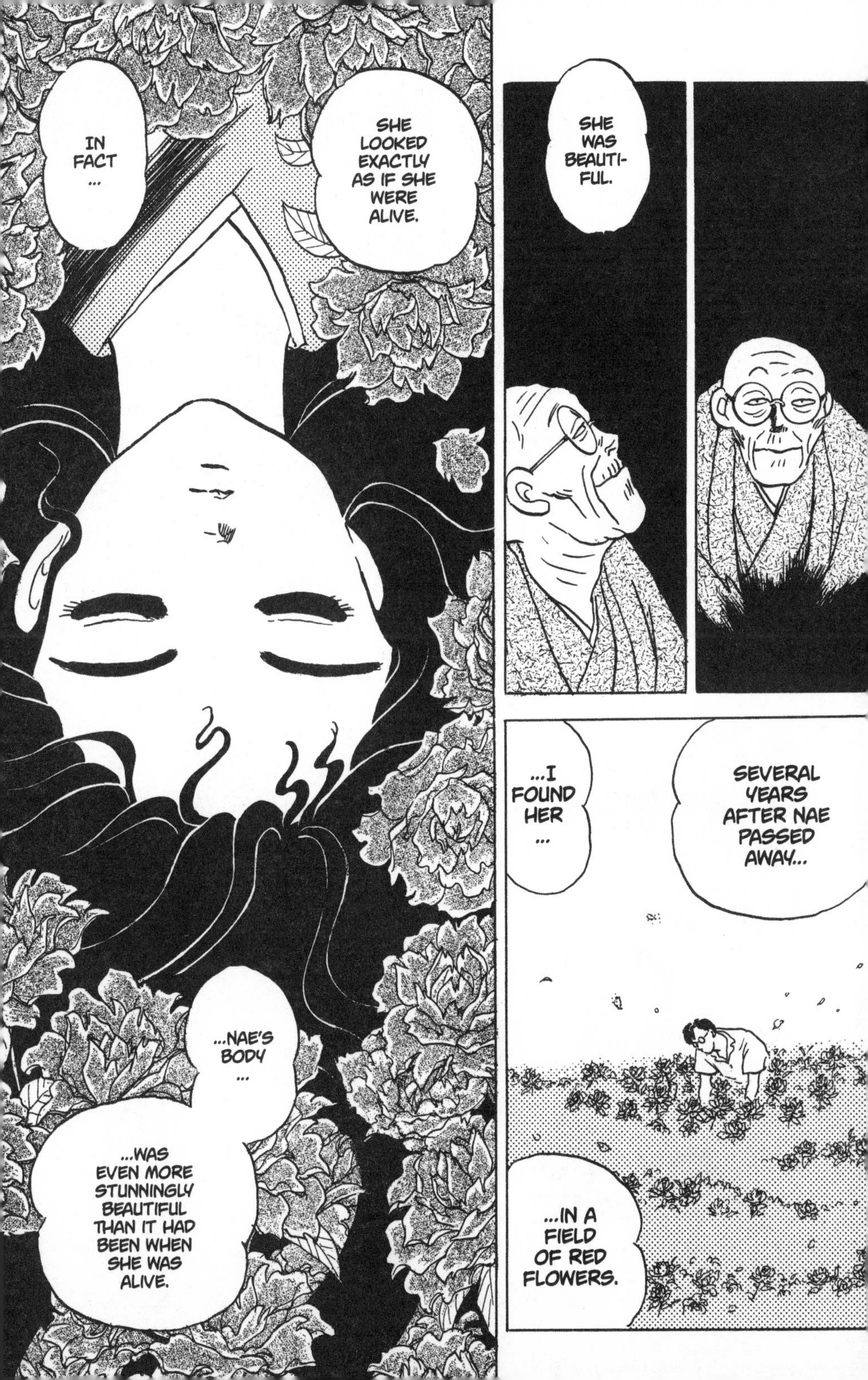
SHE WAS BEAUTIFUL.
SEVERAL YEARS AFTER NAE PASSED AWAY...
...I FOUND HER...
...IN A FIELD OF RED FLOWERS.
SHE LOOKED EXACTLY AS IF SHE WERE ALIVE.
IN FACT...
...NAE'S BODY...
...WAS EVEN MORE STUNNINGLY BEAUTIFUL THAN IT HAD BEEN WHEN SHE WAS ALIVE.

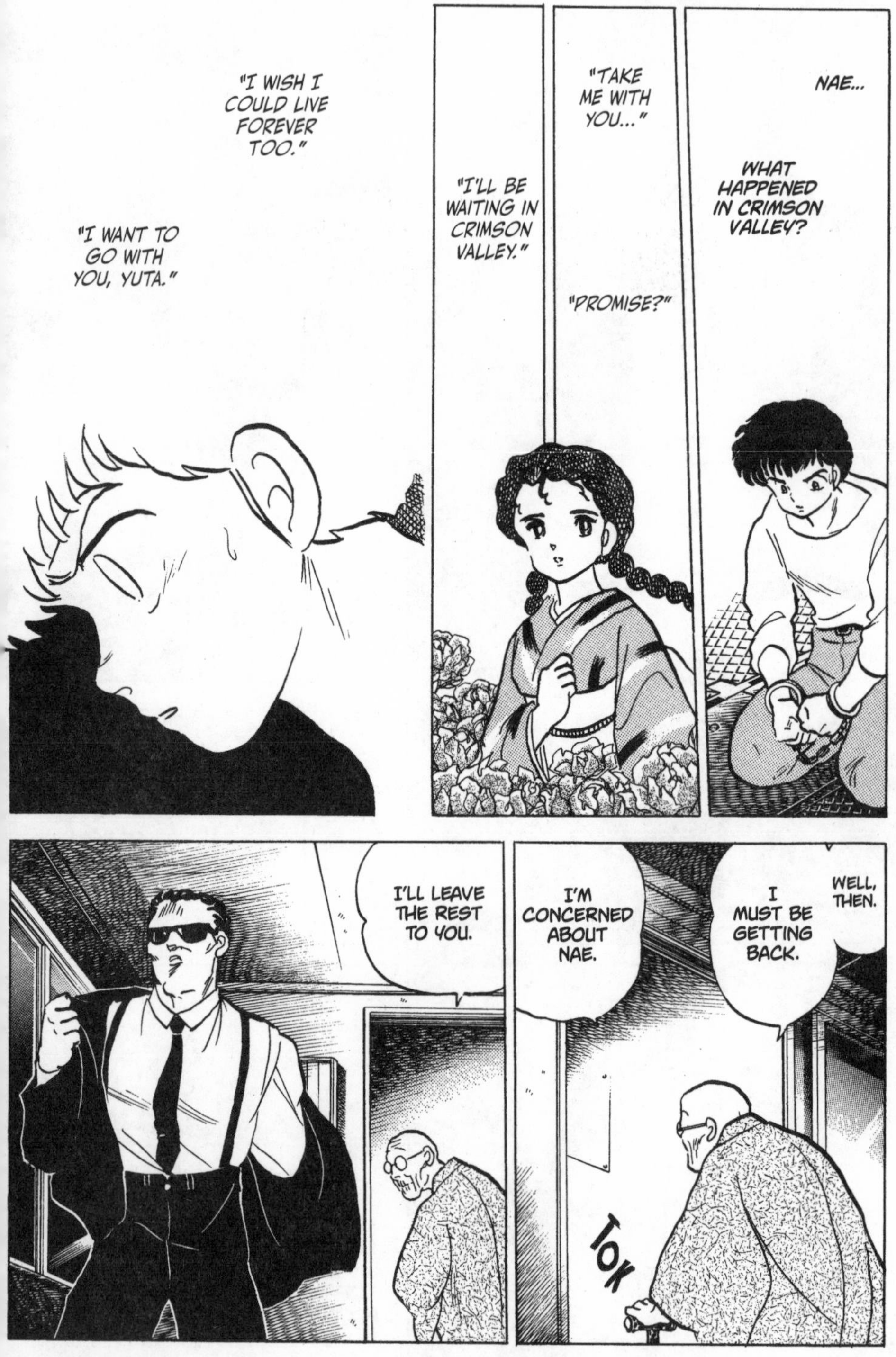
NAE...
WHAT HAPPENED IN CRIMSON VALLEY?
"TAKE ME WITH YOU..."
"PROMISE?"
"I'LL BE WAITING IN CRIMSON VALLEY."
"I WISH I COULD LIVE FOREVER TOO."
"I WANT TO GO WITH YOU, YUTA."
WELL, THEN.
I MUST BE GETTING BACK.
I'M CONCERNED ABOUT NAE.
TOK
I'LL LEAVE THE REST TO YOU.

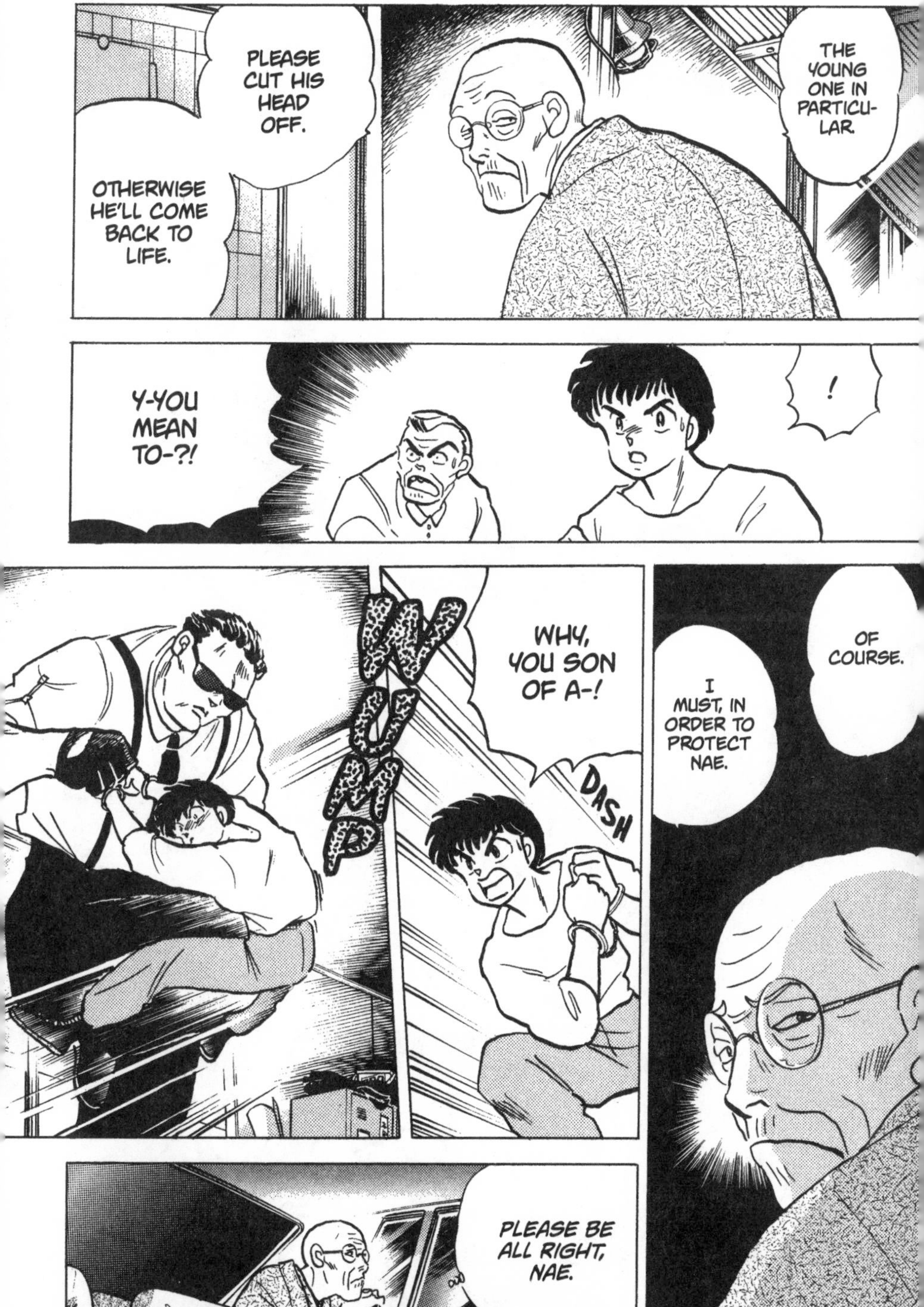
THE YOUNG ONE IN PARTICU-LAR.
PLEASE CUT HIS HEAD OFF.
OTHERWISE HE'LL COME BACK TO LIFE.
!
Y-YOU MEAN TO-?!
OF COURSE.
I MUST, IN ORDER TO PROTECT NAE.
WHY, YOU SON OF A-!
DASH
WUMP
PLEASE BE ALL RIGHT, NAE.

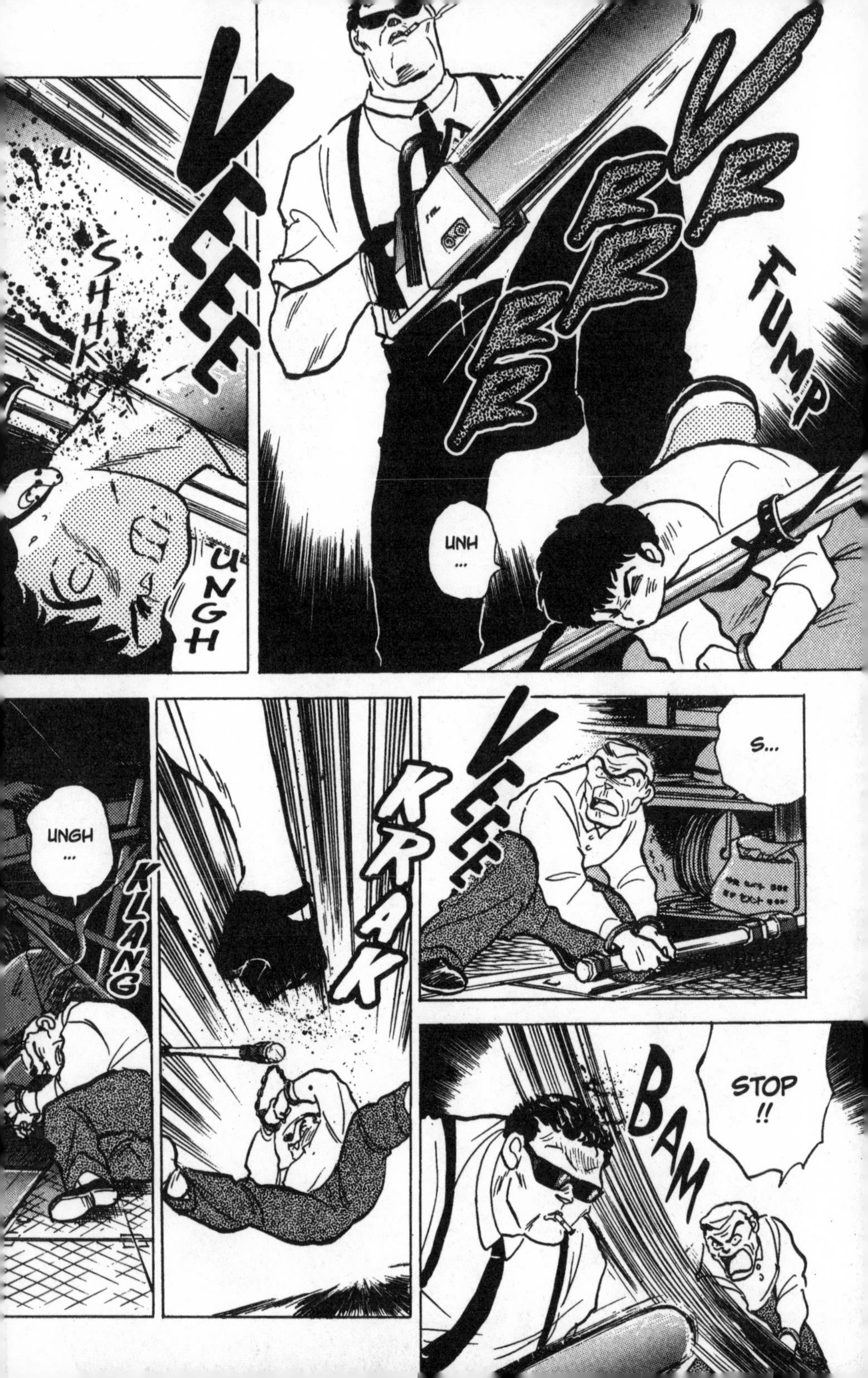
VVEEEE
FUMP
UNH ...
VEEEE
SHHK
UNGH
VEEEE
S...
BAM
STOP !!
KRAK
UNGH ...
KLANG

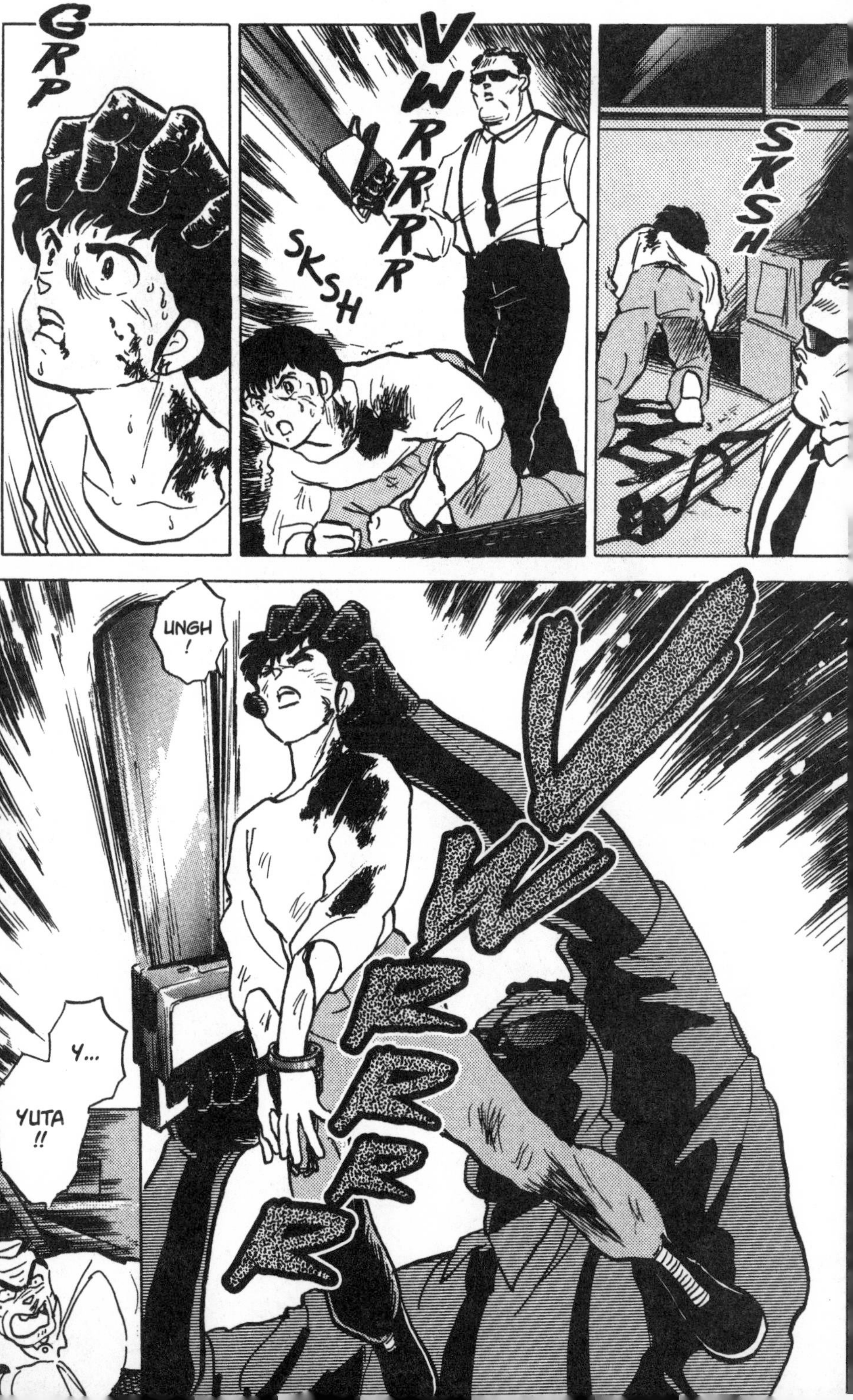
SKSH
VWRRRRR
SKSH
GRP
UNGH!
VWRRRR
Y...
YUTA!!

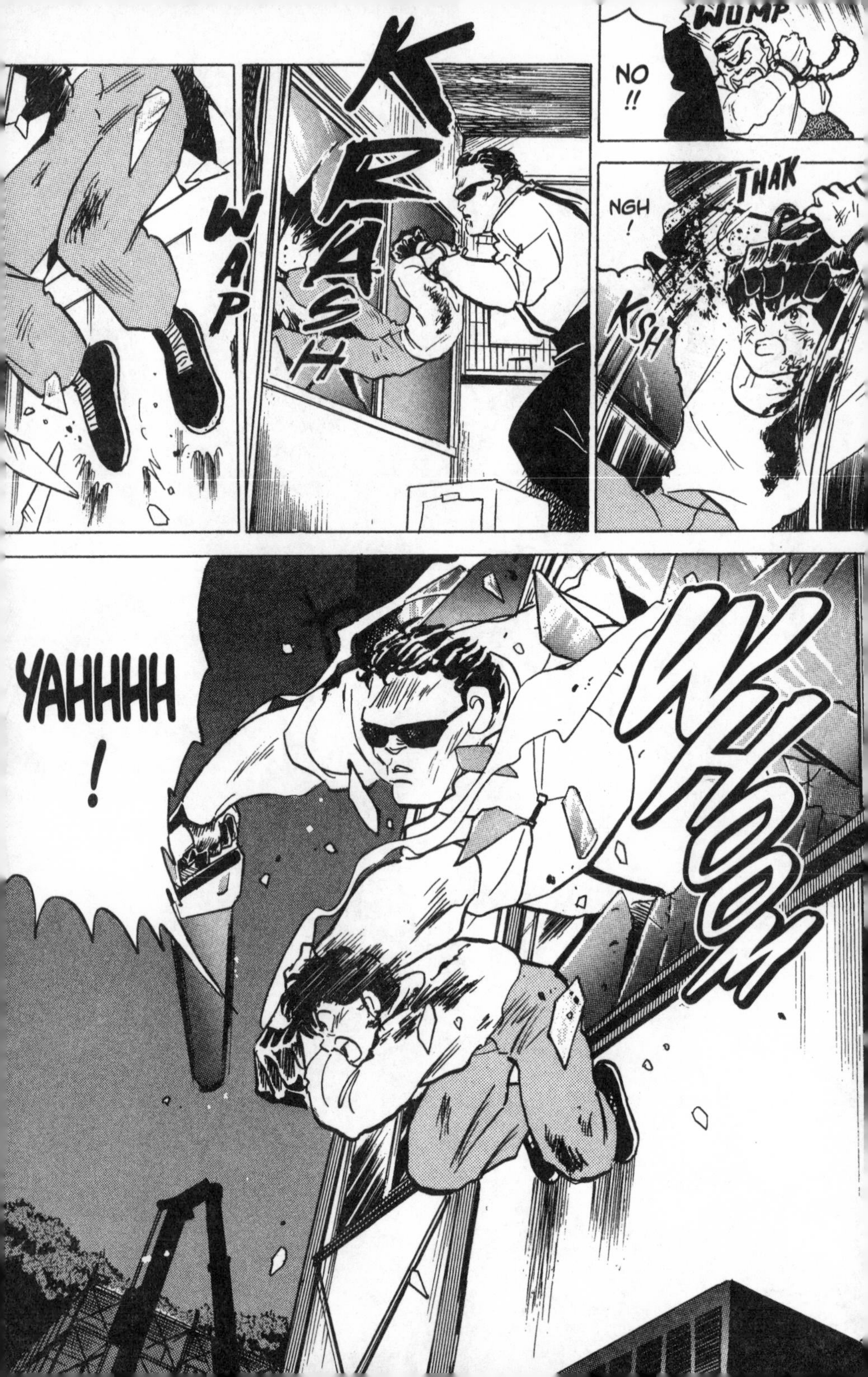
WUMP
NO!!
NGH!
THAK
KSH
KRASH
WAP
YAHHHH!
WHOOM

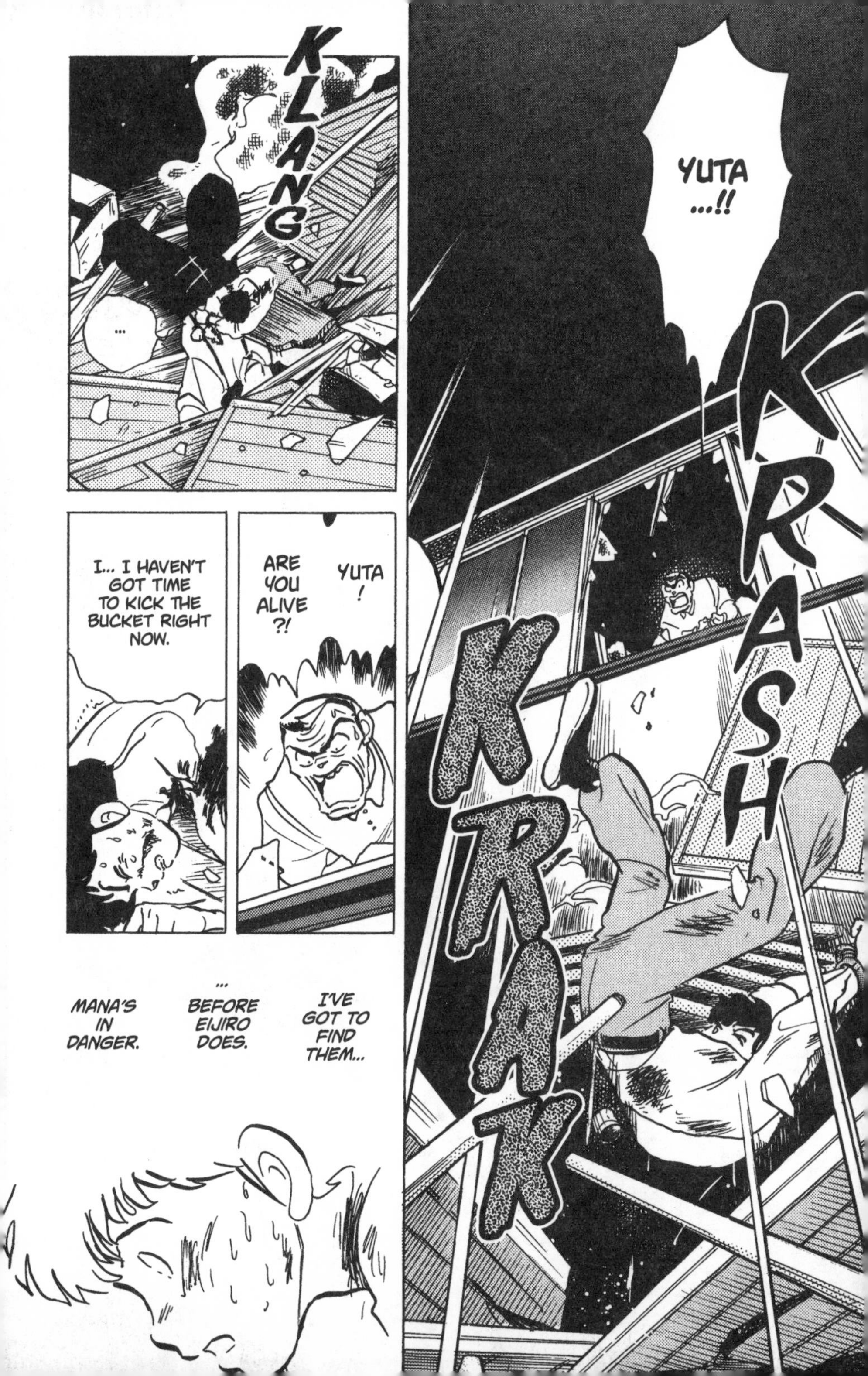
YUTA ...!!
KRASH
KRAK
KLANG
...
YUTA !
ARE YOU ALIVE ?!
I... I HAVEN'T GOT TIME TO KICK THE BUCKET RIGHT NOW.
I'VE GOT TO FIND THEM...
... BEFORE EIJIRO DOES.
MANA'S IN DANGER.

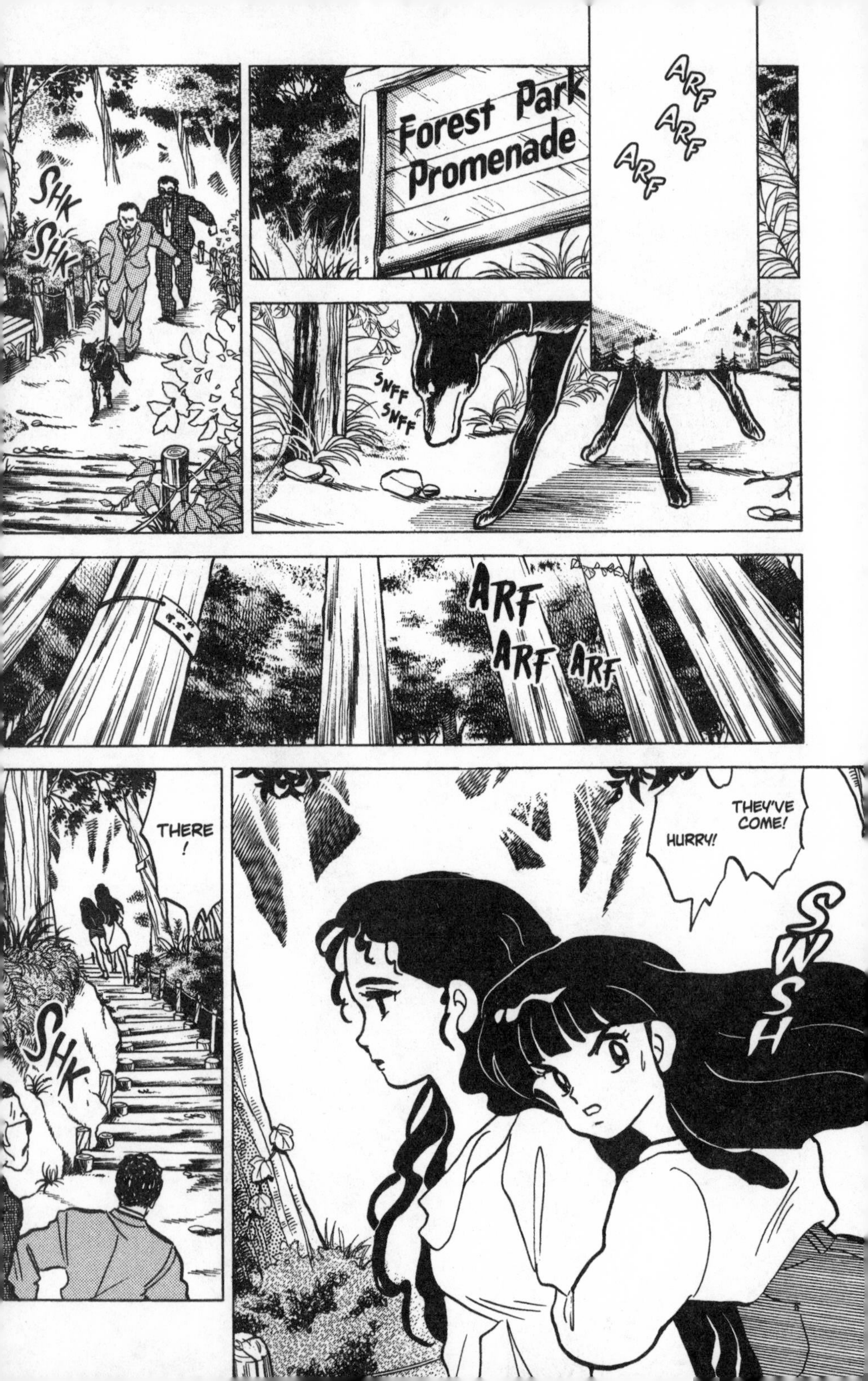
ARF ARF ARF
Forest Park Promenade
SNFF SNFF
SHK SHK
ARF ARF ARF
THEY'VE COME! HURRY!
SWSH
THERE!
SHK

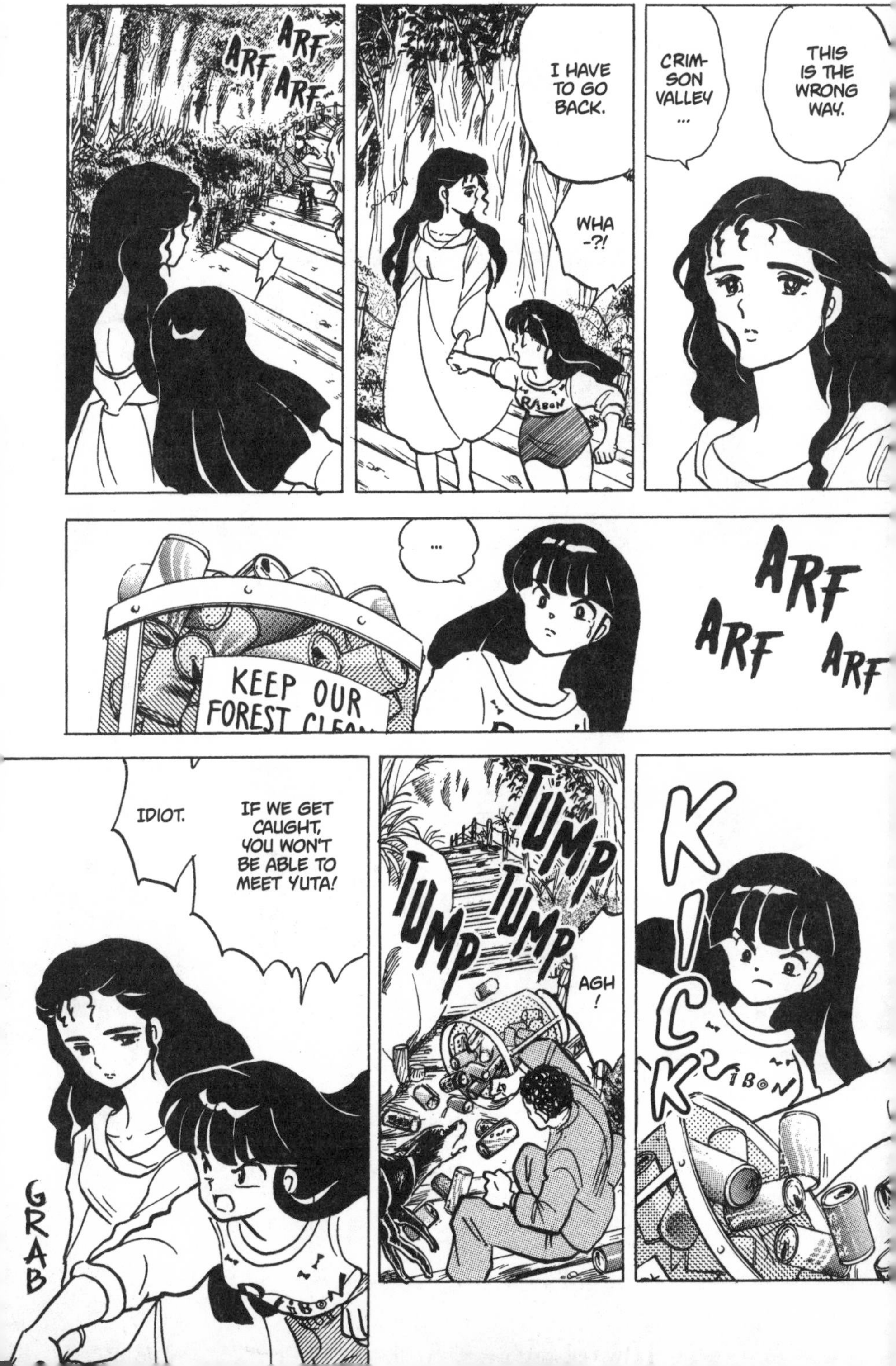

THIS IS THE WRONG WAY.
CRIM-SON VALLEY ...
I HAVE TO GO BACK.
WHA -?!
ARF ARF ARF
ARF ARF ARF
...
KEEP OUR FOREST
KICK
TUMP TUMP TUMP
AGH!
IDIOT.
IF WE GET CAUGHT, YOU WON'T BE ABLE TO MEET YUTA!
GRAB

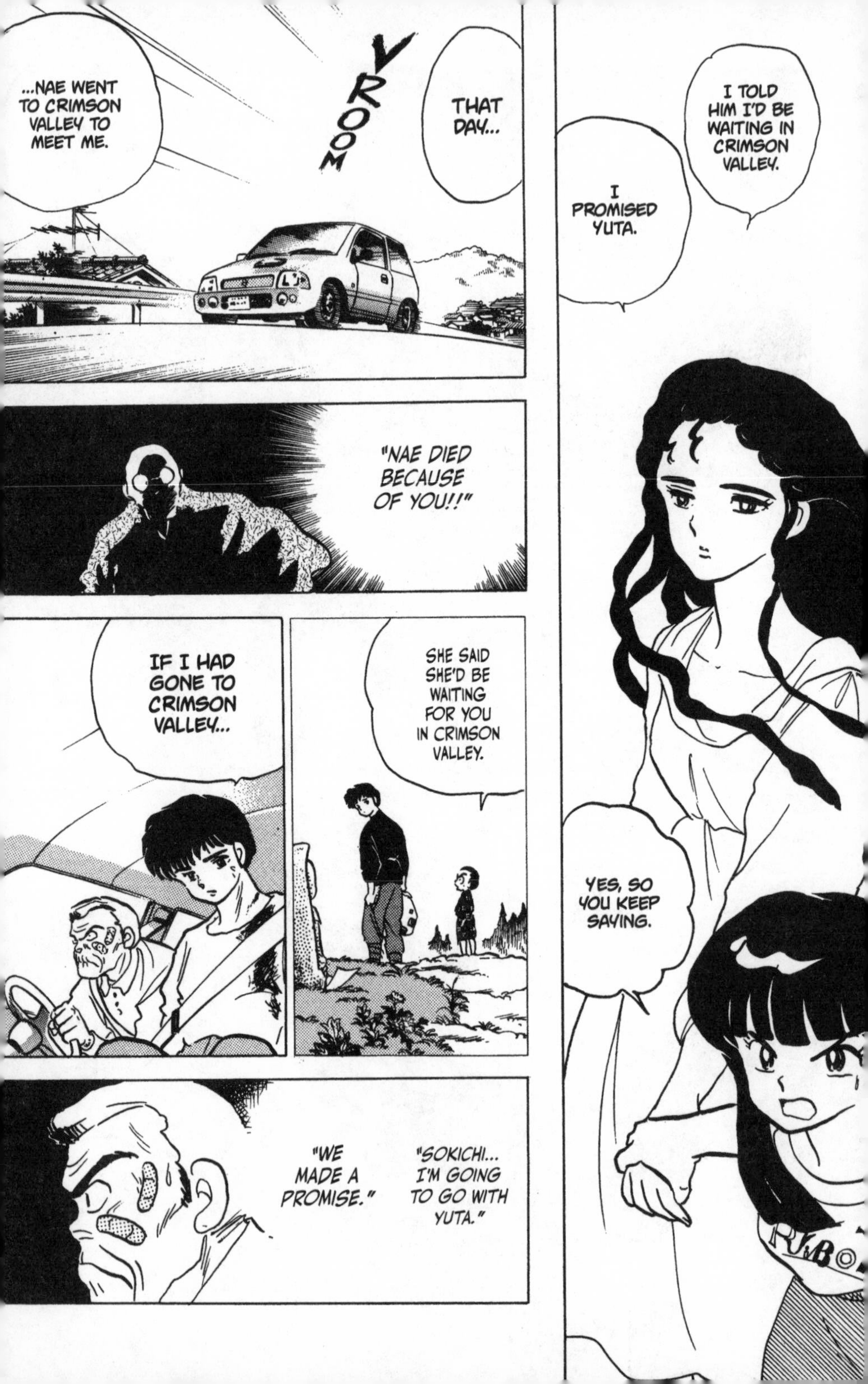
I TOLD HIM I'D BE WAITING IN CRIMSON VALLEY.
I PROMISED YUTA.
YES, SO YOU KEEP SAYING.
THAT DAY...
VROOM
...NAE WENT TO CRIMSON VALLEY TO MEET ME.
"NAE DIED BECAUSE OF YOU!!"
SHE SAID SHE'D BE WAITING FOR YOU IN CRIMSON VALLEY.
IF I HAD GONE TO CRIMSON VALLEY...
"SOKICHI... I'M GOING TO GO WITH YUTA."
"WE MADE A PROMISE."

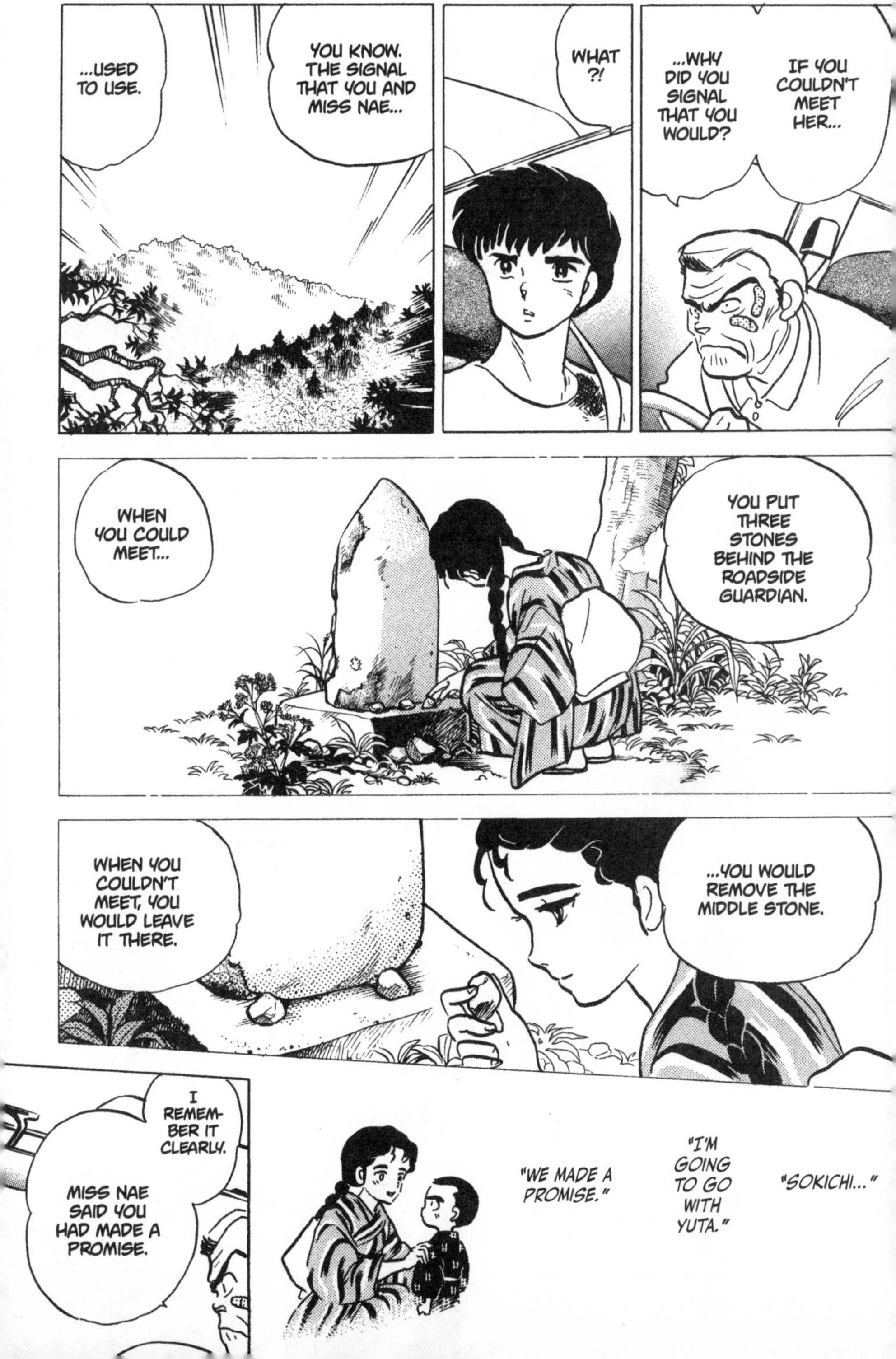
IF YOU COULDN'T MEET HER...
...WHY DID YOU SIGNAL THAT YOU WOULD?
WHAT ?!
YOU KNOW. THE SIGNAL THAT YOU AND MISS NAE...
...USED TO USE.
YOU PUT THREE STONES BEHIND THE ROADSIDE GUARDIAN.
WHEN YOU COULD MEET...
...YOU WOULD REMOVE THE MIDDLE STONE.
WHEN YOU COULDN'T MEET, YOU WOULD LEAVE IT THERE.
"SOKICHI..."
"I'M GOING TO GO WITH YUTA."
"WE MADE A PROMISE."
I REMEMBER IT CLEARLY.
MISS NAE SAID YOU HAD MADE A PROMISE.

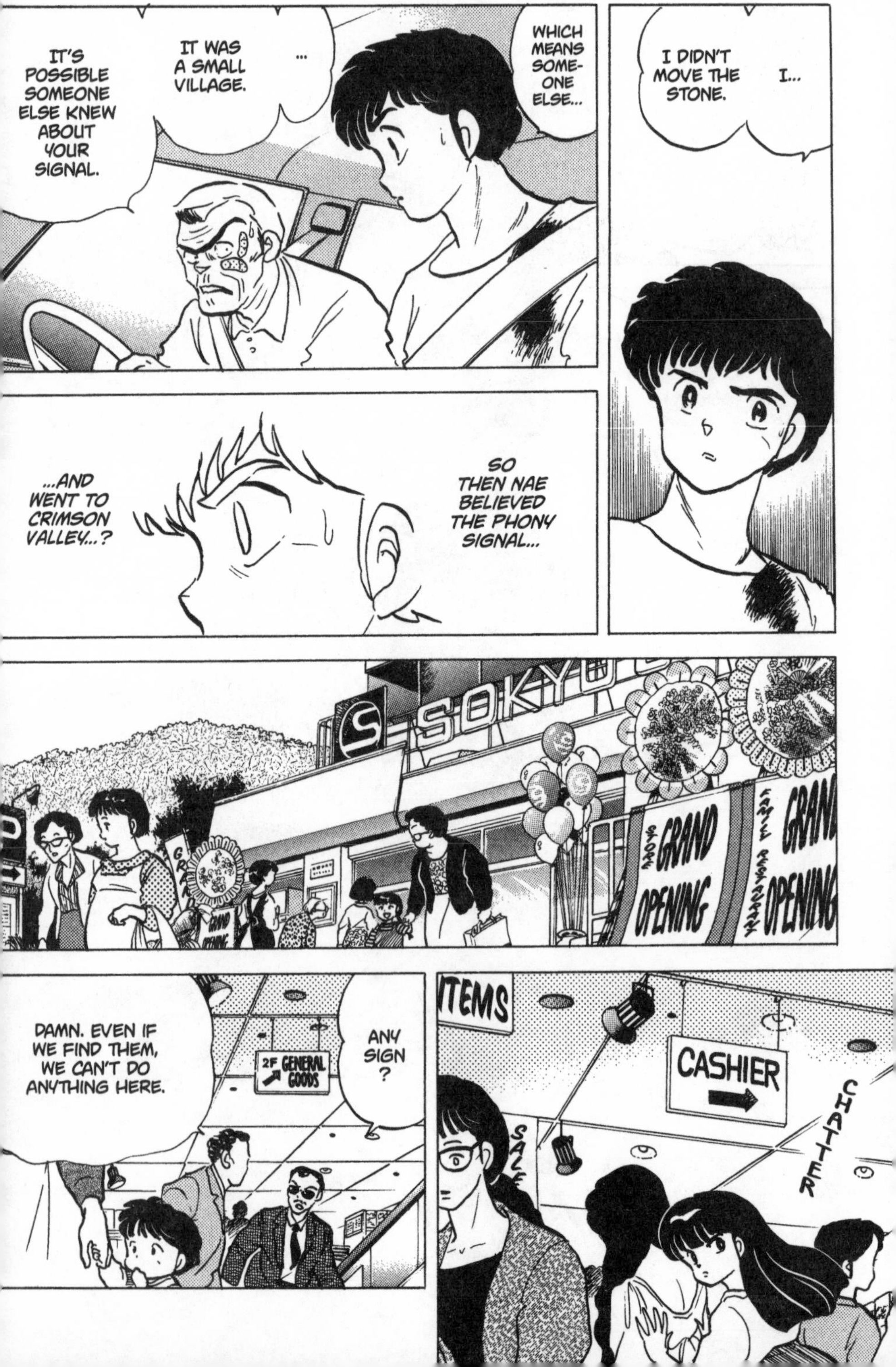
I...
I DIDN'T MOVE THE STONE.
WHICH MEANS SOMEONE ELSE...
...
IT WAS A SMALL VILLAGE.
IT'S POSSIBLE SOMEONE ELSE KNEW ABOUT YOUR SIGNAL.
SO THEN NAE BELIEVED THE PHONY SIGNAL...
...AND WENT TO CRIMSON VALLEY...?
SOKYU
FAMILY RESTAURANT GRAND OPENING
STORE GRAND OPENING
GRAND OPENING
ITEMS
CASHIER
CHATTER
SALE
ANY SIGN?
2F GENERAL GOODS
DAMN. EVEN IF WE FIND THEM, WE CAN'T DO ANYTHING HERE.

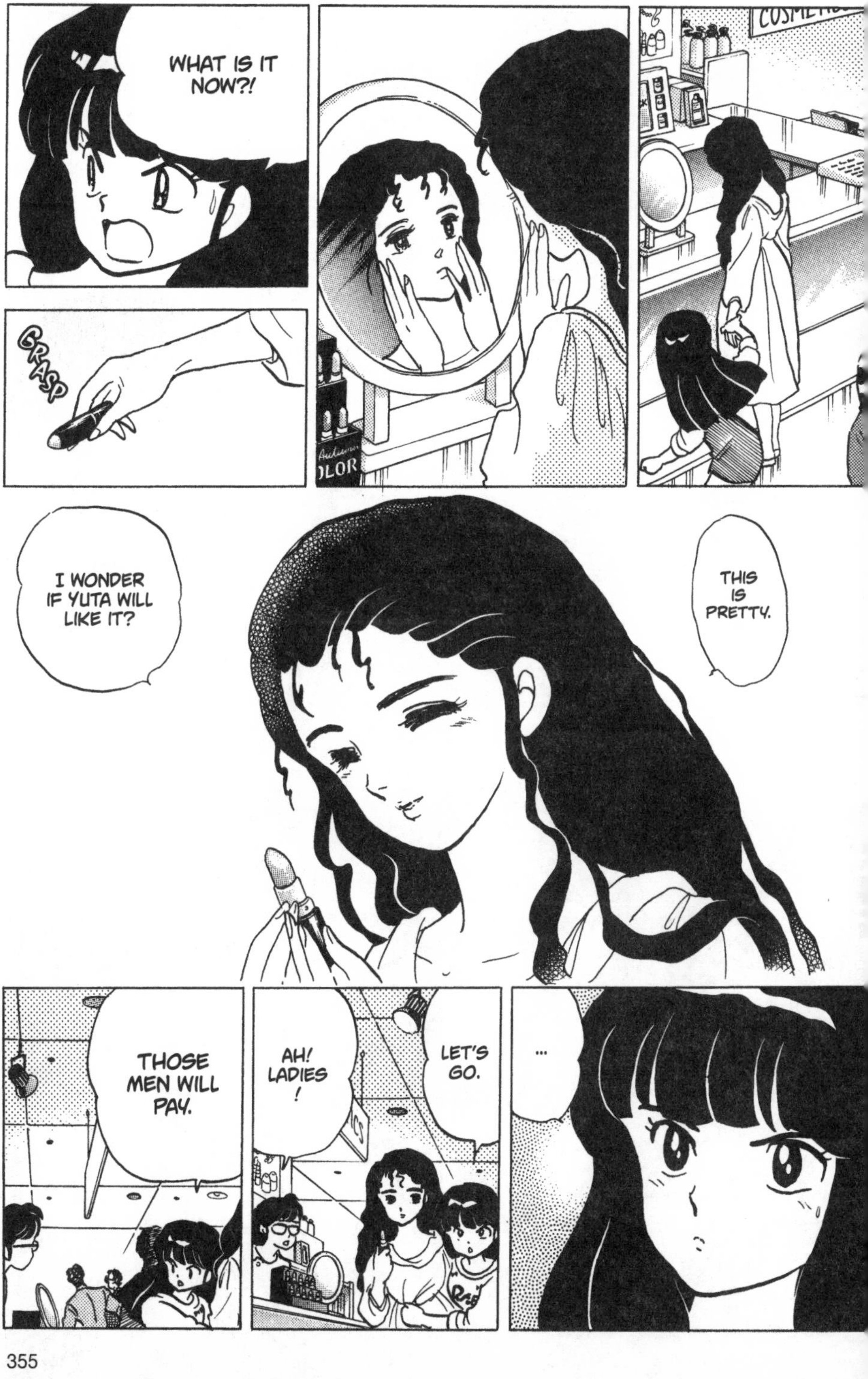
WHAT IS IT NOW?!
GRASP
THIS IS PRETTY.
I WONDER IF YUTA WILL LIKE IT?
...
LET'S GO.
AH! LADIES!
THOSE MEN WILL PAY.

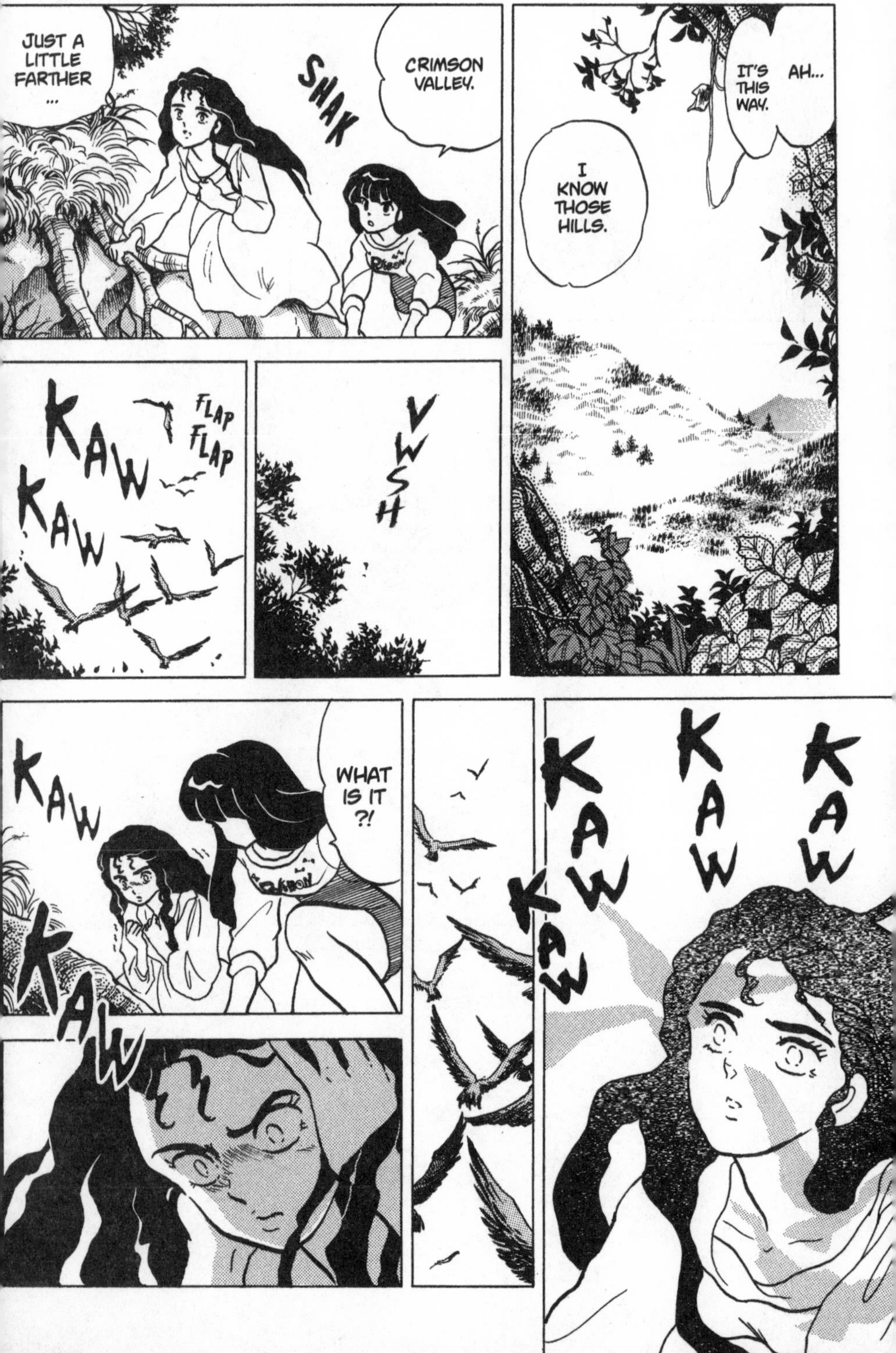
AH...
IT'S THIS WAY.
I KNOW THOSE HILLS.
CRIMSON VALLEY.
SHAK
JUST A LITTLE FARTHER ...
VWSH
FLAP FLAP
KAW KAW
KAW KAW KAW KAW KAW
WHAT IS IT ?!
KAW
KAW

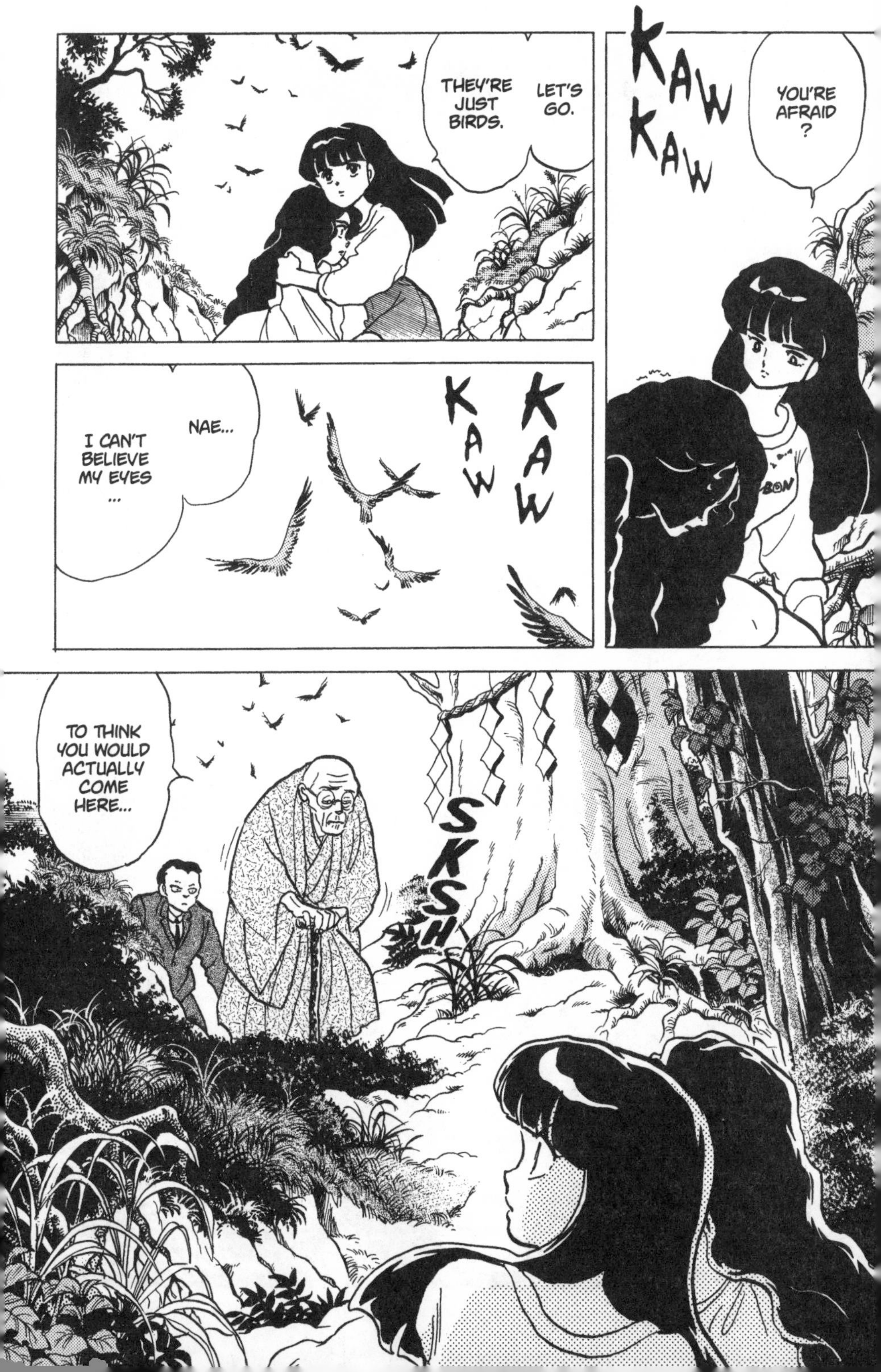
KAW KAW
YOU'RE AFRAID?
THEY'RE JUST BIRDS. LET'S GO.
KAW KAW
NAE... I CAN'T BELIEVE MY EYES...
TO THINK YOU WOULD ACTUALLY COME HERE...
SKSH

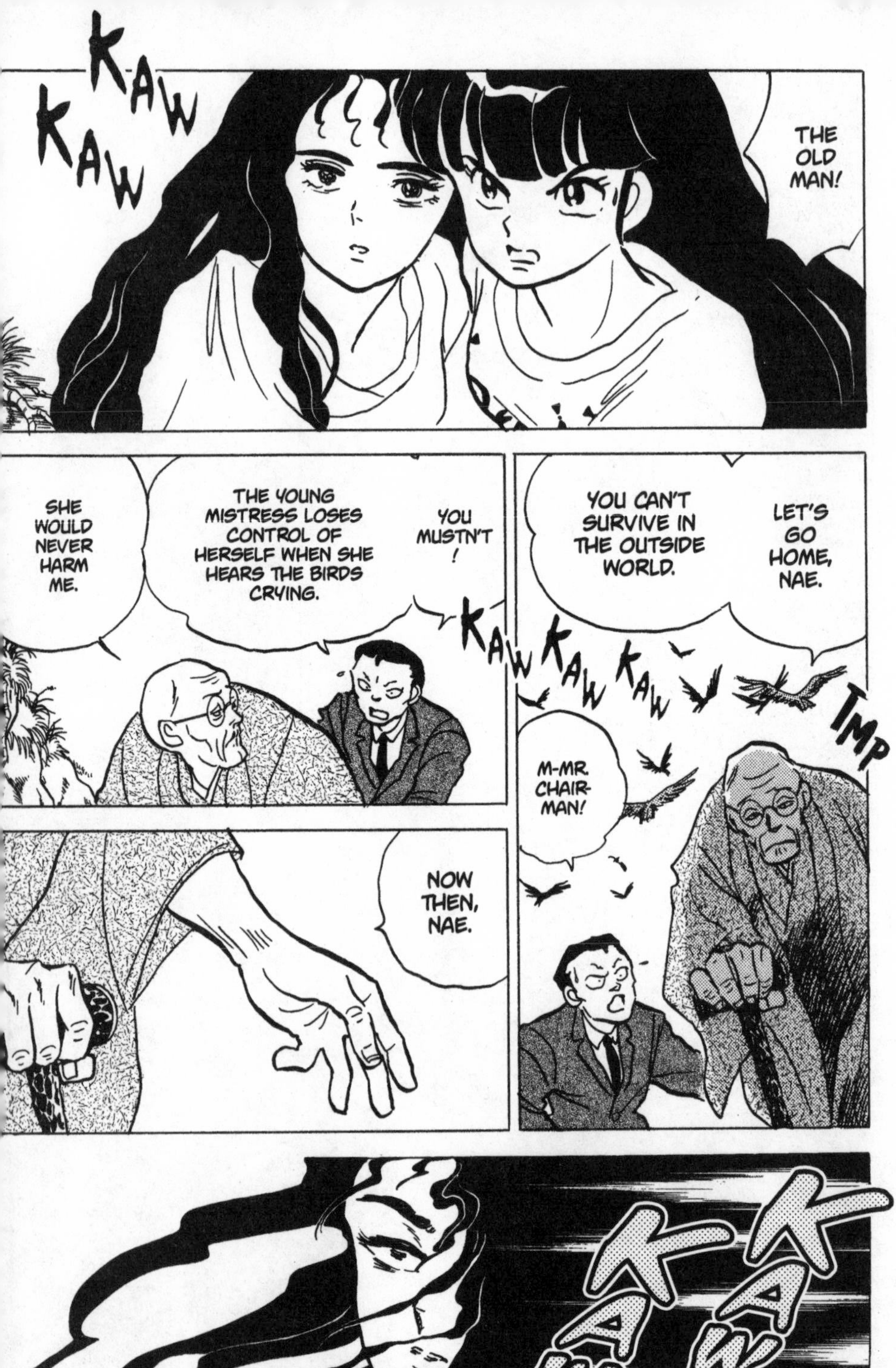
THE OLD MAN!
KAW KAW
LET'S GO HOME, NAE.
YOU CAN'T SURVIVE IN THE OUTSIDE WORLD.
KAW KAW KAW
TMP
M-MR. CHAIR-MAN!
YOU MUSTN'T!
THE YOUNG MISTRESS LOSES CONTROL OF HERSELF WHEN SHE HEARS THE BIRDS CRYING.
SHE WOULD NEVER HARM ME.
NOW THEN, NAE.
KAW KAW

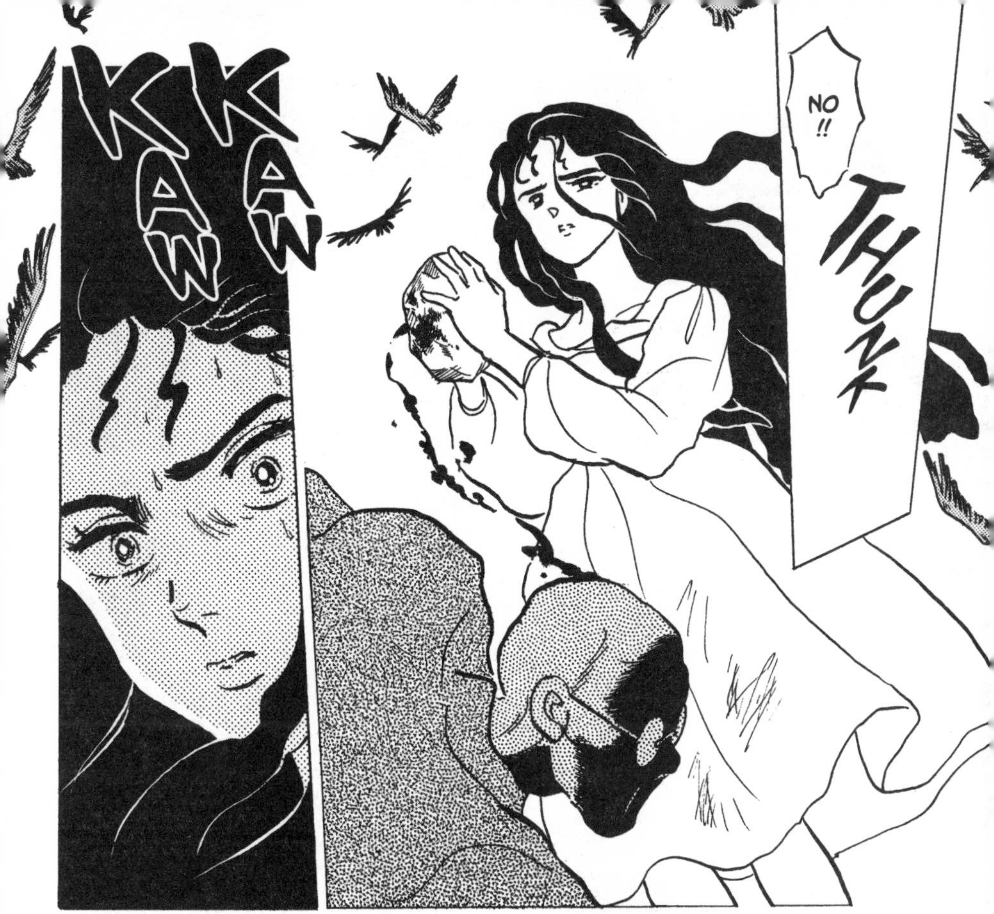
NO!!
THUNK
KKAW KAW
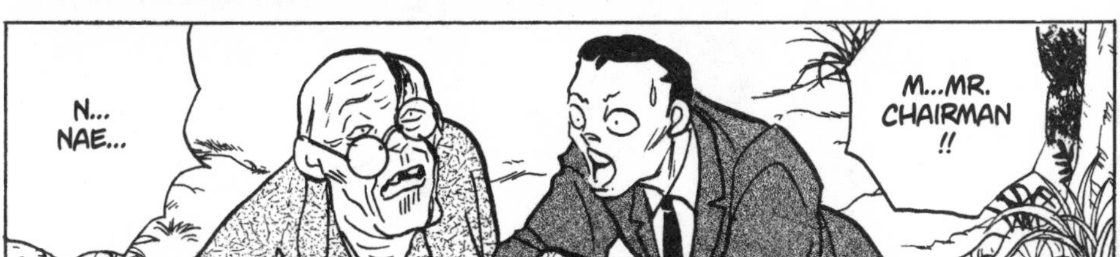
M...MR. CHAIRMAN!!
N... NAE...
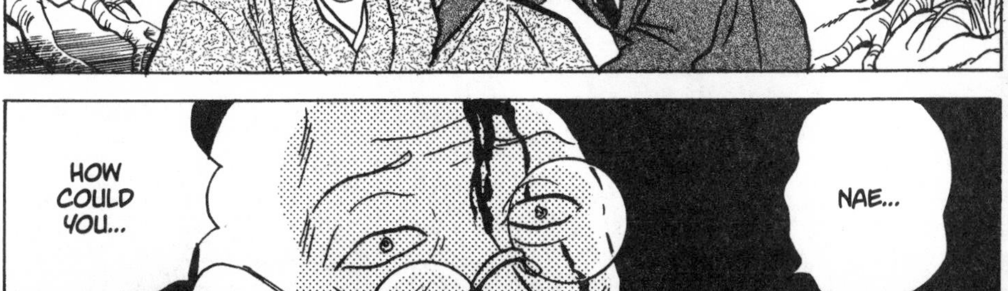
NAE...
HOW COULD YOU...

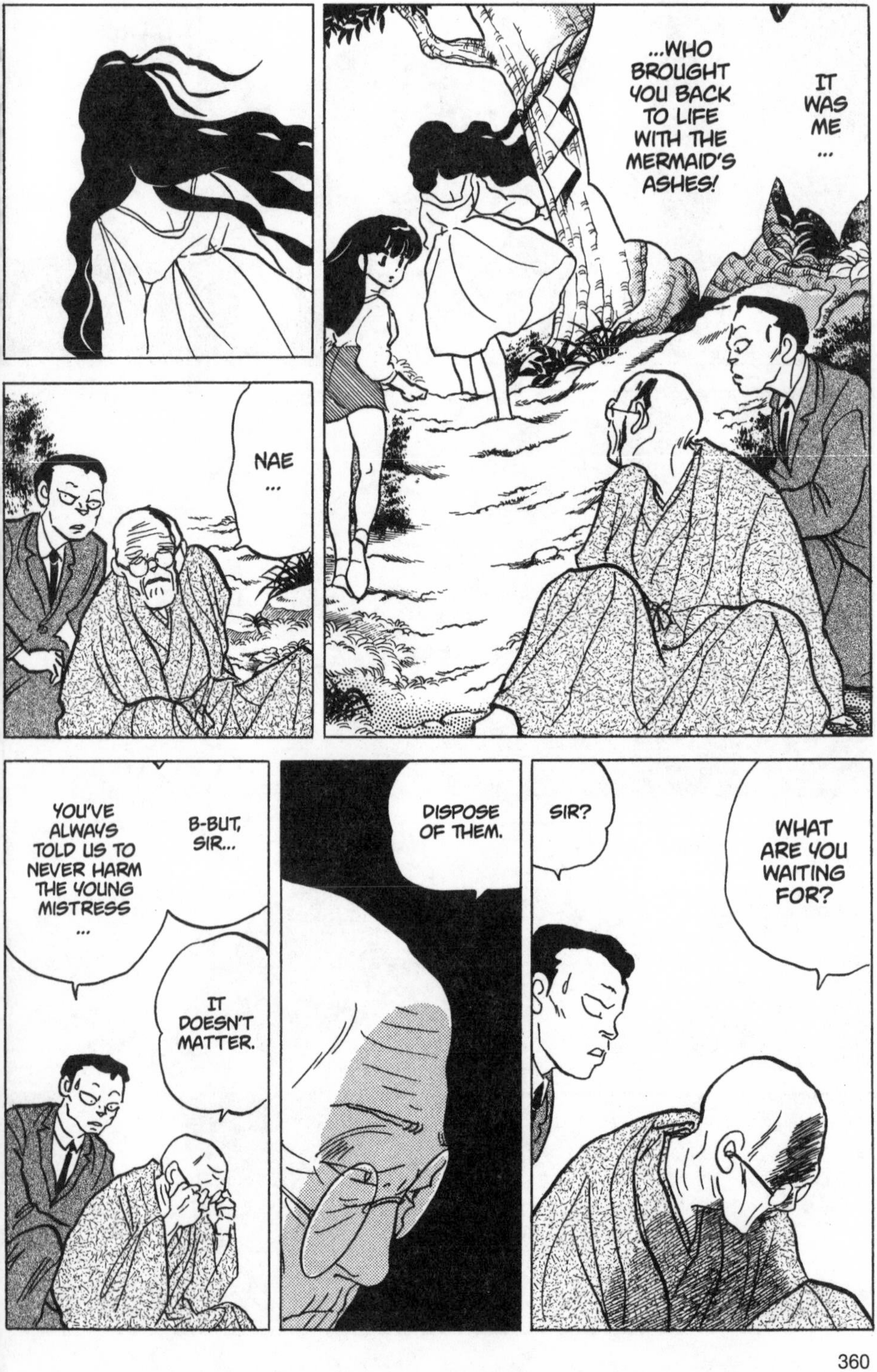
IT WAS ME ...
...WHO BROUGHT YOU BACK TO LIFE WITH THE MERMAID'S ASHES!
NAE ...
WHAT ARE YOU WAITING FOR?
SIR?
DISPOSE OF THEM.
B-BUT, SIR...
YOU'VE ALWAYS TOLD US TO NEVER HARM THE YOUNG MISTRESS ...
IT DOESN'T MATTER.

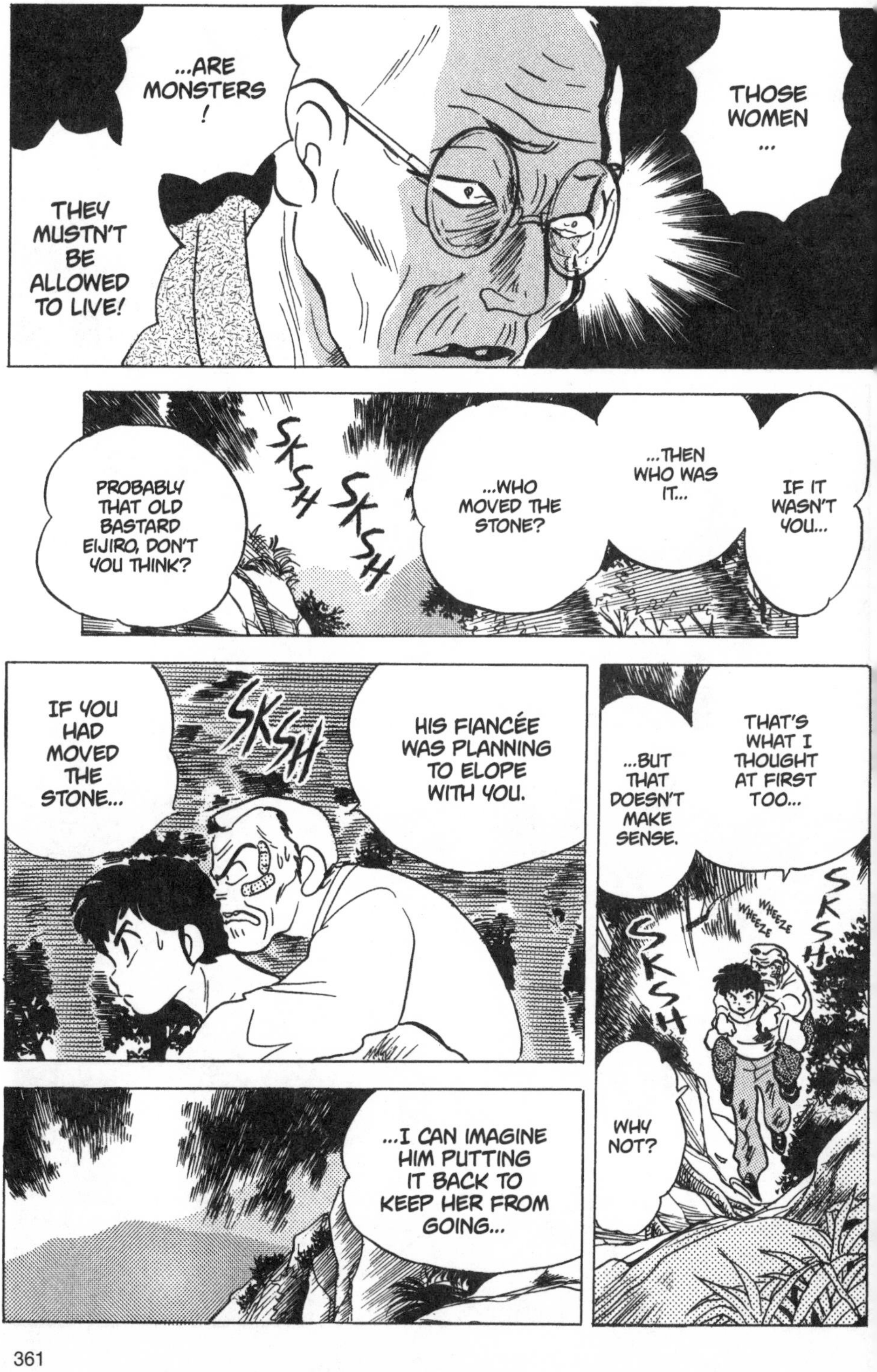

THOSE WOMEN ...
...ARE MONSTERS!
THEY MUSTN'T BE ALLOWED TO LIVE!
IF IT WASN'T YOU...
...THEN WHO WAS IT...
...WHO MOVED THE STONE?
SKSH
SKSH
PROBABLY THAT OLD BASTARD EIJIRO, DON'T YOU THINK?
THAT'S WHAT I THOUGHT AT FIRST TOO...
...BUT THAT DOESN'T MAKE SENSE.
SKSH
WHEEZE
WHEEZE
SKSH
WHY NOT?
HIS FIANCÉE WAS PLANNING TO ELOPE WITH YOU.
SKSH
IF YOU HAD MOVED THE STONE...
...I CAN IMAGINE HIM PUTTING IT BACK TO KEEP HER FROM GOING...

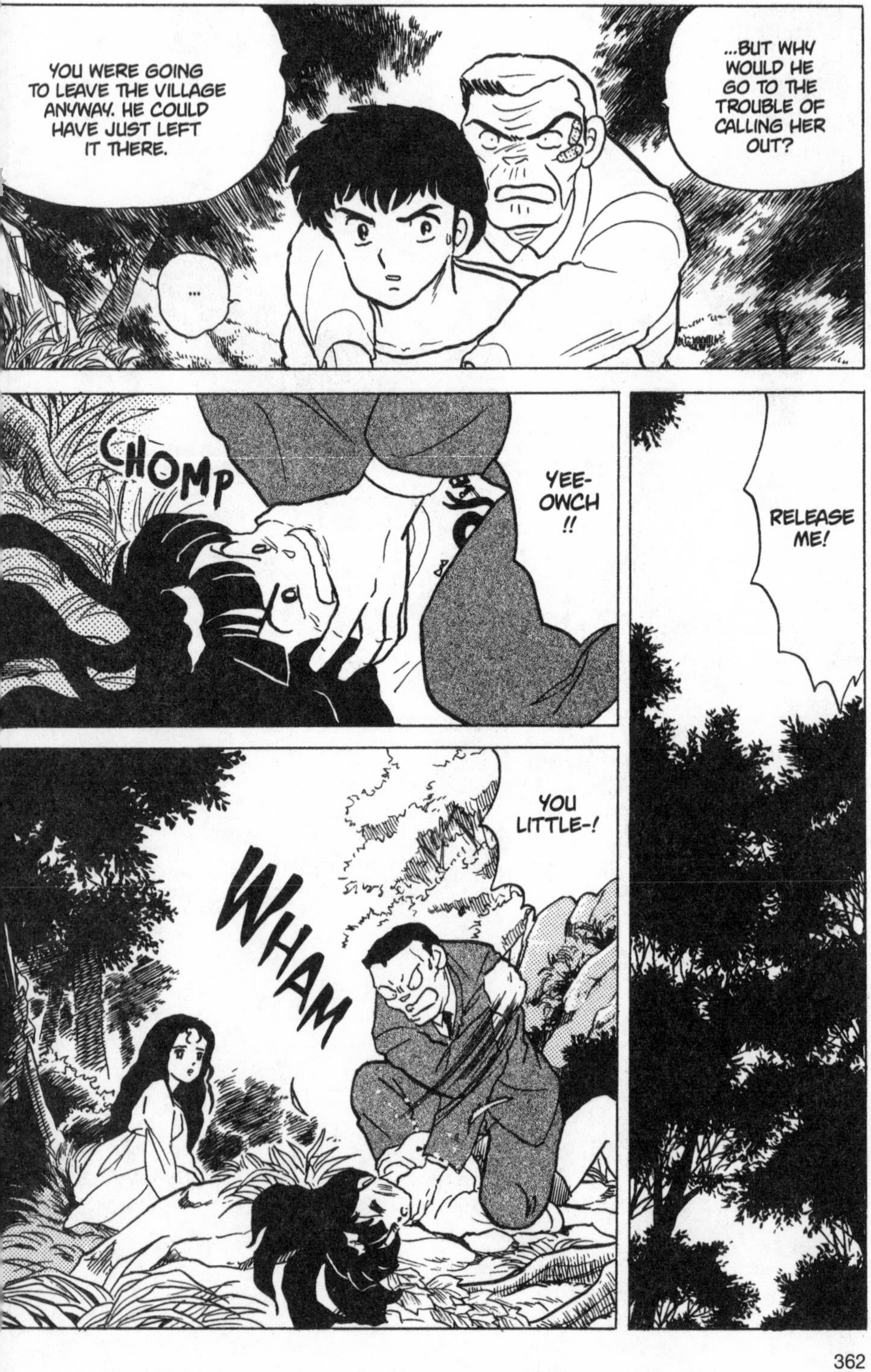
...BUT WHY WOULD HE GO TO THE TROUBLE OF CALLING HER OUT?
YOU WERE GOING TO LEAVE THE VILLAGE ANYWAY. HE COULD HAVE JUST LEFT IT THERE.
...
RELEASE ME!
YEE-OWCH !!
CHOMP
YOU LITTLE-!
WHAM

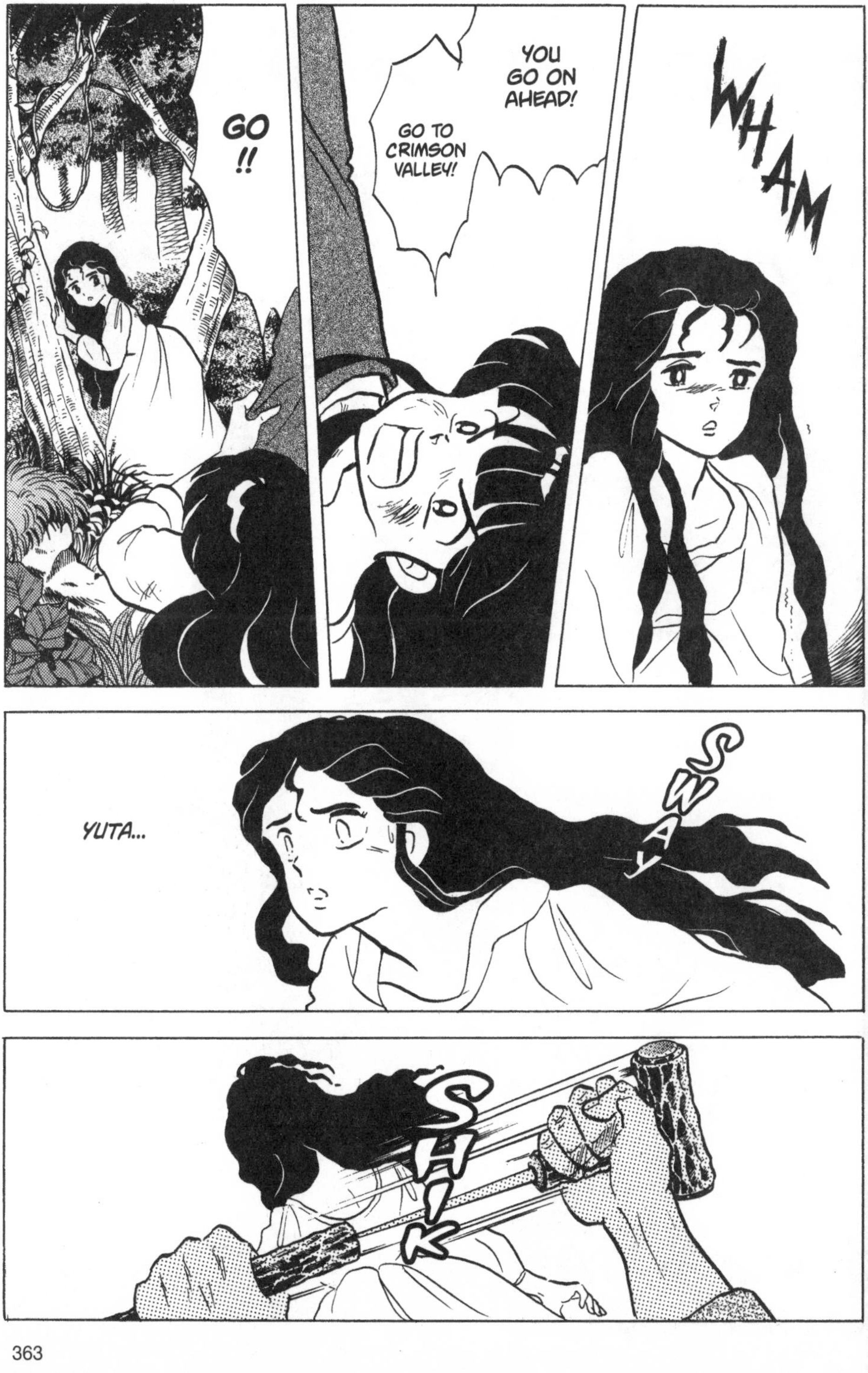
WHAM
YOU GO ON AHEAD!
GO TO CRIMSON VALLEY!
GO !!
SWAY
YUTA...
SHIK

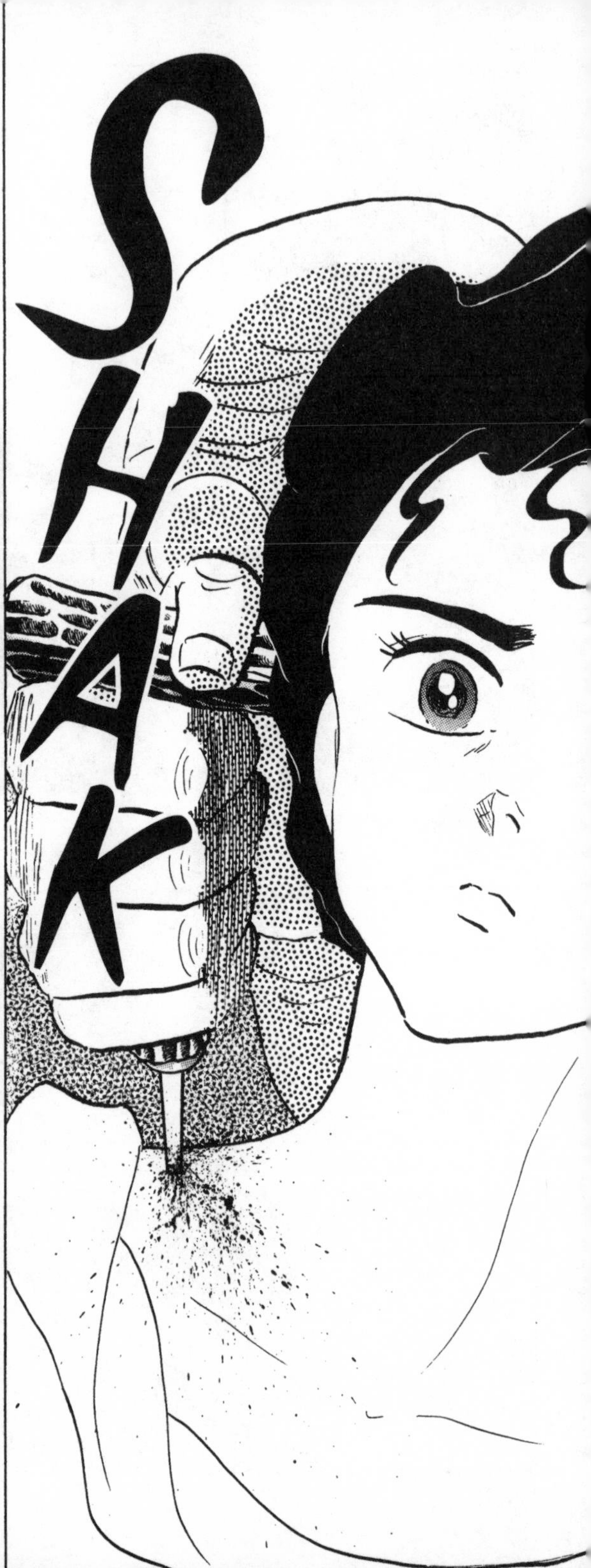
SHAK
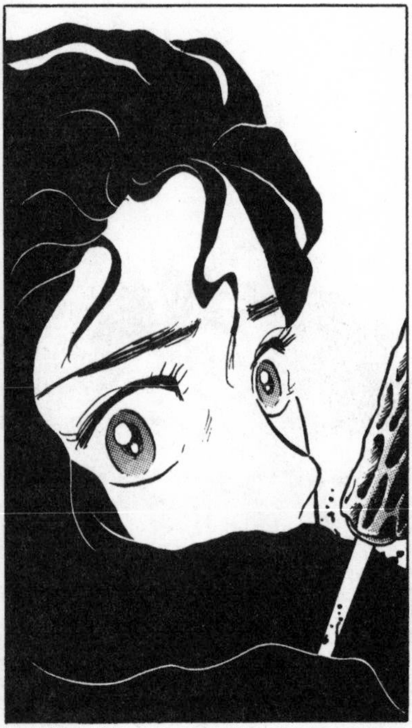
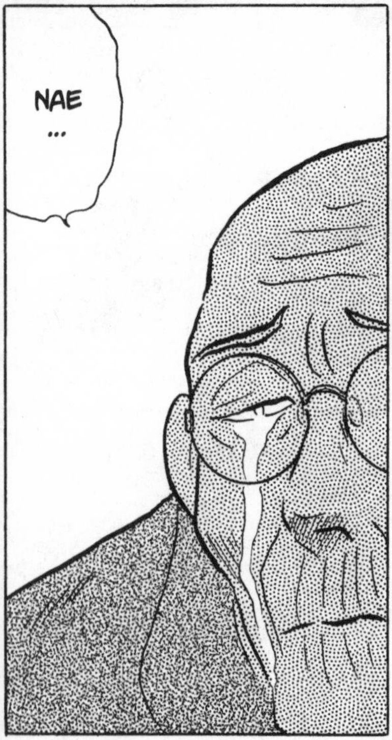
NAE ...

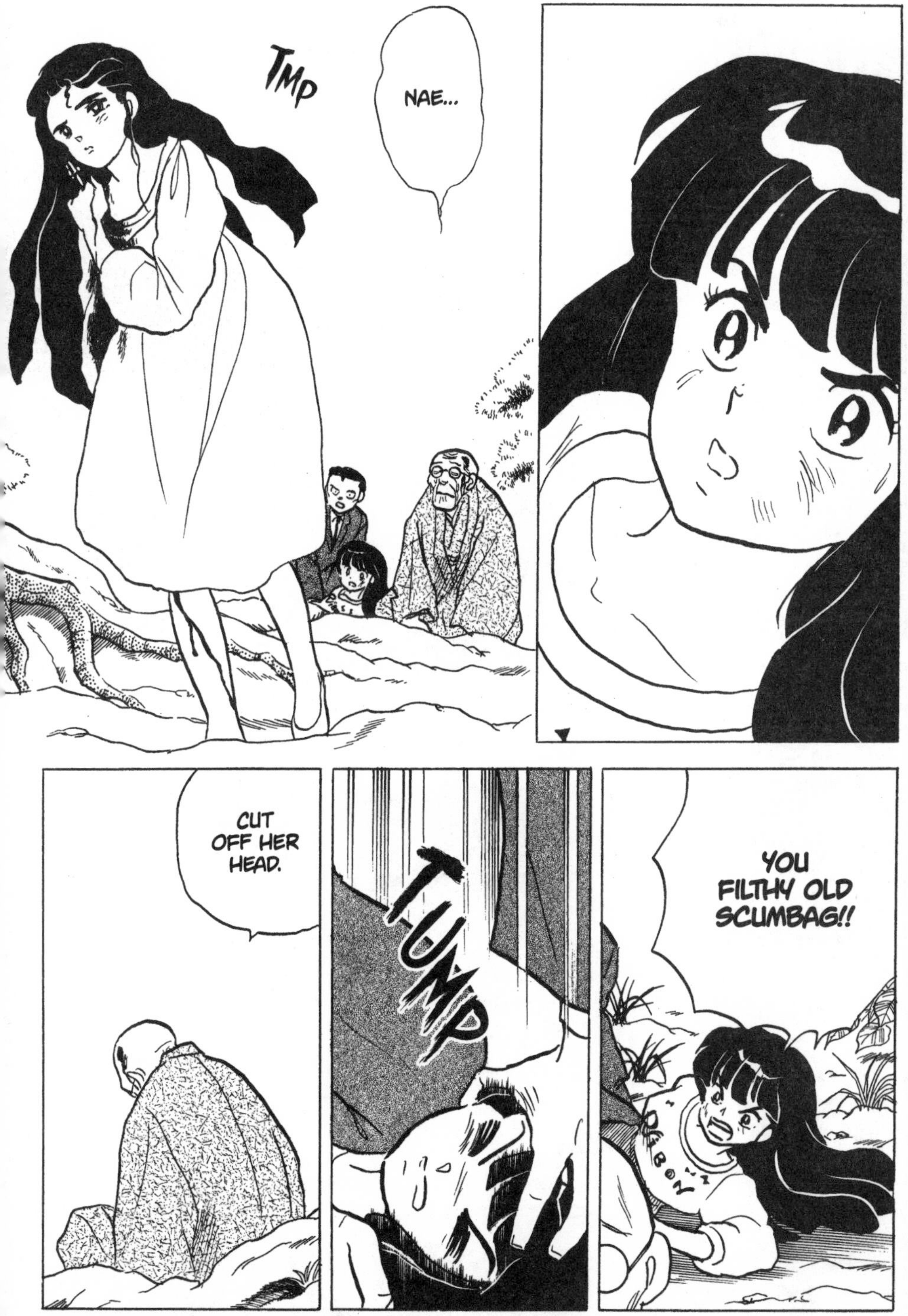
TMP
NAE...
YOU FILTHY OLD SCUMBAG!!
TUMP
CUT OFF HER HEAD.

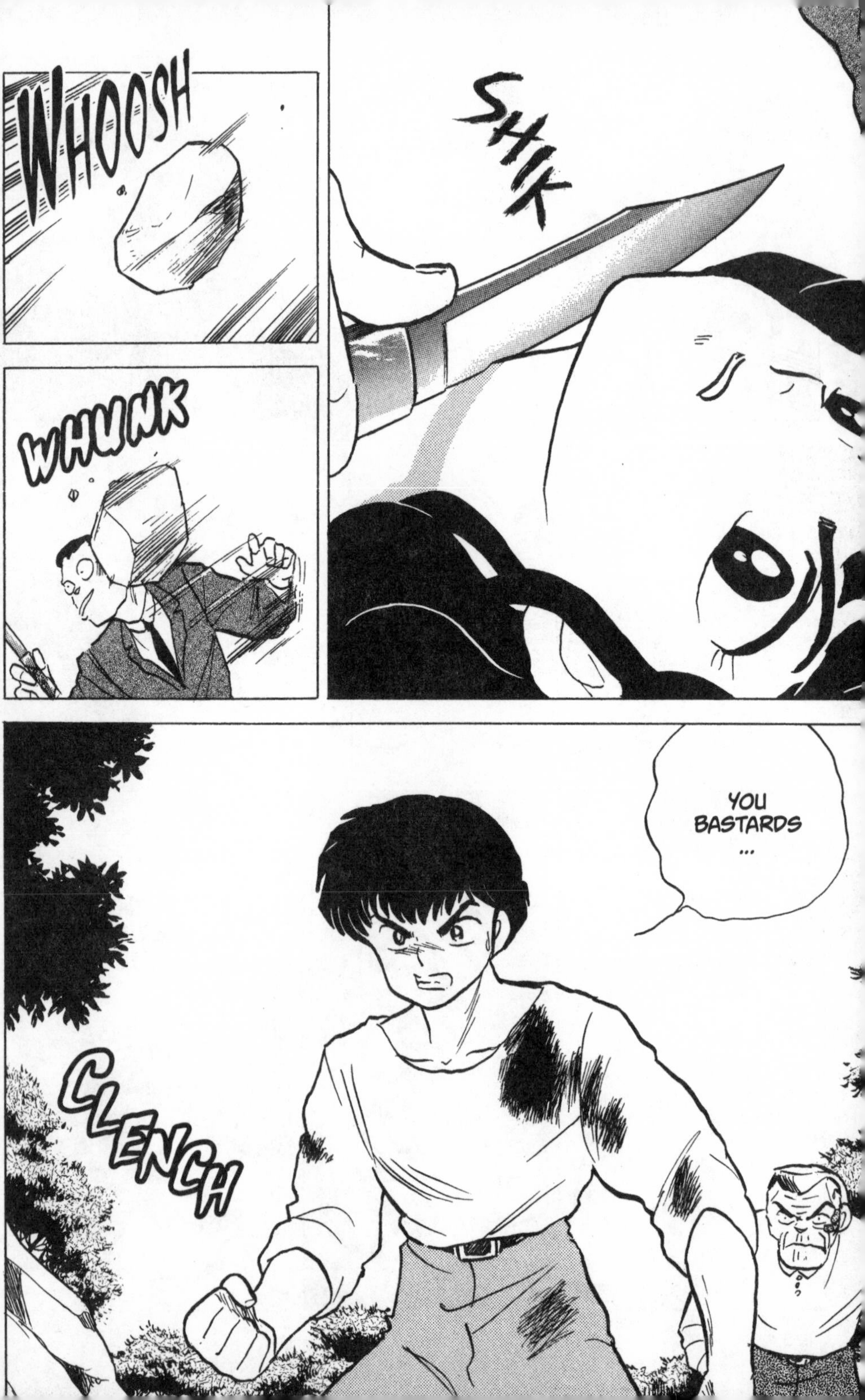
SHIK
WHOOSH
WHUNK
YOU BASTARDS ...
CLENCH

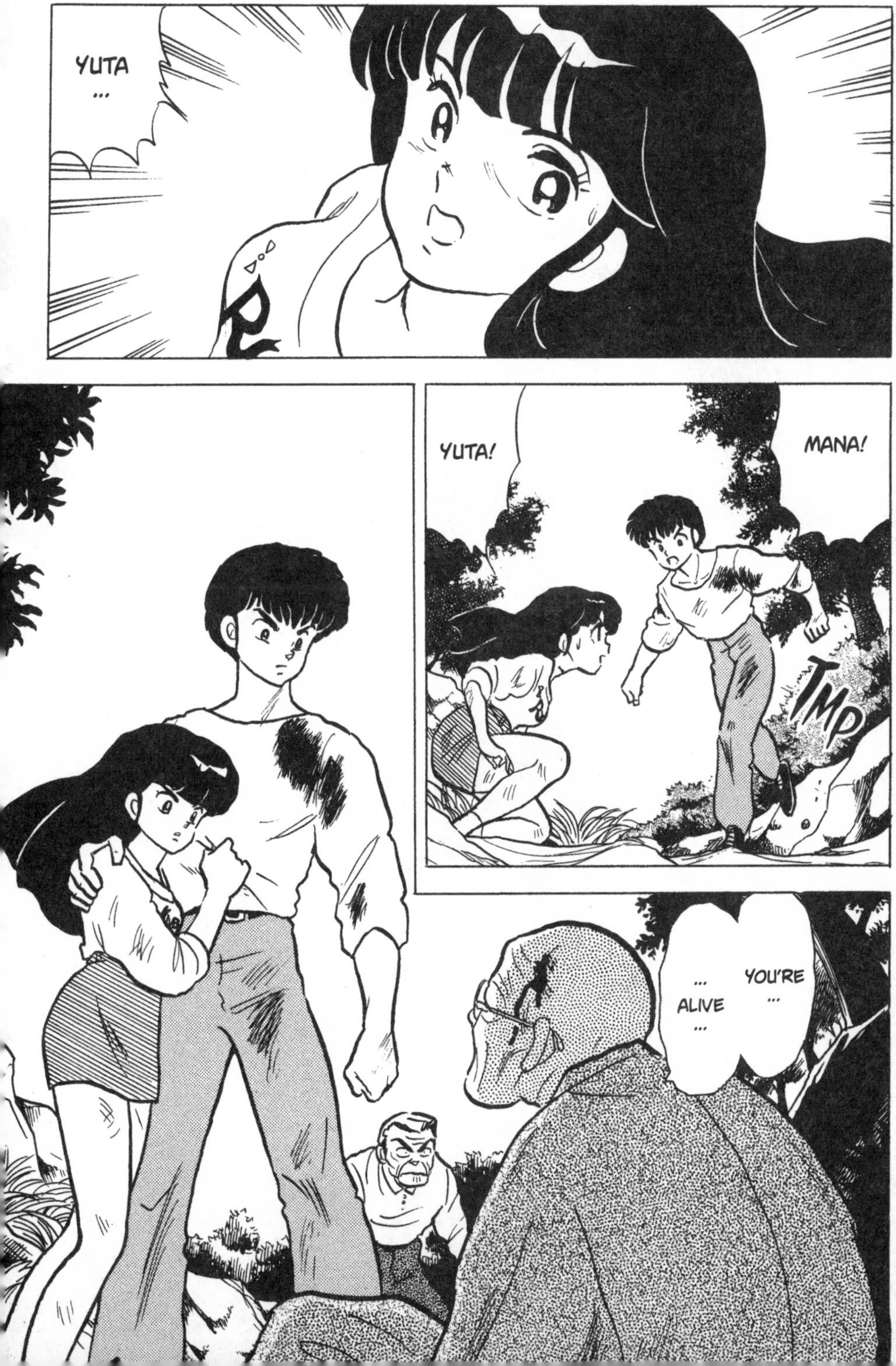
YUTA ...
MANA!
YUTA!
YOU'RE ...
... ALIVE ...

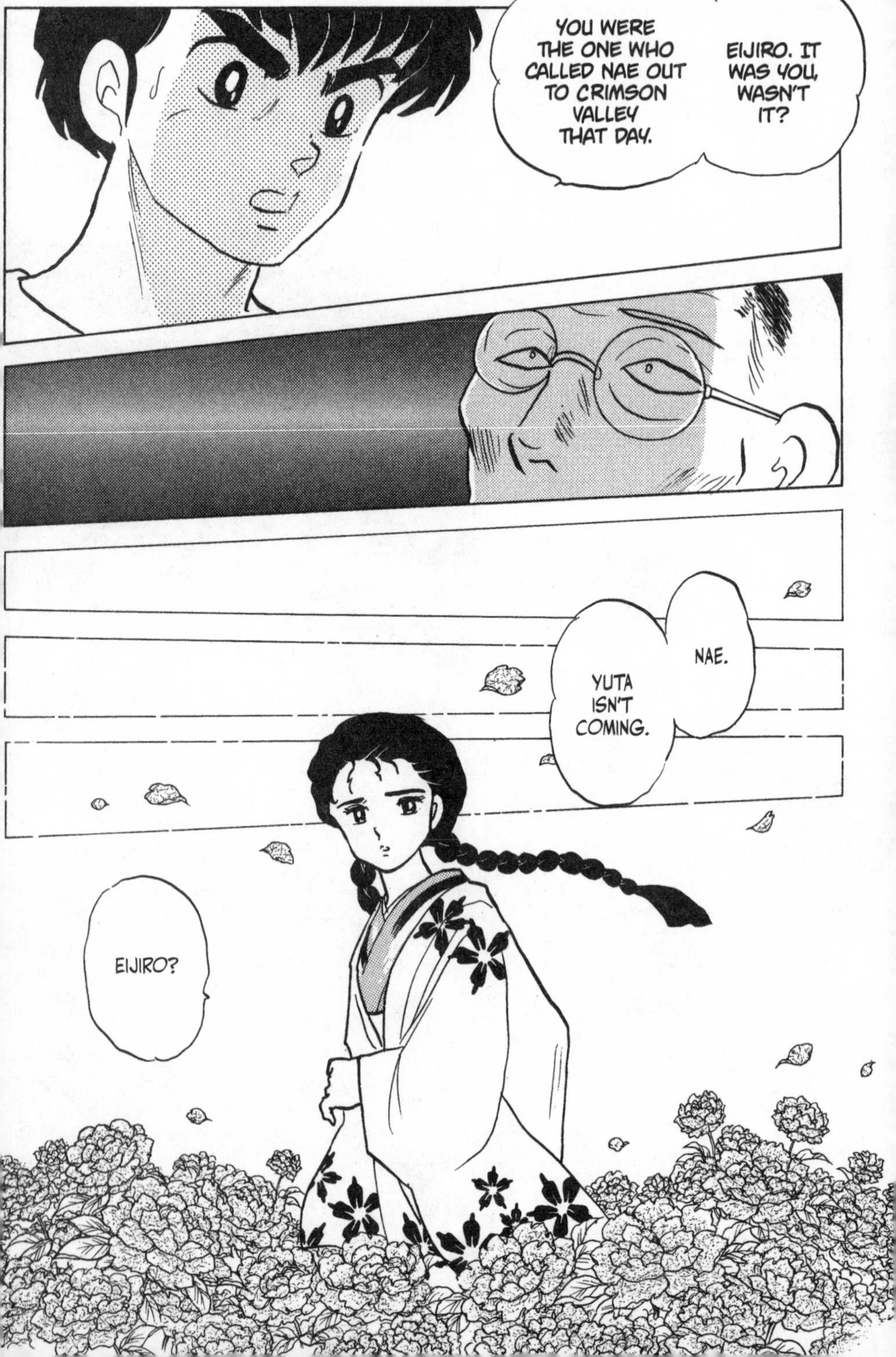
EIJIRO. IT WAS YOU, WASN'T IT?
YOU WERE THE ONE WHO CALLED NAE OUT TO CRIMSON VALLEY THAT DAY.
NAE.
YUTA ISN'T COMING.
EIJIRO?

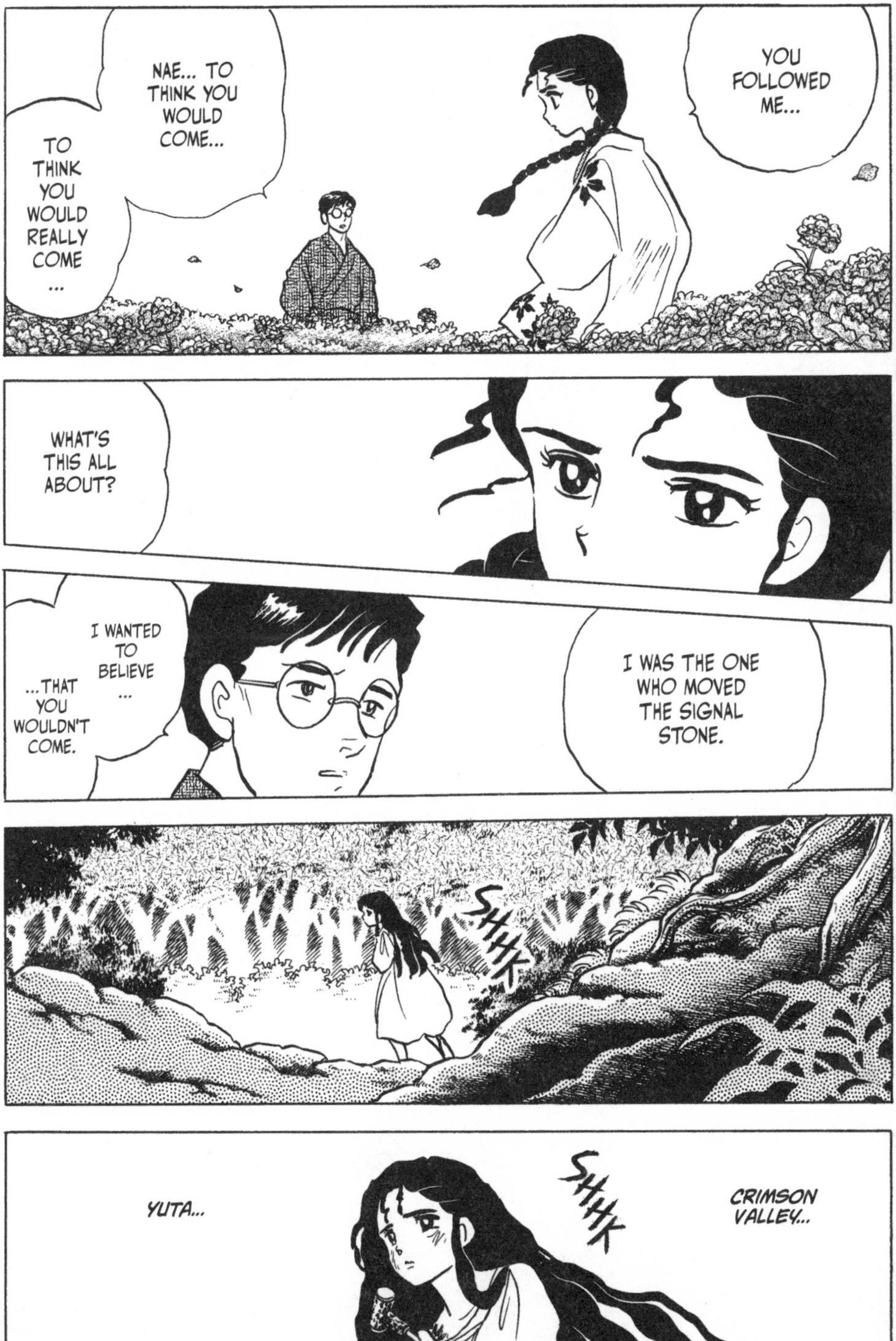

YOU FOLLOWED ME...
NAE... TO THINK YOU WOULD COME...
TO THINK YOU WOULD REALLY COME ...
WHAT'S THIS ALL ABOUT?
I WAS THE ONE WHO MOVED THE SIGNAL STONE.
I WANTED TO BELIEVE ...
...THAT YOU WOULDN'T COME.
SHHHK
CRIMSON VALLEY...
SHHHK
YUTA...

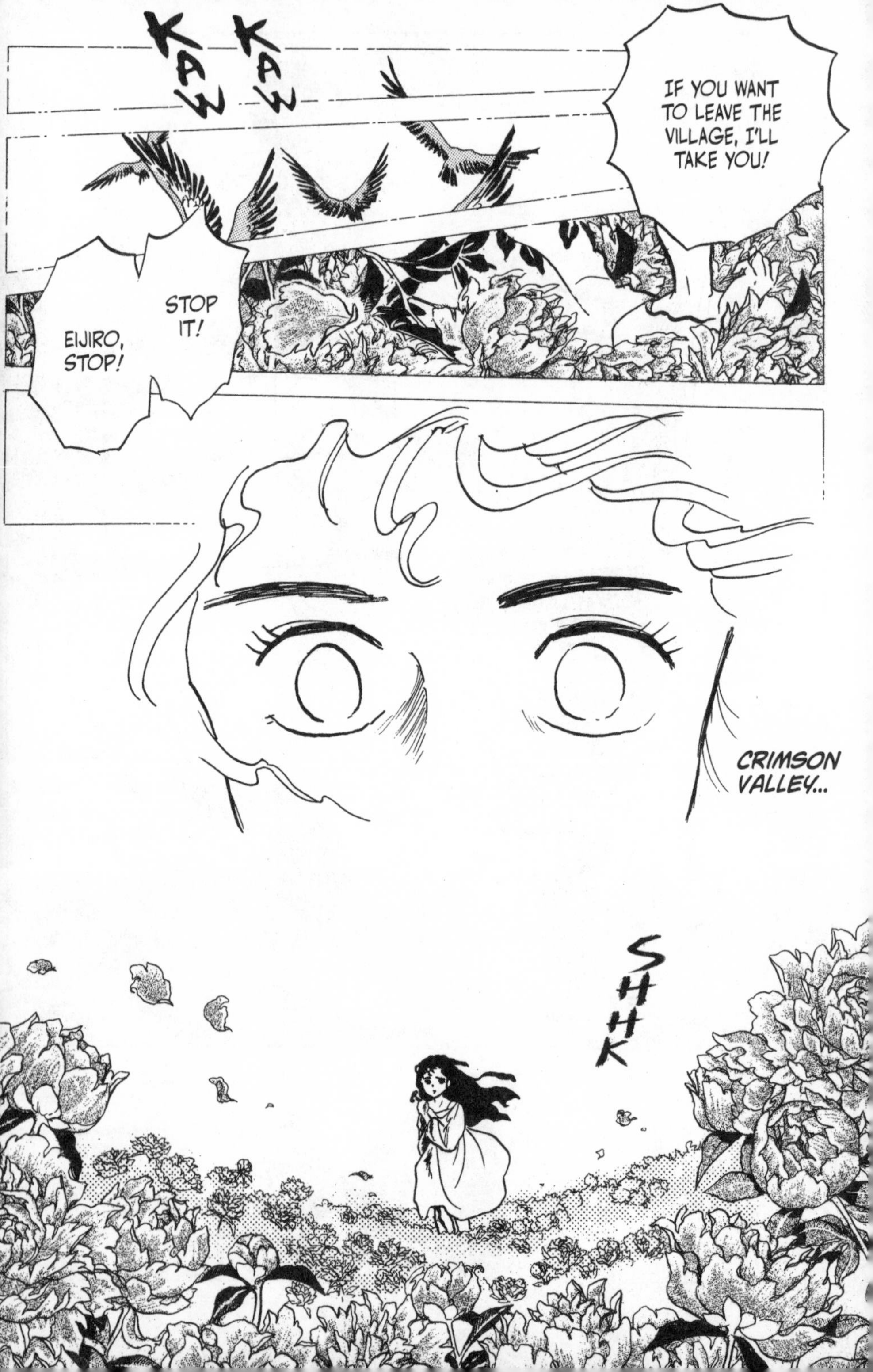
IF YOU WANT TO LEAVE THE VILLAGE, I'LL TAKE YOU!
KAW KAW
STOP IT!
EIJIRO, STOP!
CRIMSON VALLEY...
SHHK

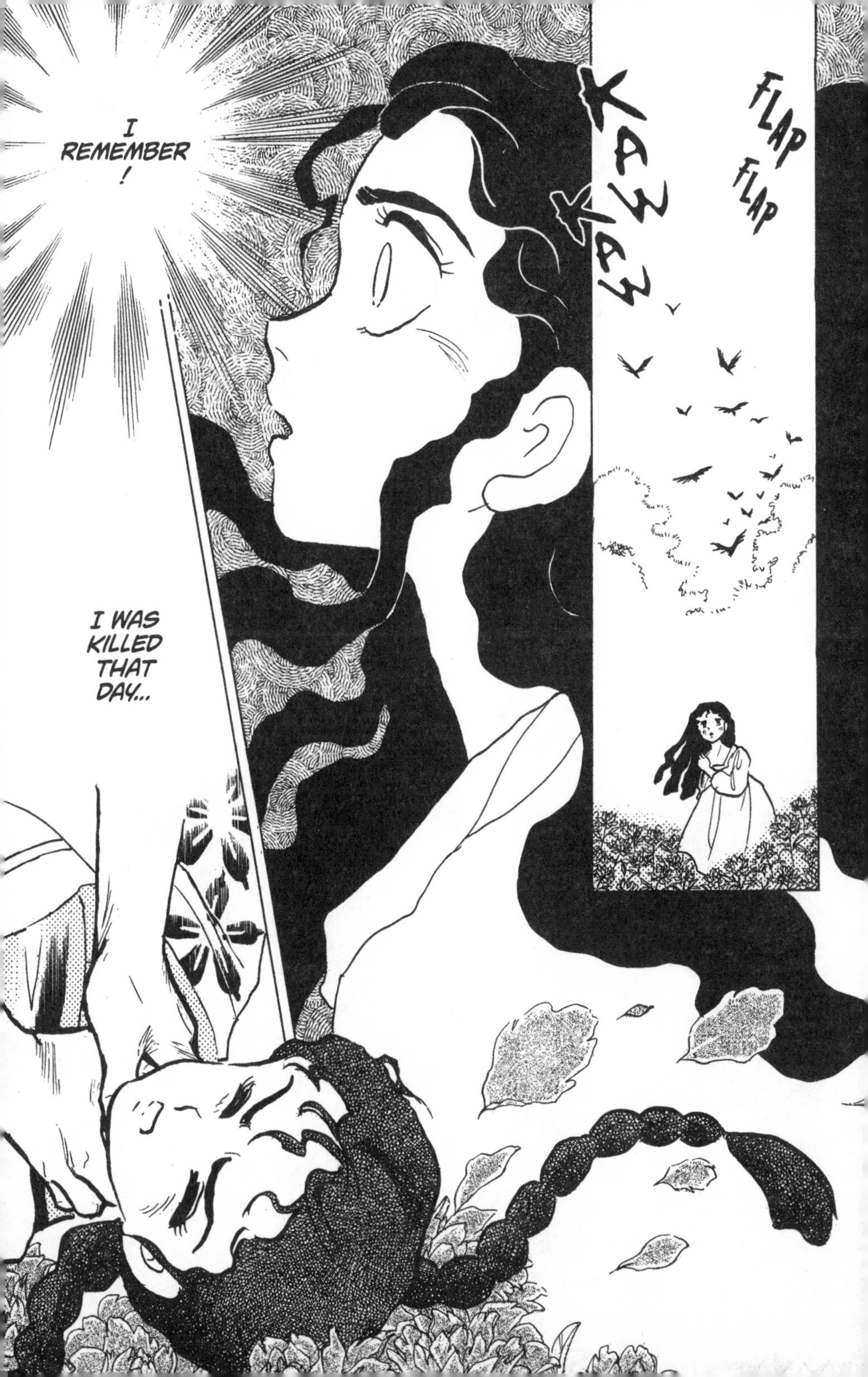
KAW KAW
FLAP FLAP
I REMEMBER!
I WAS KILLED THAT DAY...

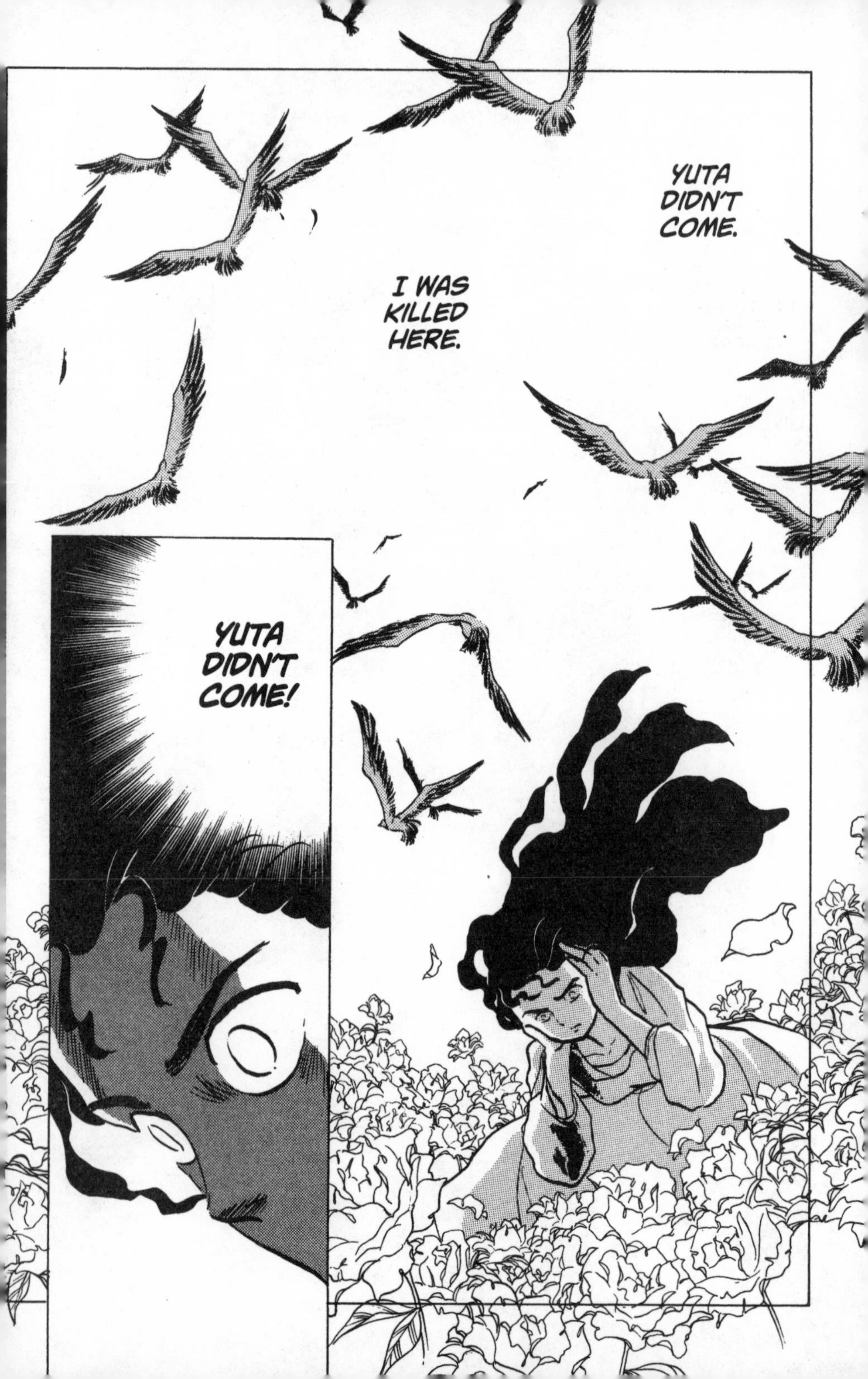
YUTA DIDN'T COME.
I WAS KILLED HERE.
YUTA DIDN'T COME!

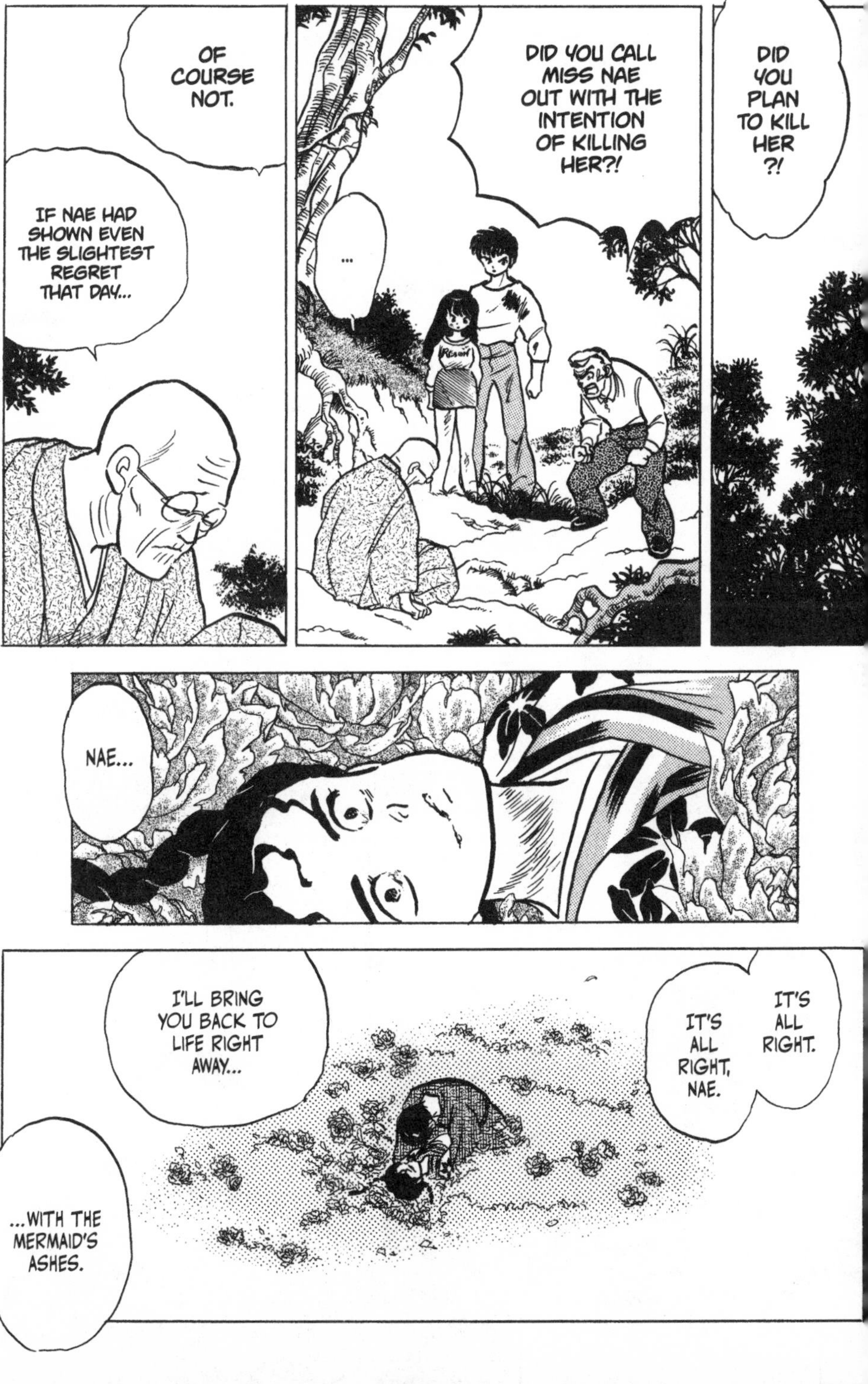
DID YOU PLAN TO KILL HER ?!
DID YOU CALL MISS NAE OUT WITH THE INTENTION OF KILLING HER?!
...
OF COURSE NOT.
IF NAE HAD SHOWN EVEN THE SLIGHTEST REGRET THAT DAY...
NAE...
IT'S ALL RIGHT.
IT'S ALL RIGHT, NAE.
I'LL BRING YOU BACK TO LIFE RIGHT AWAY...
...WITH THE MERMAID'S ASHES.

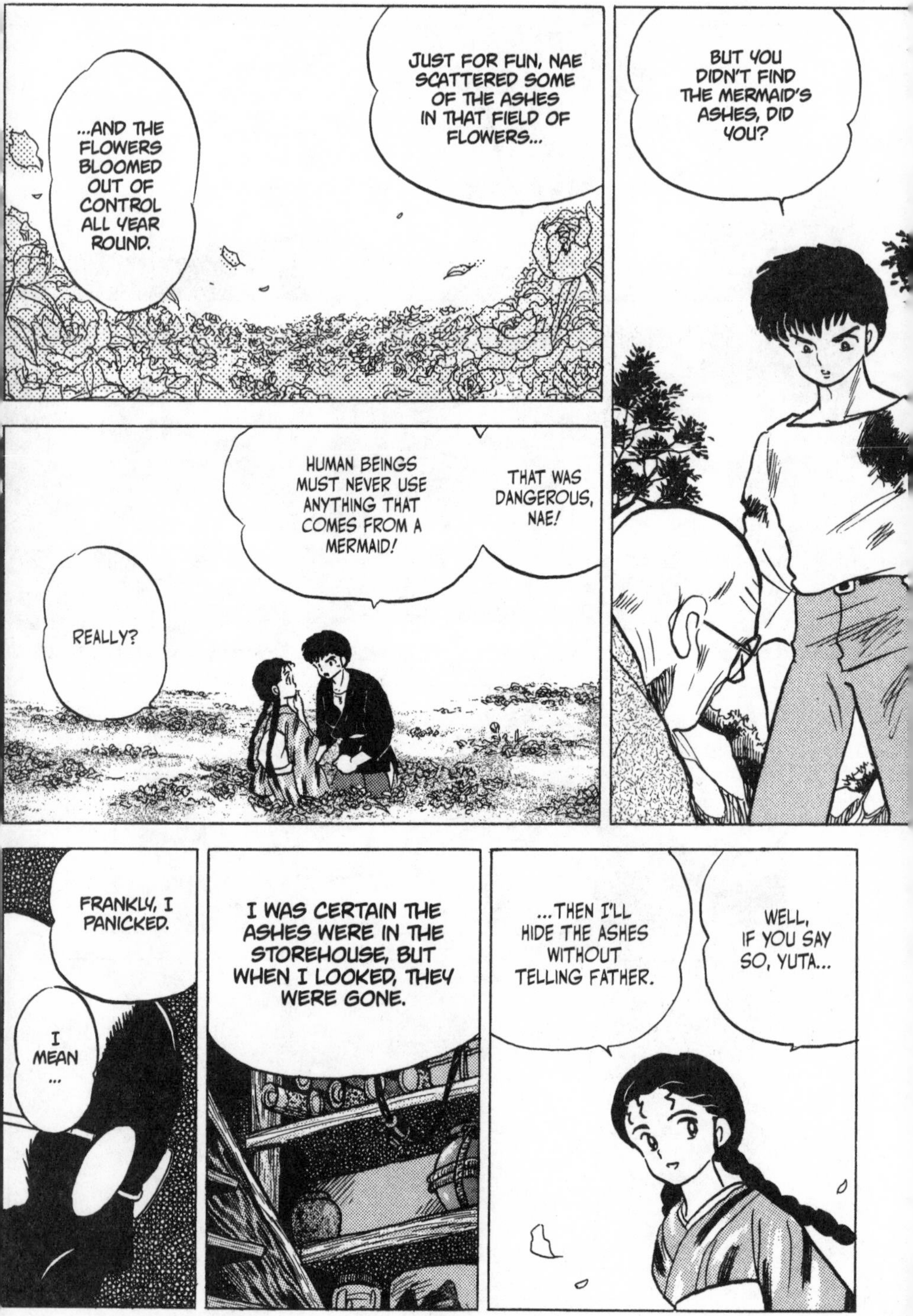
JUST FOR FUN, NAE SCATTERED SOME OF THE ASHES IN THAT FIELD OF FLOWERS...
...AND THE FLOWERS BLOOMED OUT OF CONTROL ALL YEAR ROUND.
THAT WAS DANGEROUS, NAE!
HUMAN BEINGS MUST NEVER USE ANYTHING THAT COMES FROM A MERMAID!
REALLY?
BUT YOU DIDN'T FIND THE MERMAID'S ASHES, DID YOU?
WELL, IF YOU SAY SO, YUTA...
...THEN I'LL HIDE THE ASHES WITHOUT TELLING FATHER.
I WAS CERTAIN THE ASHES WERE IN THE STOREHOUSE, BUT WHEN I LOOKED, THEY WERE GONE.
FRANKLY, I PANICKED.
I MEAN...

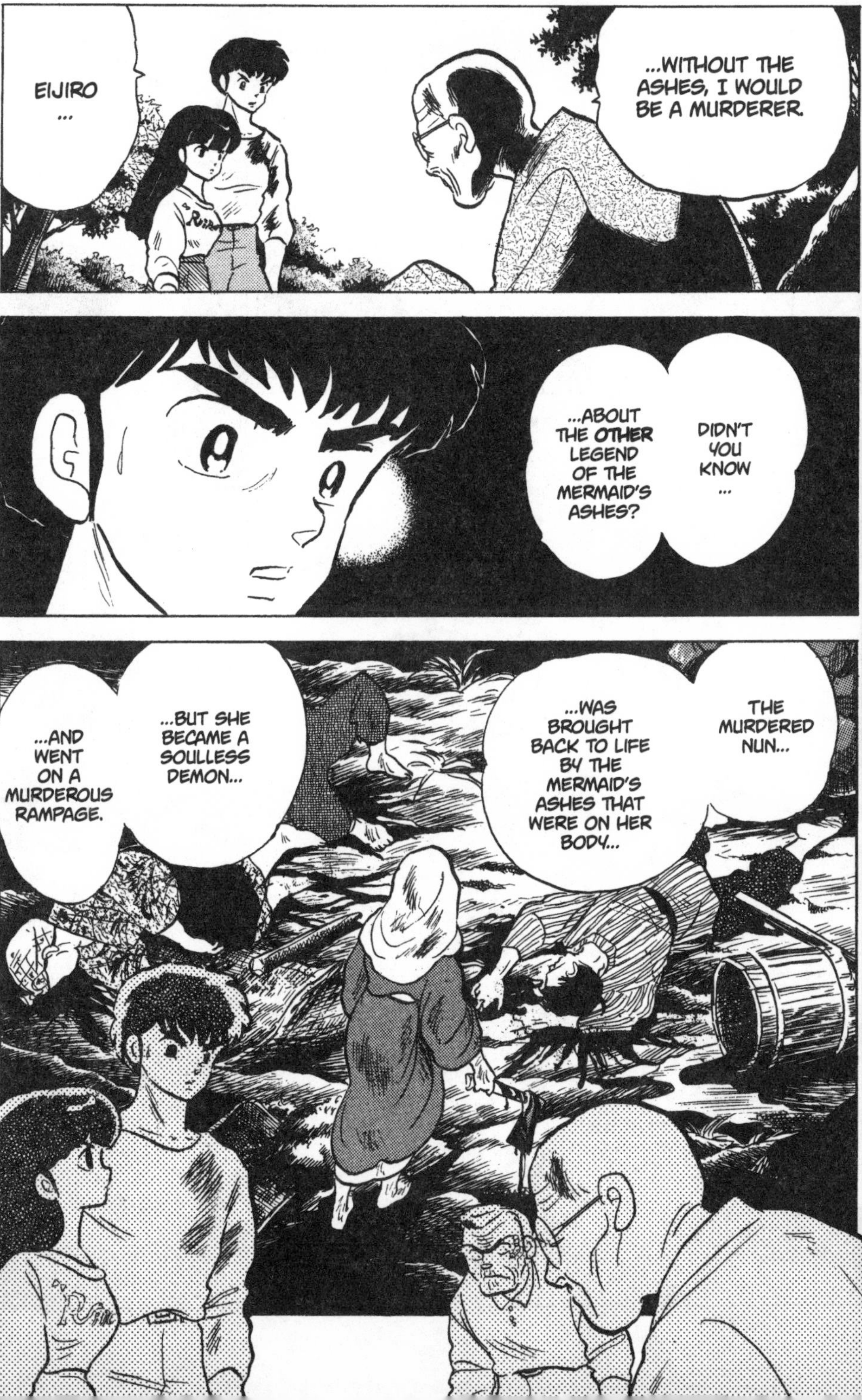
...WITHOUT THE ASHES, I WOULD BE A MURDERER.
EIJIRO ...
DIDN'T YOU KNOW ...
...ABOUT THE OTHER LEGEND OF THE MERMAID'S ASHES?
THE MURDERED NUN...
...WAS BROUGHT BACK TO LIFE BY THE MERMAID'S ASHES THAT WERE ON HER BODY...
...BUT SHE BECAME A SOULLESS DEMON...
...AND WENT ON A MURDEROUS RAMPAGE.

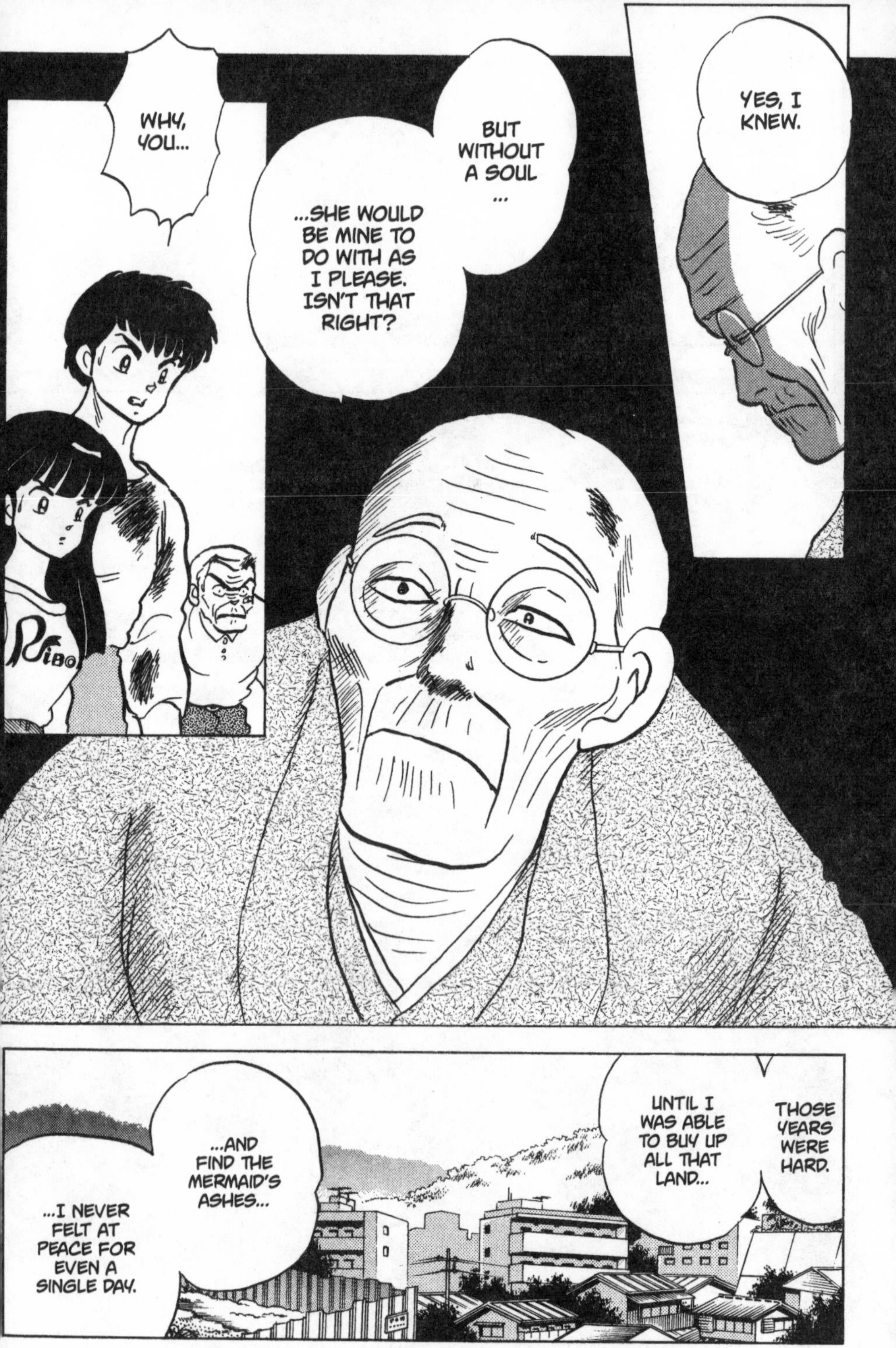
YES, I KNEW.
BUT WITHOUT A SOUL...
...SHE WOULD BE MINE TO DO WITH AS I PLEASE. ISN'T THAT RIGHT?
WHY, YOU...
THOSE YEARS WERE HARD.
UNTIL I WAS ABLE TO BUY UP ALL THAT LAND...
...AND FIND THE MERMAID'S ASHES...
...I NEVER FELT AT PEACE FOR EVEN A SINGLE DAY.

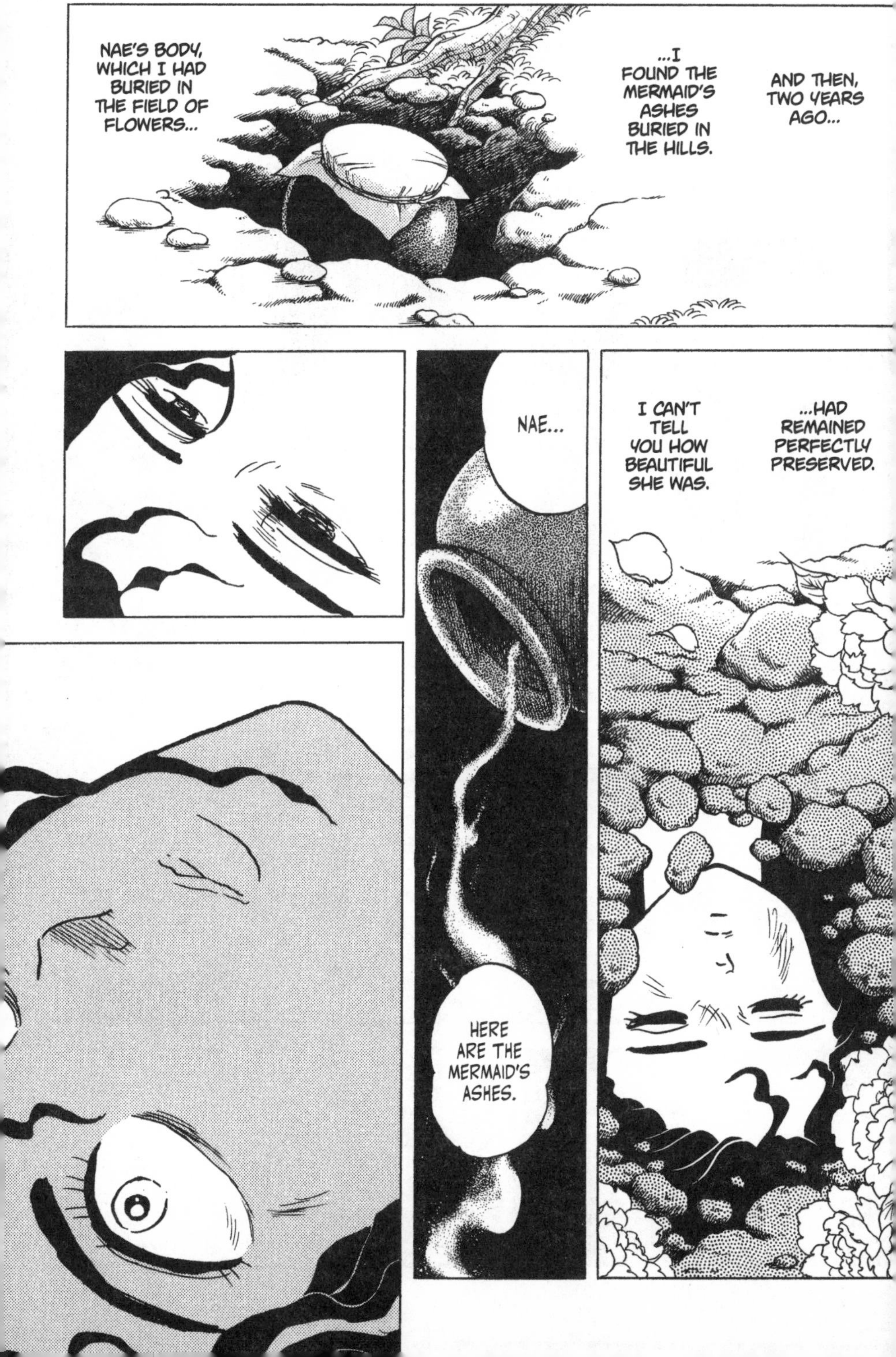
AND THEN, TWO YEARS AGO...
...I FOUND THE MERMAID'S ASHES BURIED IN THE HILLS.
NAE'S BODY, WHICH I HAD BURIED IN THE FIELD OF FLOWERS...
...HAD REMAINED PERFECTLY PRESERVED.
I CAN'T TELL YOU HOW BEAUTIFUL SHE WAS.
NAE...
HERE ARE THE MERMAID'S ASHES.

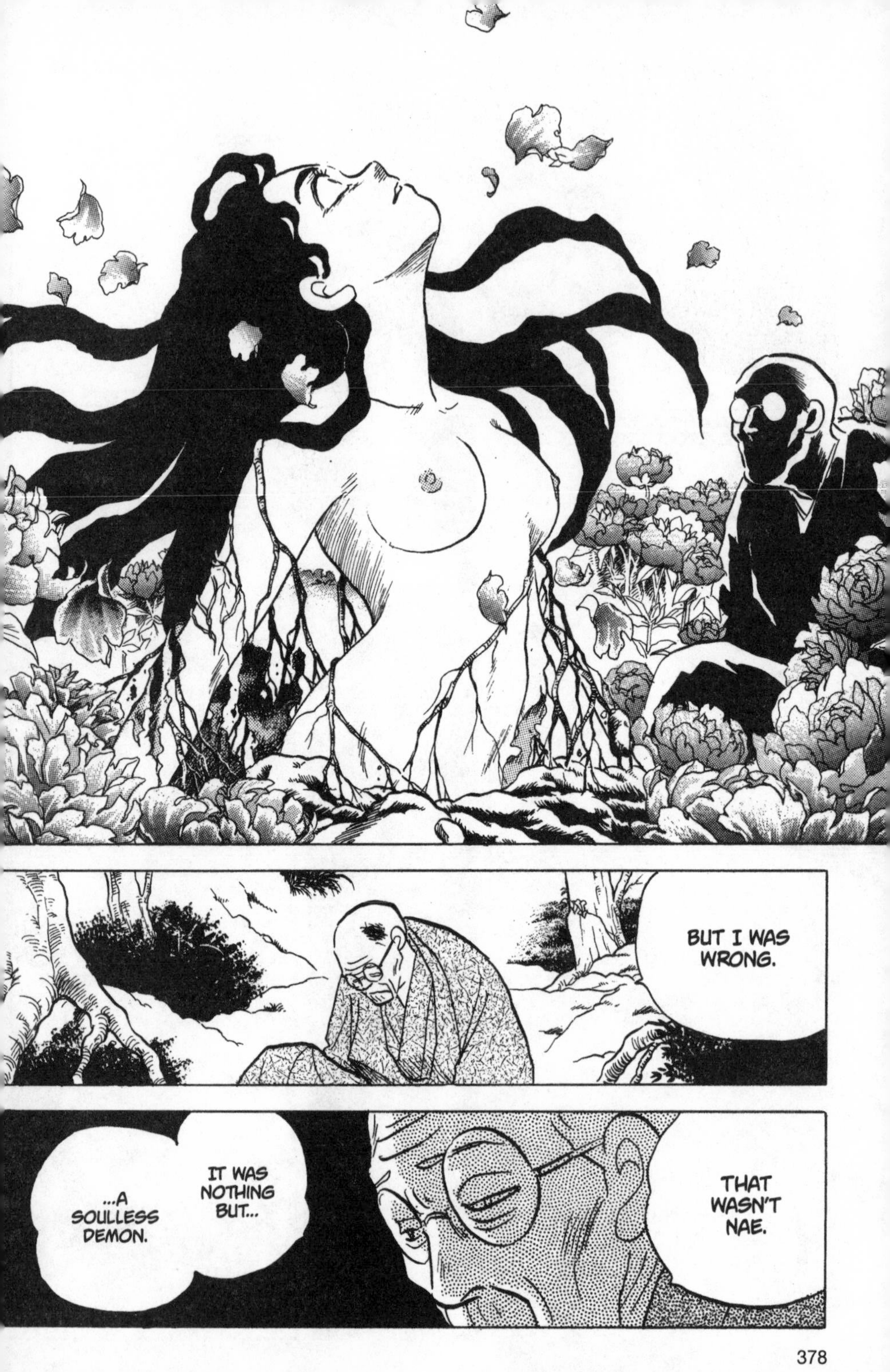
BUT I WAS WRONG.
THAT WASN'T NAE.
IT WAS NOTHING BUT...
...A SOULLESS DEMON.

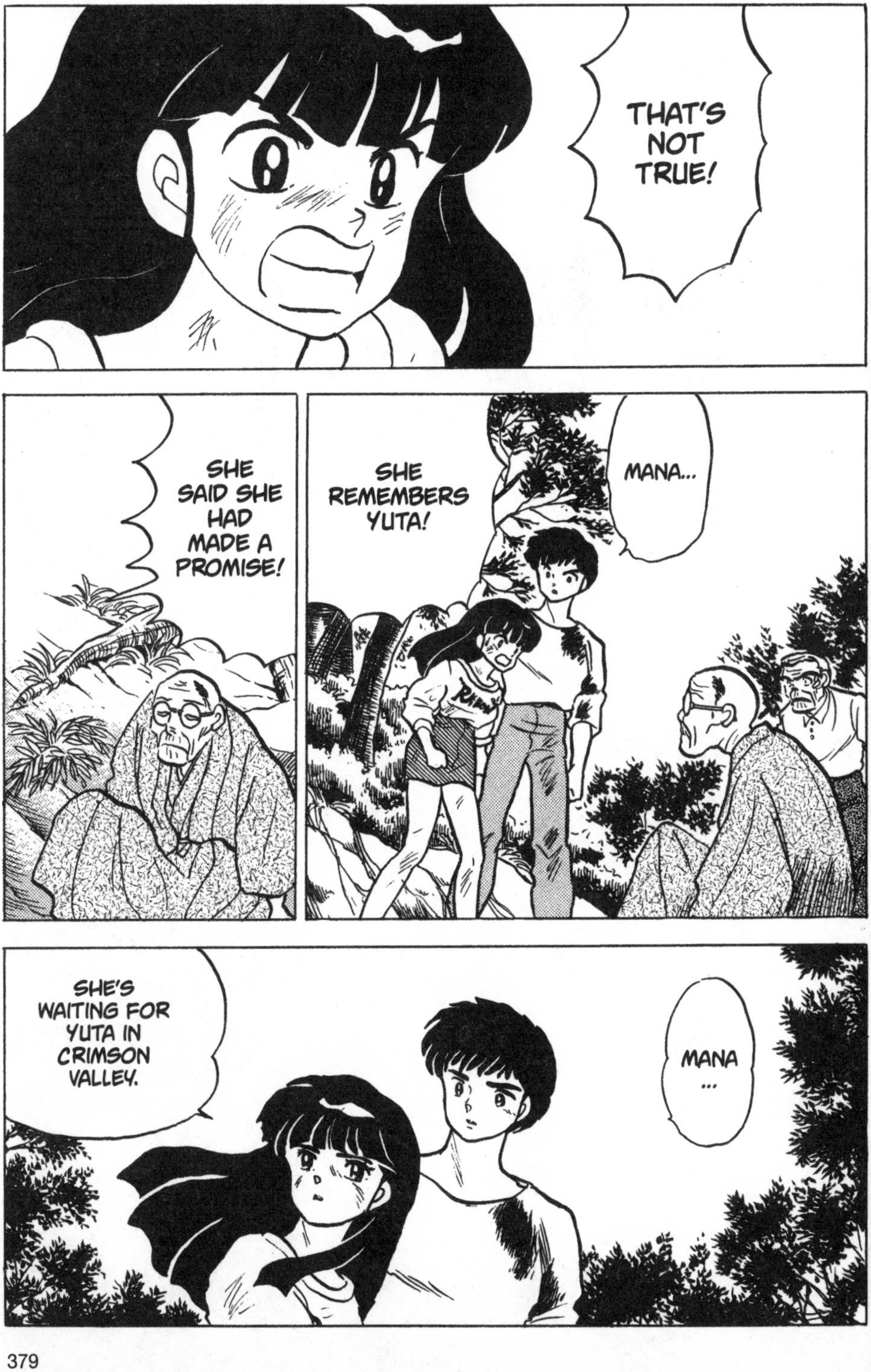
THAT'S NOT TRUE!
MANA...
SHE REMEMBERS YUTA!
SHE SAID SHE HAD MADE A PROMISE!
MANA ...
SHE'S WAITING FOR YUTA IN CRIMSON VALLEY.

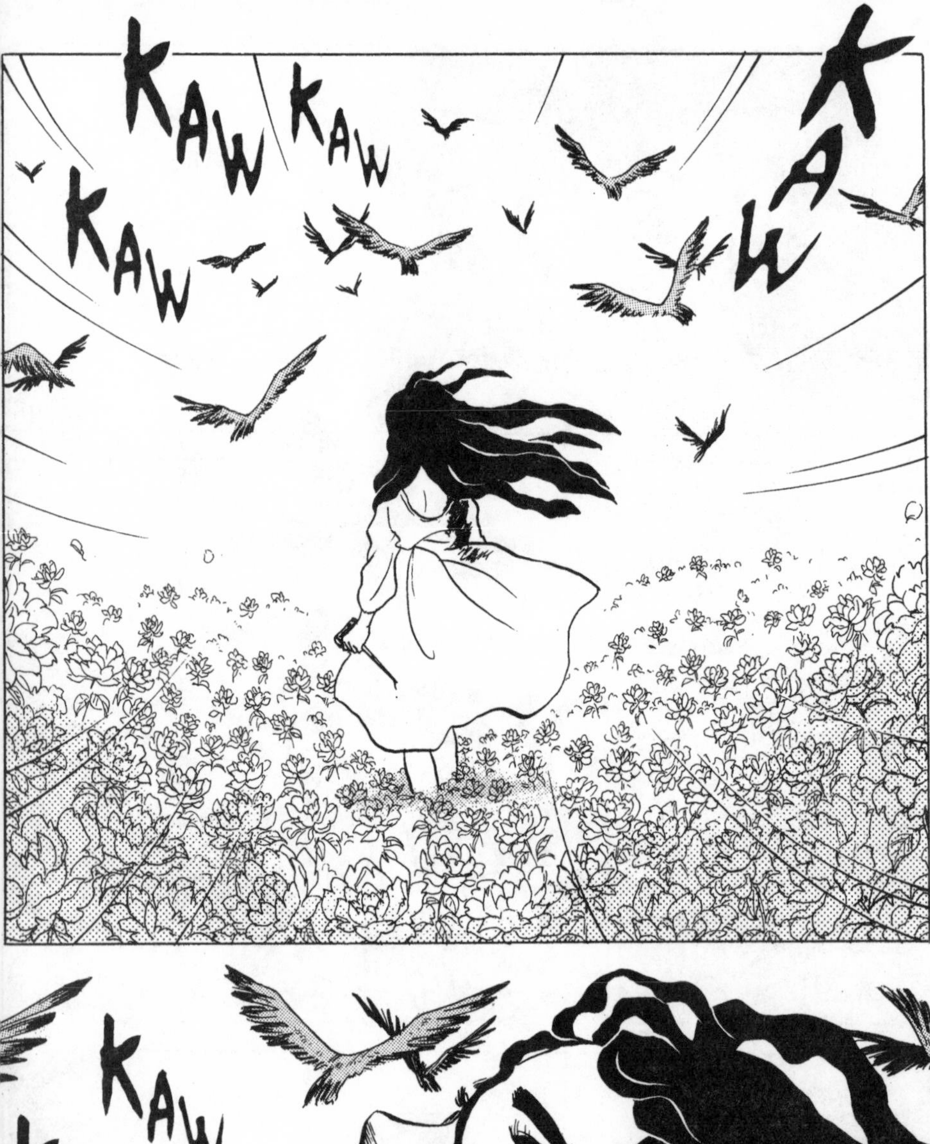
KAW
KAW KAW
KAW KAW
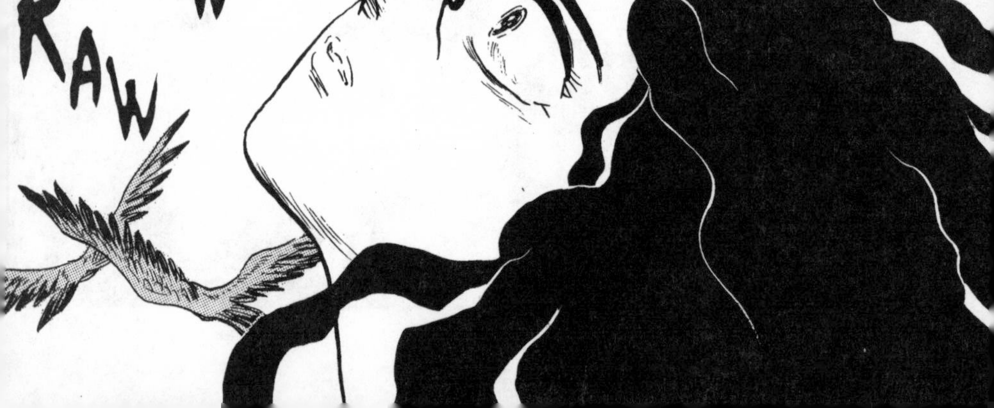
KAW
KAW

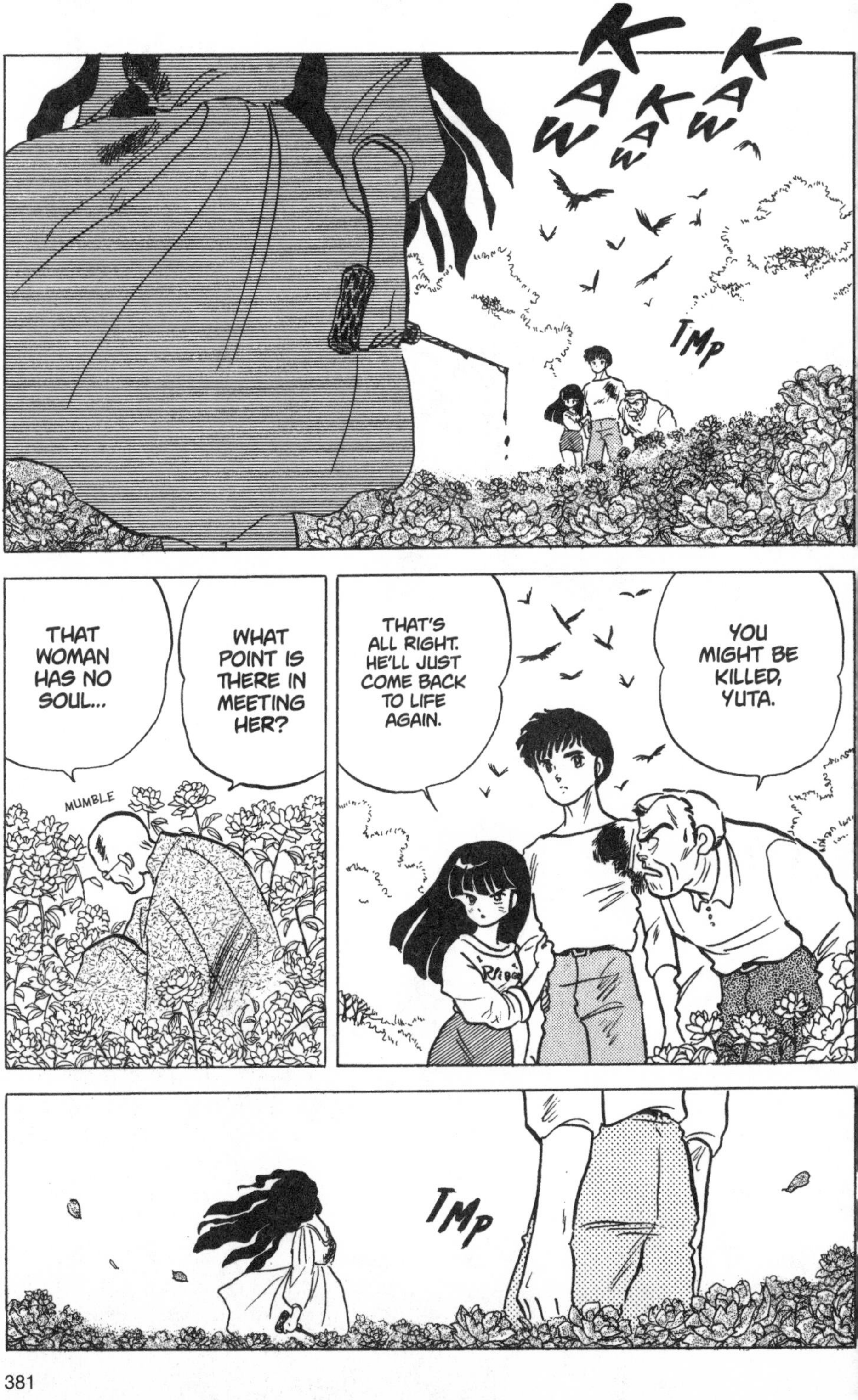
KAW KAW KAW
TMp
YOU MIGHT BE KILLED, YUTA.
THAT'S ALL RIGHT. HE'LL JUST COME BACK TO LIFE AGAIN.
WHAT POINT IS THERE IN MEETING HER?
THAT WOMAN HAS NO SOUL...
MUMBLE
TMp

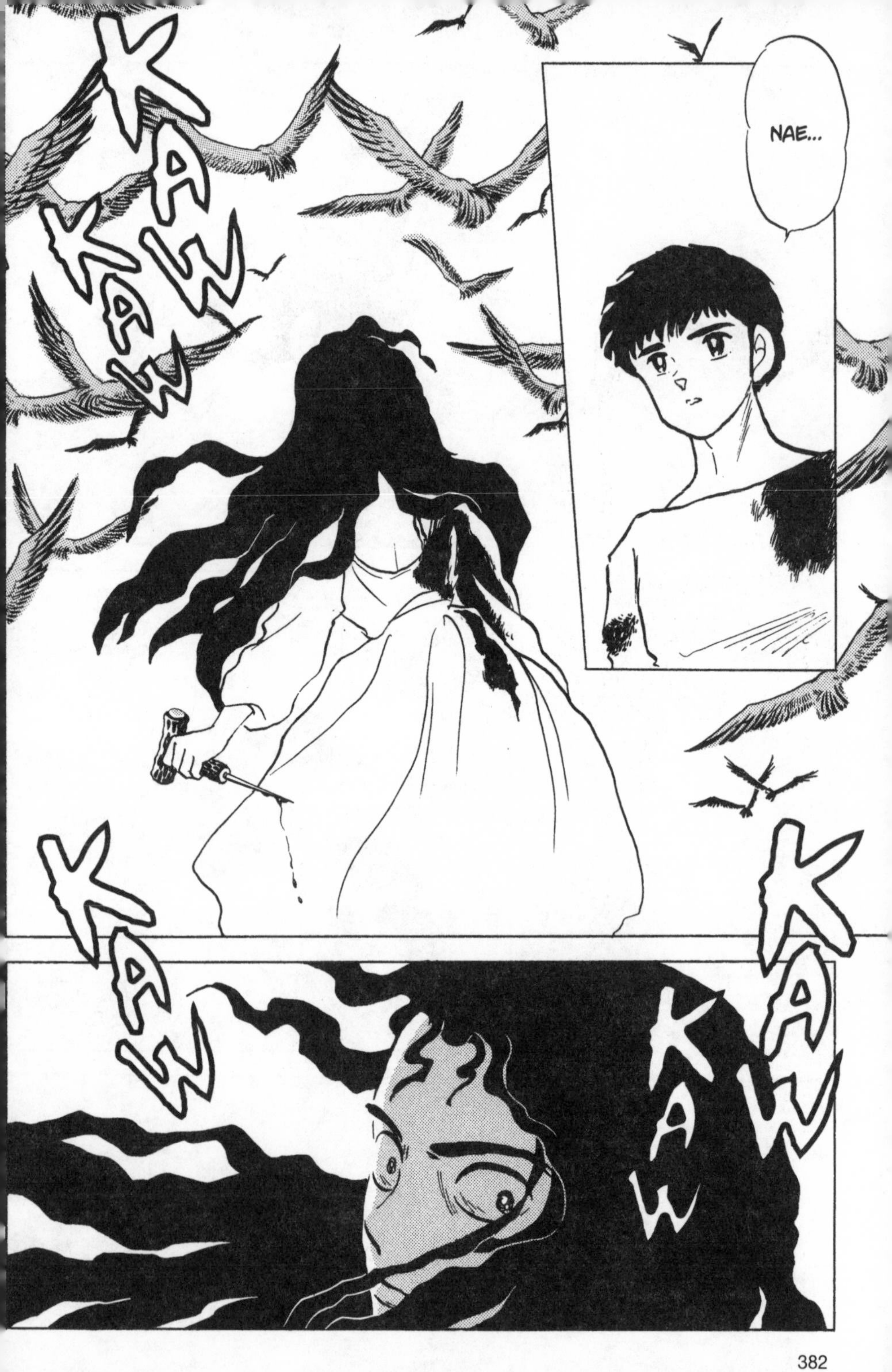
NAE...
KAW
KAW
KAW
KAW
KAW

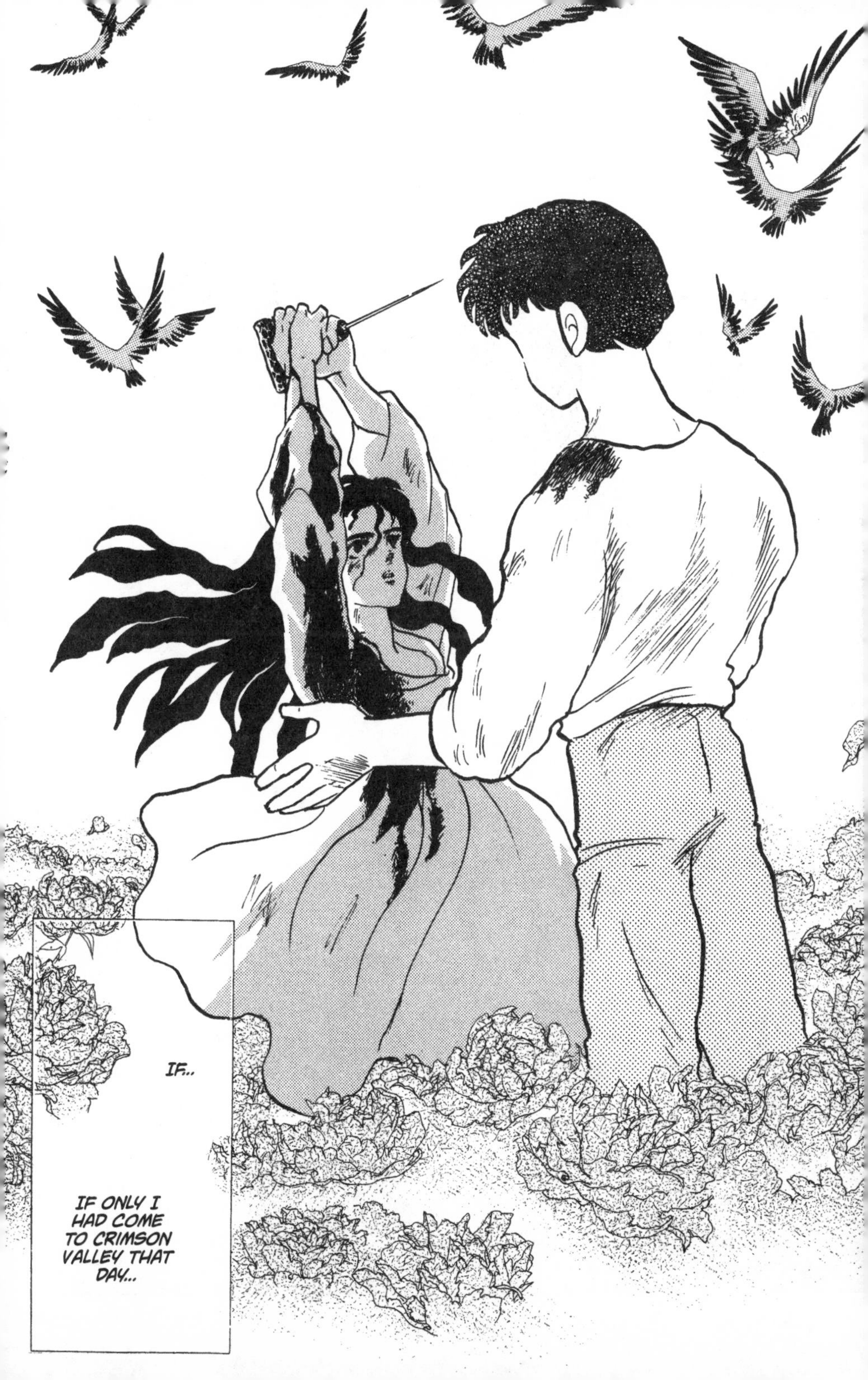
IF..
IF ONLY I HAD COME TO CRIMSON VALLEY THAT DAY...

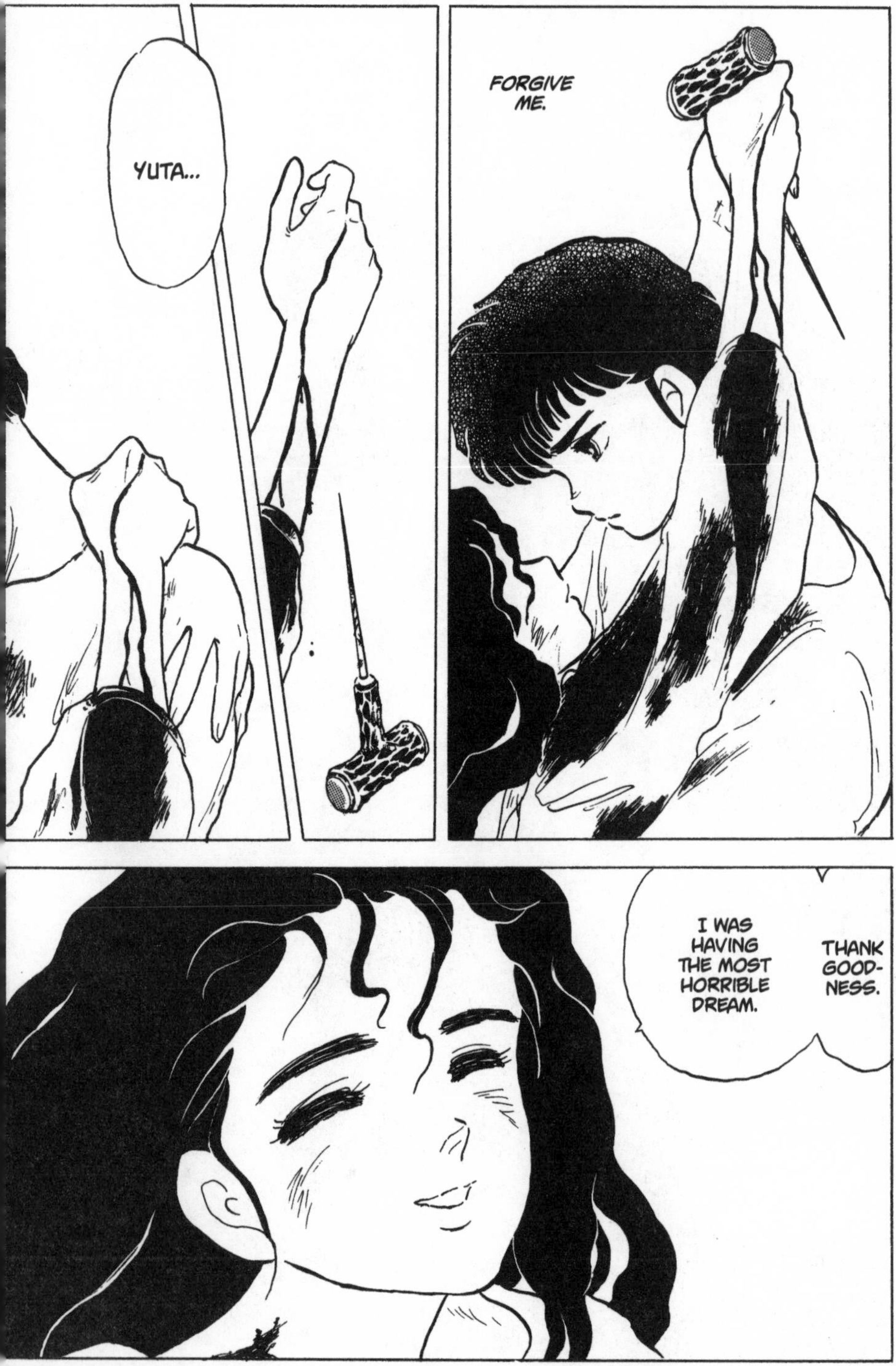
FORGIVE ME.
YUTA...
THANK GOOD-NESS. I WAS HAVING THE MOST HORRIBLE DREAM.

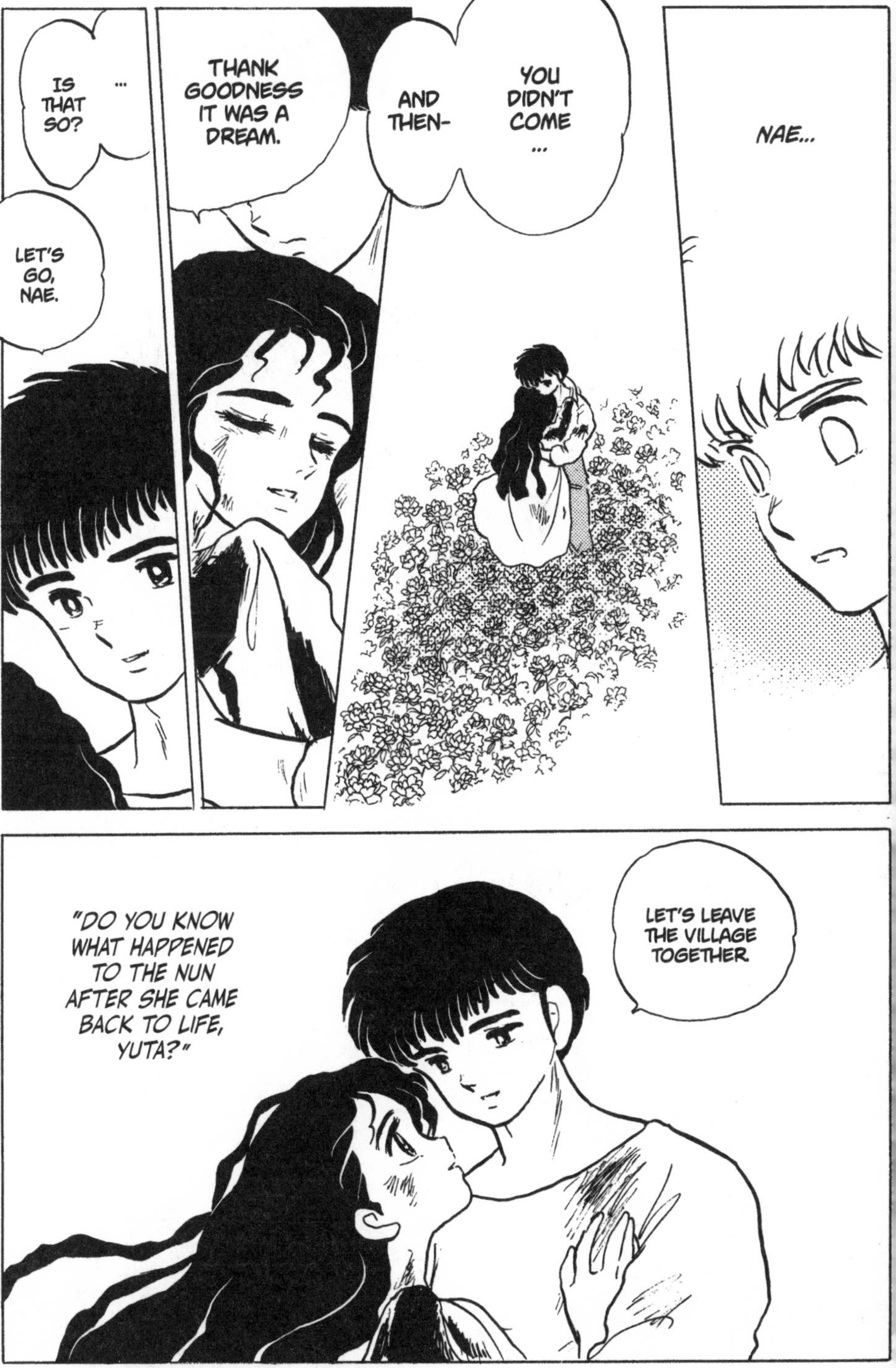
NAE...
YOU DIDN'T COME ...
AND THEN-
THANK GOODNESS IT WAS A DREAM.
IS THAT SO? ...
LET'S GO, NAE.
LET'S LEAVE THE VILLAGE TOGETHER.
"DO YOU KNOW WHAT HAPPENED TO THE NUN AFTER SHE CAME BACK TO LIFE, YUTA?"

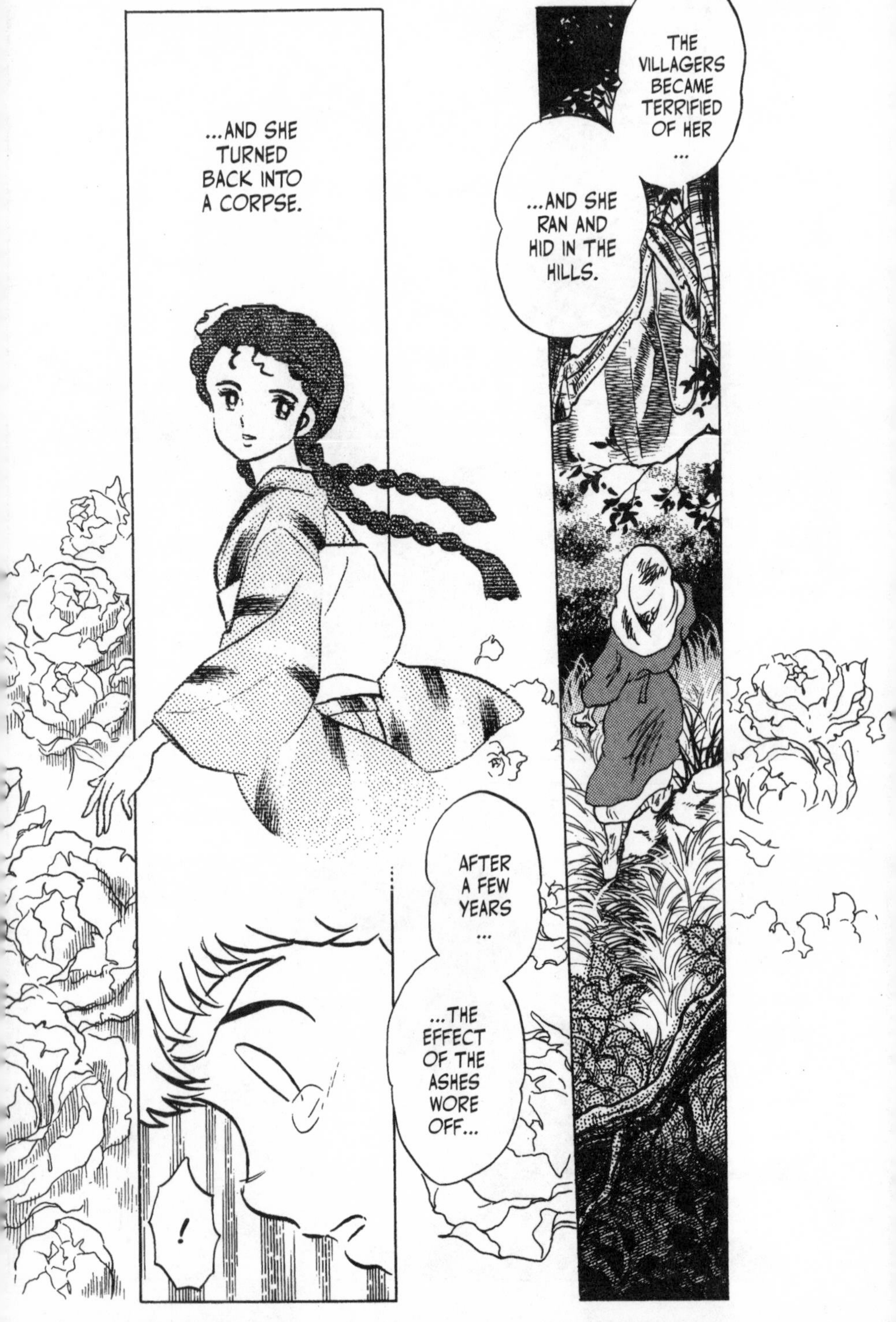
THE VILLAGERS BECAME TERRIFIED OF HER ...
...AND SHE RAN AND HID IN THE HILLS.
AFTER A FEW YEARS ...
...THE EFFECT OF THE ASHES WORE OFF...
...AND SHE TURNED BACK INTO A CORPSE.
!

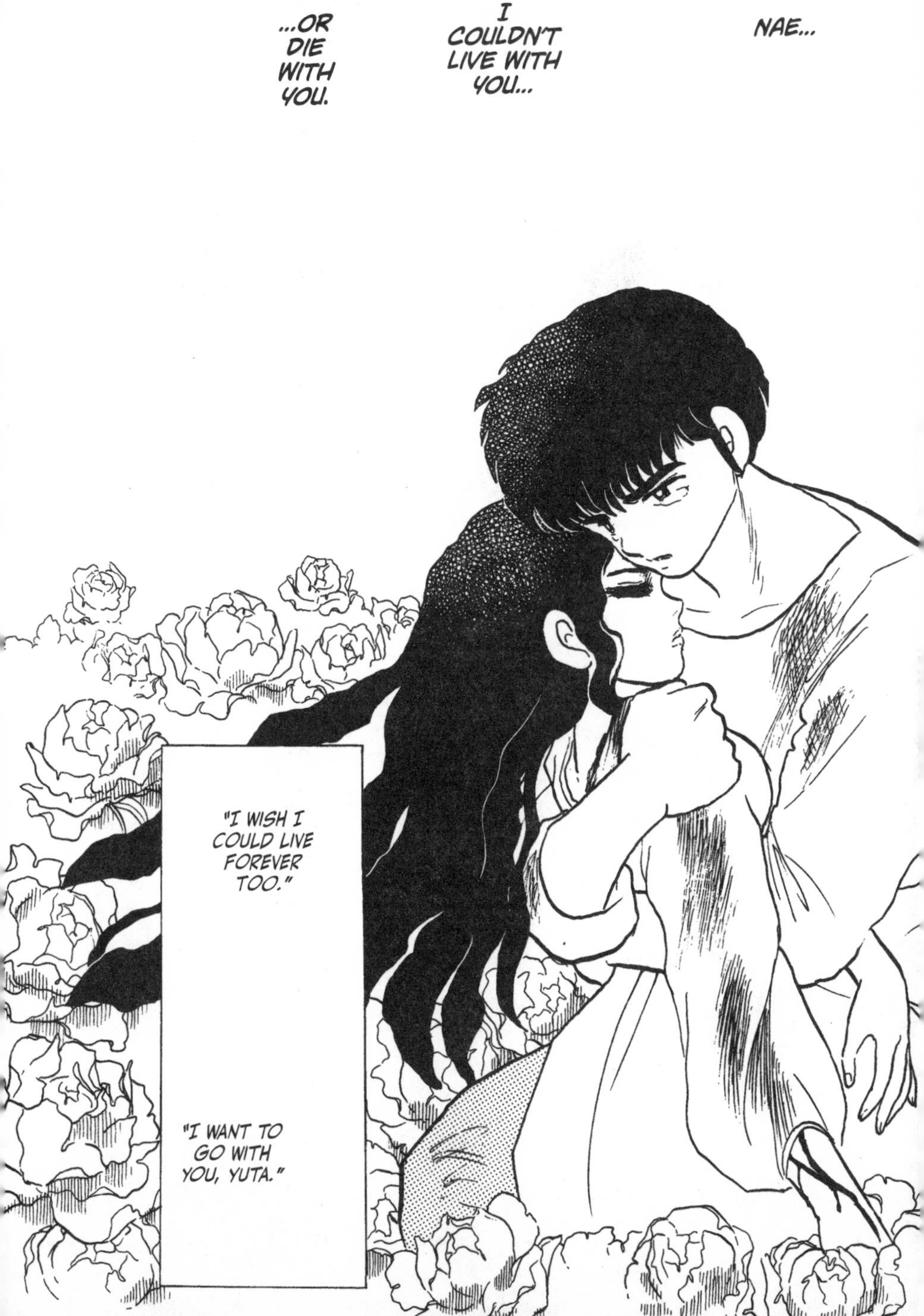
NAE...
I COULDN'T LIVE WITH YOU...
...OR DIE WITH YOU.
"I WISH I COULD LIVE FOREVER TOO."
"I WANT TO GO WITH YOU, YUTA."

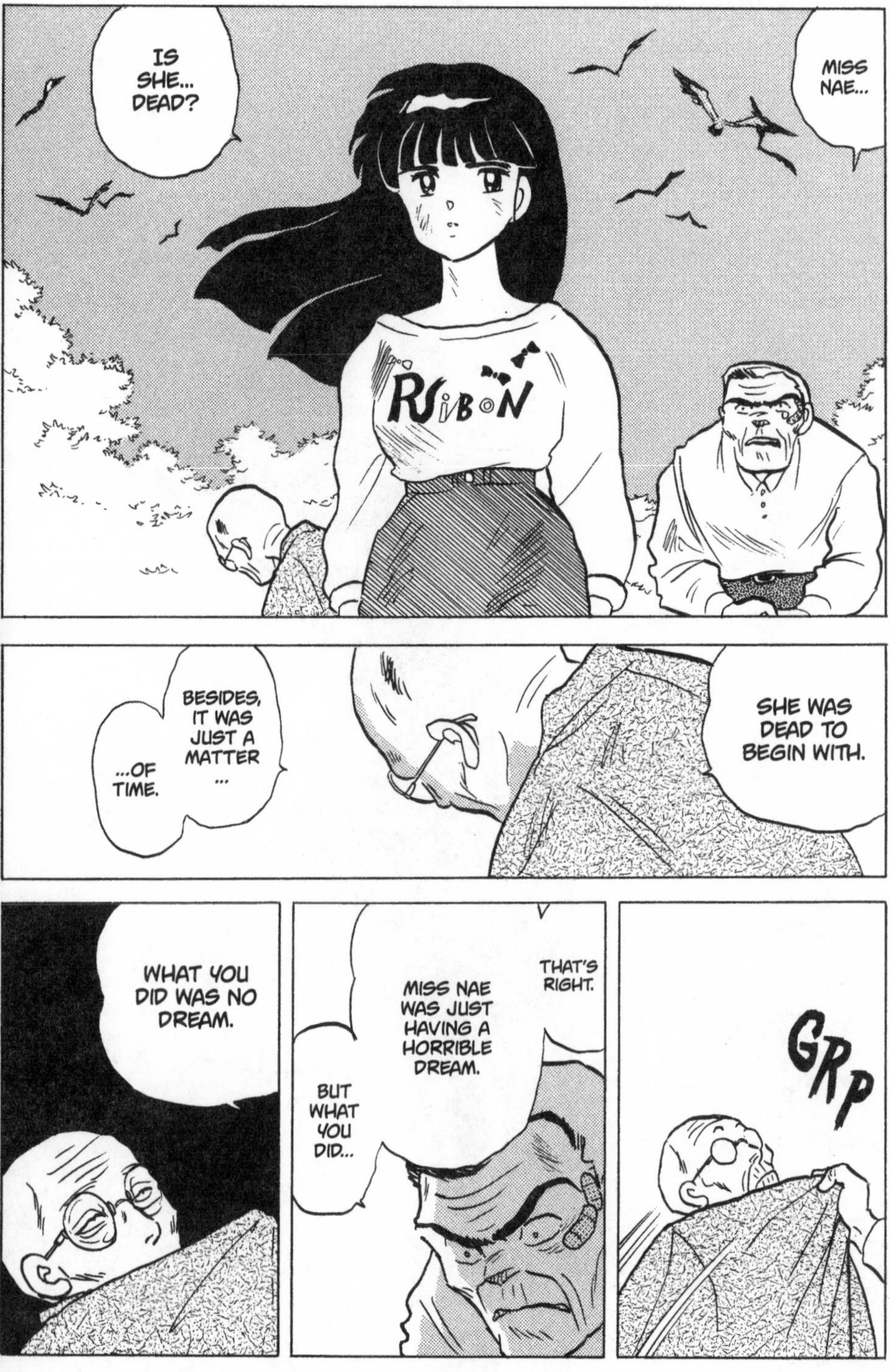
MISS NAE...
IS SHE... DEAD?
SHE WAS DEAD TO BEGIN WITH.
BESIDES, IT WAS JUST A MATTER ...
...OF TIME.
GRP
THAT'S RIGHT.
MISS NAE WAS JUST HAVING A HORRIBLE DREAM.
BUT WHAT YOU DID...
WHAT YOU DID WAS NO DREAM.

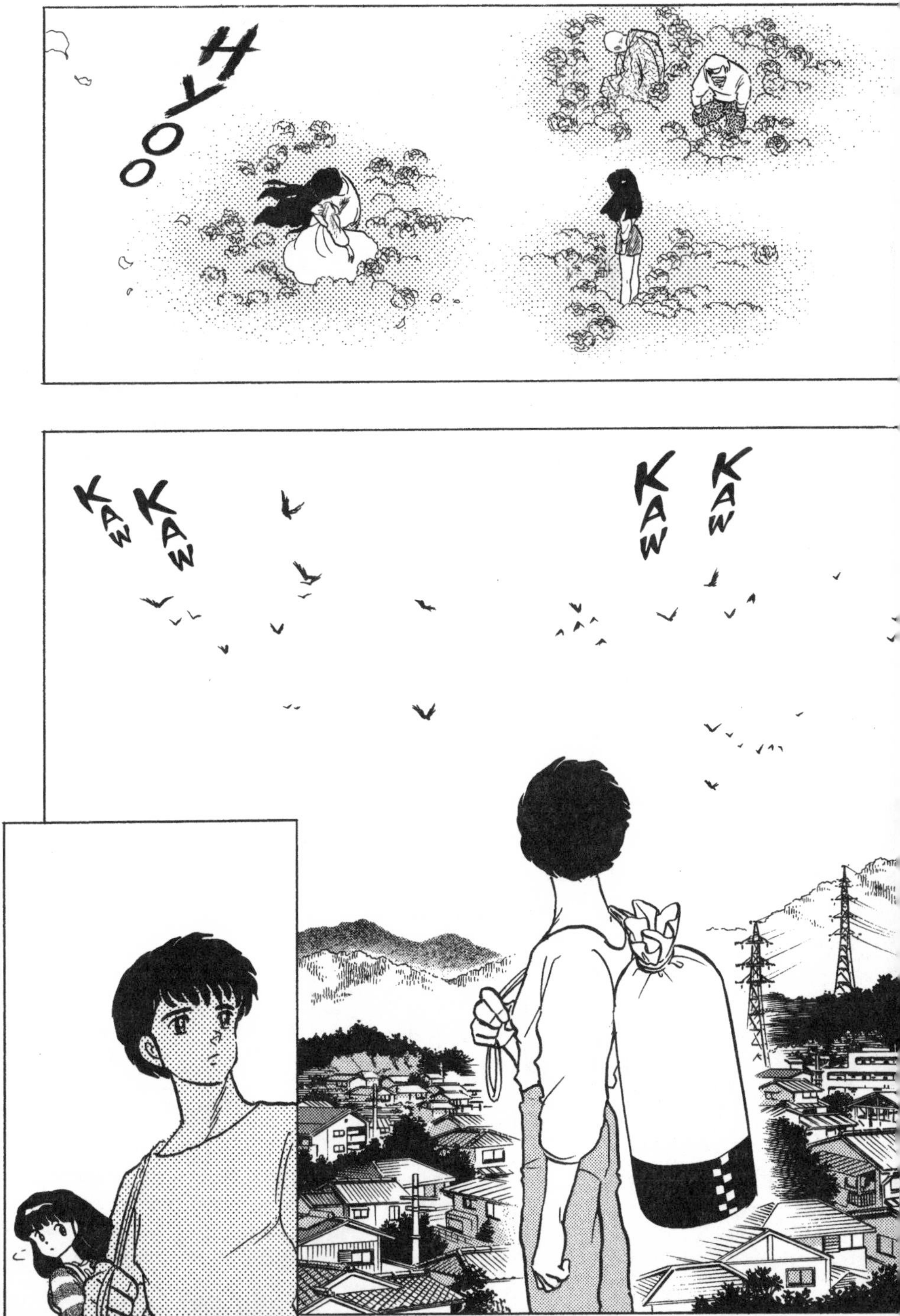
HYOOO
KAW KAW
KAW KAW

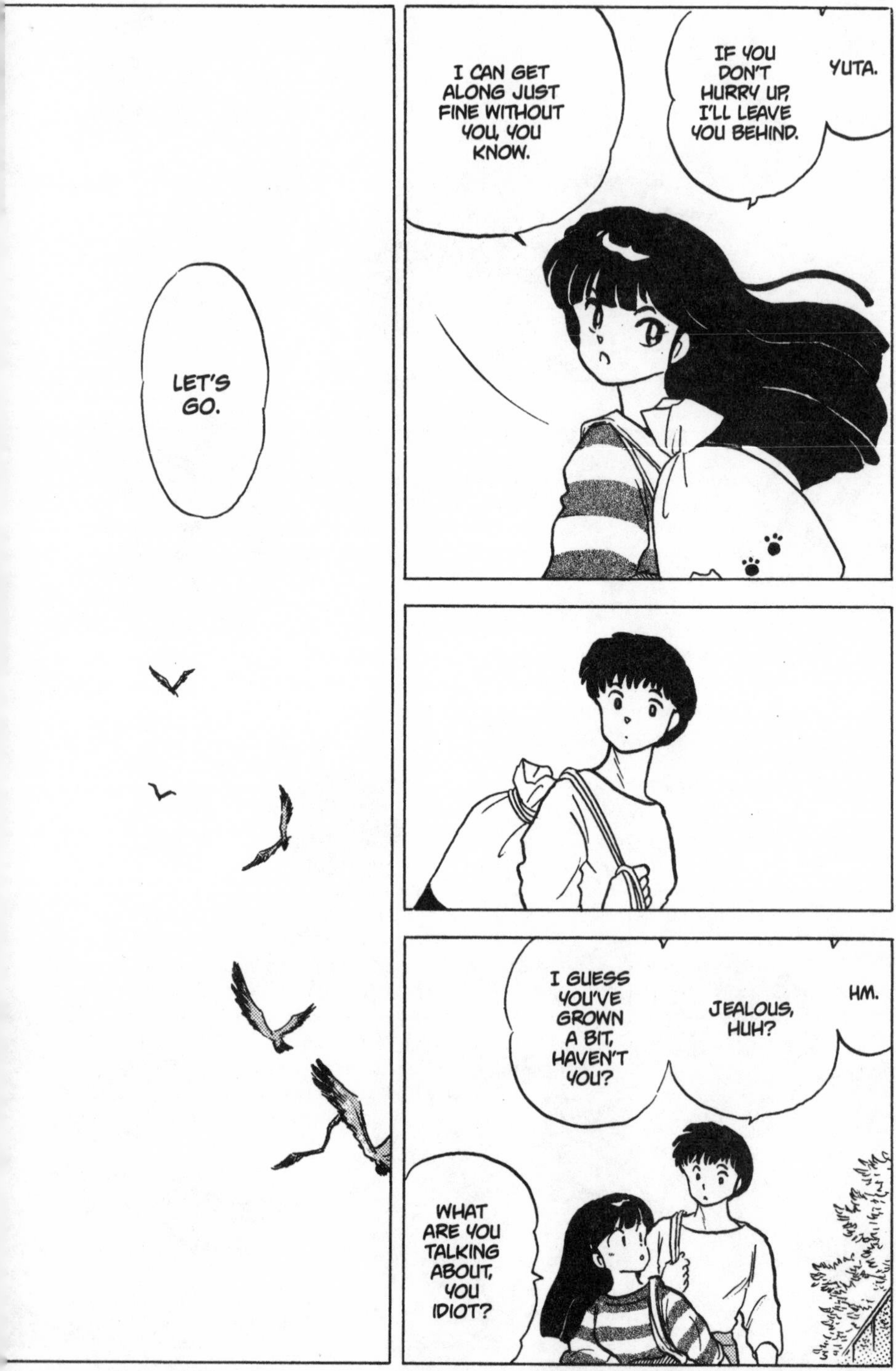
YUTA.
IF YOU DON'T HURRY UP, I'LL LEAVE YOU BEHIND.
I CAN GET ALONG JUST FINE WITHOUT YOU, YOU KNOW.
HM.
JEALOUS, HUH?
I GUESS YOU'VE GROWN A BIT, HAVEN'T YOU?
WHAT ARE YOU TALKING ABOUT, YOU IDIOT?
LET'S GO.

MERMAID'S PROMISE / THE END